THE JPS BIBLE COMMENTARY

SONG OF SONGS שיר השירים

The JPS Torah Commentary

GENERAL EDITOR *Nahum M. Sarna*
LITERARY EDITOR *Chaim Potok*

GENESIS *Nahum M. Sarna*
EXODUS *Nahum M. Sarna*
LEVITICUS *Baruch A. Levine*
NUMBERS *Jacob Milgrom*
DEUTERONOMY *Jeffrey H. Tigay*

The JPS Bible Commentary

THE HAFTAROT *Michael Fishbane*

The Five Megillot and Jonah
GENERAL EDITOR *Michael Fishbane*

JONAH *Uriel Simon*
ESTHER *Adele Berlin*
ECCLESIASTES *Michael V. Fox*
RUTH *Tamara Cohn Eskenazi and Tikva Frymer-Kensky*
SONG OF SONGS *Michael Fishbane*

THE JPS BIBLE COMMENTARY

SONG OF SONGS שיר השירים

The Traditional Hebrew Text with the New JPS Translation

Commentary by MICHAEL FISHBANE

THE JEWISH PUBLICATION SOCIETY
PHILADELPHIA
2015 / 5775

© 2015 by The Jewish Publication Society
English translation of the TANAKH © 1962, 1985, 1989, 1999 by The Jewish Publication Society
Masoretic Hebrew text, Codex Leningrad B19A, taken from Biblia Hebraica Stuttgartensia (BHS)
© 1967/77, 1983, by the Deutsche Bibelgesellschaft, Stuttgart
Synagogue adaptation and revised format © 1962, 1985, 1989, 1999 by The Jewish Publication Society

All rights reserved. *Published by the University of Nebraska Press as a Jewish Publication Society book.*
Composition by El Ot Ltd. (English text) and Varda Graphics (Hebrew text)
Adapted from the series design by Adrianne Onderdonk Dudden
Manufactured in the United States of America.

♾

11 12 13 14 15 16 17 10 9 8 7 6 5 4 3 2 1

Library of Congress Cataloging-in-Publication Data

Song of Songs = Shir ha-Shirim: the traditional Hebrew text with the new JPS translation / commentary by Michael Fishbane.
pages cm. – (JPS Bible Commentary)
Text in English and Hebrew; commentary in English.
Includes bibliographical references.
ISBN 978-0-8276-0741-5 (cloth: alk. paper) – ISBN 978-0-8276-1145-0 (pdf).
1. Bible. Song of Solomon–Commentaries. I. Fishbane, Michael A., author of added commentary. II. Bible. Song of Solomon. Hebrew. 2015. III. Bible. Song of Solomon. English. 2015. IV. Title: Shir ha-Shirim.
BS1485.53.S68 2015
223'.9077–dc23 2014027712

GENESIS *ISBN 0-8276-0326-6*
EXODUS *ISBN 0-8276-0327-4*
LEVITICUS *ISBN 0-8276-0328-2*
NUMBERS *ISBN 0-8276-0329-0*
DEUTERONOMY *ISBN 0-8276-0330-4*
Five-volume set ISBN 0-8276-0331-2
JONAH *ISBN 0-8276-0672-9*
ESTHER *ISBN 0-8276-0699-0*
ECCLESIASTES *ISBN 0-8276-0742-3*
HAFTAROT *ISBN 0-8276-0691-5*
RUTH *ISBN 0-8276-0774-6*
SONG OF SONGS *ISBN 0-8276-0741-5*

UNIVERSITY OF NEBRASKA PRESS / LINCOLN NE

In tribute to

Philip (ז״ל) and Clarice Wallock

to the love they share, and to their many contributions to family, community, and Jewish life

In gratitude to

Carol Hupping

for her extraordinary contributions to JPS

Shelley Wallock and David Lerman

for

Mona

את שאהבה נפשי
"beloved of my soul"

and for

Aderet, Abie, Ora, Tal, and Jacob,
our grandchildren,

with love

CONTENTS

PREFACE

The Song of Songs has been my intellectual and spiritual love for decades, its rhythms entering my soul and its images forging deep figures of beauty. (It is a song of love and longing—expressed in poetic dialogues; it is also a song of rupture and loss—expressed in searches within and without.) Yet my love of the Song is a young love compared to all those who have studied and interpreted the work for millennia. The ones who came before me have been my teachers and partners in private conversation, as I experienced the many ways this work has been understood and transformed by every sensibility of the Jewish soul: plain-sense, midrash, poetry, philosophy, and mysticism. The present work has tried to capture this great bounty via three main forms: the introduction (which presents the work and its creative regenerations in great detail over the centuries), the running commentary (which is built around all the forms of creativity that have emerged over the generations), and the excursus (which annotates the history of interpretation in its great depth and variety).

The introduction presents the nature of the Song of Songs and its interpretation in a linear and historical fashion. The story begins in antiquity and continues unabated into the twenty-first century. In the telling, the introduction presents the reader with many of the features that make the Song such a beautiful and powerful poetic work. It unpacks the various levels of interpretation that have rendered the Song a multivocal song of love over the millennia. The unfolding of these levels is grounded in tableaux of concrete human love (between female and male, reciprocally)—and its ongoing desire for fulfillment. In turn, this very concreteness has sponsored a spectrum of spiritual emotions (of humans for God—and God for humans), expressing many religious valences and values. Like a "rose of Sharon," the Song blossoms in delicacy and diversity.

Unlike the introduction, the commentary is arranged in an iterative and synchronous fashion. Its format allows it to operate on four levels at once. That is, each literary unit receives four levels of interpretation, in a consistently repeating sequence. The reader is invited to actively engage the discussions, verse by verse, allowing the text's plain sense to interact with other levels of meaning. For each of those levels, the full range of historical materials has been taken into account. Because those sources are sometimes arcane and complex, I have reformulated their content in contemporary terms so that the comments may address the reader in a clear and direct way.

As I surveyed and studied the works on the Song through the ages, one aspect stood out: when the comments were written by engaged authors, they intended the Song to instruct readers both intellectually and spiritually. Commentators drew from

the wealth of historical traditions and formulated their words in a personal way for their audience's instruction. I have followed their lead. My readers are invited to learn facts; but more important, they are invited to engage the text and its many voices of understanding in a personal way. My goal has been to foster a creative readership so that the Song will sing anew.

Within all levels of interpretation in the commentary, my English rendition of the Song's text is based on the New Jewish Publication Society (NJPS) translation, which is what appears with the Hebrew text. On occasion I use alternative English wording that evokes additional nuances that no single rendering can convey. Multiple renditions usefully highlight the interpretative dimensions involved in deciding upon a given passage's meaning. Meanwhile, in the textual comments I have also tried to help the reader observe the use of recurrent phrasing, grammatical forms, words, and sounds. These features are part of the Song's thick poetics; they contribute to its literary power.

As with every translation, some of the power of the original text is lost. The NJPS translation approach has led it to sometimes employ synonyms for the same Hebrew word or verbal form or to paraphrase an image or phrase. This is done for the sake of English idiom—so as not to sound too stilted or strange. To compensate for what the NJPS approach has obscured, my plain-sense commentary points out the Song's recurring terms and wordplays, and the resulting thematic cross-references.

With the other three levels of the commentary, the reader is encouraged to see how interpreters over the centuries have reshaped the Song's original meanings—sometimes focusing on a given word or phrase, but always transforming it by creative re-readings. On occasion portions of an interpretation are cited in the commentary, so that the reader can perceive how the commentators understood it; at other times, the interpretation is condensed and the verse is reformulated to reflect its new meaning.

Finally, the interested student is invited to consult and study the detailed history of the interpretation of the Song of Songs by Jewish interpreters, as laid out in the excursus that follows the commentary. Those who have read the Introduction and the commentary will be ready to engage in this intellectual enterprise—a story of the ages, revealing the Song of Songs as an expression of every aspect of the Jewish literary and religious spirit.

It is my happy pleasure to acknowledge here all the kindnesses and benefactions I have received from The Jewish Publication Society over the years; and especially the graciousness and involvement of Carol Hupping, its managing editor. She readily extended older deadlines to allow me the opportunity to do my work with care and detail. I have also (again) been fortunate to benefit from the skillful editorial interventions of David E. S. Stein. His keen and informed eye repeatedly yielded suggestions that I was compelled to consider; and I am very grateful to him for his excellent craftsmanship.

In conclusion, and filled with inexpressible gratitude, I offer some words to cherished loved ones. First and foremost, it is my greatest joy to dedicate this book to you, dearest Mona, my loving partner for a lifetime, for everything and always. You

have been fully present to all the labors and drafts of this work and so much more. What is mine is yours, in fullest measure. "You are my flower." It is also a special joy to dedicate this book to our dear grandchildren, Aderet, Abie, Ora, Tal, and Jacob, who have blessed us with their lives and love. I hope this work will enrich your lives and give you some of the pleasure of our Jewish tradition, which has so saturated my life.

Michael Fishbane
Rosh Ḥodesh 'Iyyar 5774
April 2014

ABBREVIATIONS AND OTHER CONVENTIONS

Abbreviations

AdRN	*'Avot De-Rabbi Natan*
AgS	(Midrash) 'Aggadat Shir Ha-Shirim
AhavD	*'Ahavat Dodim* (commentary by Rabbi Benjamin of Zlozetz)
Al-Fawwāl	Rabbi Joseph Al-Fawwāl
Alkabetz	Rabbi Solomon Alkabetz (author of *'Ayelet 'Ahavim*)
Anatolo	Rabbi Jacob Anatolo
Anon.	Anonymous (1 and 2)
A.Z.	'Avodah Zarah (tractate)
B.	Babylonian Talmud (Bavli)
b.	*ben* / son of
B.B.	Bava' Batra' (tractate)
Ber.	Berakhot (tractate)
B.K.	Bava' Kamma' (tractate)
B.M.	Bava' Metzi'a (tractate)
c.	century; centuries
ca.	circa; approximate date
cf.	compare
Chron.	Chronicles
Deut.	Deuteronomy
DeutR	(Midrash) Deuteronomy Rabbah
Eccles.	Ecclesiastes
Eruv.	'Eruvin (tractate)
Est.	Esther
Exod.	Exodus
ExodR	Exodus Rabbah
Ezek.	Ezekiel
fl.	*floruit*; approximate time of flourishing
Gallico	Rabbi Elisha Gallico
Gen.	Genesis
GenR	Genesis Rabbah/Bereishit Rabbah
Gershuni	Rabbi Gershon ben Avraham (author of *'Avodat Ha-Gershuni*)

Gersonides	Rabbi Levi ben Gershon (Ralbag)
Git.	Giṭṭin (tractate)
GKC	Gesenius-Kautzsch-Cowley, *Gesenius' Hebrew Grammar*
Gra	Vilna Gaon / "Gaon" Rabbi Elijah (ben Solomon)
Guide	*The Guide of the Perplexed* (by Rabbi Moses Maimonides)
Ḥag.	Ḥagigah (tractate)
Heb.	Hebrew
Hos.	Hosea
IBHS	*Introduction to Biblical Hebrew Syntax* (by Waltke and O'Connor)
Ibn Aqnin	Rabbi Joseph ibn Aqnin
Ibn Attar	Rabbi Chaim ibn Attar
Ibn Ezra	Rabbi Abraham ibn Ezra
Ibn Janaḥ	Rabbi Jonaḥ ibn Janaḥ
Ibn Sahula	Rabbi Yitzḥaq ibn Sahula
Ibn Tibbon	Rabbi Moses ibn Tibbon
Ibn Yaḥye	Rabbi Joseph ben David ibn Yaḥye
i.e.	in other words
Immanuel	Rabbi Immanuel of Rome
Isa.	Isaiah
J.	Jerusalem Talmud (Yerushalmi)
Jer.	Jeremiah
Kar.	Kareitot (tractate)
Kedushat Levi	Collected sermons of Rabbi Levi Yitzḥaq of Berdichev
Ket.	Ketubbot (tractate)
Ketonet Passim	Collected sermons of Rabbi Jacob Joseph of Polonoye
Kook	Rabbi Abraham Isaac (Ha-Kohen) Kook
Leqaḥ Ṭov	Midrash by Rabbeinu Ṭuvia ben Rabbi Eliezer
Lev.	Leviticus
LevR	(Midrash) Leviticus Rabbah / Vayiqra' Rabbah
lit.	literally
M.	Mishnah
Maggid	*Maggid Devarav Le-Yaakov* (by Dov Baer "the Maggid" of Mezhirech)
Maharsha	"Moreinu Ha-Rav" Shemu'el Eidels (commentary on *'Ein Ya'aqov*)
Maharzu	"Moreinu HaRav" Zeev Wolf Einhorn (commentary on Midrash Rabbah)
Maimonides	Rabbi Moses ben Maimon (Rambam)
Mal.	Malachi
Malbim	Rabbi Meir Loeb ben Yechiel Michel
MatKeh	*Mattenot Kehunnah* (commentary on Midrash Rabbah) by Rabbi Issachar Berman
MdRI	Mekhilta de-Rabbi Ishmael

MdRS	Mekhilta de-Rabbi Shimʿon bar Yoḥai
Me'or Einayim	Collected sermons by Rabbi Menaḥem Naḥum of Chernobyl
Meg.	Megillah (tractate)
Men.	Menaḥot (tractate)
M.Q.	Moʿeid Qatan (tractate)
MsP	Prague Manuscript
MShir	Midrash Shir Ha-Shirim
MT	Masoretic text
n.	note
Nachmanides	Rabbi Moses ben Naḥman (Ramban)
Naḥ.	Naḥum
Ned.	Nedarim (tractate)
Neh.	Nehemiah
Netziv	Rabbi Naftali Tzvi Yehudah Berlin (author of *Rinnat Shir*)
Nid.	Niddah (tractate)
NJPS	New Jewish Publication Society *Tanakh* translation
NumR	(Midrash) Numbers Rabbah
Ohal.	Ohalot (tractate)
'Or Torah	Collected sermons of Dov Baer "the Maggid" of Mezhirech
P.	Piyyuṭ
PdRE	Pirqei de-Rabbi Eliezer
PdRK	Pesiqta de-Rav Kahana
Pes.	Pesaḥim (tractate)
PesiqR	Pesiqta Rabbati
Prov.	Proverbs
Ps.	Psalms
R.	Rabbi
Radak	Rabbi David Kimḥi
Radal	Rabbi David Luria
Ralbag	Rabbi Levi ben Gershon (Gersonides)
Rambam	Rabbi Moses ben Maimon (Maimonides)
Rashbam	Rabbi Samuel ben Meir
Rashi	Rabbi Shlomoh ben Isaac
Rei'shit Ḥokhmah	Ethical treatise by Rabbi Elijah de Vidas
REzra	Rabbi Ezra (ben Shelomoh) of Gerona
Rid	Rabbi Isaac di Trani
Saadia	Saʿadia ben Joseph Gaon
Sanh.	Sanhedrin (tractate)
Sefas Emes	Collected sermons of Rabbi Yehudah Aryeh Leib of Gur
Sforno	Rabbi Ovadiah Sforno
Shab.	Shabbat (tractate)
Sheq.	Sheqalim (tractate)
Shevi.	Sheviʿit (tractate)

Shevu.	Shevu'ot (tractate)
ShṬov	(Midrash) Shoḥeir Ṭov (also known as Midrash Psalms)
SifDeut	Sifrei Deuteronomy / *Sifrei 'al Sefer Devarim*
SifNum	Sifrei Numbers / *Siphrei Bemidbar*
Song; the Song	Song of Songs
SongsR	Song of Songs Rabbah / Midrash Shir Ha-Shirim Rabbah
SongsZ	Song of Songs Zuṭa
Sot.	Soṭah (tractate)
Suk.	Sukkot (tractate)
T.	Tosefta
Ta'an.	Ta'anit (tractate)
Tan.	(Midrash) Tanḥuma
TanB	(Midrash) Tanḥuma Buber (edited by Solomon Buber)
TiqZ	Tiqqunei Zohar
trans.	translated (by); translator
Transl.	Translators (of NJPS)
v., vv.	verse, verses
Yad.	Yadayim (tractate)
YalSh	(Midrash) Yalquṭ Shim'oni
YefQol	*Yefeih Qol* (commentary on SongsR in Midrash Rabbah by Rabbi Samuel Jaffe Ashkenazi)
Z.	Zohar (including Midrash Ha-Ne'elam)
ZḤ	Zohar Ḥadash

Typographic and Location Conventions and Other Signs

a/b	sections of a biblical verse; the part before/after the *'etnaḥta*, respectively
a/b	(*following a folio*) the left/right sides of a leaf of a traditional text
c/d	columns on the right side of a book's leaf (while a/b are its left-side columns)
1.i.1	format of references to Midrash Songs Rabbah (= chapter 1; verse 1; section 1)
*	a reconstructed (posited yet unattested) form of a word

Glossary of Liturgical Terms

'Amidah	Literally, "Standing"; the main set of prayers, recited three times daily during weekdays, Sabbaths, and Festivals; recited a fourth time on Sabbaths and Festivals in the *Musaf* Service.

Kedushah	The main "Sanctification" (or Doxology) recitation, inserted into the third blessing of the *ʿAmidah*; features the threefold angelic recitation *Kadosh, Kadosh, Kadosh* ("Holy, Holy, Holy"; Isa. 6:3).
Musaf	Literally, "Supplementary"; an extra worship service added on Sabbaths, New Moons, and Festivals.
Yotzeir	A cycle of prayers and benedictions during the (daily, Sabbath, and Festival) Morning Service; follows the formal Call to Prayer (*Barekhu*) and precedes the *ʿAmidah*.

Hebrew Textual Variants (Ketiv and Qerey)

The MT's *ketiv* (written tradition) and *qerey* (recited tradition) differ from each other for occasional words; and when reading the text aloud, the *qerey* is what is traditionally followed. Where differences exist, this edition first prints that word's *ketiv* letters in small type, followed by the vocalized *qerey* letters in normal text type. (This edition's biblical text is excerpted from the *JPS Hebrew-English Tanakh* [1999], as corrected in printings through 2001. For more information on the provenance and preparation of the Hebrew text, see the preface to that volume.)

Transliteration of the Hebrew Consonants

ʾ	*ʾalef*
ʿ	*ʿayin*
b	*bet* (when pronounced with a stop, such as when it takes the *dagesh*)
bh	*bet* (spirant form; pronounced as "v"; used when needed to correspond with *bet* nearby)
g	*gimel*
d	*dalet*
h	*heh*
v	*vet* (default representation for the spirant form of *bet*) or consonantal *vav*
z	*zayin*
ḥ	*ḥet*
ṭ	*tet*
y	*yud* (consonantal only)
k	*kaf*; also *qof*, in familiar spellings of common terms and names
kh	*khaf*
l	*lamed*
m	*mem*
n	*nun*

s	*samekh* or *sin*
p	*peh* (when pronounced with a stop, such as when it takes the *dagesh*)
ph	*peh* (spirant form; pronounced as "f"; used when needed to correspond with *peh* nearby)
f	*feh* (default representation for the spirant form of *peh*)
tz	*tzadi*
q	*qof*
r	*resh*
sh	*shin*

Pronunciation Guide for Vowels

a	as in *farm*
ai	as in *Thailand*
e	as in *dent* or *quiet*
ei	as in *eight*
i	as in *bit* or *police*
o	as in *hope*
u	as in *rule*

INTRODUCTION

Songs of Love

Israelite Songs or Songs of Israel

The Song of Songs is a wondrous collection of love lyrics—songs of passion and praise between a young maiden and her beloved, nestled in the heart of the Hebrew Bible. Scenes from the natural world abound, as the young pair make their way around the countryside and invoke all they see and smell in the world to express their inner feelings and laud one another's beauty. There are plants and fruit growing in the orchards, sheep and gazelles moving on the hills, and oils and spices in profusion. Each and all convey the impressions that the loved one makes on the eye and heart.

However, readers of this love and bounty will find no references to God and Israel, the Exodus and Sinai, or any other event of the sacred history recorded in Scripture. Nor will they find references to covenant obligations and religious observance—even the love of God—in these lyrics. How can we understand this? Do these songs of human desire and delight mean just what they say? Or might they conceal some hints of sacred history and worship, and not be as secular as they seem? Readers past and present have pondered this matter and taken different positions.

Some take these songs in their most straightforward sense and celebrate their occurrence in the Bible. What could be more wondrous, they say, than robust love lyrics between a young maiden and her beloved in the national literature of ancient Israel? The heart of the maiden speaks longingly of love's fulfillment—addressing herself, her beloved, and her friends. And the youth responds in kind, with his own songs of praise—invocations to be with him in the fields, and exclamations of how her body stirs him so. Reciprocally, the pair express their love via images of flora and fauna, royal cities, and armored towers. The many expressions of love bloom and burst like the natural world all around, only to reappear in ever-new forms. In such ways the songs suggest the mysteries of love and longing, filled with pathos and possibility. How special all this is, a precious portrait of the earth and the emotions in ancient Israel!

So readers of the Song of Songs are bound to ask: How did these lyrics enter the Hebrew Bible? How were they sanctioned by the sages who culled the writings of the past and produced a sacred scripture? Did they regard these songs as straightforward outpourings of human love?[1] Or did these lyrics convey some hint of religious love found elsewhere in the Bible? We cannot know for sure; but one may well suspect that some sages looked at these love lyrics and recalled similar expressions of covenant love in the prophetic literature. After all, the ancient prophets repeatedly rendered the theme

of covenant love (between God and Israel) in terms of marriage tropes. For them, nothing so fully expressed the ideal of religious faithfulness as the bond of marriage, just as nothing so starkly manifested covenant disloyalty as "cheating" with foreign gods.

From the earliest times, this topic found expression in such prophets as Hosea, Jeremiah, Ezekiel, and Isaiah. Hosea speaks initially of faithless Israel as a harlot, who betrays her husband and children and then formulates national restoration and covenant renewal in terms of the espousals of marriage (Hos. 1:2–8; 2:20–22). Jeremiah lauded Israel for her ancient devotion and faithfulness, called it bridal love (Jer. 2:2), and was puzzled how a bride could forget her adornments and slink off with other lovers (vv. 32–33). The prophet Ezekiel spoke of covenant marriage and idolatrous betrayal in even starker terms—adding bold erotic tropes to the mix (Ezek. 16:4–14). These themes of marriage and divorce also recur in the exilic prophecies of Isaiah (Isa. 50:1; 54:4–8). The topic thus penetrated the soul of the people. It provided the strongest similes of consolation for the people in exile: "(Just) as a bridegroom rejoices over his bride, so will your God rejoice over you" (Isa. 62:5).[2]

In the light of these texts, which give explicit allegorical expression to the relationship between God and Israel in terms of love and betrayal, it was perhaps inevitable that some sages might suppose that the Song of Songs dealt with such matters as well—except that the tropes and topics found there were implicit, requiring explication for their covenant features to be seen. Thus, how the Song's earthy topics might be related to the covenant of Sinai, or to occasions of sin and rebellion, was a task for rabbinic exegesis.

Yet the possibility that the Song was a hidden allegory of covenant love would save its songs from their apparent surface sense, aligning them with various biblical and rabbinic themes. Sages imbued with this insight might even regard their interpretations of the Song as extending the concerns of the ancient prophets. Seen in this way, the Song of Songs offered a theological possibility otherwise missing in the Hebrew Bible. It offered the opportunity to present the entire history of Israel in terms of love dialogues between God and Israel.[3] Arguably through these or similar considerations, the Song entered the canon of Scripture as *the* religious lyric par excellence.

The Song of Songs is included in the third major unit of the Hebrew Bible, called Kethuvim (Writings). This collection follows the other major units, Torah (Pentateuch) and Nevi'im (Prophets, which includes the narrative "history" from Joshua through Kings). Within the Writings, the Songs of Songs has come to be grouped with the other so-called Five Scrolls: Ruth, Ecclesiastes, Lamentations, and Esther. (Actually, only the book of Esther is referred to as a *megillah*, "scroll," in ancient rabbinic sources; B. B.B. 14b.)

The Song is one of three biblical books traditionally attributed to King Solomon, along with Proverbs and Ecclesiastes. According to R. Ḥiyya Rabba,[4] the king wrote all his works at one time, in old age, and while inspired by the Holy Spirit—and the Song of Songs was the final one.[5] Another opinion, attributed to R. Yonatan, stated that the

Song was written first, then Proverbs and lastly Ecclesiastes—a sequence explained by the proclivities of the human life cycle: "When a person is young, he recites song lyrics; when he matures, he says parables; and when he becomes an elder, he speaks of vanities and follies."[6] We thus have two conflicting views concerning the Song's character: a product of romantic youth, a spirited song; and a work of elderhood, of inspired significance. The difference is between a human composition (and expression) and a divine teaching (and instruction). However, each kind of song would have to be recited and understood differently.

Attribution to King Solomon is based on our work's title ("Song of Songs, by Solomon"), and on the statement in 1 Kings 5:12 that he composed 1,005 songs (along with 3,000 parables). This consideration would place the work's composition sometime in the middle of the tenth century B.C.E. Indeed, the Song's broad geographic sweep—from Ein Gedi in the south to the mountains of Lebanon and Amana in the north—accords with the vast kingdom of Solomon's reign. But a careful reader might also note the reference to the towns of Jerusalem and Tirzah in 6:4, and wonder whether this conjunction reflects a later historical time—when the first city was the capital of the south and the second the capital of the north (after the breakup of Solomon's monarchy in 927 B.C.E.).[7]

Such a reader might also notice the many linguistic features in the Song that are rare or unattested in classic Biblical Hebrew. These include elements that became common only in the latest strata of Biblical Hebrew; or are known from Aramaic or Mishnaic Hebrew; or derive from Persian and possibly from Greek—the languages of postexilic conquerors. Such considerations, and the occurrence of many brief and often disconnected units in the Song, support the scholarly view that the Song of Songs is a collection of lyrics composed over many centuries—beginning (perhaps) in mid-tenth century B.C.E. and continuing to the fifth or fourth centuries B.C.E., when the Song achieved something like its present form.[8]

In short, the Song is a collection of love lyrics that emerged in ancient Israel over a period of centuries. Only then—as a literary whole—did this work become Scripture. (See further below.)

Ancient Rabbinic Traditions

Whatever the circumstances that led to the inclusion of the Song of Songs into the canon, there remained a strong tension between the original and its later readings. Indeed, the earliest strata of rabbinic literature preserve several accounts showing these two meanings in collision. One view deemed the Song a collection of human love lyrics, pure and simple; the other considered it a cycle of songs celebrating covenant love between God and Israel. The first of these views takes the Song in its straightforward sense, filled with erotic energy; the second reveals the temper of sober reinterpretations and a spiritual recasting of its contents.

The tension elicited by the Song is evident in a strident dictum proclaimed by R. Akiva (mid–second century C.E.), one of the most celebrated of the rabbinic sages. In an emotional outburst, he proclaimed: "Whoever trills the Song of Songs in banquet

halls—and treats it like a mere lyric (*zemer*)—has no share in the world to come" (T. Sanh. 12:10). Quite clearly there were people for whom the Song of Songs retained its erotic and suggestive meanings, and who sang it in ways that infuriated the religious elite. These carousers apparently did not know or care about any spiritual sense to the Song, and R. Akiva tried to sober them up with a theological threat. For him, the Song was no mere ditty to sing in saloons, but a work of higher caliber. How did he understand it? And what motivated him to censure these popular practices so harshly—and treat them as akin to blasphemy?

A clue is found in a tradition that reports R. Akiva's comments on the Song's special (sacred) value. This source reports an old deliberation over the ritual status of biblical books—works that would require special treatment or even restricted contact. The discussion opens with the categorical assertion that "All of Scripture 'defiles the hands'" (a technical term for those works deemed sacred and worthy of inclusion in the canon).[9] The record reveals that not all sages agreed on the status of the Song of Songs, nor of Ecclesiastes. The discussion was cut short after a participant reported that a scholarly assembly had recently ruled favorably on both books. At this point, R. Akiva proclaimed: "Heaven forbid! No Jew ever disputed the sanctity of the Song of Songs, [that he should say] it does not defile the hands; for all the ages are not equal to the day when the Song of Songs was given to Israel.[10] For all the Writings are sacred, but the Song of Songs is the most sacred of all (holy of holies; *qodesh qodashim*)—and if there was any dispute, it pertained to Ecclesiastes alone" (M. Yad. 3:5).[11]

Rabbi Akiva's proclamation is evidence of a deliberation long after the books in question had been incorporated into the sacred canon.[12] The issue at hand was whether all these works should be treated alike (viz., had the same sanctity), or whether some deserved a lesser status (presumably due to their content or lack of explicit divine inspiration). Rabbi Akiva rejected any possibility that the Song of Songs came under question, and he declared it the holiest book of all the Writings. Why did the sage make such a strong assertion?

We can infer his reasoning from elsewhere, as R. Akiva proclaimed God's "beauty" in terms of the Song's spectacular depiction of the male beloved (5:10–16).[13] Likewise, he cited 6:3 ("I am my Beloved's and my Beloved is mine") to portray the exclusive love between Israel and God.[14] Thus it is evident that he interpreted the Song in a special theological sense. For him it not only bespoke the covenant relationship between Israel and God, it also depicted God in terms even bolder than those reported by the prophet Ezekiel in his vision of the divine chariot (Ezekiel 1). If some of R. Akiva's colleagues had doubts as to the Song's sacred nature, he himself had none. In his view, it truly was the holy of holies.

Emergence of the Song as a sacred text required bold reinterpretation. Two ancient rabbinic traditions show the Song's transformation via exegesis from a series of love lyrics into a song of religious love. The first is incorporated into a comment by Abba Shaul (one generation after R. Akiva) on the verse "These are the parables of Solomon which the men of Hezekiah *he'eṭiqu*" (Prov. 25:1).[15] According to him, the king's scribes

"interpreted" those parables—presumably understanding the verb *he'etiqu* as having something to do with the transfer of one sense to another.[16]

To support this explanation, a striking account is then presented. This tradition is directly related to our present concern, because it recounts (or purports to recount) tensions concerning the status of the Song in antiquity. We are told that "originally" some authorities decided to have the Song of Songs, Proverbs, and Ecclesiastes (Solomon's books) "withdrawn" (*genuzim*) from public use because they were deemed mere "parables" and thus not worthy to be included in the sacred "Writings." This action reportedly prevailed until the "men of Hezekiah" came and "interpreted" the parables in a way that allowed these works to return to the public domain.[17] From the citations adduced, it is clear that what provoked these authorities was the suggestive language. The two passages cited from the Song are "I am my beloved's and passion for me besets him," and "Come, my beloved, let us go into the fields and lie among the henna blossoms . . . (for) there I shall give my love to you" (7:11–12); and the passages cited from the other works (Prov. 7:7, 11, and Eccles. 11:9) have a similarly bold erotic tenor. They were thus withdrawn from popular use until their content was suitably reinterpreted—most probably by allegorical meanings that "transferred" or "carried over" new (historical or didactic) meanings into the old (offensive) content.[18]

This scenario purports to convey a clash between the Song's plain sense (presumably popular among the people) and meanings deemed suitable by ancient biblical authorities. But since all the technical terms echo later rabbinic diction and practice (T. Shab. 13:2–3; B. Shab. 13b, 30b), it appears that our episode is a construction influenced by subsequent spiritual sensibilities. Indeed, the dramatic events reported by Abba Shaul palpably reflect a contemporary tension and its resolution—affecting the reception and evaluation of the Song.[19]

Another tradition shows how even the work's straightforward sense made its way into normative rabbinic pronouncements—but was subsequently subverted. The Mishnah (Ta'an. 4:8) mentions joyous festivals held in midsummer (the fifteenth of the month of Av) and again on Yom Kippur, when the young "maidens of Jerusalem" went dancing in the vineyards and called to the youths to pick a mate. On this occasion, two verses were cited from Proverbs (31:30–31) and one from the Song of Songs: "O maidens of Zion, go forth and gaze upon King Solomon wearing the crown that his mother gave him on his wedding day, on his day of bliss" (3:11). The latter recitation depicts the Song as used during popular celebrations, when young love was celebrated with prenuptial hoopla. Such celebrations may have been considerably older, for there is an ancient biblical account about annual dances next to the vineyards (Judg. 21:19–23). Perhaps these were the occasions when such love lyrics were composed and gathered into cycles of songs.

Whether the Mishnah's composer was leery of the Song's plain sense, or simply wished to insert an appropriate messianic hope to conclude the tractate (a common editorial feature in the Mishnah), the verse is again adduced—but this time with new meanings: "*On his wedding day*—this [refers] to the giving of Torah; *and on his day of*

bliss—[this refers] to the building of the Temple. May it be (re)built speedily in our time! Amen."

Once again we find the Song's original love lyrics set alongside their rabbinic reinterpretation—an interpretation of Sinai as a sacred marriage between Israel (the daughters of Zion) and God (Solomon, an ancient epithet of Divinity),[20] and of the Temple as a connubial canopy (with a messianic prayer added for good measure). We thus have one book but two Songs: one stirs interpersonal love, while the other recounts Israel's sacred history.

The songs of human love and their cultural reuses are complexly intertwined. This is the rich and fascinating history of the Song of Songs throughout the millennia of Jewish tradition. To bypass the first stages of this process (the primary text of human love), and go immediately to later interpretations (beginning with rabbinic commentaries), is to short-circuit the Song's own literary power and the spiritual work of subsequent generations. The first task is thus to learn to read and understand the Song in its own right—by figuring out what these terms are: the terms and styles of love, their modes of speech and imagination, and the meaning of the text's diverse images and scenes. Only in this way may we begin to appreciate the Song as an ancient text and not impose later issues upon its original content.

As modern readers, the ability to construe the text in its plain sense must be patiently acquired. To be sure, many later readers believed that their interpretations were latent in the text, and perhaps even its primary intention. But these readers still had to surface these meanings via diverse interpretative strategies. Thus the genius of Jewish reinterpretations is best honored by attending to their roots in, and radicalizations of, the text's plain sense. The history of the Song is the history of its dialogues of love. It therefore behooves us to examine its language of love.

The Language of Love

Some Inner-Biblical Features

The Song of Songs is a rich panoply of love songs—rich in terminology, in literary forms, and in emotional drama. It is dialogue, but a poetic one, with figures and images that intensify the speeches and demand the reader's close attention. Indeed, the Song engages the heart and mind at every stylistic turn.

It opens with a burst of emotion and desire—"Oh, let him kiss me with the kisses of his mouth!"—and sustains that intensity through its many speeches. Like this opening speech, the others occur without introduction, clarification, or specification. No narrator identifies the characters, even as the dialogues shift from one scene to another. One must discern the cues from internal features. Sometimes the maiden speaks to her beloved, to herself, or to her friends; sometimes there is direct speech or interior monologue; and sometimes a scene is reported by one character to another. On other

occasions the beloved appears in response to the maiden, on his own or with visions of her from afar. In such cases his statements about her seem like private musings. The reader tries to follow all this (and fill in the blanks) with the inner eye of imagination.

The reader also tries to follow the voice and eye of persons in love, as they express their feelings through similes and metaphors; and as their vision roams the countryside. The poetics of speech draw from a robust vocabulary of love, while employing older literary techniques in new ways. The early audience had a native competence to guide their comprehension; but later readers like ourselves must cultivate this competence—through studied attention to the Song's language, to the Bible as a whole, and to whatever can be gleaned from ancient Near Eastern literary sources.

TERMINOLOGY *Vocabulary.* We turn first to some of the "terms of love" used, marveling at their variety and boldness of expression. The maiden's words give a sense of this range and tone from the outset. She yearns for the "kisses" of her beloved's "mouth" (1:2); and refers to him as a sachet of myrrh that "lies between my breasts" (v. 11). Brimming with passion, she soon tells her beloved that she "desires" (*ḥimmadti*) to dwell in his shade and eat of "his fruit" (2:3); and then turns to her friends and asks them to give strength and sustenance in the meanwhile—for she is "love-sick" (*ḥolat 'ahavah*) for him (v. 5; which connotes being both wounded and wasted by one's feelings). Yet the maiden wishes to restrain her emotions and tells her companions neither to "stimulate" (*ta'iru*) nor "arouse" (*te'oreru*) love before the time of "desire" (*teḥpatz*) has ripened (v. 7). Perhaps she actually stimulated him under that tree at the beginning of their wooing; for toward the end of the Song she reminds him of how she had "aroused" him (*'orartikha*) under an apple tree in times past (8:5). Passion thus fills her from beginning to end; and in one of her last speeches, she proclaims that love is "strong as death," as mighty as a "raging fire" (v. 6).

The words of the youth are equally poignant—and in some cases sound a stronger erotic note. In one exclamation he tells her repeatedly that "you have enflamed my heart" (*libbavtini*; using a verb that plays simultaneously on the nouns *lahav*, "flame," and *leibhav*, "heart"; 4:9); and he goes on to speak of her as a "locked garden" and "sealed fountain"—terms evocative of her purity and chastity (v. 12), and then of her body as "branches" ripe with sweet fruit and all kinds of spices (v. 13). Her physical charms so ravish him that he even speaks of her love as "beautiful... with all its raptures" (*ta'anugim*; 7:7); and once dares admit his deepest fantasies: "Your stately form is like the palm, your breasts are like clusters. I say: let me climb the palm, let me take hold of its branches; let your breasts be as clusters of grapes, [and] your breath like the fragrance of apples" (vv. 8–9). With these words his whole heart is exposed.

POETIC STYLE *Parallelism.* The terms of love and desire in the Song do not occur in isolation, but as components of literary images shaped by poetic style. One feature of this style is a type of word repetition called "parallelism." Typically, a word or phrase (or a synonym) is repeated in a succeeding phrase—for emphasis, rhythmic intensity,

or just stylistic variety. Such repetitions work well in poetic stanzas or rhetorical speeches when speakers—perhaps a psalmist or a teacher—want to sustain or vary a certain effect or mood.

However, this poetic feature becomes more complicated in the Song, since such repetitions (or variations) occur throughout its dialogues, which purport to simulate actual speech. Little is lost—and much is gained—when the speakers seek to convey a mood through emphasis or stylistic variation. But when self-depictions or requests for information are involved, this often creates complications. For example, the maiden likens herself both to a "rose of Sharon" and to a "lily of the valleys" (2:2). Such a doubled depiction is puzzling. Is she the one or the other—or somehow both, through the deeper logic of the heart? The reader tends to choose the latter alternative and understand the double floral imagery to convey overall delicacy and tenderness, rather than specific traits.

In a similar way, when the maiden tells her friends, "I am dark, but comely . . . like the tents of Kedar, like the pavilions of Solomon" (1:5), the listener wonders how the repeated description should be construed. Two different kinds of tent may well be intended, to match the opening self-depictions. If so, the poetic stanzas convey a double simile: "I am dark—like the tents of Kedar; I am comely—like the pavilions of Solomon." In short, such stylistic figures complicate the discourse's straightforward sense.

Such poetic features must be studied with care, since they constitute the language of the heart of both the maiden and her beloved. The love talk is poetic, and must be heard as such.

Simile. Another aspect of poetic repetition is notably evident in the depictions of the loved one's body. The male or female looks at the partner with one eye and at the world of nature (or culture) with the other eye, and thus creates a stereoscopic perception: "your hair *is like* a flock of goats," he says, and "your teeth *are like* a flock of ewes" (4:2–3). Similes are the result; for similes depict two things as one, constructing a hypersense out of separate images. Here they link a part of the body with some feature in the natural world.

Yet such comparisons are often jarring; one even wonders how some serve as figures of praise. Is there beauty in comparing hair to rambling goats, or a nose to a tower? Occasionally, help comes from within the Song itself, when secondary explanations reveal more of the logic. Thus: the maiden's hair is first said to be like a flock of goats (the primary comparison), and these are said to be "streaming down Mount Gilead" (the explication). Clearly this second statement intends to fill out the flock imagery, giving the hair a more flowing character.

Nonetheless, the superimposition of a herd scene on the maiden's head is unsettling even for the most sympathetic poetic imagination. In such cases, a modern reader must pause and let the images have their primary effect—which is to create a strong sensual association between a feature of the human body and the world of nature (animals and topography). In so doing, one must try to cultivate a literary competence that appreciates the sensibilities of a shepherd's heart over the theological sense of the (modern) interpreting mind. Poetry has its meanings that reason must aspire to. We cannot

merely dissect the similes; rather, we should seek to transcend their separate parts. In so during, it is vital to let the tensions vibrate.

Allusions. In other instances, the art of allusion is uppermost: the passions of desire pulse beneath the literary surface, and erotic fantasies are conveyed only through suggestion or euphemism. Consider the image of the maiden's breasts recurring in 4:5 and 7:4. The eye of male desire, roaming up and down the female form, says that the girl's "breasts are like two fawns, twins of a gazelle, browsing among the lilies." The primary simile suggests a young girl's nubile body; the ensuing explanation, however, hints of projected desire. Lilies are the same floral image the girl had used of herself. So is the figure of "browsing" designed to convey merely a sense of her nubile body, or is something else suggested? The reader ponders these images for what they do not say—for this is a Song filled with erotic similitudes and half-suggestions.

A similar deliberation comes to mind when the youth says that the girl's "navel" is "like a round goblet—let mixed wine not be lacking!"—(and) her "belly" is like a "heap of wheat hedged about with lilies" (7:3). These figures follow a statement about the maiden's round thighs (v. 2) and precede another about her breasts (v. 4). As the gaze of male passion moves up the girl's body to the area between her thighs and breasts, it is evident that euphemistic language is used here.

We are left to consider the subtle arts of indirect discourse—of the ways a poet speaks with outward tact but conveys inner desire. The commentary will consider these matters with exegetical care.

CONVENTIONS: *Recurrent Phrases.* Another stylistic use of repetition in the Song is the refrain of *phrases* within the drama. Such repetitions function as leitmotifs. They may express changing moods in a character's inner life. A dominant case is the maiden's requests that her friends aid her in her turmoil: "I adjure you, O maidens of Jerusalem, by gazelles or by hinds of the field: do not awake or rouse love until it please." Variations occur four times, marking shifting episodes, as follows.

First and most dramatically, the maiden speaks of her "love-sick" state, depicts herself as entwined with her beloved, and urges her friends not to arouse or stimulate her feelings of love "until" (*ʿad she-*) the ripe time of desire (Song 2:5–7). The companions serve as the confidants of her inner experiences. Her adjuration concludes a series of personal statements and employs a standard double-negative formulation (*ʾim . . . ʾim*).

Second, after the maiden has pursued her beloved around town and, having found him, brought him home, she adjures her friends not to stimulate or arouse her in this state (3:1–5). Here the oath conveys the girl's desire that her friends (to whom she reports the event) not break the spell of love—and also not arouse it "while" (*ʿad she-*) it matures. While the adverbial phrase *ʿad she-* is used differently,[21] the same double-negative construction is used.

Third, the maiden again seeks her beloved and turns to her friends to enlist their help—beseeching them that if they find him first, they should convey how "love-sick" she is (5:2–8). Here there is no mention of gazelles and hinds (perhaps because this is

not an oath of desire); and the maiden's statement employs a different rhetorical sequence: "if (*'im*) you find my beloved, what (*mah*) should you tell him?—that I am love-sick [for him]." With the opening word *'im*, we might anticipate the standard adjuration; instead, we are treated to a query and request. The stylistic variation strikingly conveys the difference between this situation and the prior ones.

Finally, following a comment about a tryst in the field (7:12–14) and a statement of her desire to kiss her beloved in public and take him home (8:1–3), the maiden adjures her friends: "Do not (*mah*) awaken or (*mah*) rouse love until it please" (v. 4). She uses a rare double-negative construction that evokes a double entendre—altogether fitting for this situation. Trading on the literal sense of the word *mah* (what), the adjuration not only has the maiden explicitly warn her friends "not" to arouse her love, but also hints at a more rhetorical statement: for "what" reason would you do so, since love is so palpably aroused?

In short, the Song's variations of words or phrases can modify, intensify, or even ironize the discourse. They further demonstrate the suppleness of its poetic usage, and the different ways its audience becomes party to the "love talk."

Type-scenes. Whole episodes sometimes recur; literary images—drawn from social or literary tableaux—are reused as set-scenes. Variations of these stylistic conventions convey the differences between one situation and the next. (Examples in the Torah include the scene of a man's meeting a woman at a well, or of a matriarch in danger.) An instance of this literary feature in the Song is where the maiden lies in bed at home; and when her beloved appears (in a dream or reality) she pursues him (in fantasy or fact). There are three versions of this scene:

1. In 3:1–4, the maiden is asleep and yearning for her beloved; she then goes to search for him. Encountering the town watchmen, she asks them for his whereabouts; and when she suddenly finds him, holds him fast and brings him to her mother's home.

Perhaps this entire event is a dream sequence or a love reverie. If so, it expresses desire and the attempt to have in dream what could not be secured in reality. Alternatively, the scene may indicate that the maiden had been filled with strong dreams, which impelled her to awaken with a determination to go find her beloved—which she did.

2. In 5:2–7, the maiden is at home and asleep; but as "her heart was wakeful," she hears her beloved knock at her door and request entry. The maiden hesitates and says (to herself, perhaps, or her friends at a later time—but not to him) that she has taken off her robe and washed her feet, and thus is reluctant to go to the door. Whereupon the beloved puts his hand through the latch. Overcome with desire, she now rushes toward him—but finds that he has departed. She goes out in hot pursuit. But this time the watchmen beat her and strip off her garment.

We wonder: Is this also a dream sequence, where her passions induce conflicting feelings and even self-punishment (which in her dream she projects on the city guards)? Or is this rather an event in waking reality, where the maiden (in a half-awake state) hears her beloved's call and rushes belatedly into the night to find him, only to be

accosted and punished for wanton behavior? Or has she only imagined her beloved's presence and acted on her inner impulses, to no avail?

In any case, the poet's literary skill and psychological insight are evident. Through ambiguity and suggestion, the artist conveys the complex psychology of young love and desire.

3. In 8:1–2, the maiden wishes that her beloved were her brother, so that she might kiss him unabashedly in public and then bring him to her mother's house, where she would let him drink "the sweet wine of her pomegranate juice"!

This gemlike variant is cut to essentials. Here, where the girl's fantasies are fully expressed—in a private reverie, perhaps—many of the emotional nuances come to the fore, and the erotic innuendos are palpable.

There seems no end to the poet's literary dexterity and handling of the emotions of love. Like no other work in Scripture, the Song of Songs explores the subjectivity of desire—and the many ways it infuses all that one sees and feels.

Contrasting Uses of Love Scenes and Language

Let us now widen the aperture of our view of Israelite literary conventions about love. When employed in different genres, similar scenes can convey totally divergent concerns. The same love language can convey different valences, depending on who uses it and when.

THE SONG OF SONGS AND PROVERBS A comparison of the type-scene in 3:1–4 (discussed in the previous subsection) with Prov. 7:10–20 is an instructive case of contrastive uses of similar love language. In the Song, the maiden repeatedly "sought" her "beloved one" on her "bed" at night, and also sought him through the streets of her town—but she could not "find him" at first; until suddenly, after repeated attempts, "found" her love and quickly "seized him" and brought him home (3:1–4). This is the same beloved who, like herself, exuded an aroma of "myrrh" (1:13; 3:6), and was enjoined to celebrate with her upon their luxuriant "couch" in the fields (1:16). In another tryst, the young couple was urged to "drink" their fill of "love" (5:1).

This scene of search and seizure tallies precisely with Prov. 7:10–20, whose hortatory purpose is to warn the unwary of the wiles of false wisdom—personified as a harlot who plies her trade in the street and calls to passersby to join her in bed with the pleasures of love. The mood and setting are thus unlike that found in Song 3:1–4, yet the overall scene and the terms used are similar, suggesting two divergent renditions of one type-scene. For Proverbs depicts a woman who goes out to "grab" and kiss her prey (v. 13); and when she "finds" them, she prepares a seductive "couch" and "bed" for their pleasure—fully perfumed with "myrrh" and other spices (vv. 15–17)—bidding them to be "saturated" with "love" and "lovemaking" until the break of dawn (v. 18).[22] The negative character of this passage, with its robust vocabulary and depictions, contrasts with the words and motifs in the Song.

These contrastive uses of the vocabulary of love evidently share a common literary core. Different authors inflected them differently for their own rhetorical purposes.

Through the vocal and scenic art displayed in these cases, we get a bit closer to the languages and styles of love in biblical antiquity. Without cultivating a competence in these matters, much would be lost to us; but through attention to these details we may recover something of the affective pulse of love in olden texts—the Song of Songs in particular. (As modern readers of the Song, we are repeatedly moving from its target audience's periphery to the center, and must be ever-mindful of the task.)

THE SONG AND OTHER BIBLICAL TEXTS Terms turn in different directions, and the reader of the Song must be alert to this in order to appreciate the earthy eros its speakers express. As we have seen, the maiden repeatedly told her companions not to arouse love until its proper time of "desire" (*'ad she-teḥpatz*). This verb of passion occurs elsewhere in the context of unbridled lust—in the scriptural report of the rape of Jacob's daughter, Dinah. Not mincing words, Shechem states that his son Hamor has an insatiable "desire" or "longing" (*ḥafeitz*) for Jacob's daughter Dinah (Gen. 34:8)—just after his son had succumbed to these feelings (v. 2). The verb conveys overwhelming emotions, which result in uncontrolled passion and shameful consequence.

The example in Genesis contrasts with the positive usages in the Song, where human love and restraint are likewise involved. It contrasts even more with instances that involve divine love and consolation. In a strong formulation, God comforts Israel with the hope that she will return from exile and be called "The-One-I-Desire" (*ḥeftzibah*; Isa. 62:4). In another instance of bivalent love language, the prophet Hosea chastised Israel for acts of idolatry ("harlotry"), and warned that she will "seek but not find" the false "lovers" who have lured her astray (Hos. 2:9). These words recall the terminology of Song 3:1 ("I sought him but found him not").[23]

RABBINIC SENSITIVITY TO THE BIBLE'S LOVE LANGUAGE Biblical love language is not monolithic. It can be used in different ways for different purposes—for either base or beautiful desire, and directed to either secular or theological ends. The ancient sages were also mindful of this point. In their close study of Scripture, they collected striking instances where divine love uses earthy terms—even when the human actions resulted in base behavior. The following teaching exemplifies this point.

> Rabbi Simeon ben Lakish said: The Holy One, blessed be He, expressed love (*ḥibbah*) for Israel with three words [of passion]: "cleaving" (*deveiqah*), "desire" (*ḥasheiqah*), and "delight" (*ḥafeitzah*): "cleaving"—[as it says:] *You who did* CLEAVE *to the* LORD *your God are alive* (Deut. 4:4); "desire"—[as in] *the* LORD *did* DESIRE *you* (Deut. 7:7); and "delight"—[as in] *the* LORD DELIGHTS *in you* (Isa. 62:4). We may infer the import of these words from the [narrative about] the wicked Shechem, in the story beginning "Dinah . . . went out" (Gen. 34:1): "cleaving"—[as it says:] *His soul did* cleave *to Dinah* (v. 3); "desire"—*My son Shechem* desires *your daughter* (v. 8); and "delight"—*He had* delight *in Jacob's daughter* (v. 19).
>
> Rabbi Abba b. Elisha added two more expressions: "love" (*'ahavah*) and "speaking to the heart" (*dibbur 'al ha-leiv*): "love"—[as in] *I have* LOVED *you, says the* LORD (Mal. 1:2); and "speaking to the heart"—[as in] *Comfort you, comfort you My people, says your God,* SPEAK TO *Jerusalem's* HEART (Isa. 40:2). We also learn the import of these expressions from the [narrative about] the wicked Shechem; for it says [there]: *He* LOVED *the girl, and* SPOKE TO HER HEART (Gen. 34:3)." (Midrash Psalms, Psalm 22.22).[24]

This midrashic unit is composed of two layers. In the first, R. Simeon offers three cases of God's love for Israel whose terminology can be learned from usages in the episode of the rape of Dinah. In the second stratum, another sage adduces two additional theological terms for love that also occur in the same biblical narrative. The point is deft and the insight significant: *the language of religious love,* used of God's loving care and concern for Israel, *is not a special vocabulary, but an argot of love terms that occurs even in the most debased human situations.* This last point is given emphasis. Twice the midrash states that one may "infer" or "learn" the import of particular love terms "from" (*lemeidin mei-*) their narrative context; and this phrase alludes to one of the classic, ancient principles of interpretation taught by R. Ishmael—namely "A word [or topic] may be learned [or deduced] from its context" (*davar lammeid mei-ʿinyano*).[25] Just this is the exegetical principle employed here; and by alluding to it, the rabbinic reader is urged to note how the languages of human love may underpin even the most exalted theological formulations.

Such a point has particular bearing on the later rabbinic interpretations of the Song, where the primary terms for love used there serve altogether different theological ends. We shall explore this topic fully below. For now it suffices to stress that the language of human love arises from the heart and its passions.

Other Love Language and Lyrics in Antiquity

THE LYRICS OF EGYPT AND MESOPOTAMIA If the Song's context is Scripture, and its love language resonates with Israelite life and literature, the setting of Scripture is the ancient Near East and its sources. So situated, the Song of Songs must be viewed against the backdrop of Egyptian and Mesopotamian love lyrics composed over many centuries. Even if it is not possible to demonstrate any direct borrowings between these sources and the Song, the study of them offers many literary insights. Consider, for example, the fact that the languages of love in the Song are dialogical and expressed with figures drawn from the flora of the field and the fauna of the highlands; or that the lovers speak to one another with love epithets: she refers to him as a king or gazelle, he calls her a dove or sister; and they both descend to gardens of love and its lush fruit.

Exactly similar features recur in the love lyrics along Israel's borders. Thus they offer a comparative perspective on the types of love discourse used in Near Eastern antiquity, the role of certain figures, and the type-scenes involved. Without this comparative lens, one might miss topics that ancient readers would have noticed; but with it, one may see textual features from a larger thematic angle.

That being said, each issue must be evaluated on its own terms, for parallels have no meaning in and of themselves. They are but data in the hands of an interpreter. Moreover, comparative analysis does not diminish the value of the literatures being studied. The Song of Songs is surely a unique composition, unlike other love lyrics in the ancient world. But as we attempt to understand it on its own terms, it seems crucial to cultivate our literary competence by viewing it alongside other cultural examples of its time.

EGYPT We shall turn first to the secular love poems of ancient Egypt.[26] The most significant collections of these lyrics derive from papyri datable to the eighteenth to twentieth dynasties (fifteenth to twelfth century B.C.E.). This puts them at the temporal margin of ancient Israelite culture, and apparently prior to its literary practices. And yet there are some things to consider. Repeatedly, there are dialogues of celebration and longing between two youths, often portrayed with the epithets of brother and sister. Sometimes they speak to one another directly, and sometimes the dialogue is internal (with self-reference or reference to friends). In addition, sometimes a female speaker awaits the advent of the beloved to her home, expressing love fantasies or love-sickness; and on other occasions the beloved is described via a series of bodily features, accentuating their beauty through similes and related figures of speech. Throughout, the mood of desire is both robust and palpable. As one commentator put it, there is a "concrete realism" to these depictions and dialogues.[27]

Let us explore examples from this Egyptian love poetry side by side with similar features in the Song. The parallels help sharpen our literary gaze as readers of ancient love lyrics.

1. *I will set my face upon the outer door. Behold, my brother is coming to me . . . my heart is not silent*[28] // "I was asleep . . . Behold, my beloved knocks . . . [saying]: 'Open to me my sister, my lovely and pure one' . . . My heart was stirred for him" (Song 5:2, 4).

2. *Whenever you are seen in every glance, it is more splendid for me than eating and drinking*[29] // "O kiss me . . . for your love is more delightful than wine" (Song 1:2).

3. *I will go speedily to the brother, [and then] kiss him in front of the companions*[30] // "If only it could be as with a brother . . . then I could kiss you in the street and no one would despise me" (Song 8:1).

4. *He causes a sickness to seize me*[31] // "I am so love-sick" (Song 2:4).

5. *Would that you might come to the sister quickly, as a gazelle leaping across the desert*[32] // "Behold, my beloved comes, leaping over the mountains, bounding over the hills . . . like a gazelle" (Song 2:8–9).

6. [*The sister . . .*] *is beautiful of eyes that stare. Her lips that speak are sweet. She has not a word too much. One high of neck, one bright of breasts, real lapis lazuli is her hair. Her arms excel gold; her fingers are like lotus flowers . . . her thighs extend her perfection. Her step is pleasing when she treads upon the earth*[33] // "O now, you are fair my lovely, so fair, your eyes are like doves behind your veil. Your teeth are like a flock of goats. . . . Your lips are like crimson thread, your mouth is lovely. . . . Your neck is like the Tower of David. . . . Your breasts are like two fawns . . . browsing among the lilies" (Song 4:1–5); "Your feet are lovely in sandals. . . . Your rounded thighs are like jewels. . . . Your neck is like a tower of ivory, your eyes like pools in Heshbon" (7:2, 4–5).

Such comparisons are sufficient to highlight similar conventions of love discourse. Notable among these external features are the use of fraternal rubrics to depict the female (she is called a "sister" in both cultures), and of gazelles to indicate the swift advent of the loved one. Looking to more personal states, one will note how speakers

in these lyrics express subjective desire through interior monologue and public discourse; or how states of emotional weakness or expectation are formulated with the dynamics of erotic ardor (like love-sickness or inner turmoil). A mixture of the external and internal features comes to the fore in the ways that characters present the loved one's appearance. For the loving gaze, physical features are depicted via similes. Limbs of the body are compared with elements of the world, which are infused with subjective feelings. Literary devices focus or express these emotions, which vibrate with the distinct sensibilities of each culture. A comparative perspective helps make one a better reader, honing attentiveness to how certain type-scenes (like the appearance of a lover at the door) appear in different cultures.

MESOPOTAMIA We turn now to old Mesopotamian lyrics, specifically to love songs that have no cultic features, but are litanies of desire set in the world of nature.[34] Here, literary figures convey erotic elements by innuendo. Indeed, in many cases the terms seem to depict external actions. But on closer inspection, these are actually conventions employed to portray topics of desire. These formulations shed light on several features in the Song, which likewise seem to mean more than they say. I again present the parallels side by side:

1. *You who bloom in beauty, to the garden you go down, to the garden of fragrance go down*[35] // "Arouse O north wind.... Blow upon my garden that its fragrances may spread. Let my love come to his garden" (Song 4:16).

2. *I went down to the garden of your love*;[36] *she seeks the beautiful garden of your charms*; *the king goes down to the garden*[37] // "I have come to my garden, my sister, my bride"; "My beloved has gone down to his garden, to the bed of spices" (Song 5:1; 6:2).

3. *Your caresses are sweet; growing luxuriantly is your fruit*;[38] *may my eyes behold the plucking of your fruit*[39] // "I have come to my garden.... I have plucked my myrrh and spices"; "I went down to the nut garden... to see the budding of the vale" (Song 5:1; 6:11).

4. *Let us eat of your strength*[40]// "Let my beloved come to his garden and eat of its luscious fruits"; "I have come to my garden, my sister... eaten my honey and honeycomb" (Song 4:16; 5:1).

Quite evidently, the language of love in these Mesopotamian lyrics is artfully allusive and erotically suggestive. There is both a play of prudence and the use of certain figures to provoke the imagination. Attentive to such matters, a reader of the Song may now perceive this text with a keener eye, open to its euphemistic features. For example, in the foregoing sources, gardens are the figures for the settings of love; and eating or plucking its fruit conveys the garden's joys. It is not a reach to intuit erotic hints in these formulations. To be sure, one must evaluate each instance separately; but the overall value of noting these similarities may help cure some blind spots due to latter-day prudishness or misunderstanding. Indeed, similar euphemisms occur elsewhere in Scripture and in rabbinic sources as a matter of course.[41]

Getting Love Language Right

VOCABULARY AND SYNTAX To more fully understand the love lyrics in the Song of Songs, let us return to its vocabulary and syntax. Attending to the styles and conventions of the discourse has helped frame certain literary features and focus attention on themes and variations. But the words and verbal forms are a text's primary pivots, which one must get right in order to put it in linguistic and historical context.

Vocabulary. We noted earlier that the Song contains several layers of Hebrew, and that this has implications for the history of its composition. We now present some of these matters in more detail, beginning with the earliest evidence. This comes from the old Canaanite (Ugaritic) influences on biblical poetics and vocabulary. It shows up in single words and word pairs found in similar poetic parallelisms. Indeed, more than a dozen word pairs found in the Song also occur in the Canaanite sources.[42] For example, the Hebrew pairs *yaday* // *'etzbe'otay*, "my hands" // "my fingers" in Song 5:5, and *sadeh* // keramim, "field // "vineyards" in 7:12–13, all have exact Ugaritic parallels. Given the numerous linguistic overlaps between the latter and old biblical poetry, such parallels are hardly surprising. At the same time, many other word combinations are more rare—and thus highlight the close links with this earlier epic literature. Notably, precise Ugaritic parallels are attested for the rare pairing of *kevutzotav* with *taltallim*, "his/its locks are curly," in 5:11; and for *'arseinu* // *beiyteinu*, "our bed" // "our home," in 1:16–17.[43]

Syntax. In addition to these poetic pairs, many poetic sequences are shared by the two cultures, showing a shared stylistic background (with roots in the fourteenth to thirteenth century B.C.E.). For example, three separate phrases may be varied to produce a sequential heightening for literary effect. The basic form is: line *x* has a noun plus a direct address; line *y* uses the same noun plus a second-person verb; and line *z* replaces the preceding verb and noun with synonyms, while inverting their sequence. This pattern occurs in 4:8 ("With me, from Lebanon, O bride // With me, from Lebanon, come // leap up from the summit of Amana," etc.). This form is of Ugaritic vintage, with exact parallels in the old epic literature.[44] Such similarities point to the strong stylistic influence of this Canaanite literature, with other parallels in the liturgical poetry of Psalms. There was evidently much literary crossover. Perhaps such influences emerged through shared cultural and diplomatic contact in the early Israelite monarchy.

This shared thesaurus of language and styles in the ancient Near East is only part of the linguistic story bearing on the Song. Of equal significance are its distinctive features. More than fifty words (nouns and verbs) occur *only* in this short text (117 verses).[45] But if such features are unknown to us, the Song clearly presumes such knowledge in its audience. For example, the maiden calls herself a "guardian" of a vineyard (1:6; also 8:11–12); and her partner refers to jewelry formed in "plaited wreaths," "strings," and "spangles" of silver (1:10–11). Such terms are not otherwise known. Many unique terms refer to the budding of plants and the processes of nature at different times (2:11, 13, and 15); and a number of spices and architectural terms also have no known parallel. Such terms reveal the paucity of our knowledge about the cultural repertoire of ancient Israel, and make us realize just how limited our compe-

tence is to determine elements that most ancient readers would have known (and certainly the Song presumes such knowledge).

Furthermore, some two dozen terms otherwise unattested in the Hebrew Bible are well known from later linguistic fields like Aramaic and Mishnaic Hebrew. Phrases such as "peek through the lattices" (2:9), or "your navel is a moon-shaped vessel, may it never lack wine" (7:3), are composed of terms known to us from later sources. This suggests that they reflect features of the language that emerged or developed only after the exile (after the sixth–fifth century B.C.E.; see commentary for details). In addition, the Song includes Persian words, most famously the term *pardes*, "orchard" (4:13; it is also found in Neh. 2:8 and Eccles. 2:5, works from the latest biblical stratum), presumably postdating the Persian political domination of the region, which began in 540 B.C.E.

How can we understand all this?

The Song has been affected by several linguistic confluences.[46] Some of these (like Aramaic words or forms) hint at a vernacular that was increasingly influenced by the Aramaic language from the time of Jeremiah (in the late seventh century B.C.E.).[47] Others (like terms and styles attested in Mishnaic Hebrew centuries later) provide evidence for the emergence of a rabbinic vocabulary from the early postexilic period (i.e., the sixth to fifth century B.C.E., or later). These complex matters—to be discussed in the commentary—attest to the long history of composition and linguistic influences on the Song of Songs.[48]

The dialogues and descriptions found in the Song convey literary conventions and features whose meanings would have readily resonated with the ancient audience—for there is no hint of an archaic (or archaizing) style in the Song, or any sense that its wording was simplified for more popular comprehension. But what was accessible to the ancient audience must now be retrieved via careful deliberation. The modern reader must cultivate a new (second-order) competence from the older (now opaque) formulations. Modern meanings and expectations must be held in check, so that the full impact of the ancient text may be properly understood.

The Many Poetics of Love in Jewish Tradition

The Song of Songs has been sung and studied in every generation and every period of Jewish religious life and thought. It is the great songbook of the Jewish soul. The love lyrics of this Song are thus the font of Jewish creativity over the ages. Over the centuries, four major types of scriptural interpretation developed. Broadly speaking, these four types focused respectively on: 1. the plain sense; 2. communal and religious import; 3. personal and spiritual value; and 4. metaphysical secrets. These concerns developed in different circles and circumstances. Occasionally they were intertwined in certain presentations. But suddenly in the high Middle Ages (eleventh to thirteenth century C.E.) some groups began to prize one reading over another, or arranged them in a hierarchy—often moving from the straightforward sense to more speculative ones.

An exemplar of the fourfold hierarchy of meanings is evident in the Torah commentary of Rabbeinu Baḥya ben Asher, a Spanish scholar who knew and cited contemporary mystical traditions (fl. mid-thirteenth to mid-fourteenth century).[49] He presents a distinct scaffolding of traditions—moving from the text's plain sense, to its midrashic interpretations, to formulations of philosophical wisdom, and often climaxing with hints of mystical teachings. This hierarchy of senses reflects not only Baḥya's own proclivities, but also a new cultural interest in formulating such a hierarchy. (At this same time, a similar attempt to organize biblical knowledge and classify orders of scriptural sense developed in the Christian world. This had profound implications for the readings of the Song of Songs in its monastic schools and public preaching.[50]) A similar range of meanings began to appear in Jewish interpretations of the Song during this period, reflecting inner-Jewish values and exegetical developments.[51]

This fourfold typology will structure our approach to the Song. We thus offer a brief characterization of each type below, and follow this with a fuller account of each one's poetics and topics. The commentary is built on this exegetical foundation.

PESHAT This word became the standard term for the text's plain sense, with its focus on the grammatical meaning of terms and phrases *in their given context*. This sense is therefore not the "literal" meaning of a passage, since the plain sense includes meanings based on figurative expressions. No thoughtful reader would presume that similes or metaphors should be taken literally, for that could often lead to nonsensical results. When the beloved male likens the maiden to a "mare in Pharaoh's chariots" (1:9), no reader would take this literally, and no one would interpret the maiden's self-description as a "lily of the valleys" in factual terms (2:1). Rather, one realizes that many literary devices are employed to convey intense personal feelings. Context and mood always set the terms of interpretation, even where that leads to possibilities that a literary figure does double duty as a euphemism. Some readers may therefore push back from such conclusions, focusing on the imagery in ways that soften or bypass the erotic charge.

The *peshat* reading is the matrix of all that follows. There is no question that at this level the Song speaks about a maiden and her beloved, and presents their loving dialogues and encounters throughout the land. This guides the reader in construing any particular discourse or event in their relationship.

DERASH This is the term used for the meanings developed through midrashic exegesis. Here the ancient sages (and those who followed their lead) pondered the meaning of Scripture and discovered there theological, historical, and ethical matters reflective of their religious values and worldview. Here too was the closest reading of the words and phrases of the Bible, discovering new and striking meaning by comparing the words in one passage with those in another. For students of *derash*, the context of meaning is *Scripture as a whole*. And this was a central feature of the ancient rabbinic interpretations of the Song. All the words, phrases, and topics are interpreted in the light of Scripture as an organic unity—most especially the link between the

Song's language and the Torah. To establish these links and new meanings, the words of the Song are often broken down into new components, and then related to historical or theological concerns not stated directly in the text. The literary figures in the Song are thus deemed allegories of topics suggested or depicted in the Torah. The task of exegesis is to make this explicit.

Inevitably, different sages understood the Song's intentions or possibilities differently. Thus the *derash* interpretation offers readers a bounty of exegetical possibilities. Nonetheless, all rabbinic readers started with the presumption that the Song's maiden was a personification of the people of Israel (sometimes as individuals, sometimes as the collectivity), and that her beloved was a personification of God. This is at the core of all *derash* interpretations.

REMEZ This third level of reading was founded on philosophical interests and concerns. It deemed the words of Scripture to be hints or clues to such thematic content. On this basis, the Song was read as a philosophical allegory of the intellectual or spiritual life. The Song guides seekers of wisdom to their goals—if they know the hermeneutical keys for its interpretation. Finding these keys and knowing the secret teachings is a matter of craft and training. They cannot be discovered on the surface of Scripture in any straightforward manner, but can be perceived only in the literary figures *if* one already knows the underlying philosophical template (derived from philosophical tradition). That template is the esoteric meaning of Scripture. Typically it includes teachings about the divine origin of the human intellect or soul, and the techniques necessary for their perfection. Thus Scripture is both a book of public instruction (through its *peshat* and *derash* meanings) and a teaching for the philosophical elite. At its *remez* core, Scripture is a philosophical allegory for the mind's or soul's perfection.

Jewish philosophers deem the Song to be an ultimate expression of this secret wisdom. Depending on the allegorical template involved, the maiden could be the human intellect or the soul, engaged in a search for its divine ideal; and this divine ideal could be God in the form of the Perfect Intellect or Soul, which is personified in the Song by the youth. Thus the maiden who seeks her beloved throughout the land represents the human self striving for perfection; and the beloved who seeks her in turn, and compliments her beauty, represents God's desire for the perfection of the human being and encouragement for the seeker of truth. Likewise, budding plants might hint at the development of a person's inner virtues, or the attempt to cultivate spiritual traits and transform one's earthly nature.

Different interpreters find diverse ways to construe this hidden teaching. But all adepts of the *remez* agree that these truths are concealed in the external formulations of Scripture—the Song of Songs, in particular.

SOD A fourth approach to Scripture is mystical in aim and method. It considers the text's surface sense to be hinting at esoteric elements or events in the divine realms. Thus the entirety of Scripture is deemed a deep symbolic encoding of the most hidden and supernal truths (and reading Scripture appropriately would inspire a mystic under-

standing of these matters). As a work believed to be a most special symbolic expression of Scripture, the words of the Song (the "holy of holies" of Scripture) were read as symbolic prisms of such supernal realities. The true subject of the work (the Beloved) is thus the Godhead in all the mysterious ways Divinity constitutes or expresses one dynamic unity. Hence the Song's many dialogues and figures are all symbolic personifications of the modalities whereby Divinity seeks to realize its own inherent harmony through love. In the unfathomable depths of divine reality—which precedes our world and transcends it—creative energies pulse in inconceivably diverse combinations. These are supernal dialogues of love and longing. The Song of Songs is a verbalization in human terms of this profound truth. Thus, reading the Song is a most sacred act, which might enable the adept to ascend the spiritual worlds and conjoin with the divine truths that the text symbolizes.

From the perspective of *sod*, the Song's primary characters (the Beloved and the Maiden) are male and female modalities of Divinity. In a further mystical manner, the people Israel were believed to have a special bond with dimensions of this divine matrix—the female figure, especially. Thus their religious actions and spiritual lives take on infinite significance within the divine totality. For Jewish mystics, the *sod* is the highest of all exegetical levels and its spiritual core.

According to one famous analogy (recorded in the Zohar): *peshat* is the outer (textual) garment of Scripture; *derash* is its (more concealed cultural) body (with its theologies and laws); *remez* is the (inner) soul of this "textual being" (with hints of religious quest and truth); and *sod* is the (supernal) supersoul (of Scripture, its ultimate divine dimension).[52]

In Jewish tradition, these four types of interpretation—***peshat***, ***derash***, ***remez***, and ***sod***—are known by the (slightly scrambled) acronym of ***PaRDeS***. I present below a fuller synopsis of these modes of reading as they pertain to the Song of Songs, focusing chiefly on matters of content and poetics. (In the excursus I take up this subject again in a more detailed manner, and explore subtypes of these modes and their great diversity. This will reveal the extraordinary range of interpretations and ideas perceived in the Song over the millennia.) Most interpreters of the past melded the legacy of meanings into one or another preferred sense. The commentary in this volume is different. Building upon the history of interpretation, I cull themes and concerns from the entire legacy of the past to use as the foundation of a modern, multifaceted reformulation.

The poetics of the four main types of interpretation are considered under the following categories: (1) characters of the plot; (2) speech and discourse; (3) stylistic characteristics and types of ambiguity; and (4) coherence of phraseology and plot.

Peshat

Characters. The text's characters emerge through the various discourses and events. The main female figure is called by her male beloved "fair" and "darling" (*raʿyah*; a word that evokes "shepherdess"), and "sister" and "bride"; but also by the epithets "dove" and "purity." When the maiden speaks of herself, she uses the epithets "rose"

and "lily." However, when she speaks directly to the male she calls him "beloved," but also (more circumspectly) "the king" or "the one my soul loves."[53] The maiden uses these same terms when she refers to him with her friends at various points in the plot. Her companions play the role of intimates to whom she confides feelings or reports events, and she calls them "daughters of Jerusalem," as distinct from other women who are simply called "maidens." The youth's fellow shepherds are referred to as "friends" by both him and her. (They are on the margins of events; only once do some fellows actually speak, referring to her as "the Shulammite"; 7:1.) Subjective feelings are expressed by the addition of the personal pronoun "my" to these forms of address. This usage marks the emotions of exclusivity or the assertions of possessiveness that characterize the love between the Song's main figures.

Discourse. Discourse in the Song is both direct and indirect, and also sometimes self-referential (including interior discourse) or without reference (spoken to nameless others or as private exclamations). There are also instances of reported indirect discourse (the maiden speaks of her beloved to others, sometimes even citing statements or dialogues). These kinds of speech must be discerned in each instance, as they often shift to different topics or venues. The reader must repeatedly envision the scenes before the inner eye, and imagine their vocal tone from the content. No narrator guides the plot or marks the diverse interventions; it is not always clear when one speech cycle ends and another begins. Over the ages, readers have segmented these units differently. The Masoretes (in the ninth to tenth centuries) grouped the work's 117 verses into twenty units, three of which were separated by a major ("open") paragraph break.[54] Medieval Christian tradition (from the thirteenth century) used chapter divisions and divided the Song into eight chapters. But this division tallies only once with the rabbinic subsections (between 3:10 and 4:1). Modern interpreters have proposed many more divisions, in accordance with their literary taste and sense of style. The commentary will consider the subunits of meaning and the integration of cycles.

Poetics. We can get a sense of the book's poetics through a brief study of 2:1–2. The maiden speaks first, and her beloved responds. She says, "I am a rose of Sharon, a lily of the valleys" (2:1); and he answers, "Like a lily among thorns, so is my darling among the maidens" (v. 2). The maiden opens with a personal "I" voice, identifying herself with flowers. These metaphoric self-ascriptions intensify her delicacy; they do not specify any feature of her nature. (The pronoun, which is used once, binds the two images.)

This discourse of love just happens, without any introduction; it is presumably intended to be evocative and invite the youth's response—which he does, taking up the second flower in his own simile ("like a lily"). She is like a delicate flower among bramble, and thus distinguished among other maidens. We thus have a chained dialogue, both succinct and instructive: what she is in her own estimation is extended by his evaluation. The couple thus speaks directly to one another through figurative indirection. Elsewhere, when they depict each other's bodies, simple similes are the rule (and add no comparative judgments). These have the form "your *x* is like *y*," or "like *x* is your *y*." Metaphors such as "you have dove's eyes" (4:1) or "your navel is a round

[moon-shaped] goblet" (7:3) elide the comparative element and thus heighten the praise's force (the form is often "your *x* is a *y*"). Commentators frequently suppose an implicit comparative dimension in these cases, palpably softening the literary figure. Confronted by these metaphors, readers must ponder the poetic ambiguity.

Ambiguity. Various types of ambiguity can make the text difficult to construe. These often occur in love-talk. For example, when the maiden says, "My beloved is to me a bag of myrrh, lying between my breasts" (1:13), we wonder what this means. Is the first clause a metaphor or a simile? If a simile, she imagines him to be "like" a fragrant sachet on her chest—a kind of physical expression of his love kept near her heart. But if the expression is a metaphor, he apparently holds her in an embrace—and thus it is a literary expression of their physical intimacy. The difference is significant.

And further: one may also wonder whether the verb *yaliyn*, "lying," refers to the beloved or the bag of myrrh. It could be either. Added to the ambiguity of verbal subject is an ambiguity of tense. The verb might refer to a present or to a future action ("he lies" or "he will lie")—or even the past, for this form resembles an archaic past-tense mode.

These ambiguities produce a "strangeness" that enriches the text's poetic character. This ambiguity can be pondered but its meaning can hardly be proved decisively. As one writer aptly put it, "Strangeness . . . arouses wonder when we do not understand; aesthetic imagination when we do."[55]

Coherence. As we have seen, determining the text's coherence is often a complicated matter—whether because of the particular terms or phrases (as when metaphors may be hidden similes); or because of ambiguities in the discourse (as with euphemism or double entendre); or even because of the arrangement of speech units (and deciding how they may interrelate). Readers must give close attention to such factors and try to sort them out. Literary analysis tries to analyze and resolve the various poetic elements. Yet we must also respect the ambiguities and complexities as probably deliberate—and not rush to quick or simplified solutions.

Derash

Characters. Rabbinic (midrashic) readings of the Song make use of Scripture as a whole, with special emphasis on the Torah and its traditions. Thus the Song's main characters are God and the people Israel, personified by the beloved and the maiden, respectively. Through these central actors, the entire history of Israel contained in the Five Books of Moses is allegorically represented in the Song's imagery. It was only a matter of properly decoding the literary figures, and finding the true (best-fitting) interpretative keys to unlock the writer's (Solomon's) figurative code—a matter of ongoing discovery. Various collections of midrash preserve many examples of how the sages plumbed the Song's depths for historical and theological insights. Their diversity of opinion (and technique) provides examples of legitimate possibilities. Today's readers can study them to learn the secrets of the Song and gauge new ways to extend the rich range of interpretations.

Based on this allegorical approach, the "kisses" desired by the maiden could signify the words of God given to Israel at Mount Sinai; and the gazelle that "leaped" over the mountains could signify God Himself, who "skipped" over the centuries and shortened the time of servitude forecast in olden times.[56] Similarly, the beloved whose name was like "decanted aromatic oil" was interpreted as father Abraham, who diffused knowledge of God to the nations; and the person who asked the beloved, "How will you rest your flock at noontime?"[57] was taken to be Moses addressing God, wanting to know how God would provide guidance for the nation during the exile to come. Other persons and topics signify people or nations in the course of Israel's history. For example, the maidens who respond to fragrance, and the companions who desire to learn about the beloved, refer to potential proselytes (in the first case) and those who want to know more about the God to whom Israel is so faithful (in the second).

Discourse. The Song's discourses are reinterpreted allegorically to dramatize its new subjects (God and Israel). Sometimes short fragments of a dialogue are used; at other times longer units are developed. Sometimes a given phrase or parallel image might refer to more than one episode or topic. In such instances, these linguistic features or stylistic doublets would be interpreted as distinct historical events. The verses in 2:1–2, cited earlier, are a case in point. As noted, the maiden begins the dialogue between herself and the youth by saying that she is a "*ḥavatzelet* of Sharon." For the sages, these clauses encode multiple references to Israel and her faithfulness to God. This was done through puns that evoked new topics, and through exegetical procedures that made the seemingly straightforward terms of the Song strange and multivalent. Thus, punning on the word *ḥavatzelet* (and breaking it up into new components), we are told that Israel deemed herself "special" (*ḥavivah*) to God, who had "protected" (*ḥavui*) them when the Egyptians chased them to the Sea; and in thanksgiving she built a sacral Shrine (through the skill of Bezalel = *Be-tzal-el*) "in" (*be-*) whose "shade" (*tzeil*) He (God, *El*) would be "hidden" (*ḥavui*) from view (see SongsR at v. 1). Eliciting new verbal features from the verse's second phrase (which states that the maiden is a "lily of the valley," a *shoshanat ha-ʿamaqim*), the people also believed themselves beloved of God for other expressions of religious faithfulness—like studying (*she-shonim*) the Torah and its oral traditions even in the "depths" (*ʿamaqim*) of exile and persecution (ibid.). These multiple teachings transform the Song's language into new theological statements—each with its own coherence.

Coherence. The coherence of the discourses in *derash* readings is thus not the straightforward sense of a scriptural passage, or its relationship to some assumed external reality (the reality of the Song's characters). It is rather the coherence of new rabbinic units of instruction, drawn from the text's verbal features. With respect to the Song, the new allegorical explications (produced via creative puns and other exegetical techniques) constituted the thematic coherence of a unit. If the main focus of interpretation was to demonstrate Israel's special relationship to God (as seen above), the text could be mined for numerous possibilities that, altogether, made up the full coherence of the passage. Coherence was thus not a matter of syntactic logic (as is the case with the *peshat*), but a matter of cultural and theological significance.

Poetics. The various ways the sages unpack the Song's contents constitute its new, exegetically produced poetics. Hence the Song may have poetic layers: the primary (straightforward) layer of the figures, as articulated by the primary characters (the beloved and the maiden), and the secondary (allegorically concealed) layer of the figures, as articulated by the sages through the Song's new personas (God and Israel). For example, the youth's response to the maiden's self-depiction (he says that she is like a lily among thorns) is reinterpreted to highlight how the people Israel were repeatedly distinguished in their diverse historical settings. According to one sage, the figure of a lily among thorns referred to the matriarch Rebekah, who lived among a family of cheats (Laban and her brothers). She remained distinctive among them and was eventually extracted from their home to become a mother of the nation (SongsR 2.i.2). Another teacher interpreted the image in terms of Israel in Egypt, which was a thorn in the side of the people until God delivered them from their servitude. According to an old tradition, Israel merited this deliverance for having remained loyal to her heritage: she kept her olden dress and hairstyle, and maintained her native language and original names. These were all deemed exceptional virtues in a hostile environment, by virtue of which the people merited the Exodus.

The second case (Egypt and the Exodus) is distinct from the first one (Rebekah among her brethren); but both are now editorially combined and constitute a typological pair: the first case (Rebekah) prefiguring the second (the Exodus)—thus indicating how events in the lives of the progenitors of the nation (here a matriarch) provide the prototype for a national event (the deliverance of Israel). Other events are added to the anthological units, culminating in one that anticipates the redemption to come (called *maḥar*, "tomorrow"). All these distinct texts now assume a new cultural coherence through this editorial collection, revealing historical patterns and theological similarities that would not otherwise be seen. For *derash*, the Song's figures are thus much more than aesthetic tropes. They are parables encoding a thick cultural poetics. Through their creative interpretation, the sages imply that all this is inherent in Scripture.

Remez

The term *remez* refers to the philosophical interpretation of Scripture. It presumed that Scripture's surface sense contains "hints" or "allusions" (two glosses of the word *remez*) to a hidden or concealed content. To detect these "cues" requires both a skilled eye and informed mind, inspired by the belief that profound intellectual teachings were secreted into the public words of Scripture for the sake of persons on a higher philosophical quest. Such wisdom was not for everyone. Even able-minded philosophical seekers had to proceed with care and not rush the process through spiritual haste, incomplete preparation, or incorrect judgment. Why? Because the topics of revelation and philosophy were not always in clear accord, and the divine revelation was primary, the fundamental primer or basis for all spiritual and intellectual development. One had to build a philosophical life upon the shoulders of Scripture and Tradition, and not let one's ardor for personal perfection get in the way, clouding the profound meaning.

It was thus spiritually and intellectually dangerous to think that one could leap over the primary sense of Scripture or ignore the pedagogical processes of philosophy itself. Adepts of the *remez* believed that Moses—who was both a perfect prophet and a true philosopher—understood these complexities and took care in his formulations of Scripture to keep God's secret teachings properly concealed. Only the wise—duly trained and prepared—could decode this esoteric content and properly employ it.

The Song of Songs was also deemed a work of most hidden wisdom; and it was believed that Solomon (the wisest of the wise) encoded philosophical hints in the love lyrics of his work. These matters were kept secret for generations. But suddenly in the twelfth to thirteenth century various commentators brought these hints to light and made explicit the correlations between these esoteric matters and the Song's language. Through interpretation, this love song was shown to be a guidebook for those who sought the true love of God via intellectual or spiritual perfection. The main characters and events of the drama were adjusted accordingly.

Characters. Diverse philosophical traditions circulated in antiquity and the Middle Ages, and these informed the identification of the Song's characters. In some cases, the male beloved was deemed to be God or an angelic personification of a perfect mind; the female figure was deemed to personify the human intellect seeking to acquire intellectual perfection, or the human soul seeking spiritual purity by alignment with God. In other instances, the female speaker was seen as the Torah personified, desiring devotion; she invited and exhorted the (male) seeker to cultivate his traits though proper spiritual practices.

The Song's dialogues thus became various attempts by God or Torah to encourage and support a person's spiritual or intellectual development. Since the path was often obscure or difficult (because the soul felt ignorant about how to proceed or because one felt under the sway of strong contrary impulses), there was need for constant spiritual supervision and encouragement. Adepts of the philosophical *remez* presumed that the text's esoteric level took these challenges into account and offered guidance. They believed that the Song's hidden teaching was addressed to the individual who obeys the Law but feels all too human much of the time. The content of the Song, appropriately interpreted, was plumbed in the trust that it could guide the seeking soul—stage by stage.

Discourse. The Song's discourses offer numerous opportunities (via philosophical allegory) to instruct the student both in details positive and negative: the positive ones being the scale of values or procedures necessary for persons striving to attain mental and moral growth; the negative ones the impediments that can divert or disrupt one's progress. The exegetical task was to find the precise allegorical correlations between the text and its diverse philosophical meanings. The goal was achieved when the correspondences between the literary figures and intellectual content was deemed established and sensible in light of the philosophical program to which one was committed.

The allegorical sense unfolds via various exegetical strategies, all keyed to the particular philosophical template presumed by the interpreter. Consider the two discourses discussed earlier from 2:1 and 2 (the maiden's self-depiction as a "lily of the valley" and

the youth's praise of her as a "lily among thorns"). With respect to the first instance (2:1), R. Joseph ibn Aqnin states: "The speaking I [of '*I* am a lily'] praises her situation; and she glorifies herself and her deeds that have overcome the forces [of one's raw nature]—for these forces serve her and she is their master." And with respect to the second passage (2:2), he continues: the words "Sharon" and "valleys" (*'amaqim*) refer to what is hidden of these forces in the body, in its hidden depths (*ma'amaqav*), and what has emerged through [their transformation into] good actions. She also announces that these forces, which she called "Sharon" and "valleys," are her own lilies and her roses [i.e., the good produce of her inner state]—and she is their spiritual quality."

Poetics and Coherence. In this first case, the maiden's self-depiction is transformed into her account of personal progress. She announced, via plays on the Song's language, that she has overcome her natural state, composed of inner forces and potencies, transforming them into positive outcomes and deeds. The wordplays (between the Song and its philosophical sense) become poetic figures for the intellectual and spiritual development being praised. This is the overall philosophical content projected into the Song. Through this allegorical template, the components of the phrase assume a new coherence—as distinct features of the developing self. Coherences can also be seen among the various levels of the Song's meaning. Commenting first on the passage's verbal meaning, Ibn Aqnin notes that the flowers mentioned by the maiden are beautiful and have a lovely fragrance (*reiaḥ*). He then adduces various rabbinic interpretations that teach by analogy: like these flowers, the people of Israel produce a lovely "fragrance" (*reiaḥ*) when they perform God's commandments. At the philosophical level, the commentator brings these senses together and adds a new virtue. The adept (the maiden) is deemed most praiseworthy for having transformed her natural endowment into good actions through her inner spirituality. This reference to "her spirituality" (*ruḥaniyatiha*) verbally alludes (via the slightly different Judeo-Arabic term) to the "fragrance" in the preceding interpretations. It thus sets up a thematic progression among the levels of interpretation: starting with the natural world (and its aromas); moving to the cultural world (and its spiritual deeds); and concluding at the supreme level of spiritual self-transformation (and its cultivation of inner powers). The result is a poetic coherence of the whole sequence of interpretations.

When Ibn Aqnin turns to 2:2, he employs the same allegorical strategies and the same philosophical template. But since the speaker is now the youth, he interprets the passage to be the praise of the Active Intellect (the divine male element) for the human intellect (of the adept, represented by the maiden), and for her increasing dominance over the physical powers (the thorns) of the self. This statement transforms the literary figure from a simile of praise (the maiden is a lily among thorns) into a philosophical teaching about the relationship between the physical and intellectual parts of the self. This idea connects with the previous discussion about the maiden and her development. But such connections (between the verses) are not necessary for philosophical allegory to work. Each phrase or sentence can stand on its own terms. It is necessary only for these units to fit into the overall philosophical matrix of ideas believed latent in the text.

Sod

The mystical "secrets" of Scripture stretch the mind to its limits, because they claim to speak about topics beyond human understanding in any ordinary sense; namely, about God's self-revelation in supernal dimensions beyond space and time. This being so, there is no way that one may establish any interpretative links between the worldly symbols that occur in Scripture and the ultimate, other-worldly divine truths they encode on the basis of the received formulations of Scripture alone. One requires some disclosure of the Supernal Matrix—of which Scripture is merely a human distillation—so that their true links might be perceived through exegesis and inner vision. Such revelations from otherworldly sources was the esoteric wisdom guarded by and cultivated within mystic circles.[58] Paradoxically, the mystic Tradition (or Symbolic Code) precedes sacred Scripture (the symbolic iterations)—not only because this esoteric Tradition refers to matters that precede the creation and their symbolic embodiments in the text, but also because only through this Tradition can Scripture's *sod* be comprehended to any human degree. According to mystical sources, these esoteric traditions were transmitted orally and "in a whisper," and only to disciples who could be trusted for their piety and spiritual character.[59]

The most profound mystery was the emergence of Divinity from inconceivable depths—deemed "Without Limit" (*'Ein Sof*)—and the eternal emanation of Divinity through ten gradations (called *sefirot*). These gradations are not "outside God" in any sense, but modalities of the spiritual vitality of God in God's most fundamental forms and configurations. The highest dimension was often called the Crown (*Keter*) of this divine realm; and it contained All Being in the most spiritual of modes. The lowest gradation was designated the Diadem (*'Atarah*) or Bride (*Kallah*) of this supernal Kingdom (*Malkhut*); and it contained the totality of the divine modes in a more refracted form. Between the highest and lowest realms were spiritual structures that mediated and dispersed the divine reality. The topmost were deemed intellectual modes of the divine reality and called Wisdom (*Ḥokhmah*) and Understanding (*Binah*); below them were key value spheres called Grace or Mercy (*Ḥesed*) and Judgment or Severity (*Gevurah*). The main "Body" of the Divine Person was called Splendor (*Tif'eret*), and it expressed modes of spiritual and physical fecundity through a generative structure called Foundation (*Yesod*).

This entire divine domain is the spiritual model of the created world and of the Torah revealed at Sinai. Thus the Torah is a spiritual manifestation of the primordial emanation of God in the most supernal realms, such that all the persons and events mentioned in it symbolize (in human terms) their spiritual correlates in this ultimate divine dimension. For example, the creation of the world and the seven days of the week symbolize aspects of the most supernal emanation (from Grace to the Kingdom); the three patriarchs symbolize configurations of values within the divine hierarchy (Grace, Judgment, and Splendor); the Tabernacle and Holy Temple represent other structures of spiritual energy, and so on. An esoteric reading of every word and sentence of Scripture is thus a meditation on these esoteric matters. As earthly extensions

and embodiments of this divine reality, humans can influence these hidden realms through action and meditation—the people of Israel most profoundly. Their spiritual prototype (called the Assembly of Israel, or *Keneset Yisra'el*) was associated with the tenth or lowest of the sefirotic gradations (the Bride or Kingdom). It is first mentioned in the Talmud (B. Ber. 35b); but nothing further is known of this ancient secret.[60]

Characters. Since the Song was believed to encode all the teachings and traditions of the Torah (see the discussion of *derash*, above), mystics believed that it encoded all of the esoteric truths of Scripture as well. The principle difference between the Song and the Torah was that the Song was composed in its own symbolic key. This meant that all the Song's personalities and dialogues refer to events of love in the most supernal realms. Accordingly, the Song's central characters—deemed Solomon (*Shelomoh*) and his bride—are, respectively, a modality or manifestation of God (called "the King, the Master of Peace," *shalom*), and Israel on High (called the "Bride," *kallah*, because she was "comprised," *kelulah*, of all the superior dimensions). Because Israel on earth is connected to its heavenly form, all her actions affect the divine realm. Israel's positive religious behavior can bind her to her spiritual counterpart in heaven and, through Her, arouse divine love (in Solomon, in one of His spiritual manifestations). Correspondingly, Israel's sins can cut her off from her divine source and cause ruptures within Divinity itself. The Song of Songs encodes these and other spiritual truths through its diverse dialogues and images.

Thus the maiden's desire for the "kisses" of her beloved encode the longing of the lower divine realms (the Divine Bride = Israel) to ascend on High and conjoin with their primordial Source. The images of "oil" and "wine" similarly express profound truths about the flow of Wisdom from its supernal source. In addition, the "pavilions" and "tents" of the Song symbolize certain domains of the intradivine elements; the pure "moon" to which the Bride was likened symbolizes the reception of spiritual light from higher sources; and the maiden's "breasts" encode how Divine Wisdom nurtures the domains of Being like a primordial mother.

In many and diverse ways, the dynamics of eros expressed in the (earthly) Song were decoded as manifestations of a profound intradivine desire for the bliss of Marital Union. The imagery's boldness notwithstanding, the esoteric truths symbolized thereby were utterly spiritual and supremely transcendent.

Discourse and Coherence. As a love song within Divine Being, the Song of Songs was interpreted as expressing the longing of God (as *Shelomoh*) for *shelama' de-baiyta'*—or the harmony of all the domains of Divine Being—where love between male and female is the regular figure for such harmony and unity (ZḤ 63a). The kiss is thus the primary metaphor for conjunctions of every sort. For mystics imbued with the Song's themes and imagery, every element of divine reality (that is, every element of existence) expresses a desire to be "kissed by" (or conjoined to) the Supernal Source of All Being (Z. 2:146a–b). Many interpretations formulate this profound matter in diverse ways. Thus when the maiden depicts herself as "a rose of the valleys" (*shoshanat ha-'amaqim*), we are informed that this is the voice of the Divine Bride, symbolized as a rose, whose "six (*sheish*) leaves" constantly "change their hue" (*di-shni'at gavanha'*) from white to

red (i.e., from good to bad), and who desires to be restored to the supernal "Depths" (*ʿamiqin*) of her Ultimate Origin—called "The Most Hidden of All [or: the Hidden Source of All]"; *ʿamiqa' de-khola'*), from which the most "hidden streams [of divine sustenance] descend" (*de-naḥalin ʿamiqin nafqin*) to nourish her and (through her) all worldly existence (Z. 3:107a).

Wordplays (on *shoshanah* and *ʿamaqim*) now convey a profound mystical poetics. The terms used for earthly realities symbolically encode the most supernal matters. It is precisely this esoteric coherence that gives spiritual coherence to the Song's phrases. The multiple attempts to decode the symbolism found in the literary sources attests to the variety of insights that a given image might inspire in any mystical meditation on the Song.

In other cases, the Song's discourses convey the desire for mystical wisdom by the seekers themselves. One striking instance comes to expression in a bold reading of 1:5, "I am dark, but comely [or: I am black and beautiful]." The interpreter knows that seekers experience loss and darkness as they yearn for the light of divine truth. At such difficult times, confusion holds sway (one feels dark and lost, even as one is simultaneously aware of a higher dimension of oneself arising from the still-beautiful soul). Spiritual coherence has broken down, and the seeker needs help. "Tell me," O Beloved of my soul, "where do you dwell" (v. 7)?—where can the Source of Wisdom be found, and how may one proceed out of the morass of mental confusion? This cry of longing and despair is immediately answered (v. 8). "If you don't know" the mysteries and the path "on your own," go and seek a master—for only in this way may one find those truths which alone offer the hope of transcendent bliss and divine knowledge (ZḤ 70c). A series of subjects are then disclosed as worthy of spiritual pursuit, and hints of the path to be taken are also offered. Spiritual seekers long to dwell in the depths of divine love and "not wander" aimlessly astray, so the *sod* of the Song gives suggestions and traces a path forward.

The Song's multiple senses, as found in traditional Jewish interpretation through the ages, form the basis of the commentary, and its essentials will be reviewed again there. See further the excursus on these four levels at the back of this volume. It offers perspective on how the Song shaped Jewish thought and spiritual values over millennia, and how Jewish thought and spirituality transformed the Song into many diverse expressions of love.

The Song of Songs and Jewish Religious Practice

The study and performance of Scripture and tradition has its rhythms—daily, weekly, and annually. The recitation and study of Scripture and the enactment of prayers or rituals can be done privately and without communal involvement; but when performed in a proper public setting, with a minimal social quorum, these actions can be enhanced by special blessings and supplements, in accord with accepted norms and practices.

Every ritual community embodies the historical community of faith; thus, historical rituals and practices adapted by ongoing communities maintain and enhance this religious legacy. The recitation and performance of Scripture, and the study and enactment of its traditions, bind the generations to one another. Memory and its memorialization have ever been the thick texture of Jewish religious culture, its warp and weft.

Recitation and study of the Song of Songs has been integrated into Jewish liturgy and religious practice since late antiquity, appearing in diverse ritual settings and diverse statutory or customary forms. Over the centuries, these ritual practices varied by community. Their explanations also varied, as they were incorporated into different theological milieux.

The book is most often read during the festival of Passover and on the Sabbath day, so the following discussion will dwell on those occasions. Other ritual occasions will also be noted.

Passover

RECITATION Rules for reciting the "scroll" of Esther on (or about) the festival of Purim are spelled out in great detail in the earliest rabbinic sources (M. Meg. 1–2). In contrast, nothing is recorded from early antiquity about ritual recitation of the Song of Songs. The first known reference to its recitation is found in *Massekhet Soferim* (one of the Minor Tractates, not earlier than the eighth century C.E. in its present form; apparently composed in the Land of Israel). The times for this reading were the evenings of the seventh and eighth days of Passover, one-half read on each night (14.17).[61] The basis for standard Ashkenazi practice is first found in the *Maḥazor Vitry*, a compendium of ritual decisions and practices of the school of Rabbi Shlomoh in northern France (written in large part by R. Simḥah ben Samuel of Vitry, eleventh to twelfth century). It is written:

> One recites the scroll of the Song of Songs on the Sabbath when that occurs during the intervening days [i.e., those days between the first and second and the seventh and eighth days] of the Festival. (*Gloss 1*: But if no Sabbath occurs at this time, one recites on the seventh day of Passover.) (*Gloss 2*: Therefore we recite the Song of Songs on Passover because it refers to the redemption from Egypt; as it says, "[I have likened you...] to a mare in Pharaoh's chariots" [1:9], etc. And the entire work refers to the four exiles, if one understands [rightly]).[62]

Both the comment (by R. Simḥah) and the two glosses (by R. Isaac ben Dorbolo) indicate when the Song was ritualized and how it was related to past and ongoing Jewish history. Rabbi Shema'yah Ha-Shoshani (who lived in this region at this time, and wrote a *peshat* commentary on the Song) cites the second gloss noted above.[63] Similarly, it was the practice to recite the Song during Passover in the Mainz synagogue of R. Jacob Moellin (Maharil; sixteenth century),[64] with that recital taking place before the Torah reading (as has remained Ashkenazi custom), and "each person recited the blessing 'for the recitation of a scroll'" (a matter that later Ashkenazi authorities debated).[65] Recitation of the Song during Passover is also noted by the Spanish authority

R. David Abudirham (commonly, Abudraham; fl. 1340) as "the custom of the people... because it speaks of the redemption from Egypt—the first of Israel's servitudes; as it says, [*I have likened you...*] *to a mare in Pharaoh's chariots* (1:9)."[66] And among Persian Jews, there was a custom to recite the Song either between the *Minḥah* (Afternoon) and *ʿArvit* (Evening) prayers every day of the intervening days of Passover, or during Sabbath evenings between Passover and Shavuot.[67]

In all these communities, the recitation and study of the Song were ritual occasions to continue the obligation to speak of the redemption from Egypt, and to hope for a speedy redemption from the present exile. At such times the Targum (ancient Aramaic translation) to the Song would also have been recited (publicly) or read (individually), according to local custom. For more on the Targum to the Song of Songs, see the excursus.

PIYYUT A major engagement with the Song during Passover was via liturgical poetry (a genre called *piyyuṭ*). These poems presented the Song together with its rabbinic interpretations at various junctures of the holiday service.[68] Some of these remained part of the traditional festival prayer book (called *maḥazor*) for centuries, although they are no longer recited on a regular basis in many communities today. Notwithstanding their having fallen out of use, we possess a rich fund of materials that attests to enormous creativity, thanks especially to manuscript finds in the Cairo Genizah. One can trace diverse lines of development in these poems for more than 500 years, from the fifth to twelfth centuries in particular. Moreover, these poems extend from the Land of Israel (beginning with the great innovator of liturgical poetry, R. Yannai, and continuing with the prolific R. Eleazar Kallir in the early Byzantine period), to northern Italy and southern Ashkenaz (with such poets as R. Shlomo Ha-Bavli, R. Meshullam bar Kalonymos, R. Shimʿon bar Yitzḥak, R. Yeḥiel ben Avraham of Rome, and R. Benjamin Ha-Shelishi, among many others), in the tenth to twelfth centuries.[69]

One can hardly overstate the literary bounty, scholarship, and artistry of these compositions. Beginning with Yannai, the entire Song was commented upon in verse—with continuous citations of initial words of these verses integrated in stanzas that reformulated and condensed their classical midrashic renderings. Sometimes the citation appeared in the opening line of a stanza, sometimes at the end, and sometimes in the middle. It all depended upon the particular poem and its place in the liturgical service.

Particularly popular was the incorporation of this midrashic material into the festival *ʿAmidah* prayer, notably as an expansion of its *Kedushah* service. The cantor recited these poetic comments as part of his public repetition of the *ʿAmidah*. In addition, huge poems—hundreds of lines in length—were incorporated among the prayers and benedictions recited by the congregation during the main morning service, following the Call to Prayer (or *Barekhu*; the entire unit from the call to the *ʿAmidah* prayer was called the *Yotzeir* service, after the name of the first of these multiple prayers). In addition, cantors worked lines of the Song and its commentaries into the *ʿAmidah* recitations for the intermediate days of Passover (called *Ḥol Ha-Moʿeid*). Some

of these productions are a tour de force, in that they not only cited verses from the Song, but also added other major songs of Scripture (especially the Song at the Sea, Exodus 15, to celebrate the crossing of the Sea on the seventh day of Passover).

As an example of this poetic presentation of the Song and its teachings in the context of the prayer service, here is the opening stanza from the immensely popular *piyyuṭ* "*'Afiq Renen*" by R. Meshullam bar Kalonymos.

'Afiq renen ve-shirim	*le-nose'i 'al nesharim*
'Ashorer ke-'ozi sharim	SHIR HA-SHIRIM
'Ayom sibba' shoqeqot	*naḥani 'asiso le-hashqot*
'Ilefani dat bi-nshikot	YISHAQENI MI-NESHIKOT

I shall recite prayer and songs	To He who bore me upon eagles;
I shall sing as the singers of "My Strength"	THE SONG OF SONGS.
Most Awesome, who sated the needy;	Guided me, His elixir to drink;
Who taught me [the] Law with kisses—	MAY HE KISS ME WITH [HIS] KISSES.

In terms of poetic form, each line of the stanza begins with the letter *'alef*; and each couplet ends with a citation from the Song (here 1:1, 2), while featuring a rhyme on that phrase.

Less obvious is the deft incorporation of midrashic teachings on these verses and references to events in Israel's past. Thus the opening couplet refers to God as the One who bore Israel from Egypt on eagle's wings, a figure that precedes the revelation at Sinai (Exod. 19:4). It sings praises to God ("My Strength" alludes to such praise in the Song at the Sea; Exod. 15:2). And it lauds God through the opening words of the Song of Songs (alluding to a rabbinic tradition of its being sung by angels). The second couplet then thanks God for sustenance during the desert trek and for the revelation of Sinai ("elixir"), while playing on the second citation from the Song (and alluding to the rabbinic tradition that the commandments were all sealed with kisses).

Congregants hearing this cantorial recitation would simultaneously hear the Song framed by its rabbinic interpretations—all keyed to the core cycle of events around Passover: the exodus from Egypt; the crossing of the Sea; the song sung in celebration; the wandering in the desert; and the revelation at Sinai. The Song is the verbal matrix of this praise.

This poem (like many others recited on Passover) was inscribed in the local synagogue *maḥazor* and accompanied by figural illuminations, often alongside a citation from 4:8 ("[Come] with me (*'itti*) from Lebanon, my bride"). In such cases, the opening word *'itti* was written in larger letters under a colored figure of a bride and bridegroom sitting together in a wedding pose.[70] Surely this figure depicts the spiritual relationship (and marriage) between God and Israel, the underlying allegorical topic of rabbinic readings of the Song.[71] Hence it is likely that this verse was chosen to herald a future renewal of the exodus, when God would redeem Israel from her present exile and restore her to her homeland and to a rebuilt Temple. (This verse was cited for that purpose in early midrash, which relates that the double reference to Lebanon in that

verse conveys a double entendre: the first mention symbolizes exile beyond the land; the second symbolizes the Temple![72]) In the medieval European city of Worms, the people began their celebration of the holiday with a festive processional, during which the community-owned *maḥazor* was brought into the synagogue, placed upon the reader's desk, and opened for the congregation to see as they passed by.[73] This was a further ritual moment when the Song was central to the life and spirit of the community.

The *piyyuṭ* genre for Passover was also employed in the Babylonian east and in Spain. Particularly impressive is the ornate recitation on the Song's verses by R. Shlomo Suleiman for the first day of Passover (tenth century).[74] Relative to the liturgical tradition centered in the Land of Israel, the Babylonian-Spanish tradition reflects a different arrangement and presentation of the Song. Passover poems in medieval Spain tended to cite only brief snippets. For example, a poem by the great poet Yehudah Halevi (on the divine call to the soul to return to heaven) for the Sabbath during Passover contains only one allusion to the Shulammite. However, later in that poem, Israel twice requests that God ("The One my soul loves") not abandon her but instead come to her aid. She adds that God has for some time "turned and gone"; 5:6), and seeks Him repeatedly ("At night, upon my bed"; 3:1–2). And God's response refers to Israel as a beloved "bride," while using a language of passionate love derived from old Arabic verse.[75] That emotional sequence opens: "O splendid and pleasant one / most desired and loved (*ḥashuqah 'ahuvah*) / [My] wife of youth, (and) well-tended bride, / I have espoused you to Me in joy."[76]

Also in Spain, the master poet Ibn Gabirol composed several pieces to accompany the annual prayer for dew on Passover; one of them is saturated with phrases from the Song. It appeals to God to "send forth His sustenance" (dew) to water His garden and vineyard (the Land of Israel) and to "leap over the hills" to proclaim to His ever-expectant people the tidings of redemption—"for the winter and harsh rains have passed, and the sound of spring can be heard." In a plaintive conclusion, the poet (on behalf of the people) beseeches God to come to Zion, at this hopeful moment, and open the gates of this impoverished city (and nation). Certainly one may hear throughout the Song's joyful notes (beginning with the call for new sustenance, citing 4:13, 16; and extending to the expectation of divine advent and the birth of spring, citing 2:8, 11–12). In this poem, the rebirth of nature and the nation coalesce.[77]

Other Festivals

The Song's centrality and popularity extended to other occasions. One may note an extensive *Yotzeir* citing its verses, composed by R. Eleazar Kallir for Shavuot, and a portion of a *Kedushah* expansion for Sukkot composed by R. Pinḥas Ha-Cohen, both celebrated poets from the Land of Israel.[78]

Similarly, Ibn Gabirol composed an appeal to God to redeem His people in a reader's meditation (called *Reshut*) for Simḥat Torah.[79] In this poem, Israel first addresses God as "my beloved, white and ruddy" (Song 5:10), and refers to herself as "Your sister," whose visage is like a pomegranate (cf. 4:3, 9). The divine response refers

to her "arousal of love" (hope in redemption), and assures her that He will hasten the "time of love's" fullness (cf. 2:7). This liturgical dialogue is all the more evocative for its use of the Song and its midrashic theme of national redemption.[80]

The Sabbath

It is the custom since at least the sixteenth century—beginning in Safed—to recite the Song of Songs prior to the onset of the Sabbath. In some communities, this was done before the Friday afternoon *Minḥah* service; in others, before the *Kabbalat Shabbat* (Welcoming the Sabbath) service; and in a few locales, also on the Sabbath itself.[81]

The origin of this recitation is not certain. Undoubtedly it was rooted in kabbalistic teachings that every verse contained "profound mysteries" (Midrash Ha-Ne'elam, Z. 1:88b), and in even earlier rabbinic depictions of the Sabbath as "bride" (cf. 4:8–12; 5:1). Already the Talmud relates that R. Ḥaninah would recite at the Sabbath's onset: "Come, let us go out before [i.e., to greet] the Sabbath Queen (*Shabbat Ha-Malkah*)"; whereas R. Yannai would say: "Come, O Bride! Come, O Bride!" (B. Shab. 119a). Several striking variants are recorded elsewhere.[82]

Thus when R. Avraham Galante wrote (in his collection of "Good and Holy Practices") that "some [persons in Safed] have the practice of Welcoming the Sabbath before *Minḥah*, dressed in [special] Sabbath clothes, by reciting the Song of Songs and [immediately] thereafter the Sabbath *piyyuṭ* "Come, O Bride,'"[83] he had a rich variety of rabbinic precedents to draw upon. For him and his kabbalistic community, the Sabbath was both the sacred bride of God and of Israel, and identified with the *Shekhinah* (a supernal *and* inner-worldly aspect of God).[84]

Galante's spiritual compatriot, R. Moshe Cordovero, gave instructions on how to perform the pre-Sabbath rituals of R. Ḥaninah and R. Yannai, and to recite the Song before the *Kabbalat Shabbat* service. In his prayer book *Tefillah Le-Mosheh*, we also find a special prayer to be intoned with "great intention" immediately after the Song; and in it we find reasons given for the Song's recitation. God's favor is beseeched that the "merit" of the reading and study of the Song—with all its letters and words, including the (encoded) Divine Names in all their holy combinations—serve to make the Song's recitation a time of mercy and divine "attention," and be as if one had attained all the "wondrous mysteries" sealed in the Song, so that God might restore His *Shekhinah* to Zion as soon as possible.[85] The Song is called a "holy of holies"; its mysteries of love are deemed capable of eliciting divine love and favor for the individual and community.

A similar formulation of the Song's mysteries occurs in an influential (early Ḥasidic) handbook on prayer and the commandments, *Yesod Ve-Shoresh Ha-'Avodah*, by R. Alexander Ziskind (published in 1782). He specifies that "one should be very careful to recite the words" of the Song "with precision and without interruption," "because all of [its] verses... are arranged in the order of the hierarchy of the gradations of the supernal holy worlds."[86]

One explanation for the Song's sacred recitation has an arcane kabbalistic background. (Although little known today, it was still cited in popular nineteenth-century works on customs and in twentieth-century European prayer books.) According to a

teaching in the Zohar (1:62b), whenever the congregation responds "Amen! May His Great Name be blessed!" in the middle of the *Kaddish* prayer,[87] God is so filled with compassion that He permits three deputies to fan back the fiery smoke in Hell, giving relief to its denizens for an hour and a half. Since this exclamation is classically recited three times a day (i.e., during the three daily services),[88] the sufferers find succor for $4^1/_2$ hours per day.[89] And the powers of judgment are calmed for a weekly sum of 51 hours (that is, $4^1/_2$ hours for each of the six weekdays plus all 24 hours of the Sabbath) out of the total of 168 hours in a week. Subtracting 51 from 168 yields 117—the number of verses in the Song. Thus—we are told—Solomon composed the Song with this verse count so that if one recites it with intensity before the Sabbath, one will be "saved from the judgment of Hell" for the remaining 117 hours of the coming week. (In other words, one is protected from death for the entire week!)[90]

In short, from a work of spiritual content and rapture, the Song became a popular incantation against death and doom—its words of love stifling the fires of judgment. The kabbalistic belief that the Song could elicit divine mercy (as Cordovero averred) assumed a magic component.

Totally different is the use of phrases from the Song found in the Sabbath hymn *Yedid Nefesh* ("Beloved of [My] Soul"), composed by another Safed mystic, R. Eleazar Azikri: O my Beloved, "draw forth" your spiritual servant to Your will, that "we may rejoice in You"—"for I am soul-sick for love of You." This poignant recitation encapsulates the Song, as understood on the *derash* and *sod* levels. And spiritual seekers regularly recite it on the Sabbath day—or whenever their souls are overwhelmed with love and longing for God.

Reading the Commentary

As we have seen, the Song of Songs is a song of many songs. And as I discuss at length in the excursus, this biblical book has undergone many transformations over the course of 2,500 years. Earlier I noted how diverse groups emphasized one or another of four levels of interpretation, and sometimes even presented them in hierarchical relation. *Peshat*, *derash*, *remez*, and *sod*—these terms refer to the "plain sense," the "midrashic interpretation," the "philosophical allusion," and the deep "mystical mystery" of Scripture, respectively. These four levels of interpretation can also be understood as expressions of four aspects of the human spirit: natural experience and love; communal religion and its duties; personal spirituality and its practices; and cosmic and transcendental intuitions.

The goal of the commentary that follows is to consider each level of interpretation in its own right—and to read them interactively as multiple expressions of the human spirit. The reader is encouraged to begin with the *peshat*, treating the text's primary ground, and then to read and contemplate the other levels, depending upon taste and interest. Eventually this will allow dynamic readings of the whole, stimulating a search for more complex meaning in the Song. Perceiving the differences between the levels of

interpretation may impart a sense of wonder and delight at the capacity of the interpretative spirit to transform the Song's meanings in times past, while allowing the Song to guide the modern reader to intellectual or religious insights.

Notwithstanding the great bounty of Jewish exegesis, these interpretations are not self-explanatory or readily meaningful to a modern reader. The reason is simple. Moderns do not think in midrashic images or easily perceive the theological import of its dense comments; and moderns do not relate to the world in medieval philosophical or mystical categories—like the desire to align the mind with the Divine Agent Intellect or to conjoin the soul to a Supernal Gradation. To be truly meaningful, these modes of thought and terminology must be recast in ways that ring true to contemporary concerns and modern sensibilities. Hopefully this reformulation will also provide a new theological vocabulary and focus that can enable moderns to access the older sources in terms that make real intellectual and spiritual sense. The goal of this commentary is thus not solely to provide historical information, but also to allow the Song to become once again a voice that addresses the heart and mind. Challenging the reader to engage the text at all four levels is also an acknowledgment that moderns live at various levels of meaning and truth simultaneously—and thus allow the Song to cultivate their religious lives in this multidimensional way.

Read through this lens, the Song's truth will become the reader's own truth—built upon the historical readings of centuries of devoted and diverse readers. The content of the past is "other" and "impersonal" only when it lays no claim upon the self. It can yet become a living voice that speaks across the centuries. If this commentary "works," it will not only convey old historical and theological knowledge, but also enable a new religious temperament. It thus offers a challenge and opportunity to students of Scripture. It builds a bridge between the ancient texts and the reader. And then the reader must do the rest, transforming this act of cultural instruction into a personal spiritual exploration. In this way, the text is revealed anew.

Postscript

It takes a poet to know a poet. With most penetrating insight, the modern Israeli poet Yehuda Amichai (1924–2000) entered the mind of the "singer of the Song of Songs" (*meshoreir Shir Ha-Shirim*). In his imagination, the poet of the biblical songs was so madly in love with his beloved that he himself went mad, and roamed the countryside utterly consumed by the images of his own making—in the insane hope of finding one that might adequately represent the person he was seeking in his heart and mind. And so he went to Egypt seeking the right expression, and wrote, "I have compared you to a mare among Pharaoh's chariots," and then went up to Gilead, trying to find the right formulation for her flowing hair, and wrote, "Your hair is like a flock of goats that stream down Mount Gilead," and on and on. Crazed by love, the poet even imagined that he was Solomon himself, roaming Jerusalem and elsewhere, calling out: "Behold, you are beautiful, my dear one!" His ultimate simile was the cry "Love is as strong as death"—and with this cry he entered the truth of his image. In the power of its formulation and the depth of his love, he died, "and the *nimshal* exploded with the

mashal"; for the parable (the *mashal* "love") had been consumed by its referent (the *nimshal* "death").[91]

Entering the Song of Songs is just such a consuming reverie, even as it has been for the innumerable generations who have sought the right expression of love in and through its images. Repeatedly, and on different levels, seekers invoke new images to arrest the pulsing power of fleeting but nearly ineffable love. Still, after more than 2,500 years, words are yet added to the Song's old images, to find the most fitting *nimshal* for each and every *mashal*. The present commentary is such an effort.

Notes to the Introduction

1. See M. Margolis, *The Hebrew Scriptures in the Making*; and also "How the Song of Songs Entered the Canon."

2. On many of these texts and interpretations, see Fishbane, *Haftarot*, 11–17, 210–17, 255–62, 301–4, 310–16; and on inner-biblical transformations of the marriage theme, see my *Biblical Interpretation*, 307–14.

3. G. Cohen, "Song of Songs," proposed that the Song was understood in late antiquity (the early rabbinic period) as a positive expression of the historical love between God and Israel, to counter the negative portrayals found in the Torah (Exod. 34:14–15) and the Prophets, where the people were depicted only as whoring after false gods. I have reformulated his insight, developing it with a different emphasis (see the ensuing discussion).

4. A fifth-generation *Tanna*, respected for his editing of *baraitot* (B. Ḥul. 141a); the redactor of the Tosefta, according to Rav Sherira Gaon.

5. See SongsR on 1:1; according to *Seder ʿOlam Rabbah* 15, the inspired composition occurred near Solomon's death. Rabbi Shlomoh's comment on the reference to the Song in B. B.B. 14b remarks that in his view it was written in Solomon's old age. (However, in another version, R. Ḥiyya Rabba taught that Solomon wrote these three works separately and in a different order; see SongsR on 1:1, toward the end, and YalSh, Kings, #179.)

6. Cf. SongsR on 1:1.

7. The old town of Tirzah (Josh. 12:24) became the capital in the time of Jeroboam's secession (1 Kings 14:17); the northern capital of Samaria was established only later, by Omri (1 Kings 11:24, 28) in 876 B.C.E.

8. See further, below. But one may readily compare the succinct and significant observations of M. Segal, *Mavo'*, III, 668–84, where many of these points are made with examples. He also suggests that some of the material may derive from orally preserved wedding and dance songs that were part of old religious rituals. (This would have been part of the process of popular sanctification and canonization, in his view.)

9. The precise meaning of this term and its application to sacred scrolls has generated a vast but inconclusive literature, since rabbinic times (just how and why the texts would have this power has been debated); see especially S. Z. Leiman, *Canonization*, 104–20, for a full review of the rabbinic sources and scholarly opinions; and also the detailed proposals of S. Friedman, "The Holy Scriptures," and M. Broyde, "Defilement of the Hands."

10. In M. Yad. 3:5, *Shishah Sidrei Mishnah*, ed. Ch. Albeck (Jerusalem-Tel Aviv: Mosad Bialik and Dvir, 1959), 6, 481, the reading is *she-'ein kol ha-ʿolam keda'i ke-yom*; MS Kaufmann does not have *kol*; but it does occur in the phrase cited by Yannai in his Passover poem (ed. Rabbinovitz, 2, 273), which reads *'ein kol ha-ʿolam bah keda'i*. A. Halkin translates *kol ha-ʿolam* "all of time"; see his comment in his "Ibn Aknin's Commentary," p. 393. For other variants of this phrase, see the *derash* commentary.

11. The comment of R. Akiva seems displaced. It would seem best to follow the prior disputants and precede the tradition about the general assembly. Cf. Tosafot Yom Tov, ad loc. The present arrangement may be an attempt by his disciples to highlight his view and give it climactic force.

12. See already Leiman, 119–20.

13. The readings for "his beauty" vary; I follow the reading *navotav* cited in Z. M. Rabinovitz, *Ginze, Midrash*, 13, since it best accords with the lemma "This is my God and I shall glorify him (*ve-'anveihu*)."

14. MdRI, *Beshallaḥ, Shirah* 3; see H. Horovitz and I. Rabin, ed. (Jerusalem: Bamberger and Wahrmann, 1960), 127. See the full discussion below, pp. 301–2.

15. AdRN, 2.

16. The source offers several meanings for the verb *heʿetiqu* in Prov. 25:1. The first sense, rejected by the new proposals, is that the men of Hezekiah simply "copied" out or otherwise transmitted the "parables of Solomon." (In its primary context, this refers to the book of Proverbs alone, but it was subsequently extended to include the parables in the Song of Songs and Ecclesiastes—Solomon's three compositions, according to biblical tradition.) The first new meaning offered (in the light of the Mishnah being discussed) is that the verb means *himtinu*; that is, the tradents "prolonged," "protracted," or "extended" their deliberations on the parables. Abba Shaul then gave this suggestion the explicitly exegetical sense of the verb *pirshu*; that is, the tradents "interpreted" the parables, probably in the sense that they "extracted" or otherwise "departed" from the passage's primary sense and gave it a new meaning. The use of this verb with the sense of "interpretation" is found in older sources; cf.

SifNum (*Beha'alotekha* 78); see *Siphre*, Horowitz, ed., 74; and *Sifre*, Kahana, ed., I, 190. Lieberman has suggested that this meaning understood the biblical verb to have implied a transferred exegetical sense; that is, one "carries over" a new meaning—an intuition that comports with Greek usage and even underlies the noun *metaphor* (cf. the verb *metaphérō* and the noun *metaphorá*). Abba Shaul's usage thus comports with contemporary literary terminology. For this suggestion, see S. Lieberman, "He'arot Le-Fereq *alef* shel Qohelet Rabbah," in *Meḥqarim Be-Torat 'Eretz-Yisra'el* (Jerusalem: Magnes Press, 1991), 57–58. This meaning is accepted by Kahana; see ibid., 3, 542. In another study, Lieberman has shown how many of the ancient rabbinic hermeneutical terms have precise Greek correlates; see his *Hellenism in Jewish Palestine*, 47–82 ("Rabbinic Interpretation of Scripture").

17. Traditional and scholarly editions of "The Fathers according to Rabbi Nathan" (like the edition of Schechter, AdRN) state that the authorities were the Men of the Great Assembly. According to tradition, this "Assembly" connected the prophets with the Pharisees, whose first representative was Simon the Just (see M. Avot 1:1–2)—a period of about two centuries. Later rabbinic tradition attributed to them the editing of the books of Ezekiel, the twelve minor prophets, Daniel, and Esther (B. B.B. 15a; and see Rabbi Shlomoh, ad loc.), among other activities. But this reading introduces a confusing historical complication into the source, and is most likely a later rabbinic "correction." In fact, Schechter himself, in his edition of AdRN, A (p. 2, n. 22), approvingly adduces the reading "the men of Hezekiah" instead of "the Men of the Great Assembly" in MS. Rome (=Vat. 44); and J. Goldin, in *The Fathers according to Rabbi Nathan* (New Haven, CT: Yale University Press, 1955) introduces this reading directly into his translation (p. 5), and refers to the traditional reading as erroneous (p. 176, n. 22). Following these authorities and the sense of the passage, I have adopted the reading "men of Hezekiah" here. For the status of the Men of the Great Assembly, see note 19, below.

18. See note 16 for reasons to assume that the Hebrew verb was given a metaphorical sense.

19. The historicity of the Great Assembly was convincingly discredited by A. Kuenen, "Über die Männer der grossen Synagoge," in *Gesammelte Abhandlungen zur biblischen Wissenschaft* (Frieburg i. B.: Mohr, 1894), 125–60 (deeming it a construct based on the national assembly in Neh. 8–10); no significant rebuttal has been tendered. For a recent discussion, see J. Schiffer, "The Men of the Great Assembly," in W. S. Green, ed., *Persons and Institutions in Early Rabbinic Judaism* (Brown Judaic Studies 3; Missoula, MT: Scholars Press, 1977), 257–83. Among other instructive contributions, see H. Englander, "Men of the Great Assembly," *Hebrew Union College Jubilee Volume* (1925): 145–69; and E. Bickerman, "Viri magnae Congregationis," *Revue Biblique* 55 (1948): 397–402. And see note 17, above.

20. The name Solomon, *Shelomoh*, was deemed a reference for "The [Divine] King of Peace (*shalom*)." See the fuller explanation in the *derash* commentary.

21. Such variations will be discussed in the commentary, and demonstrate the stylistic skills of the poet.

22. Cf. the variant in Prov. 5:19.

23. Hosea's words also have a theological counterpoint when Moses tells the people that if they "seek" God with all their "soul," they shall "find" Him and be restored to their homeland (Deut. 4:30).

24. See *Midrash Shoḥeir Ṭov*, ed. S. Buber (Vilna: Romm, 1891), 192.

25. Cf. Sifra 1.2 (Baraita de-Rabbi Ishmael), in *Sifra de-Vai Rav*, ed. L. Finkelstein (New York: Jewish Theological Seminary of America, 1983), 2, 4, line 12; and see the example adduced on p. 8, lines 25–28. This edition is based on Vatican MS Assemani 66. Other editions (and commonly in prayer books) have the formulation *davar ha-lammeid mei-'inyano*; cf. *Sifra de-Vai Rav*, ed. Meir Ish Shalom (Breslau, 1905), 12 and 23.

26. I have followed the translations produced by J. White, in his *A Study of the Language*, 169–90 (appendix), along with his discussions of theme and language in chapters 2–3 of the work. The full references to the sources cited are listed there. For a consideration of the relationship of this material to the Song, see A. Lopriano, "Searching for a Common Background: Egyptian Love Poetry and the Biblical Song of Songs," in *Perspectives on the Song of Songs*, A. Hagedorn, ed., 105–35.

27. W. Wolff, "Über die Gegenstandbezogenheit des ägyptischen Denkens," *Ägyptologische Studien*, ed. O. Firchow (Berlin: Akademie-Verlag, 1955), 407–8.

28. Harris, 10, 9–12.

29. Harris, 14, 10–11.

30. Beatty, C4/4.

31. Beatty, C1/8. Cf. "I shall seek out my sister, for she is the cause of my illness" in Ostracon Nash 12, adduced by S. Israelit-Groll, "Ostracon Nash 12," p. 132, lines 4–5.

32. Beatty, G2/1.

33. Beatty, C1/2–5.

34. Earlier generations of commentators, adherents of the so-called Myth-Ritual school of ancient Near Eastern studies, sought parallels between cultic texts in Mesopotamia and the Song, on the presumption that it was a transformed ritual text. The essays of T. Meeks give a sense of this orientation; see his "Canticles and the Tammuz Cult"; "The Song of Songs and the Fertility Cult"; and "Babylonian Parallels to the Song of Songs." This viewpoint has since been discredited.

35. MAD V8.6–11. See the text edition in J. and A. Westenholz, "Help for Rejected Suitors," 202–3. Texts cited here in subsequent notes all give the full reference to the Akkadian sources and editions.

36. BM41005 obv. vii. 9. See text in W. G. Lambert, "The Problem of Love Lyrics," in *Unity and Diversity*, H. Goedicke and J. J. Roberts, ed. (Baltimore: The Johns Hopkins University Press, 1975), 104.

37. KAR 158 7. 26. See E. Ebeling, *Ein Hymnenkatelog aus Assur* (Berliner Beiträge zur Keilschrifforschung 1/3; Berlin, 1923), 1–9.

38. Kish B 472 i. 7'–8'. See in J. Westenholz, "A Forgotten Love Song," 422–23.

39. TIM IX 54 rev. 20. See A. Livingstone, *Court Poetry and Literary Miscellanea* (SAA 3; Helsinki, 1989), 36–37; and see especially the rich textual analysis in M. Nissinen, "Love Lyrics," 585–633.

40. Gilgamesh VI 68.

41. A famous instance occurs in the biblical narrative about Joseph, where the narrator states that Potiphar entrusted everything he had to his butler, Joseph—"save for the food that he ate" (Gen. 39:6). The erotic innuendo is palpable (and validated by Rabbi Shlomoh's well-known comment); and Joseph even explicates this point when he rejects the seduction by his master's wife and says that "he has not withheld anything from me *except you*" (v. 9). The evocative figure of food and eating also recurs in Prov. 30:20, with reference to acts of adultery ("Such is the way of the adulteress: she eats, wipes her mouth, and says, 'I have done nothing wrong'"). R. Assi cited this very passage to affirm that the statement in the Mishnah, "She is to eat with him on the night of every Sabbath," is in fact a "euphemism" (*lishna' me'alya'*) for sexual intercourse (B. Ket. 65b). See E. Z. Melammed, "Euphemisms and Textual Alterations in the Mishnah" [Heb.], *Lešonnenu* 47 (1983), 8.

42. For a collection of many of these, with literature cited, see Y. Avishur, "La-Ziqqah Ha-Signonit," 514–18.

43. The striking significance of this pair can be appreciated by comparison with the synonyms for "bed," *mitati // 'arsi* in Ps. 6:7. The Ugaritic and Hebrew poetic pair may break up the Akkadian expression for "bedroom," *bêt erši* (cf. TIM 9 54 r. 9b; Nissinen, 589).

44. UT 68 IV, 8–9; 49 IV, 25–27.

45. Cf. the list compiled by S. R. Driver, *Introduction to the Literature of the Old Testament* (New York: C. Scribners, 1902), 448; see the expanded list in Zakovitz, *Shir Ha-Shirim*, 18.

46. For a conspectus of elements, see F. W. Dobbs-Allsopp, "Late Linguistic Features," 27–77.

47. For early evidence of an Aramaic phrase addressed to the people, see Jer. 10:11; for evidence of the impact of Aramaic formulations on biblical Hebrew, compare Hebrew *sha-lamah* ("for why"; "lest") in Song 1:7 with Aramaic *di-lemah* in Ezra 7:23 (cf. also Hebrew *'asher lammah* in Dan. 1:10 and Babylonian Aramaic *dilmah*). See further in the commentary.

48. I offer some examples that show the shifts and changes in biblical Hebrew evident in the Song, suggesting a relatively late date (fifth–fourth century B.C.E.) for these linguistic features:

- The late *she/sha-* form ("that") is used in the Song to indicate possession after a noun and with an anticipatory pronoun. It occurs in the phrase *miṭṭato she-liShlomoh* ("Solomon's couch"; 3:7), instead of the so-called construct form found in standard Biblical Hebrew to mark possession. Compare the formulation in the Song with the classical form *miṭṭat x* (the bed of *x*) in 2 Kings 4:21. The Song's late formulation is similar to the form of the well-known rabbinic epithet *ribbono shel 'olam* (Master of the Universe).
- The phrase *ḥimmadti ve-yashavti*, "I desired and sat" (2:3) shows the late tendency to string verbs together without the so-called conversive *vav* (which would yield the form *ḥimmadeti va-'eisheiv*). To appreciate this change, compare the phrase *kerem hayah liShlomoh be-Ba'al Hamon, natan* [not: *va-yittein*] *'et ha-kerem*, "Solomon had a vineyard in Baal Hamon and assigned it . . ." in Song 8:11 with the similar topic stated by Isaiah: *kerem hayah li-ydidi be-Keren ben-Shemen va-ye'azzekeihu*, "My beloved had a vineyard in Keren Ben-Shemen and he broke (the ground) . . ." (Isa. 5:2); see A. Ben-David, *Leshon Miqra'*, 75. It is possible that this difference between early and later Hebrew forms is due to the influence of popular discourse on the Song's style.
- Late Biblical Hebrew tends to level some grammatical features, so that masculine verbs replace feminine ones (as in "the daughters praised her, *va-y'asheruha* [not: *va-te'asherennah*]"; Song 6:9); or a masculine pronoun suffix is used even when the reference is to a female (as in: "I adjure you, *'etkhem* [not: *'etkhen*], O maidens of Jerusalem"; 2:7; also Ruth 1:8). The classic construction *tze'enah u-re'eynah* ("go out and see") in Song 3:10 may be a frozen expression, from an old wedding song (see *peshat*).

49. The Torah commentary was completed by 1295. For a consideration of the mystical features in his work, see the monograph of E. Gottlieb, *Ha-Qabbalah Be-Khitvei R. Baḥya ben 'Asher*, passim.

50. Cf. the monumental work of H. de Lubac, *Medieval Exegesis*, I–III.

51. For diverse perspectives, see P. Sandler, "Le-Ba'ayat Pardes"; G. Scholem, *On the Kabbalah and Its Symbolism*, 59–64; and A. van der Heide, "Pardes: Methodological Reflections." The latter regards the emergence of a fourfold hierarchy as an inner-kabbalistic development, primarily in order to privilege the mystical reading above all others (including other readings of scriptural secrets, such as advocated in philosophical circles).

52. Paraphrasing the famous formulation in Z. 3:152a.

53. For the issues involved in possible references to "the king," see the commentary.

54. On these matters, see the classic exposition by C. D. Ginsburg, *Introduction to the Massoretico-Critical Edition of the Hebrew Bible* (1897).

55. O. Barfield, *Poetic Diction*, 177.

56. This refers to the difference between the 400 years of servitude forecast in Gen. 15 to the actual 210 years the Israelites were in Egypt according to the scriptural record. The sages (in SongsR on 2:9) resolved the contradiction by interpreting the verb *medalleig* to refer to the gracious act of God, who "skipped" over the prophesied time (rather than to the beloved as a gazelle leaping over the hills).

57. Taking *'eikhah* as "how," not "where," and *tarbitz* as a future-tense verb—all to create this new sense and query about divine providence in times to come.

58. Some believed that these sources derived from divine revelations given in primordial times to spiritual paragons like Adam or Enoch; others believed that they were granted in historical times, like the disclosures to Abraham in antiquity or the revelations granted by Elijah to mystics in medieval Provence. For the latter, at the

emergence of Kabbalah in medieval Europe, see Scholem, *On the Kabbalah*, 19–21, and *Origins of the Kabbalah*, 35–39, 238–43.

59. For this topic, see M. Idel, "'In a Whisper'."

60. See the midrashic teachings here (top of talmudic page), where it is stated that Israel's father is "the Holy One, Blessed be He," and her mother is *Keneset Yisra'el*. The relationship underwent spiritual and mystical transformations over the ages, but such aspects are not evident in this rabbinic source.

61. This reference follows the text of *Massekhet Soferim*, ed. J. Müller (Vienna: G. Bregg, 1878), p. 28, and the discussion and manuscript variants on p. 290 (at n. 70). In 14:3–4 there is also a statement that the work was to be preceded and followed by blessings—at the beginning, a blessing "for the recitation of a *Megillah*"; at the end for the commandment to recite from the "Sacred Books."

62. See *Maḥazor Vitry*, I, 304.

63. Cf. A. Grossman, "R. Shema'yah Ha-Shoshani," 38.

64. *Sefer Maharil. Minhagim*, ed. S. Spitzer (Jerusalem: Machon Yerushalayim, 1999), p. 147, paragraph 10.

65. R. Moshe Isserles, at *Shulḥan 'Arukh*, *Hilkhot Pesaḥ* 490.9, states that "the custom of the people was not to pronounce" blessings before and after the recitation of the "scrolls" (including the Song of Songs). The Mishnah Berurah, ad loc., n. 19, adduced other Ashkenazi authorities (the Taz and the Magen Avraham) who required blessings for all "scrolls" (including Ecclesiastes); and he follows this practice. Rabbi Yospe Hahn Nordlinger, in *Yosef 'Ometz* (new edition; Frankfurt-am-Main: Hermon Press, 1928), section 487, rejects the practice of the Maharil (and found in the *maḥazorim*); he concludes that "It is best to pronounce a blessing without the Name [of God]."

66. See in *Abudirham Ha-Shalem* (new edition, based on first printing; Jerusalem: Ha-Teḥiyah, 1963), 240 (dealing with the prayers for Passover; but before the discussion of practices for the intermediate days). Abudirham is mentioned by R. Moshe Isserles (see previous note), after mentioning the Ashkenazi practice for *Ḥol Ha-Mo'eid*.

67. See Melamed, *Shir Ha-Shirim*, 76.

68. A listing of *piyyuṭim* dealing with the Song of Songs can be found in the bibliography.

69. For some of the others, see Fleischer, *Piyyuṭei Shlomoh Ha-Bavli*, 378–79, where in particular the stream of tradition influenced by R. Shlomoh's *'Or Yesha'* is emphasized. R. Pinḥas Ha-Cohen was also an influential early payyetan with sections preserved of uses of the Song for various festivals (see bibliography). Fleischer, ibid., appendix 2, and p. 53, has proposed that the *Yotzeir* for Passover called *'Ashirah va-'Azammerah Shemo* is likely composed by R. Eleazar Kallir. The Passover poem citing verses of the Song by Eleazar, published by S. Spiegel in *'Avot Ha-Piyyuṭ*, 154–63, is presented by him as a work by Kallir. It is a *Shiv'ata'* for the first day of Passover that falls on the Sabbath, and is a prayer for dew (*tal*).

70. See the materials collected and discussed by G. Sed-Rajna, in *Le Mahzor Enluminé* (Leiden: E.J. Brill, 1983); see especially plates 7 and 8, figures 14–16. A listing of the *piyyuṭim* and the *maḥazor* editions, with the type of illumination, occurs on pp. 58–61. R. Meshullam's poem, *'Afik Renen*, is mentioned as no. 10; it occurred in the Worms Maḥzor, 101r, to be noted below.

71. See the various discussions by R. Bartal, "Medieval Images"; S. Shalev-Eyni, "Iconography of Love" and "*'Itti Milvanon*"; and Y. Dubrau, "*Motiv 'Iqonografi*."

72. MdRI, *Bo'*, 14. For a translation and full discussion, see my *Biblical Myth and Rabbinic Mythmaking*, 134–36.

73. See the discussion in K. Kogman-Appel, *A Mahzor from Worms* (Cambridge MA: Harvard University Press, 2012), chapter 2, and also figures 2 and 10.

74. See the publication of *Ve-'Eretz 'Atzhil Be-Shirot Menushaqot*, by V. Padwah. For the dating, see E. Fleischer, *Ha-Yotzerot Be-Hithavutam Ve-Hitpatteḥutam* (Jerusalem: Magnes Press, 1985), 191–92. Based on issues of form, he contends that R. Shlomoh preceded Saadia Gaon. The composition was discovered by M. Zulay, "Quriozim Mi-Piyyuṭei Ha-Geniza," *Sinai*, 17 (1945): 285–89. Ḥ. Schirman, *Shirim Ḥadashim Min Ha-Geniza* (Jerusalem: Israel Academy of Sciences and the Humanities, 1966), 46–47, argues that R. Shlomoh was from Babylonia.

75. For a full discussion of these matters, see the excursus.

76. See poem 150 in the D. Yarden edition of Halevi's poems, pp. 386–87; the final citation is from lines 23–26.

77. See in the D. Yarden edition of Ibn Gabirol's poems, volume II, poem 105, pp. 336–37.

78. See the bibliography under *liturgy and Piyyuṭ*.

79. See Yarden, 2, poem 86, p. 324.

80. The phenomenon of liturgical dialogues is common in these poems; see further in the excursus.

81. For a collection of sources from prayer books and ritual codes, see M. Ḥallamish, *Hanhagot Kabbaliyot Ba-Shabbat* (Jerusalem: 'Orḥot, 2006), 181–86.

82. In one case, R. Ḥaninah was said to have called upon others to go out before "the Bride and Queen"; others said, "Let us go out before the Sabbath, the Bride and Queen (*Shabbat kallah malketa'*)" (B. B.K. 32a–b). Yet another rabbinic tradition refers to the Sabbath as the people of Israel's marital partner. See GenR (edition of Theodor-Albeck) 11.8, pp. 95 f. See also the tradition found in Vayikra' Rabbah (edition of Margoliot), 27.10, p. 643, where the Sabbath is analogized (by a parable) to the "Matrona" of a King.

83. See the text published by S. Schechter, *Studies in Judaism. Second Series* (Philadelphia: The Jewish Publication Society of America, 1908), appendix A (to the chapter "Safed in the Sixteenth Century"), p. 297.

84. The most famous source for the identification of the Sabbath and the *Shekhinah* is found in Z. 2:135a–b. This passage is recited in synagogues according to the Sephardic and kabbalistic rites, where it is known as *raza' de-Shabbat* ("The Mystery of the Sabbath").

85. See *Tefillah Le-Moshe* (reprint; Jerusalem, 2004), near the conclusion of the Ninth Gate, just prior to a list of Galanti's practices and the onset of the *Kabbalat Shabbat* service. Cordovero refers to the recitation of the Song as a symbolic parable of the "passionate love" (*ḥeisheq*) of the divine gradations of *Malkhut* for *Tif'eret*; see *Shi'ur Qomah* (reprint; Jerusalem, 1966), 33d. This comment alludes to Maimonides's language and formulation in *Hilkhot Teshuvah* 10.7 (there too the terms *mashal* and *ḥeisheq* are used).

86. Gate 8, chapter 1. The original edition (Novy Dvor: Johann Krieger, 1782) was reprinted (Jerusalem: Beit Misḥar ve-Hotza'at Ha-Sefarim, 1978); the citation appears on p. 160. The preferred time of the recitation was Friday afternoon (*'erev Shabbos*); but if one didn't have the opportunity, "he should recite it on the Sabbath whenever he is able."

87. Cf. B. Shab. 119b; according to R. Yehoshua ben Levi, if a person exclaims these words with all his "strength," the sentence decreed against him is torn up. Cf. Tosafot, ad loc.

88. The three daily services include the *Kaddish* prayer at various junctures in the service, and also after Torah study.

89. For the notion that punishment in Hell ceases for an hour and a half, see Z. 3:167a.

90. See the formulation in A. Sperling (Ish Shub), *Sefer Ṭa'amei Ha-Minhagim U-Mqorei Ha-Dinim* (1896; reprinted Jerusalem: Eshkol, 1982), *'Inyanei Shabbat*, no. 256, p. 123. This kabbalistic tradition is also adduced in the Ashkenazi prayer book *'Otzar Ha-Tefillot* (Vilna: Romm, 1928), 288a and 289a, where the transmission of this tradition is credited to the *Sefer Ma'aseh Roqeiaḥ*.

91. See the poem in *Shirei Yehuda Amichai* (Jerusalem: Schocken, 2002), Volume 5, # 32, pp. 182–83. The text has also been discussed by S. Ezrahi, "'To What Shall I Compare You?,'" pp. 229–30.

THE SONG OF SONGS

שִׁיר הַשִּׁירִים

1 The Song of Songs, by[a] Solomon.

2 [b-]Oh, give me of the kisses of your mouth,[-b]
For your love is more delightful than wine.
3 Your ointments yield a sweet fragrance,
Your name is like finest[c] oil—
Therefore do maidens love you.
4 Draw me after you, let us run!
[d-]The king has brought me to his chambers.[-d]
Let us delight and rejoice in your love,
Savoring it more than wine—
[e-]Like new wine[-e] they love you!

5 I am dark, but comely,
O daughters of Jerusalem—
Like the tents of Kedar,
Like the pavilions of Solomon.
6 Don't stare at me because I am swarthy,
Because the sun has gazed upon me.
My mother's sons quarreled with me,
They made me guard the vineyards;
My own vineyard I did not guard.

7 Tell me, you whom I love so well;
Where do you pasture your sheep?
Where do you rest them at noon?
Let me not be [c-]as one who strays[-c]
Beside the flocks of your fellows.
8 If you do not know, O fairest of women,
Go follow the tracks of the sheep,

a Or "concerning."
b-b Heb. "Let him give me of the kisses of his mouth!"
c Meaning of Heb. uncertain.
d-d Emendation yields "Bring me, O king, to your chambers."
e-e Understanding *mesharim* as related to *tirosh*; cf. Aramaic *merath*.

א שִׁיר הַשִּׁירִים אֲשֶׁר לִשְׁלֹמֹה׃

2 יִשָּׁקֵנִי מִנְּשִׁיקוֹת פִּיהוּ
כִּי־טוֹבִים דֹּדֶיךָ מִיָּיִן׃
3 לְרֵיחַ שְׁמָנֶיךָ טוֹבִים
שֶׁמֶן תּוּרַק שְׁמֶךָ
עַל־כֵּן עֲלָמוֹת אֲהֵבוּךָ׃
4 מָשְׁכֵנִי אַחֲרֶיךָ נָּרוּצָה
הֱבִיאַנִי הַמֶּלֶךְ חֲדָרָיו
נָגִילָה וְנִשְׂמְחָה בָּךְ
נַזְכִּירָה דֹדֶיךָ מִיַּיִן
מֵישָׁרִים אֲהֵבוּךָ׃ פ

5 שְׁחוֹרָה אֲנִי וְנָאוָה
בְּנוֹת יְרוּשָׁלָם
כְּאָהֳלֵי קֵדָר
כִּירִיעוֹת שְׁלֹמֹה׃
6 אַל־תִּרְאוּנִי שֶׁאֲנִי שְׁחַרְחֹרֶת
שֶׁשֱּׁזָפַתְנִי הַשָּׁמֶשׁ
בְּנֵי אִמִּי נִחֲרוּ־בִי
שָׂמֻנִי נֹטֵרָה אֶת־הַכְּרָמִים
כַּרְמִי שֶׁלִּי לֹא נָטָרְתִּי׃

7 הַגִּידָה לִּי שֶׁאָהֲבָה נַפְשִׁי
אֵיכָה תִרְעֶה
אֵיכָה תַּרְבִּיץ בַּצָּהֳרָיִם
שַׁלָּמָה אֶהְיֶה כְּעֹטְיָה
עַל עֶדְרֵי חֲבֵרֶיךָ׃
8 אִם־לֹא תֵדְעִי לָךְ הַיָּפָה בַּנָּשִׁים
צְאִי־לָךְ בְּעִקְבֵי הַצֹּאן

And graze your kids*f*
By the tents of the shepherds.

9I have likened you, my darling,
To a mare in Pharaoh's chariots:
10Your cheeks are comely with plaited
   wreaths,
Your neck with strings of jewels.
11We will add wreaths of gold
To your spangles of silver.

12While the king was on his couch,
My nard gave forth its fragrance.
13My beloved to me is a bag of myrrh
Lodged between my breasts.
14My beloved to me is a spray of henna
   blooms
From the vineyards of En-gedi.

15Ah, you are fair, my darling,
Ah, you are fair,
With your dove-like eyes!
16And you, my beloved, are handsome,
Beautiful indeed!
Our couch is in a bower;
17Cedars are the beams of our house,
Cypresses the rafters.

2 I am a rose*a* of Sharon,
A lily of the valleys.

2Like a lily among thorns,
So is my darling among the maidens.

3Like an apple tree among trees of the forest,
So is my beloved among the youths.
I delight to sit in his shade,
And his fruit is sweet to my mouth.

וְּרְעִי֙ אֶת־גְּדִיֹּתַ֔יִךְ
עַ֖ל מִשְׁכְּנ֥וֹת הָרֹעִֽים: פ

9 לְסֻסָתִי֙ בְּרִכְבֵ֣י פַרְעֹ֔ה
דִּמִּיתִ֖יךְ רַעְיָתִֽי:
10 נָאו֤וּ לְחָיַ֙יִךְ֙ בַּתֹּרִ֔ים
צַוָּארֵ֖ךְ בַּחֲרוּזִֽים:
11 תּוֹרֵ֤י זָהָב֙ נַעֲשֶׂה־לָּ֔ךְ
עִ֖ם נְקֻדּ֥וֹת הַכָּֽסֶף:

12 עַד־שֶׁ֤הַמֶּ֙לֶךְ֙ בִּמְסִבּ֔וֹ
נִרְדִּ֖י נָתַ֥ן רֵיחֽוֹ:
13 צְר֨וֹר הַמֹּ֤ר ׀ דּוֹדִי֙ לִ֔י
בֵּ֥ין שָׁדַ֖י יָלִֽין:
14 אֶשְׁכֹּ֨ל הַכֹּ֤פֶר ׀ דּוֹדִי֙ לִ֔י
בְּכַרְמֵ֖י עֵ֥ין גֶּֽדִי: ס

15 הִנָּ֤ךְ יָפָה֙ רַעְיָתִ֔י
הִנָּ֥ךְ יָפָ֖ה
עֵינַ֥יִךְ יוֹנִֽים:
16 הִנְּךָ֨ יָפֶ֤ה דוֹדִי֙
אַ֣ף נָעִ֔ים
אַף־עַרְשֵׂ֖נוּ רַעֲנָנָֽה:
17 קֹר֤וֹת בָּתֵּ֙ינוּ֙ אֲרָזִ֔ים
רחיטנו רַהִיטֵ֖נוּ בְּרוֹתִֽים:

ב אֲנִי֙ חֲבַצֶּ֣לֶת הַשָּׁר֔וֹן
שֽׁוֹשַׁנַּ֖ת הָעֲמָקִֽים:

2 כְּשֽׁוֹשַׁנָּה֙ בֵּ֣ין הַחוֹחִ֔ים
כֵּ֥ן רַעְיָתִ֖י בֵּ֥ין הַבָּנֽוֹת:

3 כְּתַפּ֙וּחַ֙ בַּעֲצֵ֣י הַיַּ֔עַר
כֵּ֥ן דּוֹדִ֖י בֵּ֣ין הַבָּנִ֑ים
בְּצִלּוֹ֙ חִמַּ֣דְתִּי וְיָשַׁ֔בְתִּי
וּפִרְי֖וֹ מָת֥וֹק לְחִכִּֽי:

---

f   As a pretext for coming.

a   Lit. "crocus."

⁴He brought me to the banquet room
ᵇ-And his banner of love was over me.⁻ᵇ

⁵"Sustain me with raisin cakes,
Refresh me with apples,
For I am faint with love."

⁶His left hand was under my head,
His right arm embraced me.

⁷I adjure you, O maidens of Jerusalem,
By gazelles or by hinds of the field:
Do not wake or rouse
Love until it please!

⁸Hark! My beloved!
There he comes,
Leaping over mountains,
Bounding over hills.

⁹My beloved is like a gazelle
Or like a young stag.
There he stands behind our wall,
Gazing through the window,
Peering through the lattice.

¹⁰My beloved spoke thus to me,
"Arise, my darling;
My fair one, come away!

¹¹For now the winter is past,
The rains are over and gone.

¹²The blossoms have appeared in the land,
The time of pruningᶜ has come;
The song of the turtledove
Is heard in our land.

¹³The green figs form on the fig tree,
The vines in blossom give off fragrance.
Arise, my darling;
My fair one, come away!

¹⁴"O my dove, in the cranny of the rocks,
Hidden by the cliff,
Let me see your face,

b-b *Meaning of Heb. uncertain.*
c *Or "singing."*

4 הֱבִיאַ֙נִי֙ אֶל־בֵּ֣ית הַיַּ֔יִן
וְדִגְל֥וֹ עָלַ֖י אַהֲבָֽה׃

5 סַמְּכ֙וּנִי֙ בָּֽאֲשִׁישׁ֔וֹת
רַפְּד֖וּנִי בַּתַּפּוּחִ֑ים
כִּי־חוֹלַ֥ת אַהֲבָ֖ה אָֽנִי׃

6 שְׂמֹאלוֹ֙ תַּ֣חַת לְרֹאשִׁ֔י
וִימִינ֖וֹ תְּחַבְּקֵֽנִי׃

7 הִשְׁבַּ֙עְתִּי אֶתְכֶ֜ם בְּנ֤וֹת יְרוּשָׁלִַ֙ם֙
בִּצְבָא֔וֹת א֖וֹ בְּאַיְל֣וֹת הַשָּׂדֶ֑ה
אִם־תָּעִ֧ירוּ ׀ וְֽאִם־תְּעֽוֹרְר֛וּ
אֶת־הָאַהֲבָ֖ה עַ֥ד שֶׁתֶּחְפָּֽץ׃ ס

8 ק֣וֹל דּוֹדִ֔י
הִנֵּה־זֶ֖ה בָּ֑א
מְדַלֵּג֙ עַל־הֶ֣הָרִ֔ים
מְקַפֵּ֖ץ עַל־הַגְּבָעֽוֹת׃

9 דּוֹמֶ֤ה דוֹדִי֙ לִצְבִ֔י
א֖וֹ לְעֹ֣פֶר הָאַיָּלִ֑ים
הִנֵּה־זֶ֤ה עוֹמֵד֙ אַחַ֣ר כָּתְלֵ֔נוּ
מַשְׁגִּ֙יחַ֙ מִן־הַֽחֲלֹּנ֔וֹת
מֵצִ֖יץ מִן־הַֽחֲרַכִּֽים׃

10 עָנָ֥ה דוֹדִ֖י וְאָ֣מַר לִ֑י
ק֥וּמִי לָ֛ךְ רַעְיָתִ֥י
יָפָתִ֖י וּלְכִי־לָֽךְ׃

11 כִּֽי־הִנֵּ֥ה הַסְּתָ֖ו עָבָ֑ר
הַגֶּ֕שֶׁם חָלַ֖ף הָלַ֥ךְ לֽוֹ׃

12 הַנִּצָּנִים֙ נִרְא֣וּ בָאָ֔רֶץ
עֵ֥ת הַזָּמִ֖יר הִגִּ֑יעַ
וְק֥וֹל הַתּ֖וֹר
נִשְׁמַ֥ע בְּאַרְצֵֽנוּ׃

13 הַתְּאֵנָה֙ חָֽנְטָ֣ה פַגֶּ֔יהָ
וְהַגְּפָנִ֥ים ׀ סְמָדַ֖ר נָ֣תְנוּ רֵ֑יחַ
ק֥וּמִי לכי לָ֛ךְ רַעְיָתִ֥י
יָפָתִ֖י וּלְכִי־לָֽךְ׃ ס

14 יוֹנָתִ֞י בְּחַגְוֵ֣י הַסֶּ֗לַע
בְּסֵ֙תֶר֙ הַמַּדְרֵגָ֔ה
הַרְאִ֙ינִי֙ אֶת־מַרְאַ֔יִךְ

Let me hear your voice;
For your voice is sweet
And your face is comely."
15 Catch us the foxes,
The little foxes
That ruin the vineyards—
For our vineyard is in blossom.

16 My beloved is mine
And I am his
Who browses among the lilies.
17 When the day [d]-blows gently-[d]
And the shadows flee,[e]
Set out, my beloved,
Swift as a gazelle
Or a young stag,
For the hills of spices![f]

3

Upon my couch at night[a]
I sought the one I love—
I sought, but found him not.
2 "I must rise and roam the town,
Through the streets and through the squares;
I must seek the one I love."
I sought but found him not.
3 [b]-I met the watchmen-[b]
Who patrol the town.
"Have you seen the one I love?"
4 Scarcely had I passed them
When I found the one I love.
I held him fast, I would not let him go
Till I brought him to my mother's house,
To the chamber of her who conceived me.
5 I adjure you, O maidens of Jerusalem,
By gazelles or by hinds of the field:

הַשְׁמִיעִינִי אֶת־קוֹלֵךְ
כִּי־קוֹלֵךְ עָרֵב
וּמַרְאֵיךְ נָאוֶה׃ ס
15 אֶחֱזוּ־לָנוּ שׁוּעָלִים
שׁוּעָלִים קְטַנִּים
מְחַבְּלִים כְּרָמִים
וּכְרָמֵינוּ סְמָדַר׃

16 דּוֹדִי לִי
וַאֲנִי לוֹ
הָרֹעֶה בַּשּׁוֹשַׁנִּים׃
17 עַד שֶׁיָּפוּחַ הַיּוֹם
וְנָסוּ הַצְּלָלִים
סֹב דְּמֵה־לְךָ
דוֹדִי לִצְבִי
אוֹ לְעֹפֶר הָאַיָּלִים
עַל־הָרֵי בָתֶר׃ ס

ג

עַל־מִשְׁכָּבִי בַּלֵּילוֹת
בִּקַּשְׁתִּי אֵת שֶׁאָהֲבָה נַפְשִׁי
בִּקַּשְׁתִּיו וְלֹא מְצָאתִיו׃
2 אָקוּמָה נָּא וַאֲסוֹבְבָה בָעִיר
בַּשְּׁוָקִים וּבָרְחֹבוֹת
אֲבַקְשָׁה אֵת שֶׁאָהֲבָה נַפְשִׁי
בִּקַּשְׁתִּיו וְלֹא מְצָאתִיו׃
3 מְצָאוּנִי הַשֹּׁמְרִים
הַסֹּבְבִים בָּעִיר
אֵת שֶׁאָהֲבָה נַפְשִׁי רְאִיתֶם׃
4 כִּמְעַט שֶׁעָבַרְתִּי מֵהֶם
עַד שֶׁמָּצָאתִי אֵת שֶׁאָהֲבָה נַפְשִׁי
אֲחַזְתִּיו וְלֹא אַרְפֶּנּוּ
עַד־שֶׁהֲבֵיאתִיו אֶל־בֵּית אִמִּי
וְאֶל־חֶדֶר הוֹרָתִי׃
5 הִשְׁבַּעְתִּי אֶתְכֶם בְּנוֹת יְרוּשָׁלִַם
בִּצְבָאוֹת אוֹ בְּאַיְלוֹת הַשָּׂדֶה

d-d *Emendation yields "declines"; cf. Jer. 6.4.*
e *Septuagint reads "lengthen"; cf. Jer. 6.4.*
f *Heb.* bather *of uncertain meaning; 8.14 reads* besamim, *"spices."*

a *I.e., in a dream.*
b-b *Lit. "The watchmen met me."*

Do not wake or rouse
Love until it please!
6Who is she that comes up from the desert
Like columns of smoke,
In clouds of myrrh and frankincense,
Of all the powders of the merchant?
7There is Solomon's couch,
Encircled by sixty warriors
Of the warriors of Israel,
8All of them trained[c] in warfare,
Skilled in battle,
Each with sword on thigh
Because of terror by night.

9King Solomon made him a palanquin
Of wood from Lebanon.
10He made its posts of silver,
Its back[d] of gold,
Its seat of purple wool.
Within, it was decked with [e]love
By the maidens of Jerusalem.[e]
11O maidens of Zion, go forth
And gaze upon King Solomon
Wearing the crown that his mother
Gave him on his wedding day,
On his day of bliss.

אִם־תָּעִירוּ ׀ וְאִם־תְּעוֹרְרוּ
אֶת־הָאַהֲבָה עַד שֶׁתֶּחְפָּץ׃ ס
6 מִי זֹאת עֹלָה מִן־הַמִּדְבָּר
כְּתִימֲרוֹת עָשָׁן
מְקֻטֶּרֶת מוֹר וּלְבוֹנָה
מִכֹּל אַבְקַת רוֹכֵל׃
7 הִנֵּה מִטָּתוֹ שֶׁלִּשְׁלֹמֹה
שִׁשִּׁים גִּבֹּרִים סָבִיב לָהּ
מִגִּבֹּרֵי יִשְׂרָאֵל׃
8 כֻּלָּם אֲחֻזֵי חֶרֶב
מְלֻמְּדֵי מִלְחָמָה
אִישׁ חַרְבּוֹ עַל־יְרֵכוֹ
מִפַּחַד בַּלֵּילוֹת׃ ס

9 אַפִּרְיוֹן עָשָׂה לוֹ הַמֶּלֶךְ שְׁלֹמֹה
מֵעֲצֵי הַלְּבָנוֹן׃
10 עַמּוּדָיו עָשָׂה כֶסֶף
רְפִידָתוֹ זָהָב
מֶרְכָּבוֹ אַרְגָּמָן
תּוֹכוֹ רָצוּף אַהֲבָה
מִבְּנוֹת יְרוּשָׁלִָם׃
11 צְאֶינָה ׀ וּרְאֶינָה בְּנוֹת צִיּוֹן
בַּמֶּלֶךְ שְׁלֹמֹה
בָּעֲטָרָה שֶׁעִטְּרָה־לּוֹ אִמּוֹ
בְּיוֹם חֲתֻנָּתוֹ
וּבְיוֹם שִׂמְחַת לִבּוֹ׃ ס

4

Ah, you are fair, my darling,
Ah, you are fair.
Your eyes are like doves
Behind your veil.
Your hair is like a flock of goats
Streaming down Mount Gilead.
2Your teeth are like a flock of ewes[a]
Climbing up from the washing pool;

ד

הִנָּךְ יָפָה רַעְיָתִי
הִנָּךְ יָפָה
עֵינַיִךְ יוֹנִים
מִבַּעַד לְצַמָּתֵךְ
שַׂעְרֵךְ כְּעֵדֶר הָעִזִּים
שֶׁגָּלְשׁוּ מֵהַר גִּלְעָד׃
2 שִׁנַּיִךְ כְּעֵדֶר הַקְּצוּבוֹת
שֶׁעָלוּ מִן־הָרַחְצָה

c *Cf. Akkadian* aḫāzu, *"to learn."*
d *Meaning of Heb. uncertain.*
e-e *Emendation yields "ebony, / O maidens of Jerusalem!"*

a *Cf. 6.6; exact nuance of* qeṣuboth *uncertain, perhaps "shorn ones."*

All of them bear twins,
And not one loses her young.
3Your lips are like a crimson thread,
Your mouth is lovely.
Your brow behind your veil
[Gleams] like a pomegranate split open.
4Your neck is like the Tower of David,
Built *b-*to hold weapons,*-b*
Hung with a thousand shields—
All the quivers of warriors.
5Your breasts are like two fawns,
Twins of a gazelle,
Browsing among the lilies.
6[c]When the day blows gently
And the shadows flee,
I will betake me to the mount of myrrh,
To the hill of frankincense.
7Every part of you is fair, my darling,
There is no blemish in you.
8From Lebanon come with me;
From Lebanon, my bride, with me!
Trip down from Amana's peak,
From the peak of Senir[d] and Hermon,
From the dens of lions,
From the hills[e] of leopards.

9You have captured my heart,
My own,[f] my bride,
You have captured my heart
With one [glance] of your eyes,
With one coil of your necklace.
10How sweet is your love,
My own, my bride!
How much more delightful your love than wine,
Your ointments more fragrant
Than any spice!

שֶׁכֻּלָּם מַתְאִימוֹת
וְשַׁכֻּלָה אֵין בָּהֶם׃
3 כְּחוּט הַשָּׁנִי שִׂפְתֹתַיִךְ
וּמִדְבָּרֵיךְ נָאוֶה
כְּפֶלַח הָרִמּוֹן
רַקָּתֵךְ מִבַּעַד לְצַמָּתֵךְ׃
4 כְּמִגְדַּל דָּוִיד צַוָּארֵךְ
בָּנוּי לְתַלְפִּיּוֹת
אֶלֶף הַמָּגֵן תָּלוּי עָלָיו
כֹּל שִׁלְטֵי הַגִּבּוֹרִים׃
5 שְׁנֵי שָׁדַיִךְ כִּשְׁנֵי עֳפָרִים
תְּאוֹמֵי צְבִיָּה
הָרוֹעִים בַּשּׁוֹשַׁנִּים׃
6 עַד שֶׁיָּפוּחַ הַיּוֹם
וְנָסוּ הַצְּלָלִים
אֵלֶךְ לִי אֶל־הַר הַמּוֹר
וְאֶל־גִּבְעַת הַלְּבוֹנָה׃
7 כֻּלָּךְ יָפָה רַעְיָתִי
וּמוּם אֵין בָּךְ׃ ס
8 אִתִּי מִלְּבָנוֹן כַּלָּה
אִתִּי מִלְּבָנוֹן תָּבוֹאִי
תָּשׁוּרִי ׀ מֵרֹאשׁ אֲמָנָה
מֵרֹאשׁ שְׂנִיר וְחֶרְמוֹן
מִמְּעֹנוֹת אֲרָיוֹת
מֵהַרְרֵי נְמֵרִים׃

9 לִבַּבְתִּנִי
אֲחֹתִי כַלָּה
לִבַּבְתִּינִי
באחד בְּאַחַת מֵעֵינַיִךְ
בְּאַחַד עֲנָק מִצַּוְּרֹנָיִךְ׃
10 מַה־יָּפוּ דֹדַיִךְ
אֲחֹתִי כַלָּה
מַה־טֹּבוּ דֹדַיִךְ מִיַּיִן
וְרֵיחַ שְׁמָנַיִךְ
מִכָּל־בְּשָׂמִים׃

b-b *Apparently a poetic figure for jewelry; meaning of Heb. uncertain.*
c *See notes at 2.17.*
d *Cf. Deut. 3.9.*
e *Emendation yields "lairs"; cf. Nah. 2.13.*
f *Lit. "sister"; and so frequently below.*

11Sweetness drops
From your lips, O bride;
Honey and milk
Are under your tongue;
And the scent of your robes
Is like the scent of Lebanon.

11 נֹפֶת תִּטֹּפְנָה
שִׂפְתוֹתַיִךְ כַּלָּה
דְּבַשׁ וְחָלָב
תַּחַת לְשׁוֹנֵךְ
וְרֵיחַ שַׂלְמֹתַיִךְ
כְּרֵיחַ לְבָנוֹן׃

12A garden locked
Is my own, my bride,
A fountain locked,
A sealed-up spring.
13Your limbs are an orchard of pomegranates
And of all luscious fruits,
Of henna and of nard—
14Nard and saffron,
Fragrant reed and cinnamon,
With all aromatic woods,
Myrrh and aloes—
All the choice perfumes.
15g-[You are] a garden spring,
A well of fresh water,-g
A rill of Lebanon.

12 גַּן ׀ נָעוּל
אֲחֹתִי כַלָּה
גַּל נָעוּל
מַעְיָן חָתוּם׃
13 שְׁלָחַיִךְ פַּרְדֵּס רִמּוֹנִים
עִם פְּרִי מְגָדִים
כְּפָרִים עִם־נְרָדִים׃
14* נֵרְדְּ ׀ וְכַרְכֹּם
קָנֶה וְקִנָּמוֹן
עִם כָּל־עֲצֵי לְבוֹנָה
מֹר וַאֲהָלוֹת
עִם כָּל־רָאשֵׁי בְשָׂמִים׃
15 מַעְיַן גַּנִּים
בְּאֵר מַיִם חַיִּים
וְנֹזְלִים מִן־לְבָנוֹן׃

16Awake, O north wind,
Come, O south wind!
Blow upon my garden,
That its perfume may spread.
Let my beloved come to his garden
And enjoy its luscious fruits!

16 עוּרִי צָפוֹן
וּבוֹאִי תֵימָן
הָפִיחִי גַנִּי
יִזְּלוּ בְשָׂמָיו
יָבֹא דוֹדִי לְגַנּוֹ
וְיֹאכַל פְּרִי מְגָדָיו׃

5 I have come to my garden,
My own, my bride;
I have plucked my myrrh and spice,
Eaten my honey and honeycomb,
Drunk my wine and my milk.

ה בָּאתִי לְגַנִּי
אֲחֹתִי כַלָּה
אָרִיתִי מוֹרִי עִם־בְּשָׂמִי
אָכַלְתִּי יַעְרִי עִם־דִּבְשִׁי
שָׁתִיתִי יֵינִי עִם־חֲלָבִי

Eat, lovers, and drink:
Drink deep of love!

אִכְלוּ רֵעִים שְׁתוּ
וְשִׁכְרוּ דּוֹדִים׃ ס

g-g Emendation yields "The spring in my garden / Is a well of fresh water."

v. 14. חצי הספר בפסוקים

2 [a]I was asleep,
But my heart was wakeful.
Hark, my beloved knocks!
"Let me in, my own,
My darling, my faultless dove!
For my head is drenched with dew,
My locks with the damp of night."
3 I had taken off my robe—
Was I to don it again?
I had bathed my feet—
Was I to soil them again?
4 My beloved [b]took his hand off the latch,[b]
And my heart was stirred [c]for him.[c]
5 I rose to let in my beloved;
My hands dripped myrrh—
My fingers, flowing myrrh—
Upon the handles of the bolt.
6 I opened the door for my beloved,
But my beloved had turned and gone.
I was faint [d]because of what he said.[d]
I sought, but found him not;
I called, but he did not answer.
7 I met the watchmen[e]
Who patrol the town;
They struck me, they bruised me.
The guards of the walls
Stripped me of my mantle.
8 I adjure you, O maidens of Jerusalem!
If you meet my beloved, tell him this:
That I am faint with love.

9 How is your beloved better than another,[f]
O fairest of women?
How is your beloved better than another[f]
That you adjure us so?

2 אֲנִי יְשֵׁנָה
וְלִבִּי עֵר
קוֹל ׀ דּוֹדִי דוֹפֵק
פִּתְחִי־לִי אֲחֹתִי
רַעְיָתִי יוֹנָתִי תַמָּתִי
שֶׁרֹּאשִׁי* נִמְלָא־טָל
קְוֻצּוֹתַי רְסִיסֵי לָיְלָה׃
3 פָּשַׁטְתִּי אֶת־כֻּתָּנְתִּי
אֵיכָכָה אֶלְבָּשֶׁנָּה
רָחַצְתִּי אֶת־רַגְלַי
אֵיכָכָה אֲטַנְּפֵם׃
4 דּוֹדִי שָׁלַח יָדוֹ מִן־הַחֹר
וּמֵעַי הָמוּ עָלָיו׃
5 קַמְתִּי אֲנִי לִפְתֹּחַ לְדוֹדִי
וְיָדַי נָטְפוּ־מוֹר
וְאֶצְבְּעֹתַי מוֹר עֹבֵר
עַל כַּפּוֹת הַמַּנְעוּל׃
6 פָּתַחְתִּי אֲנִי לְדוֹדִי
וְדוֹדִי חָמַק עָבָר
נַפְשִׁי יָצְאָה בְדַבְּרוֹ
בִּקַּשְׁתִּיהוּ וְלֹא מְצָאתִיהוּ
קְרָאתִיו וְלֹא עָנָנִי׃
7 מְצָאֻנִי הַשֹּׁמְרִים
הַסֹּבְבִים בָּעִיר
הִכּוּנִי פְצָעוּנִי
נָשְׂאוּ אֶת־רְדִידִי מֵעָלַי
שֹׁמְרֵי הַחֹמוֹת׃
8 הִשְׁבַּעְתִּי אֶתְכֶם בְּנוֹת יְרוּשָׁלִָם
אִם־תִּמְצְאוּ אֶת־דּוֹדִי מַה־תַּגִּידוּ לוֹ
שֶׁחוֹלַת אַהֲבָה אָנִי׃

9 מַה־דּוֹדֵךְ מִדּוֹד
הַיָּפָה בַּנָּשִׁים
מַה־דּוֹדֵךְ מִדּוֹד
שֶׁכָּכָה הִשְׁבַּעְתָּנוּ׃

a In vv. 2–8 the maiden relates a dream.
b-b Meaning of Heb. uncertain.
c-c Many manuscripts and editions read "within me" ('alai).
d-d Change of vocalization yields "because of him."
e See note at 3.3.
f Or "What sort of beloved is your beloved?"

v. 2. ר׳ דגושה

¹⁰My beloved is clear-skinned and ruddy,
Preeminent among ten thousand.
¹¹His head is finest gold,
His locks are curled
And black as a raven.
¹²His eyes are like doves
By watercourses,
Bathed in milk,
b-Set by a brimming pool.-*b*
¹³His cheeks are like beds of spices,
g-Banks of-*g* perfume
His lips are like lilies;
They drip flowing myrrh.
¹⁴His hands are rods of gold,
Studded with beryl;
His belly a tablet of ivory,
Adorned with sapphires.
¹⁵His legs are like marble pillars
Set in sockets of fine gold.
He is majestic as Lebanon,
Stately as the cedars.
¹⁶His mouth is delicious
And all of him is delightful.
Such is my beloved,
Such is my darling,
O maidens of Jerusalem!

6 "Whither has your beloved gone,
O fairest of women?
Whither has your beloved turned?
Let us seek him with you."
²My beloved has gone down to his garden,
To the beds of spices,
To browse in the gardens
And to pick lilies.
³I am my beloved's

10 דּוֹדִי צַח֙ וְאָד֔וֹם
דָּג֖וּל מֵרְבָבָֽה׃
11 רֹאשׁ֖וֹ כֶּ֣תֶם פָּ֑ז
קְוֻצּוֹתָיו֙ תַּלְתַּלִּ֔ים
שְׁחֹר֖וֹת כָּעוֹרֵֽב׃
12 עֵינָ֕יו כְּיוֹנִ֖ים
עַל־אֲפִ֣יקֵי מָ֑יִם
רֹֽחֲצוֹת֙ בֶּֽחָלָ֔ב
יֹשְׁב֖וֹת עַל־מִלֵּֽאת׃
13 לְחָיָו֙ כַּעֲרוּגַ֣ת הַבֹּ֔שֶׂם
מִגְדְּל֖וֹת מֶרְקָחִ֑ים
שִׂפְתוֹתָיו֙ שֽׁוֹשַׁנִּ֔ים
נֹטְפ֖וֹת מ֥וֹר עֹבֵֽר׃
14 יָדָיו֙ גְּלִילֵ֣י זָהָ֔ב
מְמֻלָּאִ֖ים בַּתַּרְשִׁ֑ישׁ
מֵעָיו֙ עֶ֣שֶׁת שֵׁ֔ן
מְעֻלֶּ֖פֶת סַפִּירִֽים׃
15 שׁוֹקָיו֙ עַמּ֣וּדֵי שֵׁ֔שׁ
מְיֻסָּדִ֖ים עַל־אַדְנֵי־פָ֑ז
מַרְאֵ֙הוּ֙ כַּלְּבָנ֔וֹן
בָּח֖וּר כָּאֲרָזִֽים׃
16 חִכּוֹ֙ מַֽמְתַקִּ֔ים
וְכֻלּ֖וֹ מַחֲמַדִּ֑ים
זֶ֤ה דוֹדִי֙
וְזֶ֣ה רֵעִ֔י
בְּנ֖וֹת יְרוּשָׁלָֽיִם׃

ו אָ֚נָה הָלַ֣ךְ דּוֹדֵ֔ךְ
הַיָּפָ֖ה בַּנָּשִׁ֑ים
אָ֚נָה פָּנָ֣ה דוֹדֵ֔ךְ
וּנְבַקְשֶׁ֖נּוּ עִמָּֽךְ׃
2 דּוֹדִי֙ יָרַ֣ד לְגַנּ֔וֹ
לַעֲרוּג֖וֹת הַבֹּ֑שֶׂם
לִרְעוֹת֙ בַּגַּנִּ֔ים
וְלִלְקֹ֖ט שֽׁוֹשַׁנִּֽים׃
3 אֲנִ֤י לְדוֹדִי֙

---

g-g   Septuagint vocalizes as participle, "producing."

And my beloved is mine;
He browses among the lilies.

4 You are beautiful, my darling, as Tirzah,
Comely as Jerusalem,
a-Awesome as bannered hosts.-*a*
5 Turn your eyes away from me,
For they overwhelm me!
Your hair is like a flock of goats
Streaming down from Gilead.
6 Your teeth are like a flock of ewes
Climbing up from the washing pool;
All of them bear twins,
And not one loses her young.
7 Your brow behind your veil
[Gleams] like a pomegranate split open.
8 There are sixty queens,
And eighty concubines,
And damsels without number.
9 Only one is my dove,
My perfect one,
The only one of her mother,
The delight of her who bore her.
Maidens see and acclaim her;
Queens and concubines, and praise her.

10 Who is she that shines through like the
dawn,
Beautiful as the moon,
Radiant as the sun
a-Awesome as bannered hosts?-*a*

11 I went down to the nut grove
To see the budding of the vale;
To see if the vines had blossomed,
If the pomegranates were in bloom.
12 *a*-Before I knew it,
My desire set me
Mid the chariots of Ammi-nadib.-*a*

a-a Meaning of Heb. uncertain.

וְדוֹדִי לִי
הָרֹעֶה בַּשּׁוֹשַׁנִּים׃ ס

4 יָפָה אַתְּ רַעְיָתִי כְּתִרְצָה
נָאוָה כִּירוּשָׁלָםִ
אֲיֻמָּה כַּנִּדְגָּלוֹת׃
5 הָסֵבִּי עֵינַיִךְ מִנֶּגְדִּי
שֶׁהֵם* הִרְהִיבֻנִי
שַׂעְרֵךְ כְּעֵדֶר הָעִזִּים
שֶׁגָּלְשׁוּ מִן־הַגִּלְעָד׃
6 שִׁנַּיִךְ כְּעֵדֶר הָרְחֵלִים
שֶׁעָלוּ מִן־הָרַחְצָה
שֶׁכֻּלָּם מַתְאִימוֹת
וְשַׁכֻּלָה אֵין בָּהֶם׃
7 כְּפֶלַח הָרִמּוֹן
רַקָּתֵךְ מִבַּעַד לְצַמָּתֵךְ׃
8 שִׁשִּׁים הֵמָּה מְלָכוֹת
וּשְׁמֹנִים פִּילַגְשִׁים
וַעֲלָמוֹת אֵין מִסְפָּר׃
9 אַחַת הִיא יוֹנָתִי
תַמָּתִי
אַחַת הִיא לְאִמָּהּ
בָּרָה הִיא לְיוֹלַדְתָּהּ
רָאוּהָ בָנוֹת וַיְאַשְּׁרוּהָ
מְלָכוֹת וּפִילַגְשִׁים וַיְהַלְלוּהָ׃ ס

10 מִי־זֹאת הַנִּשְׁקָפָה כְּמוֹ־שָׁחַר
יָפָה כַלְּבָנָה
בָּרָה כַּחַמָּה
אֲיֻמָּה כַּנִּדְגָּלוֹת׃ ס

11 אֶל־גִּנַּת אֱגוֹז יָרַדְתִּי
לִרְאוֹת בְּאִבֵּי הַנָּחַל
לִרְאוֹת הֲפָרְחָה הַגֶּפֶן
הֵנֵצוּ הָרִמֹּנִים׃
12 לֹא יָדַעְתִּי
נַפְשִׁי שָׂמַתְנִי
מַרְכְּבוֹת עַמִּי־נָדִיב׃

v. 5. שני טעמים

7

Turn back, turn back,
O maid of Shulem!
Turn back, turn back,
That we may gaze upon you.
"Why will you gaze at the Shulammite
In[a] the Mahanaim dance?"
2 How lovely are your feet in sandals,
O daughter of nobles!
Your rounded thighs are like jewels,
The work of a master's hand.
3 Your navel is like a round goblet—
Let mixed wine not be lacking!—
Your belly like a heap of wheat
Hedged about with lilies.
4 Your breasts are like two fawns,
Twins of a gazelle.
5 Your neck is like a tower of ivory,
Your eyes like pools in Heshbon
By the gate of Bath-rabbim,
Your nose like the Lebanon tower
That faces toward Damascus.
6 The head upon you is like [b-]crimson wool,[-b]
The locks of your head are like purple—
[c-]A king is held captive in the tresses.[-c]
7 How fair you are, how beautiful!
O Love, with all its rapture!
8 Your stately form is like the palm,
Your breasts are like clusters.
9 I say: Let me climb the palm,
Let me take hold of its branches;
Let your breasts be like clusters of grapes,
Your breath like the fragrance of apples,
10 And your mouth like choicest wine.
"Let it flow to my beloved as new wine[d]
[c-]Gliding over the lips of sleepers."[-c]

a *With many manuscripts and editions; others read "like." Meaning of entire line uncertain.*
b-b *So Ibn Janah and Ibn Ezra, taking* karmel *as a by-form of* karmil: *cf. 2 Chron. 2.6, 13; 3.14.*
c-c *Meaning of Heb. uncertain.*
d *See note at 1.4 end.*

ז

שׁוּבִי שׁוּבִי
הַשּׁוּלַמִּית
שׁוּבִי שׁוּבִי
וְנֶחֱזֶה־בָּךְ
מַה־תֶּחֱזוּ בַּשּׁוּלַמִּית
כִּמְחֹלַת* הַמַּחֲנָיִם׃
2 מַה־יָּפוּ פְעָמַיִךְ בַּנְּעָלִים
בַּת־נָדִיב
חַמּוּקֵי יְרֵכַיִךְ כְּמוֹ חֲלָאִים
מַעֲשֵׂה יְדֵי אָמָּן׃
3 שָׁרְרֵךְ אַגַּן הַסַּהַר
אַל־יֶחְסַר הַמָּזֶג
בִּטְנֵךְ עֲרֵמַת חִטִּים
סוּגָה בַּשּׁוֹשַׁנִּים׃
4 שְׁנֵי שָׁדַיִךְ כִּשְׁנֵי עֳפָרִים
תָּאֳמֵי צְבִיָּה׃
5 צַוָּארֵךְ כְּמִגְדַּל הַשֵּׁן
עֵינַיִךְ בְּרֵכוֹת בְּחֶשְׁבּוֹן
עַל־שַׁעַר בַּת־רַבִּים
אַפֵּךְ כְּמִגְדַּל הַלְּבָנוֹן
צוֹפֶה פְּנֵי דַמָּשֶׂק׃
6 רֹאשֵׁךְ עָלַיִךְ כַּכַּרְמֶל
וְדַלַּת רֹאשֵׁךְ כָּאַרְגָּמָן
מֶלֶךְ אָסוּר בָּרְהָטִים׃
7 מַה־יָּפִית וּמַה־נָּעַמְתְּ
אַהֲבָה בַּתַּעֲנוּגִים׃
8 זֹאת קוֹמָתֵךְ דָּמְתָה לְתָמָר
וְשָׁדַיִךְ לְאַשְׁכֹּלוֹת׃
9 אָמַרְתִּי אֶעֱלֶה בְתָמָר
אֹחֲזָה בְּסַנְסִנָּיו
וְיִהְיוּ־נָא שָׁדַיִךְ כְּאֶשְׁכְּלוֹת הַגֶּפֶן
וְרֵיחַ אַפֵּךְ כַּתַּפּוּחִים׃
10 וְחִכֵּךְ כְּיֵין הַטּוֹב
הוֹלֵךְ לְדוֹדִי לְמֵישָׁרִים
דּוֹבֵב שִׂפְתֵי יְשֵׁנִים׃

v. 1. בנוסח אחר "במחלת"

11I am my beloved's,
And his desire is for me.
12Come, my beloved,
Let us go into the open;
Let us lodge [e]among the henna shrubs.[e]
13Let us go early to the vineyards;
Let us see if the vine has flowered,
If its blossoms have opened,
If the pomegranates are in bloom.
There I will give my love to you.
14The mandrakes yield their fragrance,
At our doors are all choice fruits;
Both freshly picked and long-stored
Have I kept, my beloved, for you.

11 אֲנִי לְדוֹדִי
וְעָלַי תְּשׁוּקָתוֹ׃ ס
12 לְכָה דוֹדִי
נֵצֵא הַשָּׂדֶה
נָלִינָה בַּכְּפָרִים׃
13 נַשְׁכִּימָה לַכְּרָמִים
נִרְאֶה אִם־פָּרְחָה הַגֶּפֶן
פִּתַּח הַסְּמָדַר
הֵנֵצוּ הָרִמּוֹנִים
שָׁם אֶתֵּן אֶת־דֹּדַי לָךְ׃
14 הַדּוּדָאִים נָתְנוּ־רֵיחַ
וְעַל־פְּתָחֵינוּ כָּל־מְגָדִים
חֲדָשִׁים גַּם־יְשָׁנִים
דּוֹדִי צָפַנְתִּי לָךְ׃

8 If only it could be as with a brother,
As if you had nursed at my mother's breast:
Then I could kiss you
When I met you in the street,
And no one would despise me.
2I would lead you, I would bring you
To the house of my mother,
Of her who taught[a] me—
I would let you drink of the spiced wine,
Of my pomegranate juice.

ח מִי יִתֶּנְךָ כְּאָח לִי
יוֹנֵק שְׁדֵי אִמִּי
אֶמְצָאֲךָ בַחוּץ
אֶשָּׁקְךָ
גַּם לֹא־יָבוּזוּ לִי׃
2 אֶנְהָגְךָ אֲבִיאֲךָ
אֶל־בֵּית אִמִּי
תְּלַמְּדֵנִי
אַשְׁקְךָ מִיַּיִן הָרֶקַח
מֵעֲסִיס רִמֹּנִי׃

3His left hand was under my head,
His right hand caressed me.
4I adjure you, O maidens of Jerusalem:
Do not wake or rouse
Love until it please!

3 שְׂמֹאלוֹ תַּחַת רֹאשִׁי
וִימִינוֹ תְּחַבְּקֵנִי׃
4 הִשְׁבַּעְתִּי אֶתְכֶם בְּנוֹת יְרוּשָׁלִָם
מַה־תָּעִירוּ ׀ וּמַה־תְּעֹרְרוּ
אֶת־הָאַהֲבָה עַד שֶׁתֶּחְפָּץ׃ ס

5Who is she that comes up from the desert,
Leaning upon her beloved?

5 מִי זֹאת עֹלָה מִן־הַמִּדְבָּר
מִתְרַפֶּקֶת עַל־דּוֹדָהּ

e-e Or "in the villages."

a Emendation yields "bore"; cf. 6.9; 8.5.

Under the apple tree I roused you;
It was there your mother conceived you,
There she who bore you conceived you.

6Let me be a seal upon your heart,
Like the seal upon your hand.^b
For love is fierce as death,
Passion is mighty as Sheol;
Its darts are darts of fire,
A blazing flame.
7Vast floods cannot quench love,
Nor rivers drown it.
If a man offered all his wealth for love,
He would be laughed to scorn.

8"We have a little sister,
Whose breasts are not yet formed.
What shall we do for our sister
When she is spoken for?
9If she be a wall,
We will build upon it a silver battlement;
If she be a door,
We will panel it in cedar."
10I am a wall,
My breasts are like towers.
So I became in his eyes
As one who finds favor.

11Solomon had a vineyard
In Baal-hamon.
He had to post guards in the vineyard:
A man would give for its fruit
A thousand pieces of silver.
12I have my very own vineyard:

b Lit. "arm."

תַּחַת הַתַּפּ֙וּחַ֙ עֽוֹרַרְתִּ֔יךָ
שָׁ֚מָּה חִבְּלַ֣תְךָ אִמֶּ֔ךָ
שָׁ֖מָּה חִבְּלָ֥ה יְלָדַֽתְךָ׃

6 שִׂימֵ֨נִי כַחוֹתָ֜ם עַל־לִבֶּ֗ךָ
כַּֽחוֹתָם֙ עַל־זְרוֹעֶ֔ךָ
כִּֽי־עַזָּ֤ה כַמָּ֙וֶת֙ אַהֲבָ֔ה
קָשָׁ֥ה כִשְׁא֖וֹל קִנְאָ֑ה
רְשָׁפֶ֕יהָ רִשְׁפֵּ֖י אֵ֑שׁ
שַׁלְהֶ֥בֶתְיָֽה׃*
7 מַ֣יִם רַבִּ֗ים לֹ֤א יֽוּכְלוּ֙ לְכַבּ֣וֹת אֶת־
הָֽאַהֲבָ֔ה
וּנְהָר֖וֹת לֹ֣א יִשְׁטְפ֑וּהָ
אִם־יִתֵּ֨ן אִ֜ישׁ אֶת־כָּל־ה֤וֹן בֵּיתוֹ֙ בָּאַהֲבָ֔ה
בּ֖וֹז יָב֥וּזוּ לֽוֹ׃ ס

8 אָח֥וֹת לָ֙נוּ֙ קְטַנָּ֔ה
וְשָׁדַ֖יִם אֵ֣ין לָ֑הּ
מַֽה־נַּעֲשֶׂה֙ לַאֲחֹתֵ֔נוּ
בַּיּ֖וֹם שֶׁיְּדֻבַּר־בָּֽהּ׃
9 אִם־חוֹמָ֣ה הִ֔יא
נִבְנֶ֥ה עָלֶ֖יהָ טִ֣ירַת כָּ֑סֶף
וְאִם־דֶּ֣לֶת הִ֔יא
נָצ֥וּר עָלֶ֖יהָ ל֥וּחַ אָֽרֶז׃
10 אֲנִ֣י חוֹמָ֔ה
וְשָׁדַ֖י כַּמִּגְדָּל֑וֹת
אָ֛ז הָיִ֥יתִי בְעֵינָ֖יו
כְּמוֹצְאֵ֥ת שָׁלֽוֹם׃ פ

11 כֶּ֣רֶם הָיָ֤ה לִשְׁלֹמֹה֙
בְּבַ֣עַל הָמ֔וֹן
נָתַ֥ן אֶת־הַכֶּ֖רֶם לַנֹּטְרִ֑ים
אִ֛ישׁ יָבִ֥א בְּפִרְי֖וֹ
אֶ֥לֶף כָּֽסֶף׃
12 כַּרְמִ֥י שֶׁלִּ֖י לְפָנָ֑י

You may have the thousand, O Solomon,
And the guards of the fruit two hundred!

13 O you who linger in the garden,[c]
A lover[c] is listening;
Let me hear your voice.
14 "Hurry, my beloved,
Swift as a gazelle or a young stag,
To the hills of spices!"

הָאֶ֤לֶף לְךָ֙ שְׁלֹמֹ֔ה
וּמָאתַ֖יִם לְנֹטְרִ֥ים אֶת־פִּרְיֽוֹ׃

13 הַיּוֹשֶׁ֣בֶת בַּגַּנִּ֔ים
חֲבֵרִ֥ים מַקְשִׁיבִ֖ים
לְקוֹלֵ֥ךְ הַשְׁמִיעִֽינִי׃
14 בְּרַ֣ח ׀ דּוֹדִ֗י
וּֽדְמֵה־לְךָ֤ לִצְבִי֙ א֣וֹ לְעֹ֣פֶר הָאַיָּלִ֔ים
עַ֖ל הָרֵ֥י בְשָׂמִֽים׃*

תם ונשלם תהילה לאל בורא עולם

c *Heb. plural. Meaning of verse uncertain.*

v. 14. סכום הפסוקים של הספר 117 וחציו 4.14

COMMENTARY TO THE SONG OF SONGS

Four Levels of Commentary: Peshat, Derash, Remez, and Sod

For the reader's convenience, the following treatment summarizes the discussion of these topics in the Introduction and in the excursus. It also explains the main features of the particular commentary that follows.

Peshat

Peshat marks the plain sense of a verse or passage. As with any text, the Song's dialogical or dramatic units compose its discourse, which conditions how *peshat* readers view a given passage. Then they construe the text through a combination of its philological and semantic sense; syntactic and metaphorical nuance; and literary style and structure. Consequently, in each successive analysis within this *peshat* commentary, the literary units are clarified first, the language and phraseology second, and the stylistic and poetic features third. A summary review concludes each of the larger units.

The *peshat* commentary incorporates all available information; it is drawn from traditional Jewish commentators who employ this approach, as well as from contemporary critical scholars who study Semitic languages, ancient Near Eastern literatures, and archeological artifacts. These considerations imbue readers with greater literary and cultural competence.

Because of the *peshat* level's complexity, the term "plain sense" is often a misnomer. Each element of the Song requires studious evaluation and careful consideration. For example, the opening verse proclaims this work "a Song (*shir*) of Songs (*shirim*)," relating it to King Solomon. Given the stated literary genre connected to this royal person, we readers expect a certain coherence. However, as the composition unfolds, the full nature of this *shir* becomes manifest: it is an anthology of poetic lyrics expressing human love and desire—marked by dramatic dialogues, evocative imagery, and diverse settings. In effect, each speech and scene is a mini-song, even as each literary unit is a cluster of diverse lyrical dialogues. Since the scenes and speeches shift unannounced, the reader is often puzzled by the identity of the speakers and the sequence of events. Interpretative judgments are required at every turn. This characteristic has elicited vastly different evaluations of the composition over the generations.

The relationship of the Song to King Solomon ("which is Solomon's," *'asher li-Shlomoh*) is itself open to interpretation. For some, the title refers to his authorship, linking it to a biblical report that this king composed numerous songs and parables (1 Kings 5:12). Those who attribute Song of Songs to Solomon claim that its figures depict a courtship between him and a maiden. Hence the various references to "the king," "his chambers," the "pavilions of Solomon," and a royal "wedding day." Others interpret the Song as a love drama between a "shepherd" boy and a young girl, aroused when they first see one another—he while pasturing his sheep, she while tending "vineyards" (Ibn Ezra). These figures are the surface sense.

Given the internal discontinuities of speakers and scenes, others have supposed that the references to the king (and his possessions) are simply stylistic, a kind of heightened love-talk. This supposition is supported by ancient Near Eastern love lyrics that use the figure of a king as a trope for a male lover. If so, the references in the Song to a king, "his chambers," and "his couch" are stylized literary devices used to portray the moods of love—its noble character and its earthy core. Similarly, the depictions of the girl as a guardian of vineyards or in conversation with companions are also interpreted to convey the settings and intimacies of love. The precise reality of the figures and landscape thus fade before the emotions of love and its modes of literary realization.

The *peshat* commentary adopts such a reading. It narrows the cast of characters to only a maiden and her beloved, while taking the diverse expressions of love as fluctuations of their relationship. Similarly, their companions and friends function as confidants or foils for the protagonists' self-expression. According to this reading, the maiden stands at the center of all the action. She repeatedly initiates events through desire and search. Indeed, her expressions of feeling and passion are among the most remarkable aspects of this lyric. Through her words and states of love, the reader is carried across an evocative landscape of town and field, entering the heart of desire. According to the *peshat*, the Song's arch-theme is ***human love and desire***.

Derash

Derash marks the midrashic reflections that various rabbis composed from antiquity to the present. These works are distinguished by their allegorical treatments of the biblical book. Typically they interpret the Song's principal characters, dialogues, and literary figures in terms of the relationship between God and Israel, as recorded in the Torah. They also interpret in terms of Jewish life from later times, subsequent to the Second Temple's destruction (70 C.E.). The midrashic units emphasize the major events of ancient Israelite religious history: the lives of the patriarchs and matriarchs, the exodus from Egypt, the revelation at Sinai, and the building of the Tabernacle. These treatments also highlight the central concerns of classical Judaism: the status of written and oral Torah, the ongoing study thereof, and religious observance.

Viewed in the light of midrash, the Song provides a literary prism for teaching Jewish traditions and ideals. Thus Abraham becomes a model of faithfulness under duress; the Exodus offers examples of life under (political and religious) servitude; and the revelation at Sinai is the occasion to emphasize the particular virtues of the oral Torah (Tradition). Throughout, the discourses between the maiden and her beloved are reformulated in terms of the relationship between the people Israel (known as *Keneset Yisra'el*) and God. According to the ***derash***, the Song expresses ***covenant love for God*** and aims at ***national redemption***.

Midrashic collections display the range of rabbinic creativity. Every phrase in the Song warrants the spotlighting of Jewish values or themes. Furthermore, they usually treat each topic via multiple approaches.

Midrashic teachings accumulated as sages studied the Torah from Sabbath to Sabbath, and as they produced homilies for the Sabbath and Festivals. Other rabbis subsequently collected the earlier output, arranging it according to the Song's verse

sequence. These anthologies thus provide insights into the Jewish religious and cultural mentality over many centuries (from the second to fifth centuries C.E., especially).

According to the prologues added to the anthology called Songs Rabbah, it was King Solomon himself who (by divine inspiration) composed the Song in order to teach Torah in public—with the aim of clarifying dense or elliptical formulations in the Torah narrative through creative and expansive figures. Solomon's purpose was thus deemed pedagogical at its core. Yet since there is no obvious correlation between the Song's words and the Torah's topics, the rabbinic discourses proceed to elucidate Solomon's authorial intent. In so doing, they invariably assume that the Song's figures are allegorical parables of the Torah narrative. Building upon prophetic precedent, the rabbis added their own distinctive theological insights. The result is that the Song and the Torah reciprocally illuminate one another. The Song expresses figuratively the love relationship between God and Israel as narrated in the Torah; and the Torah's episodes are correspondingly reflected in the Song's mirror of love.

The *derash* commentary employs the multifaceted midrashic tradition. The units of interpretation tend to follow the topics of prior generations. However, because the sages often expressed themselves in an archaic and condensed style, this commentary usually presents their ideas in a modern idiom. Similarly, it presents the diversity of rabbinic topics in terms of spiritual tensions and themes. In this way, I hope to nurture the living spirit of *derash*.

Remez

Remez marks an allegorical interpretation in terms of individual spirituality. It presumes that a yearning for personal perfection is the true goal of the self. Thus *remez* interprets the Song's characters with respect to the human intellect or soul—and in particular to striving for divine wisdom or spiritual perfection. In this light, the Song provides a literary prism for the intellectual or religious quest. Its images specify aspects of the ideal path—and pitfalls along the way. Most notably, the Song expresses *the personal love for God* and aims at *individual perfection and redemption*.

(Such readings counterpoint national and historical interpretations of religious love and collective redemption, as featured in a *derash* approach. But a counterpoint is neither a contradiction nor a negation. Religious persons thrive at both levels. As my *derash* commentary reflects, the rabbis occasionally treated personal goals and spiritual ideals also within the framework of communal and historical tradition.)

The figures of the Song provide the *dramatis personae* of the issues that different commentators wished to emphasize. For example, the work has been deemed the work of King Solomon (*Shelomoh*) in his own striving for intellectual or spiritual perfection (*sheleimut*). Accordingly, the maiden is his soul or intellect that is yearning for contact with its divine source—portrayed by the youth or the king. Interpreted this way, the dialogues present an extended series of discourses dealing with (human) longing and (divine) encouragement. The various side discourses between the maiden and the "daughters of Jerusalem" reflect inner dialogues between the soul and other parts of the self (sometimes positive elements of the soul, at other times negative aspects of one's nature). Hence the seeker called Solomon is comprised of an earthly and undeveloped

side, along with a more developed, divine dimension (of soul or intellect). The latter strives to contact and deepen the connection with its divine counterpart (which may be the Active Intellect of medieval philosophy, or some higher aspect of the individual "Solomon").

Alternatively, interpretations that regard "Solomon" as God view the beloved as a personification of the Divine Intellect that counsels the human soul or mind, represented by the maiden. The Song is thus a spiritual drama: the maiden seeks and develops; she also stumbles and withdraws. Meanwhile, the beloved exhorts and demands, but he also seems to disappear or withdraw. The various oscillations fill the Song.

The *remez* commentary mines this rich (medieval) lode of traditional interpretation. However, no one type of symbol system is imposed, since it is the variety of this striving that displays the treasure of this tradition overall. Even so, the terminology of this tradition requires special consideration. Occasionally, the bygone medieval psychology will be referenced in its terms. More frequently, the latter will be reformulated with contemporary correlates (especially with respect to a spiritual quest and emotional self-regulation). The goal is to present the wisdom of the older sources in a contemporary religious idiom. In this respect, the Song offers a challenge and an opportunity: a challenge to continue the path developed by our forebears, and an opportunity to do so in an authentically modern manner.

Sod

The *sod* marks the mystical level of interpretation. It reveals supernal "secrets" or "mysteries" concerning Divinity. Other terms (*raz* and *nistar*) refer to the "esoteric" or "hidden" layers of Scripture. Initially, these matters were reserved for small and restricted circles; but by the thirteenth century many teachings were revealed to the wider public in a more explicit fashion. Interpretations of the Song appear in both forms. Exemplary of the first type were the mysteries about Divinity deemed encoded in the image of the Beloved described in Songs 5:10–16. Whereas many rabbinic sages interpreted this bodily depiction as an allegory of an incorporeal Divinity, a separate tradition believed that this figure hinted at a cosmic image of God—altogether inconceivable by ordinary perception. This figure was called *Shi'ur Qomah*, or "Measure of the [Divine] Body," the knowledge of which initiated one into eternal life.

Public teachings of the Song's secrets took diverse expression. Exemplary are the verse-by-verse interpretations produced by R. Isaac ibn Sahula and R. Ezra ben Solomon, as well as the Zohar's teachings on nearly every Song verse, scattered throughout that anonymous mystical work. All these interpretations were rooted in exegetical meditations based on the esoteric truths of Jewish theosophy—specifically, the emanation of the Godhead from the most hidden recesses of Infinite Reality (*'Ein Sof*) into a series of supernal gradations (*sefirot*). This emergence was formulated in a rich range of symbolic terms and images, beginning with the most recondite Crown (*Keter*) and supernal Knowledge (*Ḥokhmah*) above, and descending through such forms as royal Splendor (*Tif'eret*) and sovereign Kingship (*Malkhut*). According to Rabbi Ezra, the Song concealed diverse movements within this divine realm, particularly the desire of the lower gradations to ascend to their supernal source. The text's dialogue is thus

deemed an *intradivine discourse* between these gradations—lower ones in search of ascension, higher ones beckoning and acknowledging the process. A mystical adept who read the Song in this spirit could contemplate these movements and participate in their dynamism.

The mystics marked the divine gradations by gender (male and female). The Zohar identified the central pillar called Splendor (*Tif'eret*) with a masculine dimension, and the lowest domain, Kingship (*Malkhut*), with a feminine one. This allowed for a bold mapping of the Song's erotic discourses upon these supernal domains. Furthermore, inasmuch as *Malkhut* was also identified with *Keneset Yisra'el* (the Community of Israel), older rabbinic readings of the Song (as an allegorical discourse between God and Israel; see *derash*, above) likewise attained a supernal dimension. Most notably, the nation's longing for redemption from exile was understood in terms of restoration of a divine harmony fractured by human sin and evil. In short, mystics believe the Song of Songs to be *a love song within Divinity*—yearning for ultimate balance or harmony *and* desiring Israel to take part in this reality. The dialogues and the imagery are variously construed so as to disclose this truth.

The mystics also correlated the divine gradations with symbols (of nature or culture) derived from scriptural passages. For example, the budding of nature featured in the Song symbolically expresses the awakening of intradivine longing on High, and the arousal of the human self for spiritual fulfillment on earth. To the mystic, such symbolic readings possess cosmic and personal significance—eternal and ever vital. Indeed, their profound potential may enable a contemporary reading of the Song in the spirit of *sod*. In the Zohar, the spiritual companions repeatedly seek the Song's secrets, listening attentively to each other for insights. Each generation must crack its code with the yearning of its own spirit and voice.

Modern seekers may take counsel from the mystics' endeavors in their quest for spiritual inspiration. In this way, the older commentaries may offer a symbolic language for *personal spiritual desires*. Similarly, these discourses carry the self toward more *transpersonal possibilities*: the self hears God's call as the call of Being itself, and yearns for participation in the divine totality. From this perspective, the dialogues reflect our cosmic aspirations to expand awareness and perspective.

In the *sod* commentary, I use insights from the traditional sources as repositories of earlier insights *and* as resources for contemporary spiritual life. In so doing, I continue the path paved by prior masters of this tradition. They likewise tapped older sources for new veins of spiritual ore. The goal is to be guided by spirits greater than our own, as we receive from them flashes of insight about the mystery of God. Each reader must determine the resonance of the symbols of Jewish mystical tradition (Kabbalah) with exegetical patience and spiritual integrity.

CHAPTER 1:1–17

First Words, First Encounters

This passage is subdivided into four units, according to Masoretic tradition.[1] These are marked by a series of dialogues between a young maiden and her beloved, and a series of rapidly shifting scenes. The dialogues open on the high pitch of desire, expressed by a female voice to a male.[2] In subsequent speeches, this maiden apparently speaks not only to her companions about her relations with a "king" (vv. 4, 12) in home environments, but also to a shepherd, who tends sheep in the pasture (vv. 7–8) and meets with her in the fields (vv. 16–17). Some regard these differences as due to a triangle relationship: the king and his harem maiden, who loves a shepherd. Others unify the plot and consider the king an epithet for the beloved male, as in ancient Near Eastern love lyrics (see below). The longing expressed at the outset (v. 2) comes to an emotional resolution at the end (vv. 15–17).

The maiden is the dominant voice in the Song overall, and in this passage in particular. She inaugurates conversations to her beloved, to her companions, and seemingly to herself as well. Her addressee's identity is often difficult to determine. At other times, it is explicit—named by group ("daughters of Jerusalem"; v. 5) or love epithets ("you whom I love so well"; v. 7; or "my darling"; vv. 9, 15).

In the fullness of emotion, both she and he express their feelings through figures of speech and types of comparison. She compares him "to" (*le-*) the finest oil (v. 2); he compares her "to" (*le-*) a royal mare (v. 9). Some of these figures are charged with passion (as when she says that "my beloved is to me a bag of myrrh lodged between my breasts" (v. 13), and the reader must be ready to detect allusions and euphemisms.

This opening segment sets the tone of love, the tone of voice, and the tenor of imagery for the entire work. Engaged in deducing the vocal proceedings, the reader becomes a participant.

Superscription (v. 1). The Song proper is preceded by an ascription of the work to Solomon. Alternatively, it announces the work's subject: "concerning Solomon." (Both possibilities are discussed below.) Superscriptions are independent of the work itself and should be evaluated separately.

Unit 1 (vv. 2–4). A maiden speaks about or to her beloved, in dialogues that emphasize womanly desire and the beloved's great appeal. This section has two parts. The first (vv. 2–3) opens with her statement of desire about "him" (v. 2a)—a third-person reference that suggests she is speaking to herself or her friends. This turns into a direct address, in which she extols his impact upon her and other maidens: both she and they "love" him.

In the second part (v. 4), the maiden in turn exhorts the beloved to "draw" her nigh (v. 4), rejoices that he has done so (perhaps to her friends), and commends the delights of love. Here, again, both she and the other women "love" him.

Unit 2 (vv. 5–8). This unit begins the trope of the maiden's search, which characterizes her longing throughout the Song. This section has two parts. In the first (vv. 5–6), she speaks to her friends and describes her dark complexion. This feature, she says, is due to a quarrel with her brothers, who made her tend the vineyards in the blazing sun. In saying so, she both counters their potential derision over her appearance—and adds that she has not tended her "own vineyard."

This statement seems like an allegory of the maiden's own desire to love; indeed, this phrase provides the transition to the second part (vv. 7–8), in which she suddenly addresses her beloved, asking him where he pastures his sheep. In response, he tells her to go out and follow the tracks of sheep near the "tents of the shepherds" (v. 8). This reference to tents links up with her earlier self-description (v. 5).

Unit 3 (vv. 9–14). This section likewise has two parts. In the first (vv. 9–10), the beloved addresses the maiden and offers a description praising her beauty. Presumably, this episode occurs after the maiden has found her beloved among the flocks.

In the second part (vv. 11–12), the maiden muses (to an indeterminate addressee) that she has been aroused by her beloved; she goes on to proclaim (twice) that "my beloved is to me" like myrrh and henna between her breasts. Thus the beloved embodies sensual aroma, while the figure has a suggestive tenor.

Unit 4 (vv. 15–17). This section contains a duet of love: each person separately proclaims the beauty of the other (vv. 15–16). Then the maiden speaks for them both and exults about their hideaway (vv. 16–17). Their union in the woods concludes the first cycle of lyrics.

The opening section of the Song introduces themes that recur throughout. The desire for kisses (v. 2) recurs at the end (8:1); the love by the maiden and her friends for the beloved (vv. 3, 4) is found again (6:1–3); her self-identification with a vineyard (v. 6) is echoed in the beloved's remark (8:12); and reference to the lad's companions (v. 7) brings the book to a close (8:13).[3] Retrospectively, these features will give the cycle of Songs a thematic cohesion.

1 The Song of Songs, by Solomon.

א שִׁיר הַשִּׁירִים אֲשֶׁר לִשְׁלֹמֹה׃

Peshat

SUPERSCRIPTION (1:1)

1:1. The Song of Songs The phrase *shir ha-shirim* is constructed like other superlatives in Scripture: "holy of holies" (*kodesh ha-kodashim*); "vanity of vanities" (*havel havalim*; Eccles. 1:2); and "King of kings" (*melekh malkhayya*; Ezra 7:12). As such, it denotes an element distinctive among its kind—i.e., this Song is the best "of all songs" (Immanuel). On this basis, the Song has been deemed exceptional since rabbinic antiquity ("the most praiseworthy of songs, the most exalted of songs, the most superior of songs"; SongsR 1.i.11). Building on this evaluation, Rashbam called it "the most praiseworthy of all (*she-be-khol*) the songs."[4] Rabbi Tamakh adds the element of function, suggesting that the composition is named Song of Songs "because it is the most superlative of these songs—whose purpose was to arouse the passions of lover and beloved for one another."

At the same time, the phrase can indicate a song compilation. Rabbi Tobiah b. Eliezer put it thus: "Why . . . the plural? Because [the Song] is composed of many songs, both early and late" (Leqaḥ Ṭov; similarly Malbim). As such, our Song is a lyric anthology deriving from various periods.

In Scripture, the term *shir* can denote both a "Song of Ascents" (Psalms 120–34) and the victory recitation of Deborah (Judg. 5:12), just as the variant word *shirah* can designate both a victory hymn (Exod. 15:1) and a chant celebrating the discovery of water in the desert (Num. 21:17–18).[5] More pertinent is that Isaiah sings a "song of my beloved for his vineyard" (*shirat dodi le-karmo*; Isa. 5:1–7).[6] In contrast, "bawdy songs" (*shir 'agavim*)[7] are erotic ditties sung by one "who has a sweet voice and plays skillfully" (Ezek. 33:32).[8]

by Solomon Attributed to (*'asher li-*) Solomon. The superscription may thereby indicate that this song was the best of all the known songs of Solomon, which reportedly numbered 1,005 (1 Kings 5:12).[9] Possibly this reference, and the subsequent remark that Solomon spoke about the cedars of Lebanon and of animals and birds (v. 13)—metaphorical topics found abundantly in the Song—inspired our superscription. Likewise, authorship was often announced at the head of a biblical book or psalm. For example, the words "The proverbs of Solomon" precedes the book of Proverbs (1:1), and "Of [or: concerning] Solomon" precedes Psalm 72 (72:1).

Alternatively, "concerning Solomon" (Transl.). The attribution formula uses the relative pronoun *'asher* (of, concerning) for stylistic emphasis, as against the use of *she-* elsewhere in the Song. But this variant provides no clue to the ascription's meaning.[10] Others have proposed that the superscription indicates that whereas Solomon sang these songs, he did not actually compose them all (Netziv).[11] The old rabbinic comment that the work was "copied" by King Hezekiah and his circle is indeterminate in this regard (B. B.B. 15a).[12] Solomon's authorial role is unspecified.

Stylistics. The superscription is marked by strong alliteration: *shir ha-shirim 'asher li-Shlomoh*. This feature accounts for the use of *'asher* here instead of *le-*, which serves the same function in Psalms (see Ibn Ezra on Ps. 20:1 and 100:1).

Derash

1:1. The Song of Songs As expressed in the title (*The* Song of Songs), this composition's quality is deemed exemplary: "the most praiseworthy (*meshubaḥ*)" or "most exalted (*mesulsal*) of songs" (SongsR 1.i.11)[13]—being in style and content like finely sifted grain (*solet*). Rabbi Akiva raised his esteem for the Song's quality to another level when he said that it was the "most holy" of the works in the Writings, and that "all the ages (*kol ha-'olam*) are not equal to (*ke-da'i*) the day when the Song of Songs was given to Israel" (M. Yad. 3:5). For

it is unique: at once Israel's love song "for Solomon" (*li-Shlomoh*)—a rabbinic name for God as the master of "peace" (*shalom*) (B. Shevu. 35b)[14]—and a song of God's love for Israel (SongsR, ibid.). The Song is a veritable duet of covenant love.

Indeed, "if the Song of Songs had not been given in the Torah (Scripture), it would have been sufficient (*ke-da'i*) to guide the world!" (AgS; cf. SongsZ).[15] That is, the principle of love (God for the world, and the world for God) would have generated spiritual and moral norms sufficient to regulate existence. In its present manifestation, the Song reveals the heartbeat of love that animates the world and Torah. Creation and freedom are the gifts of love; and just laws and human dignity are their social expressions. Law seeks to regulate love; love keeps law sacred.

Remez

1:1. The Song of Songs The Song's varied poetic figures offer the possibility of expressing the spiritual longing of the soul in all its complexity. This process requires a great multitude of songs—some to orient present desires, others to reclaim past experiences, and still others to express yearning and hope. The seeker is guided by such models.

The phrase also conveys the incompleteness of any articulation, and the need to formulate it with diverse (and intersecting) images (Al-Fawwāl).[16] Religious language strives to find the most proper or guiding expression, through images drawn from worldly things. The images of the Song serve as prisms to help the adept recall spiritual heights, cultivate their inner eye, and induce new imaginative possibilities.

by Solomon Solomon (*Shelomoh*) is a model for the human quest for spiritual integration (*sheleimut*). Reading the testimony of a celebrated seeker cultivates the heart for love of God (Sforno), while arousing a deeper inwardness (of soul) within one's embodied being (Malbim).

Sod

1:1. The Song of Songs This Song is the song of all songs, embracing the totality of existence—each element in its particular voice, and all together in manifold concord. As such, this Song is the veritable "principle of all the Torah" (*kelala de-khol 'oraita*; Z. 2:143b–144a). In spiritual terms, this principle is the God-given charge of life that not only drives each organic and natural element toward self-realization or enhancement, but also drives human consciousness to an awareness of the divine dimension that informs all Being (ZḤ 62b). The opening verse is thus a call to realize that each worldly song (or expression of life) is linked to all other songs (of existence), and that their totality expresses the supernal harmony of the divine whole (Kook)[17]—*Shelomoh*-Solomon symbolizing the inherent *shalom* of All (AhavD 9b). It is both a spiritual declaration and a contemplative ideal.[18] And so, if each song (or particularity of existence) is holy, the Song of all songs (or the panoply of Being) is the holy of holies. Attention to this infinite chorus consecrates the earth as a shrine of divine immanence.

2 Oh, give me of the kisses of your mouth,
For your love is more delightful than wine.

2 יִשָּׁקֵ֙נִי֙ מִנְּשִׁיק֣וֹת פִּ֔יהוּ
כִּֽי־טוֹבִ֥ים דֹּדֶ֖יךָ מִיָּֽיִן׃

Peshat

1. A MAIDEN'S DESIRE (1:2–4)

This section begins with an expression of the maiden's desire (v. 2a). It bespeaks her longing for her beloved (she yearns for "the kisses of his mouth"). The initial words of desire are followed by a direct address of loving praise (vv. 2b-3), wherein she requests that he take her away (v. 4a). The subsequent phrase is oblique. Suddenly the maiden states that the king "has taken" her to his chambers (v. 4b). If a real king is implied, there is special urgency in the girl's appeal to her true beloved. The companions (daughters of Jerusalem) hear the girl's words and say that they shall celebrate her good fortune. But if this king is in fact her beloved shepherd, the maiden projects her desire to be taken to his chambers as a realized event; and her friends respond in expressions of joy (comparing him to wine, as she did earlier; v. 4c).

The first alternative presupposes a love triangle; the second a succession of emotions as desire and reality interpenetrate. Rashbam was alert to these oscillations: "Sometimes the bride recites her song (*meshoreret*) as if she is speaking to her beloved; and sometimes she recounts to her companions that he is not nearby." His "as if" is significant as an attempt to resolve the successive shifts in addressee. Ibn Ezra adds that the maiden's expressed desire for her beloved's kisses is "as if she is speaking to herself." His comment suggests that the private language of fantasy is involved. In context, this alternative seems more psychologically vibrant and thematically coherent than the first. Each choice is consequential.

2. Oh, give me of the kisses of your mouth Literally, "Let him give me of the kisses of his mouth!" (Transl.).[19] The verb *yishaqeini* expresses volition or desire.[20] It articulates the speaker's intense longing for a kiss ("Would that he [come and] kiss me"; see Rashbam).[21] Apparently it is an aside that marks his absence.[22] These words inaugurate this song of love, marking its character.

The reader is drawn into this maiden's intimate subjectivity and becomes a partner to the Song's emotions. Every expression of intimacy is seen or heard. The reader is thus an all-present audience, a counterpart to the all-seeing and omniscient author.

For The initial wish is now justified, without losing the tenor of intimacy.

your Longingly, the maiden now speaks to the absent lover,[23] evoking his presence in personal terms (*dodekha*). The contrasting pronouns concretize her twofold consciousness: he is absent in fact but present in her heart. Alternatively, the maiden's initial expression of desire is disrupted by the beloved's sudden appearance.[24]

love The noun *dodim* suggests intimacy and physicality. It is used elsewhere to indicate sexual behavior (Ezek. 16:8, 23:17; Prov. 7:18). It is part of a vocabulary of eros that complements the maiden's desire for kisses.

more delightful than wine This figure exalts physical love, deeming it *ṭovim* ("better" or "more delightful")—that is, emotionally more intoxicating than other stimulants. It also suggests that his love is "sweeter" to her than wine. The word *ṭov* implies this double sense. Ancient Ugaritic texts denote "choice wine" in similar terms (*yn ṭb*).[25]

This is merely the first instance where an emotional state is compared to an element (or product) of the natural world, providing an objective basis for subjective feelings. This simile also introduces a quality of value into the feeling state, and the sense of an inward reality (love) as having been incorporated from without.

Derash

2. give me of the kisses of your mouth At the center of covenant love stands Mount Sinai, the classic site of a revelation whose words are like kisses—sealing a bond for all generations

(SongsR 1.ii.2).[26] Each kiss of the decalogue inspires its recipients with the tasks of Tradition, whereby the formative words of Torah are lovingly reformulated to meet the social and spiritual realities of life.[27] The oral tradition strengthens and guides the people toward a godly life. The cry *yishaqeini* ("Let Him kiss me") is the voice of each and every worshiper (for the task is individual and collective) who eagerly wants to receive the kisses (*neshiqot*) of Torah—whose study is like armament (*nesheq*), strengthening spiritual resolve; whose contents connect (*mashiq*) to the heart, purifying human nature; and whose goal is the subtle touch (*mashiq*) of the sacred, revealing God's presence (SongsR 1.ii.5, end).[28]

This spiritual process renews Sinai at every moment. It longs for the kiss of confirmation that blesses one's life path. It desires an attentive dedication to the work of the ancestors, who felt the divine kisses and resolved "to do" and "to hear" all that is given by God's kiss of life (cf. Exod. 24:7).[29] The flow of creation thus reveals anew the tasks of Sinai; the duty to respond becomes a timeless imperative.

For your love is more delightful The clause *ki ṭovim dodekha* is an ecstatic explanation of the express desire for "kisses," namely, both God's written Torah and oral Torah—as established here by the plural formulation.

Alternatively, the *dodim* constitute God's expression of "love" through "the words of Torah," easily explicated by exegesis because they are philologically related or "similar" (*domin*) to one another—like "breasts," *dadim*;[30] "companions," [*ye*]*didim*; or "close relatives," *dodim*[31] (SongsR 1.ii.2).[32]

Through these puns, the language of Torah shows its deep integral resonance, whereby its words are inherently drawn to one another for reinterpretation (whether by word association or similarity—even by the traditional methods of exegetical correlation, as noted by Radal). As love binds, so do the words of Torah recombine and elicit new laws and insights.

more delightful than wine Sages including R. Yoḥanan trump the preceding point by asserting that loving "interpretations" (*dodim*) of Torah are even "better than wine"—meaning, better than the Torah itself (SongsR 1.ii.2):[33] that is, the traditional "words of the sages" (*soferim*) exceed in both value and pleasantness (*ṭovim*) the very words of the Torah (revelation)—since they can transform the body of one who imbibes it, even more than wine does (SongsR 1.ii.3).[34]

Another reason the oral tradition is so exalted (suggests R. Tanḥum) is because the severity (*ḥamurim*) of its regulations safeguard the formulations of the written Torah. These traditions may transcend even Scripture in sense and application (SongsR 1.ii.2; J. Ber. 1:4; B. Eruv. 21b).[35] Love of Torah produces the love of Tradition, its guarantee—even as love of Tradition guards the love of Torah, its source.

Remez

2. ***Oh, give me*** An alternative rendering of *yishaqeini*, "Let him kiss me," reflects the two poles of spiritual reference: the unnamed God, in hidden depths ("Him"), and the personal self ("me"), aroused in passionate longing (Ibn Tibbon; Immanuel).

kisses of your mouth Spiritual realization is ever partial and fragmentary. The honest seeker knows that the goal is to make contact with some modality "of" (or "from") the great divine mystery—with something that remains hidden and other ("His"), even as one dares to imagine the connection in terms knowable and human ("mouth").

"Kisses" boldly express the intensity of the longing for contact with God (Rambam),[36] despite human finitude (Al-Fawwāl).[37] The kiss represents the desired infusion of divine reality into the human self—the yearning for spiritual transformation. It is a moment of meeting that silences speech.

your love is more delightful Each seeker proclaims some hierarchical relationship between the divine and the earthly. How exactly is God "more"? As the depth and ground of physical reality (Ps. 24:1)? As life's source or creative spirit (Ps. 104:30)? As the Lord of All (*'adon ha-kol*) or the Wisdom of All Being? Or is God still far "more" (and "other") than such

expressions? The answer focuses one's spiritual life, affecting religious consciousness at every point. (Cf. Immanuel; Al-Fawwāl; Malbim.)

Should characterizations of God be formulated in positive terms, or by their negation? Philosophers and seekers have differed profoundly. The perplexity is deep. How can religious language and images say the unsayable, or hint at the "more"? In religious terms, what does the phrase "more delightful *than*" say and not say simultaneously?

Sod

2. ***give me of the kisses of your mouth*** The spiritual quest begins with great longing, marked by absence and otherness (as marked by the third-person Hebrew pronoun). It wishes for contact with Divinity, symbolized by a kiss. Spiritually understood, the kiss is the co-infusion of breath or spirit between one being and another (*ruḥa be-ruḥa*, Z. 1:64a, 70a). It is thus an overcoming of transcendent distance ("his mouth") by immanent presence ("your love"). The speaker yearns for a connection to the divine whole—the kiss being the expressive figure for such contact and the desire to transcend individuality for a Higher Unity (Z. 2:146a). Poignantly, the seeker wishes to be infused by this godly reality (Ibn Sahula). The cry of love is an opening of the heart (Rei'shit Ḥokhmah 2:24).

your love... more delightful God's love is beyond worldly delights, symbolically denoted as wine. The seeker wants God more than all earthly pleasures (Kedushat Levi), for the reality of God bestows a fullness of awareness and joy exceeding evanescent delights (AhavD 15a–16a). The yearning for transcendence is not a nullification of the world but rather its transfiguration through a consciousness of Divinity infusing all things (ibid., 20b). This is a spiritual transformation of the everyday. Thus when seekers exult in God's love as "more delightful" (*ki ṭovim*) than wine, listeners may perceive in their words an allusion to the primal light infusing creation (called *ki ṭov*, "very good" in Gen. 1:4)—and to the spiritual sense that a divine radiance illumines the created order (REzra). This radiance is the "truly good" that shines through the world of experience. A seeker strives to see the world in its light.

[3] Your ointments yield a sweet fragrance,
Your name is like finest oil—
Therefore do maidens love you.

[3] לְרֵ֙יחַ֙ שְׁמָנֶ֣יךָ טוֹבִ֔ים
שֶׁ֖מֶן תּוּרַ֣ק שְׁמֶ֑ךָ
עַל־כֵּ֖ן עֲלָמ֥וֹת אֲהֵבֽוּךָ׃

Peshat

3. The figures of allurement continue. She claims that his qualities exude from his being like a fragrant scent.

Your ointments yield a sweet fragrance His oils are sweet (*ṭovim*) to her sense of smell.[38] In this unusual Hebrew construction, the initial particle *le-* is the so-called dative of reference;[39] it means "with respect to" or "with regard to" the fragrance.[40] Cf. Num. 18:8, where *le-moshkhah* (literally, "for attracting") denotes "for the purpose of" an ointment. Rashbam regards the prefix *le-* as an abbreviated form of *le-ma'an*, with a similar sense. It is not directly translated here.

ointments Saadia Gaon notes that their function was to be a stimulant, thus implying an erotic effect.

Your name is like finest oil Literally, "*shemen turaq* [is] your name (*shemekha*)." Like the proverb *ṭov shem mi-shemen ṭov* ("a good name is better than fragrant oil," Eccles. 7:1), the maiden likens her lover's name to a special oil. The exact force is uncertain. If *turaq* is a verbal noun (presumably a past causative *hof'al* of the stem *r-y-q*, "to empty out"), then the Beloved's name is likened to "decanted" oil (i.e., of a high quality, as noted in SongsR 1.iii.20).[41] However, that reading is undercut by a grammatical mismatch:[42] the *tu-* prefix is feminine, while the noun *shemen* is masculine. One solution is that *turaq* is a brand of oil (so Ibn Ezra);[43] another sees it as the oil's place of origin—named Turaq (so Tamakh). These solutions skirt the grammatical problem.

Three other suggestions are plausible. The first one contends that the received term has been garbled and should be restored to the noun *tamruq* ("ointment," as in Est. 2:3, 9, 12). The new noun would function like a descriptive adjective and mean that the oil has an ointment-like quality (cf. the proposal of the Gra).[44] A second solution is that *turaq* be emended to (the verbal noun) **muraq*, which would refer to the oil's "flowing" nature.[45] This reading underlies the Septuagint version and is nearly confirmed by the Qumran fragment 6QCant, which has the letters *mr-* (before a lacuna).[46] The third possibility is that the *tu-* prefix preserves an archaic, rare masculine causative form (cf. Deut. 33:3 and Ramban's comment).[47]

Therefore do maidens This rationale confirms the lass's personal experience: her subjective emotions have a public resonance. The admiring women are designated as "maidens" (*'alamot*), without further identification. With this assertion, the youth's appeal is justified as a social fact.

love you The vocalization of *'aheivukha* is similar to that of other stative verbs of desire (cf. Immanuel; *ḥafeitz*, "desire," Gen. 34:19). This expression of love thus conveys a "state" or condition of being.

Stylistics. The comparison of name and oil (*shemekha–shemen*) is alliterative, linking sound and sense. The *sh-* sound also echoes the words for songs (v. 1) and kisses (v. 2), thus giving the three verses a recursive intensity.[48] The maiden gives two rationales to convey the beloved's erotic impact. The first is marked by the word *ki* ("for" or "indeed") in verse 2b; the second by *'al ken* ("therefore") in verse 3b. Through these features, the maiden's remarks have rhetorical intensity and exclamatory force.

Derash

3. This verse celebrates exemplary human faithfulness. Abraham was the archetype. He was like one who decanted the perfume of good deeds from one container to another (taking *shemen turaq* as this decanting; cf. Peshat), thereby inspiring others to serve God[49]—others like the converts or "maidens" (*'alamot*) of the

nations (SongsZ; AgS), who come to "love" God and to leap "with great alacrity" (*be-ʿalmut u-vi-zrizut*) to perform acts of sacred service, even rejoicing in the "hidden aspects" (*ʿalumot*) of divine providence, in this and future "worlds" (*ʿolamot*) (SongsR 1.iii.3).[50] Abraham's heirs then gave new expression to spiritual life through the Torah and Tradition: they decanted the 613 commandments into the world, wafting fragrance into the world through their acts of devotion and righteousness (cf. Tan., *Yitro*, 3).[51] These devotees are called the "maidens" who "love" God and the truths of Tradition. Infused by its fragrance, they have consecrated themselves to deeds of sacred service for the near and far.[52]

Remez

3. Your ointments yield a . . . fragrance The seeker "senses" God through spiritual traces in the self or the world (Malbim), picking up other residues from deposits in Tradition (Ibn Tibbon; Immanuel). These are all deemed *ṭovim*—matters both "sweet" and "good." Such a perception is both ontological and theological. God's good fragrance is embedded in the world's being; and this reality offers traces of a more transcendent good. The seeker must make this correlation.

Your name is like finest oil The seeker thinks about God analogically ("like"), this being the limit and the hope of "naming" God within the world of things. The panoply of existence offers hints of God-derived intelligibility, and these are constructed by the human intellect as hints for spiritual insight (Ibn Aqnin). The Name is symbolic of the Divinity addressed; it is at once sayable and unsayable. In the first aspect, something is articulated—directing consciousness toward the transcendent; in the second, we know that this formulation substitutes for a wholly ineffable reality. (The proffered analogies cast the Name as a stand-in both personal and distant.)

Sod

3. Your ointments yield . . . fragrance The flow of divine giving through the totality of existence is like the scent of fine oil (REzra)—a spiritual quality exuded by worldly substance. It is poured (*turaq*) into all things and gives each thing its unique quality or name[53]—all these names pointing to God's ineffable Name ("Your name"). Human language parses existence with names, giving things their particular distinction. The Divine Name is their transcendental aggregate, and indescribably more.

As the source of all naming and being, God is hidden (*ʿalumot*) in a most ultimate transcendence (ZḤ 65a)—toward which spiritual seekers turn as "maidens" (*ʿalamot*) in "love" (Ibn Sahula).

In this yearning for divine transcendence, God is addressed as "you." Divinity—the focus of a personal quest—is invoked as a person. Love longs to be personalized, for it arises in a human heart. This yearning brings God into presence. In consequence, the kiss is expressed as an aromatic infusion of divine creativity into world-being (*ʿolamot*). If this new image is more tangible, it nevertheless remains symbolic of a more ultimate truth—the ineffable mystery of the Divine Name: "I shall be as I shall be" (Exod. 3:14).

4 Draw me after you, let us run!
The king has brought me to his chambers.
Let us delight and rejoice in your love,
Savoring it more than wine—
Like new wine they love you!

מָשְׁכֵ֖נִי אַחֲרֶ֥יךָ נָּר֑וּצָה 4
הֱבִיאַ֨נִי הַמֶּ֜לֶךְ חֲדָרָ֗יו
נָגִ֤ילָה וְנִשְׂמְחָה֙ בָּ֔ךְ
נַזְכִּ֤ירָה דֹדֶ֙יךָ֙ מִיַּ֔יִן
מֵישָׁרִ֖ים אֲהֵב֑וּךָ׃ פ

Peshat

4. Draw me after you The maiden continues speaking to her beloved, shifting from desire to demand. She implores him (with an imperative), hoping for a shared getaway ("let *us* run").

The king has brought me If this reference is to a third party, it provides the provocation for her beloved to rescue her. The sudden shift to the past tense must be correlated with these possibilities. If the girl has turned to her beloved, she urges haste because another man ("king") has already taken me away. Alternatively, this remark is a private thought expressing the realization of her desires for her beloved "king" (perhaps stated to her companions). The whole matter is indeterminate (perhaps intentionally so) and serves to convey the intensity of shifting emotions and emotional states. The lass is in a tizzy: interpersonal references collide and produce a tangle of feelings.[54]

Let us It seems that the maiden again appeals to the beloved.

Savoring it more than wine Literally, "let us proclaim your love more than wine (*mi-yayin*)." This assertion echoes her initial comparison, when she said that "your love" is better than wine (*mi-yayin*; v. 2). She now adds that they shall enjoy it together.

Savoring In this context, the verb *nazkirah* surely means more than "proclaiming" a quality; it conveys the sense of inhaling a smell (Ibn Janaḥ, Ibn Ezra, Radak, Immanuel).[55] Elsewhere, the related noun *'azkarah* denotes the odor of the incense offering (Lev. 2:2, 9); and in Lev. 6:8 this term's referent is characterized as a *reiaḥ niḥoaḥ*, or "sweet-smelling savor"—thus underscoring the link in the Song to the *reiaḥ* ("fragrance") of the beloved's oils

(v. 3). See also Hos. 14:8, where restored Israel is likened to a great cedar "whose scent (*zikhro*) will be like the wine of Lebanon," thereby highlighting the link in v. 4 between aroma and wine. The usage of the stem *z-k-r* is thus part of a rich vocabulary of scents. The maiden's "sense" of her beloved is tangible.

Like new wine This translation understands the noun *meiysharim* as related to *tirosh* ("wine"; cf. Aramaic *merath*). Indeed, the term is elsewhere used with wine to indicate its good or proper flow (Prov. 23:31). Here, however, it would be better to construe *meiysharim* in its usual sense ("rightly"; see Ps. 58:2), so that the following word ("they love you") refers back to its occurrence at the end of verse 3. The author thus highlights the beloved's effect on the maidens.[56] Nonetheless, in the context of the preceding comparison with wine, a verbal play with *tirosh* is likely at work.

Stylistics. As compared with the poetic lines of verse 3, the four clauses of verse 4 have a narrative character. Each phrase develops the content further, rather than intensifying it through repetition. The fifth phrase ("rightly [or: like new wine] they love you") is the concluding refrain, in poetic parallelism with the final refrain in verse 3. Public love is doubly marked, denoted by the shared love of all the women (*'aheivukha*), in verses 3–4. By contrast, her more private love for him is also doubly marked—in a distinctive way (as *dodekha*)—in verses 2 and 4.

In terms of sound, the adverb *meiysharim* sustains the *sh*- continuo and evokes the superscription and its multitonal cluster: *shir ha-shirim*. Meanwhile, the *m-sh* cluster (of *meiysharim*) produces a tonal chord with *moshkheni* (draw me) at the start of verse 4, and with *shem* and *shemen* in verse 3. Thus the semantic sense

is thickened by internal rhymes. The result is a lyric song in every sense.

Derash

4. *Draw me* Having exulted in God's Torah and its spiritual "kisses" of life-giving direction, *Keneset Yisra'el* (the people) yearns for the joy of divine companionship: O God, seize our longing soul and draw it into the divine chambers, where exultation and intimacy may be joined!

In this plea (*moshkheini*), the sages discovered traces of divine graces already received—thereby transforming the imperative into words of thanksgiving. Hence "we shall run after You" in devotion because "You caused your *Shekhinah*" to dwell among us in the Shrine (*mishkan*); You brought us into the land of good "dwelling" (*mashkenuta*); and You received our sins in "deposit" (*mashkon*) for future repentance (SongsR 1.iv.4).[57] Praise now trumps petition.

Alternatively, it is God whose command of *moshkheini* asks the nation at Sinai to provide guarantors who will embody the "deposit" (*mashkon*) of enduring commitment—lest the present recipients of Torah fail to redeem its true value. A succession of ancestors is invoked, but God rejects them all due to sundry sins or failures of faith. Only children who study the Torah in simplicity are acceptable; only through them will the Torah be firmly established and guaranteed. Transmission of Tradition to future generations is thus essential. Children sit at the covenant's center (SongsR 1.iv.1; cf. Tan., *Vayigash* 2).

These two voices of "draw me"—Israel's and God's—reflect two sources of religious initiative. The voice of Israel is the human voice, in search of divine presence; it is the pathos of religious longing for spiritual intimacy—the cry of prayer. By contrast, the voice of God is a transcendent voice, calling to the human spirit for renewal and responsive openness; it is the revelation of possibility. The two voices meet in the heart of the individual.

The king has brought me to his chambers After the plea for divine intimacy, the people report the response: they were taken into God's chambers (a figure for the consummation of covenant love, and for the hidden mysteries of Torah; SongsR 1.iv.2).[58] And then in a heartbeat, the graced ones exult ("let us rejoice"), expressing their spiritual bliss *bakh* ("in You"). Initially God is referred to with a term of majesty ("the King"); and then, with a shift of focus to the Source of this bounty, God is addressed in personal terms. The word "in You" means "in *Your* salvation, in *Your* Torah, in reverence for *You*" (SongsR 1.iv.3; YalSh, Song, #982; Ibn Aqnin).[59] Torah mediates the religious love of God.

These two teachings stand at theological poles: direct religious feeling (a concrete sense of divine immanence) and indirect engagement with God (through Scripture and Tradition), respectively. If the first is a *modus vivendi*, focused on emotional experience, the second is a *modus operandi*, focused on embodied action.

The overall movement of the verse is also instructive. It begins with reverence for the transcendent God, "King" of the universe, and continues with love for the immanent God, the "You" of divine presence[60]—experienced in the world and in language. For Israel, the words of Torah and Tradition combine awe and intimacy: the holy tasks, undertaken with reverence, and the dutiful deeds, performed with love.

Remez

4. This verse articulates stages of the quest that follows the identification (v. 3) of a spiritual goal. Desire achieves a momentary realization. (But it is only one moment on the spiritual path. Soon the self falls back into everyday consciousness and self-centeredness; v. 5.)

Draw me after you The self desires an initiative from the divine source (Al-Fawwāl), expressing longing and readiness for heavenly beneficence (Sforno; Ibn Tibbon). The self wants to be more than itself; it wants to be drawn Godward into a higher actualization (Immanuel).

let us run A more intensified confirmation of the relationship with God.

The king A more reflective awareness of the relationship's awesome reality—shifting from the personal "You" to this more austere designation. After the personal petition, transcendence reasserts itself.

brought me to his chambers Expressing the personal sense of being spiritually resituated—a condition that the seeker savors...

more than wine The adept returns to an earlier image (v. 2), again extolling the divine relationship above all earthly pleasures.

Sod

4. ***Draw me after you*** We seekers yearn for a divine initiative that responds to our spiritual desire for God—and will draw us toward transcendence. This is expressed in personal terms; thus, first: "draw *me*"; then: "after You *we* shall run" ('Or Torah). Touched by God, the soul cultivates its spiritual resources (felt as a collection of energies—the self as "we") that must be integrated and devoted to divine service. Feeling this prompt as the call of divine sovereignty, the soul responds with joy (Ibn 'Attar).

brought me to his chambers Feeling taken into the realm of divine kingship, the soul proclaims an intention to harness its resources and devote them ("us") to God—*bakh*, "to You" (Kedushat Levi; AhavD 24b). There is now no scattering of energy or separation of the worldly from the godly, only the devotion of all things to God and godliness (Ketonet Passim). The desired summons (*moshkheini*, "draw me") widens in scope. Having focused its energies on divine service, the soul wishes to be taken into the transcendent Tabernacle (*miskhan*) of God (ZḤ 65b) and filled with the bounty of divine presence. Affirming its devotion, the soul adds: *meisharim 'aheivukha*, meaning that all its being is set to "love You (God) properly," and serve You "uprightly" (Ibn Sahula; REzra).

5 I am dark, but comely,
O daughters of Jerusalem—
Like the tents of Kedar,
Like the pavilions of Solomon.

5 שְׁחוֹרָה אֲנִי וְנָאוָה
בְּנוֹת יְרוּשָׁלָם
כְּאָהֳלֵי קֵדָר
כִּירִיעוֹת שְׁלֹמֹה׃

Peshat

2. A CONFESSION AND A QUERY (1:5–8)

This unit has two parts. Part 1 (vv. 5–6) opens with a woman addressing the "daughters of Jerusalem," telling them that she is dark but comely—like tents and pavilions. She bids them not to despise her for this, since she is sunburnt from long hours in the vineyards. The imagery thus shifts to her present condition and appearance. Self-conscious of her visage, she blames her brothers and exclaims that she has not (yet) tended her own vineyard (v. 6b). This phrase is a double entendre. Palpably, the "vineyard" is both a specific place and a figure for her person. Motivated by her distraught state, the maiden seeks fulfillment in love.

In part 2 (vv. 7–8), the maiden suddenly turns to her beloved and asks him "where" he will "pasture" his flock "at noon," lest she wander among the sheepfolds. He tells her to follow the tracks of the flock to the shepherds' tents—where they could meet (as they do, in the next unit).

Where this dialogue occurs, and how it continues the preceding scenes, is unclear. Perhaps her prior request—that he take her away—was a call of desire (following the opening wish); and she now renews that desire by asking him where he might be found. The words about her physical and emotional condition would thus function as an interlude.

5. I am dark, but comely The talk turns autobiographical. The maiden provides a self-depiction: *sheḥorah 'ani ve-na'vah*. As in the many self-descriptions that will follow, it focuses on subjective evaluations—attentive to inner states, tender in comparisons, and full of fervor.

but Commentators have puzzled over the force of this conjunction (*ve-*). Alternatively, "black *and* beautiful" (Immanuel). In context, the two attributes seem like variants of the same sense of self. Her exterior presentation (of darkness) is thus complemented by its evaluation (being beautiful). As she formulates it, her darkened pigment is the result of circumstance (stated in v. 6). Moreover, the striking occurrence of the personal pronoun between the two qualities heightens the stress on her skin color, which is then explained. Thus: "dark am I, *yet* comely." Having been subjected to the sun's glare, she is not what she seems.

comely The adjective *na'vah* is either a deliberate pun or a blend of two verbal stems. The main element is derived from the verbal stem *'a-w-h* (cf. Ps. 132:13), such that the word is a presumed *nif'al* participle connoting "desire" (Ibn Ezra). But the stem *n-'-h* also imposes itself and adds the quality of "beauty." By means of this doubled form, the maiden is rendered a double charm—lovely to sight and appealing to sense.

O daughters of Jerusalem The maiden addresses herself to figures who serve as intimates of her private feelings.

Like the tents . . . /Like the pavilions The two similes compare the (dark but beautiful) maiden to tents both dark and lovely. The first quality (dark) is to be linked to the nomadic tents of Kedar (Gen. 25:13; Ps. 120:5), presumably made of black goatskin; the second (beautiful) is connected to the pavilions of Solomon, presumably made of a lush woven fabric. This construal would separate the qualities but conjoin their effect.[61]

Stylistics. The qualities are linked by the particle *ve-*, and both are followed by two similes in succession. The reader may construe the structure in two ways. Read horizontally, as a series of elements, the two qualities are successively specified—thus: I am dark but beautiful—like the tents of Kedar, like the pavilions of Solomon;

but read vertically, as two parallel pairs, the similes evoke two distinct images—thus: I am dark like the tents of Kedar, but beautiful like the pavilions of Solomon.

Derash

5. ***I am dark*** After the expressions of covenant love, *Keneset Yisra'el* (the people) turns to self-examination. Recipients of divine grace, the people reflect on their worthiness. The pairing "dark" ***and*** "comely" evokes two kinds of self-evaluation (SongsR 1.v.1).[62] Together they highlight God's ever-gracious regard: even if the people feel dark and unworthy toward themselves (*bifnei 'atzmi*), they are lovely and beloved before their creator (*bifnei qoni*). God's love is a transforming reality. It is a gift of pure acceptance, revolutionizing self-perception.

Alternatively, this polar evaluation (dark-comely) reflects Israel's religious history. Though rebellious and unbelieving in Egypt and worshiping an idol (the golden calf) at Mount Sinai, the people also demonstrated religious commitment at these places—performing circumcision and the paschal offering in Egypt, and also proclaiming their loyalty at Sinai ("We will faithfully do"; Exod. 24:7; cf. MdRI, *Beshallaḥ* 4). This polarity inspired insights into the spiritual dynamics of ritual time. Said R. Levi b. Ḥayta, though the people be "dark" during the days of the week, or throughout the year, they may hope in a restoration of their "beauty"—both weekly on the Sabbath, and annually on Yom Kippur (SongsR 1.v.2). At these times, the dark shadows of sin may be removed through the restorative power of sacred occasions. If these moments are duly cultivated, the self may achieve a new spiritual harmony: derived from a radiant strength within (*mi-bifnim*), and not beset by events without (*mi-baḥutz*).

Remez

5. ***I am dark, but comely*** The self has returned to itself in its subjectivity. It draws upon personal experience to assess its mixed or complex nature.

Like the tents...pavilions The self-evaluation is analogized to external things, both pedestrian and royal. Aware of body and soul—natural reality and spiritual potential, respectively—the self feels itself as combining a lower, earthly condition and a higher, holy longing for integration or perfection (*sheleimut*). (Cf. Sforno; Al-Fawwāl.)

Sod

5. ***dark, but comely*** In the trembling before God's awesome transcendence, we seekers confess. "Dark" refers to our bodily nature; "comely," to our cultivated soul. The phrase is thus a declaration of worthiness.

This affirmation is then elaborated in a more figurative manner, when we seekers state that our outer nature enshrines a spiritual center—like a "pavilion" protecting some inward wholeness (*Shelomoh-shalom*). This inner quality is the spiritual axis that orients the self and directs a spiritual intention toward the world. The soul strives to sustain a balance between the inner and outer during life's vagaries. The declaration is thus also an assertion of spiritual purpose.

Spiritual inwardness transfigures one's physical being like a transcendent light piercing natural embodiment (Ibn Sahula). Since a person's externality may block the higher light (ZḤ 69d), the spiritual task is to access this light and sustain its presence. This is the inner beauty noted by the speaker. Its achievement requires self-discipline.

6 Don't stare at me because I am swarthy,
Because the sun has gazed upon me.
My mother's sons quarreled with me,
They made me guard the vineyards;
My own vineyard I did not guard.

6 אַל־תִּרְא֙וּנִי֙ שֶׁאֲנִ֣י שְׁחַרְחֹ֔רֶת
שֶׁשֱּׁזָפַ֖תְנִי הַשָּׁ֑מֶשׁ
בְּנֵ֧י אִמִּ֣י נִֽחֲרוּ־בִ֗י
שָׂמֻ֙נִי֙ נֹטֵרָ֣ה אֶת־הַכְּרָמִ֔ים
כַּרְמִ֥י שֶׁלִּ֖י לֹ֥א נָטָֽרְתִּי׃

Peshat

6. Don't stare at me Addressed to her companions, the maiden beseeches them not to look disapprovingly or mockingly at her (Rashi; Ibn Ezra; Rashbam). Hebrew *tir'uni* (literally "see me") functions like the related verb *le-ra'avah* in Ezek. 28:17 ("to stare; to hold in contempt"). Rashi also applied this sense to the verb *ra'u* in 1 Sam. 6:19;[63] see also his comment on *kotzerav* in B. Sot. 35a.

swarthy *Sheḥarḥoret* is a reduplicated noun based on the element *shaḥor* ("dark"). It alludes to her self-depiction as *sheḥorah* (v. 5). The precise force of the variant has been debated: Ibn Janaḥ considers the reduplication an intensification of quality;[64] whereas Ibn Ezra suggests that the form marks its diminishment (like *yeraqreq*, "light green"; also Immanuel; Rid).[65] The context suggests a darker hue, prompting her self-justification. Deftly, *sheḥarḥoret* also puns on the verb *shaḥar*, "seek, see, look out for" (see Prov. 7:15). It thereby reengages the verb *tir'uni*, "deride me," with its core meaning of "see, behold." The poet thus doubly marks the key issues of darkness and sight.

gazed upon me This rendering of *shezaftani* follows Rashbam (adducing Job 28:7) and captures a correlation between the prior mention of contemptuous "seeing" (by the maidens) and the sun's present deleterious "shining" or "gazing." Figuratively, the verb connotes being "scorched" or "burnt" (Ibn Aqnin; Immanuel).

My mother's sons The term denotes full siblings. This is the first of the maiden's three references to her mother (cf. 3:4 and 8:1).

quarreled with me Hebrew *niḥaru bi*, "were angry with me." The verb is a *nif'al* perfect from the stem *ḥ-r-h*, "burn." The vocalization is an alternate of *neḥeiru*. The word choice puns on "be hot" (Job 30:30) and also alludes to her coloring. Thus: she became sunburnt (*sheḥarḥoret*) because of their hot anger.

Stylistics. The sound cluster *ḥ-r* is dominant in this verse. It is marked in *sheḥarḥoret* and *niḥaru*. This tonal conjunction joins her present state to a past event.

made me guard Or "assigned me as a guard (*noṭeirah*)." This participial usage is more common in Aramaic; Hebrew usage prefers *natzar* (2 Kings 17:9). This formulation was presumably chosen to convey the added nuance of "anger" (as in Lev. 19:18, "bear a grudge"; Jer. 3:5, "hate"). That is, the brothers' anger made her a guard; she became an embodiment of their fury. The feminine form *noṭeirah* is a variant of the more common *noṭeret* (cf. *yoleidah* and *yoledet*, which denote a childbearing woman in Isa. 13:8 and Lev. 12:5, respectively).

My own vineyard I did not guard The maiden bemoans her condition. The statement suggests a figurative sense: she has not taken care of her personal needs.[66] (She proceeds to do so.) On the syntactic construction, see at 3:7.

Derash

6. Don't stare at me Having turned from self-criticism to a reflective inner-wisdom, the speaker bids others do likewise. Criticism should be balanced and not based on the shadow (*sheḥarḥoret*) of appearances—be these occasional sins or spiritual lapses by others (SongsR 1.vi.1). Generations of sages emphasized the need for good will, employing this verse to decry internecine malice and recrimination, by connecting the phrase "my mother's (*'immi*) sons" who "quarreled with me" with "the members of my people (*'ummati*)" en-

gaged in social contention (SongsR 1.vi.4). Citing biblical cases, they rebuked cultural discord and those who undermined religious life and its institutions (the "vineyard"; SongsR, ibid.). *Keneset Yisra'el* is that body politic that is injured by the fractiousness of its own siblings.

Remez

6. Don't stare at me Speaking perhaps through an interior dialogue, which presents self-judgment through the figure of external eyes (the stare of the Other).

Because the sun has gazed upon me That is, because of the self's exposure to the natural world and its glare.

My mother's sons quarreled Natural proclivities have induced inner conflict (Immanuel; Ibn Aqnin).

My own vineyard I did not guard The self realizes that it has squandered time and talent. The task must change; care for the world must be complemented by care for the inner self or "spiritual form."[67] This is the light within. (Wine imagery again inspires a reflection on personal priorities; cf. v. 2.)

Sod

6. Don't stare at me The speaker confesses to a dark night of the soul. She confesses to an impermeable darkness produced by the blaze of exterior forces (symbolized by the natural light of the sun) and the volatility of interior qualities (symbolized by the anger of siblings). The spiritual self has become lost in external tasks (Ketonet Passim), leaving its virtues unattended (Ibn Sahula) and desecrated (Elimelekh of Lizensk).[68]

The soul returns to itself with the recognition that it has not protected its "own vineyard." The work of self-cultivation is thus a spiritual healing of inner conflicts and recognition that the fallow field is one's "own." The self feels its own dark side and affirms this as a positive spiritual act. The divine stimulus has produced a deeper self-scrutiny (TiqZ 60b). Emboldened, the soul reengages its destiny.

7 Tell me, you whom I love so well;
Where do you pasture your sheep?
Where do you rest them at noon?
Let me not be as one who strays
Beside the flocks of your fellows.

7 הַגִּ֣ידָה לִּ֗י שֶׁאָֽהֲבָה֙ נַפְשִׁ֔י
אֵיכָ֣ה תִרְעֶ֔ה
אֵיכָ֖ה תַּרְבִּ֣יץ בַּֽצָּהֳרָ֑יִם
שַׁלָּמָ֤ה אֶֽהְיֶה֙ כְּעֹ֣טְיָ֔ה
עַ֖ל עֶדְרֵ֥י חֲבֵרֶֽיךָ׃

Peshat

7. ***Tell me*** Suddenly the maiden addresses her beloved. Without transition, the scene and focus shift dramatically. From a monologue with her companions, filled with her self-presentation, the maiden now engages her beloved in dialogue.

you whom I love A most heartfelt expression, literally "whom my soul [or: entire being] loves" (*she-'ahavah nafshi*). Indeed, it is precisely her *nefesh* (or entire self) that is overwhelmed by his presence in 5:6 and 6:12. A related sense of *nefesh*, expressing deep feelings for another person, occurs in the context of both male-female passion (Gen. 34:3) and male-male friendship (1 Sam. 20:17).[69] As earlier, the maiden is forthright about intimate emotions and unabashed in their expression.

Where Her desire is for an imminent rendezvous—elsewhere.

Where . . . / Where The doubling of the query intensifies her longing. The two phrases supplement one another ("pasture" // "rest them") as a twofold thread of inquiry.[70] The interrogative that inquires about location is usually *'eifoh* ("where") rather than *'eikhah*, as Ibn Ezra noted.[71] In 6:1, the interrogative *'anah* ("where [to]") is used to denote a similar query in search of the beloved.

Let me not be as one who strays The literal force of *shallamah 'ehyeh ke-'oṭyah* is interrogative: "For why should I be as one . . . ?" The formulation *shallamah* (similar to *she-lamah*; Rid) is a variant of *'asher lamah* (cf. Dan. 1:10), both possibly based on the Aramaic construction *di-lamah* ("for why"; found in Ezra 7:23).

The maiden's self-designation is difficult. If the word *'oṭyah* (or possibly *'oṭiyah*, like *bokhiyah*, "cry," in Lam. 1:16) derives from the verbal stem *'-ṭ-h* ("to cover"), one may construe her statement as not wishing to be like some "cloaked" woman (and perhaps mistaken as a harlot; cf. Gen. 38:14–15, where Tamar conceals herself at the crossroads).[72] However, the Greek, Syriac, and Targum versions all have some verb meaning "go astray." The frequent use of the Aramaic verb *ṭ-'-y* with this sense (cf. Targum Neofiti to Gen 21:14 and Exod. 14:3) supports the frequent emendation of MT *'oṭyah* to **ṭo'yah* (or **ṭo'iyah*)—meaning a person "who strays" or a "wayward person." This change is unnecessary if the Hebrew verb itself means "cast away," yielding "like a wanderer" as supposed by Anon. 1 and 2, as well as R. Shema'yah Ha-Shoshani (and cf. the Gra).[73] This sense is suggested by 1 Sam. 25:14 and Isa. 22:17.

Beside The preposition *'al* conveys the sense of "nearby." In context, it may mean "high" or "above"; that is, she would be high above the flocks or concealed from the other shepherds' view (as in a secret tryst; so Immanuel).

Derash

7. ***Tell me, you whom I love*** The speaker turns back to God after self-reflection; but this pause was sufficient to lose contact with the divine presence. Such are the vagaries of spiritual consciousness that even a devoted religious sensibility can easily be set adrift. In this instance the question "Where do You pasture your sheep?" conveys a longing for God's Presence, that the self not "stray" in despair (cf. *'oṭyah* in the Peshat). As the voice of *Keneset Yisra'el*, this appeal expresses the anxieties of historical reality. Though carrying the memories of Sinai in her heart, the people are tormented by national suffering, and wonder "where" God is and how God shepherds their lives.

Alternatively, Moses is speaking; and he asks God, "Tell me, concerning this people whom I love," how can it endure the heat and sun of historical oppression? (SongsR I.vii.1). Or he is pleading: "Tell me" how You will provide leaders for the people and shepherd them in the ensuing subjugation and exile! (ibid. vii.2).[74]

Remez

7. Tell me The self now undertakes care for its soul, turning its attention toward the Beloved One. But this self has lost direction. It seeks a path (through the world and selfhood) to where God and the spiritual realities reside.

Where do you rest This is a question asked outwardly; but it is also directed to the soul's inwardness, where its powers might find "rest" (spiritual tranquility).

Let me not be as one who strays Renewal of the soul begins with this sense of loss and being lost—off one's true path (Ibn Aqnin). From this place of longing, the soul's question has arisen ("Tell *me*") and posed its request for spiritual direction (Malbim; Immanuel).

In response to this ardor, an answer somehow rises—and is heard (see next verse).

Sod

*7. **Tell me, you whom I love*** The return to spiritual life is a complex blend of absence and presence. The driving force of "love" restores the search for God; but its inner hesitations leave the soul lost and disoriented. This crisis is formulated as a double question: where (*'eikhah*) is the place from which You, God, emanate care for all Being (as a shepherd)?—and why (*lamah*) should I, Your seeker, be a wanderer who "strays" afield? The self has lost its spiritual direction; Divinity has receded in ambiguous absence. Embedded in the first question is the quest for the mysterious "how" (*'eikhah*) of divine providence (Z. 3:17b; Ibn Sahula); concealed in the second is the supplication: "let me not be" lost forever among the other seekers ("your fellows").[75] The soul appeals for spiritual direction. How and where, LORD, do You shepherd Being? The lonely soul ponders in perplexity. How can the Unknowable be known, or the Endless found?

8 If you do not know, O fairest of women,
Go follow the tracks of the sheep,
And graze your kids
By the tents of the shepherds.

8 אִם־לֹא תֵדְעִי֙ לָ֔ךְ הַיָּפָ֖ה בַּנָּשִׁ֑ים
צְאִי־לָ֞ךְ בְּעִקְבֵ֣י הַצֹּ֗אן
וּרְעִי֙ אֶת־גְּדִיֹּתַ֔יִךְ
עַ֖ל מִשְׁכְּנ֥וֹת הָרֹעִֽים׃ פ

Peshat

8. The beloved's response has a narrative quality: "If you do not know . . . follow the tracks . . . and graze . . . by the tents." The formulation twice employs an ethical dative (*teid'ei lakh*, "know—for your benefit"; *tze'i lakh*, "go forth—for your benefit"); but adds no further directions. Details of his whereabouts are lacking. But when the pair are next mentioned, they are face to face in loving dialogue.

graze your kids As a pretext for coming (Transl.).

Stylistics. The negative *'al tir'uni* ("don't stare at me"; v. 6) has its positive counterpoint in *'eikhah tir'eh* ("where do you pasture?"; v. 7). The maiden speaks the first phrase to the women, the second to her beloved. This alliteration conjoins the maiden's concerns: her physical state and her desire. The alliterative pair *Shelomoh* ("Solomon"; v. 5) and *sha-lamah* ("for why"; v. 7) has a similar effect.

Derash

8. If you do not know Answers to these queries are addressed to the nation and Moses, the "fairest of women." To those who feel the loss of direct providence, the answer of the Song is to follow the "tracks" (*'iqvot*) left by tradition. Just these may provide the imprint of a holy life, and enable the people ("kids") to find stability in the schools ("tents") of their teachers (the "shepherds"). Study and the instruction may thus provide a path of hope (B. Shab. 33b; cf. Z. 3:17b).

The answer offered to Moses (archetypal leader of the nation) is that the people may transcend personal sufferings by casting an eye to portents of the future. They should "go forth" and learn about hints of the "end" (the future time; *'aqeiv*) from the "traces" (*'iqvei*) left by past acts of divine care (SongsR 1.viii.3).

Rabbi Akiva recalls in this connection God's providence in the desert wandering, when the "clouds of the divine glory" (*Shekhinah*) enveloped the people like sheltering "booths" (*sukkot*; Lev. 23:43). Sustained by this memory, the people may be consoled by the old prophecy of Isaiah, which seems to echo this event—when it promises that God would again provide a shelter (*sukkah*) for the spiritual benefit of the people (Isa. 4:6; SongsR; ibid.; GenR 48.10).

Rashi neutralizes this expectation; he focuses instead on the righteous ancestors, saying that their Torah practices would protect and guide the nation—confused and unable to know where to turn in their historical travail. If R. Akiva focuses on a model of divine care, Rashi emphasizes human conduct. Both views find support in Scripture and Tradition.

Remez

8. The adept is told to heed both public tradition and personal uniqueness, in order to find the path toward the One who awaits.

If you do not know The self's not-knowing is confirmed and answered (Ibn Tibbon).

Go follow The voice instructs the seeker to heed other seekers ("sheep") and traditional teachers ("shepherds") (Immanuel; Ibn Aqnin). The imperative *tze'i lakh* invites listeners to "go out of" (or transcend) themselves—beyond one's prior presumptions and misdirection, to new paths on the spiritual journey.

graze your kids The voice also calls the self to release one's hidden soul-potential. This instruction is directed to what is most personal and distinct about one's spiritual self.

Sod

8. ***If you do not know*** An answer is addressed to the soul. "If you do not know"—*lakh*, on your own, then "go" forth—*lakh*, from your own limitations, and follow the way of other seekers. Seek the clues and "tracks" that have guided their way. The self is called to self-transcendence in its quest for divine transcendence. It is called to a higher wisdom (ZḤ 70b). Where the inner vineyard is not sufficient, one must follow the external traces of God's gifts wherever they lead.

To discern how God shepherds Being, one must become a shepherd oneself—and learn how others seek these mysteries. One may take counsel from the "dwelling places" (*mishkenot*),[76] or portals where God has become manifest to human consciousness. Just these are the "tabernacles" (*mishkenot*) of the *Shekhinah* in our world.

This teaching is both revealing and concealing. It merely points a way forward; it does not provide explicit answers. To perceive the flow of Being, one must enter the flow of life and follow the examples of others who have done likewise. This is a going-forward with discernment, guided by shared wisdom. Because the soul has strengthened itself with new spiritual purpose, she is called the "fairest of women" (Ibn Sahula). This is an inward beauty set upon a disciplined path.

⁹I have likened you, my darling,
To a mare in Pharaoh's chariots:

9 לְסֻסָתִי֙ בְּרִכְבֵ֣י פַרְעֹ֔ה
דִּמִּיתִ֖יךְ רַעְיָתִֽי׃

Peshat

3. PRAISES AND RESPONSES (vv. 9–14)

This subsection joins several topics. It presents dialogues of descriptive praise. The male compares the maiden to a mare of Pharaoh's chariots, splendidly studded and outfitted (vv. 9–11); and he calls her "my beloved" (ra'yati), thus alluding to the shepherding language she used earlier ("where do you pasture, tir'eh?"). Perhaps in response to the royal imagery, the maiden suddenly makes a strikingly bold, evocative statement—presumably to her friends (v. 12). Privately expressed, the reader overhears this intimacy.

9–11. The beloved addresses the maiden, in the first of several encomiums. She had described herself as black yet beautiful and compared herself to tents. He now compares her to a mare among Pharaoh's steeds (caparisoned in finery)—an image evoking vigor and vitality.⁷⁷ Linking the two comparisons, one commentator suggested that the male is responding to her self-designation as black—a black mare being the most beautiful (Anon. 1).

The sequence has three parts. In the first, the beloved invokes the image ("to a mare," *le-susati*), then stresses its role as a literary trope ("I have likened you"; v. 9). The second part takes up the general figure and offers details about her cheeks and her neck (v. 10). These features serve as a metonym for her entire body. The final part goes further, and refers to the gems and fine tooling.

9. likened This verb *damah* recurs in 2:9, 17; 8:14. It evokes the notion of similarity. Ezekiel employs it when comparing the king of Egypt to a mighty tree (31:2–3, 8). Isaiah uses it to stress God's incomparability (40:25 and 46:5).

my darling Literally, "my friend." The noun *ra'yah* is an alternate feminine form of **rei'ah* (whose plural is *rei'ot*, Judg. 11:38). There are two masculine forms as well, *rei'a* and *rei'eh* (see 2 Sam. 13:3 and 15:37, respectively).

Deftly, the word evokes both the Hebrew term for grazing and the Aramaic word for desire (cf. Ezra 5:17; Targum Neofiti employs it to render *ḥashaq*, "set His heart," in Deut. 7:7).

mare The noun *susati* is a feminine absolute with a suffix; the *-i* ending is arguably an old genitive case-marker that (following a preposition) had almost entirely dropped out of use by the classical Hebrew period. According to Ibn Ezra: "The (final) *yod* is supplemental, like *melei'ti mishpat* ("filled with justice"; Isa. 1:21)."⁷⁸

in Pharaoh's chariots That is, outstanding even among a group of select horses (so Rashbam, following Rashi).

Derash

9. The plea for God's presence is answered with words of loving regard. They allude to the salvation from Egypt—suggesting that Israel was like a mare of God's providential care that led the enemy to doom (SongsR 1.ix.6).

Alternatively, these events were tokens of hope (Leqaḥ Ṭov). In addition to the imagery (mare), the theological power of these words lies in the epithet "my darling" or "Beloved" (ra'yati), which expresses the special role Israel has played in sustaining the world order. God calls her *ra'yati* because she is *ra'yeta' de-'olami*—the "provider of My world"—the people who gives moral stability and spiritual worth to the creation, through her acceptance of divine sovereignty and the enactment of Torah (SongsR, 1.ix.6). When Israel affirmed divine lordship at Sinai (proclaiming "We will do and obey," Exod. 24:7), they affirmed a commitment to divine unity and covenantal law. Their collective proclamation of God's sovereignty affirmed the ideals of monotheistic transcendence and its promises of religious harmony (beyond sectarian divisions) and of social utopia (beyond ethnic discord). Sinai

thus marks Israel's commitment to the ideals of a habitable creation and a moral order at every level. Ethics is deep ecology.

Remez

*9. **I have likened you, my darling*** In the soul's quest, its new beginning is confirmed. The question for direction has opened a new spiritual moment. For whereas the seeker had earlier compared itself to tents and pavilions as markers of its twofold nature (v. 5), it is now likened by its Beloved to a royal "mare"—that is, its spiritual majesty is affirmed through the image of a horse "in Pharaoh's chariots." For the seeking self, this depiction might confirm that its physical aspects—its earthly being—are harnessed toward higher goals (Malbim). Care for one's vineyard (v. 6) is thus dramatized in a more energetic image (Al-Fawwāl). The feminine voice that recuperates its task through a figure of growth and care (for the vineyard) is replaced by a figure of vigor and nobility. The self is thus envisioned from two perspectives.

Sod

*9. **I have likened you, my darling*** The approbation continues. The soul is now deemed "my darling" (*ra'yati*)—to confirm her desire to know where God "shepherds" (*tir'eh*; v. 7) Being, and to underscore the instruction that she should "shepherd" (*re'i*) her flock among other "shepherds" (*ro'im*; v. 8)—who are also in search of God's presence.

To further mark her new state, the soul is compared to "*My* mare in Pharaoh's chariots" (Ibn Sahula).[79] Suddenly the soul is addressed as a person. The soliloquy of love has become a dialogue. The questing self has been taken up in love.

These words of acceptance ("*My* darling") are like a kiss from the divine Beloved.

10 Your cheeks are comely with plaited wreaths,
Your neck with strings of jewels.
11 We will add wreaths of gold
To your spangles of silver.

10 נָאו֤וּ לְחָיַ֙יִךְ֙ בַּתֹּרִ֔ים
צַוָּארֵ֖ךְ בַּחֲרוּזִֽים׃
11 תּוֹרֵ֤י זָהָב֙ נַעֲשֶׂה־לָּ֔ךְ
עִ֖ם נְקֻדּ֥וֹת הַכָּֽסֶף׃

Peshat

10. comely The beloved's adjective for the maiden's beauty (*na'vu*) echoes her self-depiction (*na'vah*; v. 5). The two units are thus brought into dramatic correlation.

plaited wreaths The rare noun *torim* may denote something circular (cf. Num. 13:25)—like a hoop or ring; or something in rows (cf. Est. 2:12)—like a braid or pendant. The ornament designated as *turru* in Akkadian may refer to a string of gems.[80]

11. We will add Literally, "we shall make for you" (*na'aseh-lakh*). This inclusive language echoes the maiden's own earlier exclamation, "we shall rejoice in you" (*nismeḥah-bakh*; v. 4).

Stylistics. The three-part structure utilizes two types of poetic parallelism. In verse 10 the adjective ("beautiful," *na'vu*) comes first and governs the ensuing sets of comparison ("*x* in *y*"), which supplement one another. The first formulation emphasizes the female body as a whole; the second, the ornaments around her face. Verse 11 includes a future ornament, adding a supplement ("*x* with *y*"). Both the maiden's countenance and her bodily form hold the male in thrall.

Derash

10. plaited wreaths... strings of jewels The imagery of praise shifts to features of physical beauty, set off by ornaments: *torim... ḥaruzim*. These decorations evoke and celebrate Israel's transformation into a Torah-centered people.[81] The "cheeks" allude to Moses and Aaron: as cheeks were created for speech, so were these two created to speak "in *torim*"—that is, "in the two Torahs, [both] the written and oral" (SongsR 1.x.1; YalSh, Song, #583). The topic is extended to include ongoing study. Just as the sages expound the *halakhah* of these Torahs and explore (*la-tur*) their wisdom (Eccles. 1:13), their disciples' expositions are like "strings (*ḥaruzim*) of jewels," which "link" (*ḥorezim*) the words of Torah to the words of the Prophets, and the words of the Prophets to those of the Writings. Through such acts, which conjoin the language of Scripture in new combinations, "the words rejoice as when they were [first] given at Sinai" (SongsR 1.x.2; and J. Ḥag. 2:5).[82]

According to R. Yehudah, this verse and the next allude to the classic threefold division of Scripture. Here, *torim* refers to Torah, and *ḥaruzim* (which can also mean "poetic verses") refers to the Prophets. See the next comment.

11. wreaths of gold... spangles of silver Heb. *torei zahav... nequdot ha-kasef*. Rabbi Yehudah noted: "The *torei zahav* refer to the Writings, and the *nequdot ha-kasef* refer to the Song of Songs, whose every word is simultaneously sealed and specified (*ḥatumah... mesuyyamah*)" (SongsR 1.xi.1; see above at v. 10).[83] Paradoxically, the Song's words are sealed shut (their plain sense is obscure), yet their import is spelled out (their hidden connotation is apparent via an associative reading). This dual character gives the Song its allusive, riddling aspect—and its capacity to elicit meanings of unexpected significance.[84]

Remez

10. Your cheeks are comely The imagery of praise shifts. The seeker is now depicted as comely and bedecked with ornaments. The first phrase echoes the initial self-depiction (v. 5); and if the seeker expressed a hesitant assertion ("black *but comely*") of self-worth, the Beloved now praises the person's development without qualification. Such praise is enhanced by refer-

ring to additional qualities (Malbim). Thus the self as a whole is initially commended, and then various aspects of its being (or appearance) are singled out.

11. We will add The developing self is not passive but participates in its own spiritual augmentation (Ibn Aqnin; Al-Fawwāl). The pronoun "we" suggests that as the seeker progresses, the self's attainments are neither appropriated (undeservedly, from without) nor bestowed (unmerited, from within). That is, the occurrence of the "we" suggests a mutuality of giving and receiving: what is taken is given, and what is offered is received. The two realms coalesce—for the moment.

wreaths of gold . . . spangles of silver These stand for the new attainments: *torei zahav* and *nequdot ha-kasef*. From the perspective of the questing self, this means that there must be a certain (proper) "order" (*tor*) in our growth toward God and spirituality, and that the seeker must balance the sequences of self-development and shapes of human "desire" (*kissuf*), on the one hand, and the quality of spiritual goals longed for, on the other (Malbim; Immanuel; Al-Fawwāl; Ralbag). This accord (marked as "we" in the text) correlates inner processes with transcendent realities.

Sod

10–11. Your cheeks are comely The spiritual achievement of the seeker is confirmed. She had spoken of her beauty (*na'vah*; v. 5), and it is now seen as such (her "cheeks" are *na'vu*).

A special radiance frames her face: her hair is more than a natural plait; her neck sparkles bright as a jeweled aura. Love of the Beloved has transformed the seeker and adorns her natural state (Ibn Sahula). Wondrously, the radiance of love has bestowed "wreaths of gold" and "spangles of silver" to her being.

Receiving these words of bestowal ("we shall *make* for you," *na'aseh lakh*; v. 11),[85] the seeker feels reborn. She hears these words as a sign of her re-creation (cf. *na'aseh 'adam*, "Let us make a creature"; Gen. 1:26).

The word *lakh* completes a progression. In verse 8, it marked the seeker's lack of spiritual knowledge and the charge to transcend one's naturalness in quest of God. It now underscores the gift of self-renewal—a heavenly grace "for *you*." On the path of spiritual development, each individual must go *le-fum'orḥoi*, "in their own (personal) way" (ZḤ 72b).

12 While the king was on his couch,
My nard gave forth its fragrance.

12 עַד־שֶׁהַמֶּ֙לֶךְ֙ בִּמְסִבּ֔וֹ
נִרְדִּ֖י נָתַ֥ן רֵיחֽוֹ׃

Peshat

12–14. The maiden's response evokes odors and spices that exude from the body and field. These connote intimacy and eros.

*12. **While*** Temporal clauses starting with *'ad she-* occur frequently in the Song (similar to *be-'od she-*), as here;[86] elsewhere, this construction apparently denotes "until" (as if *be-khol 'od she-*; cf. 2:7).

the king Tamakh understands this as an epithet of loving admiration.

couch The noun *meisev* is mentioned in B. Shab. 63a, where it denotes a couch for reclining at meals—and is employed as a sexual euphemism (Rashi).[87] This connotation is intimated by our passage as well.

nard An aromatic of the genus *Nardostachys*, otherwise mentioned only in 4:13–14, which famously evokes desire (Immanuel)—and thus an erotic overtone here. It is listed among the spices of the priestly incense offering in B. Kar. 6a.

Derash

12. Rabbi Meir applied the royal reference to God (the King of kings) and proposed a historical reading of this verse: even while God was still resting upon Mt. Sinai to commune with Moses, the people gave off the odor (*reiaḥ*) of sin, due to their worship of the golden calf.[88] Thus the speaker is countering the Beloved's praise with a confession of sin (Rabbi Shlomoh).

Rabbi Yehudah rejected this view. Rather, the Song may be "interpreted" (*doreshin*) only in "praise" (*shevaḥ*) of the people of Israel—and never to their detriment. Hence he explained the verse as saying that while God was still at Sinai, the people averred: "All that the LORD said, we will faithfully do"—literally "we shall do and hear" (Exod. 24:7)—and thus emitted a "good fragrance" before the King (SongsR 1.xii.1).[89]

The positions of R. Meir and R. Yehudah reflect two poles. One focused on the paradox of sin: "even as" God's presence was with the people, they undermined their oaths of loyalty; the other focused on the paradox of commitment: "even before" the people "heard" the Law or comprehended its consequences, they asserted their readiness to "do" it.

Remez

*12. **While the king was on his couch*** The dialogue is disrupted, and the speaker reflects on the space between the self and its ideal. The "king" is set over there, separate; the self, embodied by its "nard," wafts "forth its fragrance" from here. The self is stimulated and emits its longing toward the object of desire. This image counterpoints the initial figure of the Beloved Other as itself suffused in a wafting fragrance (v. 3).

Sod

*12. **While the king was on his couch*** The soul responds to the Beloved. Addressed in personal terms, she remains cognizant of God's Majesty (cf. v. 4). The voice that pierces the heart seems to come from beyond—as from a divine king enthroned on High. The religious sense feels God's transcendence—and feeling it, responds. But this sensibility is beyond language; hence the self can merely exude its love as the silent fragrance of inner feelings.

Compactly, this image denotes the experience's complexity. On the one hand, the soul asserts that "my nard gave forth *its* fragrance" (*reiḥo*)—that is, it states that the feelings of love come from itself (at this moment). On the other, the speaker also avers that this fragrance comes from God (it is *His* fragrance; *reiḥo*)—that is, the soul has been suffused by divine love and responds with the gift of love *that it has been given* (Z. 1:30a).

In this way, the speaker affirms that the response is genuine. God's gracious gift of Being evokes a response in kind: creatures turn to God through the resources bestowed upon them. The *reiaḥ* of God's ointment, proclaimed as good (v. 2), is now experienced. A sense of union is suggested; and the divine-human poles are suddenly correlated (Ibn Sahula). Though God still remains beyond and apart, a turning toward intimacy has begun.

13 My beloved to me is a bag of myrrh
Lodged between my breasts.
14 My beloved to me is a spray of henna blooms
From the vineyards of En-gedi.

13 צְר֨וֹר הַמֹּ֤ר ׀ דּוֹדִי֙ לִ֔י
בֵּ֥ין שָׁדַ֖י יָלִֽין׃
14 אֶשְׁכֹּ֨ל הַכֹּ֤פֶר ׀ דּוֹדִי֙ לִ֔י
בְּכַרְמֵ֖י עֵ֥ין גֶּֽדִי׃ ס

Peshat

13. a bag of myrrh Rashbam remarks: "Now the two of them lie on their bed and speak to one another... [She saying:] 'My Beloved is sweet to me—he who lies[90] with me and places his head between my breasts like a sachet of myrrh.'"[91] Flasks with oils were worn by women in rabbinic times (M. Shab. 6:3).

between my breasts Anon. 1 interprets *beiyn shadai* here to mean: "When he is between my breasts; [this being] a euphemism."

14. vineyards of En-gedi These were well known even in later Roman antiquity, as documented in diverse sources.[92]

Derash

13–14. These verses articulate the intimate relationship between *Keneset Yisra'el* and her Beloved (*dodi*). The expressions of love focus on various plants of symbolic significance. Interpreted historically, the figures apply to the patriarchs, who displayed three paradigms of religious devotion.

bag of myrrh According to Rabbi Azariah, *tzeror ha-mor* refers to Abraham. Just as this plant is a premier spice, which gives off its best fragrance when burnt, so was this patriarch the foremost of martyrs, whose fealty to God was first displayed when he was thrown in the fiery furnace of the Chaldeans for destroying their local idols (SongsR 1.xiii.2; and GenR 38.13). Remaining steadfast, he endured this travail ("suffering," *tzeror*) by being as scented as *mor* when tested and burnt. Abraham is thus a model of martyrdom for those who are put to death by fire.

Other explications make a similar point. Just as one who gathers *mor* has his hands embittered (*mitmarmerot*) in the process, so did Abraham "suffer" (*memarmeir*) and "undergo torment with suffering" in order to sanctify God in the world (SifDeut, *Ha'azinu* 311; GenR 57.4; SongsR, ibid.). His acts are extolled as paradigmatic expressions of love, now recounted by *Keneset Yisra'el* to her Beloved. Myrrh symbolizes spiritual commitment, which is kept close to one's bosom.

spray of henna blooms The phrase *'eshkol ha-kopher* refers to Isaac, in recognition of his loyalty to God when "bound upon the altar" (Gen. 22:9–14). Like a sacrificial offering, Isaac's suffering atoned for the people—the henna blooms (*kopher*) signaling "atonement (*mekhapper*) for Israel's sins" (GenR 56.8–9; SongsR 1.xiv.1).[93] Thus Isaac's fortitude had profound consequences—even for future generations.[94] During the Roman and Christian persecutions, Jews could turn to the deeds of their ancestors as models of faithfulness, martyrdom, and vicarious suffering. Such images have resonated for subsequent generations similarly beset by persecutions and suffering, and by the need for models of sacrifice and intercessory atonement after the Temple's destruction. The example of Isaac is recited to God daily in the morning liturgy, annually on Rosh Hashanah, and also on special penitential occasions (like the Ten Days of Penitence and the Ninth of Av).

Rabbi Berekhiah points out the sages' capacity to provide atonement for the people through their devoted study of Torah. For the verse refers to the atoning (*mekhapper*) power of "a person who is infused" (*'ish she-ha-kol bo*) with the works of Scripture and Tradition (SongsR 1.xiv.2). The scholar is like a priest; devotion to learning is like a sacrificial gift. Here again is a Jewish response to the mystery of atonement in times after the Temple—elevating the ritual act (*'avodah*) of study to a supreme cultic status.

vineyards of En-gedi The phrase *karmei ein-gedi* applies to the patriarch Jacob, in his

filial piety. For readers disturbed by his deception of his blind father (Gen. 27:6–29), this passage offers a portrait of his inner state (SongsR 1.xiv.1): when Jacob went to Isaac to receive the blessing, he did so with a "blushing face" (*kerum panav*), while concealed in the skins of a "goat" (*gedi*).

Remez

13–14. My beloved to me is The interior discourse continues and compares the Beloved (embodiment of the quest) to the perfumes of nature—"myrrh" (v. 13) and "henna blooms" (v. 14). The couplet expresses the seeker's transfixed state: the Beloved is both near and physically close to the self, as well as other and physically distinct from it ("set among the fields"). The sense of a loving appropriation ("to *me*") is thus internally split. The seeker feels both nearness to and distance from a spiritual center. Put differently: the religious goal has both an inward and an other-directed component—a matter mirrored by use of the pronoun "my" for the Beloved, who dwells within the heart and mind; and by use of the verb "is" to introduce the image of comparison, since the Beloved is perceived through the lens of creative representations.

Sod

13. My beloved to me The human speaker continues in response to the divine initiative. The voice exults to whoever would hear. Her Beloved remains other, but He has entered her heart. This is the mystery of spiritual love. What was distant has come near. God is now a presence.

The "bag (*tzeror*) of myrrh / Lodged between my breasts" symbolizes this intimacy. The wholly other, ever remaining so, is also a personal reality. The initiative of God, a grace unexpected and infusing (v. 12), is transformed into a personal truth, exciting the heart and expanding the mind (AhavD 50a–51a).[95]

Earlier, in expectant hope, God's love was called "*Your* love" (*dodekha*; vv. 2, 4)—for it was all desire and wish. God is now addressed as "*My* Beloved" (*dodi*)—for His emanation fills the self. This intimacy is the wondrous thing "hidden away" (*tzarur*) as a "shape" (*tzurah*) of Divinity in the depths of the heart (REzra).[96]

14. My beloved to me The speaker exults further. Now the experience and its token are identified with "henna blooms / From the vineyards of En-gedi." The change in imagery is symbolic and significant. Having tended her own vineyard (cf. v. 6) and heeded the instruction to lead her "kids" (*gediyotayikh*), or spiritual qualities, along the tracks of other seekers (v. 8), the speaker has achieved success. God has infused her with His love and has met her through the attributes she has cultivated. (In token of this fact, she plucks blossoms from the "vineyards of En-*gedi*.") Spiritual realization is achieved not in the tents of other shepherds (with their models or proclivities), but through one's own traits.

This truth is placed as a sign upon her breast. Deftly the speaker obscures whether the divine "*is*" or "is *as*" this spice. Once again, an interior truth is memorialized through a concrete expression: a sign upon her heart.

15 Ah, you are fair, my darling,
Ah, you are fair,
With your dove-like eyes!

הִנָּ֤ךְ יָפָה֙ רַעְיָתִ֔י 15
הִנָּ֖ךְ יָפָ֑ה
עֵינַ֖יִךְ יוֹנִֽים׃

Peshat

4. THE LOVERS' DUET (VV. 15–17)

In the opening cycle's final unit, the loving couple dialogue. Now face to face, he praises her beauty and doves' eyes; and she echoes his words with praise for their love hut. All distance overcome, the poet intimates a consummation of their love.

Masoretic tradition carries this unit through 2:7. However, 2:1–7 seems to be a separate discourse and focuses on a house—not a bower. We shall treat it separately, as a postlude to the present passage.

15. In response to her love-talk, the Beloved answers. She has just referred to him as *dodi* ("my beloved"); now he calls her *ra'yati* ("my darling"). He proclaims her beauty (*hinnakh yafah*, "Ah, you are fair") twice, with ascending intensity.

With your dove-like eyes The metaphor *'einayikh yonim* literally means "your eyes are doves." This rendering recasts it as a simile. The point is that her eyes are soft and appealing (Immanuel).

Derash

15. *you are fair…you are fair* In response to Israel's faithfulness, God responds doubly: you are "fair" through the performance of the commandments, and "fair" from deeds of loving kindness. Alternatively: you are "fair" through the fulfillment of positive religious duties, and "fair" for your rejection of prohibited acts (SongsR 1.xv.1).[97] Loveliness is thus a spiritual quality. Religious commitment transforms the appearance and nature of the doer.

dove-like eyes Israel is extolled further. Just as a dove is both "pure" and "modest" and "loyal" to its mate, so is Israel pure in its religious and personal comportment—loyal to God and to the institution of marriage (SongsR 1.xv.4). These eyes are mirrors of the national soul, praised for inner and outer piety.

Remez

15. *Ah, you are fair* The longing for spiritual realization is now answered by a call from the divine to the soul (Malbim), exulting: Behold, *you* are fair! The self feels addressed and confirmed in its development (Immanuel; Ralbag). Having cultivated its spiritual nature, the self is no longer subject to the harsh gaze of self-judgment (v. 6), but now has opened the inner eye of spiritual perception—a quality called here "dove-like eyes."

Sod

15. *you are fair* The final dialogue externalizes the experience just depicted. The soul hears the Beloved call her "beautiful" (*yafah*)—twice, to underscore the event's intensity.

This beauty is conveyed by her "dove-like eyes." Why the eyes? Perhaps to confirm her spiritual gaze and accentuate her insight. The soul has moved through the visible world, yearning for spiritual vision. And this has become a reality. The eyes are the pools in which God has been refracted into her purified soul—and this realization is confirmed as beautiful (Ibn Sahula). Emboldened, she celebrates His beauty as well.

16 And you, my beloved, are handsome,
Beautiful indeed!
Our couch is in a bower;
17 Cedars are the beams of our house,
Cypresses the rafters.

16 הִנְּךָ֨ יָפֶ֤ה דוֹדִי֙
אַ֣ף נָעִ֔ים
אַף־עַרְשֵׂ֖נוּ רַעֲנָנָֽה׃
17 קֹר֤וֹת בָּתֵּ֙ינוּ֙ אֲרָזִ֔ים
רחיטנו רַהִיטֵ֖נוּ בְּרוֹתִֽים׃

Peshat

16–17. The maiden echoes his words, but her intensification is different. She states, "[You are] truly (*'af*) lovely" (v. 16), and then adds: "truly (*'af*) our couch (*'arseynu*) is in a bower." She describes their "home."

16. ***And you... are handsome*** She reciprocates, proclaiming his beauty (*hinnekha yafeh*) in terms that correspond precisely to what he has just told her (*hinnakh yafah*, "Ah, you are fair").

couch The noun *'eres* corresponds to *bayit* ("house, home") in the next verse. This word pair occurs in Ps. 132:3 and in Ugaritic texts (*bt // 'rs*).[98] The pairing here is suggestive. In an Akkadian love lyric, the two words are conjoined (as *bet erši*) with the explicit sense of "bedroom" (or place of anticipated lovemaking).[99]

in a bower Literally, "a splendid [overgrowth of trees]."

17. ***Cypresses the rafters*** Both words are unique in the Bible: *berotim* ("cypresses") is an Aramaic form of *beroshim* (used as a building material in 1 Kings 6:15); *rahiṭeinu* (reading with the Qerey; literally "our *rahiṭim*") may be related to an Aramaic verb meaning "to run," and to the Syriac word for a "beam" (*rahaṭa'*)—and would thus denote the beams that run across a ceiling (cf. Rashbam). In this outdoor setting, it would refer to the extended limbs of the trees overhead.

Rabbinic tradition, possibly derived from this passage, records the custom of planting a cedar sapling upon a boy's birth, and a cypress upon a girl's, and subsequently using these trees for their bridal bower (B. Git. 57a).

Derash

16. ***And you... are handsome, / Beautiful indeed!*** *Keneset Yisra'el* now responds in turn, expressing her own great love. God having deemed her *yafah* ("fair") twice, Israel now proclaims her Beloved Lord both *yafeh* ("handsome") and *na'im* ("beautiful"). The praise of God is not redundant, but progressive and climactic (SongsR 1.xi.1). Moreover, the text varies its two terms of male beauty, punctuating the second with the exclamation *'af* ("indeed"). This gasp says it all: descriptive terms for God are mere gestures, pointing toward eminence; the evocative gasp of the worshiper reveals the soul, unloosed in shuddering wonder at sheer divine splendor.

Our couch is in a bower This love song rises toward ecstatic consummation, as the people speak of their spiritual union with God ("*our* couch"). This "couch" is the Temple. Its sanctuary was the locus for God's indwelling (Ibn Aqnin) and thus a font of earthly bounty (AdRN, A, 1; SongsR 1.xvi.3; Rashi). Indeed, the Ark (with its staves) was deemed a virtual marital bed for God's fructifying presence (cf. B. Yoma 54a).[100]

The Temple thus marks the spatial and spiritual nexus of God's conjunction with Israel; it symbolizes their covenant marriage. In a world without the Temple, God dwells in the bosom of the nation as it is focused on holiness, and the heart of the worshiper intent on purity.

17. ***our house*** This confirms the temple imagery, since the word *bayit*, "house," has indicated a Temple since biblical times.

Cypresses the rafters The clause *rehiṭeinu berotim* likewise alludes to the Temple, for "the

place (*makom*) where the priests ran (*rehuṭim*)"—while performing their rituals with alacrity—was overlaid with cypress (SongsR 1.xvii.2; cf. 1 Kings 6:15).

R. Yoḥanan adds a personal touch, suggesting that this passage teaches worldly practice (*derekh 'eretz*): when building a house, cut its ceiling beams from cedar and run (*meraheiṭ*) its rafters with cypress wood. This implied analogy between the Temple and one's home also works in reverse: we should make our home like a temple, through the acts of sanctity performed therein.

Remez

16. And you, my beloved, are handsome The longing soul can only mirror the praise. All else would be superfluous, since its own beauty is derived from its longing and love for the Beloved. The soul is shaped by its spiritual imagination. What it projects outward as the ideal reciprocally forms its interior beauty. This unexpected spiritual bond closes the distance that the self felt when it sensed that its "king" lay far beyond, on "*his* couch" (v. 12). It now says that "*our* couch is in a bower." The pronouns "my" and "his" have become "our." The couch is shared and the plants of the field grow upward, forming a bridal canopy above them. This is the longed-for spiritual communion. Loss and longing have been overcome. The two meet as one.

17. Cedars are the beams The bower is now more fully depicted. The myrrh and sprays have become cedars and cypresses—the supports and crossbeams of shared love. The world, as it were, forms the canopy of this spiritual bond. The two are within, joined in mutual confirmation. The song has moved from separation and hope to unity and presence. Love has been fulfilled.

Sod

16–17. And you...are handsome Can one truly call God handsome? Aesthetic beauty suggests a sacred analogue. The seeker's soul is drawn upward to a great transcendent beauty; and also drawn downward to the bounty of all immanent splendor. "Beautiful indeed!"—is all the heart can muster.

Experiencing this bounty intimately, the soul dares use inclusive language. Referring to the Beloved in her soul, she says: "*Our* couch ...*our* house...*our* rafters."[101] The soul's proclamation of love has deepened into an intimacy felt in the chambers of her heart (REzra).[102] Not wanting to rupture this communion, the soul uses the plural pronoun "our." Her heart has been not nullified but enhanced; and it expresses itself in an ecstatic proclamation of relationship. The words express gratitude for a God-given grace. Transcendence has become immanence, swelling the heart.

CONCLUSION

The opening segment is comprised of several scenes, marked by changes in voice, style, imagery, and setting. Matters are often ambiguous. No rubrics indicate the speakers, and no narrative voice provides transitions and identifications. The Song is entirely composed of discourses (internal monologues and external dialogues), and the venue must be inferred from these speeches. If the text served as a libretto for dramatic enactment, the performance would clarify speakers and setting. It would also signal moods and musings, settings and suggestions.

The passage moves from the maiden's private statement of desire ("give me the kisses of your mouth") to her public evocation of its realization ("Our couch is in a bower"). There is thus a dramatic movement from physical separation to connection, and from wish to its culmination. As the episodes unfold, the odors become increasingly bold. At first the beloved's scent is smelled by the maiden and her companions—these being his bodily oils; by the end, he is the odor upon her body. And as the scenes shift, the locale moves from palace imagery (and the maiden's desire), to the shepherds' tents (and an encounter with the beloved), to the bower of the field (where they meet in conjoint harmony). Her own beauty is successively marked as well. At the outset, she asserts

it with qualifications ("I am dark, but comely") with proofs by simile; later, upon meeting the beloved, he extolls her beauty through similitudes of natural force and decoration ("I have likened you . . . to a mare"); and in their concluding dialogue, he simply calls her "fair" with "dove's eyes"—the image and person are co-infused.

At the end, love and longing are realized. The poet mediates their expression with direct but discrete language. The reader is thus party to great intimacies, but only in a stylized manner. Formulated with subtle indirection and the circumspection of simile, the physical force of love is evoked by the spiritual mystery of speech. External reality and the poet's imagination interact. The poetry speaks directly and indirectly. This is love-talk at its most artful.

CHAPTER 2:1–17

Love in Its Proper Time

This second cycle is subdivided into four units, according to Masoretic tradition.[103] As in the first cycle, the maiden and her beloved are the principal characters. At the beginning, they engage in a dialogue of mutual admiration. Then they appear separately: she in her account of the joys of love, he in his request that she join him in the fields. Toward the end, they again speak in a duet, after which she gives a farewell directive. These units join internal states of feeling with external conditions of reality, through personal statements and figures drawn from the natural world.

Once again, the maiden and her emotions predominate. She initiates the discourses; portrays events to others; and concludes the cycle with her words. Ostensibly this unit continues the intimacies of love found at the end of the first cycle,[104] which suggests a thematic progression in the anthology. But this presumption is complicated by the shift of venue after the initial dialogue. The maiden now reports that she has been taken to a "house of wine" (v. 4). This motif borders on the metaphoric, suggesting the sphere of love and its great intoxication. It conveys a different tone than the espousals in the bower (1:13–17); and it is addressed to her friends.

2 I am a rose of Sharon,
A lily of the valleys.

ב אֲנִי֙ חֲבַצֶּ֣לֶת הַשָּׁר֔וֹן
שֽׁוֹשַׁנַּ֖ת הָעֲמָקִֽים׃

Peshat

1. WORDS OF LOVE AND LONGING (2:1–7)

This section has two parts, with subsections. The first part (vv. 1–3) is a dialogue between the maiden and her beloved. She states that she is a lily (or rose; v. 1), whereupon he reformulates this depiction in superlative terms (v. 2). She then offers a comparative image of her own, portraying her beloved as a mighty tree, whose shade and succor she ardently desires (v. 3).

In the second part (vv. 4–7), the maiden first addresses her friends and tells them that her beloved brought her to a "house of wine" and that his love has overwhelmed her (v. 4); she then urges them to sustain her with condiments, as she is ravished by emotions (v. 5). The maiden depicts an embrace in her beloved's arms (v. 6); she then adjures her friends not to arouse or disturb her love prematurely (v. 7). This request engages her companions as confidants, a role they repeatedly play. At the center of this passage is the word *'ahavah*, "love"—a core term of the Song and expressive of the maiden's emotions.

2:1. I am a rose...A lily The maiden begins with a self-depiction (MsP; Rid).[105] The figure is doubled, in accord with poetic parallelism. She calls herself a "*ḥavatzelet* of the coastland (the Sharon), a *shoshanah* of the valleys." Interpreters have puzzled over which plants are meant. (The terms' conjunction provides no added clue to meaning, since they function as a poetic pair.) One view identifies the *ḥavatzelet* with the narcissus, which grows both in the lowlands and highlands (B. Ber. 43b; Targum; Saadia; Ibn Janaḥ); another relates it to the colchicum, a multipetaled plant that flowers before the winter rains (like the plant called *ḥabatzillatu* in Akkadian). Still others identify *ḥavatzelet* as the crocus.[106]

As for the second plant, Ibn Ezra and Immanuel of Rome linked it to the rose, possibly because its petals are surrounded by thorns, as here (v. 2). But reference to "thorns" may indicate thistles surrounding the plant in the field.[107] Thus some have suggested the black lily (*Lilium candidum*).[108]

No consensus exists, and all one can confidently assert is that the flowers mark her delicacy and allure.[109] As both plants were known for their blossoms (Isa. 35:1–2; Hos. 14:6–8), the evocation of budding suggests her solicitation of the beloved's love.[110]

Derash

2:1. Floral imagery helps formulate the two poles of Israel's existence: suffering and study. The two botanic figures provide verbal prisms through which memory and hope were expressed.

I am a rose of Sharon *Keneset Yisra'el* (the people) proclaims herself a *ḥavatzelet ha-sharon* ("a rose of Sharon") because she is "most Beloved" (*ḥavivah*) of God:[111] "hidden" (*ḥavuyah*) in the "shadow" (*tzeil*) of Egypt (protected during servitude), Israel was eventually redeemed and sang a song (*shirah*) of thanksgiving.[112] Subsequently, she was protected (*ḥavuyin*) from the shadow cast by Pharaoh's army at the Sea, and shielded "in the cranny of the rock" (Song 2:14) at Mount Sinai (SongsR 2.i.1).[113]

Recalling these images, Israel awaited God's providential "shade" (*tzeil*; v. 3) from ongoing oppression. The language of this verse also shaped spiritual resistance. It is a deeply felt belief of Israel that it is protected (*ḥavuy*) by Torah and Tradition (Leqaḥ Ṭov).

A lily of the valleys This second phrase, *shoshanat ha-'amaqim*, reinforces the above point. It too acknowledges the "depths" (*'imqei*) of persecution that cast a "shadow" over national existence; and it confirms that "study" (*shoneh*) of the "depths" (*be-'imqah*) of Torah will sustain the people in their travail (Leqaḥ Ṭov).

Remez

2:1. I am a rose...A lily The self (or soul) exclaims its sense of identity (Ibn Tibbon).[114] Her character confirmed by the Beloved (1:9–11, 15), the seeker proclaims: "I *am* a rose." Love may cultivate one's nature, which flourishes like a flower. The sense of self-worth has changed. Earlier, apart from her Beloved, the self said: "I am black but comely." Now, having begun to cultivate her soul, there is a change in self-characterization. The figure of the rose expresses this new self-in-the-making (Immanuel).[115]

Sod

2:1. I am a rose of Sharon The soul identifies with tender flowers of the "valleys" (*'amaqim*). Gone is her sense of a dual nature (compared to tents; 1:5) and absent her sense of wandering (in quest of the Beloved; 1:7). Confirmed in love (1:9–11, 15), the soul feels rooted in the divine depths (*'amaqim*), where it absorbs spiritual sustenance from on High (Z. 3:107a). These depths symbolize the vastness of Divinity, pulsing through the natural orders and sentient reality. Such depths cannot be plumbed or fully fathomed—so primordial and imponderable are they (Z. 2:63a–b). As a tender plant, the seeker feels embedded in this divine ground—a fragile manifestation of its infinite vitality, in symbiosis with the ever-new gifts of God (REzra).[116]

[2]Like a lily among thorns,
So is my darling among the maidens.

2 כְּשֽׁוֹשַׁנָּה֙ בֵּ֣ין הַחוֹחִ֔ים
כֵּ֥ן רַעְיָתִ֖י בֵּ֥ין הַבָּנֽוֹת׃

Peshat

*2. **Like a lily*** In contrast to her metaphoric self-representation ("I *am*"), the male picks up the second term (*shoshanah*) and transforms it into a simile ("you are *like*"). She is a delicate flower surrounded by thistles (note the form: *ke-* . . . *bein* . . . *ken*; "like . . . among . . . so"). Such is her exemplary nature (Rid). As compared to her aromatic softness, other girls are like dried barbs (Rashbam).

Derash

*2. **Like a lily among thorns*** God responds to Israel's self-characterization and extols it through historical examples. Among the ancestors, the matriarch Rebekah stands out. She represents the moral quality of righteousness (a "lily") among the "thorns" of deceit (symbolized by Laban the Aramean, *'arami*—so designated because he was an inveterate "deceiver," *rama'i*). The sages thus proclaim ethical deportment a foundational national trait (SongsR 2.ii.1). Other virtues include the capacity for loving-kindness (*gemilut ḥasadim*); knowing proper behavior in times of sorrow and joy; and the ability to recite the requisite blessings on various occasions (SongsR 2.ii.4).[117] In these cases, the "thorns" mark the qualities of crassness or ignorance, whereas the "lily" symbolizes gentleness and good deeds (SongsZ).

The sages again praise the people's capacity to withstand suffering:[118] just as a lily resists the hot northerly winds and the bruises of surrounding thorns, remaining upright and pointed to heaven, so does Israel resist oppression and remain committed to God (SongsR 2.ii.5–6). Faithfulness is added to Israel's virtues. Faith, religious knowledge, and moral integrity delineate the supreme ideals.

Remez

*2. **Like a lily among thorns*** The seeker's statement confirmed, the Beloved repeats and extends her words. She is not just a lily of the valley (her personal view), but a lily among thorns (the Beloved's assessment). This comparison acknowledges the spiritual growth and transformation of the self (Ibn Aqnin). The seeker's spiritual character, her existence in the valley, is acclaimed. The soul's love of God and transcendent ideals sustain her, despite harsh circumstances. Secure in her identity, the soul blossoms and matures. These developments are implied by the flowering of the lily (Malbim). Her inclination and rising toward God is a kind of "theotropism."[119]

Sod

*2. **Like a lily*** The soul feels self-contained ("I am"), not relative to anything. It is only the voice of the Beloved that initiates comparisons ("like"). Unique to herself, this soul is also distinguished when compared to others. All the other "maidens" (seekers of the Beloved; 1:3) are like thorns among blossoms. The compliment confirms her spiritual qualities. Like a lily seeking light above while sending tendrils into the earth below, the soul is grounded in its moral body, with a godly spirit soaring beyond: both at once.

3 Like an apple tree among trees of the forest,
So is my beloved among the youths.
I delight to sit in his shade,
And his fruit is sweet to my mouth.

3 כְּתַפּ֙וּחַ֙ בַּעֲצֵ֣י הַיַּ֔עַר
כֵּ֥ן דּוֹדִ֖י בֵּ֣ין הַבָּנִ֑ים
בְּצִלּוֹ֙ חִמַּ֣דְתִּי וְיָשַׁ֔בְתִּי
וּפִרְי֖וֹ מָת֥וֹק לְחִכִּֽי׃

Peshat

3. She responds and compares him to a luxuriant tree in the forest (using a similar literary form: *ke-...be-...kein*).[120] In the first part of the image, only the fruit is indicated; but the continuation makes clear that a tree is intended (Ibn Ezra). The figure is thus an ellipse (Rashbam).

apple tree The longstanding presumption that *tappuaḥ* is an apple tree has been put in doubt by historical botanists: first, because the cultivated apple was unknown in antiquity; and second, because wild apples were bitter and acidic.[121] Hence the fruit in question has been linked to the lush apricot (*Prunus armenicaca*).[122] Significantly, the maiden stresses the sweetness of the fruit's juices.

I delight to sit in his shade She, the "flower," seeks her beloved "tree."[123] The figure and terms are suggestive.[124] The conjunction of verbs in *ḥimmadti ve-yashavti* captures her ongoing desire to be settled near this arbor, beneath his overarching shade (*tzilo*).[125] The unique *pi'el* use of the verb *ḥamad* ("desire") suggests an intensification of the longing;[126] and the use of two verbs in this form connotes a past-continuous tense, indicative of her ongoing emotions.

In a botanic image used to convey the restoration of Israel to her homeland, the prophet Hosea (14:6–8) speaks of the people as a *shoshanah* that will settle under the boughs of a cedar, and "sit in its shade" (*yoshevei be-tzilo*). The shared imagery suggests a fixed motif. In the prophetic image especially, the verb connotes not only sitting but also ongoing dwelling and bounty.

his fruit The imagery remains suggestive. Beneath him, she incorporates his fruit (*piryo*) and savors his sweet savor. His nurture is her sustenance.

Stylistics. The two comparative figures use the form *ke-...kein*, punctuating the clauses with an assertive claim. The conjunction of the maiden's self-identity as a *ḥavatzelet* is audibly linked to her desire to be ensconced *be-tzilo*, in his shade. The alliteration reinforces her desire to have him nearby.

Derash

3. *Keneset Yisra'el* now proclaims God's transcendence and her "delight" to "sit in his shade" and taste "his fruit." Rabbi Yose b. Zima (SongsR 2.iii.1) perceived a twofold valence. On the one hand, the Song exalts God over all other gods; on the other, it glorifies Israel over other nations. For the latter rejected the "apple tree" (God) and its apparent lack of "shade" (they denied divine providence), whereas Israel desired this "shade" and delighted in its benefits (the fruit of Torah).[127] By exalting her Lord, Israel proclaims her theology; and by decrying the nations, she asserts religious dedication. The figure of "delight" (or "desire") adds a tone of spiritual passion; the imagery of "fruit" (or "benefit") marks a Torah-centered spirituality.[128]

The arbor image inspired other links between God and Israel. Rabbi Aḥa perceived a comparison between the way an apple tree buds and Israel's commitment to the covenant at Sinai (SongsR 2.iii.2): just as an apple tree produces buds before its leaves, so did Israel determine to "do" God's will before "hearing" it (Exod. 24:7). The botanic figure suggests a mode of *imitatio dei* (spiritual analogy between God and Israel). For like an apple tree produces buds prior to its leaves, thereby expressing its inherent fruitfulness, so God is an effective power even before humans perceive this reality in the world. This teaching thus offers a threefold correlation between nature, culture, and theology.

Remez

3. Like an apple tree among trees Love is a duet, an intimate reciprocity. It is expressed here by the interchange of rhetorical figures. After the prior dialogue (vv. 1–2), the soul answers the Beloved's comparison with her own—though now in revealing terms. She feels small and delicate, sunk in earthly nature; but she regards her Beloved as correspondingly high and stately, ascendant toward heaven. The image of a lordly tree reflects these sensibilities.[129] Her feelings extend to a desire for protection and nurture, as she now states:

I delight to sit...And his fruit The divine nurture so desired is twofold. The soul wants spiritual shade conducive to growth (Immanuel),[130] for it would otherwise wither in the glare of natural reality. It also desires providential sustenance conducive to self-transformation, for it would otherwise shrivel of its own resources. The soul thus tells her Beloved that it is both the fact of His being (or protective presence) that offers her spiritual well-being, and the gifts of His being (or instructive presence) that provide sustenance. Both features are needed. Turning outward, the soul (or intellect) wants the reality of the divine (the Beloved) and all its spiritual benefactions (Al-Fawwāl).[131] It wants to "taste and see how good the LORD is" (Ps. 34:9). The tree's transcending eminence and the succor of its fruit represent such a presence and bounty.

Sod

3. Stimulated by the prior simile, the soul in turn compares her Beloved to a "tree." For the fragile spirit, identified with a lily, God is height, protection, and sustenance. Divinity extends upward from the ground of being—like a cosmic tree, illimitable in elevation and omnipresent in outbranching extensions. All that grows is nurtured by its sap, flowing in all directions (Ibn Sahula).[132] Like a lily under an arbor, God gives the soul protective "shade" and the "fruit" of life. The heart, humbled by the awesome *tremendum* of Divinity, exudes gratitude for its providential gifts. Inspired by nature, the soul regards itself as sheltered and sustained by the cosmic whole. Just earlier, trees were a figure for an arbor of the heart (1:17). They now assume their natural height—symbols of transcendence, pointing beyond while protecting below. The soul deems such care a spiritual "delight."

4 He brought me to the banquet room
And his banner of love was over me.

4 הֱבִיאַ֙נִי֙ אֶל־בֵּ֣ית הַיָּ֔יִן
וְדִגְל֥וֹ עָלַ֖י אַהֲבָֽה׃

Peshat

4–7. The scene shifts. Suddenly the woman speaks to her companions and reports her situation. Speaking allusively, she says that her beloved has brought her to the house of wine, his banner of love upon her (v. 4). So appraised, the friends are bidden to sustain her with nourishments (v. 5). The maiden now depicts the love scene that dominates her imagination (an image of entwined selves; v. 6). She then adjures them to sustain her arousal and let it peak in due course.[133] Sitting with them, she is bereft of her beloved. In this state, her thoughts become consuming fantasies—until the sound of his arrival comes nigh (v. 8).

4. ***banquet room*** Literally, "the house of wine," a condensed form of *beit mishteih ha-yayin* ("the house of the drinking of wine"; Est. 7:8).[134] It marks the setting of love as a place of intoxication. The image may well be euphemistic.

his banner of love was over me This statement complements the first clause, indicating the intensity of the love (*'ahavah*) experienced.

banner The *degel* is a standard held upright[135] (in that respect it is like the prior image of a fruit tree—likewise depicted above her); or perhaps like a canopy of love (his "banner" being a metonym for his erotic presence, real and fantasized). But this term has puzzled commentators and induced alternate explanations. Among these is the proposal that *diglo* ("his banner") is actually a verbal noun, attested in Akkadian, meaning "(visual) regard."[136] On this view, the phrase asserts that the beloved's attention was focused on the maiden. This interpretation has the merit of highlighting the intimacy's visual quality;[137] but the verb is otherwise unknown in Biblical Hebrew.

Derash

4. *Keneset Yisra'el* confesses to spiritual intimacy. The initial longing for Torah and Tradition (the kisses; 1:2) was succeeded by the people's desire for God's providential care and the internalization of divine wisdom. The Song now celebrates both features. Preeminent is the founding moment at Sinai—a place that R. Yehuda compared to a wine cellar containing a precious elixir (SongsR 2.iv.1). Such is the sustenance of Torah.

He brought me to the banquet room God "brings" (initiates) the people "into" this sphere of instruction. The spatial orientation is horizontal, marking its progressive incorporation of divine truths—providential for the soul.

And his banner of love was over me This clause, *ve-diglo 'alay 'ahavah*, shifts to a vertical axis, marking God's transcendent eminence. From this height, God "gave" (*natan*) the "banners" (standards) of Torah (that is, commandments and good deeds), which the people received with "great love" (SongsR 2.iv.1; Ibn Aqnin).

The love expressed is bilateral—a divine instruction given, and a gift received. The key verbs ("gave" and "received," *natan* and *qibbalti*) express this dynamic. Properly channeled, such divine love infuses the self with spiritual passion and sustenance. But it may also overwhelm an individual and elicit diffuse expressions. Thus R. Yona taught tolerance for any student of the *halakhah* (religious law) who misconstrued the traditional rules of analysis—if that misunderstanding or "oversight" (*dillugo*; following Maharzu) was a result of an exuberance of "love" (*'ahavah*) for God (SongsR ibid.; B. Shab. 63a). Rabbi Aḥa even has God say that if a person improperly pronounced a scriptural word, "his mispronunciation" (*dillugo*) remains "Beloved to Me" (*'alay*).[138]

Remez

4. ***He brought me to the banquet room*** The soul desires transformation. Ingesting the divine wisdom is not sufficient. The soul does not merely want to incorporate spiritual nurture and cultivate inner perfection. It wants

more: it wants to be spiritually incorporated *within* the transcendent order (the "banquet room"). The active soul wants to be transformed by spiritual bliss. This great desire is palpably realized here. Suddenly the soul shifts from its sense of self and identity ("*I am*" a rose) to being the recipient of a divine action (the king "*brought me*" into the realm [banquet room] of spiritual love). With this movement, the divine-human relationship intensifies (Ibn Tibbon)—a development that transforms the self within and without.

His banner of love was over me This clause marks the transformation of self—both the effusion of divine love into the soul (from without),[139] and the emotions of love transfusing the heart (from within). The spiritual sense of having been brought *into* the divine realities and of having been overwhelmed *by* them are progressive and complementary expressions of the same spiritual truth: progressive, because the movement into the divine chambers results in an intensified experience of spiritual love; and complementary, insofar as the movement into a spiritual space is also the infusion of that reality into the self. The two are effectively one. They flow from two distinct but converging perspectives.

Sod

4. *He brought me* The speaker reports the rapture of mystical love. The verb "brought" signals the impulse of the experience; the "banquet room," the spiritual lift that Philo deemed a mystical inebriation.[140] The precedence of the third person ("*He* brought"; "*His* banner") over the first ("*me*;" "over *me*") highlights the otherness of the experience. What is the overwhelming presence of Divinity here? It is love: *'ahavah*. The soul has been subordinated to God's infusing love—and testifies to its force.

5 "Sustain me with raisin cakes,
Refresh me with apples,
For I am faint with love."

5 סַמְּכ֙וּנִי֙ בָּֽאֲשִׁישׁ֔וֹת
רַפְּד֖וּנִי בַּתַּפּוּחִ֑ים
כִּֽי־חוֹלַ֥ת אַהֲבָ֖ה אָֽנִי׃

Peshat

*5. **Sustain me with raisin cakes*** The maiden implores her friends to aid her in this state of love. The plural verb *rappeduni* has the strong sense of "strengthen me" (Ibn Ezra adduces an Arabic cognate).[141] Two kinds of food are mentioned that presumably were known to heal, stimulate, or arouse. The first is called *'ashishot*, which is used neutrally in 2 Sam. 6:19. Whatever its ingredients, it evokes the verb *'ashash* ("to strengthen"; Ibn Aqnin).[142] This edible was thus some kind of "energy booster," and is used here to suggest some support for or inducement of love (this would also be the presumptive role of the *'ashishei 'anavim*, grape/raisin cakes mentioned in Hos. 3:1).

apples Whatever the effects of *tappuḥim*, this term evokes the *tappuaḥ* to which she just compared her beloved. The fruit thus functions as a displaced figure; the *tappuḥim* sustain her in his absence—"they" standing in for "he."

For This clause justifies her demand. It is introduced by *ki*, which here is equivalent to the rabbinic Hebrew *harei she-*, "for indeed; surely" (Rashbam).

faint with love Perhaps intentionally, the formulation *ḥolat 'ahavah* is multivalent and emotionally evocative. Once again, *'ahavah* is the dominant emotion (as in v. 4). The present translation expresses the diminishment of physical strength (for the stem *ḥ-l-h* in this sense, see Judg. 16:17). Hence the foods are presumed to be medicaments requested for her invigoration (Rid).[143] But this is not certain. The state of being "love-sick" (Rashbam) could indicate her overwhelming passion (as in Mic. 1:12). On this view, the foods are love potions or stimulants to condition her for his advent. Or perhaps she is "wounded" by assailments of love (implying the stem *ḥ-l-l*).[144]

Derash

*5. **Sustain me with raisin cakes*** *Keneset Yisra'el* desires God's ongoing presence. This takes two forms: the majesty of divine manifestation and the gift of divine instruction. The yearning for a living encounter with God regards Sinai as the precedent for such an encounter. Hence the request for *'ashishot* ("raisin cakes") was interpreted as a request for the twofold character of God's manifestation in "fire" (*'eish*) at Sinai (*'ashishot* being construed as *'eish-'eish*): one fire marking the appearance of God on High (the fire burning "to the heart of heaven"; Exod. 19:11); the other, God's holy presence on earth (the fire of God's descent upon the mountain; v. 18).[145] Desire for the divine teachings applies these fires to the written and oral Torahs—the core of Judaism. In this vein, some construed the request for *'ashishot* to denote Israel's desire to be strengthened (*me'oshashot*) by the *halakhot* (legal norms); and the request for apples as signifying her love for the *haggadot* (theological teachings)—whose taste is so appealing (SongsR 5.i.1; Leqaḥ Ṭov).

The religious spirit longs for spiritual experience and sustainable life forms. For some, the two are at odds and remain an unresolved tension. Others seek to internalize the "fire" of Sinai as the spiritual source of a religious practice infused with fervor.

For I am faint with love The sufferings of love may evoke two sensibilities. In one mode, when Israel says that she is "love-sick" (*ḥolat 'ahavah*), she declares that her fate results from steadfast devotion to God and Jewish tradition. On this view, the verse encodes Israel's belief that "the nations of the world bring torments (*ḥala'im*) upon me *because of my love for You*" (taking the suffering as a consequence of unflagging commitment; SongsR ibid.). The

other mode shifts from the human component to the divine, wondering whether "the illness [or: suffering; so Rashi] that You (God) bring upon me [is] *in order to make me Beloved to You*" (taking the link between suffering and love to be a theological pedagogy; ibid.). The heart of Israel has struggled with both understandings. Joined together, they may have a reciprocal influence: the steadfastness of love becoming a spiritual condition for religious purification; and the depths of suffering offering training in spiritual resolve.

Remez

5. ***Sustain me . . . For I am faint*** The self reflects on the intensity of its spiritual bliss in the present. Overwhelmed by the gift of love, the soul asks the Beloved (source of its virtues and love), or those who serve His purposes, to sustain it with "raisin cakes" and "apples"—with something of the new bliss (the cakes) and the old benefits (the apples). Spiritual passions feel like a painful wound, a love-sickness (*ḥolat 'ahavah*; Rambam;[146] Al-Fawwāl); and the need for a remedy and sustenance is insatiable. The God-given bounty of the world provides the means to assuage this spiritual ache. Emptied of other concerns, the self wants to be filled by God's love (or its earthly tokens)—continuously and completely.

Sod

5. ***Sustain me*** The soul has succumbed to divine love. She calls her cohorts to sustain her with gifts—that she may endure. The force of love is marked by the sense of an emotion that is "over me" (REzra). During this intense experience, the seeker requests not recovery but care. Touched by ecstasy, our soul feels "faint." The self is both less and more than it was: less, because it has been diluted by an infusion of divine presence; and more, because of this spiritual enhancement. Overcome by God's reality, our soul seeks to sustain this state—and let it mature in its own way. Only then will this love properly infuse our spiritual demeanor. Stimulated by an ecstasy that transcends natural experience, the self wants to cultivate an inner strength for its preservation (Z. 1:98b–99a; Ibn Sahula). The request for food may thus symbolize the reception and internalization of spiritual practices—be these study, contemplation, or ritual performance (AhavD 62a–b). In part proxies, they also cultivate the receptive heart.

6 His left hand was under my head,
His right arm embraced me.

6 שְׂמֹאלוֹ תַּחַת לְרֹאשִׁי
וִימִינוֹ תְּחַבְּקֵנִי׃

Peshat

6. The image of entwined figures is an old motif for physical intimacy. It is found in an ancient Sumerian text depicting a sacred marriage rite;[147] and an iconographic image of a male lover placing his left arm under a woman's head—while his right arm encircles her in embrace—appears on a terra-cotta figurine from the early second millennium B.C.E.[148]

was This clause is actually verbless; it gains its temporal sense from the next, parallel clause.

embraced Grammatically speaking, *teḥabbeiq* is an old preterite form (denoting a past occurrence) that only looks like a classical future-present verb.[149] Rashbam perceived this temporal aspect and suggested that the maiden was referring to an earlier tryst in the bower (also Rid). Choice of this archaic form may be deliberate, to hint also of the maiden's present fantasy and future desire: "Let [or: May] his left hand be..." (MsP).[150] It intimates a temporal continuity of emotions.

Derash

*6. **His left hand... His right arm*** *Keneset Yisra'el* characterizes God's relation with her as a sustaining, providential presence. Rabbinic tradition spells this out. For some, the "left hand" symbolizes the first tablets, given to guide the people (Exod. 24:12; 31:18) but broken after the sin of idolatry (the golden calf); whereas the "right arm [or: hand]" symbolizes the second ones, given only after the people's forgiveness (Exod. 34:28). This view perceives an ongoing divine pedagogy. The first tablets contained only the Decalogue, initially deemed sufficient; the second ones were more detailed, and orally elaborated to guide the repentant nation. That is, alongside the Torah, Israel was given "*halakhot*, *midrash*, and *aggadot*"—the full oral tradition (ExodR 46.1). The sages thus express their view of Torah and Tradition as successive divine gifts, increasingly detailed, to shape Israel's spiritual life and reform its human nature.

Ritual and prayer are cases in point. Thus the two arms symbolize the ritual objects of "fringes (*tzitzit*) and *tefillin* (phylacteries)," or the liturgical "recitation of the *Shema* and the *'Amidah*-prayer" (SongsR 2.vi.1). God's reality is ongoing through ritual life—the practical commandments being ways of remaining mindful of spiritual tasks and integrity. The divine "hands" powerfully symbolize the embodied nature of religious life—and its role in focusing the human mind on the highest values.

Remez

6. The soul's request for sustenance is complemented by its sense of divine care. The soul has given up ordinary needs for higher values—and feels supported in the process.[151] This is depicted as a total embrace, a figure more personal and tangible than being in a room (v. 4). A room is a sphere of protective enclosure, whereas an embrace is an intimate entwinement. The self is still aware of itself and the divine Other (denominated by the pronouns "my" and "His"). But there now is a sense that the self is somehow joined to divine reality. The soul reports this spiritual experience as a loving embrace.

Sod

6. The speaker depicts in human terms the spiritual transport noted earlier. It is a figure of erotic intimacy. The Beloved's left arm under the seeker's head—there is face-to-face presence; the right arm embracing her—there is direct contact. This is an image of intimate entwinement, symbolizing the oneness of love (Z. 1:28a). There is now ineffable bliss: the most transcendent has become the most immanent. Opposites conjoin; the two are as one.

7 I adjure you, O maidens of Jerusalem,
By gazelles or by hinds of the field:
Do not wake or rouse
Love until it please!

7 הִשְׁבַּ֨עְתִּי אֶתְכֶ֜ם בְּנ֤וֹת יְרוּשָׁלַ֙͏ִם֙
בִּצְבָא֔וֹת א֖וֹ בְּאַיְל֣וֹת הַשָּׂדֶ֑ה
אִם־תָּעִ֧ירוּ ׀ וְֽאִם־תְּעֽוֹרְר֛וּ
אֶת־הָאַהֲבָ֖ה עַ֥ד שֶׁתֶּחְפָּֽץ׃ ס

Peshat

*7. **I adjure you . . . / By gazelles or by hinds of the field*** This oath invokes the energies of nature by means of two erotic images, the gazelle and the hind.[152] The association of an *'ayelet* (roe) with love occurs in Prov. 5:19, likewise in a charged erotic image. Here the terms are plural (*bi-tzva'ot 'o be-'aylot ha-sadeh*), which evoke a counterpoint with (oaths customarily taken in the name of?) "the LORD of hosts" (*tzeva'ot*) or the Almighty God (*'el shaddai*).[153]

Perhaps her formula uses an old Israelite incantation recited as a love charm (a related type occurs in ancient Mesopotamia).[154] This would also explain the subsequent references to the arousals.

By gazelles This reference prefigures the maiden's designation of her beloved as a gazelle (in vv. 9, 17). The image connotes erotic energy; indeed, it was so used in an ancient Mesopotamian potency incantation (e.g., "By the love [power] of the gazelle . . . copulate with me").[155]

you, O maidens The addressee, though female, is referred to by the masculine plural pronoun *'etkhem*, which suggests that the oath formulary is generic. This would also explain the masculine plural verbs by which she proceeds to address her female friends.[156]

Do not The repeated oath formula *'im–'im* (literally "if . . . if") has the force of a double negative (i.e., "do not . . . or"); cf. Saadia. Such a construction evolves by a transformation of the conditional clause into its consequence (thus: *if* you do this or that, then the following will result; hence, do *not* do it!).

Do not wake or arouse / Love until it please The precise import of this appeal is uncertain. On one possibility, the maiden beseeches her friends neither to arouse nor disturb love *while* it is in force; on another, they are requested to refrain from any interference *until* the time is ripe. The difference depends on how one construes the temporal phrase *'ad she-* ("while; until") in this passage. In the first instance, their love has become an event; in the second, it has not yet been stimulated or occurred (see further Immanuel). The oath's erotic imagery (see above) supports the second alternative. In this regard, the verbs *ta'iru* and *te'oreru* seem to indicate an emotional, erotic arousal (for the verbal variants, cf. *ha'ir* and *'orer* in Isa. 42:13 and Song 8:5, respectively).[157] That is, the verbs have the force of an incantation for arousing love. Significantly, *'ahavah* ("love") is personified and governs a verb of eruptive desire (i.e., "until desire comes," *'ad she-yagi'a ḥeifetz*; Immanuel). Possibly, such verbal charms were accompanied by stimulants believed to arouse love (see below). If so, the maiden's prior request for aid has nothing to do with medicinal support, but is rife with innuendo and desire.

wake or rouse The verb *ta'iru* is causative (*hif'il*) in form; the verb *te'oreru* is a *pi'el* of a middle-weak verb (the so-called *pollel* form). The effect of this verb doubling is a further intensification of meaning (Rashbam). In Isa. 51:9, the same verb *'uri* is used to invoke or appeal to the divine arm to "arise" again—as in ancient times, when it destroyed the sea serpent Tannin ("Dragon"); the related verb *'oreir*, in Job 3:8, is also used to "arouse" the dragon Leviathan.

Stylistics. Verses 4–5 and 6–7 are two speeches in parallel form. The first clause of each is descriptive (vv. 4 and 6), and addressed to the female companions; the second clause of each is an imperative of action (vv. 5 and 7), related to acts of love. Further, the first clause in each group uses the particle *ve-* ("he brought me . . . *and* his banner"; "his left hand . . . *and* his right," in vv. 4 and 6); whereas the second clause in each is marked by parallelisms ("sustain me with *x*" // "refresh me with *y*"; "deer" // "hinds";

"awaken" // "arouse," in vv. 5 and 7). The combined effect is to create a twofold intensification. The concluding phrase, "until it please," stands syntactically outside the double adjuration concerning the arousals of love; it functions like an exclamation point. It is the semantic and topical climax of the maiden's speech.

Derash

7. ***Do not... until it please*** Since antiquity, this passage has been applied to messianic impulses. Love and its longings—spiritual and national hopes—must be deferred "until" their proper time.[158] According to R. Ḥelbo, God adjured Israel "not to rebel against the kingdoms; not to force the end-time; not to reveal their mysteries to the nations; and not to go up from the exile en masse [literally: like a wall]" (SongsR 2.vii.1; cf. B. Ket. 111a).[159] The first, second, and fourth adjurations have clear political implications and seem designed to inhibit premature messianic awakenings; the third may allude to esoteric messianic calculations.[160] Rabbi Oshaya spoke for many generations when he stated that God tells the exiles: "Wait for me—and I shall make you like the host of the heaven."[161] Such a view valorizes divine providence and constrains human initiative; but it also blurs the line between pious restraint (reliance upon God) and impious passivity.

What spiritual lesson does deferral teach? Perhaps a humble attentiveness to the events of the everyday, without imposing human will thoughtlessly or reducing the mystery of life to pragmatic assessments. The religious spirit must live "in the between," spurred by ideals without giving them (undue) messianic warrant. Prophecy may point to the future; but it cannot pinpoint it. The conditions of deferral may constrain idolatrous presumptions, both spiritual and political.

Remez

7. The soul yearns to sustain the most sacred moment. Turning inward, she urges her worldly qualities ("maidens of Jerusalem") not to disrupt this experience of "love until it please!"[162] The self perceives, while still enthralled, that this state should not be disturbed (Malbim)[163] but allowed to mature. The soul's achievement of intellectual insight or spiritual transport is thus experienced as incomplete, and the self wants it to complete its inherent development (Ibn Tibbon; Ralbag).[164] But this beginning has elicited a new consciousness. The soul is now able to perceive the Beloved's advent (see v. 8).

Sod

7. ***I adjure you*** The helpers of the soul are addressed—not by a command for direct action (as in v. 5), but by a request for inaction through an oath. Under the impress of mystical love, the soul invokes restraint: "do not wake or rouse" this love *while* it is in a state of desire.[165] The soul confesses its ecstasy and the need to sustain it. She begs her friends neither to break the spell of love nor interfere with its rhythm. Supernatural love can abide no natural intervention. That is why she invokes "gazelles" and "hinds of the field"—these animals symbolize natural love and its stimulation.[166] But spiritual love is of a different, more transcendent kind (Ibn Sahula).

8 Hark! My beloved!
There he comes,
Leaping over mountains,
Bounding over hills.

8 קוֹל דּוֹדִי
הִנֵּה־זֶה בָּא
מְדַלֵּג עַל־הֶהָרִים
מְקַפֵּץ עַל־הַגְּבָעוֹת׃

Peshat

2. THE BELOVED'S ADVENT (vv. 8–13)

This is one episode in two parts. In the first, the maiden anticipates her beloved's advent, which seems like the leap of a deer—to which she compares him (vv. 8–9). Her earlier adjuration (by the hinds of the field) will soon materialize. This present moment is marked by the adverb *hinneih* ("here, now").

The second part (vv. 10–13) reports the beloved's presence and his call to the maiden to join him in the fields. This moment is likewise marked by *hinneih* (v. 11).

*8. **Hark! My beloved!*** In this phrase (*qol dodi*), the present translation takes *qol* as an exclamation, marking the beloved's impending arrival. Alternatively, *qol* has its usual meaning of "voice" or "sound" and is combined in a construct chain with *dodi* (yielding "the voice of my beloved"; Rashbam).[167] Aroused to her beloved's voice, she reports this to her companions. The stark initial use of *qol* here would be elliptical: "[I hear] the voice" (of my Beloved); cf. Luzzatto on Isa. 40:3.

There he comes In the clause *hinneih zeh ba'* (literally "Behold, he is coming"), the adverb *hinneih* marks temporal imminence ("just now"), while the pronoun *zeh* indicates "that one" and refers to "my beloved."[168] Combined, they highlight the suddenness of the Beloved's appearance.[169] If the previous phrase is a construct chain, then *hinneih zeh ba'* means "Indeed, he [or: it (his voice)] is [now] coming," with *hinneih* marking the moments of advent and perception.

The verb *ba'* is a participle, indicating present actualization.[170]

Leaping . . . Bounding The character of the beloved's entrance is specified by these two participles. The verb *meqappetz* ("leaping") is a unique use of the *pi'el* form; surely it emphasizes springing up (cf. Ibn Ezra on Lev. 11:21); the verb *medalleg* ("bounding") is used for deer (Isa. 35:6). The fleetness of deer is a trope applied to humans (2 Sam. 2:18; Hab. 3:19).

Derash

*8. **Hark! My beloved!*** Attentive waiting prepares the heart for the advent of God. It comes suddenly. For midrashic tradition, *qol* here signals both the "sound" and "voice" of an impending spiritual connection—contracting the awaited future into the emergent "now." Old expectations and constraints may evaporate in the concrete moment of redemptive reality. Some suggested that the miracle of the Exodus was that God "skipped" over prophetic and historical impediments (literally "hills") and reduced the forecast years of bondage—sending Moses (the "Beloved") after only 210 years, instead of the 400 years predicted in Gen. 15:13.[171] Alternatively, the "voice" of redemption was a sudden grace that yanked the people—mired in "evil deeds" or "false worship"—to a new spiritual freedom (SongsR 2.viii.1–2). Servitude may dull the spirit; and then, against all expectation, something happens: deaf ears hear, blind eyes see, and loose hands find strength. Such momentous suddenness is a heavenly opening: "Hark! My Beloved comes!" (See next comment.)

Rabbi Yitzḥak (SongsR 2.ix.1; cf. PdRK 5.8) intensified the announcement that *dodi ba'* ("my Beloved comes") by reading the term *dodi* as an anagram (*deo-deo*) and interpreting it (in light of the Hebrew verb *ba'*) as encoding the Greek plural imperative *deui, deui* ("Come! Come!").[172]

Remez

8. ***Hark! My beloved!*** The soul engages in intellectual or spiritual preparations (Ibn Tibbon); but the moment of realization happens independently. The self tries to remain patient and sustain its spiritual focus until the time is ripe (Sforno)—when it suddenly senses the long-awaited moment: "There he comes, Leaping over mountains." A new reality penetrates the field of perception. The seeking self knows this to be more than subjective desire, though it remains somewhat distant—like the slow shaping of insight. The heart knows intuitively: it is the advent of the Beloved. Love has ripened.

Sod

8. ***Hark! My beloved!*** In this spiritual situation, the soul brims with anticipation. For the attentive spirit, the word *qol* ("hark") conveys a call to attention,[173] an arousal of alertness (TiqZ 6b). The Beloved remains an exterior reference point ("behold *zeh* [this one] comes"). The time of waiting is fraught with intensity, within *and* without. As an inner experience, the voice is a sharpening of religious consciousness—something is happening; and as an external matter, the oncoming reality throbs with vibrant images ("leaping" and "bounding"). The spiritual call cuts through all worldly constraints and rivets the seeker's attention (Ibn Sahula).

9 My beloved is like a gazelle
Or like a young stag.
There he stands behind our wall,
Gazing through the window,
Peering through the lattice.

9 דּוֹמֶה דוֹדִי לִצְבִי
אוֹ לְעֹפֶר הָאַיָּלִים
הִנֵּה־זֶה עוֹמֵד אַחַר כָּתְלֵנוּ
מַשְׁגִּיחַ מִן־הַחַלֹּנוֹת
מֵצִיץ מִן־הַחֲרַכִּים׃

Peshat

*9. **like*** The maiden uses the verb *domeh* to indicate a comparison, suggesting that her beloved personifies the creatures of the field. It also recalls the beloved's use of this term in 1:9, and it anticipates her subsequent usage in 2:17.

gazelle...young stag She likens her beloved to two types of deer (*tzevi* and *'ofer ha-'ayalim*). This gives poignancy to her prior adjuration by the "gazelles" and "hinds of the field" (*tzeva'ot* and *'aylot ha-sadeh*; v. 7). The time of love is ripe, and the beloved comes with the energy of a young buck.

There he With his advent in the maiden's domain, she again says *hinneih zeh*, now referring to his physical proximity.

stands In this striking figure, the beloved stretches like a buck on his hindquarters and peers into her dwelling.

Gazing...Peering Two participles indicate the present aspect of the event. Both verbs use the preposition *min* to suggest looking "through" the windows. A comparable term will mark the appearance of the maiden's face "through" (*mi-ba'ad*) her framing locks (see 4:1).[174]

Stylistics. Verses 8–9 convey two moments in the beloved's advent, each marked by the phrase *hinneih zeh* ("There he...") plus a participle. Each one features a complementary parallelism that intensifies the action. In the first, the preposition *'al* ("upon") recurs; in the second, the preposition *min* ("through"). These images of advent effect scenic augmentation and further conjoin the two verses.

Derash

*9. **My beloved is like a gazelle*** *Keneset Yisra'el* anticipates God's arrival. The figure concretizes the mood. Just as a gazelle bounds from place to place, so has God come in successive manifestations on Israel's behalf: to Egypt, to the Sea, and to Sinai. With this image, the people anticipate God's immediate advent (SongsR ibid.) and even beseech it (see previous comment).

There he stands behind our wall Rabbi Yose develops the divine appearance at Sinai (see above). "Wall" refers to the boundary set up at the mountain to separate God from the people (Exod. 19:12); the subsequent acts of "gazing" and "peering," to God's descent upon Sinai and speech to the people (SongsR 2.ix.2). And the next phrase (v. 10), "My Beloved spoke thus to me," marks the opening words of the Decalogue ("I am the LORD"). In this way, the images of the Song mark the biblical sequence of divine revelation.

Alternatively, the divine advent marks God's manifestations at the "walls" of the synagogues and study halls whenever Jews recite the *Shema* or study in public. Ritual recitation elicits a reciprocal act of divine presence. In this vein, the Beloved's acts of gazing and peering represent God's manifestation between the shoulders of the priests (standing before the Ark to recite the priestly blessings) and through their fingers, which are spread like "the lattice"—through which the *Shekhinah* appears (ibid.; PesiqR 15.9; and B. Ḥag. 16a, with Rashi).

The people's spiritual institutions (synagogues and study halls) are the sites of God's ongoing presence in this era[175] between the

archetypal times of national founding and the final messianic redemption. Sacred history includes all the moments of daily life where the ordinary may be transfigured through religious practice.

tween them, the soul dares refer to the wall as "*our* wall." They two (divine and human) remain apart. But there is now a connection. This experience cannot be doubted, and the soul proclaims it aloud (v. 10).

Remez

9. My beloved is like a gazelle How does one name this moment? Echoing itself, the soul cries with jubilation—"*my* Beloved"—and then reuses a figure from that just-experienced moment, when it had a sense of the Beloved's love and adjured itself ("By gazelles . . .") to let this experience mature (v. 7). That trace is now a reality. And yet it is still only sensed through a conceptual filter—the figure of likeness. Simile is the veil of distance and appropriation. It is the humble gesture of positive theology—and the limit of poetic song. Beyond this is silence.

There he stands behind our wall The simile is concretized by a sense that the loved one is "gazing" from without and "peering" toward the soul.[176] As earlier, when its spiritual achievements were confirmed (vv. 9–10), the soul feels seen and confirmed by a gaze (Sforno).[177] The Beloved is now a tangible presence for the self. Despite the barrier be-

Sod

9. My beloved is like The emergent reality is formulated by a series of analogues. These similes sharpen the sense of actuality. The figure is initially referred to by the demonstrative pronoun *zeh* ("he," v. 8; literally "this one"), and then by images of animal energy and swiftness. In the process, the figure is personalized. The soul senses the presence of transcendence—an external reality felt as standing and "peering through" the self's enclosure. The natural self protects itself by a "wall"; the heart seeks to pierce beyond—through the "window" of the spirit (Ibn Sahula). Transcendence hovers and slowly penetrates; but only to the aroused sensibility. To the open heart, transcendence is perceived in and through the world. It is not something wholly beyond, but just "this" unnamable object nearby. Eyes and heart washed clean, the seeker senses God's presence (cf. Z. 2:9b).

10 My beloved spoke thus to me,
"Arise, my darling;
My fair one, come away!

10 עָנָה דוֹדִי וְאָמַר לִי
קוּמִי לָךְ רַעְיָתִי
יָפָתִי וּלְכִי־לָךְ׃

Peshat

10–13. Following the maiden's announcement of her beloved's words (v. 10a), his speech is framed by the invocation "Arise, my darling . . . come away" (vv. 10b and 13b). His call contains two imperatives. The first of these is justified (*ki*, "for now; because"), recalling her earlier accounting to her friends ("*ki*, for, I am faint with love"). The immediacy is punctuated by *hinneih* ("now," v. 11), followed by a succession of statements indicating the revival of nature in the spring. This unit correlates the ripening of nature with the readiness of love.

Derash

10. Arise . . . come away According to R. Azariah, the two imperatives mark the appeals of Moses and Aaron to the people in Egypt, imploring them to "arise" (*kumi lakh*, physically and spiritually; SongsR 2.ix.5; PesiqR 15.10) and "come away" (*lekhi lakh*).[178] Speaking thus, these leaders followed scriptural precedent: first, when God called Abraham to "Go forth (*lekh lekha*) from your land" (Gen. 12:1); and later when Jacob heeded the exhortation of his parents "and went" (*va-yeilekh*) to Paddan Aram (Gen. 28:7; SongsR ibid. and PesiqR 15:11).

These verbal tallies give a historical dimension to the exhortations to the nation in Egypt; and also give *Keneset Yisra'el* a personality. She is called the "daughter" of these ancestors and bidden to follow their example and depart for their homeland with obedient alacrity. The eye of midrash perceives striking correlations in Scripture.

Remez

10. My beloved spoke thus to me The prior experience is that of "my Beloved"; and now this sense of presence is replaced by a direct address.

Arise The soul is called to arise and follow: to ascend to a higher level and come away (*lekhi lakh*).[179] Is it ready for the journey? Perhaps an echo of the divine call to Abraham has shaped the listener's consciousness. Does it hear in this call a trace of God's ancient address to that spiritual pilgrim to "come forth" (*lekh lekha*) to a new beginning? Like that great forebear, the present seeker must respond from the depths. I must come forth with my fullest being (Ibn Tibbon). Nothing partial will do.

Sod

10. My beloved spoke thus to me An answering now, because the soul feels personally addressed ("to me").

Arise, my darling . . . come away! The soul is bidden to ascend to its spiritual possibilities (*lakh*—"for your sake") and, like Abraham, to go forth to a new beginning (*lekha*—"for your sake"; Rashi at Gen. 12:1). The soul is called to transcend its own limits and enter the world with all the spiritual possibilities that await.[180]

11 For now the winter is past,
The rains are over and gone.
12 The blossoms have appeared in the land,
The time of pruning has come;
The song of the turtledove
Is heard in our land.
13 The green figs form on the fig tree,
The vines in blossom give off fragrance.
Arise, my darling;
My fair one, come away!

11 כִּֽי־הִנֵּה הסתו הַסְּתָיו עָבָר
הַגֶּשֶׁם חָלַף הָלַךְ לֽוֹ׃
12 הַנִּצָּנִים נִרְאוּ בָאָרֶץ
עֵת הַזָּמִיר הִגִּיעַ
וְקוֹל הַתּוֹר
נִשְׁמַע בְּאַרְצֵנוּ׃
13 הַתְּאֵנָה חָנְטָה פַגֶּיהָ
וְהַגְּפָנִים ׀ סְמָדַר נָתְנוּ רֵיחַ
קוּמִי לכי לָךְ רַעְיָתִי
יָפָתִי וּלְכִי־לָךְ׃ ס

Peshat

11. The sequence begins with the passing of the cold, wet season—the verse's two clauses (about the winter and its rains) being complementary in nature (Riq).

winter This period is called *setav*, indicating the winter or rainy season (thus distinct from modern Hebrew "autumn"). This is the common sense in Aramaic (cf. Targum Onqelos at Gen. 8:22, where *ḥoref*, "winter," is translated *sitva'*).

12. The blossoms... The song The imagery evokes the character of the spring: the blossoms (*nitzanim*) are seen, and the voice or song (*qol*) of the turtledove is heard. Nature awakens in sight and sound.

time of pruning Or "singing" (Transl.). This clause *'eit ha-zamir higgi'a* bridges the verse's other two clauses. It is a play on the noun *zamir*.[181] Pointing back to the first clause, it refers to pruning (see Lev. 25:3; Rashbam);[182] pointing toward the last clause, it refers to singing (see Isa. 24:16; Rashi; MsP; Ibn Ezra; and Rid).[183] These activities are inseparable emblems of springtime.

13. The green figs form on the fig tree Literally, "The fig [tree] forms its green fruit." The noun *te'enah* can denote either the tree or its fruit; here it must be the former.

green figs The fig is presented at the initial stage when the unripe fruit is in formation. The verb *ḥaneṭah* ("formed") indicates something like a primary "swaddling" of the seed (cf. Gen. 50:2); the plural noun *pagim*, which in the Bible occurs only here, denotes "the fruit before it has ripened—as in Arabic" (Ibn Ezra).

The vines in blossom The phrase's unusual syntax follows the pattern of *ki ha-se'orah 'aviv ve-ha-pishtah giv'ol,* "for the barley was in the ear and the flax was in bud" (Exod. 9:31; Ginsburg).[184]

in blossom The noun *semadar* is found only in the Song; it marks the budding of the vine (Ibn Janaḥ; Ibn Ezra) or budding in general (cf. Targum Jonathan on Isa. 18:5).[185]

give off fragrance The vines' palpable perfume (*natenu reiaḥ*) reinforces the likelihood that the previous clause indicates that the figs are likewise ripening and beginning to exude an aroma. Both odors add to the aphrodisiac atmosphere. Moreover, the echo of *natan reiḥo* ("gave forth its fragrance") in 1:12 gives this image an added overtone (see above; and 7:14, below).

Stylistics. The male's speech is framed by an *inclusio*—the opening exhortation is repeated at the end. In both cases, the phrase is chiastic in structure ("arise, my *x* | my *x'*, and come away"). The appeal to go (*lekhi*) addressed to her (*lakh*) is repeated, which connotes insistent imploring.

Depictions of nature's revival are multiple. The fixed pattern is noun-plus-verb, with occasional augmentation. This sequence directs attention first to a feature of nature, then to the

transient characteristic emphasized (the passing of winter, the emergence of buds, and the smell of grape blossoms). In verses 11 and 12a the parallelisms are asyndetic (without any conjunction); whereas the clause in verse 12b opens with the conjunction *ve-* ("and"), and the parallel pair in verse 13 is similarly conjoined. In the first case, the conjunction joins seeing and hearing; in the second, the conjunction indicates the end of a series.

Derash

11–13. These verses continue the preceding historical vectors, providing reasons and motivations. Thus "the winter has passed" (v. 11) indicates that the 400 years of bondage decreed in the time of Abraham (Gen. 15:13) has expired (SongsR 2.xi.1);[186] "the rains are over" intimates that the most intense period of servitude is complete—this being 86 years (according to R. Tanḥum, SongsR ibid.; cf. Radal at PdRE 48), which tallies the time from the birth of Miriam to the Exodus[187] with the 86-day period of the heaviest winter rains (falling from the 17th of Ḥeshvan to the 15th of Shevat; see Radal). The announcement (v. 12) that "the blossoms (*nitzanim*) have appeared in the land" means that the two victors (*ha-natzoḥot*),[188] Moses and Aaron, have made their appearance in the land of Egypt (SongsR 2.x.4); and the "the time of pruning" (*'eit ha-zamir*) announces that the time for the "cutting off" of Egyptian idolatry has come, and that the occasion for the "song" of salvation has arrived (ibid. xii.1; for the dual valence of *zamir*, see Peshat). Finally, "the green figs" (v. 13) stand for "the sinners of Israel," who were enamored with Egyptian ways and refused to change (remaining unripe; SongsR 2.xiii.1); whereas the "vines in bloom" refer to those who repented and were redeemed at the Exodus (being of good "fragrance"; ibid.).

Midrashic tradition developed a close correlation between the patterns of nature and the historical and spiritual life of Israel. This is more than a transformation of natural cycles into historical sequences. It allowed teachers to think with natural metaphors and concretize the birth of the nation and its redemptive flowering. Jews celebrate these correlations annually with the recitation of the Song on Passover. Ordinarily the planes of natural and historical existence are kept separate: one being earthly experience, the other cultural memory. On this festival, they are joined in mind and heart.

Remez

11–13. The voice that addresses the soul ("My Beloved") speaks now of the changing seasons. What might this mean to the seeker? Is it an allusion to temporality and the need to take stock? Or might it mean that the Beloved acknowledges that the soul has begun to ripen and emit a spiritual fragrance (Ibn Aqnin)?[189] If so, the sequence of natural growth suggests a certain sequence of growth (Ibn Tibbon), since spiritual development requires time and cultivation (Al-Fawwāl). For the individual rooted in natural existence[190] and yearning for a higher wisdom, the imagery of cold rains and sprouting shoots may suggest the often fruitless desolation of spiritual beginnings, and the slow growth of new habits and thoughts (Malbim).

Simultaneously, the imagery is also a prism for the natural self that experiences itself as reborn—like a budding flower or fragrant fruit. The soul senses its emergence and growth, its spiritual awakening and transformation (Ibn Aqnin; Al-Fawwāl). Now the awakened inner eye has a glimmer of truth (Immanuel). Through labor and grace, the soul gains insight and ascends the spiritual ladder toward God (Malbim).

Sod

11. For now the winter is past This "now" (*hinneih*) is spiritually correlated with "there (*hinneih*) he comes" in verse 8. The sudden immanence is depicted by the Beloved's voice. The first word spoken to the heart is that the winter "is past"—the period of spiritual dormancy is "over and gone" (*lo*—that is, "for its part"). The time is now. Beyond any "why" (Rilke), a new spiritual reality has beckoned.

Exile and isolation near their end (REzra). The soul may ascend to spiritual maturity (Ibn Sahula).

12. ***The blossoms have appeared*** The rebirth of the soul is a budding from its earthliness; for one doesn't rescind embodiment on the spiritual path.[191] Natural processes offer a valid analogue to the soul's renaissance. There is now a coming into appearance (sight); a pruning of excess (spiritual discipline); and a joyful exuberance of speech (song). All this is the new configuration: a breaking into view; a harnessing of possibilities; and a bursting of sound. All the senses are transfigured. A spiritual restoration is at hand (REzra); a spiritual maturation is occurring (Ibn Sahula).

13. Worldly bounty further intoxicates the senses: "figs form," with aromas and succulent seeds; "the vines . . . blossom" and exude "fragrance." These are signs that one's soul is coming to fruition. A Voice bids the soul to hasten. The earlier call resounds (v. 10), in the very same terms. Between that first call and the second (v. 13) was an explanation (*ki hinneih*, "For now [or: behold]"; v. 11). This is the flicker of rationality that tries to justify the event. At the core is a divine call—transcendent and exacting. Can the soul respond? Can it develop (Ibn Sahula)? Can one's entire being become a song of divine praise (Z. 1:97a–b)?

14 "O my dove, in the cranny of the rocks,
Hidden by the cliff,
Let me see your face,
Let me hear your voice;
For your voice is sweet
And your face is comely."

14 יוֹנָתִ֞י בְּחַגְוֵ֣י הַסֶּ֗לַע
בְּסֵ֙תֶר֙ הַמַּדְרֵגָ֔ה
הַרְאִ֙ינִי֙ אֶת־מַרְאַ֔יִךְ
הַשְׁמִיעִ֖ינִי אֶת־קוֹלֵ֑ךְ
כִּֽי־קוֹלֵ֥ךְ עָרֵ֖ב
וּמַרְאֵ֥יךְ נָאוֶֽה׃ ס

Peshat

3. AN ENTREATY (V. 14)

The Beloved again speaks to the maiden, but the setting is more ambiguous. He describes her as concealed and expresses his desire to see and hear her. This verse may thus be a further exhortation to the maiden in her room (Rashbam). Or if this speech follows his earlier appeal, they are now together in the fields but she (coyly or modestly) remains hidden from him—like a dove in the crags. The shift in imagery suggests a new venue.

14. O my dove The beloved invokes his fair one.

in the cranny... Hidden She is doubly concealed—in the recesses of the rocks and the outcropping of the cliffs. She is now depicted not in her terms (such as a lily) but his own. To him, she is like a dove perched afar, inaccessible. His terms for her location are standard (cf. Jer. 49:16 and Ezek. 38:20, respectively). Poetic parallelism gives them an intensified force of height and hiddenness.

Let me see your face... hear your voice The beloved calls to her with desire and urgency.

For your voice... comely To make his meaning clear, he adds an explanation (introduced with *ki*): your voice (*qol*) is sweet and your appearance beautiful (*na'veh*). His words may thus appeal to her—should she recall her own expectation of his *qol* (in v. 8) and her self-depiction as *na'vah* (in 1:5).

Stylistics. The appeal is threefold: a depiction of the dove he desires; an appeal for her manifestation; and a justification of this request. Each element is formed by a parallelism. In the first case, the dove is "in an *x* of *y*" (twice), giving the location in two different but related aspects; in the second, the particle *'et* links a verb to its object (twice); and in the third case, adjectives of desire complement the physical features (twice). In the final justification clause, the two features are linked by the conjunction *ve-*. This gives the statement a descriptive and logical appeal. It resumes the topics of the preceding call in inverse order (there: "your face... your voice"; here: "your voice... your face").

Derash

14. my dove, in the cranny of the rocks The Beloved continues to address Israel, now called *yonati*, "My dove." This designation highlights one of Israel's two spiritual traits: tender and faithful like a "simple dove" (Hos. 7:11), when it comes to piety and loyalty toward God (SongsR 2.xiv.1); she can also be like a lion or wolf (Gen. 49:9, 27), when nations try to destroy or inhibit her religious practices (ibid.; GenR 99.4; 100.9). Faith and fortitude enable historical continuity. They are projected here through polar figures: the tender spirit of the dove, and the tough resolve of the lion. Both are Israel.

Alternatively (in terms of past memories and present experiences), Israel is like the dove, which fled to a crevice before a hunter's arrow, where it flapped its wings to call her owner to the rescue—just as Israel fled before the Egyptians and hid in the crevices of the Sea until she shouted to God, who rescued her (SongsR 2.xiv.2–3; and MdRI, *Beshallaḥ*, 2). And for R. Yose, this figure portrays Israel's plight among the nations. In defiant loyalty, they raise their voice in study and prayer and maintain a life of kindness and good deeds (SongsR

ibid., 5). Such cases project the power of prayer (in petition and praise) and deeds (in obedience and generosity) as life principles for the dove's heirs.

Remez

14. in the cranny The self is suddenly ambivalent. It seemed ready for spiritual and intellectual growth. But there remains resistance. The soul hides among the "rocks" of the known and the stable. It fears the *seiter ha-madrigah*—all that is "hidden" and concealed by the higher stages of knowledge and experience (for the self also knows that what appears as a "cliff" is a projection of stability, concealing levels of possibility).

Let me see your face The hesitant self is attentive to the challenge. It hears a call that it cannot deny. Is this the Beloved who beckons (Malbim)?[192] Or is it the inner voice of the courageous self?

On the precipice of this beginning—having been called but still hesitant—the seeker totters. Is the "cranny" like an abyss of the spirit? The individual must determine such matters and make a decision.

Sod

14. Suddenly, a crisis. The Beloved became manifest and summoned the soul. But the yearning is disrupted; the soul has withdrawn. What seemed to appear (*nir'u*) and be heard (*nishma'*)—signs of the soul's development—is suppressed. Retreating to the crannies, the soul hides from view. And thus the Beloved beseeches with pathos: "Let me see (*har'ini*) your face / Let me hear (*hashmi'ini*) your voice." Why this concealment (*seiter*) at the onset of spiritual ascendance (*madreigah*; cf. Z. 1:84b)?[193] Does the soul fear the spiritual unknown? Is there a sense of unworthiness that has cast it back?

15 Catch us the foxes,
The little foxes
That ruin the vineyards—
For our vineyard is in blossom.

15 אֶחֱזוּ־לָנוּ שׁוּעָלִים
שׁוּעָלִים קְטַנִּים
מְחַבְּלִים כְּרָמִים
וּכְרָמֵינוּ סְמָדַר׃

Peshat

4. FEARS AND FLIGHT (VV. 15–17)

This concluding group of speeches has two parts. The first is a dual appeal by the maiden and her beloved (to others? to themselves?) to catch foxes (v. 15); the second is the maiden's farewell discourse to her beloved, reasserting her sense of their mutual commitment (vv. 16–17). The first speech seems to climax their appearance in the vineyard. The fact that she then urges him to flee suggests a meeting out of the public eye. She bids him leave as he came—like a gazelle.

15. Catch us the foxes The plural imperative *'eḥezu lanu* conveys the sense of seizing or grabbing for one's benefit (cf. 2 Sam. 2:21).[194] A similar form occurs with *'ehevu*, "love" (in Ps. 31:24).[195] This verse's ending suggests that the act ("catch") is somehow intended to serve the couple, to protect their blossoming vineyard (*semadar*). Hence it is unlikely that this call is an appeal to youths (or the maidens' brothers), for this would imply that the couple are public in their love and share a vineyard. More likely, the vineyard is symbolic of their relationship; and the wild foxes concretize the libidinous impulses that pervade the unit. The forces of nature not only surround the pair, but infuse them as well. With masterful control, the poet speaks by suggestion and allusion. The reader must determine the phrase's nuance.[196]

Derash

15. Catch . . . the foxes, / The . . . foxes An old tradition interpreted this verse as recompense against the Egyptians. Scheming like foxes (*shu'alim*), they determined to destroy the Israelite firstborn by drowning in the sea; hence they were similarly punished by drowning in the "swells" (*sha'alim*) of the Sea—measure for measure (SongsR 2.xv.1).[197]

With a more pedagogical purpose, Rabbi Berekhiah identified these "*young* foxes" with the "four . . . *young* ones of the earth" (Prov. 30:24)—these being the four empires that subjugated the Jews in antiquity (Babylon; Persia; Greece; and Edom [Rome]); he then stated that they "destroyed the vineyards" (the people Israel)[198] because the latter's "bloom" was unripe (ibid. xv.3). That is, the people were insufficiently prepared to withstand the influences that infiltrated and ravaged their spiritual inheritance. Only the cultivation of their moral and spiritual life, and the increase of fortitude, would enable the Jews to counter the pressures and the allure of other religions and cultures. This sage's words ring true for later eras. Ripening must be nurtured from within one's native ground; and spiritual vigilance must be acquired and sustained.

Remez

15. Catch us the foxes The Beloved speaks to the soul as to a partner, telling it to proceed with firmness and seize those elements of doubt that may "ruin the vineyards" it has so arduously cultivated (Immanuel).[199] Surely the soul remembers its earlier determination to care for itself (deemed a vineyard, 1:6). So perhaps there is a realization that something more profound is involved; namely, that God is implicated in the spiritual development of the human being. This possibility is hinted at by the Beloved himself, when he turns to the soul and says: "*our* vineyard is in blossom." This suggests that the human soul is not simply engaged in a private spiritual exercise, but that its work somehow engages the divine reality. This realization affects the spiritual task as a whole. The Beloved announces that the soul is not alone—for the soul also belongs to God. The words "our vineyard" are thus a charged theological metaphor.

Sod

15. The soul offers a clue to its flight. It calls to itself and to God to seize some destructive forces that "ruin the vineyards" (the site of the soul) just when it—newly gifted with God's grace (*our* vineyards)—is "in blossom" (v. 13). Has something plundered the soul's purity (Ibn Sahula)? Or do these words express terror before the *mysterium tremendum*—a sense of insignificance before God's unsurpassable mystery? The cry is assertive: "Catch us (*lanu*—that is, for *our* sake) the foxes." The soul needs help. Its spiritual sustenance requires assistance.

16 My beloved is mine
And I am his
Who browses among the lilies.

16 דּוֹדִי לִי
וַאֲנִי לוֹ
הָרֹעֶה בַּשּׁוֹשַׁנִּים׃

Peshat

16. My beloved is mine... Who browses among the lilies The maiden affirms their mutual love directly (Ibn Aqnin).[200] He is hers and she is his—he who pastures (*ro'eh*) among the lilies. The epithet has their love in mind, through an allusion to her self-depiction (v. 1) and his occupation (1:7). In her heart she is for him both a vineyard and a field of lilies. His browsing thus has erotic overtones, stated obliquely by a double entendre.[201] This depiction of the beloved follows the innuendos of verse 15.

Derash

16. My beloved is mine / And I am his This proclamation of mutuality ("[he] is mine," *li*; and "[I] am his," *lo*) expresses the theological relationship between God and Israel. This phrase encapsulates a spiritual duet, as Jewish destiny pairs (respectively) God's instruction, words of Torah, and obligations of sanctity with Israel's national tradition, a life of study, and the practice of virtue. Scripture offers diverse theological forms of this duet: LORD–people; father–son; shepherd–flock; protector–defender (SongsR 2.xvi.1); and Tradition has concretized these images in multiple modalities: prayer, midrash, and the poetic imagination.

Religious practice sets the demanding tasks of holiness; and Israel responds with faithful loyalty (Rashi). For Israel, the covenant outlines a pattern of life governance, like a "shepherd (*ro'eh*)" guiding one through the complex conditions of existence.

Generations also meditated upon this image in the face of persecution. Some dared read the phrase "who browses (*ha-ro'eh*) among the lilies" in terms of God's providential testing of Israel through suffering (*ro'a*), challenging them to deeper spiritual resolve (MatKeh) and to assert spiritual strength amid the broken vessels (*qanqanim mero'a'im*) of existence (cf. SongsR ibid., 2).[202] The religious person's task is to remain ever true to spiritual imperatives. This is Israel's antiphon to God's call.

Remez

16. My beloved is mine Hearing this, the self turns from doubt and hesitation. It is now ready to receive what is given (Ibn Tibbon). The soul realizes that the Beloved is not separate from itself and participates in its quest in some unfathomable way.

Who browses among the lilies Who is searching for the soul. And thus the soul feels sought and found all at once. There is a holy beckoning to the self ("lily") from the hidden depths. It now knows (and avers) that it is not alone.

Sod

16. My beloved is mine The soul counterpoints its anguish with an assertion of its positive commitment, despite all. The proclamation expresses reciprocity. For has not the Beloved beckoned, and has she not indicated her readiness (Z. 2:20a)? Surely he has come, the one who "browses among the lilies" and gathers the soul that had proclaimed itself (from the outset) a lily!

17 When the day blows gently
And the shadows flee,
Set out, my beloved,
Swift as a gazelle
Or a young stag,
For the hills of spices!

17 עַד שֶׁיָּפ֙וּחַ֙ הַיּ֔וֹם
וְנָ֖סוּ הַצְּלָלִ֑ים
סֹב֩ דְּמֵה־לְךָ֨
דוֹדִ֜י לִצְבִ֗י
א֛וֹ לְעֹ֥פֶר הָאַיָּלִ֖ים
עַל־הָ֥רֵי בָֽתֶר׃ ס

Peshat

17. When the day blows gently The ecstatic proclamation (v. 16) is cut short by parting words. She exhorts him to leave "when" (or "before"; *'ad she-*) the day blows its morning breezes and daybreak's shadows dissipate (Immanuel).[203] It is a lingering, last word of love. A temporal clause, introduced by *'ad she-,* marks the onset of their separation, while echoing the maiden's earlier adjuration to her friends (v. 7). If the first use of this formula anticipated the beloved's advent, it now denotes his departure.

Set out More precisely, "turn away" (MsP).

Swift as a gazelle She urges him to flee quickly. His departure echoes his sudden advent (v. 8). Earlier, she imagined him to "be like (*domeh*) a gazelle" (v. 9); he now leaves "like" one.

For the hills of spices This rendering equates the difficult phrase "hills of *bater*" with the parallel "mountain of spices (*besamim*)" in 8:14, when she again urges her beloved to flee. The noun *bater* is obscure. (Based upon the verbal stem *b-t-r*, "to split," Targum, Rashi, and Ibn Ezra render in terms of "jagged" or "cleft" mountains; cf. Gen. 15:2.) Yet one may suppose that it also has a figurative aspect. For this couple, their love and desire infuse all features on earth.

Derash

17. When the day blows . . . And the shadows flee This is God's word to Israel regarding the future of judgment and salvation: abide in faith and wait *'ad she-yafuaḥ ha-yom*, "*until* the day blows" and the dark "shadows" of exile recede. This echoes the divine admonition not to engage in acts of restoration "*until* love's desire [is nigh]" (*'ad she-teḥpatz*; v. 7).[204] The challenge to wait is poignant, given the expressions of divine love found throughout this section. Hence the first caution is supplemented by a promise. The imperative to "set out [or: turn]" (*sov*) and be like a gazelle "on the hills of spices" (*beter*) is a divine promise that at the "end" (*sof*) time, God will hasten like a gazelle for the redemption of Israel—not least "because of the promises made to Abraham at the Covenant between the Parts (*betarim*; Gen. 15:17–18)" (SongsR 2.xvii.1). In a midrashic flash, separation is reformulated—and loss becomes hope.

Rabbi Berekhiah focuses on the punishment and final vindication of Israel—"the day" (*ha-yom*) refers to the Day of Judgment (Leqaḥ Ṭov, citing Mal. 3:19; also YalSh, *Song*, # 986).[205] The scenario is this: God will initially send a "fiery blast" (*'afiaḥ*) against Israel and refine them of their sinful dross. After this, God promises to turn toward the people in mercy and wreak judgment against the evil kingdom (Rome)—not least because of their brutal persecution of the Jews at Beitar (in the Galilee), where the emperor Hadrian cruelly murdered hundreds of thousands of people.[206]

Thus this verse offers two tokens of hope: the ancient promise given to Abraham, because of his faithfulness even before he had progeny; and a reference to the martyrs of Beitar, because of whose blood the progeny of Abraham will be vindicated. Israel may therefore be consoled and fortified by noble acts of allegiance (personal and collective) throughout their history. The closing phrase offers hope that nothing is lost when nothing is forgotten.

Remez

17. When the day blows gently Is the soul ready to continue its spiritual journey? It wants the divine spirit to blow "gently" and linger forever. But the soul realizes that this intimacy will pass and the glare of the everyday will return.[207]

Set out Anticipating this loss, the soul requests that the Beloved "turn back [or: return]" (*sov*) to it through those very forms that once depicted His presence:[208] the images of the "gazelle" and "young stag"—figures of erotic ardor (v. 7) and of intimacy's advent (v. 9). The soul knows that these images are but virtual presences. But it hopes that they shall be like arrows of the heart, eliciting the one she awaits in longing. This request is a prayer.

Sod

17. When the day blows gently Rather, "Before the day passes."[209] The soul knows the reality of time (Z. 1:99b; Ibn Sahula)—beset with impairments that might inhibit its spiritual growth (Z. 3:43a). Hence its climactic call to the Beloved not to abandon her, but rather turn (*sov*)[210] and hasten "as a gazelle" to her aid. The Beloved is also summoned to "be as" (*demeih lekha*) a "gazelle." This language emerges from the spiritual depths and restores the soul to its proper balance. With this figure, the heart evokes its earlier sensibility—when (sensing the advent of the Beloved) it proclaimed that "My Beloved is like (*domeh*) a gazelle" (v. 9). That sensibility was filled with tangible presence; and now the soul feels it again. She had hidden from the call; now she reclaims her spiritual destiny. She cries: "Turn swiftly to the break-back hills!"[211]—where I have withdrawn in readiness for You.[212] The response is not given. The words hang in the air.

CONCLUSION

The scenes shift from motif to motif and dialogue to dialogue. The initial setting of the field gives way to a house of wine, whose walls provide the enclosure through which the beloved beckons the maiden to emerge—which she does in the final scenes. In each unit the lovers are imagined or vivified by reference to elements of nature: the lily and the tree; the gazelle and the stag; the dove; and perhaps also the foxes. These images govern the discourses. Three types of representation are indicated: metaphors (as in "I am a lily"); similes (as in "like an apricot tree"); and more formal terms of likeness (as in "compared to a gazelle").

Nature plays also an actual and figurative role. It is the concrete time of blooming, when the beloved calls his beloved to join him in the fields. These bud bursts variously suggest an awakened human eros: grapes blossom (*semadar*), as does the couple. There is thus a dramatic correlation between these two states of nature: the outer world of growth and the inner world of passion. The poet directs our attention to this conjunction in other ways as well. To mark the imminence of springtime, we find the adverb *hinneih* ("behold, now!") marking the season, even as this term was used earlier to indicate the beloved's advent. The world is palpably new: the awakening of seeds and passions are two parts of this process. By establishing this correlation, the poet suggests powerful human feelings in a delicate and figurative manner. Nature is altogether suffused by love, while love is grounded in earthly energies.

CHAPTER 3:1–11

Inner Experience and Shared Joy

The third cycle of lyrics is composed of three units. These comprise two long scenes and one bridging element. The first unit (3:1–5) portrays the maiden alone and longing for her beloved, whom she eventually finds and brings to her mother's home. Speaking autobiographically to her female companions, she details her impulses and recites her adjuration about the proper timing of love. By contrast, the concluding unit depicts a grand marital procession, with references to the wealth of Solomon and the king himself on his wedding day (though the bride and groom are not named). Speaking like a herald, an anonymous voice announces this entourage and invites the maidens of Jerusalem to come and celebrate (vv. 7–11).[1] The middle section (v. 6) hangs in the balance. Its speaker sees a scented woman ascending from the desert; but the query of her identity is not answered. The reader will ponder if and how these units are related.

Contextually, this cycle continues the previous one. That one ended as the maiden bid her beloved depart; this one opens with her pining for him and seeking their reunion in a city. The subsequent units are episodic (the reference to a mysterious woman and to the royal entourage); but no ligatures bind them into a unified narrative, and no details identify the characters involved. Since the first and third units counterpoint the beloved and a king, one might suppose that two persons are involved, with the maiden caught betwixt and between—in love with the one, perhaps taken by the other (on this view, the fragrant woman is a transitional figure). But there is no indication that the maiden has been removed or induced from her love nest to be a royal bride.

Alternatively, the wedding scenario portends (perhaps as projected fantasy) the connubial culmination of the maiden and her beloved. On this account, the editor-poet apparently adapted an old wedding song to new ends.[2] The result is a triptych formed from older motifs: (*1*) a lonely lass scouring the town for her beloved, whom she eventually finds and rejoins; (*2*) a scented woman seen ascending from the steppes; and (*3*) a hymn praising "the wedding bed of Solomon," with hoopla about the groom and marriage crown. Read sequentially, the love and dreams of the sweethearts materialize in a figurative form. Alone with her beloved, the maiden feels like a queen—stately and scented, and her bed seems like a kingly couch—bedecked in love. For her beloved is her king, and she his queen upon their bed of love. Imagination is a virtual reality; dreams of marriage project royal splendor into their humble hearts.

3 Upon my couch at night
I sought the one I love—
I sought, but found him not.

ג עַל־מִשְׁכָּבִי בַּלֵּילוֹת
בִּקַּשְׁתִּי אֵת שֶׁאָהֲבָה נַפְשִׁי
בִּקַּשְׁתִּיו וְלֹא מְצָאתִיו׃

Peshat

1. THE LONGINGS OF LOVE (3:1–5)

The maiden recounts her nightly desire for her beloved (v. 1), impelling her to seek him outdoors (vv. 2–3). The sequence begins in her bedroom, moves to the streets, and ends with her bringing him to her mother's house (v. 4). At each juncture there are two leitmotifs: the first is the language of seeking and finding, in various combinations; the second is the reference to the beloved as "the one I love" (*she-'ahavah nafshi*), repeated four times (vv. 1–4; with a climactic reference to *'ahavah* at the end). These two motifs work in tandem. Love is once again the catalyst, as in the previous cycle, where the epithet "the one I love" first occurs (1:7).

The lass reports this escapade to her friends (Rid), now that she has found her beloved (v. 4)—but before the consummation of their love, since she again adjures them against its premature arousal (v. 5). The companions again serve as aides in the enterprise of *'ahavah*. The recurrence of the adjuration scene gives poignancy to the drama of desire.

3:1. Upon my couch at night The maiden's report begins *in medias res*, without any prior clarification. We thus catch the conversation in process. The maiden speaks of herself in bed (*mishkavi*), beset nightly with yearnings for her beloved (MsP).[3] The plural form *ba-leylot* ("at night") has a frequentative aspect—night after night, or nightly (cf. Ps. 92:3; 16:7)[4]—an iteration that underscores the maiden's ongoing passion.

I sought . . . I sought The report intensifies: *biqqashti . . . biqqashtiv*; the verb for seeking is repeated, while coupled with its failure ("found him not"). Those two verbs set the tone and tension for the entire scene.

the one I love . . . him The initial seeking refers to the beloved in personal terms; the next two references to him substitute the third-person object pronoun (*biqqashtiv ve-lo' metza'tiv*), signaling his distance. The epithet thus evokes his presence in her heart, while the pronoun marks the reality of his absence.

Derash

3:1. Upon my couch at night The Hebrew plural *ba-leiylot* evokes the dark "nights" of history, when Israel endured exile and oppression. For some, the "couch" (*mishkav*) also symbolizes this suffering (or spiritual illness)—occasionally relieved by the light of divine consolation (SongsR 3.i.1). Others consider the couch a figure for spiritual lassitude,[5] as a result of which *ba'u leiylot*, the "nights" of oppression "came" successively and unremittingly (ibid.).[6] According to these sages, suffering increases with the abandonment of Torah and Tradition.

The heart struggles with such comments, trying to find God and religious meaning within the inexplicable events of existence. One strives to remain faithful to religious teachings during the eclipse of apparent meaning. A possible solution is to accept that spiritual tremor and transform it into a meditative reflection (an inward "seeking" upon one's "couch"), in hopes of strengthening or restoring religious commitment. The yearning for the "Beloved" marks this possibility. Religious acts and spiritual questions may keep ideals in mind even when the heart is in despair or confusion. Tragedy buckles the community; but uplift may begin in the soul of individuals, and extend from there toward others.

Remez

3:1. Upon my couch Apart from her Beloved (2:17), the soul retreats into meditative seclusion. In the dark of "night," shut off from everyday distractions, the self turns inward.[7] It has repeatedly "sought the one" it "loves"[8]—through recollection, imagination, and yearning (Immanuel; Malbim).[9] In such ways, the seeker has tried to make the spiritual goal present to mind and heart. But the void of absence remains. The Beloved remains elusive, and the soul is overcome with longing.

I sought, but found him not The self has entered a cycle of seeking, with no result. A great emptiness separates the lonely, inward "I" from its spiritually distant goal (called "him"). A powerful pathos impels it. Loss defines the self and the corresponding quest to fill this void.

Sod

3:1. Upon my couch at night The soul is alone, cut off from spiritual clarity ('Or Torah 36c). Past achievements suddenly fade and spiritual gains are unsettled. Perhaps nagging doubts prevail, or perhaps focus wanders. Suddenly there is a dark "night" of the soul. Desire has lost traction, and the quest seems beyond attainment. Is this mere laziness or lack of will (Ibn Sahula)? Or is a deeper rupture involved, an alienation from one's spiritual center (Z. 3:42a–b)?

But despite the emptiness, all is not lost. There is still a yearning for divine reality. The self "seeks"—initially to no avail. Dislocated, adrift, the soul cannot "find" insight. However, love of God and sense of spiritual loss prods it forward.

2 "I must rise and roam the town,
Through the streets and through the squares;
I must seek the one I love."
I sought but found him not.

2 אָק֤וּמָה נָּא֙ וַאֲסֹובְבָ֣ה בָעִ֔יר
בַּשְּׁוָקִים֙ וּבָ֣רְחֹבֹ֔ות
אֲבַקְשָׁ֕ה אֵ֥ת שֶׁאָהֲבָ֖ה נַפְשִׁ֑י
בִּקַּשְׁתִּ֖יו וְלֹ֥א מְצָאתִֽיו׃

Peshat

2. *I must rise and roam* The cohortative tone in *'aqumah na' va-'asovevah* is self-imploring more than compulsive;[10] the particle *na'* enforces this aspect, for it conveys respect. The mood is thus intensely volitional. A similar first-person cohortative form occurs in Gen. 27:4; another with the particle *na'* is found in Exod. 3:3 (*'asurah na' ve-'er'eh*, "I must turn aside and look [at this marvelous sight])." The arising is joined to the roaming via the conjunctive particle *ve-*, correlating them emotionally and physically. The depiction conveys the realism of an actual event (Rid).[11] We are left to wonder how much is dream, how much waking fantasy (Immanuel), and how much is actual occurrence (Rashbam; MsP).[12]

the town That is, "throughout the town" (*bha-'ir*), as clarified by the subsequent reference to the streets and squares. In this sense, "the town" is the general location and is given first. This locale replaces the home, even as the seeking outdoors replaces the maiden's inner yearning.

I must seek The verb *'abhaqshah* continues the cohortative mood. Deftly, the poet splits the first two verbs from this one, inserting the (general) place of wandering (the town) after this pair; then, after adding two other (specific) places of her search (the markets and streets), the poem indicates her quest's object ("the one I love"). This sequence has an incremental effect. The anticlimax turns expectation into despair: "I sought him but found him not."

Derash

2. *I must rise and...seek the one I love*
The people are determined to respond to their historical darkness. For the sages, religious renewal (seeking "the One I love") begins with

a search for a proper leader or teacher—a quest that leads through the byways of the world, broad and narrow. The search arises as a necessity ("I must"), giving purpose even when the "One" "sought" is "not found." Finding the right leader or teacher is not simple. Such a person must have the vision to guide, and the integrity to be trusted. Ancient models are Moses in Egypt and Daniel in Babylon (SongsR 3.iii.1; iv.1–2). The arousal of this spiritual desire is a sign of personal transformation. It must withstand despair, for it develops within the darkness itself. National renewal is a task for one and all; the reorientation of individual *teshuvah* (literally, "turning") is a beginning, not the end (Ibn Yaḥye).

Remez

2. *I must rise* The soul exhorts itself to "rise and roam the town"—to "seek the one I love" (the Beloved) in the forms of spiritual truth scattered or concealed throughout the world. More than mere desire, an inner necessity compels the soul (Ralbag). Its bursting outward is a counterthrust to ignorance and despair. But the result (reported to oneself, in an interior monologue) is futile: "I sought, but found him not." The repetition of this phrase intones a litany of loss. The self is spiritually empty and its quest vacuous. The spiritual goal seems both elusive and absent. The word "not" is definitive. Past achievements and present intentions lead nowhere. At such times, one needs a spiritual guide (Ibn Aqnin)—for direction, if not a conclusive answer.[13]

Sod

2. *I must rise* A decision is required. Impelled outward, the soul seeks its goal. But the self is mired in ego: everything is wrought

from the "I" ("*I* must arise"; "*I* shall roam"; "*I* must seek"). Self-assertions consume the self and block the search. "*I* sought but [*I*] found him not." Nothing changes until the self can transcend itself (self-centeredness) and seek spiritual counsel.

3 I met the watchmen
Who patrol the town.
"Have you seen the one I love?"

3 מְצָאוּנִי הַשֹּׁמְרִים
הַסֹּבְבִים בָּעִיר
אֵת שֶׁאָהֲבָה נַפְשִׁי רְאִיתֶם׃

Peshat

3. I met the watchmen Literally, "The watchmen met me" (Transl.). Moving impulsively in search of her beloved, the maiden is found (*metza'uni*) by the watchmen (MsP), an event that counterpoints her desire to "find him" (*metza'tiv*).

Who patrol The portrayal of the watchmen as those "who circumambulate" (*ha-sovevim*) provides a second counterpoint to the maiden's wandering (*'asovevah*; v. 2).

the one I love The epithet says it all. To her, he is (in name and being) *she-'ahavah nafshi*!

Derash

3. I met the watchmen These are the "guardians" (*shomerim*) of the people—leaders like the tribe of Levi who "guarded" (*shameru*) God's teaching (Deut. 33:9). All Jewish leaders begin with this dual task: to guard and oversee the people, by guarding and imparting the Torah and Tradition. Moses is the paradigm of the tribe of Levi—both teacher and interpreter of the sacred word. Daniel is a prophetic prototype—both reader and decoder of inscrutable signs (SongsR 3.iv.2). True guardians also beseech the mercy of Heaven, out of love for their people. Such was the greatness of Moses (Exod. 32; Targum) and the merit of Daniel (Dan. 9; SongsR, ibid.). Because of these traits, the community turns to such guides (and their historical heirs; Leqaḥ Ṭov) and asks: have you found what my heart truly seeks?

Remez

3. I met the watchmen To find its way, the soul now seeks counsel from those who are *shomerim*—"guardians" of spiritual truth.[14] Wisely, it places itself in a situation where these watchmen may find or meet her in the course of the search.[15] The initial attempt at self-reliance is aborted. The second move accepts the necessity of assistance in the spiritual quest (through persons, books, or tradition). And then the question is reformulated: "Have you seen the one I love?" This "one" is the object of the personal search; but it is not a wholly subjective reality. It is known to other seekers, as well, who may give assistance—if asked.

Reformulating the question is crucial, and offers a breakthrough. For now—after the soul has sought guidance—the Beloved becomes manifest. Turning the question into a public matter lifts one from pure subjectivity toward the objective spiritual goal. One may seek and ask in personal terms; but one also has to learn to be guided by a shared tradition and common language. One must learn how to find instruction.

Sod

3. I met the watchmen Suddenly the self reaches outward—to guardians of the spiritual path. Its core question is a turning point: "Have you seen the one I love?" The question remains personal ("I"); but now another self is addressed ("you"). This changes matters dramatically and substantively. The question presupposes that the Divine Beloved is a reality that may be formulated in public terms, and is not a private illusion. This does not mean that the Divine Other is nameable as such. It remains "the *One* I love." But it does mean that the search for God is part of a broader theological quest. The heart asks if the others have had spiritual success: "Have *you* seen the One I love?" This seeing is not something external, but an inner apperception. The self seeks guidance.

4 Scarcely had I passed them
When I found the one I love.
I held him fast, I would not let him go
Till I brought him to my mother's house,
To the chamber of her who conceived me.

כִּמְעַט֙ שֶׁעָבַ֣רְתִּי מֵהֶ֔ם 4
עַ֣ד שֶֽׁמָּצָ֗אתִי אֵ֤ת שֶׁאָֽהֲבָה֙ נַפְשִׁ֔י
אֲחַזְתִּיו֙ וְלֹ֣א אַרְפֶּ֔נּוּ
עַד־שֶׁהֲבֵיאתִיו֙ אֶל־בֵּ֣ית אִמִּ֔י
וְאֶל־חֶ֖דֶר הֽוֹרָתִֽי׃

Peshat

4. The maiden continues her account, saying that it was just after ("scarcely") her run-in with the watchmen "when" she "found (*matza'ti*) the one I love." The two temporal clauses—*kim'at she-* ("scarcely") plus *'ad she-* ("when")—convey an emotional sequence.[16] Her response is swift and sure: she holds him tight.

I held him fast . . . would not let him go . . . brought him The account has a threefold sequence: the first pair of verbs conveys the result of the longing—not just a seizing but a holding on (the stylistic pattern "*X* but not *Y*" mirrors the prior seeking but not finding); the third verb conveys a temporal aspect and the place of conveyance—marking time by the clause *'ad she-* ("until") and stressing that she has brought him home. The emotional mood of loss and separation are balanced by the physical (and psychological) act of holding and retaining.

I brought him to my mother's house . . . the chamber Notably, the maiden initiates the action. Bringing her beloved into an enclosure varies a fixed motif. In this instance we read *havei'tiv 'el-beiyt 'immi ve-'el-ḥeder horati*; whereas in 2:4, her beloved brought her to the house of wine (*heivi'ani 'el beiyt ha-yayin*); and in 1:4, the king brought her to his chambers (*heivi'ani ha-melekh ḥadarav*). The location here is doubly marked: to (*'el*) her mother's house; to (*'el*) the chamber of she who bore her.[17]

The second image has an erotic tinge (MsP; Rashbam).[18] Most likely, it suggests that mothers provided young girls with intimate information (cf. 8:2). With this event the couple's fantasy is fulfilled, in fact or fantasy. The enclosure of the home protects the embraces of love. The external search has become a private affair; pining thoughts in bed have become a realized proclamation.

Derash

4. *Scarcely had I passed them* The struggle for spiritual renewal may pass by (*'avar*) or ignore the very resources that can guide the quest—a transgression (*'aveirah*) or oversight that requires renewed focus. The individual casts about, hoping to "find" what has been so ardently sought—and "hold it fast" and bring it into the deepest recesses of one's self. For the ancestors, the Exodus from Egypt was also a wandering toward spiritual fulfillment; a long-term passage through the desert until they arrived at their "mother's house"—Sinai, the spiritual birthplace of the people (interpreting *'immi*, "my mother," as *'ummati*, "my nation").[19] There, they entered "the chamber of she who conceived me" (*horati*)[20]—the Tent of Meeting, the place where (according to tradition) Israel was inducted into rabbinic "instruction" (*horayyah*) and its obligations (SongsR 3.iv.1; LevR 1.10).[21] For each worshiper, this historical process is paradigmatic. Jews must each find their rebirth in the womb of tradition (cf. LevR 1.12). Guided by teachers ("watchmen"; v. 3), the community may cultivate religious wisdom.

Remez

4. *Scarcely had I passed* The self attests to the mystery of insight. Having learned how to seek (preparation), the Beloved has somehow been "found" (realization). Suddenly contact with "the one I love" is a tangible reality, and this gift is "held fast" and "brought . . . to my mother's house." That is, the self must transform the spiritual reality found in the external world—and make it personal. It must become part of the reborn self:[22] "brought . . . to the chamber of she who conceived me." This is

vital. The spiritual reality is first formulated and found in communal or traditional terms, but then cultivated and reframed in internal and individual ways. Bringing the Beloved inward is a rebirth of the spirit and the spiritual life. The chamber of the lonely soul (v. 1) becomes the house of the Beloved—a womb of renewal. The clauses of this verse thus mark the seeker's (progressive) spiritual transformation.[23]

Sod

4. *Scarcely had I passed them* The rhythms of the spirit are mysterious. Spiritual direction must be guided, but its forms are various and may come unexpectedly. In this case, the soul was not aware that its search had changed until after the request for help. The cry of the heart opened its inner eye. In the briefest instant, everything changed—a moment called *kim'aṭ*—"scarcely"! Scarcely had one reformulated the quest than a new light dawned. The guardians do not answer the soul's question. They are rather the occasion for a revelation. Suddenly, there is wisdom: the Divine is not hidden in a cosmic beyond, but found here and now. The search for "the One I love" must come from within (cf. 1:7). The truth dawns by asking the right question.

In that moment, so swift in advent, the soul found its Beloved and "held him fast." For the questing soul, this is a seizing upon the Truth and taking it within. This gestation is a rebirth. The momentous finding incorporates the self into the womb of divine wisdom—a divine "mother," source of spiritual instruction (Z. 3:40b; Ibn Sahula).[24] Taken beyond itself, the soul is opened to the vastness of divine reality. This awakening is a spiritual event.

5 I adjure you, O maidens of Jerusalem,
By gazelles or by hinds of the field:
Do not wake or rouse
Love until it please!

5 הִשְׁבַּעְתִּי אֶתְכֶם בְּנוֹת יְרוּשָׁלַ͏ִם
בִּצְבָאוֹת אוֹ בְּאַיְלוֹת הַשָּׂדֶה
אִם־תָּעִירוּ | וְֽאִם־תְּעוֹרְרוּ
אֶת־הָאַהֲבָה עַד שֶׁתֶּחְפָּץ׃ ס

Peshat

5. Having reported her achievement to her friends, the maiden again appeals to them to respect love's tempo and neither disturb nor arouse it "until (*'ad she-*) it please!" (cf. 2:7).[25] This term echoes its use in the preceding verse. In both cases, it introduces a temporal sequence. The repeated verbs for her feelings of love (*she-'ahavah*; "[the one] that I love") conclude with a reference to "the love" itself (*ha-'ahavah*). This quality is the central theme of the Song (see 8:6 for its climactic formulation).

Stylistics. The narrative report is driven by repeated and interlocking verbs (seeking and finding); and the actions are expressed through diverse kinds of parallelism (marking emphasis and progression). Repeatedly, a final clause caps the discourse. For example, verse 4 develops with two temporal clauses—introduced by *kim'at she-* and *'ad she-*, respectively—and then portrays the result dramatically with a perfect verb ("I held him fast," *'aḥaztiv*) and a future of intent ("but I would not let him go," *ve-lo' 'arpennu*). The latter phrase provides a segue to another temporal clause (*'ad she-*), which reports that the maiden has brought her beloved homeward. The maiden's dramatic monologue carries the rhythms of all action and emphasis. It is not mere gossip or intimate chatter, but a song of songs depicting the force of love.

Derash

5. ***I adjure you, O maidens*** See above at 2:7. The nation must prepare for redemption with spiritual fortitude,[26] but Jews must not force the end based on fleeting impressions or inconclusive signs of the times. They must abide in patience. The admonition not to arouse love "until (*'ad she-*) it please" echoes "until (*'ad she-*) I brought him to my mother's house" in verse 4, but offers a counterpoint. The danger of imagining the goal achieved (found and held fast) is the danger of presumption and pride. Our verse counsels caution against such idolatries of the spirit (false truths for the self, or a messianic impulse for the nation; Gershuni).

Remez

5. ***I adjure you, O maidens*** The self has retrieved its lost Beloved, and some communion is tangible. As earlier (2:7), the soul adjures itself (its nature and temperament) not to disturb this experience of love; it is determined to let it be—"until *it* please." The soul cautions itself with restraint. Love has its own tempo. The moment of mystery may be anticipated; but it must be cultivated with patience, to be properly fulfilled (Immanuel).[27]

Sod

5. ***I adjure you*** See at 2:7. At the moment of transformation, the soul adjures its supporters not to disturb the balance. Spiritual gains are fragile; nothing should be done to impair them (REzra). In this adjuration, the soul cautions its companions and itself.

6 Who is she that comes up from the desert
Like columns of smoke,
In clouds of myrrh and frankincense,
Of all the powders of the merchant?

6 מִי זֹאת עֹלָה מִן־הַמִּדְבָּר
כְּתִימְרוֹת עָשָׁן
מְקֻטֶּרֶת מוֹר וּלְבוֹנָה
מִכֹּל אַבְקַת רוֹכֵל׃

Peshat

2. A QUESTION OF APPEARANCE (v. 6)

In this unit, a woman ascends from the desert, exuding spices and myrrh (v. 6). The image bridges the restless lass in the previous unit and the wedding entourage in the next unit. Given that she addressed the "daughters of Jerusalem" with her oath (v. 5), it is perhaps these women who provide the choral voice that projects her glory as one who ascends in myrrh.

*6. **Who is she that comes up*** A query is posed regarding a female: *mi zo't*, "Who is this [woman]?"[28] A similar one recurs later when the maiden's spectacular nature is observed (6:10); and also in the account of her manifestation in tandem with her beloved (8:5): "Who is this that comes up from the desert, leaning on her *dod*?"[29] Such questions suggest amazement (see Immanuel).[30]

from the desert Given its brevity, this is presumably a literary figure marking the woman's emergence into the social world. Therefore it should not be taken literally—either to determine the exact locale, or to speculate as to why a bride should come up from this place.[31]

Like columns of smoke The comparison to *timerot* (a plural noun) marks her progressive ascension. Although this noun is rare in Scripture, MsP adduces the related verb *metammer* ("ascend") in rabbinic sources (B. Yoma 28b).

In clouds of myrrh As she "comes up" she seems "like" a column of fragrant smoke wafting upward. The verb *mequṭṭeret* denotes the spices on her body, which characterize her being. This form (*pu'al* participle) of the verb is unique in Scripture.

Of all the powders The phrase *mikkol 'avqat* (*rokheil*) supplements the prior reference to the myrrh and frankincense. Her manifestation evokes the effusion of aromatic perfumes: *all* of the merchants' "spices" (Immanuel). The noun *'avqat* (in construct) suggests dried, ground-up leaves; it is related to the word *'avaq*, "dust" (cf. Deut. 28:24). The spices are thus a powder (Rashbam, following Menaḥem b. Saruq).[32] Cf. Radak.

Derash

*6. **Who is she that comes up*** The desert is a place of transition, between Egypt and the land of promise. It is also a place of imponderables, positive and negative. The midrashic tradition captures this complexity in the query of the Beloved. God asks: Who is this one *ha-'olah* from the desert? Is this the nation "who went up" (*ha-'olah*) to Canaan from the desert after years of disobedience, to find favor and renewal once again? In which case, Israel is a people marked by transitions and transformations. Acts of disobedience resulted in destruction and "death" (*silluqah*) in the desert (Num. 14:35; SongsR 3.v.1).[33] Only subsequently is there restoration. The question thus induces reflections on Israel's oscillating nature and the cycles of the spirit.

On the other hand, the wilderness generation was also "distinguished" (*'illuyah*) by acts of divine grace. They were "raised up" and "made notable" by the gifts of Torah, sacred service (ritual worship), and the designation of special worthiness. *Keneset Yisra'el* ascends to its homeland (physically and spiritually), bearing its "goodly gifts" (*matanot ṭovot*) into the present (SongsR, ibid.).[34] Just *who* is *this one* that ascends (then and now)? Will they realize their God-given traits and gifts? The query awaits an answer.

Like columns of smoke The simile compares the ascension of Israel to columns of smoke. This figure evoked memories of God's

cloud of glory and the column of fire that protected the nation in the desert (SongsR 3.v.2). It also recalled the spiral of smoke that arose from the staves of the Ark, protecting the people from poisonous serpents (ibid.; revising MdRI, *Beshallaḥ, petiḥta*, and SifNum, *Beha'alotekha* 83)[35] and striking fear into Israel's enemies.[36] The nation is again the beneficiary of God's care (SongsZ). Ascending from the desert, perfumed in glory, Israel is ready to fulfill her destiny. God will join her on His chariot of love (v. 7).

In clouds of myrrh and frankincense *Keneset Yisra'el* is guided twofold: by the mystery of God in her midst (above) and by the deeds of her ancestors. Once again, the "clouds of myrrh" (*mor*) recall the merits of Abraham, who suffered for God and "gravely suffered" (*memarmeir*) in sanctification of the divine name (SongsR 3.v.2; discussed above at 1:13); and the "frankincense" alludes to the purity of Isaac's self-sacrifice (*she-nitqareiv*) upon the altar (SongsZ)—another expression of martyrological dedication. (The third patriarch, Jacob, is specified in the next phrase.)

Of all the powders of the merchant *Keneset Yisra'el*—the embodiment of Jacob-Israel—was deemed uniquely fragrant; for she was comprised in her entirety (the entire people of Israel) of exemplary devotion (*mi-kol*, "of all," being understood as summative, indicating a totality of fragrant "spices"). And what was this merit? It was that Jacob's "bed" was "without blemish"; that is, his progeny remained faithful to God and true worship. (According to tradition, before this patriarch's death, all the "sons of Israel" averred religious loyalty, saying: "Hear, O Israel [father Jacob!], the LORD is *our* God, the LORD alone!")[37] In this way they exemplified the faithfulness of their ancestors.

Another trait must distinguish Israel. In addition to the purity of faith, there must be purity of speech. Just as Jacob-Israel could be distinguished "from all" (*mi-kol*) the "powders" (*'avaq*) of the merchants (*rokheil*), so must the people Israel keep far "from" the "dust" or mere semblance (*'avaq*) of "tale-bearing" (*rekhilut*). If evil speech harms by its slightest trace (*'avaq*; B. B.B. 165a), its repair must be through healing words (cf. B. Yoma 44a).

Remez

6. ***Who is she that comes up*** Who speaks? Is it the Beloved addressing the soul (Ibn Tibbon), which has now risen from its lowliness toward the transcendent ideal? Or is this the reflective discourse of the self, so imbued by the thrall of love (vv. 4–5) that it feels itself ascendant—as if "from the desert" of its nonbeing? Somehow this inner voice appears as the outer confirmation of the Beloved. The two conjoin. In this bounty of restored love, the soul is transfigured in the very substance of its being. A mere touch of transcendence suffices to transform one's consciousness.

Sod

6. ***Who is she that comes up*** The transformed soul, opened to the divine reality, evokes marvel. The heart wonders and asks, "Who is *this* that ascends?" The demonstrative pronoun (*zo't*) does double duty. It marks something inchoate and impersonal ("this"), but also something figural and personal ("she").[38] There is a spiraling ascendance "from the desert" of the soul. Something is taking shape. To what may it be compared? Perhaps to spices ("myrrh and frankincense") that waft upward as a fragrant aggregate ("all [*kol*] the powders"), *kelulah mi-kol* ("comprised of them all"; REzra). The ascendant self seems spiritually whole and integrated. Its soul is like an incense offering, rising to heaven.

7 There is Solomon's couch,
Encircled by sixty warriors
Of the warriors of Israel,

7 הִנֵּה מִטָּתוֹ שֶׁלִּשְׁלֹמֹה
שִׁשִּׁים גִּבֹּרִים סָבִיב לָהּ
מִגִּבֹּרֵי יִשְׂרָאֵל׃

Peshat

3. CEREMONIAL SPLENDORS (vv. 7–11)

The couch of Solomon appears. The temporal adverb *hinneih* (here rendered as "there is"; literally, "behold!" or "here now") marks its sudden manifestation. The depiction has two parts. The (marital) couch (*miṭṭato*) is depicted first, surrounded by a warrior-guard for nighttime protection (vv. 7–8). After this, a palanquin (*'apiryon*) is denoted (vv. 8–9); it is another term for this ensemble of love. It is deemed "inlaid with love" (*ratzuf 'ahavah*). The song of the couch ends with an ecstatic call to the maidens of Zion to go and see King Solomon wearing the crown made by his mother.

The depiction of this entourage may sustain and stimulate the maiden's feelings. In so doing, they would also project the latent desire of the couple—who envision their future wedding in olden terms. Like an allegory of hope, their desires are fit into filigrees of fancy. As suggested earlier, this unit may derive from an old marriage song.

7. Solomon's couch The syntactic construction *miṭṭato she-li-shlomoh*—literally "his couch, that [one] of Solomon"—is not found in early Biblical Hebrew.[39] The formulation gives added personal emphasis (compare the similar form *karmi sheli*, "my vineyard," in 1:6 and 8:12); it occurs also in biblical Aramaic and in mishnaic Hebrew.

This couch is one of the cases where the narrator mentions King Solomon's possessions.[40] According to Rashbam, Solomon (the author) used his own property as a model.

Remez

7. There is Solomon's couch In its new state of mind, the self feels a new inner reality. The "couch" (*mishkav*) of lonely introspection and longing (v. 1) has become like a "chamber" (*ḥeider*) housing the Beloved (v. 4). And this transformed soul reciprocally feels like a "couch" (*miṭṭah*) of this divine beneficence—personified here as Solomon (*Shelomoh*), the quality of spiritual integration (*sheleimut*) so much desired. This transcendent harmony suddenly seems immanent to the self, as if the soul were "encircled by sixty warriors"—protecting this treasure with newfound strength. So gifted, the soul is ready to withstand the impact of external reality.

Derash

7. There is Solomon's couch A voice proclaims (*hinneih*; "there") the presence of God upon His throne—Solomon (*Shelomoh*) being the divine King "of peace" (*she-ha-shalom shelo*). Suddenly the Beloved appears upon the divine chariot to receive Israel, ascending with spiritual devotion (v. 6). The moment of communion seems near: the long-awaited moment of covenant renewal.

Is this not also the ascension and renewal of Israel through Torah study, performance of the commandments, and deeds of loving-kindness? Such actions may transfigure the mundane world, through the light of religious purpose. The ascendance of Israel, carried by the forms of religious action, also raises the world toward God and holiness; and the sanctification of the everyday, like a divine chariot, raises the striving self (Israel) toward transcendence. In such ways the aura of divine immanence is perceived, radiant with harmony (*shalom*).

Sod

7. There is Solomon's couch Suddenly there is an identification: "behold"—*hinneih*—"there"! It appears like Solomon's couch. But

who or what is that? Perceived spiritually, this "Solomon" is the symbolic perfection of self—a human image of King Solomon, the divine perfection. Hence this "couch" is the human soul in spiritual consort with its divine potential. Having just received instruction (v. 4), the soul ascends to a new level. But it remains vulnerable to the challenges of worldly reality. Thus it is "encircled" by "warriors"—protectors of the spirit—who guard it from harm (Z. 1:37a). Actively engaged, these helpers support spiritual integration in all the phases of life (Ibn Sahula).[41]

8 All of them trained in warfare,
Skilled in battle,
Each with sword on thigh
Because of terror by night.

8 כֻּלָּם֙ אֲחֻ֣זֵי חֶ֔רֶב
מְלֻמְּדֵ֖י מִלְחָמָ֑ה
אִ֤ישׁ חַרְבּוֹ֙ עַל־יְרֵכ֔וֹ
מִפַּ֖חַד בַּלֵּילֽוֹת׃ ס

Peshat

8. ***trained in warfare / Skilled in battle*** These phrases characterize the guards. The terms are technical expressions. The designation *'aḥuzei ḥerev* means "trained in warfare" (not the literal "handlers of a sword"), in light of cognate uses of this verb for skilled behavior in Ugaritic[42] and Akkadian.[43] Correspondingly, *melummedei milḥamah* means "trained" or "practiced in warfare" (cf. 2 Sam. 22:35), in the sense of someone "learned" in its arts.[44]

Because of terror by night The military guard functions as protectors of the bridal pair on their marriage night. Rabbinic sources stress a need for protection at this occasion (cf. B. Ber. 54b and PdRE 12).[45]

Derash

7–8. For the sages, the image of a divine throne, encircled by a heavenly host, was a model for ritual life on earth. The transcendent pole (the throne world) has its immanent counterpart in the Ark of the synagogue and the priestly blessings bestowed upon the people. Thus the heavenly "couch" (*miṭṭah*) of divine sanctity is embodied on earth by the priestly "tribe" (*maṭṭeh*) of Levi; and the sixty "warriors" (*gibborim*) on High are exemplified below by the sixty letters of the priestly blessings (Num. 6:24–26), recited by the priests to "strengthen" (*megabberin*) the people with spiritual fortitude.[46] The merit of this recitation may bring peace and blessing to its listeners, even as their amen may vanquish the "terrors" in their heart (SongsR 3.vi.6). A mysterious sanctity infuses the earthly liturgy, drawn from supernal models.

Remez

8. ***All of them trained in warfare*** The sense of inner support is a deep resolve. It is the realization of the need to care for these acquired values and enhance them by training—through meditative exercises that will help protect the insights and emergent perfections from ruin (Ibn Aqnin), from "the terrors of the night." This phrase, which echoes the soul's earlier turmoil "at night" (v. 1), may arise from the seeker's unconscious. For the recurrence of a dark night of the soul is always a possibility. One can easily slip into this state of loss and ignorance (Ibn Aqnin). Only training in spiritual alertness may offer the hope of resilience, bolstered by prior achievements.

Sod

8. ***All of them trained*** The self requires protection against all the happenings that may disrupt the spiritual quest or decenter the soul. Spiritual integration requires an utmost vigilance. What is most worrisome? The inner "terror" of the "night." Recall the opening image of the soul, "upon *my couch* by *night*" (v. 1); wasn't this event just such a dark drift of the soul? Recalling it, the soul knows it must protect itself from spiritual loss and despair (Ibn Sahula). It must remain alert and keep focus on the transcendent goal.

9 King Solomon made him a palanquin
Of wood from Lebanon.
10 He made its posts of silver,
Its back of gold,
Its seat of purple wool.
Within, it was decked with love
By the maidens of Jerusalem.

9 אַפִּרְיוֹן עָשָׂה לוֹ הַמֶּלֶךְ שְׁלֹמֹה
מֵעֲצֵי הַלְּבָנוֹן׃
10 עַמּוּדָיו עָשָׂה כֶסֶף
רְפִידָתוֹ זָהָב
מֶרְכָּבוֹ אַרְגָּמָן
תּוֹכוֹ רָצוּף אַהֲבָה
מִבְּנוֹת יְרוּשָׁלִָם׃

Peshat

9. palanquin The noun *'apiryon*[47] refers to a kind of canopied bed whose supports and cushions were overlaid with gold and silver (v. 10). This depiction recalls the beds of gold and silver in Persian banquet halls (Esther 1:6; called *miṭṭot*), whose floors (*ritzpah*) were inlaid with gems. In a marvelous touch, our poet concludes his description of the couch with the comment that its inner seat was *ratzuph 'ahavah* ("inlaid by love"; here "decked with love")[48]—possibly a deliberate transformation of *ratzuph 'avanim* ("inlaid with gemstones").[49]

The etymology of *'apiryon* is unclear. It arguably derives from Greek *phoreion* ("sedan chair") via Aramaic (where *purya'*, among other variants, means "bed"; cf. B. B.B. 9a). It may have been used here—as a variant of *miṭṭah*—to allude to the stem *p-r-y* and its sense of fruitful progeny (Ibn Aqnin;[50] cf. Gen. 1:28, *peru u-revu*, "be fruitful and multiply").[51] Rid also notes that this loveseat is the place where the couple will rejoice together. The Hebrew formulation *'apiryon* is a noun preceded by an initial *'alef* (cf. *'etzba'* and *'arba'*), which was added to break up the initial consonantal cluster.

10. Its back More precisely, *rephidato* indicates the tooling or inlay of the bedding (cf. Job 17:13). The reader can readily hear an allusion to the maiden's prior request to be "supported" (*rappeduni*) by sweetmeats (2:5). By this overtone, the erotic character of the couch is further intimated.

Derash

9. King Solomon made him a palanquin The chariot of the King is the symbolic locus of Israel's encounter with God. The sages offered five separate (but interrelated) interpretations. The "chariot" symbolizes the Ark, the Tabernacle, the Temple, the world, and the Temple on High. Each represents a spiritual setting where divine presence may be sought and love of God expressed (SongsR 3.vii.1–viii.1–4). And each one offers a model for meditative reflection. The Ark symbolizes the most contracted point of God's presence on earth: spheres of sanctity containing tokens of religious instruction. One must cultivate a priestly sensibility to approach such a site, purifying both mind and heart to receive its teachings.

The Ark is the point of all points, the inner core of the Tabernacle and Temple (and all synagogues) (cf. M. Kelim 1:1). Such sanctuaries circumscribe sacred space; they teach Jews how to stand in holiness before God. They are paradigms for comportment throughout the world, wherever Jews live and learn. Walking in the world is transformed when Jews carry the teachings of the Ark in their hearts; then the world's neutral space becomes sacred, and they hear the call to attend to the mysteries of existence. The spoken words of Torah and Tradition cultivate attunement to this more silent speech. Filled with wonder and gratitude, the heart is raised to the ineffable Temple of God, embracing all being.

10. He made its posts of silver The appointments of the palanquin are detailed. Its diverse features evoke parallels with the Tabernacle of old. The palanquin had posts of "silver," a back of "gold," and a seat of "purple." Similar materials were found in the Tabernacle: its hooks and bands (for the hangings) were made of "silver" (Exod. 27:10–11); its planks overlaid with "gold" (ibid. 26:29); and its cur-

tain woven from "purple" yarn (v. 31) (SongsR 3.viii.1–2).

Solomon's carriage also contains an interior "decked with love." Rabbi Azariah perceived here an allusion to the *Shekhinah* (divine presence), which descended to the Tabernacle to confirm divine love for Israel. And just as human love is not limited in time and space, God's immanence is a transcendent bestowal, unlimited and omnipresent. Like ocean waters that flood the crevice of a cliff without diminishing the sea's volume, the glory of God fills the Tabernacle without diminishment (ibid., 2; NumR 12.4). According to R. Gamliel, there was "no space . . . where the *Shekhinah* was absent" (PdRK 1.2). The gift of presence is a gift of love.

This theology of space invites reflection. Divine omnipresence is an indwelling of sanctity, an infusion of each point of the world with transcendent meaning. When the Jewish heart becomes a chariot for God, a spiritual sanctuary "overlaid with love," there is no worldly space where sacred possibilities are absent.

Remez

9–10. King Solomon made him a palanquin . . . decked with love Transformed by its new spiritual sensibility, the self reflects on this godly "couch" within. It is like a royal throne of the finest materials. Is this "palanquin" not the transfigured heart of the seeker, constructed through soul work (Ibn Tibbon)?[52] The spiritual work aimed at the perfection of the intellect and heart is a nurturing through love. The Beloved gives the soul the gifts necessary for its presence; and these benefits are then cultivated by spiritual labor and heavenly grace.[53] This is the mystery of spiritual exercises and their realization. The gift of divine love is primary. It arouses the soul and sets it on its path.

Sod

9. King Solomon made him a palanquin The soul meditates further. It perceives that its own integrated being ("a couch of Solomon") is integral to a higher order—even to the most supernal reality (the "palanquin" of "King Solomon"), which emanates a spiritual effulgence over all being.

wood from Lebanon[54] This symbolizes the radiance (*libbun*, literally "heating until glowing white"; REzra) of the supernal reality—the hidden light that allows all existence to be manifest. The soul seeks this source. It longs to see all things in the light of God.

10. He made its posts of silver The soul envisions the palanquin as the realm of Divinity (Z. 1:29a). It is like a cosmic sanctuary, wondrously "decked (*ratzuf*) with love." Suddenly the soul perceives the source of its love in the Source of Love itself. At the chariot's center is the burning (*ratzuf*) passion of love, kindled by the "daughters of Jeru-*salem*"—the heavenly helpers of spiritual wholeness (*sheleimut*) (Ibn Sahula). Love is thus revealed as the root principle of all yearning and striving. Illumined by this spiritual source, there is no earthly passion that cannot be transfigured for divine service (AhavD 99b).

11 O maidens of Zion, go forth
And gaze upon King Solomon
Wearing the crown that his mother
Gave him on his wedding day,
On his day of bliss.

11 צְאֶינָה ׀ וּרְאֶינָה בְּנוֹת צִיּוֹן
בַּמֶּלֶךְ שְׁלֹמֹה
בָּעֲטָרָה שֶׁעִטְּרָה־לּוֹ אִמּוֹ
בְּיוֹם חֲתֻנָּתוֹ
וּבְיוֹם שִׂמְחַת לִבּוֹ׃ ס

Peshat

11. This chorale seems like an old antiphon, perhaps originating in the monarchy of Solomon himself, and then enacted for all grooms on their wedding day, when crowned with a diadem.

crown The *'atarah* indicates a bridal wreath.

go forth / And gaze The odd form *tze'eynah* (instead of *tze'nah*, "go forth") undoubtedly mimics *re'eynah* ("and gaze").[55] The combined actions form a verbal pair. The gaze is similarly doubled ("at Solomon"; "at the crown"), as is the occasion of celebration ("on his wedding day"; "on his day of bliss"). This invocation to behold the groom is the wedding song's climax.

On his day of bliss Literally, "on the day of the rejoicing of his heart." This phrase qualifies "his wedding day." It is an ancient figure for happiness without reserve—willingly engaged.[56] With a robust legal usage throughout the ancient Near East, it gives added nuance to this wedding formulation.

Stylistics. Units 1 and 3 are complex combinations of elements. Each unit uses incremental features to poetic effect, punctuating topics with additions or supplements. Though different in content, they form a diptych: the young pair newly rejoined (unit 1), and the marriage entourage and celebration (unit 3). Earlier, thematic reasons were offered for their combination; here we highlight their correlations. These features intensify the relationship between the two parts. (See table below.)

Derash

11. O maidens of Zion, go forth / And gaze The event invites beholders. "Zion" (*tziyyon*) refers to those who are distinguished (*metzuyyanim*) by religious qualities; they are called to behold God's glory and the diadem bestowed upon Him.[58] Those individuals who merit this vision are marked by a transcendent awareness: through insight and practice they understand that God, called *Shelomoh*, is to be extolled by the attributes of His Name: the One called Peace and Harmony establishes order and

Verbal Correlations between Two Units

Unit 1		***Unit 3***	
v. 1	*ba-leylot* ("at night")	v. 8	*ba-leylot* ("by night")
v. 2	*va-'asovevah* ("must roam")	v. 7	*saviv* ("encircled")
v. 3	*re'item* ("have you seen?")	v. 11	*u-re'eynah* ("and gaze")
v. 4	*'aḥaztiv* ("I held him fast")	v. 8	*'aḥuzei* ("skilled")
v. 4	*'immi* ("my mother")	v. 11	*'immo* ("his mother")
v. 5	*benot* ("maidens")	v. 10	*benot* ("maidens")
	ha-'ahavah ("love")		*'ahavah* ("love")
Note also:			
v. 1	*mishkavi* ("my couch")	v. 7	*miṭṭato* ("his couch")[57]

harmony (*sheleimot*) throughout the created world. The sun, moon, and stars were created without "blemish" or diminishment (SongsR 3.xi.1 and PdRK 1.3); they follow their heavenly courses without strife or competition (PdRK, ibid.). The balance of "peace [or: harmony]" (*shalom*) in existence is such that contradictory elements coexist within the same universe.[59] Spiritually endowed persons attain this realization, being able to transcend limited perceptions and to intuit greater wholes and harmonies. In so doing, they cleave to God "with joyful heart" (Gallico).

the crown . . . his mother / Gave The crown envisioned by the *metzuyyanim* is a symbol of the divine majesty proclaimed by the people at Sinai. On that "wedding day" God and Israel entered a spiritual covenant of enduring significance. Proclaiming commitment, Israel became a mother of future generations. Meditating further, R. Eleazar taught that Solomon's "mother" (*'immo*) is none other than God's (*Shelomoh*) own "nation" (*'ummato*) (SongsR, ibid., 2; PdRK 1.4). The covenant begins with an acclamation of divine sovereignty. All the people proclaimed the sovereign lordship of God; and those who daily cultivate a deeper sensibility may also perceive this lordship throughout the world. For them, all being is robed in majesty and the divine crown is the aura of each element.

Remez

11. O maidens of Zion, go forth / And gaze The self reaches a climax of ecstasy (Ibn Tibbon). It calls upon its highest qualities (Ralbag)—all that makes it distinguished (*metzuyyan*)—to behold its new state of being (Ibn Aqnin).[60] The call of the self (to itself) to "go forth and gaze" is now an invocation for the opening of its seeker's inner eye. The sense of the indwelling traits of "Solomon" (e.g., wisdom; integral being) is intensified by an imperative to expand one's awareness of this spiritual enthronement. Earlier, when the soul felt reborn, this inner transformation was expressed through the image of a mother's chamber (v. 4)—a symbolic womb of divine wisdom. The experience of transcendent reality is now imagined as a mother's beneficence—a bestowal of perfection (*Shelomoh-sheleimut*) upon the self. Emboldened, the soul formulates worldly images to convey what it has experienced: the soul reborn through transcendent love.

This experience of heavenly beneficence elicits another teaching for the self: humility before the divine bounty so graciously given. The call to the various dimensions of the soul (the "maidens of *Tziyyon*") is an assertion of the importance of modesty (*tzeniyyut*) at all times—for the reception of these gifts and the quest for their attainment (Al-Fawwāl)[61] or realization (Immanuel).[62]

the crown that his mother / Gave him on his wedding day The trait of "Solomon"—the perfected intellect or soul—is nurtured by even higher divine sources. These are the sources of wisdom and enlightenment that flow to the human mind and soul. The moment of spiritual conjunction resembles a sacred marriage in one's deepest being. Marital communion is thus the apt figure for the highest yearning of the human soul (Malbim): for an overcoming of selfhood and the realization of one's divine potential (Immanuel; Al-Fawwāl). Like an *'atarah* ("crown"), the soul is encircled by this sense of inclusion.[63] At this occasion, the sense of time is suspended. But it will return when and wherever the soul is faced with challenges in daily life. How spiritual achievements may be sustained by the newly integrated self is a task for consciousness and attentive action.

Sod

11. O maidens of Zion, go forth Such is the charge the soul imposes on itself. Turning inward, it calls upon the daughters of its spirit—those marked by special excellences (*tziyyunim*; AhavD 101b)[64]—to gaze into this divine reality (King Solomon) and behold the "crown" of love given by their "mother," the engendering principle of God (Z. 2:100b). This Mother is the primordial womb of love in which all human love is conceived and nur-

tured. Through its grace, the soul may even ascend to crown God with love in connubial ecstasy—on the "day" of its conjunction with Divinity (REzra). In contact with this divine source, the soul is simultaneously crowned with supernal blessings (ZḤ 15b).

CONCLUSION

The main parts of this chapter convey two modes of love. In the first, verses 1–5, a maiden recounts her own yearning for her beloved, in a dream state upon her bed, whereupon she was impelled to search for him—whether in dream or reality we do not know. The desire to have and to seize the beloved compels her behavior, as does the desire to possess love, even where she admonishes restraint and respect for its character (v. 5). Love is thus a force that may dominate the self and overwhelm one's emotional attention in every way. In this unit, the self is entangled in love's bonds—a theme resumed from prior chapters. By contrast, verses 6–11 depict a more distant visual field for the objects of love: the appearance of an aromatic woman (v. 6), and then a detailed portrayal of a wedding entourage, with evocations of the splendor of a king and his nuptial crown. This tableau conveys regal elegance and is more a report of exterior display than inner emotions.

The first account is filled with anxiety and the desire to have and to hold; the last is rich in fragrance and opulence, a bit beyond reach. Love is comprised of both modalities. For some the dominant issue is seeking and seizing the object of love; whereas others enjoy love with more restraint and an aesthetic eye. Perhaps the maiden combines both types—loving simply and secretly in the privacy of her home; but dreaming of a grander transformation of the symbols of love in public places. If the first type shows love in its earthly and immanent aspects; the second heightens its noble and transcendent stature. Every heart should know both.

CHAPTER 4:1–5:1

The Beautiful Maiden, So Praised

The collection of songs in 4:1–5:1 is divided into two units, according to Masoretic tradition. The first is the beloved's praise of the maiden's beauty (vv. 1–7). The second, in which he remains the speaker, has four parts: he invites the maiden to join him in the hills (v. 8); he refers to her effect upon him (v. 9); he celebrates her sweet love (vv. 10–11); and he depicts the lass as a lush garden—in response to which she invites him to enter this place, which he does (4:12–5:1). Throughout this cycle, the male's initiative and voice predominate.

The songs of praise are spoken with rapid intensity. Figures drawn from the natural world prevail. Some images are vibrant and direct; others are more suggestive and hint of intimate relations. It is one thing to say that the maiden has doves' eyes or breasts like fawns, another to say that he will take himself "to the mount of myrrh." Even such cases show degrees of suggestion. To say that his darling is a garden with aromatic plants is one thing; it is quite another for her to wish that the winds blow upon "my garden." Such similes and metaphors evoke the feelings of love, and variously hold the line of discretion.

4 Ah, you are fair, my darling,
Ah, you are fair.
Your eyes are like doves
Behind your veil.
Your hair is like a flock of goats
Streaming down Mount Gilead.

ד הִנָּ֤ךְ יָפָה֙ רַעְיָתִ֔י

הִנָּ֖ךְ יָפָ֑ה

עֵינַ֣יִךְ יוֹנִ֔ים

מִבַּ֖עַד לְצַמָּתֵ֑ךְ

שַׂעְרֵךְ֙ כְּעֵ֣דֶר הָֽעִזִּ֔ים

שֶׁגָּלְשׁ֖וּ מֵהַ֥ר גִּלְעָֽד׃

Peshat

1. IN PRAISE OF HER (4:1–7)

The maiden is depicted in terms of nature and culture: goats and sheep; crimson thread and pomegranates; and a tower decked in grandeur. The beloved focuses first on her head and face, then upon her neck and breasts. These images elicit his desire to proceed onward, so enchanting is she. The opening evocation (of beauty) recurs at the end (vv. 1 and 7).

1. Ah...Ah The opening gasps render *hinnakh* (an adverbial emphatic *hinneih* with a suffixed feminine pronoun). With these exclamations, the lad conveys the immediacy and allure of his love. Her beauty is a true rapture.

you are fair... you are fair This evocation is doubled with intensifying effect:[1] the first indicates his feelings (she is his "darling"), the second introduces an image of her beauty ("doves' eyes"). He also repeats the language of their first tryst (1:15). Previously he had limited himself to one image; now he lets his desires produce successive figures of her loveliness.

Behind The compound preposition *mi-ba'ad le-* conveys the sense of something peering out "from behind [a barrier]" or "from within [an enclosure]" (*mi-bi-fnim*, Rashi, Ibn Ezra;[2] *bi-fnei*, Rashbam). For a similar preposition, see Gen. 26:8.

veil The meaning of the noun *tzammah* is uncertain. Since antiquity, it was taken to refer to a veil,[3] although this is not the common word for it.[4] Some commentators render likewise (Saadia; Rashbam). The usage in Isa. 47:2 depicts the uncovering of a garment;[5] there, the phrase *galli tzammateikh* may mean "expose your veil" or "...head covering" (MsP).[6] By contrast, others explain the word to refer to the bands or ornaments that "bind" (*metzam-metzeim*) the hair (Menaḥem b. Saruq; Rashi; Rid),[7] or to the bound (or twisted) hair that frames the face (Ibn Ezra). However, the latter interpretation does not comport with the ensuing image.

Streaming down The verb *galshu* suggests a flowing motion and may be related to the movement of water (as in Ugaritic).[8] Some kind of fluid agitation is also indicated in B. Pes. 37b.[9] By contrast, the Septuagint (here and at 6:5) perceives a manifestation or appearance—a sense found also in Ibn Ezra. Rashi suggests that it indicates the laying bare of the hillock (due to the trampling flock).[10] But this would be an odd image of female beauty.

Stylistics. The verse is replete with phonetic density: *she-galshu; galshu me-har gil'ad; mi-ba'ad...gil'ad.* Such tonal intensity heightens the semantic features.

Derash

4:1. Ah, you are fair This "repetition" of praise (*kaphul u-mekhupal*, in the formulation of YalSh #984),[11] emphasizes Israel's spiritual beauty (SongsR 4.i.1). Her natural state is transfigured by religious practice. The twofold praise ("fair"; "fair") highlights several virtues. Israel is "fair" by virtue of her observance of (1) the fixed divine commandments *and* the impromptu acts of interpersonal kindness; (2) the positive *and* the negative commandments; (3) the commandments performed at home *and* in the field (that is, the ritual preparation of bread dough in the house *and* the

allocation of grains for the poor in the field);[12] and (4) the recitation of both the *Shema* and the *'Amidah* prayers.

Piety is a practice that transforms the performer, heart and body. It refashions the soul and extends outward (through the body) to the world. The ensuing images detail this matter, feature by feature.

Your eyes are like doves The importance of "eyes"—windows to the world and portals to the soul—is emphasized first. They direct our limbs and their purposes (SongsR 4.i.2): we may focus on God and spiritual perfection,[13] or be buffeted by events and material desires. In the first case, the eye is honed and vision purified; in the second, the eye swells with earthly desires. We must choose. The purity and constancy of the dove are exemplary. Loyal to their companion and to their brood, doves are symbols of spiritual and familial faithfulness (ibid.). Eyes are also the fonts of perception and assessment. They thus symbolize the importance of judgment in personal (Ibn Aqnin) and cultural life (cf. YalSh #988 regarding courts of law).

Behind your veil This suggests the traits required for proper assessment. If a figure of enclosure (*tzammateikh*) is intended (see Peshat), the image commends the virtue of modesty (Ibn Aqnin) in our comportment (the way that our eyes see and evaluate the world). Alternatively, the focus is on the self's being bound or connected (*metzummatim*) to God and to our neighbor through the commandments (YalSh #988). Such acts of concentration include restraint and self-withdrawal (*tzimtzum*) before the claims of others, and the need to balance their needs with our own (Leqaḥ Ṭov). Israel's virtues include a resilient commitment to cultural continuity, despite being repeatedly put in straits (*tzametu*) by their enemies (Lam. 3:53). One particular virtue is the contraction (*tzimtzum*) of private needs for the larger social good (Leqaḥ Ṭov).

Streaming down Mount Gilead The maiden's hair elicits the first of several references to historical events. First noted is Israel's passage through the Reed Sea, whose streaming wall of water mounted up like a "monument of witness" (*gal 'eid*) for all nations to see and take note (SongsR 4.i.3). The nation's beauty is thus testimony to her providential deliverance by God; the flowing (*galshu*) of her hair a monument (*gal*) to the miracle of national birth.

Remez

1. Ah, you are fair, my darling The soul's progression toward the Beloved (depicted in chapter 3) is transformative. A spiritual beauty exudes from her entire physical being, visible to all (Malbim). The onlooker beholds in wonder and tries to capture this splendor in worldly terms. The gasp of astonishment is expressed in the exclamation "Ah, you are fair." But the heart wishes to specify the vision in detail. The result is the sequence of similes that link the features of the body to the external world.Each feature has been cultivated and refined, and this gives them a wondrous aspect. Even so, the Beloved's list is exemplary. The similes suggest there is more to say. The vision of love exceeds one's capacity to speak. Excess is the sign of love, and the language of love overflows throughout.

Who speaks here? Is it a divine voice (as most medieval commentators supposed), boldly praising the soul for its development of spiritual qualities (Immanuel)? On this reading, the features of the soul are personified through bodily images. Alternatively, the speaker is the inner self, aware of its inner transformations and spiritual enhancement. On this reading, the soul knows that it has been transfigured and beholds itself, as it were, through its inner eye (a self-perception opened by a heightened spiritual consciousness). Is a decision required? Both possibilities are necessary: the sense of external (divine) praise objectivizes the subjective (human) sense of the soul; and the inner soul projects its felt achievements outward. Where the "heavenly" muse ends and "human" musing begins is a mystery.

Your eyes are like doves After the initial exclamation of beauty, the physical specifics are detailed from head to toe. The soul shines through the body in all its parts (Ibn Aqnin;

Ibn Tibbon; Malbim).[14] Yet the face is the most compelling feature of personal presence. One sees the eyes that behold; and one feels the other through their gaze. The eyes seem "like doves behind your veil." They convey a focused attentiveness, but what they perceive remains concealed.[15] This concealment is the soul's inner eye. The onlooker perceives this. Contact with this person's inner being is mediated by the power of the eyes. The soul revealed thereby cannot be denied.

Your hair is like a flock of goats The perspective widens. The eyes are framed by hair that flows like goats "streaming down" a mountain. The image conveys an undulating softness. The hair frames the eyes at the facial center, yet the center gives way to an animated horizon of height. The soul's hidden beauty reveals a flowing transcendence in its outward aspect; and this perception is conveyed by an image of a streaming flock. Likeness both approximates and invokes. It expands the consciousness of the beholder.

Sod

4:1. Ah, you are fair Cultivation of spiritual traits—exemplified in the previous song cycle by the seeker's ascent from inner solitude ("the desert") to spiritual espousal ("his wedding day")—now gives her body a visible beauty. Her inner worthiness radiates outward. But before the eye can detail its perceptions, the heart exclaims its joy. The words "you are fair" celebrate this feeling.

Your eyes The Beloved beholds the seeker's spiritual gaze. The eye sees creation's wonders via a cultivated inwardness (ZḤ 31a–b). It requires a "concentration" of visual attention (*tzimtzum*, symbolized by her veil, *tzammateikh*) and a sense of inner purpose (AhavD 104a). Balanced in the soul, the two eyes join the material and the spiritual aspects of existence (Alkabetz), alternating in emphasis according to circumstances.

Your hair The seeker deepens her quest of God through the totality of her earthly being. The Beloved acknowledges this through a succession of similes that correlate her body with elements of nature.[16] The first of these comparisons associates her hair with "a flock of goats streaming down" the "mount." This cascading flow evokes the seeker's vitality—an effusion that transforms her appearance. Her spiritual energy extends into the world's own dynamism. The two are correlated by simile.

2 Your teeth are like a flock of ewes
Climbing up from the washing pool;
All of them bear twins,
And not one loses her young.

2 שִׁנַּיִךְ כְּעֵדֶר הַקְּצוּבוֹת
שֶׁעָלוּ מִן־הָרַחְצָה
שֶׁכֻּלָּם מַתְאִימוֹת
וְשַׁכֻּלָה אֵין בָּהֶם׃

Peshat

2. ***like a flock of ewes*** The present translation renders *ha-ketzuvot* so as to accord with the alternate idiom in 6:6 (where a flock of *reḥeilim*, "ewes," is seen as coming from the washing pool).[17] The noun *ketzuvot* can designate "shorn" animals (2 Kings 6:6) or things of a "similar shape" (1 Kings 6:25); both features are evoked by the extended figure here.[18] The image of the maiden's teeth as being like shorn sheep (for their whiteness) picks up the first sense (Rashbam); the animals' depiction later in this verse as *mat'imot* ("well matched"; in the present translation: "bear twins") evokes the second (Rashbam; Rid). Thus, any single-word rendering into English obscures the simile's double entendre.

All of them . . . And not one loses her young For the image conveyed by *she-kullam . . . ve-shakkulah 'ein bahem*, see the next comment. The iterative and punning language (*shekullam* // *ve-shakkulah*) stresses the totality of the maiden's perfection. This, together with the negation of faults, anticipates the concluding words of this depiction: *kullakh yafah . . . u-mum 'ein bakh*, "Every part of you is fair . . . [and] there is no blemish in you" (v. 7). The two phrases form a phonemic and thematic bond.

not one loses her young More figuratively accurate: the ewes bear twins "without mishap." Such a rendition simultaneously captures the successful birth process and the fact that the teeth (the subject of the comparison) are in good order or shape (Rid). The context requires this adverbial sense. The figure of twins, indicating order or similarity, recurs in verse 5, where the maiden's breasts are compared to fawns moving in tandem.

Derash

2. ***Your teeth . . . like a flock*** Successive images further evoke Israel's sacred history. Her teeth, compared to "a fixed (*qetzuvot*) flock of ewes," were associated with the "fixed words" (*millin qetzuvin*) of ancient prophecy, whereby the people were promised to leave their servitude with the "spoil of Egypt" (presumably, the "great wealth" promised Abraham's heirs in Gen. 15:14;[19] SongsR 4.i.3). This flock is also portrayed as ascending "from the washing pool," a figure for the nation's purification when they emerged from the Sea and recited "words" of praise (Exod. 15:1). (According to the sages, the people's panic before the Egyptian horde in Exod. 14:10–13 showed a lack of faith that warranted purification.[20]) The historical paradigm directs attention to the transforming effect of personal repentance (Netziv). The soul may also be renewed by Torah study (YalSh #988) and strengthened by teachers of tradition (Leqaḥ Ṭov).

Remez

2. ***Your teeth are like a flock of ewes*** The face continues to transfix the onlooker. Teeth are seen next, glistening like ewes "climbing up from the washing pool." The horizontal pattern (of the teeth) evokes something ordered and purified—emerging individually and together, whole and perfect. The teeth also shape speech, through which the soul's inwardness comes to expression.

Sod

2. ***Your teeth*** Her mouth is also evocative—beginning with the teeth, which convey a sense of order. Like shorn sheep, the things of the world are stripped of externality and perceived in terms of deeper relationships (*mat-'imot*).[21] No rupture (*shakkulah*)[22] rends the interlocking whole (Z. 3:137a).[23] Like the eyes, teeth also mark a transition between inner and outer realms. Being the place where the world is incorporated through food, they are symbolic of the spiritual ingestion of reality (Ibn Sahula);[24] and as the barrier of speech, teeth also symbolize the need to articulate thoughts in appropriate ways (Alkabetz). For the spiritually developed self, attuned to the world and its tasks, the body is a means for expressing inner vision.

3 Your lips are like a crimson thread,
Your mouth is lovely.
Your brow behind your veil
[Gleams] like a pomegranate split open.

3 כְּחוּט הַשָּׁנִי שִׂפְתֹתַיִךְ
וּמִדְבָּרֵיךְ נָאוֶה
כְּפֶלַח הָרִמּוֹן
רַקָּתֵךְ מִבַּעַד לְצַמָּתֵךְ׃

Peshat

3. ***Your mouth*** Commentators have suggested that *midbareikh* means "your speech," from the stem *d-b-r*, "speak" (Rashi; Rashbam; Immanuel). However, the depiction emphasizes body parts; and the parallel word in the preceding bicolon is "your lips." Hence this word most likely means "your mouth" and is constructed on the *miqṭal* pattern, which conveys the locus of something (like *mizbeiaḥ*, "the place of slaughter; altar"). Thus *midbar* indicates the place of *dabhar*, "speech, word."

Your brow... like a pomegranate Possibly the rare noun *raqqah* (here rendered "brow") designates one's "temple" (Ibn Ezra; cf. Judg. 4:21–22 and 5:26); or "cheek" (Rashi; Rashbam; Ibn Aqnin) or "cheekbone" (Immanuel). The latter interpretations derive from the Aramaic figure in B. A.Z. 30b (*rimonei de-'apei*, "the pomegranates of the face").

Derash

3. ***lips... like a crimson thread*** Historical interpretations continue. The maiden's lips recall Israel's Song at the Sea (Exodus 15)—her "beautiful (*na'veh*) words" (see the Peshat on *midbareikh*) evoking the people's glorification of God ("This is my God, and I shall praise Him (*ve-'anveihu*)"; ibid., v. 2). The appearance of "her brow (*raqqateikh*) behind the veil (*tzammateikh*)" also recalls the "modest and pious" (*metzummatim*) people of Israel,[25] who arrived at Sinai "empty" (*rayqan*) of merit, yet "bound themselves" (*metzamtzimim 'atzmam*) to God with every word (*dibbur*) of the Decalogue (SongsR 4.iv.1).

Guided by precedent, successive generations similarly bind themselves to teachers of Torah. These heirs of Sinai are like the "crimson thread" that borders the covering of the Ark. Just as this coverlet marks gradations of sanctity, so the words of the sages delineate the sacred by teaching and interpreting the words of tradition (LṬov). A thread of hope is woven by such language, renewing the words of Sinai and preserving them for future generations.

Remez

3. ***Your lips are like a crimson thread*** The gaze now fixes on the red-rimmed lips that frame the "mouth," so incomparably "lovely" (there is no simile here).[26] It is the second, lower zone of the face that is now praised. Beneath the eyes and sight (perception), the mouth is the orifice of speech (communication). The two eyes and lower mouth thus suggest a triangle, a geometric center within the face. Gradually the speaker's gaze widens and the viewer takes in the cheekbones or temples (see Peshat) "behind your veil"—twin features that frame the face "like a pomegranate split open." The shift to fruit imagery evokes the sense of taste, supplementing those of shape and color. The fair one is thus tangible to external sensibilities, revealing qualities nurtured in her innermost being (Immanuel).[27] Through her beauty, the onlooker is gifted with a new perception of the world.

Sod

3. ***Your lips... Your mouth*** The gaze shifts to the mouth, conveyer of words and meaning. The unusual use of the word *midbar* as "mouth" evokes its more common homonym, "desert." The overlapping senses carry weight. The desert's silent emptiness merges with the virtues of speech: the desert symbolizes poverty

in nature, whereas the mouth marks the bounty of culture. Properly used, speech ascends from silence to transmit the gifts of wisdom (Z. 1:10b and ZḤ 3b).[28] Thus the modalities of speech carry the soul in its train—in matters great and small (Ibn Sahula). In this sense, the mouth is a measure for the soul (Alkabetz).[29] One must guard it carefully.

4 Your neck is like the Tower of David,
Built to hold weapons,
Hung with a thousand shields—
All the quivers of warriors.
5 Your breasts are like two fawns,
Twins of a gazelle,
Browsing among the lilies.

4 כְּמִגְדַּל דָּוִיד צַוָּארֵךְ
בָּנוּי לְתַלְפִּיּוֹת
אֶלֶף הַמָּגֵן תָּלוּי עָלָיו
כֹּל שִׁלְטֵי הַגִּבּוֹרִים׃
5 שְׁנֵי שָׁדַיִךְ כִּשְׁנֵי עֳפָרִים
תְּאוֹמֵי צְבִיָּה
הָרוֹעִים בַּשּׁוֹשַׁנִּים׃

Peshat

4. *Built to hold weapons* In the phrase *banuy le-talpiyyot*, the meaning of the otherwise unknown word *talpiyyot* is uncertain. The present rendering is periphrastic (based on the image portrayed), where the tower is decked with weapons. The Septuagint simply transliterated the word (perhaps taking it as a place name). The Song may be engaging in wordplay when it proceeds to state that this tower is "hung (*taluy*) with a thousand (*'eleph*) shields." Such a depiction seems to portray *talpiyyot* as if formed by a combination of these words (VERB + NOUN). More likely, the etymology derives from the verbal stem *l-p-'* (found in Arabic)[30] or *l-p-y* (Aramaic),[31] suggesting that what is mentioned is a structure built in "courses" or layers. As for the imagery, note the depiction of shields or military gear hung on city walls in Ezek. 27:10–11 (with the same verb) and the contemporary Tyrian and Assyrian renditions of this practice.[32]

Derash

4. *neck . . . like the Tower of David* The neck binds the head (with its eyes and mouth and mind) to the body (with its heart and limbs). Thus it may embody several virtues. The "neck" may thus be a personal channel of *celebration*, transforming feelings of gratitude and voicing them in praise and prayer. The psalms of David are exemplary; hence the maiden's neck is compared to his tower (*ke-migdal david*). Boldly, the simile is reformulated. Divided as *kemi-gdal*, the phrase is heard as proclaiming "how much" (*kamah*) David "enhanced" (*giddeil*)[33] the glory of past events (SongsR 4.iv.3). A case in point is his celebration of God's act of "splitting" the sea into multiple parts, enabling the people to pass through (Ps. 136:13).[34]

Built to hold weapons The tower's function is specified, but the noun *talpiyyot* ("to hold weapons") is obscure (see the Peshat). For the sages, it alludes to the book of Psalms—comprised ("built") of the words of "many mouths" (*piyyot harbeih*); it was produced by a "mound" (*teil*) of "mouths" (*piyyot*).[35] It was the product of ten authors (as credited in the title lines of various psalms), with David serving as master singer and anthologist (SongsR 4.iv.2).[36] Psalms is the nation's songbook, comprised of multiple voices. This is its beauty (*yafyafit*) (ibid., 6).

Hung with a thousand shields The depiction continues: *'elef ha-magein talui 'alav*. The neck's uprightness symbolizes the virtue of rectitude. Accordingly, the Torah was not given until the thousandth (*'elef*) generation from the creation—namely, the generation of Moses. (This is based on reading Ps. 105:8 as "He [God] commanded the Word *for* the thousandth generation.") If later generations enjoyed the Torah's benefits, it was by virtue of the merit, or rectitude, of Moses—who was Israel's "shield," and for whose sake the Torah had been "hung" (*talui*) or "held" in promise (SongsR 4.iv.6).[37] Indeed, Moses's merit protected the people at the sea, at Sinai, and at the crossing of the Jordan (ibid., 1–4). All was "dependent" (*talui*) upon him and his merit. Other righteous persons fulfilled this role in later generations (ibid.; see below). They too drew their strength from God Most Exalted (*'aluf*), *The* Shield (*ha-magein*) and Stay of Creation.[38]

All the quivers of warriors Literally, the "armaments of the warriors" (*shilṭei ha-gibborim*). A third virtue is thus suggested. Mediating between the passions and one's will, the neck may also symbolize submission to the Good—the act of humility and restraint before the proper deed. Exemplary are the righteous ones, who strive to "dominate" (*sholeiṭ*) or rule (*yit-gabbeir*) their natural instincts (*yitzro*; ibid.). This virtue is the ability to overcome natural temperaments (desire, anger, and pride) and direct them to higher goals. On this topic, Ben-Zoma asked (M. Avot 4:1): "Who is mighty (*gibbor*)?" and answered: "One who conquers his instincts (*yitzro*)." Maimonides famously elaborated on these matters.[39] The virtue is dominance over one's natural endowment—its redirection and transformation, not its denial or suppression. This capacity is also deemed part of the "spiritual beauty" of Israel.

5. ***Your breasts are like two fawns*** Crucial for the ongoing beauty of Israel is the spiritual nurture of future generations. Her cultural body includes two fundamental sources of such sustenance: Torah and Tradition, as transmitted and interpreted by teachers. Moses and Aaron are exemplary: each "filled Israel" from these sacred fonts. Just as breasts sustain a suckling with milk ("All that a mother eats the suckling eats;" B. Yoma 75a)[40], these men sustained Israel with the teachings of Torah (SongsR 4.v.1).[41] The chain of Tradition is crucial. Here too Moses and Aaron are models: "All the Torah that our master Moses learned (from God) he taught to Aaron" (ibid.; from B. Ned. 38a).

The matriarch Sarah is the exemplar for the intimacy of religious education. Through the milk of her breasts, we are told, many foreigners were transformed: some were infused with reverence for God (*yir'ei shamayim*; GenR 53.9); others were converted (TanB, *Vayeira'*, 38). This use of suckling imagery is striking, since it suggests that Sarah's endowment was spiritual and that she transmitted this quality through her true being. She thus exemplifies a transfigured naturalness. In mystical literature, suckling marks the reception of esoteric wisdom (see Sod).

Browsing among the lilies Exemplifying Israel's spiritual resistance in times of crisis are the midwives Shiphrah and Puah, who sustained or "nurtured" (*ro'ot*)[42] the children of Israel ("the lilies") in Egypt after the decree of death (Exod. 1:13). This heroic pair was identified with Jochebed (Moses's mother) and Miriam (his sister). See SongsR 4.v.2; based on B. Sot. 11b and ExodR 1.13.

Remez

4. ***Your neck is like the Tower of David*** The viewer's gaze moves downward, and the imagery shifts from nature to culture. The neck is a vertical column connecting head and body—the two poles of thought and action. The perfected soul conjoins them; and the point of conjunction is physically marked by the neck (Immanuel; Ibn Aqnin).[43] Hence the neck is likened here to the Tower of David—that is, a threefold connector: between the natural world and cultural ideals, between earthly forms and messianic possibilities, and between reality and hope. Like a tower rising from earth to heaven, the self seeks transcendence. Perhaps the viewer also senses the tension: the yearning upward and the constraints of nature. The need to be vigilant is marked by the "weapons" and "warriors" arrayed along the walls.[44] The seeker must negotiate many stages (physical and mental) on the way to spiritual integration.[45] David's tower is the embodiment of this achievement.

5. ***Your breasts are like two fawns*** The torso is now depicted and specified by the breasts. This feature has inner and outer aspects. Seen from without, the robed breasts suggest an inner softness; and in their outlined movements, they hint of fawns "browsing among the lilies." Thus the fawns symbolize the spiritual Beloved, who has become part of this "lily of the valleys"—the seeking soul (Ibn Aqnin).[46] The image integrates the seeker and the sought, depicting their coincidence as if from without. Both are conjoined in the seeker, as a growth of soul in her body—the breasts

suggesting a nubile formation of inner sustenance. The soul had sought spiritual counsel (cf. 1:7; 3:3), and these insights are maturing within. This is perceived by the inner eye (the eye of insight) and the gaze of others. The breasts are thus a metonym for the Beloved, for a hidden movement near the heart.

Sod

4. ***Your neck*** The emphasis shifts to verticality and stature. The neck serves to bridge what is above (mind and mouth) and below (heart and body). The neck thus symbolizes the alignment of these elements. The shift to cultural similes (e.g., "the Tower") marks another dimension in the self's constitution, namely, the need for proper practices to guide self-development (Z. 1:74b; ZḤ 28a). In this regard, the tower evokes stability (Ibn Sahula), a pole of transcendence amid the swirl of existence.

5. ***Your breasts*** The body gives and receives nurture. Expressing sustenance to others, it receives in kind from all orders of existence. The breasts symbolize this duality. This sustenance is both material and spiritual. As something material, it points to the interdependence of all beings—the elements of existence being correlated in myriads of ways; and as something spiritual, it signals that transcendence and immanence are also interconnected—the highest and lowest actually being integral to one another (AhavD 100b). The breasts are thus "twin" fonts from one aquifer. Physical sustenance is conjoined to cosmic and spiritual yearnings, even as the latter come to expression in worldly life. One aspect of spiritual training is to understand how the self is suckled from such primordial bestowals (TiqZ 14a).

6 When the day blows gently
And the shadows flee,
I will betake me to the mount of myrrh,
To the hill of frankincense.

6 עַד שֶׁיָּפ֙וּחַ֙ הַיּ֔וֹם
וְנָ֖סוּ הַצְּלָלִ֑ים
אֵ֤לֶךְ לִי֙ אֶל־הַ֣ר הַמּ֔וֹר
וְאֶל־גִּבְעַ֖ת הַלְּבוֹנָֽה׃

Peshat

*6. **When the day blows gently*** This clause, like 2:17, indicates the cool of the morning when "the shadows flee." In this instance the youth speaks to the maiden and refers to his going out upon the "mount of myrrh" and "hill of frankincense." The imagery has erotic overtones—evocative of the woman's figure and fragrance. Earlier he compared her body to elements of nature; now her body is a virtual element of nature, aromatic and alluring.

Derash

*6. **When the day blows gently*** See at 2:17. The imagery of a blowing (*yafuaḥ*) wind elicits traditions of Abraham's circumcision of himself and his family (GenR. 47.7; TanB, *Va'eira'* 4). The wafting "scent" of this act was deemed an incense offering, able to evoke divine mercy. The "mound" of myrrh and "hill" of frankincense further specify this rite. The mass circumcision performed by Joshua after the Israelites crossed the Jordan (Josh. 5:2–9) was linked to this meritorious precedent (SongsR 6.1; NumR 14.12).[47] Spiritual life has relied upon obedient self-sacrifice for the sake of future generations.

mount of myrrh Abraham is the "foremost of the righteous," on account of the sacrificial devotion he displayed with his son Isaac on the mountain (Genesis 22; SongsR 4.vi.2). ("Myrrh" [*mor*] is associated with this patriarch's "suffering" [*memarmeir*].[48] On a similar link between myrrh and Abraham, see above at 1:13.)

hill of frankincense Isaac's sacrificial devotion on the altar follows his father's precedent (ibid.).[49]

Remez

6. The speaker addresses the self in words used earlier (2:17). Whereas the soul then anticipated a loss of immediacy and requested the gift of images to substitute for the Beloved's presence, the Beloved now announces an end to their conjunction (Malbim)[50]—speaking of his imminent departure "to the mount of myrrh" and "the hill of frankincense." But weren't these figures just used to depict the soul's fragrance (3:6)? Might the Beloved be suggesting a renewal of contact in the future, so long as the soul retains its fragrance and higher calling?[51] Perhaps the speaker uses the soul's own words to suggest that the withdrawal is not total and the period of separation may forge a deeper bond. So understood, the figures address the soul subliminally. At this deeper level, they counter despair and prepare for a new call (v. 8).

Sod

*6. **When the day blows gently*** The soul hears a call. The Beloved says: When the shadows lift and you perceive truth more clearly, I shall ascend to a higher spiritual plane—to the heights of *levonah* ("frankincense"), symbolic of the luminous purity of supernal Wisdom (*lavan* = "white"; cf. REzra). By saying, "I will betake me" (*'eilekh li*; literally, "I shall take myself") to the "hill of frankincense," the Beloved hints at a transcendent realm beyond the seeker's present station: a realm for God Alone. Hearing this, the soul is made aware of a higher divine dimension—beyond conceptual forms, for which an intoxicating fragrance is the spiritual symbol.

7 Every part of you is fair, my darling,
There is no blemish in you.

7 כֻּלָּךְ יָפָה רַעְיָתִי
וּמ֖וּם אֵ֥ין בָּֽךְ׃ ס

Peshat

7. ***Every part of you*** Hebrew *kullakh*. Having enumerated each detail (*peraṭ*) of the maiden's beauty, the lad concludes with an emphatic summation (*kelal*) (Rid).

Stylistics. The dominant literary device is the applied figure: metaphor and simile. The features of the woman are compared to elements of nature and of culture, noting their characteristic and especially visual aspects. Viewed separately, these are a series of separate images; taken together, a kaleidoscope unfolds—the panoply of nature in the lover's sight. Three patterns are dominant:

1. Metaphor: "you are *X* + DEPICTION" (v. 1a, the doves' eyes)
2. Simile: "your *X* is like *Y* + DEPICTION that does *Z*" (vv. 1b–2, and 5);
"like *X* is your *Y* + DEPICTION" (vv. 3–4)

Thus verses 1b and 2a have the same form, "your *X* is like *Y*," but the poet may expand the *she-* clause (that) with a supplemental pair (each echoing the *she-* clause): *she-kullam* X // *ve-shakkulah* Y (v. 2b); or the *Y* element may be expanded before the depiction (v. 5, where *ha-* corresponds to "that"). In the pattern "like *X* is your *Y*," the poet adds elements via a conjunction, a preposition, or a descriptive verb (vv. 3–4, respectively)—and extends the pattern by a descriptive parallelism (v. 4b regarding the "shields"). The poet also adds an account of the lad's intentions in verse 6, after describing the lass and before the conclusion.

The beloved's words of praise are framed by an *inclusion*. That is, the opening exclamation of loveliness is repeated at the end—the initial emphasis on manifest presence (*hinnakh*, "Ah, you," or "Behold, you are;" v. 1) is highlighted with summative effect at the conclusion (*kullakh*, "every part of you;" v. 7). The initial praise is repeated for emphasis; the final proclamation specifies in general and particular ("every part . . . no blemish").

Complementing these stylistic features are phonemic resonances, adding further density of sense. The following seven instances are exemplary: *ra'yati* and *ha-ro'im* (vv. 1, 5); *mi-ba'ad*, *ke-'eder*, and *gil'ad* (v. 1); *she-galshu* and *gil'ad* (v. 1); *she-'alu* and *'alav* (vv. 2, 4); *she-kullam*, *shakkulah*, *kol*, *kullakh* (vv. 2, 4, 7); *mat'imot* and *te'omei* (vv. 2, 5); and *talpiyot* and *taluy* (v. 4).

Derash

7. ***Every part of you is fair*** The final praise is cumulative. According to R. Shim'on bar Yoḥai, this reference recalls the unity of Israel at Sinai,[52] when they jointly accepted the covenant (saying "*We* shall do and *we* shall hear"; Exod. 24:7)—and were physically and spiritually transformed (SongsR 4.vii.1; LevR 18.4). The people undertook that commitment without any inner conflict (*ḥalluqei leiv*). As a concluding word of praise, this proclamation also has future import: Israel is and will be "fair" and "without blemish" through its performance of the tasks and virtues just specified.

Remez

7. ***Every part of you is fair*** The initial impression (*hinnakh yafah*, "Ah, you are fair"; v. 1), segmented into several parts to celebrate them individually, is repeated in the conclusion. It marks a climax of sorts. Having reported the spiritual beauty of several aspects of the soul (Malbim), the Beloved ends with a grand encomium: *kullakh*, "every part of you," has been perfected; "there is no blemish in you." The soul has achieved integral wholeness (Ibn Aqnin; Ibn Tibbon),[53] within and without. The speaker sees the outward beauty of the soul and proclaims its spiritual perfection.

Sod

7. ***Every part of you*** The Beloved concludes these praises with an echo of the initial exclamation (v. 1). Now the fullness of perfection is stressed: "every part of you" is without "blemish." These words mark the seeker's readiness for new spiritual achievements (Ibn Sahula). Being without blemish, the adept is ready to realize a deeper level of growth (TiqZ 52a–b). The radiant outer body is attuned to a spiritual inwardness—to what is ***bakh***, "in you" (Alkabetz). This purity must now be developed.

8 From Lebanon come with me;
From Lebanon, my bride, with me!
Trip down from Amana's peak,
From the peak of Senir and Hermon,
From the dens of lions,
From the hills of leopards.

8 אִתִּי מִלְּבָנוֹן֙ כַּלָּ֔ה
אִתִּ֥י מִלְּבָנ֖וֹן תָּב֑וֹאִי
תָּשׁ֣וּרִי ׀ מֵרֹ֣אשׁ אֲמָנָ֗ה
מֵרֹ֤אשׁ שְׂנִיר֙ וְחֶרְמ֔וֹן
מִמְּעֹנ֣וֹת אֲרָי֔וֹת
מֵהַרְרֵ֖י נְמֵרִֽים׃

Peshat

2. A LOVE CALL (vv. 8–11)

This section has three parts, with different moods and styles. Each part uses the newly introduced epithet *kallah* ("bride"). In the first discourse (v. 8), the lad urges the lass to join him and spring (like an animal) to his presence. The figures dramatize a desire for immediate closeness. The second part (v. 9) evokes her effect upon him. He twice tells her that she has "captured" his "heart." The verb's sound evokes a pounding heart (*libbavtini*), infused with passionate intensity. The third part (vv. 10–11) emphasizes her loveliness. His words echo hers in 1:2. The unit begins and ends with a reference to the Lebanon (vv. 8, 11), encasing it in a literary *inclusio*.[54]

8. From Lebanon come with me; / From Lebanon . . . with me! English syntax is not as plastic as Hebrew in its word order. Here, the initial Hebrew clause actually opens with the evocative *'itti*, "with me," followed by the spatial figure and a reference to the "bride"; the second begins in the same way, but concludes with the verb *tavo'i* ("come"). This sequence underscores the emotional valences at play—rising from conjoint action ("with me") to a double climax ("bride," "come"). There is a circular effect as well, since the final invocation (*tavo'i*) echoes the initial preposition (*'itti*), which puns on the Aramaic feminine imperative *'ati*, "come." The poetic structure is *a-b-c // a-b-d*, where *c* is the epithet and *d* is the verb.

Trip down The verb *tashuri* is doubly evocative. It evokes animals "springing" or "leaping" from the heights, as in Hos. 13:7.[55] The verb also evokes "viewing" or "looking [down]," as in Num. 23:9; 24:17 (Ibn Ezra; Radak).[56] Indeed, the poet twice notes the peaks (*ro'sh*) of the mountains to indicate elevation. Thus *tashuri* connotes both raw action and keen sight.

Amana's peak Part of the Anti-Lebanon mountain range (north and west of Damascus). These mountains are mentioned with Lebanon in Assyrian inscriptions, where they are named Ammananu.[57]

Senir Apparently another name for Hermon; cf. Deut. 3:9 (Transl.).

Stylistics. The three doublets ("with me"; "peak"; paired mountain redoubts) give the call a dramatic quality. The iteration of *'itti* governs both *tavo'i* and *tashuri*. The maiden is asked to come and leap with him from the peaks. For him, she embodies the elemental energy of nature. The words *tashuri and ro'sh* have an inverse tonal pattern: *sh-r* and *r-sh*.

Derash

8. From Lebanon . . . with me Covenant love transfigures the experience of history. The Song sings the consolations of divine providence and prophecy. The poles of loss and hope are joined. "Lebanon" marks the sacred center from which the people descended into Egypt, and to which they shall ascend from exile (MdRI, *Bo'*, 14).[58] Poignantly, the Beloved affirms a shared destiny with Israel. Their diminishments are entwined. The sufferings of Israel mark an eclipse of Divinity in history (through the blinding evils of persecution); whereas the restoration of Israel marks a corresponding spiritual effulgence (through the enhancement

of goodwill on earth). The phrase "*with* Me" (*'itti*) signifies this complex interconnection.

Rabbinic tradition underscored the point through dramatic figures of God's sympathetic care and love for Israel (MdRI, *Bo'*, 14; ExodR 23.5; SongsR 4.viii.1).[59] These images entered the soul of subsequent generations and were revivified in later periods—inspiring spiritual resistance and heavenly consolation in desolate times. Rabbi Ishmael reports that holy tears flowed from God's arm in heaven, withdrawn in sympathy for Jewish sufferings in antiquity (3 Enoch 38 A).[60] In his Warsaw Ghetto diary, R. Kalonymos Shapira (the Piazeczner Rebbe) gave expression to a similar divine pathos.[61] In his words, God bears human pain with a silent cry.

Trip down from Amana's peak Faith (*'emunah*) is an elevation of the spirit, a spiritual height (*ro'sh*) from which one may see (*tashuri*) life from a broader perspective. The Beloved calls Israel to attain this viewpoint. The heart of faith sings (*tashuri*) in gratitude for wonders large and small—earthly miracles in the maze of life. At the national level, Israel broke into song (*shirah*) at the very beginning (*me-ro'sh*) of her life of faith (*'emunah*; Exod. 14:31); and on account of this song (Exodus 15) she will again sing (*tashir*) at the time of her redemption (YalSh, #988; cf. SongsR 4.viii.2; following J. Shevi. 6:1).[62] Until that time, one must attain the right "measure" (*teshurah*) of hopeful possibility.[63] Memory must be sustained in the everyday, as a trace of hope amid the ordinary routine.

Amana's peak . . . Senir . . . Hermon The names of these mountain peaks evoke the patriarchs—exemplars of faith and devotion (SongsR 4.viii.3): "Amana" denotes Abraham, who sustained his "faith" (*'emunah*) over many trials; "Senir" denotes Isaac, who "refused to be broken" (*soneh . . . nir*) in his trial on Mount Moriah;[64] and "Hermon" denotes Jacob, whose descendants were the priests, Levites, and kings of Israel.[65] The verse thus catalogues a genealogy of faithfulness and leadership (cf. Rashi).

Remez

8. The speaker calls to the soul, addressing it from some shared elevation—suggesting an acknowledgment of the soul's achievement of height (spiritual eminence). The soul is also called "my bride," alluding to the spiritual marriage mentioned earlier (3:11). All this confirms the soul's transformation, but not the end of its spiritual development. The seeker must now descend from the heights to which it had ascended in solitude. It must put the spiritual quest's purity to the test. The Beloved promises to remain a guide ("come *with me*"); but the spiritual risk must be undertaken. (The soul remains silent. It needs further strengthening and inducement.)

Lebanon That is, the clarity (*lavan*, literally, "whiteness") of true insight. The soul must descend from the singular moments of pure vision, to the complexities of the everyday.

Amana's peak That is, the steadfastness (*'emunah*) of true commitment. The soul must descend from the intensification of faith, to the challenges of earthly life (Sefas Emes).[66]

dens of lions . . . hills of leopards The threats that cause one to lose spiritual direction. The seeker must overcome fear and solidify its spirit—lest the challenges of life ruin its purposes (Ibn Tibbon; Immanuel).[67]

Sod

8. ***From Lebanon come with me*** A new challenge occurs. The seeker is called to actualize God's transcendental reality on earth. Having glimpsed an aura of Divinity (with the passing of false consciousness; v. 6), the task is now, with God's help ("*with* Me"), to give this insight worldly expression: to "come" into the world and "behold"[68] its bounty with the eye of spiritual awareness. In this way, one may bring a perception of transcendental harmony ("Lebanon"; see at v. 6) into the world of diversity and thought. The one neither effaces nor

negates the other. Rather, the two are held in living correlation. The fact that normal worldly distinctions are not ultimate ones—for they are transcended by the pinnacle of "Lebanon" (REzra)—does not diminish their distinctive claims. The seeker is therefore bidden by God: *'itti* ("come with Me")—with spiritual mindfulness (Ibn Sahula); *tashuri* ("venture forth"[69])—with spiritual courage from the heights of Amana (the peaks of "faith," *'emunah*),[70] and strive amid the world's challenges (the impulses that lurk like "lions" in one's heart, or rear up like untamed "leopards"). This is the task for the transformed mind.

9 You have captured my heart,
My own, my bride,
You have captured my heart
With one [glance] of your eyes,
With one coil of your necklace.

9 לִבַּבְתִּנִי
אֲחֹתִי כַלָּה
לִבַּבְתִּינִי
באחד בְּאַחַת מֵעֵינַיִךְ
בְּאַחַד עֲנָק מִצַּוְּרֹנָיִךְ׃

Peshat

*9. **You have captured my heart*** The verbal form *libbavtini* (derived from the noun *leivav*, "heart") suggests that the maiden has "taken away" the beloved's heart (Rashi),[71] with no "remainder" (Ibn Ezra). Denominative verbs in the (intensive) *pi'el* often have such a privative sense.[72] Alternatively, the verb (also nominally derived) indicates that the lad's heart has been "pierced" (so Ibn Janaḥ, adducing the rabbinic expression *'orot levuvin*, "pierced" or "punctuated leather," in M. A.Z. 2:3).[73] That is, our phrase is an ellipse for the girl's eye being like a piercing arrow.[74] The first possibility is preferable, since the youth has "lost his heart" to the maiden. The verb *libbavtini* plays on the "flame" (*lehavah*) of love as well as its "heart" (*leivav*)-stopping aspect.

My own, my bride Literally, "my sister, bride." This is a figure of intimacy, perhaps taken from traditional marital epithets.[75] The term *'aḥot* (sister) connotes a close relationship, like the use of *bat* (daughter) in the marriage hymn of Psalm 45 (v. 11). The terms *'aḥot* and *kallah* also occur separately in the Song (5:2 and 4:8, respectively). Their conjunction here, *'aḥoti khallah*, is evocative.[76]

With one The masoretic *ketiv* (written textual tradition) is *b'ḥd*, while the *qerey* (recitation tradition) is *be-'aḥat*.[77] The latter is more grammatical.

With one [glance] of your eyes The elliptical construction captures her penetrating glance; the next clause continues the ellipsis.

necklace The (plural) noun *tzavveronim*, which occurs only here, is surely derived from the word *tzavva'r*, "neck" (cf. v. 4). The nominal form is often used for decorative ornaments; cf. *pa'amon* ("bell," Exod. 28:34; plural in Exod. 39:25) and *saharonim* ("crescents," Isa. 3:18).

Stylistics. The poetic structure is cumulative: "VERB-*X* + EPITHET // VERB-*X* + one OBJECT-*A* // one OBJECT-*B*." Note the successive replacements, building to the climactic (third) colon.

Each of the three cola share a phonemic cluster: *'aḥoti* ("my sister"); *be-'aḥat* ("with one"); *be-'aḥad* ("with one"). Cola 2 and 3 are also conjoined by *'einayikh* ("your eyes") and *'anaq* ("coil" or "link"). The alliteration *libbavtini* and *levanon* links the inner state (of the heart) with the outer world of nature (the mountain range).

Derash

*9. **You have captured my heart*** The Beloved exults *libbabhtini* in response to Israel's beauty and faithfulness. Surely this unusual verb conveys an intensification of feeling, as revealed by the two spellings of the Hebrew word for "heart": *leibh*, spelled with one letter *bet*, connotes halfheartedness—a lack of complete or true faith; *leibhabh*, spelled with two, connote wholeheartedness—a full commitment.[78] According to an old comment, the doubled *bet* here marks the people's deep devotion to God, making them so Beloved. Several types of heartfelt devotion exemplify Israel's spiritual growth and constancy. If Israel was characterized by "one heart" in Egypt, having engaged in false worship and being of little faith,[79] their subsequent performance of the rites of circumcision and the paschal offering denotes their redoubled commitment and devotion. Similarly, if the people expressed doubt and rebellion at the Sea (see above at vv. 2–3), their faithfulness at Sinai was doubly proclaimed

with the words "we shall do *and* we shall hear" (Exod. 24:7; SongsR 4.ix.1). In His praise, the Beloved now attests to Israel's spiritual transformation. Such growth may begin with a sudden opening of the "eye"[80] (the "glance" mentioned in our verse) and be established even by one mitzvah (Gra).

Remez

9. ***You have captured my heart*** The Beloved goes beyond descriptive praise (vv. 1–7) and solicitation (v. 8), and now expresses the total effect of the seeker upon him. He confesses that "my heart" is no longer my own, for you have "captured" it. This is more than physical capture. The verb *libbavtini* suggests that the seeker's love has magnified the Beloved's own heart (*leibh*)—doubled it (so to speak) by its inclusion in his own. Perhaps the Beloved conveys something of the mysterious magnification of love that occurs when there is spiritual mutuality. And perhaps when one partner is a human soul, the love that throbs in its heart enhances the qualities of love in the depths of Divinity, so that this enhancement returns to the soul and confirms it reciprocally. The soul perceives in the words of the Beloved an attestation of the truth of its love, allowing it to grow in spiritual worth. The Divine Beloved thus gives the soul confirmation of its value. This is love requited at the deepest level.

My own, my bride The soul is connected to the Beloved in a way that transcends all familial and marital bonds. For she is not "my own [or: a sister]" in fact—only in figural intimacy; and she is not a "bride" either, except in the metaphorical sense of having entered a spiritual union with her Beloved. This double designation is doubly false literally, even as it expresses a profound truth about their spiritual relationship. Through these figures, the Beloved asserts that the soul is intimate with divine matters. Having become a devotee of God, it has been transfigured.

With one** [**glance**] **of your eyes The pulse of love radiates from the eyes, as the Beloved had intimated earlier (v. 1). But now the description of the eyes conveys their personal effect. These eyes are not just "your eyes" and compared to those of a "dove"; they are like darts of light that convey the subject's inner radiance. With the merest glance, they transfix what they alight upon. The self retains its intimacy behind the veil; for all is not seen. However, its impact changes (captures and enhances) those it beholds, who feel its visual presence. The soul need not speak words of love. It is sufficient for it just to be, so greatly has it grown in spiritual power.

Sod

9. ***You have captured my heart*** The seeker feels the pull of higher mysteries—"captured" by a spiritual longing that draws it upward (Ibn Sahula). The divine voice objectifies this experience.

one** [**glance**] **of your eyes Once again, "eyes" symbolize spiritual perception. (They were praised as a portal of awareness; v. 1.) This special perception is the capacity to see the things of the world from the transcendent perspective of "Lebanon" (v. 8). It marks an extension of consciousness, of higher wisdom (Ibn Sahula).

10 How sweet is your love,
My own, my bride!
How much more delightful your love than wine,
Your ointments more fragrant
Than any spice!

מַה־יָּפ֥וּ דֹדַ֛יִךְ 10
אֲחֹתִ֣י כַלָּ֑ה
מַה־טֹּ֤בוּ דֹדַ֨יִךְ֙ מִיַּ֔יִן
וְרֵ֥יחַ שְׁמָנַ֖יִךְ
מִכָּל־בְּשָׂמִֽים׃

Peshat

10. *How sweet...How...delightful* The parallelism employs the evocative *mah yafu... mah ṭovu* (literally, "how beautiful...how good [or "sweet," when used with wine]"). Both expressions are complemented by *dodayikh* ("your love"): the first proclaiming its addressee ("my own, my bride") and the second introducing a comparative element ("than wine"). The structure is ABC // ADC. This comparison is further expanded. Having said that her love is more delightful than wine, he adds (*ve-*) that the fragrance of her oils exceeds all spices. These terms (love, goodly fragrance, ointments, and wine) first occur in the maiden's initial speech (1:2b–3a). The beloved's reapplication of the literary figure is striking. The first exclamation, *mah yafu*, recurs in 7:2; the second, *mah ṭovu*, famously occurs in the blessing of Balaam in Num. 24:5 (*mah ṭovu 'oholeykha ya'aqov*, "How goodly are your tents, O Jacob!").

Derash

10. *How sweet...my bride* The praise of *Keneset Yisra'el* continues, emphasizing her bridal status. Rabbi Samuel bar Naḥman observed that the word "bride" occurs ten times in Scripture (six times in the Song; four times in prophetic literature); and it is paralleled by ten references to God's majestic garments (SongsR 4.x.1).[81] His correlation evokes a deep bond between the Beloved and His "spouse."[82] Their spiritual relationship is expressed via the Ten Commandments (ibid.) and the "fragrant ointments" of study and prayer (Netziv).[83]

Remez

10. *How sweet is your love, / My own, my bride!* The intensity of feeling is repeated, and the twin designations "my own [or: sister]" and "bride" again convey a many-splendored spiritual love. The speaker pointedly underscores this by the plural construction *mah yafu dodayikh*: the soul's "loves" are altogether "sweet" (literally, "beautiful") in every sense.

more delightful your love than wine The adjective used with *dodayikh* ("your love") is *ṭovu* ("sweet") when joined with wine, but something "good" and proper as well.[84] The formulation alludes to the soul's initial address to the Beloved (1:2); and thus we have a hint of a profound reciprocity. Loving rightly—and channeling it toward spiritual ends—transforms the self who loves. The Beloved confirms this. Such loving affects the quality of the soul's being as well.

Your ointments more fragrant The seeker had initially characterized the Beloved as having "ointments" of a "sweet fragrance" (1:3). This compliment is now returned. Love is shaped by the ideal of love; the human soul, by its divine and spiritual ideals. Drawn forth by Love, the self is transformed by the quality of its desire.

Sod

10. *How sweet is your love* That is, the soul's love of the ultimate. This verse's words echo the seeker's own praise at the outset (1:2–3). They thus confirm the soul's journey toward God in its own terms, as it strives for a sense of "the mystery of the [true] integral wisdom" (Ibn Sahula).[85] The seeker has yearned to perceive earthly existence as partaking of the source of all (Alkabetz; cf. AhavD 131b). It is now blessed in terms of its own desire: "How sweet is *your* love."

11 Sweetness drops
From your lips, O bride;
Honey and milk
Are under your tongue;
And the scent of your robes
Is like the scent of Lebanon.

11 נֹ֫פֶת תִּטֹּ֫פְנָה
שִׂפְתוֹתַ֫יִךְ כַּלָּ֫ה
דְּבַ֤שׁ וְחָלָב֙
תַּ֣חַת לְשׁוֹנֵ֔ךְ
וְרֵ֥יחַ שַׂלְמֹתַ֖יִךְ
כְּרֵ֥יחַ לְבָנֽוֹן׃

Peshat

11. Sweetness drops... Honey and milk He praises the sweetness of her mouth ("your lips"; "under your tongue"). The expression *nofet tiṭofenah* ("sweetness drops") is alliterative and suggests the dripping of honeycomb—a figure of female allure (cf. Prov. 5:3). After this double praise, the poet turns to the fragrance of her garments (introducing a simile of scent and comparing the smell of her clothes to the Lebanon), another figure of female appeal (cf. Ps. 45:9).

the scent of Lebanon In a striking interpretation, Rashbam reads *reiaḥ ha-levanon* as referring to (the cedar) trees that emit *levonah* (frankincense)! These trees are a metonym for the region. Cf. Hos. 14:7, *ve-reiaḥ lo ka-levanon*, "and its scent is *like* [the mountains of] Lebanon."

Stylistics. The two expressions (vv. 10–11) are hyperbolic. The first offers a superlative, the second a simile. Their poetic structure is similar: "*A // B* + and the fragrance/scent (*ve-reiaḥ*) + OBJECT," the latter then being treated in comparative terms: *mei-* and *ke-*, respectively.

The internal rhyme: *nofet tiṭofenah siftotayikh* (v. 11) mimics the dripping of the honeycomb from the maiden's lips.

Derash

11. Sweetness drops Two forms of speech characterize Israel's heritage. One is prophetic instruction. In Scripture, beginning with Moses, such speech mediates divine instruction for present and future times (SongsR 4.xi.1). Thus, *nofet tiṭofnah*—sweet instruction (Torah) will continue to instruct through inspired prophets. This includes instruction in the primary teachings and the ongoing critique of the people's behavior.

From your lips After the Written Torah comes the Oral Torah of Tradition. This, too, is a teaching for contemporary and ensuing times. It guides the people by discourses crafted with rhetorical pleasantness (*'areivim*; ibid.). With this second type of speech, authority shifts to the sages, duly inspired by Scripture. "Since the time when the Temple was destroyed, prophecy was removed from the prophets and [instruction] given to the wise" (B. Meg. 17b).[86] Sage wisdom is a more socially stable form of pedagogy—less inclined to messianic outbreaks.[87] Nevertheless, both ideal types (sage wisdom and prophecy) oscillated in significance over the ages.[88] For some, prophecy was even a means to angelic legal instruction (the "Holy Spirit");[89] for others (like Maimonides), prophecy was deemed the capstone of philosophically perfected wisdom.[90]

Honey and milk... under your tongue Rabbi Berekhiah taught that whereas some legal issues may be bitter (difficult or contentious) under one's tongue, halakhic instruction that is sweet as honey and fluid as milk can enhance receptivity and resolve (SongsR 4.xi.2).[91] The mode of instruction is thus crucial for ongoing tradition. One must also know if or when to teach certain subjects. This pertains especially to esoteric matters, which should be kept secret ("under your tongue") and not proclaimed in public (B. Ḥag. 14a; and see Sod). All instruction in these matters must be careful and carefully cultivated, to safeguard their content from (ignorant) trivialization or (crass) misinterpretation.

Remez

11. your lips...your tongue The initial depiction of the maiden's beauty centered on her eyes and lips (vv. 1, 3). The claim of the eyes was underscored earlier in this expression of admiration (v. 9). Now the lips receive special praise. The emphasis is on their scent. The inner mouth likewise conveys tangible qualities, as the Beloved now avers. This twofold image imparts a twofold truth. The lips manifest sweet, flowing speech into the world; even so, a concealed sweetness remains "under" the tongue[92]—an interior virtue, not publicly shared. Nevertheless, it informs speech in the deepest way.

your robes... like the scent of Lebanon The power of spiritual love has an exuding fragrance that pierces the outer garments. Earlier, the Beloved exhorted the seeker to descend from the heights of Lebanon (v. 8)—a deep interior state of purity. We now learn that the qualities of that elevation remain palpable. The scent flowing within the soul is perceived from without: it is like the exterior qualities of "Lebanon"—also a state of grandeur and elevation (cf. v. 8).

Sod

11. Sweetness drops / From your lips More than a means of proper speech (v. 3), the lips have a sweetness that derives from a transformed consciousness. The ideal is not merely for me to achieve higher knowledge as a private achievement, but to do so in a way that enables others to sense the depths of wisdom concealed in my words (Ibn Sahula). In this way, others may be perfected as well (Alkabetz). Such is the interpersonal dimension. The seeker is also praised for how the spiritual ideal is articulated to the Beloved. This is the transpersonal aspect. Insights derived from heaven (the "scent of Lebanon") enter the heart and are revealed by speech. An interior sweetness is manifest in human communication and prayer. The first draws others to transcendence through dialogue; the second may open the self to higher levels of awareness (ZḤ 45b). The ideal is to join inner truth and outer expression (Alkabetz).

12 A garden locked
Is my own, my bride,
A fountain locked,
A sealed-up spring.

12 גַּ֥ן ׀ נָע֖וּל
אֲחֹתִ֣י כַלָּ֑ה
גַּ֥ל נָע֖וּל
מַעְיָ֥ן חָתֽוּם׃

Peshat

3. THE GARDEN OF DELIGHTS (4:12–5:1)

The imagery shifts to a garden with a spring. The maiden is identified with these features: the first (spices and fruit) suggests her fertility; the second (a locked or sealed well) suggests her virginity. To him, her body is a lush growth, fertilized by freshets of water within and without (v. 15). She is his garden, and he wants to be infused by her fragrance and bounty (v. 16a). In response, she beckons his advent (v. 16b); and he enters "his" garden and imbibes its smells and tastes. A chorus celebrates this (5:1).

The vibrant metaphoric imagery has parallels in ancient Near Eastern love lyrics.[93] The figures of the maiden as a closed and fertile garden, and as a verdant tree with aromatics, as well as her appeal to him to enter "his" garden and eat there, are rife with erotic overtones (Immanuel).[94] With succinct directness, Anon. 1 bluntly states that the imagery "depicts the act of love" (*ti'eir ma'aseih 'ahavah*).

12–16. The description is in two parts. At the outset, the maiden is compared to a garden and then to a spring and well (v. 12). The focus is the garden, emphasizing its verdant branches and fragrant spices (vv. 13–14). The second focus is the spring and well, first emphasizing the flowing waters (*nozlim*; v. 15); then, returning to the garden theme, the beloved invokes the winds to blow upon his garden and waft (*yizzelu*, from the same verbal stem; v. 16) its spices.[95] The two parts are thus entwined.

*12. **A garden locked . . . A fountain locked*** The paired phrases *gan na'ul* and *gal na'ul* are alliterative. The second noun, *gal*, indicates an uprush of water, as suggested by its conjunction with *ma'ayan* ("spring"). The term "*gullot* of water" in Josh. 15:19 apparently indicates the same feature. The figures connote the maiden's virginity, her body inaccessible.[96] Garden imagery is a recurrent feature in ancient Near Eastern love lyrics, where it suggests the body of a woman and marks the place of lovemaking.[97] This literary convention comes to vibrant life in the evocative comparisons of these verses (vv. 12–16).

Derash

*12. **A garden locked / Is . . . my bride*** The imagery suggests sexual chastity and spiritual purity—virtues lauded for *Keneset Yisra'el*, God's bride (SongsR 4.xii.1). According to R. Huna, this passage marks certain restraints that distinguish the people Israel, and for which they merited redemption from Egypt. Two deal with the concern to maintain national and spiritual identity, by using Hebrew names and preserving their linguistic heritage; a third deals with moral and ethical probity, by not abusing speech through falsehood or slander; and a fourth involves family values, by not engaging in sexual impropriety (ibid., following LevR 32.5). This caution applies to both females and males—these being the "locked garden" and "sealed fountain," respectively (ibid.; also Leqaḥ Ṭov and Ibn Aqnin).

Remez

*12. **A garden locked / Is my own, my bride*** For a third time, the designation "my own, my bride" recurs. But the imagery shifts from sweetness and scent to fertile nurture. The seeker (or soul) is initially called a "garden locked"; then "a fountain locked, a sealed-up spring." A garden lies on the earth's surface; whereas a fountain-spring rises from its depths. Each provides a special source of benefit. The first offers fruit and spices (vv. 13–14); the second, life-giving waters (v. 15). Their conjunction is intensified by the shared verb "locked."

This term conveys a sense of enclosure and bounty. Through spiritual labor, the soul has cultivated its inner virtues and become self-contained. At the same time, this centering allows the self to provide spiritual gifts to others. Love has cultivated both qualities, impelling the soul to further development. The soul is no longer deemed "like" something in nature (v. 11), but "is" a manifestation of its qualities (v. 12). The soul has matured and become whole.

Sod

12. A garden locked The seeker is praised for her proliferation of insight. Transcendental perceptions enrich the self as a "locked garden" (containing fructifying bounty), and as a "sealed-up spring" (its inner nourishment). Such mysteries provide resources for further spiritual development (Z. 1:32b; 63a). This verse's two figures symbolize the outer and inner world of spiritual understanding: "garden" pointing to an integrated consciousness of the world, and "spring" suggesting an inward harmony of mind.

Portrayal of the seeker as garden-and-spring conveys two other spiritual truths. Like a garden, the self must maintain clear boundaries, so that personal insights are not depleted; and like a spring, its inner resources must sustain its capacities and renew them. The spiritual self must learn to cultivate and coordinate the two aspects, while engaged in thoughtful self-examination (Alkabetz).

¹³ Your limbs are an orchard of pomegranates
And of all luscious fruits,
Of henna and of nard—
¹⁴ Nard and saffron,
Fragrant reed and cinnamon,
With all aromatic woods,
Myrrh and aloes—
All the choice perfumes.

שְׁלָחַ֙יִךְ֙ פַּרְדֵּ֣ס רִמּוֹנִ֔ים 13
עִ֖ם פְּרִ֣י מְגָדִ֑ים
כְּפָרִ֖ים עִם־נְרָדִֽים׃
נֵ֣רְדְּ ׀ וְכַרְכֹּ֗ם 14*
קָנֶה֙ וְקִנָּמ֔וֹן
עִ֖ם כָּל־עֲצֵ֣י לְבוֹנָ֑ה
מֹ֖ר וַאֲהָל֑וֹת
עִ֖ם כָּל־רָאשֵׁ֥י בְשָׂמִֽים׃

v. 14. חצי הספר בפסוקים

Peshat

13. limbs The noun *shelaḥim* refers to an orchard's "branches" (Ibn Ezra)[98]—hence more broadly, its "trees."[99] The word is unique to this passage and presumably a variant of the equally rare *sheluḥot* ("branches") in Isa. 16:8. Here Anon. 1 emphasizes the erotic element; Ibn Parḥon suggests that *shelaḥim* indicates the maiden's uncovering of her body, which has the aroma of an orchard.[100]

orchard The designation *pardes* (whence the English word "paradise") comes from Persian, first occurring in late biblical texts (cf. Neh. 2:8) and indicating some kind of (special) park. Here it is filled with profuse and varied spices.

Stylistics. Verse 12 reiterates the term *naʿul* ("locked"), and its structure develops its point incrementally: "garden locked + FEMALE EPITHETS"; "fountain locked + sealed spring." The sounds of the first epithet, *'aḥoti* ("my sister"), are intoned in the concluding verb, *ḥatum* ("sealed"). Alliteration in verse 13 highlights the theme of fertile fruit: *pardes*, *peri* ("fruit"), *kepharim* ("henna"). The abundance of spices is reiterated four times in vv. 12–13 by a structure that joins two elements by the preposition *ʿim* ("[along] with").

14. A sequence of fragrances are mentioned. According to Rashbam, the sequence from nard through cinnamon refers to spices that grow from plants (suggested by the conclusion "aromatic woods"), and the pair "myrrhs and aloes" refers to spices that grow in the earth (suggested by the conclusion "choice perfumes").

Derash

13. Your limbs Interpreting the obscure *shelaḥayikh* (see Peshat) as *shilluḥayikh*, "your Exodus [or: "your sending forth"]," continues the interpretation of verse 12, by deeming sexual restraint a reason for which the people merited redemption (cf. MatKeh). Correspondingly, the nation was espoused in covenant marriage at Sinai, and received the Torah as her "bridal gifts" (cf. *shilluḥim* in 1 Kings 9:16). Yet another view reads this verse as a prophetic promise: that Israel's present dispersion ("your far-flung exile, *shilluḥayikh*") will be gathered, and she *shall become* like a bountiful orchard (SongsR 4.xiii.5; see MatKeh).

14. All the choice perfumes The scent imagery continues in verses 10–11 and 13. Israel both is and shall be a garden of spices, exuding the cultivation of its spiritual practices (Ibn Yahye).

Remez

13–14. Your limbs are an orchard The soul as a garden is epitomized by its extensions; specifically, it is an orchard laden with "fruits," "aromatic wood," and "perfumes."[101] This verdant beneficence evokes both its cultivated development and the bounty accrued. In a

similar fashion, the soul is a cultivated aspect of one's inner being, worked on and brought to fruition. Another characteristic of the garden is that it is rooted in the earth and produces diverse plants. It may therefore also symbolize a human soul that is both grounded and ascendant—a cultivated immanence seeking spiritual heights.[102] Self-care is precious. The soul is a holy garden.

Sod

13–14. ***Your limbs are an orchard*** The seeker exudes great bounty, via the metaphors of fragrance and fruit. The self is not just "like" the flourishing of the outer world; it "is" in fact a being of overflowing vitality. Love and longing have shaped the seeker in the Beloved's image. The present depiction abounds in Edenic splendor, for something primordial has been gained. The seeker smells the holy fragrance of Being and is filled with its qualities.

14. This verse mentions thirteen aromas of the garden, which symbolize the thirteen attributes of divine blessing—to be acknowledged via the thirteen words of praise enunciated daily by the Jew in the morning service, in the *Yishtabbaḥ* prayer (Z. 2:132a).[103]

15 [You are] a garden spring,
A well of fresh water,
A rill of Lebanon.

15 מַעְיַן גַּנִּים
בְּאֵר מַיִם חַיִּים
וְנֹזְלִים מִן־לְבָנוֹן׃

Peshat

15. *[You are]* ***a garden spring, / A well of fresh water*** The first phrase's references combine the images of garden and of spring mentioned at the outset (v. 12). Now the lad adds the topos of a well of fresh (literally "living") water, which resumes the earlier theme of a fountain (ibid.). Presumably the initial identification of garden and fountain applies here as well.

Derash

15. *[You are]****...A well of fresh water*** Rabbi Yoḥanan observed that the word *be'eir* ("well") occurs forty-eight times in the Torah, corresponding to the forty-eight ways by which the Torah is acquired (SongsR 4.xv.1; based on the list of spiritual virtues in Pirqei Avot 6:5–6).[104] This praise of Israel (present and future; see v. 13) refers to the cultivation of its distinctive property—Torah.[105] The result is that the people shall become a "living" expression ("well") of Torah. Through Israel, the tradition will flow: each teaching like the tributaries of a stream "from Lebanon" (ibid.); each new instruction making it "like Lebanon" (fully "clarified," *melubban;* cf. YalSh #988).

Remez

15. *[You are]* ***a garden spring*** Complementing the garden imagery is this reference to a spring and "well of fresh water (*mayim ḥayyim*)." Both draw from sources below the earth, hidden treasuries that support life (*ḥayyim*). This garden (the soul) is nurtured from primordial depths. Put more allegorically: the soul has descended to its deeper dimensions and found the source of its bounty within (Ibn Tibbon; Malbim)[106]—in response to the love and voice (divine stimuli) that beckon her from beyond, to heavenly possibilities (Ibn Tibbon).

Sod

15. *[You are]* ***a garden spring*** The praise concludes as it began, affirming the seeker's resources. Having received streams flowing from "Lebanon," the self is both a spring of fresh water and a "well" of *mayim ḥayyim*—filled with the "waters of life." The self has incorporated gifts from transcendental sources and cultivated an inner reservoir of purity and vitality (ZḤ 15a).[107] The final metaphor marks the soul's achievement.

16 Awake, O north wind,
Come, O south wind!
Blow upon my garden,
That its perfume may spread.
Let my beloved come to his garden
And enjoy its luscious fruits!

16 עוּרִי צָפוֹן
וּבוֹאִי תֵימָן
הָפִיחִי גַנִּי
יִזְּלוּ בְשָׂמָיו
יָבֹא דוֹדִי לְגַנּוֹ
וְיֹאכַל פְּרִי מְגָדָיו׃

Peshat

16. Awake, O north wind . . . Blow upon my garden It seems that the lad is still speaking. He refers to the maiden as his garden. He calls upon the winds to spread this garden's fragrances upon him.[108]

Let my beloved come The maiden responds to his call in similar terms: he has invoked the wind to "come" (*bo'i*); she now invites him to "enter" (*yabho'*).

Rashbam prefers to see all of verse 16 as the maiden's words, importuning the wind to blow upon her so that her fragrance may reach her beloved and induce him to approach. The imagery harks back to prior evocations about blossoming nature and love.

enjoy More precisely, "eat." The verb is provocative (cf. the sexual euphemism in Gen. 39:6 and B. Ket. 65b).

its luscious fruits That were mentioned in verse 13.

Derash

16. Awake, O north wind The Beloved's celebration of Israel culminates in messianic promises. According to R. Eleazar, this call to the elements to "awaken" (*'uri*) alludes both to the future "arousal" (*yit'oreru*) and ingathering of exiles from the "north" (based on Jer. 31:8), as well as the "arousal" of the messianic king from the north (based on Isa. 41:25 and its related verb *ha'iroti*) and rebuilding of the Temple in the "south."[109] Through this exegetical perception, the Song elicits ciphers of hope for national renewal (SongsR 4.xvi.1). It brings hopes for a restoration of the "garden" (homeland; Temple) to a historical peak. Nature is transformed into a figural agent connoting spiritual and national arousal.

Let my beloved come to his garden Israel responds to her Beloved's words of promise. For the sages, it expresses the people's desire for God's advent to her ("his garden"; ibid.). This is an appeal for divine immanence. It has two poles: the personal and spiritual, and the national and cultic. Stressing the first, Gallico understood this verse as Israel's request for God's spiritual presence in her heart—a garden where God may enjoy the fruit of her love, expressed through the commandments. Stressing the second, others read this verse as an appeal for God's restoration of the Temple—a garden where God may enjoy the sacrifices ("eat of its fruit") offered in gratitude and joy (Targum; Leqaḥ Ṭov; Rabbi Shlomoh).

Remez

16. Awake, O north wind Imbued by the confirmation of its growth, the soul is inspired to ascend further. Older terms are used and transformed. The self now proclaims to its innermost spirit: "Awake (*'uri*)!" It is a call of arousal and readiness that echoes its own earlier words of restraint and caution: "Do not arouse (*ta'iru*) or disturb (*te'oreru*) love until it please." The moment of realization has come. Love need not be deferred. The soul exhorts itself, for it is ready to receive love's beneficence (Ibn Tibbon).[110]

Come, O south wind If the north wind represents the inner spirit called to arousal,[111] the south wind represents the spiritual forces that exhort the self from without. Earlier, the

Beloved called upon the soul to "come" (*tabho'i*) with him from the heights of Lebanon (v. 8). This call is now echoed in the self's call to her Beloved to "come" (*bo'i*) and "blow upon my garden." This garden is the soul's region of cultivated spirit, ready for further inspiration. It is also the space of self-being, prepared to receive the fragrant breath of heaven.

A further echo is evoked. Earlier, the image of the "gently blowing" (*yafuaḥ*) breeze betokened the Beloved's imminent withdrawal (1:17; 4:6). The soul now reiterates these words in joy, calling upon her heavenly source to "blow" (*hafiḥi*) upon her and stimulate the spiritual bounty. This call boldly importunes the "Beloved" to "come to his garden and enjoy its . . . fruits!" The human soul is now a benefactor. Near the outset of the Song, the soul had sat beneath the lofty shade of her Beloved and extolled the taste of His fruit (*piryo*). Now, at this moment of spiritual achievement, the soul feels like a ripened fruit (*peri*), a source of sustenance. Love wants to share. It wants to give what it has received.

Sod

16. Awake, O north wind The seeker responds with an imperative evoking arousal (*'uri*), hinting that now is the time when love may be aroused (*ta'iru*; cf. 3:3). The seeker's command responds to the Beloved's exhortations, particularly the implied invitation to meet in the "hills of frankincense" (the transcendental realms) when the shadows pass and the day "blows" (*yafuaḥ*) its beneficent breeze (v. 6). With these words in mind, the seeker yearns for Divinity's advent from concealment. Hopefully, truths that are "hidden," *tzafun*, within and beyond—as hinted at by the "north wind," *tzafon* (Z. 3:3a)[112]—will "blow" (*hafiḥi*) into or inspire her soul ("garden") with a supernal fragrance (cf. REzra).[113] The self anticipates a higher wisdom. So readied, she says: "Let my Beloved come" and partake of His bounty. This is the conjunction long desired. Proactive in love, the self awaits God's gifts. This transformation into humble receptivity is expressed with joyful expectation.

5 I have come to my garden,
My own, my bride;
I have plucked my myrrh and spice,
Eaten my honey and honeycomb,
Drunk my wine and my milk.
Eat, lovers, and drink:
Drink deep of love!

ה בָּ֣אתִי לְגַנִּ֮י
אֲחֹתִ֣י כַלָּה֒
אָרִ֤יתִי מוֹרִי֙ עִם־בְּשָׂמִ֔י
אָכַ֤לְתִּי יַעְרִי֙ עִם־דִּבְשִׁ֔י
שָׁתִ֥יתִי יֵינִ֖י עִם־חֲלָבִ֑י
אִכְל֣וּ רֵעִ֔ים שְׁת֥וּ
וְשִׁכְר֖וּ דּוֹדִֽים׃ ס

Peshat

5:1. I have come His acceptance of her invitation (*ba'ti*) closes the dialogue of call-and-response regarding entry (begun with *tavo'i*, 4:8; and continued in 4:16).[114]

I have plucked... Eaten... Drunk The Beloved extols the pleasures of his love. The first verb, *'ariti*, means "gathered" (cf. Ps. 80:13; M. Shevi. 1:2; and B. B.M. 89b, with Rashi). The spices and wine allude to verses 10 and 14; the honey and milk to verse 11. Thus the elements of the discourses are integrated.

Eat... and drink A chorus echoes and affirms the lad's words.

Drink deep of love Literally, "be drunk on love."

Derash

5:1. I have come to my garden The Beloved responds to Israel's invitation.[115] According to R. Simeon b. Yosinah, the text writes *ganni* ("my garden") and not *gan* ("garden"), to indicate that this is God's bridal bower (*ginuni*; SongsR 5.i.1).[116] And then, alluding to an older tradition, this garden attains far deeper significance: it is also the Garden of Eden—the primary earthly locale of the Shekhinah (divine presence) before sin caused its heavenly withdrawal; and the Temple—the locale of this renewed presence, as an expression of messianic restoration (PdRK 1.1). On this view, the spices and libations refer to the offerings of the renewed shrine. Two modes of messianic hope thus conjoin: the restorative mode—marked as the Garden of Eden; and the utopian mode—marked as the rebuilt Temple. The primordial and the prophetic are the two faces of hope.[117]

Remez

5:1. I have come to my garden The soul is not just "*a* garden" (v. 12), but "*my* garden"—the realm of the Beloved. The soul is ready for reinvigoration, and the Beloved accepts the call. The advent has a trace of the primordial—a return to the Garden of Eden and a restoration of the soul.

I have plucked... Eaten... Drunk She whose love was sweeter than wine (v. 10), and who emanated myrrh and spice (vv. 10, 14), is now received and absorbed by the Beloved. This ingestion confirms that the soul has achieved the worth of the ideal, and has become perfected in a worthy manner (Immanuel).[118] The person of spiritual value is permeated by the spirit. She is truly "my own, my bride!"[119]

Eat, lovers, and drink From somewhere a choral chant resounds, celebrating this holy union and imploring: "drink deep of love!" Love is the cherished expression of purified desire. It gives and receives; it is concrete and spiritual. To have become the bride of this Beloved is the soul's true wish; and with this conjunction it tastes the harmony that binds all things to their divine source—at once the center of the soul and the soul of all being.

Sod

5:1. I have come to my garden The Beloved responds. There is now a divine advent to the garden—a figure redolent with nuance. It is both the inner space of spiritual cultivation—the soul, and the outer space of divine creation—the world. The Beloved comes to the soul through the world and its bounty, perceived in its God-rich splendor. Divine immanence births our spiritual consciousness. All is seen and felt anew; all is replete with godly beneficence. The spiritual bounty so minutely portrayed in 4:10–15 is both external and internal. The world is reborn for the awakened soul; the gifts of God are the munificence that enlivens all Being with potential. But these come to fruition only for the cultivated spirit. The Beloved's advent to the garden stands for the actualization of the divine powers within.

Divine bounty flows from the heavenly heights to the world below. The self must incorporate that flow to develop spiritually and physically. The twofold ideal of *le-qayyema' nafsha'* is both the cultivation of one's soul and the sharing of gifts (spiritual, ethical, and material) with other beings—from this spiritual source (Z. 1:164a).[120] A self that can receive and nurture these gifts can become a "bride" (*kallah*) of God—infused by the divine whole (*kelulah mi-kol*; REzra), and filled with an attentive care for others (Ibn Sahula). "Eat, friends, and drink"—says the self of its offerings to others; "drink" from the resources of "love." The soul wants to give to the world what it has received. Through such reciprocity, the self becomes an "offering to God" (Z. 1:239b).

CONCLUSION

In what is in essence a long speech by the Beloved (with only a brief concluding word by the maiden and by a chorus), a range of evocative wooing takes place. He extols her beauty and body—never able to say it all, and only by similitude; he invokes her companionship in the woodlands, as he invites her to bound with him outdoors; he tells her of his ravished heart, smitten by her merest glance; and he exudes pleasure over her smells, comparing her to a lush garden. These speeches give way to a final remark that acknowledges their mutual intoxication and bids them have their fill of love. The fruits incorporated are a sensual delight—products of nature and figures of desire. Once again a unit concludes with hints of intimacy. Through such tropes of worldly bounty, the song evokes the flush of desire.

CHAPTER 5:2–6:3

In Quest of the Marvelous Beloved

The song cycle in 5:2–6:3 is one entity, according to Masoretic tradition. It opens with a report of the maiden in a state of dreamy wakefulness awaiting her beloved; it concludes with her request that her companions join her search for him. This framework is filled with diverse images, dialogues, and moods—portraying internal states and external realities.

In the initial unit (5:2–8), the maiden reports a series of nighttime events to her friends. The sequences that she recounts have a dreamlike realism, recalling an earlier nocturnal experience (3:1–4). Having searched for her beloved but failed to locate him, she enlists their aid to seek his whereabouts. Should they find him, they are enjoined to say how love-sick (or wounded) she is.

Passion and expression fill the unit. The text combines concrete reality and dream fantasy; the episodes express a stark psychological realism dominated by conflicting feelings (desire and its repression; passion and its activation; and the turmoil of loss and quest). All the images are erotically charged.

Hearing this engaging account, the companions ask the maiden to describe her beloved (v. 9), so that they might recognize him. With passionate precision she describes his body from the head down (vv. 10–16). This depiction engages her friends, who join the search (6:1). The cycle closes with a reference to her beloved's whereabouts, and a declaration of their mutual love (6:2–3).

2 I was asleep,
But my heart was wakeful.
Hark, my beloved knocks!
"Let me in, my own,
My darling, my faultless dove!
For my head is drenched with dew,
My locks with the damp of night."

2 אֲנִי יְשֵׁנָה
וְלִבִּי עֵר
קוֹל ׀ דּוֹדִי דוֹפֵק
פִּתְחִי־לִי אֲחֹתִי
רַעְיָתִי יוֹנָתִי תַמָּתִי
שֶׁרֹּאשִׁי* נִמְלָא־טָל
קְוֻצּוֹתַי רְסִיסֵי לָיְלָה׃

v. 2. ר׳ דגושה

Peshat

1. A NIGHTTIME ESCAPADE (5:2–8)

The maiden speaks in the first person. The unit begins with the pronoun *'ani* ("*I* was asleep"; v. 2) and ends with the same word ("that love-sick am *I*"; v. 8). Within that frame, she punctuates her actions with verbs expressing personal agency ("*I* did *x*"). Everything is depicted from her point of view, yielding a series of emotional and physical states. As such, this unit echoes her earlier confession, "On *my* couch at night, *I* sought the one *I* love" (3:1).

*2. **I was asleep, / But my heart was wakeful*** The maiden reports to her companions (Rid) a twofold state of consciousness—a dream state still alert to the sound of her Beloved's advent (which either calls her to wakefulness or occurs within the dream; Tamakh).[1] The remark attests to the way her beloved was on her mind;[2] it is akin to the state of seeking her beloved nightly (3:1). The reference to her "heart" refers to her emotional awareness; and the adverb *'er* ("wakeful") suggests a state of arousal or readiness for love, comparable to the feelings invoked in the adjurations of 2:7 and 3:5 (*'im ta'iru ve-'im te'oreru*, "do not wake or arouse" love). These allusions underscore the maiden's heightened agitation.

Hark, my beloved knocks! The precise meaning of *qol dodi dofeiq* is uncertain. As in 2:8, *qol* suggests either a vocative of alertness (here, "hark") at the knocking of her beloved, or the "sound" of the knocking along with his call to her. As an event in the real world, the term elicits her wakefulness; as an event in her mind, it marks her sense that the beloved is present. Perhaps the maiden cannot distinguish these realities. The poet has artfully contrived the report to be ambiguous in this regard. For her, inner experience is an expression of external intention; and external events are a confirmation of inner desires. Impelled by both, she "hears" her beloved beckon—knocking at the door of her heart.

For my head is drenched with dew The symbolic innuendos are palpable. Hardly, one thinks, would her beloved refer to the dewy wetness of his hair simply to describe his morning advent. Rather, for her he is himself this sensuous moisture coming toward her home (and heart), just as she is the dripping, flowing myrrh of her response to him. If the scene depicts his physical presence, she evokes him with all the erotic suggestiveness of her desires, the embodied fulfillment of her arousal for him at night. His words actualize her vision of him. Reciprocally, she will soon (vv. 11–12) describe him with some of the same terms that he uses here.

For This renders the particle *she-*, reminiscent of the maiden's self-description as swarthy "because (*she-*) the sun has gazed upon [or: burnt] me" (1:6).[3] It governs also the next clause.

head The letter *resh* of *ro'shi* is punctuated, as sometimes occurs (cf. Ezek. 16:4; 1 Sam. 1:6).[4]

drenched The verb *nimla'* (literally, "filled") governs both the dew and the dampness (i.e., the lines' structure is: A filled with B // C [filled] with D).

locks The noun *qevutzot* refers to the "ends of" (*qetzot*) the hair (Ibn Ezra).[5]

damp of night This renders *resisei laylah*. The first term occurs only once more in Scripture (Amos 6:11); it is a geminate noun with the sense of "soak" (note the verb *la-ros* in Ezek. 46:14, meaning "to moisten" flour; Ibn Ezra). This noun occurs also in Aramaic (thus *revivim*, "rain droplets," in Deut. 32:2 is rendered *resisei malqosha'* in Targum Onqelos).

Derash

2. I was asleep, / But my heart... wakeful The dual state of consciousness suggested by this phrase educed several cultural reflections. Each reflects a different polarity. In one case, *Keneset Yisra'el* (the people Israel) confesses to a spiritual somnolence (*yesheinah*) with regard to the commandments—*though* she remains wakeful (*'eir*) with regard to deeds of loving-kindness (SongsR 5.ii.1). This remark contrasts failure to perform divine obligations with a heart attentive to human needs. More negatively, another reflection presents the speaker as failing to perform acts of public charity—*though* retaining a desire to do the good (ibid.). The directing consciousness (the "I") has lost its spiritual alertness; yet something still pulses within, an inner arousal evoked by the voices of tradition (Sforno). Just this small awakening may turn the heart to its spiritual tasks—and an alertness that "neither slumbers nor sleeps" (Leqaḥ Ṭov and YalSh #988; citing Ps. 121:4).[6]

my beloved knocks The soul is attuned to the divine call, which is manifest in diverse forms. For historical tradition, this may be personalized in a prophetic figure—like Moses (SongsR 5.ii.2), who actualizes a divine agency and directs the people's heart toward redemptive action. Moses serves as a spiritual exemplar who exhorts the people to do what is necessary in preparation for the divine redemption to come (see next comment). The external form (or mode) of the divine call correlates with the inner arousal (or capacity) to hear and respond to its challenge. For students of the textual tradition, the divine call to the reader is the ever-new manifestation of meaning from ever-sacred words. One Hasidic master even called this personal capacity to respond the soul's "Elijah principle"—it being the harbinger of a breakthrough in spiritual consciousness (Me'or 'Einayim).[7]

Let me in The sages understand *pitḥi li* (literally, "Open up for me") as a divine call to repentance: to open the heart so that a divine dimension may enter. Rabbi Yissa said: "The blessed Holy One said to Israel: 'My children, open for Me an opening of repentance [as small] as the eye of a needle, and I shall open for you openings [big enough] for calves and wagons to pass through'" (SongsR, ibid.).[8] The significance of this meager (human) initiative was deemed sufficient for the bounty of (divine) redemption. The call to "open" is thus the call for an awakened self-transformation—this being the root of redemption. On the public plane, the figure of Moses is paradigmatic; on the private plane, he symbolizes the God-like call to spiritual consciousness, via psychological self-reflection and contemplation of tradition.

my own Literally, "my sister" (*'aḥoti*). The call to Israel begins with a term of familial intimacy to convey the emotional bond between the people and God—established at the time of the nation's formation. Thus the term *'aḥoti* is understood to commemorate how the people "united" (*nit'aḥu*) with God in Egypt through "two commandments: the blood of the paschal offering, and the blood of circumcision" (SongsR 5.ii.2; Leqaḥ Ṭov).[9]

Israel is also called *ra'yati* ("my darling") to recall how the nation "befriended" (*riy'u*) God at the Sea with their proclamation "My God" (Exod. 15:2).[10] Israel is then called *yonati* ("my dove") to indicate that she "became a special" (*nitztayyenu*) people through the *mitzvot* at Marah (Exod. 15:25)—just as a dove is "special" (*metzuyyenet*) among birds. And the people was ultimately called *tammati* ("my pure one") to recall how they "became faultless" (*nittammemu*) at Sinai, proclaiming with wholehearted devotion to "do" and to "hear" all of God's commandments (Exod. 24:7; SongsR, ibid.).

Presented sequentially, these four figures underscore the unfolding covenant relationship between God and Israel (from Egypt to Sinai) through epithets of love. Alluding to their faithful past, God beckons Israel to remain spiritually alert in the present.

For my head is drenched with dew This image continues the previous sequence. The reference to the Beloved's "head" (*ro'shi*) soaked in "dew" is correlated with Ps. 68:9, whose image of the earth "shaking (*ra'ashah*)" and the heavens "dripping" evokes the revelation at Sinai (Targum and ShṬov, ad loc.; SongsR, ibid.). This personification of the Beloved in terms of God's advent to Sinai inaugurates a sequence of events. The original call to covenant—received with alacrity—correlates with the present call to covenant renewal, rife with complex dynamics (see below).

Remez

2–8. This episode records a twofold dynamic: a profound spiritual alertness alongside an ambivalence due to the complexities of the spiritual quest (Ralbag).[11] Ostensibly, this tableau recalls 3:1–2 (when the speaker sought the Beloved at night). But this occasion is different. Whereas the earlier episode follows an account of the Beloved's departure (2:17), such that absence and longing are uppermost in the seeker's heart, this one follows a scene of intense spiritual communion (4:16–5:1). Ostensibly, the Beloved remains present in the speaker's mind.

2. ***I was asleep / But my heart was wakeful*** The seeker experiences a dual state of consciousness. The surface mind, ordinarily concerned with the self and ego, was stilled, while in a deeper level of meditative awareness (Al-Fawwāl).[12] The self has withdrawn from worldliness and cultivated a mindfulness of spiritual matters (Ibn Aqnin; Sefas Emes).[13] Sleep symbolizes the quieting of consciousness; and wakefulness, the focalization on matters of ultimate concern (Rambam).[14] In the latter state, one hears with an inner ear.

Hark, my beloved knocks! The soul is in a state of readiness when the spiritual event occurs: *qol dodi dofeiq*. Each word is significant. The word *qol* signals both a spiritual arousal ("hark") and the "sound" of a "voice" that addresses the self. For the seeker, this call is the voice of "*my* Beloved" (*dodi*)—who "knocks," as if from without (Malbim)[15]—but who is simultaneously felt within, as the "throbbing" (*dofeiq*) of spiritual emotion. There is no mere inside or outside: the Beloved's voice fills the seeker entirely; the heart is wholly attuned to a call that takes over the self. The invocation is heard: "Let me in . . . my faultless dove." The self—in meditative wakefulness—suddenly feels the presence of the Beloved beseeching a more intensified indwelling.

For my head is drenched with dew The Beloved tells the seeker that he is suffused with spiritual bounty—the dew upon his head suggesting a higher divine consciousness. The Beloved announces that the quality of mind and spirit the seeker has longed for is imminent. It stands just beyond. But is the seeker truly ready (Ralbag)?[16] Can the adept allow this reality to pervade the self (Ibn Aqnin)?[17] A moment of truth has arrived.

Sod

2. ***I was asleep*** The soul dreams of this divine advent, and of its own capacity to give. As earlier (3:1), the quiet of night is a time of longing (5:1), a time of inwardness in the seclusion of one's room (*Guide* III:51).[18] The "I" (the interrupting ego) has been stilled so that one's "heart" can achieve a "wakeful" (*'er*) alertness. In such a state one may perhaps hear the divine "knock" and "call" to the soul.

my heart was wakeful This is an appeal for an opening toward God (Z. 3:33b), a turning toward supernal wisdom (REzra). The Divine comes from the transcendent heights (a "head . . . drenched with dew") and enters the heart. New awareness floods the soul. Divine reality calls from the fullness of being (ZḤ 24b).[19] The "call" was inaudible to the inner exile (self-alienation) of the mind. It now breaks into consciousness as a spiritual manifestation.

3 I had taken off my robe—
Was I to don it again?
I had bathed my feet—
Was I to soil them again?

3 פָּשַׁ֙טְתִּי֙ אֶת־כֻּתָּנְתִּ֔י
אֵיכָ֖כָה אֶלְבָּשֶׁ֑נָּה
רָחַ֥צְתִּי אֶת־רַגְלַ֖י
אֵיכָ֥כָה אֲטַנְּפֵֽם׃

Peshat

3. The maiden explains why she did not initially respond to his call. The image reflects her anxiety at the realization of her emotional and sexual desire. (Some commentators take this as her statement to her beloved,[20] in which case it is both evocative and inciting,[21] referring to her nakedness in bed with washed legs.)

The counterpoint to her disrobing is her reluctance to get dressed again; the counterpoint to the washed extremities is her concern not to "soil them" (*'aṭannefeim*). This verb has strong connotations; for though found nowhere else in Scripture, it is commonly used in rabbinic Hebrew with the sense of "pollute" or "be defiled"; cf. B. Nid. 29b (Ibn Ezra deemed it a type of *ge'ul*, or defilement; notably, the biblical phrase *nego'alu ba-dam* in Lam. 4:14 is rendered *'iṭanafu ba-dam*, "were defiled in blood," in the Targum).[22]

The motif of a lover rejected at the door recurs in ancient Egyptian love poetry.[23]

Derash

*3. **I had taken off my robe*** The nation's response to God's call to repentance expresses hesitation and demurral. As hesitation, the remark conveys a lack of spiritual readiness to "open" the self (national and personal) to God; as demurral, it reveals a sense of unworthiness. Disrobing and washing dramatize the work of spiritual preparation. On the one hand, a voice of hesitant withdrawal is suggested, in the belief that spiritual work needs privacy and separation—and would be "soiled" if it touched the ground (so to speak) of everyday reality. On the other hand, a voice of self-judgment is suggested in the belief that spiritual preparation was incomplete and still bore the traces of past impurity (verb: *ṭanneif*)—whether the stain of impure worship, due to physical exile (SongsR 5.iii.1), or impure devotion (or: inner desires; Gra), due to the exilic ambience.

Such responses convey the dynamics of religious psychology: a fear of engagement and the justifications involved. The ensuing statement provides a counterpoint. Despite human withdrawal, God "nevertheless" (*'af 'al pi khein*; SongsR, ibid.) puts forth His hand, palpably immanent.

Remez

3. The soul expresses its ambivalence. Through the figure of disrobing, the self indicates an act of retreat and hesitation. This is the negative counterpoint to the state of being "asleep" (v. 2a). If the positive aspect of this state was a turning from the world toward an intensified consciousness of the Beloved, the other aspect (now expressed) is a retreat from the immediacy of this presence. On the one hand, the self wants this presence and desires it; on the other, it is fearful of losing personal identity. Both emotions occur simultaneously. The maiden's interior monologue expresses a pull to the natural self, coincidental with the emergence of a new (overwhelming) personal reality.

The pathos of these competing emotions is captured by the ensuing perplexities. At first, the self thinks aloud: I have returned to my natural state and divested myself of my new spiritual garment (achievement); "was I to don it again?" Could I regain what I have lost? But then the opposite thought occurs—and the self also wonders: "I had bathed my feet" (engaged in intellectual and spiritual self-purification); "was I to soil them again" (and lose all that I had strived for)?

Sod

3. I had taken off my robe At lower levels of spiritual development, these words may convey hesitation (cf. Peshat and Remez).[24] Here, they express an assertion of achievement. Hearing the call, the soul says: I am ready; I have removed (*pashaṭeti*) the impediments of false images (ZḤ 4b);[25] and I have purified my thoughts of disruptive attractions (Alkabetz)[26]—"so how" (*'eikhakhah*) could I fail to care for my soul? It would be folly to return to a lower consciousness (AhavD 151a). But without attentiveness, this achievement can in fact be lost (REzra).[27]

4 My beloved took his hand off the latch,
And my heart was stirred for him.
5 I rose to let in my beloved;
My hands dripped myrrh—
My fingers, flowing myrrh—
Upon the handles of the bolt.

4 דּוֹדִי שָׁלַח יָדוֹ מִן־הַחֹר
וּמֵעַי הָמוּ עָלָיו:
5 קַמְתִּי אֲנִי לִפְתֹּחַ לְדוֹדִי
וְיָדַי נָטְפוּ־מוֹר
וְאֶצְבְּעֹתַי מוֹר עֹבֵר
עַל כַּפּוֹת הַמַּנְעוּל:

Peshat

4–5. By changing the terms for the door's lock along with the imagery, the poet infuses the maiden's words with a complex psychological nuance. She is aroused by the insertion (real or imagined) of his hand through the keyhole—but simultaneously restrained within the locked enclosure, even as she bounds toward him with hands dripping myrrh.

took his hand off the latch Alternatively, "stretched his hand through the door"[28]—a charged image. Both the verb *shalaḥ* and the preposition *min* convey penetration. The clause's object (*ḥor*; here "latch") actually means "hole" (cf. Isa. 11:8), hence the figure is highly evocative. Strikingly she uses this expression of insertion regarding the male's advance. His action evokes an emotional (even erotic) response (Riq).

my heart was stirred for him More precisely (and provocatively), *mei'ai hamu 'alav* connotes "my innards were stirred on account of him."

bolt This word for closure (*man'ul*) evokes the earlier depiction of the maiden as a "garden locked" (*na'ul*). Evocatively, she speaks of herself as putting her hand on this item.

Derash

4. ***My beloved took his hand*** Whereas the Beloved's call was deflected by a verbal excuse, the appeal expressed through the image of the hand (*yad*) (inserted *through* the door hole[29]) elicits a corresponding physical response: "my innards (*mei'ai*) were stirred (*hamu*)."[30] The concreteness of the Beloved's presence stimulates the emotions (Netziv) and bypasses rationalizations. The imagery also evokes a historical precedent. At the crossing of the Reed Sea, all the people saw God's mighty hand (*yad*) (Exod. 14:31)—including the unborn fetuses in their mothers' wombs (*mei'ei 'immam*), which became like a transparent lens (YalSh, Song, #988)—as they were collectively reborn as a nation. The new event betokens a spiritual rebirth, if the nation can respond. For the hesitant heart, the hand cannot be forceful but must reach out in a gentle beckoning. Thus does God coax Israel to respond—attuned (*hamu mei'ai*; Jer. 31:20)[31] to the people's emotional state (SongsR 5.iii.1).

5. ***I rose*** *Keneset Yisra'el* now responds, rising to the occasion (SongsR 5.v.1). The addition of the personal pronoun "I" to the verb (Hebrew *qamti 'ani*, not merely *qamti*) dramatizes the action, highlighting the actor (YefQol). The people thus "open" themselves to their Divine Beloved "in repentance" (SongsR, ibid.). The verse continues the theme of call-and-response.

flowing myrrh The figure captures a complex dynamic. Reaching out to the door latch with fingers like "flowing (*'oveir*) myrrh (*mor*)," the maiden demonstrates that her "rebellious" (*meri*) spirit (of hesitation) had "passed" (*'avar*) and would no longer impede her religious responsiveness—a passing experienced as divine forgiveness (*'oveir* [*'al pesha'*]; Exod. 34:6; SongsR 5.vi.1). Still, some hesitation remained, with the result that the longed-for spiritual fulfillment suddenly "turned and passed away (*'avar*)" (v. 6). The two acts are correlated. The divine call hung in abeyance, in the absence of a proper response; the manifestation of the hand was similarly withdrawn, due to the maiden's prevarications and delayed response. Such is the mystery of the spiritual life. When negative

sensibilities or traits block the openings of hope, the call of renewal fades into silence and tangible possibilities disappear.

Remez

4. ***took his hand off*** The inner ambivalence is externalized. As the self thinks to withdraw (to what is common and known), the Beloved does so reciprocally.[32] But as this feeling empties the self of its desire to change, it is counterpointed by an interior movement that pulses outward: "And my heart was stirred for him" (*hamu mei'ai*—my whole inner being was in turmoil). The self is thrust back and forth. Then, suddenly, the balance is tipped.

5. The self ascends toward its higher calling and initiates the next spiritual move (Ibn Aqnin; Ralbag; Malbim).[33] The action sequence underscores the psychological dynamics involved. After an initial hesitation, the seeker rises to let the Beloved enter. But in the interim, and with the slightest hesitation, the Beloved has withdrawn his hand from the door—leaving the seeker empty-handed, with "hands" and "fingers" filled with unrequited desire ("myrrh").[34] Action for action: the two are locked in a complex interchange.

Sod

4. ***My beloved took his hand*** The phrase expresses the ambiguities in the soul.[35] Is the hand (divine presence) about to be withdrawn "from" the latch (a loss of spiritual reality), or is it beckoning "through" it (a new possibility)?[36] The heart is tense due to these options' significance. On the one hand, the "heart" is "stirred"; on the other, it wonders whether it can devote itself wholly to spiritual service (Z. 1:87a). One must answer decisively (Alkabetz). The "latch" symbolizes the heart's opening. It marks the boundary between the enclosed self (the self-referential ego) and a God-directed consciousness. The "hand" embodies the summons.

5. ***I rose to let in my beloved*** This is a rising toward deed, a movement of readiness "to open" (*liftoaḥ*) to the Beloved. The call ("open to me") and response mirror each other. As the soul moves toward the bolt separating it from God, her "hands" and "fingers" (figuratively) "flow" with the "myrrh" of her transformed being (4:14). The action takes place in the depths of consciousness. Her rising is an elevation of mind and heart, in response to the challenge to live with spiritual integrity. Alacrity and action are required. Love has come; it cannot be denied.

6 I opened the door for my beloved,
But my beloved had turned and gone.
I was faint because of what he said.
I sought, but found him not;
I called, but he did not answer.

6 פָּתַ֤חְתִּֽי אֲנִי֙ לְדוֹדִ֔י
וְדוֹדִ֖י חָמַ֣ק עָבָ֑ר
נַפְשִׁי֙ יָֽצְאָ֣ה בְדַבְּר֔וֹ
בִּקַּשְׁתִּ֙יהוּ֙ וְלֹ֣א מְצָאתִ֔יהוּ
קְרָאתִ֖יו וְלֹ֥א עָנָֽנִי׃

Peshat

6. had turned and gone If her beloved had departed in fact, *ḥamaq ʿavar* connotes that he disappeared (Rashi),[37] turned away, or distanced himself (Ibn Ezra; Immanuel);[38] whereas if she is recounting her fantasy, the image connotes his elusive presence—a figure of her desires. In either case, the poet has produced a striking counterpoint, juxtaposing her expectant reaching out with "flowing myrrh" (*mor ʿoveir*) to his having gone "away" (*ʿavar*). With fine effect, the same verb conveys the dissipation of embodied emotions—tangible to her and projected onto the beloved.

I was faint because of what he said More likely, *nafshi yatze'ah bhe-dabbero* conveys her great despair. She who has referred to him repeatedly as *she-'ahavah nafshi*, "the one whom my soul loves," now laments that "I nearly died when he spoke to me" (cf. Gen. 35:18)—in the sense that her pining soul had all but withered (see Ps. 84:3) and departed at the sound of his voice. She is overwhelmed.

I sought . . . I called More precisely, "I sought *him* . . . I called *to him*"; he is the reiterated object of her longing. With this, there begins a second seeking for the beloved (cf. 3:2).

Derash

6. my beloved had turned This divine turning is experienced as a *hesteir panim* (Gallico), or withdrawal of presence; and the soul went "faint" at the loss of "what he said." Timing is everything; the call does not linger indefinitely. Thus the seeker follows the traces of the call outward (into the world), having lost them in the depths of the heart. At present, there is only divine silence. The divine spirit has withdrawn (Gra). There is only human longing and the unanswered call (SongsR 5.vi.1).

Remez

6. I opened the door for my beloved Though the seeker accedes to the Beloved's request (to "open" for him); the moment has been squandered. The Beloved "had turned and gone." To be sure, the Beloved is still present in the seeker's heart; but the concrete immediacy has faded with the display of ambivalence. All that remains is a trace of the Beloved's presence and voice, lingering in the soul now empty and bereft: "I was faint because of what he said." A spiritual moment has passed; a precious opportunity lost (Ralbag). The self is now cast upon its prior loneliness and desire. Resorting to old words and ways, it says: "I sought . . . I called." But to no avail. Only loss remains. The Beloved is no longer a personal presence. What is left is the mark of presence in the object pronouns "he" and "him": "(I) found *him* not; *he* did not answer."

Sod

6. I opened the door The climactic moment of opening (*pataḥti*). It follows both the outer call (v. 2) and the inner determination to respond (v. 5). But instead of presence, there is absence: "my Beloved had turned and gone." How may we understand this? Had the soul dallied, this withdrawal could express its inability to respond to the challenge (ZḤ 24b). But the soul cultivated a readiness to respond. And still, in the event, nothing is at hand—only abandonment. Why? Perhaps for pedagogical reasons; perhaps the divine absence may prod

the soul to higher levels, beyond images and words (substitute presences). Perhaps it may induce the soul to deal with failure as part of spiritual growth (AhavD 154a–b).[39]

I was faint Literally, "my soul went out at his word." This is the inner spiritual reaction to the call, expressed earlier through the figures of the rising and seeking body. Now this expiry expresses a necessary emptying of selfhood, a divestment of spiritual presumptions. This is the challenge. "I sought" and "called"—says the soul—but there was naught. The religious seeker must transcend spiritual certitude, and realize the absolute otherness of Divinity—beyond cultural forms and language. One must give up even the images that bring God to mind and heart. Confident certitude is a false consciousness, akin to idolatry. Divinity shall be as it shall be. One cannot possess it. This passing away of presence into absence is the truth of the Truth.

7 I met the watchmen
Who patrol the town;
They struck me, they bruised me.
The guards of the walls
Stripped me of my mantle.

7 מְצָאֻנִי הַשֹּׁמְרִים
הַסֹּבְבִים בָּעִיר
הִכּוּנִי פְצָעוּנִי
נָשְׂאוּ אֶת־רְדִידִי מֵעָלַי
שֹׁמְרֵי הַחֹמוֹת׃

Peshat

7. ***I met the watchmen*** Literally, "the watchmen found me" (as in 3:3; Transl.)—this being the ironic counterpoint to her wanting to find him.

They struck me... bruised me... Stripped me In this escapade she does not ask his whereabouts (as she did in 3:3). Now she is a maiden caught in a compromised situation; the figure of stripping off clothes connotes the public shaming of a wanton woman (cf. Ezek. 16:39; Hos. 2:5). At a psychological level, the image recalls her earlier act of disrobing at home (v. 3). Thus the watchmen seemingly enact a punishment for her earlier state of naked desire; that is, their public action evokes her self-judgment at such feelings. Within the dreamlike atmosphere of the report, the cultural and emotional connotations fuse.

mantle The noun *redid* refers to some kind of mantle or veil, as in Isa. 3:23.[40] In the Targum, this noun translates *tze'if* ("veil") in Gen. 24:65; 38:14, 19.[41]

Derash

7. ***I met the watchmen... They struck me*** Present loss evokes past memories. Roaming about, the maiden is bereft, having left God's word unheeded. Suddenly a deep cultural memory comes to mind, regarding the "watchmen" (*shomerim*) of the Song, who "patrol [or: move about]" (*sovevim*) the town, rendering blows: they recall the tribe of Levi, who "guarded" (*shameru*) God's word (Deut. 33:9) and moved "from gate to gate" to punish the rebels after the golden calf apostasy (Exod. 32:27). The "stripping" of the maiden's cloak also recalls the ruin of national pride, when the "walls" of Jerusalem were toppled (SongsR, ibid.). Historical events are thus strategically evoked. For the sages, the Song is a prism that elicits past memories into present consciousness.

Remez

7. An ironic reprise of an earlier scene (3:3). Now the self's ambivalence is at issue, and the watchmen incriminate it with wounds ("they struck me, they bruised me")—these being both the torments of conscience (within) and the despair over lost truths (without).[42] Accosted in the public realm, even "the guards of the walls"—all the self-judgments of the soul—"stripped me of my mantle." The self cannot cover her shame. She had taken off her spiritual robes, and now every attempt to conceal her natural body is rudely removed. Her headlong flight is frenetic and unfocused—the opposite of a careful quest of the spiritual virtues. Thus the guards "trash" this makeshift mantle, leaving the self both exposed and desolate.[43]

Sod

7. ***I met the watchmen*** Literally, "the watchmen met [or: found] me." This marks the challenge. There are many blocks to higher wisdom (ZḤ 21a). The tree of true life is guarded by an impassable flame—this being our human limits, our mortality (Ibn Sahula). These impediments may result in misprisions of Torah, of reading its teachings in our own image and for personal benefits (Alkabetz). These matters "bruise" the soul, until one can achieve a new spiritual focus (REzra). Only then may the soul perceive the benefits of this process: namely, that these wounds "strip" the self of the "mantle" that covers its self-serving assumptions. One must pass through this travail to find transcendent wisdom.

8 I adjure you, O maidens of Jerusalem!
If you meet my beloved, tell him this:
That I am faint with love.

8 הִשְׁבַּעְתִּי אֶתְכֶם בְּנוֹת יְרוּשָׁלָ͏ִם
אִם־תִּמְצְאוּ אֶת־דּוֹדִי מַה־תַּגִּידוּ לוֹ
שֶׁחוֹלַת אַהֲבָה אָנִי׃

Peshat

8. I adjure you Once again the maiden employs an adjuration formula. Here it speaks not of imminent arousal (as in 2:7; 3:5) but of her desire that the women tell the beloved of her consuming love—should they find him. Deftly, the particle *'im* of the oath formula now conveys contingency ("if"). Here it denotes the subjunctive mood and its state of wishful longing.[44]

faint with love See at 2:5. The condition of being "love-sick" now expresses the maiden's distraught state at her beloved's absence.

Stylistics. As 5:2–8 moves from a dream state to a search in the streets, an encounter with watchmen, and an adjuration, it parallels the scenario in 3:1–5. The stylistic similarities and variations between the two accounts are notable. (See table below.)

These corresponding scenes intensify the drama of the maiden in the Song.[45] Each case portrays its topic with a different rhythm, emphasis, and psychological nuance. Altogether, they form a diptych of recurrent desire and longing.

Stylistic effects add to this narrative intensification and convey mounting emotions. One device is the doubling of parallel terms, as in verse 3: I had done *A*, "was I [then] to (*'eikhakhah*) do *B*"? // I had done *X*, "was I [then] to (*'eikhakhah*) do *Y*?" Another such device splits an action and its result by inserting the conjunction *ve-* ("and") after an initial action verb and before the report of a physical response. This pattern occurs in verses 4–5a: "My beloved stretched his hand . . . , *and* my innards were aroused" // "I arose to open . . . , *and* my hands were dripping myrrh."

Meanwhile, recurrent words emphasize the key issues involved: *pataḥ* ("open") in verses 2, 5, 6; *matza'* ("find") in verses 6, 7, 8; and as noted above, *'avar* in verses 5 ("flowing") and 6 ("gone").

Sound patterns reinforce the textual coherence. Notable instances are: *pitḥi li 'aḥoti* ("Open for me, my sister") in verse 2; and *'aṭannefeim* ("[was I to] soil them?") linked to *naṭefu* ("dripped") in verses 3 and 5, respectively.

Derash

8. I am faint with love Lost and wandering, the roaming is a physical and spiritual exile. Accordingly, the maiden's adjuration evokes a longing for redemption (SongsR 5.viii.1). Distant from God, the maiden requests her companions' intervention. But patience and restraint are required. Recalling the paradigm

Stylistic Similarities and Variations in the Nighttime Accounts

3:1	"Upon my couch at night"	5:2	"I was asleep but . . . awake"
3:2	"I must arise and roam" (*'aqumah ve-'asovevah*)	5:5	"I rose (to let in)" (*qamti [liftoaḥ]*)
	"I sought him" (*biqqashtiv*)	5:6	"I sought him" (*biqqashtihu*)
3:3	"the watchmen found me" (*metza'uni ha-shomerim*)	5:7	"the watchmen found me" (*metza'uni ha-shomerim*)
3:4	"scarcely had I passed them" (*kim'at she-'avarti mei-hem*)	5:6	"but my beloved had . . . gone" (*ve-dodi . . . 'avar*)
3:5	"I adjure you . . . do not" (*hishba'ti 'etkhem . . . 'im*)	5:8	"I adjure you . . . if" (*hishba'ti 'etkhem . . . 'im*)

of Egyptian servitude, when the people pined for redemption, tradition emphasizes the need to wait—in hope—despite the sufferings of exile (Rashbam).[46] The people's call is like an act of prayer, beseeching God for salvation and healing. Feeling cut off, they need spiritual helpers—friends and teachers who may understand her longing and give it a proper formulation. The self awaits a sign (Netziv).

Remez

8. Stripped of the conceits of false desire, the seeker calls upon its companions (the "maidens of Jerusalem") to look out (with her) for her Beloved. Should they see him, she urges them to say that she is "faint with love." This weakness is not the wound of nearness, but a love-sickness due to absence. She is wounded by loss; and by squandering the reality that had beckoned.[47]

Sod

8. The seeker exults. Suddenly, the watchmen have been replaced by the "maidens of Jerusalem." The negative traits (which impede yet instruct) have been transformed into positive qualities. Knowing that the quest for spiritual achievement is ongoing, the soul addresses its inner resources and tells them that it is "faint with love" (Z. 1:122a).[48] With these words the seeker reaffirms its commitment to theological search, despite its turmoil and the tenuous nature of its achievements. The seeker has accepted the challenge. The wounds of love now commit one to live with the fragility of human language when dealing with ultimate matters. Theological images must be chosen with care. Images of Divinity may guide the soul—but not fill it with verbal idols.

9 How is your beloved better than another,
O fairest of women?
How is your beloved better than another
That you adjure us so?

9 מַה־דּוֹדֵךְ מִדּוֹד
הַיָּפָה בַּנָּשִׁים
מַה־דּוֹדֵךְ מִדּוֹד
שֶׁכָּכָה הִשְׁבַּעְתָּנוּ׃

Peshat

2. THE COMPANIONS' QUESTION (v. 9)

9. ***How is your beloved better than another*** Or "What sort of beloved is your Beloved?" (Transl.). The formulation is both alliterative and intensifying: *mah dodeikh mi-dod*. The question marker (*mah*) generates the query; the succeeding comparative (*mi-*) formulates its force. In this way, the beloved is distinguished from all others. The query is repeated—a deliberate intensification. The first question speaks to the maiden of "her" beloved, highlighting the comparative element; the second continues with an explanation clause (introduced by *she-*, "that") that evokes the maiden's prior adjuration.

Derash

9. ***How is your beloved better than another...?*** Bewildered by her religious steadfastness—even in times of tribulation and loss—the nations pose this query to Israel. They ask: "How is your God distinguished from other gods?" (SongsR 5.ix.1). So goes a homily composed by R. Akiva, where the question posed is likewise not a matter of abstract theology, but an astonishment at Israel's readiness to die for their Beloved One (MdRI, *Beshallaḥ, Shirta* 3). The people prefer death to conversion or apostasy—as during the Hadrianic persecutions, 132–35 C.E., when R. Akiva himself died a martyr.[49] What inspires such resolve?

Remez

9. Enjoined by her passion, the companions wish to learn more of the Beloved's qualities. They want to know how he is most superior (Malbim).[50] Their question offers the self a new opportunity to reformulate her spiritual goal and bring the Beloved before her mind's eye. And a reformulation it is—significantly different from the earlier imagery of trees and fruit; of stags and deer; and of myrrh and henna blossoms. With precision, she portrays the Beloved in statuesque splendor, detailing his spiritual qualities in bodily terms (Al-Fawwāl).[51]

Sod

9. ***How is your beloved better*** This question exposes the theological task. The challenge is to pose a vision of the Beloved that can raise consciousness to ultimate matters. The goal is to produce images of God that exceed their own limits—that say and unsay simultaneously. Can this be done? Can a vision be constructed out of longing, which somehow turns earthly words into a ladder of ascent? Has the trial of absence resulted in a new mode of absence—such that (paradoxically) the literary expressions may be inwardly perceived as the concealments of a more (ultimate) inconceivable presence? If the seeker can measure up, the quest may rise to a higher plane (Ibn Sahula; Alkabetz).[52]

[10] My beloved is clear-skinned and ruddy,
Preeminent among ten thousand.

10 דּוֹדִי צַח וְאָדוֹם
דָּגוּל מֵרְבָבָה׃

Peshat

3. IN PRAISE OF HIM (vv. 10–16)

Responding to the friends' reference to "your beloved" (*dodeikh*), the maiden produces an ecstatic depiction, beginning with a personal proclamation about "*my* beloved" (*dodi*). She concludes in the same vein, "such is my beloved, such is my darling" (*zeh dodi ve-zeh rei'i*; v. 16). Within this framework, she depicts him from the top of his head down (head, eyes, cheeks, lips, hands, belly, thighs), as the eye of her praise runs "from above to below" (Rashbam, following Tan., *Ki Tissa'* 18).[53] The features vary in kind. They are presented in terms of qualities like color (white, red, black) and value (gold, ivory, sapphire); and with references to birds (raven, dove), flowers and spices (lily, myrrh), and stately trees (cedar).

10. My beloved is clear-skinned and ruddy, / Preeminent The maiden opens with general praise (of his complexion, pure white with a reddish hue) and an exclamation of his exceptional stature (*dagul mei-revavah*, "preeminent among ten thousand"). Her conclusion will have a similar character, denoting eminence and uniqueness (v. 15).

Derash

10. My beloved is clear-skinned The response moves in two theological directions. One focuses on divine actions on Israel's behalf. God was *tzaḥ* (or pure and compassionate) for them in Egypt and at the Sea, but *'adom* (red-faced and punitive) against the Egyptians at the same time (SongsR 5.x.1). The focus is on the divine attributes of mercy and judgment; and Israel commits to God in gratitude for such beneficence. This is the response of historical theology. By contrast, R. Akiva presented a personal theology that portrayed God in anthropomorphic terms (see previous comment).[54] Adducing "This is my God" (Exod. 15:2), this sage proclaims his spiritual allegiance to Divinity. His is a mystical theology of presence and vision—a theology of rapture that inspired his martyr's death with the words of the *Shema* and love of God on his lips (B. Ber. 61b).[55]

Remez

10–16. This passage's account begins with a general depiction (v. 10), and then continues with specifics. Upon a first impression, the visual details portray merely external features (Ibn Tibbon).[56] But the description is also driven by personal feelings of love ("*my* Beloved"). The one sought for has objective, public features—visible to all; and subjective, private ones—known to the seeker. Both elements give the depiction its power.

10. My beloved is clear-skinned and ruddy The self begins to describe the Beloved. These features reflect both His external appearance and the impression He makes on her heart. For colors convey spiritual values; artists and seekers know this well.[57] White and red reflect the poles of heaven and earth: the purity of transcendence, and the tactility of immanence, respectively. The Beloved is thus "preeminent" (*dagul*) here and beyond, in any assembly and by any comparison; but also tangibly present—as the seeker knows, for "his banner (*diglo*) of love" is upon her (2:4). Such is the Beloved One: universal and particular at once—an ideal.

Sod

10–16. To imagine the divine reality in the form of a person is to envision the spiritual dimension through the figure of a human body: a supernal projection of mind, height, and extension—but also of value, character, and action. To configure the Divine in human terms is to "shape" absolute being with vitality, purpose, and foundation; and to bless personhood and accord it a divine-like dimension. To be

sure, personhood is not the only imaginable form that may be ascribed to Divinity. Nonetheless, it is one of the most meaningful ways that humans experience God in relation to human life and its purposes. Thus if theopoetic boldness dares humanize the transhuman, it confers infinite value to human life and action. Daring to say the unsayable, such figural projections are a response to the Divine Name: I Shall Be What I Shall Be (Exod. 3:14).

10. My beloved is clear-skinned and ruddy Literally, "pure-white and red"—a unity that imagines a conjunction of qualities. Since color conveys appearance and form, this combination joins the pure ground of the seeable (white) with vibrant specificity (red). Considered theologically, Divinity is initially evoked through an image that conjoins (imperceptible) "absolute being" (white) with (perceptible) "finite manifestation" (red) in infinite magnitudes.[58] The subsequent phrase ***dagul mei-revavah*** spells this out. Deemed "preeminent among ten thousand," Divinity is most eminent among the infinities of Being. Rising beyond plenitude, the Divine is inherently invisible, yet visible through hints of qualities in the created world (thus: white and red); and descending into plenitude, Divinity is also infinitely refracted throughout world-being, by virtue of the vitality that inheres therein (thus also: red and white). In this first depiction, Divinity is imagined as a conjunction of opposites—a most transcendent singularity, beyond quality and quantity (Alkabetz).[59]

11 His head is finest gold,
His locks are curled
And black as a raven.
12 His eyes are like doves
By watercourses,
Bathed in milk,
Set by a brimming pool.

11 רֹאשׁוֹ כֶּתֶם פָּז
קְוֻצּוֹתָיו תַּלְתַּלִּים
שְׁחֹרוֹת כָּעוֹרֵב׃
12 עֵינָיו כְּיוֹנִים
עַל־אֲפִיקֵי מָיִם
רֹחֲצוֹת בֶּחָלָב
יֹשְׁבוֹת עַל־מִלֵּאת׃

Peshat

11. finest gold This depiction combines two words for gold: *ketem paz* (see Lam. 4:1 and Ps. 19:11, respectively). A variant occurs in the depiction of a heavenly being in Dan. 10:5, whose loins were girded with *ketem 'uphaz.*[60] That figure appeared radiant, flashing like precious minerals or metals—his body like beryl, his arms and legs like bronze. A further indication of the statue-like aspect of the beloved is Daniel's description of Nebuchadnezzar's statue as having a head of "fine gold" (*dehav ṭav*), with "its breast and arms were of silver; its belly and thighs, of bronze; its legs were of iron" (Dan. 2:32–33). Evidently, public statuary has influenced her portrayal.

His locks Her word *kevutzotav* echoes the lad's self-depiction in 5:2b.

are curled The adjective *taltallim* characterizes his hair, but the word is unique. Rabbi Shlomoh construed it to mean *teluyim*, implying locks "hanging [down]" or "curled" (the reduplicated noun suggests entwined hair). Alternatively, we can infer the sense of "piles" from an old description of a handsome Nazirite, which states that "his locks were arranged in *taltallim*" (i.e., "heavily bunched" or "matted"). Apparently our word's syllabic reduplication was interpreted as akin to *tillei tillim*, "piles"; cf. Riq. See B. Ned. 9b.

like doves . . . Bathed in milk Speaking of the beloved's irises within the whites of their pupils. The verb has a present-active aspect.

Set by a brimming pool More precisely, "sitting in a pool (*millei't*)." That is, the dove-like irises are like gems fixed in their setting. Cf. Exod. 28:17, *u-millei'ta vo millu'at 'even*, "you shall set in it mounted stones" (Ibn Ezra); and also verse 14 below, where the beloved's hands are like "rods of gold, studded (*memulla'im*) with beryl." This verb, too, has a present-active aspect.

Derash

11–16. The ancient sages transposed the following passage—the bodily praise of the Beloved—into praise of the Torah. In this way, they rendered anthropomorphic features of God as dynamic aspects of Torah and interpretation. Old esoteric notions concerning Torah as the *Shi'ur Qomah* or "bodily form" of Divinity (i.e., the Torah's being conceived of as a mode of divine embodiment;[61] or God deemed manifest through the textual forms of the Torah) stand behind these portrayals.[62] Through this bold transposition, the later mystical teaching that "Torah and God [and Israel] are one" finds early expression.[63] Torah study is thus not only an engagement with God's will but also a relationship with divine reality as such (revealed in the Torah). In this way, the age-old Jewish belief that a relationship with God may be achieved through Torah study is highlighted and intensified.

Halakhic masters as diverse as Maimonides and R. Ḥayyim of Volozhin, and mystical sources as varied as the Zohar and Hasidic texts, all share this fundamental conviction. Whereas the former masters emphasize the ideal of a spiritual conjunction (*deveiqut*) with God through the principles of reason and will expressed in Torah, the latter focus on a mystical conjunction with the vitality of Divinity as emanated into the Torah and its teachings. The bodily form of the Beloved in this passage elicits early

expressions of these ideals. A reinterpretation of their enduring value is offered below.

11. His head The "head" connotes height, spiritual transcendence, and origins. Divinity as "head" connotes ultimate transcendence and source. For Jewish religious consciousness, Torah is a manifestation of this transcendence, raising the mind and the spirit toward it. "The wise person—[who] has his eyes in his head (*ro'sho*)" (Eccles. 2:14)—is both attentive to the concrete world at hand and to the traces of transcendence at "its head" (or source).[64] If raising human consciousness to its divine source is a spiritual ideal, doing so through Torah is a Jewish ideal. Torah is thus placed as the font of all cultural wisdom, as a worldly formulation of divine wisdom. The Song calls it "His head" (*ro'sho*), thereby directing attention to Torah's spiritual eminence.

His locks are curled This phrase specifies the inherent potency of scriptural language. The word *qevutzotav* ("his locks") can be revocalized as *qotzotav*, which alludes to *qotzei ha-'otiyot* (a scribe's ornamental flourishes on "the tips of the letters" in a Torah scroll). Thus R. Eliezer and R. Joshua said that from even these "minutest marks" (or "crowns"),[65] a sage may derive *taltallim* (taken as *tillei tillim*), "many mounds" of interpretation (LevR 19.1; B. Eruv. 22b).[66] Rabbi Azariah added that these *kotzim* (scribal "marks") are like textual "thorns," impeding understanding[67]—to "be resolved" by those who devote themselves to study from "morning to evening" (*mashḥir u-ma'ariv*—playing on the words *sheḥorot ke-'oreiv*, "dark as a raven"; LevR, ibid.). Through devoted study, God, Torah, and Israel are conjoined—this being one of the deepest convictions of living Judaism.

12. eyes... like doves The Beloved's eye directs its gaze outward; what directs the eye is the Torah. It is the same for Israel. On the cultural and spiritual centrality of eyes—both for legal judgment and spiritual direction in one's life—see at 4:1.

By watercourses Following the two senses of the noun *'afiq*—"water-channel" and "might" (Ps. 42:2 and Job 40:18, respectively)—leads to two diverse interpretations. As the "eyes" guiding the nation (see 4:1), the Sanhedrin (and all courts of law) "channel" the Torah as a resource for community benefits, just as the "teachings of Torah 'strengthen' those who engage in them for all purposes" (SongsR 5.xii.1). In both cases, water is the dominant trope. It metaphorically transforms nature and its effects into religious terms. This homiletic application underscores the social and individual benefits of Torah.

Bathed in milk Continuing the theme of Torah study, this image points to the Torah scholars' examination of laws (*halakhot*), to cleanse them of error and remove doubts or confusion (SongsR, ibid.; Leqaḥ Ṭov; YefQol). They clarify the words of Torah in terms of new human situations. This is one of the tasks of scholarship.

Set by a brimming pool This figure of doves alighted by a pool (*millei't*)[68] evokes scholars who study "the bounty of Torah" (*melei'atah shel torah*)—who study Torah's fullness,[69] so that its teachings may "fill" (*memallei'*) the many needs of life (cf. YefQol, SongsR 5.xii.2). The ideal of Torah living is to produce a culture "filled with justice" (*mellei'ati mishpaṭ*; Isa. 1:21).[70]

Remez

11. His head The account shifts from the personal "my" to the objective "his." The self begins with the head, which signifies eminence and height, mind and value.[71] The physical body thus inspires meditative insight; and embodiment leads to reflective contemplation. Positive images have the capacity to focus the mind and guide thought. This has always been a theological and spiritual challenge. In this instance, the figure of the head (*ro'sho*) turns attention to supreme origins. The seeker must attempt to fix this in his or her mind. Worldly occurrences may then become occasions for considering the wondrous enchaining of elements, from above to below; or for looking beyond their base uses to higher purposes. This is a beginning (*rei'shit*) of wisdom,

and may lead to reverence for God. Mindfulness of beginnings—of potentiality and influence—is a spiritual exercise.

*12. **His eyes*** The eyes channel thought and symbolize spiritual insight for the seeker (Malbim). At the interpersonal level, a shared gaze is a conjunction of perspectives; it is the beginning of an alignment of worldviews. To turn from another's gaze is to deny the other's presence; but to be empathic requires us to internalize another's perspective. The eyes are thus a crucial meeting point. At the personal level, eyes guide our viewpoint and orientation; and they shape a sense of depth and relationship. For the seeker, this includes opening the inner eye and becoming mindful of origins. "The wise one has his eyes in his head (*be-ro'sho*)" (Eccles. 2:14). This passage connotes more than mere attention or alertness. It suggests that the wise keep their eyes "on what is above"—on what is primordial and supernal, namely wisdom and God (see Z. 3:187a). This spiritual practice seeks to attain and maintain a transcendent vision.[72]

Sod

*11. **His head is finest gold*** The eye of imagination is drawn upward, envisioning height. The head is exemplary,[73] gemlike and refined. Awesome and transcendent, the personal tone ("*my* Beloved") becomes impersonal and referential ("*his* head"). What can be said directly? One can indicate Divinity only by imaginative hints and analogies. There follows the sense (through the figure of hair) that aspects of divine radiance descend as "curled locks"—intangible emanations, as it were, of this precious core.[74] The word *qevutzotav* ("locks") even suggests to the mystical mind that every jot and tittle of Being (every *qotz*) embeds modalities of divine wisdom (Z. 3:79b).[75] Such a mind senses infinite traces of meaning in the creation, these being the imaginable and seeable shapes of transcendent reality, which human beings interpret as signs of significance.

The reference to the locks "black as a raven" (*sheḥorot ke-'oreiv*) hints at the oscillation of dawn (*shaḥar*) and dusk (*'erev*)—the play of light and shadow that illumines and impedes our perceptions. The mystical imagination thus conceives Divinity as a luminal radiance that descends and thickens as shapes of significance to our consciousness—emanated aspects, so to speak, of an absolute transcendence that can be symbolized as pure gold. Such transcendence is like a glowing deep within the unfolding qualities of reality: mysteriously one and many to the mind's eye.

*12. **His eyes*** The focus shifts: the irises are "like doves" at a "pool" (*mill'eit*). Complementing transcendence, the divine eyes convey providential oversight (Ibn Sahula)—an all-encompassing vision. Attributing eyes to Divinity means that all worldly deeds and thoughts are believed to be seen and known. The Whole (*mill'eit*; stem: *m-l-'*, "to be full") is thus deemed absolutely present to God—nothing is concealed.

13 His cheeks are like beds of spices,
Banks of perfume
His lips are like lilies;
They drip flowing myrrh.
14 His hands are rods of gold,
Studded with beryl;
His belly a tablet of ivory,
Adorned with sapphires.

13 לְחָיָו כַּעֲרוּגַת הַבֹּשֶׂם
מִגְדְּלוֹת מֶרְקָחִים
שִׂפְתוֹתָיו שׁוֹשַׁנִּים
נֹטְפוֹת מוֹר עֹבֵר׃
14 יָדָיו גְּלִילֵי זָהָב
מְמֻלָּאִים בַּתַּרְשִׁישׁ
מֵעָיו עֶשֶׁת שֵׁן
מְעֻלֶּפֶת סַפִּירִים׃

Peshat

13. They drip flowing myrrh This description of the lips (*noṭefot mor ʿoveir*) echoes the maiden's earlier depiction of her hands and fingers as "flowing with myrrh" (*naṭefu mor... ʿoveir*), when she rushed to open the latch for her beloved (v. 5).

Derash

13. His cheeks...spices The Beloved's speech emits fragrance—the Torah's spiritual qualities. Human discourse replicates its divine source. Thus the cheeks (*leḥayav*) of Torah students emit fragrant scents through the labor (*laʿayin*)[76] of devoted study. And since the meaning (*ṭaʿam*) produced by any one student is different from those of another, Torah has an ever-new fragrance and taste (*ṭaʿam*; SongsR 5.xiii.1).[77]

Banks of perfume Devoted students are like "banks" or towers (*migdelot*) of learning—filled with Torah, Mishnah, *talmud*,[78] *halakhah*, and *ʾaggadah*. Such persons have "lips like lilies" (*shoshanim*), because they are ever repeating (*shonim*)[79] their studies. Overflowing, their learning "drips" like "flowing myrrh" (*mor ʿoveir*)—refreshed by constant repetition (*ʿoveir... ve-ḥozeir*) and clarification (*u-mvareir*). (See SongsR, ibid.)

14. His hands That is, the two tablets of the covenant, given at Sinai. Being like "rods of gold," they evoke the words of Torah, which are like "finest gold" (Ps. 19:11), "studded [or: filled]," *memullaʾim*, with gems (SongsR 5.xiv.1–2, following J. Sheq. 6:1).[80] Correspondingly, a student filled with Torah and inlaid by its explications is like a living Torah—with hands reaching into the world, giving and receiving. Hands mark the agency of spiritual action, whereby the teachings of Torah extend into the world—to transform it and derive new insights from these encounters.

His belly The Beloved's midsection is compared to Leviticus ("the Torah of the priests"), the middle book of the Five Books of Moses. Its laws of sacrifice and purity are as tough as "ivory studded with sapphires" (*shein meʿullefet sappirim*)—which can "wear out (*meʿolefet*) the strength" of students who try to hone its hardness. Tough and fixed, these laws sharpen the mind and, in the process, purify the spirit. They transform the student who appropriates them (SongsR 5.xiv.3).

Remez

13. His cheeks The face conveys presence and inner disposition. It is a focal point of expression. As a spiritual ideal, it exudes one's inner nature. The divine "face" is therefore more than a visual feature. It is a spiritual quality of regard. Similarly, the human face reveals both heart and soul. Meditating on the quality of face is a contemplation of presence—both the manifest details of existence, and how they are received or seen; but also the more concealed or hidden realities, and how they may be engaged or valued. The "face" is therefore public and private; seen and unseen. A visage is iconic. For the seeker, God may be not only the face of

spiritual reality (as seen in the inmost heart); God may also be the effacement of all images (as perceived by insight). Attunement to the face and facets of existence leads to higher awareness. Raising and shining the face are signs of blessing—a bestowal of light and peace (Num. 6:24–26).[81]

*14. **His hands*** Symbolic of action as such, and of praxis as a means for personal perfection (Immanuel). Hands extend into the world, in all directions. They may give or receive, withhold or restrain. They are thus iconic. To open the hands is to offer sustenance and acceptance; to close them is to be stingy and rejecting. The self has to choose. Moreover, the hands are not independent actors. The kind concerns of the head and eyes and face may settle in the hands; or they may be thoughtless and blind and disregarding. Focusing on the work of one's hands can therefore be a spiritual practice. Then they will be elevated for holiness. And this serves the sacred. For God's hands may be deemed the gifts of creation, when creation is nurtured; or they may be withdrawn or fall fallow when not uplifted by human care. "May the work of our hands be rightly formed" (Ps. 90:17) is thus a prayer of the seeker—directed to God and one's heart.

Sod

*13. **His cheeks*** The vision converges downward, along the curves of the face toward the mouth. The eyes and mouth form an inner triangle within the half-circles of the cheeks. Thus the divine face evokes the mystery of geometric planes and figures, deep structures manifest in the panoply of existence. The face of Being, gift of God, exudes growth and smell and flow. Like the beard of a youth, "spices" hedge round about; and like the words of love, breath carries sound like perfumed "myrrh." How wondrous is the countenance of things, its sights and sounds, emerging from the creative depths of Divinity.

Such is the rapture conveyed by this verse. God's face evokes the mystery of multiplicity—the ever-new appearance of things. The image of the "lilies" (*shoshanim*), whose color changes (*meshaniya gavanha*) from red to white, evokes the ever-shifting features of worldly existence—modalities of Divinity, mysteriously one and many (Z. 1:221a).

*14. **His hands*** Below the face (marking spiritual presence) are the hands and arms, reaching toward the world. Like the head, these hands are of "gold"—golden "rods" extending like radiant rays, and "studded" (*memulla'im*) with gemstones. Hence they too are symbolic of fullness or totality (stem: *m-l-'*). Hands and arms, as the means of giving and receiving, offer anthropomorphic images for divine beneficence—pulsing through the material and spiritual realms of existence, assuming the shapes of plants and animals and human beings. Hands and arms are also the attributes of receptivity—whereby cosmic energies recirculate for the ongoing sustenance of the greater Whole.

His belly As the center of physical gravity, the belly shines like "sapphires." It connotes the torso's axis, joining the upper and lower halves of the human. It thus symbolizes the mysterious axis of Being, through which divine creativity emanates vitality anew each day. Radiating into creation, God's gift of Being is one and many. And we may think this through our body.

15 His legs are like marble pillars
Set in sockets of fine gold.
He is majestic as Lebanon,
Stately as the cedars.

15 שׁוֹקָיו֙ עַמּ֣וּדֵי שֵׁ֔שׁ
מְיֻסָּדִ֖ים עַל־אַדְנֵי־פָ֑ז
מַרְאֵ֙הוּ֙ כַּלְּבָנ֔וֹן
בָּח֖וּר כָּאֲרָזִֽים׃

Peshat

15. He is majestic...Stately More precisely, *mar'eihu...baḥur* conveys that "his appearance" is "distinguished" (emphasizing his incomparability; see above at v. 10). Thus the passive participle *baḥur* connotes both the Beloved's unique appearance (Ibn Ezra; in 1 Sam. 9:2 Saul is similarly deemed *baḥur va-ṭov*, "splendid and comely")[82] as well as his youth. (The twofold sense is elicited also in Jer. 48:15, *mivḥar baḥurav*, "the best of its youths.")[83]

Derash

15. His legs The Beloved's "legs" (*shoqav*) "are like marble pillars" (*'ammudei shesh*)—symbolic of the "world" that God "desired" (*nishtoqeiq*) to create and then founded in "six" (*shesh*) days. Like these world pillars,[84] "set in sockets of fine gold," the words of Torah establish a universe of Torah values (LevR 25.8; NumR 10.1; SongsR 5.xv.1).[85] Torah is the foundation, supporting tradition in all its forms. In this way, Torah students are God's partner in making the world a place of values and holiness.

Remez

15. His legs The axis of the human body is vertical; for we are not animals. Standing upright, we may think and see and act with perspective; for uprightness is also a characteristic of values and rectitude. Legs thus symbolize a balanced and measured life. They are iconic of physical stability and movement, and of settled virtues and decisive outreach. At a spiritual level, legs also connote the grounding of values and the way the bodily form mediates between heaven and earth. As a figure for God, legs symbolize the foundations of existence, rising from the material and earthly to the spiritual and transcendent. This issue must be perceived and cultivated within the soul. The ideal of "Lebanon" (*levanon*) is thus symbolic of the "clarification" (*libbun*) of insight and the "purification of [moral and intellectual] virtues" (*libbun ha-middot*) (Immanuel).[86] This is the "majestic" vision to be sought; for such is the appearance (*mar'eihu*) of the Beloved—to the seeking and purified eye and mind.

Sod

15. His legs Firmness and solidity in mass ("like marble pillars"), radiance and effulgence in aspect ("sockets of fine gold"), and a sense of foundation upon which all depends (Ibn Sahula). The body stands on the earth (its immanent ground) and rises toward heaven (its transcendent goal)—transferring energy and meaning from above to below. It provides an image of Divinity, mysteriously joining the infinitudes of heaven and earth.

sockets of fine gold Taken together, verses 11, 14, and 15 depict a golden gleaming from head to foot.

the cedars The imagery shifts to the cedars of Lebanon, "majestic" in height and "stately" in appearance. Somehow, while depicting Divinity—Source of all Being—older associations come to mind. Perhaps the speaker's heart recalls when it compared the Beloved to "trees in the forest" (2:3);[87] or it remembers the call to join the Beloved "from" the high peaks of "Lebanon" (4:8). The heart's longing has interrupted the spectacle of the eye—and the insight of memory takes over.

16 His mouth is delicious
And all of him is delightful.
Such is my beloved,
Such is my darling,
O maidens of Jerusalem!

16 חִכּוֹ מַמְתַקִּים
וְכֻלּוֹ מַחֲמַדִּים
זֶה דוֹדִי
וְזֶה רֵעִי
בְּנוֹת יְרוּשָׁלָֽם׃

Peshat

16. His mouth is delicious . . . delightful The maiden returns to a focus on his sensual appeal (as in v. 13). This comment (*ḥikko mamtaqqim . . . maḥamaddim*) alludes to her earlier statement (2:3) that "I delight [or: have desired]" (*ḥimmadti*) to sit in the shade of his tree, whose fruit "is sweet to my mouth (*matoq le-ḥikki*)."

all of him is delightful The maiden's comment—*kullo maḥamadim*—reciprocates his earlier exclamation of her total beauty (*kullakh yafah*; 4:7). Thus do these speakers complement one another: she, undulating and soft like the natural world; he, stately and firm like a statue (v. 15).

Stylistics. The maiden repeatedly says, "his *X* is," which corresponds to the lad's praises ("your *X* is") in 4:1–7 (and so below in 6:4–7 and 7:2–10). This account uses two patterns of description. For metaphors: "his *X* is *Y* + DEPICTION" (vv. 11, 13b–15a); for similes: "his *X* is like *Y* + DEPICTION" (vv. 12a, 13a, 15b). In verse 11, the first pattern is employed in intensification: "his *A* is *B* // his *X* is *Y* + DEPICTION." In verse 12, the second pattern intensifies via expansion: "his *X* is like *Y* + DEPICTION"—and two additional characterizations. Through these styles, the poet modulates feeling and intensity.

Derash

16. His mouth is delicious The Torah's mouth is the font of instruction, calling on the worshiper to seek God and turn from sin (Amos 5:4; Ezek. 18:27, 32). "Is there a mouth of greater sweetness than this?!" (SongsR 5.xvi.1; Ibn Aqnin). The word "delicious" (*mamtaqqim*) occurs in the plural because appreciations of the Torah differ person by person—in many and diverse ways (Netziv).

With this exultation, the praise of God and Torah reach a climax. Spatially, this praise moves from "above to below" (from head to foot), whereas depiction of the maiden will move in the opposite direction (7:2–8). Thinking theologically, R. Berekhiah said that the human praise descended from high to low because God "was in the transcendent heights and manifested His presence (*Shekhinah*) on earth"; whereas the corresponding depiction of Israel ascends in its account, "since she was in the lowest state, and He will raise her up in the future" (SongsR 5.xvi.6). This account also conveys messianic hope. Whereas God moves from transcendence to immanence, in response to Israel's beckoning love, the people are promised ascendance and restoration.

Remez

16. Memory is unloosed in the seeker, and older experiences come to the fore. Earlier, the self had said that the Beloved's "fruit is sweet to my mouth" (*matoq le-ḥikki*) (2:3). This image now returns, transformed: "his mouth is delicious" (*ḥikko mamtaqqim*).[88] Furthermore, with her Beloved in mind, the seeker echoes his words of praise. Previously, he had concluded his encomium by saying that "every part of you (*kullakh*) is fair" (4:7); and she now concludes her depiction of the Beloved by exulting that "all of him (*kullo*) is delightful."

Such is . . . / Such is As if to mark her words' validity, she ecstatically adds: *zeh . . . zeh*, "this! . . . this!"—as if pointing. The overwrought heart can only gesture. Nothing more can be said.

Sod

16. ***His mouth*** The imagery of the tree continues, and with it other memories. Earlier, when the soul first sought her Beloved, she said that "his fruit is sweet (*matoq*) to my mouth (*ḥikki*)," and "delighted" (*ḥimmadeti*) to "sit in his shade" (2:3). Now this sensibility (of taste and sustenance and protection) recurs in a phrase evoking it all: "His mouth (*ḥikko*) is delicious (*mamtaqqim*) and all of him is delightful (*maḥamadim*)." The similarity is clear (see Z. 3:74a).[89] But so is the difference. Initially this imagery evoked the soul's longing for the Beloved's nurture. The praise is now for the splendid Otherness of the Beloved, whose qualities are of singular worth.

There is perhaps another memory trace. Earlier, the Beloved referred to the seeker as "completely" (*kullakh*) lovely (4:7).[90] The compliment is now returned in joy—"all of him" (*kullo*) is splendid and delightful. Filled by its divine source, the soul finds its voice and almost names the nameless. After the cascade of depictions, the seeker concludes: "Such" (*zeh*) is the Beloved One. Operating mostly beyond language, this pronoun simply points toward God. This unseen deictic gesture is a fitting closure to an attempt to envision the invisible and make reference to it.

6 "Whither has your beloved gone,
O fairest of women?
Whither has your beloved turned?
Let us seek him with you."

ו אָנָה הָלַךְ דּוֹדֵךְ
הַיָּפָה בַּנָּשִׁים
אָנָה פָּנָה דוֹדֵךְ
וּנְבַקְשֶׁנּוּ עִמָּךְ׃

Peshat

4. SEEKING THE BELOVED (6:1–3)

In response to her friends' query (6:1), she answers that he has gone down to "his garden" (v. 2). In the context of her own just-stated ignorance, this response is puzzling. Presumably it expresses her conviction that he is seeking her as well (cf. 4:16 and 5:1).

6:1. The maiden's depiction has put the companions in thrall, so they ask her (twice) where her beloved has "gone" and "turned" (*'anah halakh ... 'anah panah*)—for they wish to "seek him" with her (v. 1).

Derash

6:1. Whither has your beloved gone Theologically and psychologically, the palpable sense of divine absence stimulates the yearning for renewed presence. The seeker holds the Beloved in her heart and mind, and the depiction of His beauty and virtues elicits a corresponding desire in the bystanders.

Rabbinic tradition deems the question of absence a taunt regarding divine providence. In the double query and movement ("Whither has your Beloved gone (*halakh*) ... turned (*panah*)?"), the first verb refers to past divine activity, when God accompanied Israel "from Egypt to the Sea [and thence] to Sinai"; the second verb marks the withdrawal of this sustaining care (SongsR 6.i.1).[91] To this presumption of a hidden or absent God, Israel's response is indignant. Despite appearances, she claims a "portion" in God, due to their covenant bond. And this gives her hope: "Wherever He is, He shall come to me!"[92]

Keneset Yisra'el thus asserts her special relationship to God, maintaining trust in His providential care (Netziv). The challenge to faith is overcome by a more insistent determination. Maintaining the covenant in dark times is a triumph of spiritual will. It may even sustain the people's soul. In this way, paradoxically, the divine covenant elicits its own providential benefits.

Remez

6:1. Whither has your beloved gone After the evocation of the Beloved's qualities (5:10–16), the search resumes (Immanuel; Malbim). But the seeker may wonder whether the images used truly direct consciousness to the desired goal (Al-Fawwāl).[93] This is not a trivial matter. It is a concern for every spiritual quest. The double question (where has your Beloved *gone*—and where has he *turned*?) queries the theological worth of images or similes used to direct the soul. The companions function here as personifications of this perplexity. The query itself has value, since it demonstrates the desire for integrity and honesty. Hence it signals a rebirth of the soul, taking counsel with itself. In this the question is a sign of spiritual awakening. The soul wishes to employ all its resources to find or recover the One who is absent. The collective form "Let *us* seek [him with you]" marks this fact. Previously the seeking was done by the self alone, until it came upon (and was seized by) outer guardians (3:2–4) and inner recriminations (5:7). Now both of these capacities (spiritual counsel and psychological concerns) conjoin in a desire for a steady and thoughtful spiritual development (Ralbag). One grows term by term; question by question.

Sod

6:1. Whither has your beloved gone Voices arise in the soul, expressing its quandary. The seeker wants God, but God cannot be found. Religious life has now narrowed to a question: "Whither" has the Beloved "gone" (*halakh*); and whence has He "turned" (*panah*)?[94] The double formulation arises from a twofold crisis. Divine presence seems both hidden from view and concealed in mysteries. Absence is all. The mind is hampered by its own nature. Attempts to locate God fail. Inner desire is frustrated by incomprehension; disorientation leads to vapid conceptions. Who could know the place of Divine Glory? Who could name or find God?

Faced with this reality, what can a seeker do? Perhaps turn this realization into a spiritual practice. It would then (paradoxically) be the very incomprehensibility of God that must be held in mind. The spiritual task would be to contemplate the very "whither" and whence of all concealment (TiqZ 22a).[95] The soul must meditate on the necessary withdrawal of all language and understanding into silence. This is more than negative theology or the negation of God talk. Rather, it transforms the mind through an imponderable and infinite question. The question of "Whither?" turns the mind toward its limits—and beyond that, to a shuddering wonder. Each formulation of the question peels away spiritual presumptions and paves a passing into Mystery. This shift in consciousness makes all the difference. From the depths of the soul comes an answer—a holy intimation.

2 My beloved has gone down to his garden,
To the beds of spices,
To browse in the gardens
And to pick lilies.

2 דּוֹדִי֙ יָרַ֣ד לְגַנּ֔וֹ
לַעֲרוּגֹ֖ת הַבֹּ֑שֶׂם
לִרְעוֹת֙ בַּגַּנִּ֔ים
וְלִלְקֹ֖ט שֽׁוֹשַׁנִּֽים׃

Peshat

2. Her reply is redolent with her desire for him. He must surely be seeking her—"to browse" (*li-r'ot*) with her (his "darling," *ra'yati*; 2:10, 13) and pluck her to him like a "lily of the valley" (2:1). The place in question is thus a place of desire, a location in her heart as much as any actual field.

to his garden That is, to her (cf. 4:16–5:1).

to pick Ancient Akkadian love lyrics often add plucking to the vocabulary of love, thus giving our passage other allusions of intimacy.[96]

Remez

2. Emboldened by the query, the soul responds with insight. Seeking is the beginning of finding. And thus the self says: "My Beloved *has gone* to His garden"—to the spiritual aspect of my inner being (Immanuel; Malbim); and in so doing, He has turned "to browse" there (and "pick lilies")—to conjoin with the seeker. The garden as a figure for the self was first intimated in 4:12–5:1, and browsing among the lilies as a figure for spiritual conjunction echoes 2:2, 16, and 4:5. The soul is ready to proclaim its love once again.

Derash

2. ***My beloved has gone down to his garden*** Somehow, *Keneset Yisra'el* asserts knowledge of God's whereabouts and His modes of presence. She claims that He is now immanent and near to His people Israel (*ganno*, "*His* garden")—she being His fragrant "bed of spices" in this world (R. Yose); and that He has come "to browse in the gardens" of their synagogues and study halls—made fragrant through Torah learning (YefQol), and "to pick lilies"—gathering those who have remained "righteous" (despite circumstances) at death (SongsR 6.ii.1; Leqaḥ Ṭov). Such divine presence is different than in the past, yet no less personal or involved. God is now drawn to those engaged in prayer and learning—expressing love of God in ritual life; and to those engaged in righteous deeds—meriting divine glory after death (Ibn Aqnin). Prayer, study, and good deeds become pillars of a God-centered religious life—modes through which God is brought to spiritual presence.

Sod

2. ***My beloved has gone down*** Pondering the mystery (v. 1), the soul proclaims that the Beloved has descended to "His garden"—to the seeking soul itself! Somehow, through the very query of "Whither?" the self has located the Divine in its own depths. The self knows that this garden is its spiritual core, and the "beds of spices" (*'arugot ha-bosem*) its exuding love. The fragrance of love emerges from the soul's deep longing ("like a hind yearning [*ta'arog*]," Ps. 42:2) for fulfillment (Z. 3:68a). Aroused, the seeker feels the stirring of the Beloved within—there "to browse" in the garden of her soul, to "pick" its "lilies." For is she not the lily of the valley (2:1)? And has He not browsed there before (2:16)? Perhaps this picking is a gathering of the soul's qualities (Z. 3:263a),[97] or an acknowledgment of the virtues cultivated in the mind and heart (REzra).[98] Unexpectedly, the self has a sense of God's reality. Presence now fills the heart.

3 I am my beloved's
And my beloved is mine;
He browses among the lilies.

3 אֲנִ֤י לְדוֹדִי֙
וְדוֹדִ֣י לִ֔י
הָרֹעֶ֖ה בַּשּׁוֹשַׁנִּֽים׃ ס

Peshat

3. This statement echoes that in 2:16. She goes out to find him because she already has him within.

Derash

3. ***I am my beloved's*** See at 2:16. This phrase reinforces spiritual intimacy and exclusiveness. It is a strong assertion of covenant love, a proclamation of identity (Gallico).

Remez

3. The self now asserts the Beloved's reality in its soul (Ibn Aqnin).[99] It feels the growing inwardness and actuality of this truth and proclaims this in terms of spiritual mutuality: I am my Beloved's *and* my Beloved is mine. What is more: "he browses among the lilies." With these words, the self's renewal is confirmed. The double formulation (being loved and giving love) confirms an entwined spiritual relationship *and* a sense of the Beloved's presence—as emotional reality and personal truth.[100] Of the two, the second is the core from which this reciprocity is experienced and confirmed. Feeling this deeply, the "voice" of this truth addresses the soul (vv. 4–10).

Sod

3. ***I am my beloved's*** This cry of affirmation—proclaiming in ecstasy an experience of the divine presence (v. 2)—echoes an earlier moment of presence (2:16). The heart thus cites itself, knowing the deep bond between itself and the Beloved.

A shift has occurred. Earlier, the soul had asserted: "my Beloved is mine," and then added: "and I am his." This formulation bespeaks a lower spiritual stage: one that sought to possess Divinity—and through that possession to feel possessed. But now, having endured the night of divine absence, and having come to terms with God's infinite Otherness, the soul simply affirms its devotion to God—and by that act knows that the Beloved is a presence that "browses" in her being ("lilies"). This is no theological having, but rather the spiritual disposition of "being there" for God. With this reorientation, the soul becomes a conduit for the divine gifts pervading existence (REzra).

CONCLUSION

The cycle moves from desire to desire. Beginning within the maiden's room and the dreamy recesses of her heart, her beloved's presence (in mind and body) draws her outward into the streets and ultimately toward the garden of lilies (where he browses). The figures of her desires assume a palpable presence: first as a sensed voice and perceived hand; subsequently in robust images conveyed to the companions. In this way she fills their hearts with figures of his beauty, projected from her inner eye of longing. Her impassioned inwardness infuses outward reality, from beginning to end. The name of this passion is called "love," and its compelling character is (again) the theme of sensuous song.

CHAPTRR 6:4–10

The Maiden, Lovely and Luminous

This cycle is composed of two units, according to Masoretic tradition. The first is verses 4–9, in which the beloved proclaims his darling's beauty. Each evocation highlights her physical appeal though sensuous similes (vv. 4–7), with the final series extolling her as incomparable—even among the noblest ladies (vv. 8–9).

The second unit is verse 10, in which another (choral) voice beholds her luminous appearance and reiterates her splendor.[1] Whereas the beloved addressed the maiden directly, using the second person "you," the chorus beholds her from a distance, asking "Who is this?!" in a rhetorical exclamation. For both parties, she is "awesome"—like a heavenly spectacle (vv. 4b and 10b).

These units repeat and echo earlier material, while introducing variations and innovations. The depiction of the maiden in 6:4–7 is almost a replica of 4:1–3, with the concluding elements in verses 8–9 adding a new point of uniqueness. In addition, the query "Who is this?" in verse 10 echoes 3:6, adding new emphasis on her luminosity. The similarities display a convergence among the book's scenes; the divergences highlight this moment of praise.

The images ascend climactically, moving from figures of nature and culture to the heavenly lights at the end.

⁴ You are beautiful, my darling, as Tirzah,
Comely as Jerusalem,
Awesome as bannered hosts.

⁴ יָפָ֨ה אַ֤תְּ רַעְיָתִי֙ כְּתִרְצָ֔ה
נָאוָ֖ה כִּירוּשָׁלָ֑͏ִם
אֲיֻמָּ֖ה כַּנִּדְגָּלֽוֹת׃

Peshat

1. SO PRAISEWORTHY, AGAIN (6:4–9)

The beloved depicts the maiden's beauty. It begins with a proclamation of praise (v. 4) and spells this out in detail (vv. 5–7). The conclusion exclaims her loveliness to all who behold her—and reports their praise (vv. 8–9).

4. *You are beautiful, my darling, as Tirzah*
This phrase echoes 4:1, but with a difference. Earlier, the beloved opened with *hinnakh yafah*, "Behold, you are beautiful..." (there rendered "Ah, you are fair")—marking her presence (*hinneih* + SUFFIXED PRONOUN). Now the statement of beauty comes first and is followed by the pronoun in direct address: *yafah 'at*.

This reconfirmation of her beauty introduces two comparisons. The first says "you are A (my darling) as TOWN-X"; the second adds a condensed parallel: "[you are] B as TOWN-Y." Whereas in the initial overture the double evocation of her beauty (*hinnakh yafah*) was followed by a metaphor of doves' eyes (4:1), here the single evocation of beauty is followed by a series of similes. The first two invoke prominent towns, and the third offers a general climax ("awesome as z"). In addition, the present depiction defers the image of doves to the end (v. 9), while referring to the maiden's eyes after the towns—and stressing their impact (v. 5a).

as Tirzah...as Jerusalem The maiden is compared to two major towns: Tirzah, the capital of the Northern Kingdom (from the reigns of Jeroboam son of Nebat to Omri; see 1 Kings 14:17 and 16:23, respectively); and Jerusalem, the capital of the southern territory (from the time of David to the exile). These places represent (by metonymy) the entire country. The maiden's beauty is thus deemed all-encompassing, like the twin capitals of the land. As a love simile, the mention of Tirzah may also express the maiden's favor and appeal via allusion to the

verb *ratzah* (cf. Ps. 85:2, "O LORD, You desire Your land," *ratzita...'artzekha*);[2] Jerusalem may similarly convey a sense of her perfection or harmony by alluding to the noun *shalem* ("whole"). These qualities enhance the urban analogies.

Awesome as bannered hosts The phrase *'ayummah ka-nidgalot* is difficult. This rendering is similar to Ibn Ezra's statement that it refers to an awesome sight "like [military] camps—which have banners (*degalim*)."[3] That is, this third element of the portrayal likewise indicates some majestic sign. Something of this visual reality is conveyed in Ps. 20:6, "We shall set up banners (*nidgol*) in the name of our God" (NJPS "arrayed by standards...") ; and the Septuagint presented this sense through the word *tetagmenai*, "ranked [orders]." Thus, the phrase invokes a remarkable sight, "awesome as spectacular things." The same word recurs in verse 10 regarding astral phenomena, brilliant in appearance.[4]

As the poet conveys it, the beloved is attuned to the maiden's own sense of him, for he speaks in similar terms to how she spoke of him: "his banner (*diglo*) of love" is upon her (2:4); and she sees him as a "preeminent" (*dagul*) figure (5:10).

Derash

4. *You are beautiful...as Tirzah* The speaker suddenly shifts. Israel's avowal of reciprocal love (v. 3) is answered. Now the Beloved praises the people and compares them to two great towns. These places serve as symbolic prisms of the past and present ideals of divine-human relations. Interpreting the verse in terms of temple worship, R. Judah b. Simon deemed "Tirzah" (*tirtzah*) an allusion to Israel's endearment to God through her sacrificial "offerings," whereby she "found favor" (*nitratzeh*) with Him (SongsR 6.iv.1; with Tan., *Bemidbar* 12).[5]

The people were also called "comely as Jerusalem," since they brought their "holy gifts" to be eaten throughout that sacred city.[6]

This passage was also interpreted in terms of Israel's covenant performance: "You are beautiful... as 'Tirzah' (*tirtzah*): you are beautiful when you are pleasing (*retzuyah*) to Me" through deeds of piety (SifDeut 36, *Va'etḥannan* 6, end).[7] Beauty is therefore a spiritual quality acquired through the mitzvot. The proclamation of the Beloved ("you are") is thus something progressive; the comparative particle *ke-* ("as") highlights the yet-distant ideal. Tradition changes the self, as one embodies the tasks and virtues of a God-centered life.

Remez

4. ***as Tirzah... as Jerusalem*** The inner self is reborn and aware of its highest aspect—now doubly designated as Tirzah ("Most Favorable; Desirable")[8] and Jerusalem ("Foundation of *Shalem*; Perfection"). What the self hears within, as if from the Beloved without, is that its deepest "desire" and most inward "perfection" are coming to realization. Before this moment, the self merely felt the Beloved's "banner" (*diglo*) upon it (2:4). But now this love is celebrated as the "awesome bannered hosts" (*nigdalot*)—a reality in its own right. Inner truth has become so palpable that it is confirmed from without.

Sod

4. ***You are beautiful... as Tirzah... as Jerusalem*** In response to the soul's proclamation, a divine voice confirms the seeker's beauty. It is manifest at every level of her being (Z. 3:197b).[9] The praise is symbolic and incremental. Like great cities and looming towers, she is beautiful as Tirzah (*tirtzah*): for her spiritual will (*ratzon*) has become acceptable (*nirtzah*) in focus and intent;[10] as lovely as "Jeru*salem*": for she has become perfected (*shalem*) by her spiritual preparations; and as awesome as "bannered hosts" (*nigdalot*): for she has ascended in spiritual height (*gadlut*) like fortress turrets on display.[11] The sequence of movement—from inner mind (will), to total being (wholeness of body and spirit), and then to a transcendent quality (eminence)—intensifies appearance: from beauty and loveliness to majestic awe. The self had perceived this transformation subjectively (v. 3), but now—upon hearing the divine voice—knows it as an objective reality. The external depictions are thus expressions of internal states.

5 Turn your eyes away from me,
For they overwhelm me!
Your hair is like a flock of goats
Streaming down from Gilead.
6 Your teeth are like a flock of ewes
Climbing up from the washing pool;
All of them bear twins,
And not one loses her young.
7 Your brow behind your veil
[Gleams] like a pomegranate split open.

5 הָסֵבִּי עֵינַיִךְ מִנֶּגְדִּי
שֶׁהֵם* הִרְהִיבֻנִי
שַׂעְרֵךְ כְּעֵדֶר הָעִזִּים
שֶׁגָּלְשׁוּ מִן־הַגִּלְעָד׃
6 שִׁנַּיִךְ כְּעֵדֶר הָרְחֵלִים
שֶׁעָלוּ מִן־הָרַחְצָה
שֶׁכֻּלָּם מַתְאִימוֹת
וְשַׁכֻּלָה אֵין בָּהֶם׃
7 כְּפֶלַח הָרִמּוֹן
רַקָּתֵךְ מִבַּעַד לְצַמָּתֵךְ׃

v. 5. שני טעמים

Peshat

5. Turn your eyes away... For they overwhelm me! The maiden's gaze is too much to bear (Rashi; Rashbam; Riq). At her merest glance, the youth is undone, so he begs her to turn aside. Such is the effect of her eyes.

In chapter 4, it was only after the full depiction of the girl's beauty that the lad said "you have stirred [or: weakened] my heart" (*libbavtini*) with but "[a glance of] one of your eyes" (v. 9).[12] Here, reference to the girl's eyes precedes the bodily description. The poet has reused the topos with striking variation.

Turn... away from me The force of *haseibi* (turn away) is stressed and inflected: *mi-negdi* ("away from me").[13]

overwhelm Other than here, the causative verb *hirhibh* occurs only in Ps. 138:3, with a similar emotional effect. Consequently, Ibn Ezra glosses that her eyes "are too strong for me." In Isa. 60:5, the conjugation *rahabh* means to "tremble." The Syriac cognate has the same force (and the causative means "to frighten").[14] In Job 26:12, the sea monster named Rahab is a turbulent and presumably terrifying force.

5b–7. The descriptive sequence that follows is similar to 4:1–5 (eyes, hair, teeth, temple). But while in the first sequence the eyes appear through the locks (or veil), in the second they are simply overwhelming. Further, the first account features the lips, mouth, and breasts, whereas in the second these features are absent; and if in the first the neck is compared to the Tower of David (near the end of the list), in this unit there is no mention of the neck, while the image of towns or ramparts occurs at the outset.[15]

Stylistics. The comparative elements may be charted as shown in the table below.

Comparison of the Elements in Two Passages

4:1–7		*6:1–5 + 9*	
v. 1a	doves	v. 9	(my) dove
vv.1b–2	hair; teeth (well-formed)	vv. 5b–6	hair, teeth (ewe-like)
v. 3a	lips; mouth		—
v. 3b	temple	v. 7	temple
v. 4	neck (towerlike)	v. 1	— (towns)
v. 5	breasts		—
v. 9	(awesome) eyes	v. 2	(awesome) eyes

The rhetorical structure in verses 5–6 is "TOPIC + SIMILE + EXPLANATION"—the latter marked by the relative pronoun *she-*, "which" or "that."[16] Such clarification gives a narrative and descriptive character to the similes that proclaim her beauty (cf. 4:1–2). And the *she* sound occurs five times, keeping this element in the ear and mind.

Derash

*5. **Turn your eyes*** This refers to God's pathos in view of Israel's fasting when confronted with sorrows—real or anticipated. That is, *haseibi ʿeinayikh* suggests *haseibi ʿonyeikh* (or *ʿinnuyeikh*), "turn your suffering" away from me—as I, God, am overcome with love and fond remembrance of your loyalty, when you accepted My kingship in olden times. It is not now the "eyes" that "overwhelm" the speaker (God), but the "fasts" (*taʿaniyyot*) that diverse persons (pious,[17] elders, and children[18]) proclaim and duly "afflict themselves" (*mitʿannim*) which so "overwhelms Me" (*hirhivuni*)—and "cause Me to restore" this nation,[19] which "exalted Me" (*hirhivuni*) and "established Me as [Divine] King" at Sinai (SongsR 6.v.1; Ibn Yaḥye).[20] According to the sages, Israel's suffering has effects. Their acts of exegesis formulate a bold theology of pathos.

*5–6. **like a flock of goats... like a flock of ewes*** Israel's loyalty at Sinai (see previous comment) evokes the sins and virtues of their wilderness sojourn. The "goats" mark the people's indecent behavior at Shittim, when they sinned at Baal Peor (Num. 25:1–9), whereas the "ewes" mark their resistance to sexual misconduct during the war against Midian (Numbers 31) (SongsR 6.v.1, end; and vi.1, beginning). The verse thus encodes a historical sequence—the trials and triumphs of covenant love.

The ensuing imagery supports this reading, since the goats are said to stream "down," as if in degeneration, whereas the ewes correspondingly ascend "up," from the (ritual) pools. Such a contrast carries cultural associations, found in a talmudic comparison: goats are shameless, since their small tails are unable to cover their gender; whereas ewes are more modest, since their larger tails more fully cover their sex (B. Shab. 77b, as elaborated by Rabbi Shlomoh, s.v. *mekhassin*).

*7. **Your brow... like a pomegranate*** The imagery shifts from animal comparisons to the fruit of a pomegranate, which serves to exalt Israel's piety upon their return from the Midianite war. As in the previous verse, the emphasis is on sexual morality and restraint. The maiden's brow (*raqateikh*) covered by a veil or scarf (*tzammateikh*) indicates that even persons devoid or "empty" (*reiqanim*) of merit are "full" of good deeds (like a pomegranate filled with seeds)—since they exhibited sexual restraint in tempting circumstances, "constrained" (*metzummatim*) by their virtue (SongsR 6.vii.1).

Remez

5–7. The praise repeats the celebration of flowing hair, perfect teeth, and gleaming brows—again compared to animals and fruit, these being the figural correlatives of the self's harmony, perfection, and radiance. This is an old-new beauty, lost and regained. Repetition reinforces the soul's identity, affirming it at a deeper level.

Sod

*5–7. **Your hair... Your teeth... Your brow*** Older memories rebound in this account of beauty (echoing 4:1b–3). Yet appearances seem different at later stages of life. (This account does not refer to the mouth and speech as in 4:3a, nor to the neck and breasts as in 4:4–5.) It is now the flowing hair, the order of the teeth, and the symmetrical temples that grab attention. Is this selection a way of shifting the gaze from the eyes to rhythm and order and enclosure? The correlations evoked by similes are just such balanced forms; sight and insight are joined in spectacular ways. Thought rises on the wings of likeness.

8 There are sixty queens,
And eighty concubines,
And damsels without number.
9 Only one is my dove,
My perfect one,
The only one of her mother,
The delight of her who bore her.
Maidens see and acclaim her;
Queens and concubines, and praise her.

8 שִׁשִּׁים הֵמָּה מְלָכוֹת
וּשְׁמֹנִים פִּילַגְשִׁים
וַעֲלָמוֹת אֵין מִסְפָּר׃
9 אַחַת הִיא יוֹנָתִי
תַמָּתִי
אַחַת הִיא לְאִמָּהּ
בָּרָה הִיא לְיוֹלַדְתָּהּ
רָאוּהָ בָנוֹת וַיְאַשְּׁרוּהָ
מְלָכוֹת וּפִילַגְשִׁים וַיְהַלְלוּהָ׃ ס

Peshat

8–9. This is the second part of the Beloved's encomium. He now mentions a multitude of women and proclaims that the maiden is unique and incomparable, inducing great praise.

8. ***sixty . . . eighty . . . without number*** This numerical progression begins with the most noble women and continues with the concubines and maidens. The numbers are typical. Sixty was the number of heroes that stood guard around the bed of Solomon in 3:7. And the numbers of sixty and eighty are decade multiples of the common rhetorical sequence 3 and 4.[21] The phrase "beyond number" (*'ein mispar*) is a standard biblical locution (Judg. 7:12).

9. ***Only one*** The clause *'aḥat hi'*, is stated twice: initially with a personal epithet, then with respect to her family. The first epithet is stated directly, as a private possession; the second relates the maiden "to" (*le-*) her kin. The repetition of the clause enforces the declaration.

mother . . . her who bore A fixed poetic pair. Cf. Jer. 50:12.

delight More precisely, "radiant one"; the adjective *barah* adds a shining quality, as also in verse 10 (where it is used with the sun). In this context, *barah* is also correlated with *tammah* (*tammati*, "my perfect one"), with both conveying the quality of physical and spiritual purity (for the latter, see Ps. 24:4 and Job 1:1, respectively).

Stylistics. The literary structure of verse 9a is "*x* is (my) *y* + (my) *y′* // *x* is (she) to (her) *z* // (she is) *y″* to (her) *z′*." (Hereby, *x* is repeated exactly; *y′* and *y″*[21] are parallel terms, as noted above; so are *z* and *z′*.) The pattern begins with personal intimacy and extends to familial relations; *'aḥat hi'* is repeated at the outset, underscored by *barah hi'* at the end. The stylistic pattern is "NUMBER + PRONOUN," which gives emphasis, as also at the start of verse 8. The threefold *hi'* (she) marks the key person.

Maidens Literally, "daughters" (*banot*), resuming "the damsels" (*'alamot*) mentioned in verse 8.

Maidens . . . Queens and concubines Relative to verse 8, the sequence of women is reversed, while these "maidens" are singled out with two verbs ("see and acclaim"); the two other types of women have only one verb ("praise"). The suffixed pronoun *-ha* ("her") occurs with all these verbs, reinforcing attention on the object of praises.

acclaim . . . praise The verbal sequence *va-y'asheruha* // *va-yhalleluha* is a fixed poetic pair; it is famously used to glorify a woman of valor in Prov. 31:28.

Derash

8–9. ***sixty queens . . . damsels without number*** This panoply of the royal court is compared to Israel: grand ladies are many in number, but she is a singular and "perfect one," whom all "acclaim" and "praise."[22] This comparison evokes the virtues of Israel among the nations. Several contrasts underscore Israel's

status. They include cultural heritage, in that Israel has uniquely preserved its ancestral "script and language" (Est. 8:9); they also include familial lineage, in that while some nations know their paternal line, and others their matrilineal descent, only Israel has preserved all the records "of their ancestral houses" (Num. 1:18) (SongsR 6.viii.1).

Israel, God's dove, is "one" and whole—the "pure" descendent of the matriarchs "who bore her." The patriarchs were likewise special: Abraham was "one" (Ezek. 33:24)—uniquely chosen at the beginning of his journey; Isaac also was "one" and special "to his mother"; and Jacob was the "delight of her who bore" him. Faced with these virtues, the nations "acclaim" Israel, as the courtiers had praised Joseph in Egypt (Gen. 41:38) (SongsR 6.ix.1).

By proclaiming Israel's cultural and genealogical continuity in the Song, the sages infuse these traits with the qualities of religious loyalty and love. They also depict language and family as crucial buffers against assimilation and a disrupted heritage. And they portray the ancients as a model for their descendants. Scriptural exegesis now serves cultural continuity.

Remez

8–9. Earlier, when the self was compared to a tower, the image was enhanced by various kinds of armor (4:4). Now, in the context of two royal capitals (Tirzah and Jerusalem, v. 4), the praise mentions "queens" and "concubines" and "damsels without number" (v. 8), who fill these places with splendor. But the one now gazed upon exceeds them all. She is "one and only," a "perfect one"—the object of much "acclaim" and "praise" (v. 9). This spiritual self has become an exemplar of perfection. As the core of the body, the soul enhances the physical self. It is like a unique being—"the only one of her mother"—deep within. So speaks the Beloved, browsing among the lilies of the soul: she is so singular and spectacular (Ibn Tibbon; Ralbag),[23] so beyond compare.[24]

Sod

*8. **There are sixty queens*** The voice of praise charts a sequence that climaxes in celebration of this unique soul (v. 9). The portrait of a royal entourage extends to "damsels (*ʿalamot*) without number." What is suggested? At one level, the images betoken the kingdom of the outer world, filled with all the aspects of life that reveal the mystery of Divinity (Z. 2:14b). At another, these images signify the more concealed (*neʿelamot*) aspects of reality (Alkabetz), infinitely disposed in the depths of Being—like worlds within worlds (*ʿolamot*). The inner eye sees both and understands their correlation. Just this is the seeker's wondrous capacity. The Beloved is preeminent among the myriad realms of Being; correspondingly, the soul is unique among God's innumerable creations.

*9. **Only one is my dove*** The spiritual self knows that this myriad of reality (v. 8) is One, integrated by the soul's eye (Z. 1:124b–125a). It is out of this "perfect" or perfected spiritual perspective that the self keeps all things in ever-new harmony. The inner eye sees that all being derives from God, as if from the womb of a supernal, cosmic mother—this also being the matrix of the soul. And so the self hears praise of its specialness ("my dove is: one and only"; *ʾaḥat hi*: *yonati*), because it has come to perceive the hidden truth of unity in multiplicity ("my dove: all is one"; *yonati: ʾaḥat hi!*). The soul's perfection engenders a new awareness, and this perception is part of its uniqueness.[25] Cleansed in vision, the soul sees all as one; for it is itself a luminous ray of the Creator "who bore her."[26] The soul is like an earthly daughter of an all-engendering mother (Ibn Sahula)—the supernal womb of Being.

10 Who is she that shines through like the dawn,
Beautiful as the moon,
Radiant as the sun
Awesome as bannered hosts?

10 מִי־זֹאת הַנִּשְׁקָפָה כְּמוֹ־שָׁחַר
יָפָה כַלְּבָנָה
בָּרָה כַּחַמָּה
אֲיֻמָּה כַּנִּדְגָּלוֹת׃ ס

Peshat

2. A HEAVENLY AURA (v. 10)

This verse poses a query about someone who shines like the astral bodies on High. The speaker is not indicated. Its references to the maiden as both "awesome" and "shining" echo verses 4 and 9, respectively—suggesting a speaker who has heard the beloved's praises. The echo also reinforces the praise.

10. Who is she The query *mi zo't* echoes 3:6, where it likewise marks a female's notable appearance. The stylistic feature is rhetorical. It serves to proclaim and extol, not request information.

shines . . . Radiant The maiden is depicted like an earthly goddess with a nimbus.

Awesome as bannered hosts A final simile: she is *'ayummah ka-nidgalot*. The phrase harks back to the youth's comment in verse 4, where it highlighted her spectacular appearance. There is a similar (though climactic) effect here. Given the preceding imagery of celestial illumination (Immanuel), *nidgalot* now denotes something like the starry courses or banners (and phalanxes) of the heavenly hosts. For good reason, this image has been taken to mean "brilliant stars."[27] With the reiteration of this phrase, the speeches of this cycle conclude as they began, in praise of the spectacular maiden.

Derash

10. Who is she that shines The praise of Israel invokes astral glory: beyond compare to the things of this world, she is exalted as light itself—as a beacon that "shines like the dawn, beautiful as the moon, radiant as the sun, [and] awesome as the bannered hosts" of heaven.[28] The question "Who?" gives the praise transcendent worth. This wondrous one—the glorified bride of God—is a resplendent presence evoking marvel. She is like a heavenly light, an incomparable "Who?!" The sages try to specify this light; but to no avail. She shines in both daylight and nighttime, spangled in heaven and awesome to behold (SongsR 6.x.1). This is God's own halo, the earthly Queen of Torah. Spiritually renewed, Israel has a heavenly stature (NumR 2.4).

Remez

10. Who is she that shines The self is a spectacle of radiance, an aura illumining the world and the heart (Ibn Tibbon; Immanuel).[29] She is pure and glorious to behold (Malbim). The praised one is even like an astral being, "awesome as bannered hosts."[30] In the thrall of this presence, only a question is appropriate. *Who is she?* The query is one of gasping wonder. In a struggle to name it, the question is transformed into an exclamation: Who is she?—One who irradiates the firmaments!

Sod

10. Who is she that shines The spectacle of the soul evokes wonder. It shines like the "dawn," brightening the horizon; it "is beautiful" as the "moon," shining in the morning sky; and it is "radiant" like the "sun," rising along the arc of heaven. She seems celestial: like the queen of heaven, decked in the aura and jewels of the sky, "awesome as" the "bannered hosts." Out of the inner dark of spiritual loss, the soul radiates the aura of its spiritual restoration (Z. 1:170a). The soul glows like the orbs of heaven (sun and moon)—a twofold illumination that joins the human realm to the cosmos beyond (Z. 2:126b).[31] Spiritual development irradiates

the self and is evident to all. "Who is she?!"—a question and exclamation in one. She is transcendent—and reveals something that transcends all worldliness.

CONCLUSION

The two units respond to the maiden: initially in the voice of the male, then in the voice of a chorus. Both express praise, with the second reinforcing the first. She had gone in search of him (6:1–2); he now sees her and sings her praises (vv. 4–9). He is overwhelmed—blinded by her beauty. Recovering somewhat, he can only repeat past praises. For him, she is beyond compare. The choral query confirms that the maiden (in quest of her beloved) has appeared to view. It adds: she shines with pure splendor. Through her beauty, the beloved sees the world in new ways. Such are the sights and insights of love.

CHAPTER 6:11–7:11

Love Overwhelming

This diverse collection of speeches comprises one entity, according to Masoretic tradition.[1] It is composed of four units. Identification of the voices involved depends on the reader's sense of the dramatic flow, the relations between events, and the play of language. The first task is to assess the content, then access its coherence.

The first presumptive unit is 6:11–12. Both verses are marked by the "I" voice, indicating a first-person experience. In the first instance (v. 11), a person reports entry to a garden to see if budding has occurred. There follows (v. 12) a sudden emotional event wherein the speaker feels conveyed to a chariot. The nature of this event is obscure, and the speaker's identity is not specified.

The second presumptive unit is 7:1. In it, a "we" voice abruptly calls to the maiden to "turn" or "return" so that the speakers may behold her. In response, she asks why they would gaze upon her as a dancer in a whirl. In this dialogue, the group's identity is not indicated, and this exchange's relationship to the prior report is uncertain.

The third unit is 7:2–10a. It begins with a celebration of the girl's physical beauty, moving upward from her feet to her head and hair (vv. 2–6). The speaker is not identified. One may suppose that it is again the beloved (as in the past). This supposition is reinforced by the ecstatic male exclamations that follow these depictions (in the "I" voice; vv. 7–10a).

The fourth and final unit (vv. 10b–11) comprises the maiden's response to these encomiums. Upon hearing such love-talk, she twice calls the speaker *dodi* ("my Beloved"), confirming that he was the one who just described her beauty. They are again entwined in the passions of love.

As the narrative sequences develop, the identity of character and scene is progressively easier to discern. The opening units are more perplexing. Two threads of discourse may be considered.

1. A speaker reports going down to the garden (6:11). If this is the maiden,[2] searching for her beloved (cf. 6:2), one may suppose that she is overwhelmed by his sudden presence and finds herself (somehow) "set"—physically or emotionally—in his "chariot."[3] Alternatively, the maiden reports her wandering, but when suddenly overcome with despair at his absence, she gets into this vehicle and starts to leave the scene.[4] On either explanation (her encounter with him or her exit), the speakers in 7:1 beseech the lass to "turn" or "come back." They want to continue to enjoy her beauty. This reconstruction of events makes sense if the beloved's words of praise in 6:4–9 are the reason for her heightened state, and if the query of her luminous appearance in 6:10 is a choral proclamation of her appearance in the garden.

On this view, the lad's praise and the girl's reaction are simultaneous events (presented sequentially).

2. Another interpretation attributes the voice in 6:11–12 to the male who, having seen the advent of the maiden to his place (and praised her appearance, 6:4–9), now muses that he has gone to the garden to see if the plants have budded (perhaps alluding to her anticipated presence). In this setting, bewildered by desire, the youth feels "set" within a chariot. Somehow this figure indicates the object of his passions—the beautiful maiden (see below). Onlookers (a male chorus) behold this event and proclaim their wish to gaze upon her (7:1). Brought together once again, the pair engages in wooing with increasingly explicit erotic innuendos (7:2–10a, and 10b–11). This reconstruction accounts for the sequence of episodes and speeches from 6:4–7:11 in a sustained way (the beloved youth being the primary actor). I have adopted it below.

[11] I went down to the nut grove
To see the budding of the vale;
To see if the vines had blossomed,
If the pomegranates were in bloom.

11 אֶל־גִּנַּת אֱגוֹז יָרַדְתִּי
לִרְאוֹת בְּאִבֵּי הַנָּחַל
לִרְאוֹת הֲפָרְחָה הַגֶּפֶן
הֵנֵצוּ הָרִמֹּנִים׃

Peshat

1. OVERWHELMING EMOTIONS (6:11–12)

The lad reports (to himself, or his friends) that he had gone down to the garden to view the budding of its fruit when, suddenly overwhelmed by the fantasies and reality of his desires, found himself in a "chariot of love"—his longings fulfilled.

6:11. I went down to the nut grove He "goes down" to a garden, as in verse 2. It is here called a *ginnah* (there, a *gan*). The term is found also in Esther 1:5; 7:7–8, where it refers to a royal garden or arbor of some kind.[5] The nut called *ʾegoz* is mentioned only here; it is possibly the Persian walnut (*Juglans regia*), which may have grown in ancient Israel.[6] This nut presumably refers to the trees of this type ("grove"), just as the *pardes rimmonim* in 4:13 refers to a pomegranate orchard.[7] The ensuing references in this verse to *rimmonim* and *gefanim* probably also refer to an orchard or arbor of pomegranates and vines, respectively. Recall that the *tappuaḥ* in 2:3 was among the "trees of the forest," hence also designating an apricot orchard.[8]

The image of going down and into a lush fruit garden is evocative. It recalls the garden tableaux in 4:12–5:1. The figure of a person descending to a garden recurs in ancient Near Eastern love lyrics, with explicit erotic innuendos.[9]

To see... To see The verb *lirʾot* ("to see") recalls *lirʿot ba-ganim*, "to browse in the gardens" (v. 2).[10] It occurs twice: the first time with respect to the buds generally, then with respect to growth specifically on vines and pomegranates. The examination of the buds is introduced by the preposition *be-*, to mark the direction of the vision. The beloved has gone to inspect the sprouts and flowers.

budding of the vale The expression *ʾibbei ha-naḥal* is literally "the buds of the wadi [or: brook]." The singular noun (**ʾeiv*, "bud") occurs in Job 8:12, where it indicates a time of growth and sprouting.[11] Similarly, the festival of Passover occurs "in the month of *ʾabhibh*" (Exod. 34:18; Deut. 16:1), the springtime of budding.[12] Cf. the agricultural notice in Exod. 9:31: *ki ha-seʿorah ʾabhibh*, "for the spelt was in bloom." In Aramaic, the noun *ʾaneibh* means "fruit" generically (Dan. 4:9).[13]

Tamakh connects the natural imagery to the emotional event. He observes that the spring is a time of passion and lovemaking, hence the youth goes down to the garden "to see" if the buds of spring have emerged, "because of his great yearning for her." Assyrian love lyrics likewise evocatively refer to garden fruits as "full of voluptuousness"; and, in particular, the word *inbu* ("fruit") indicates erotic appeal and sexuality.[14]

if... blossomed, If... in bloom These clauses are introduced by the interrogative *ha-* (before the verbal action), to mark the speculation. This prefix occurs explicitly in the first instance, but implicitly in the second ("to see *ha-fareḥah... heineitzu...*"). Its absence before the second verb is undoubtedly for phonetic reasons (*ha-heineitzu* being difficult to pronounce).

The imagery recalls 2:12–13, which reports buds (*nitzanim*) shooting up (v. 12) and vines beginning to blossom (*semadar*; v. 13). A similar expression occurs in Gen. 40:10; referring to his dream about a vine, Pharaoh's cupbearer states: *ve-hiʾ khe-foraḥat ʿaletah nitzah*, "It had barely budded" (literally, "and it was like a blossom [whose] bud had shot up").

Derash

11. I went down to the nut grove Earlier (v. 1), the nations asked Israel where her Beloved had turned, and she responded that "He has gone down to his garden"—to attend her prayers and study. Now the Beloved accounts for His own whereabouts,[15] changing the garden imagery to a nut grove, and the lilies to vines.

Why is Israel compared to a nut (*'egoz*) grove? Among the various answers, the theme of learning is foremost. Just as this nut, when pruned, regenerates with improved quality, so will those who prune their wealth and support "the laborers of Torah" receive divine beneficence in recompense. And just as the tree of this nut protects its fruit, so will the people who "hold fast to the words of Torah" (the tree of life) be sustained (SongsR 6.xi.1; PesiqR 11). Thus spiritual benefits accrue to those who study Torah and support its scholars.

Earlier, the "garden" symbolized religious study and worship; now "the vines" similarly refer to synagogues and study halls; and "the pomegranates" evoke children engaged in study, seated in rows "like the seeds of a pomegranate" (SongsR, ibid.). Such religious behavior draws God into worldly presence, for the Lord on High cares for the cultivation of Torah on earth. Indeed—according to another tradition—it is because of this learning that God sustains the world (B. Shab. 119a).

Remez

11. I went down to the nut grove Who speaks? Is it still the Beloved who has descended into the heart, to see if the "vines" of this garden "had blossomed"?[16] Or is it perhaps the self, turning inward to inspect its own spiritual growth (Immanuel)?[17] The transformation of the soul is perceived within and without; for true self-examination looks upon one's development with an outer eye. This process stimulates further desire for self-realization, and this emotion overwhelms the self (v. 12).

Sod

11. I went down to the nut grove Emboldened, the soul continues its pilgrimage. With a divine center to orient it, a new task is crucial: not to seek Divinity in the silent darkness, beyond language and concepts, but to descend to the core of things, beneath their external layers (Z. 1:19b). The spiritual task is to enter the multiple aspects of reality (like the quadrants of a nut) and integrate its parts—without destroying the husks that protect its inner qualities from harm (Z. 2:14b). This task requires finesse and courage, to penetrate the depths of one's heart into its hidden or repressed parts, and then to raise them toward higher purposes—without destroying their inherent vitality and value (ZḤ 17b). Can we do this? Can we descend to the mysterious font of life, to "see" the nature of its "budding" and "bloom"? This is an engaged attending and watching—but also a kind of peering from beyond, for there is no clear or certain vision of these primal truths for creatures of flesh and blood (ZḤ 9d).[18] And yet just this is the soul's daring task: to attempt to look past appearances and perhaps perceive things at their root.[19]

12 Before I knew it,
My desire set me
Mid the chariots of Ammi-nadib.

12 לֹ֣א יָדַ֔עְתִּי
נַפְשִׁ֣י שָׂמַ֔תְנִי
מַרְכְּב֖וֹת עַמִּי־נָדִֽיב׃

Peshat

12. *Before I knew it, / My desire set me* The phrasing of *lo' yada'ti nafshi samatni* is ambiguous. The present translation follows the Masoretic punctuation. It interprets the first clause as the youth's statement of bewilderment (but since *lo' yada'ti* simply means "I did not know," the adverb "before" was added to convey the lad's lack of awareness);[20] and it explains the second clause in terms of the emotional catalyst at work (*nafshi* conveys a sense of self and desire; cf. 1:7). That is, the beloved was suddenly overcome with desire (presumably at the sight or fancy of the maiden), and felt himself "set" (*samatni*, literally "[it] placed me") "mid [or: in] the chariots of Ammi-nadib."[21] What this means is unclear.

Another resolution seems necessary, since the clause *lo' yada'ti nafshi* occurs in Job 9:21 as an idiom meaning "I did not know myself" or "I was beside myself."[22] The words thus suggest a particular psychological state,[23] conveying a mood of emotional intensity. But this leaves the subsequent verb *samatni* without an explicit subject (i.e., "*x* set me"). One may therefore assume that the word *nafshi* does double-duty.[24] Read with the prior idiom, it marks the lad's distraught state (his loss of self); and read with the ensuing verb, it marks his emotional sense of being transported. The syntactic effect is striking. The poet has deftly formulated the beloved's remark to fuse his bewildered state (clause 1) with a feeling of being impelled by inner forces (clause 2). For though the emotional impulse certainly came from his own being (*nafshi*), it also felt like a force acting upon him (*samatni* marks this sense). The jagged and jarring syntax thus renders an altogether unsettling experience.

One is left to explain the sense of being "set" in a chariot. Given the youth's emotional turbulence, one may suppose that he sees the world in terms of his inner feelings; and thus any real chariot is transformed into a figural expression of his desires. Perhaps he still has in mind (and heart) the mare in the "chariots" of Pharaoh to which he had likened his lass (1:9). Looking outward through the eye of desire, he sees and senses a loveseat—an external image of his inner passions.[25] The chariot is thus an erotic euphemism,[26] revealing and concealing his feelings for the maiden.[27]

set me The syntax is clipped, without a preposition to mark the indirect object. The beloved just feels "put" there.

chariots This plural form of the noun, *markevot*, is arguably a poetic intensification, used to convey the youth's emotional ardor. It is hard to imagine a convoy of chariots on the scene. Moreover, the rendering "mid the chariots" softens the emotional experience of the youth "set" in this context.

Ammi-nadib Rendering the designation *'ammi(y) nadibh* as a proper name, as also the Septuagint and Targum. Alternatively, this is a phrase depicting a quality of the chariot in question. If so, it is presumably a stylistic inversion of the expression *nedibh 'am* (cf. *nedibhei ha-'am* in Num. 21:18),[28] and thus this chariot belongs to a "nobleman of the people" (the final *yod* in *'ammiy* being a frozen marker for the old genitive case ending).[29] Construed figuratively, it tells us that this chariot is elegant—finely tooled and appointed (like the palanquin of Solomon, 3:10).[30]

Derash

12. *Before I knew it* As the voice of Israel, this statement echoes her prior response to the nations (when she challenged their insinuation of divine abandonment; v. 1). Just as in Egypt, when mired in servitude, the people were the beneficiaries of divine grace—turning them into free persons "before" they "knew it"—so now *Keneset Yisra'el* tells the nations

that although she is presently in travail of exile, nevertheless, "before" she might even "know it," her Beloved God will come and rescue her (SongsR 6.xi.1; ShṬov 22).[31] Alternatively, although Israel presently "wanders" in "exile" (*nad galut*), in the future—thanks to God's grace—she will be awesome "as the bannered hosts" (*nidgalot*; 6:4, 10) (SongsR 6.x.1).

Moments of national and spiritual renewal may be anticipated in hope, and cultivated by religious practice; but the gift itself is a divine grace, which comes with transcendent suddenness. Human readiness is natural; the miracle of redemption is supernatural—something truly "other."

Ammi-nadib For the sages, *'ammi nadiv* is an epithet of divine grace, which will raise Israel to the heights—even to the "chariots" of God's heavenly realm. One sage reads the noun *'ammi* (my nation) adverbially, as *'immi* (with me)—that is, God went with me (*'immi*) graciously (*nadiv*), and thus "I" (Israel) was revived (SongsR, ibid., end).

Remez

12. ***Before I knew it*** It is surely the self that speaks here, overcome by renewed "desire" for self-realization. The force of this desire has put the self "amid the chariots of Ammi-nadib": through the "beneficent gift" (*nadiv*)[32] of one's spiritual Source, the "Giver" par excellence (Al-Fawwāl; Malbim)[33]—who works through the forms of one's cultural heritage. This dual dimension is called Ammi-nadib. The component *nadiv* underscores the unrequited "gift" coming from the Beloved; whereas the word *'ammi* emphasizes the emergence of spiritual truth through traditional (*'am* as "nation") and personal (*'ammi* as "my people") wisdom. The soul is both singular and aggregate (Ralbag): nurtured by generations of teachings and cultivated by the individual self. It is given "before" all knowing, waiting to be taken up and transformed. For spiritual truth to be active and present, the soul must be ready and receptive. There is no other way.[34]

Sod

12. ***Before I knew it*** Suddenly, the quest is transformed. As if without knowledge (beyond mind), our desiring "soul" (*nafshi*)[35] was "set" among God's "chariots"—Ammi-nadib, the "Gracious Divinity of my people."[36] The redemptive hope of the shining dawn (v. 10) seizes the soul and thrusts it beyond ordinary thought, into the realm of transcendent Divinity. These chariots are thus not only God's wings (the spiritual words and thoughts that 'transport' the self to higher planes of consciousness) but also the carriers of divine reality on earth (through the language and forms of culture). Our verse recalls a mystical moment, re-presented here in the language of our "people."[37] Hoping to see, we are blessed with insight; intending to act, we are acted upon—beyond all saying. We achieve wisdom though an ineffable whisper (Alkabetz). It happens in the mind's depths—*before I knew it*.

7 Turn back, turn back,
O maid of Shulem!
Turn back, turn back,
That we may gaze upon you.
"Why will you gaze at the Shulammite
In the Mahanaim dance?"

ז שׁ֤וּבִי שׁ֙וּבִי֙
הַשּׁ֣וּלַמִּ֔ית
שׁ֥וּבִי שׁ֖וּבִי
וְנֶחֱזֶה־בָּ֑ךְ
מַה־תֶּֽחֱזוּ֙ בַּשּׁ֣וּלַמִּ֔ית
כִּמְחֹלַ֖ת* הַֽמַּחֲנָֽיִם׃

v. 1. בנוסח אחר "במחלת"

Peshat

2. A CALL TO THE MAIDEN (7:1)

The maiden is suddenly addressed by a group of bystanders, who beseech her to "turn" about or back, so they can gaze upon her. The meaning of the verb is ambiguous, as is the speakers' motivation. Her response has a tone of indignation, treating their request as manifesting their desire to stare at a dancer.

7:1. Turn back, turn back The double command is repeated twice. The first appeal is augmented by a reference to her (as "the Shulammite"; see below); the second call adds their motivation ("that" or "so that" they may look at her). The fourfold imperative *shuvi* ("turn") expresses intensity. If the maiden is moving away (either having found the beloved or despairing his presence), the call beseeches her to "return" or "come back" so that they can enjoy her presence. If she is engaged in some dance movement (whirling in joy at her reengagement with the beloved), the call requests that she continue her movements, so enchanting is she to behold.

The rhetorical form "[TWO IMPERATIVES] + [PERSONAL NAME] // [(THE SAME) TWO IMPERATIVES] + [REQUESTED ACTION]" occurs also in Judg. 5:12, in the call to Deborah to arise and recite a song.[38]

O maid of Shulem! The speakers refer to her by the designation *ha-shulammit*, and she refers to herself similarly in the response. The meaning is uncertain. It may designate a place; she is "the one of Shulem" (Ibn Ezra). Given that an earlier name for Jerusalem was Shalem (Gen. 14:18; Ps. 76:3), it has been supposed that this may be the reference here (Ibn Ezra). Alternatively, the title designates a quality. If so, the formulation (a passive participle) is an epithet for her "perfected" beauty (Ibn Aqnin; Tamakh).[39] But it is unlikely that she would so designate herself—unless her response is ironic, mimicking the group's language.

Why will you gaze... / In the Mahanaim dance? The force of the query *mah teḥezu* is "why would you gaze?" (or "for what reason?"). It poses a rhetorical challenge to the group's request. Alternatively, it conveys the maiden's rebuttal: "how could you gaze at me *ki-mḥolat ha-maḥanayim*"? On this view, the maiden is responding to the gaze's character, which appears to look at her "*as* [one engaged in] the dance of Mahanaim." Given that *maḥanayim* is a dual, this designation may refer to a dance involving "two camps" or to "two sets" of dancers whirling around.[40]

In the... dance Apparently because of the elliptical formulation (*ki-mḥolat*, "as [one performing] a dance"; rather than a more straightforward *ke-meḥollelet*, "as one dancing"), our translators preferred a minority reading found in many manuscripts and editions, which differs by one similarly shaped letter: *be-* ("in"), rather than *ke-* ("as, like").[41] Thus she refers to the dance that she is engaged in—and that the audience wants to keep viewing. However, the Masoretic formulation offers a sharper edge to the girl's remark and provides a counterpoint to the ensuing similes expressed by her beloved.

Derash

7:1. Turn back, turn back The fourfold call to the Shulammite (Israel) evokes the challenge of the four "kingdoms" that ruled Israel in antiquity (Babylonia, Persia, Greece, and Rome). Subjected to each, the people were repeatedly induced to "turn back" from their ancestral ways and assimilate into the dominant culture. Ancient sages heard in this entreaty attempts of alien cultures to weaken Jews' religious resolve as a minority "in their midst" (GenR 66.2) or "under their dominion" (SongsR 7.i.1).[42] The proper countercheck is spiritual resistance, whose imperative was deemed encoded in Israel's name: *Shulammit* (The Whole One). Thus the people are exhorted to maintain their cultural integrity. Only in this way will they "enter" subjugation "in peace" *be-shalom* (whole) and likewise emerge with their identity intact.[43] Inscribed in Israel's identity, as it were, is the charge to resist threats to their heritage with "wholehearted" vigor.

maid of Shulem This is the Shulammite, *Keneset Yisra'el*. She is "perfectly" loyal to God (see above and Ibn Aqnin),[44] through her inherent resources and commitments. She is also the "nation" in whom God's "peace" (*shalom*) dwells,[45] who receives the divine blessing of "peace" (Num. 6:26);[46] and who will be restored to her homeland, a "habitat of peace" (*neveih shalom*; Isa. 32:18)[47] (SongsR, ibid.; Leqaḥ Ṭov). Theologically speaking, Israel's loyalty and divine care intertwine. The people first "made peace between herself and God" at Sinai, when they accepted a covenant commitment of a life infused with religious values. God reciprocally assures her value to Him through promises of sustenance and survival (physical and spiritual). (See SongsR, ibid.).[48]

That we may gaze The nations entreat the Shulammite (Israel) to join them, puzzled at how they remain loyally "devoted to Him" (*meshallemim lo*)—even to death (*mavet*) (SongsR 7.i.2). They thus ask her to explicate her name, *Shulammit*, now interpreted as her destiny: *meshullemet la-mitah*, "devoted to death" (on God's behalf)![49] Israel repeatedly resisted opportunistic allures threatening her survival—and proved ready to pay the supreme price. Such is the case here. The nations entice the people to assimilate via promises of material success—so that all will "gaze" (*ve-neḥezeh*) upon her. The enticement is to "turn" from loyalty to God and Tradition for the opportunity to become "the admiration of all" (*ḥezyateih de-'alma'*).

Why will you gaze *Shulammit*-Israel resists temptation. She answers the nations: "Wherefore (*mah*) would you" entice me with such blandishments?! She justifies her resistance with ancient precedents. Despite their trials, neither Abraham nor Isaac became disloyal, and Jacob was even greeted (after his trials with Laban) by "angelic troupes" (*maḥanayim*).[50] How, then, could such worldly promises prove enticing, or even be compared to "the Mahanaim dance"—God's own "dance" (*ḥulah*)—promised to the righteous "in the future" (SongsR, ibid.; ShṬov 48:14.5)?[51] Such a promised encirclement of divine love "transcends death" itself (Ps. 48:15; *'al mut*) and provides a shield of courage against despair. With this ancient promise in mind, "the maidens (*'alamot*)"—that is, Israel—continue to "love" God with a life-transcending love, even "unto death" (*'ad mavet*).[52] Bound to a transcendent vision and sustained by divine promises, Israel has remained loyal to God and religious values.

Remez

7:1. Turn back, turn back This twofold call reflects a tension. The soul can turn in two directions: it can continue its spiritual progress toward the Beloved; or it can turn back, having achieved a certain level of self-realization. It is now betwixt and between—and must choose. The experience of bliss amidst "the chariots of Ammi-nadib" marks a peak moment on the soul's journey (Ibn Tibbon),[53] even if there is need for further development (Immanuel; Malbim).[54] And so the seeker must now decide whether to build on its spiritual achievements and ascend to yet higher levels (Ralbag).[55] Perceiving the challenge in positive terms, the

soul hears itself addressed as the "maid of Shulem"—as one engaged in self-perfection (*sheleimut*), a soul mate of Solomon, the Perfect Beloved. From this perspective, the soul-in-progress feels confirmed. A higher Voice desires to "gaze upon" it.

But there is also ambivalence. Something human tugs at the soul to "turn back" to its earthly self—to integrate its perfections and return to the world. Should the soul be induced to continue its journey and be absorbed in its private perfections; or should it heed the call of the earth and try to actualize its enlightenment in society with other persons? Should the soul remain alone and flee to the Alone, in a self-focused spiritual quest; or should it join the work of the worldly community? The tension between contemplation and activism requires a decision. One ideal is solitude; the other, communal solidarity.

Why will you gaze The self is modest and uncertain, pondering the spectacle her presence makes. She wonders why others (the Beloved or humans) would wish to gaze upon her while she oscillates "in the Mahanaim dance" (moving between "two realms" of reality—the divine and the worldly—unresolved; Ibn Aqnin and Malbim).[56] Beset by humility and irresolution, she wonders why one would or should take notice. Her spiritual perplexity is fundamental, and she, like every seeker, must resolve it. The words of praise offers the self an external perspective as it tries to determine how to fulfill its destiny.

Sod

7:1. Turn back, turn back Spiritual life is not constant. Positive experiences of Divinity can suddenly give way to doubt—about personal worthiness or spiritual capacity (Alkabetz). These aspects are implied here: the soul seeking perfection (the "Shulammite") suddenly recoils and needs to be summoned anew. The fourfold imperative "turn back" (*shuvi*) is that summons: heard from without, as an external challenge; and also from within, as a personal exhortation. Feeling fragmented and unsure, the self must try to integrate all aspects of reality: the earthly and transcendent; and the physical and spiritual. Each of these (four) aspects requires specific attention, and one must "turn" to each and all as they present themselves—receiving what is given with a deliberate but "quiet composure" (*shuvah va-naḥat*; cf. Isa. 30:15) (Ibn Sahula).

That we may gaze The object of regard is indicated by an ambiguous preposition, *be-*, which yields either "upon you" or "within you." As for the "gaze," it indicates the process of self-examination. That is, all components of the self must undergo scrutiny. Given the bivalent preposition, the focus is twofold: we must attend to our character's external expressions (looking "upon" the self and the way it realizes its purposes); and we must also examine the internal aspects of our being (looking "within" ourselves and our spiritual formation).

Why will you gaze The soul hears this challenge and feels compromised. Turning inward, the query *mah* poses the issue: "why" should the self believe itself capable of the task, since life is filled with a swirl of situations that spin about "like a dance"? And "how" could one ever find a balance point between one's internal being and the external challenges of existence? (Those are the "two camps" of reality, as signified by "Mahanaim"; see Peshat.)

2 מַה־יָּפוּ פְעָמַיִךְ בַּנְּעָלִים
בַּת־נָדִיב
חַמּוּקֵי יְרֵכַיִךְ כְּמוֹ חֲלָאִים
מַעֲשֵׂה יְדֵי אָמָּן׃

2 How lovely are your feet in sandals,
O daughter of nobles!
Your rounded thighs are like jewels,
The work of a master's hand.

Peshat

3. DESCRIPTION AND DESIRE (vv. 2–10a)

This unit is composed of two parts. The first (vv. 2–6) opens with an exclamation of beauty (*mah yafu*, "how lovely"), initially lauding the maiden's feet in sandals, and then proceeding upward to the thighs, navel, belly, breasts, neck, eyes, nose, and head. This sequence follows the male gaze of delight, from the shape of her foot to the flow of her hair—"from below to above" (Rashbam).[57] After the initial reference, each of the remaining features is complemented by a characterization. The eye beholds the maiden's body, with supplemental topics and sights found in nature. This ocular aspect dominates; no sense of smell or touch is mentioned.

Struck by her robust beauty, the speaker complements his initial praises in the second part of his discourse (vv. 7–10a). He begins with an ecstatic proclamation of the joy of love and the loved one (*mah yafit u-mah na'amt 'ahavah ba-ta'anugim*; "How lovely and fair you are, O love, among the pleasures!"). Enraptured by his own depiction, he speaks of her in heightened terms. Now likening her body to a palm tree and her breasts to (fruit) clusters, he expresses his desire to mount that tree, hold the clusters, and imbibe her intoxicating aroma. Hearing this, the maiden is reciprocally enthused and continues his expressions of passion (v. 10b, see below).

There is a poignant progression to the speeches. The maiden has just tartly retorted the group's request with her query (*mah teḥezu* . . . ; v. 1). The negative character of this gaze is initially countered by the beloved's evocation of her visible beauty: *mah yafu* ("how lovely!") in verse 2, and later by his enunciation *mah yafit u-mah na'amt 'ahavah* in verse 7. The maiden responds to the different quality of these expressions and reacts in kind. Her tart response to the group is transformed by the lad's exclamations of love—and she answers with passion.

*2. **your feet*** The praise begins with her feet (*pe'amayikh*), possibly in response to the preceding dance allusion. The term primarily evokes movement (the Septuagint translates it as "your steps"); it may also evoke sound (cf. Judg. 5:28, *pa'amei markevotav*, "the clatter of his chariot steeds").[58]

O daughter of nobles! The designation *bat nadiv* echoes the reference to *'ammi nadiv* in 6:12, reinforcing the speculation that the poet used the chariot there euphemistically to evoke and express his feeling for the maiden. In context, the present evocation seems more than a heightened epithet. In the verbal echoes we hear tones of desire.

rounded The speaker begins with reference to the circular turn or turning point (Ibn Ezra) of the thighs. The adjective *ḥamuq* is unique to this passage.

like jewels The comparison to *ḥala'im* ("jewels") may be due to their rounded shape (cf. Prov. 25:12), or because her thighs seem well formed and finely tooled. The beloved's eye imagines more than it can see. His depictions (here and subsequently) characterize a double gaze: her outward appearance, and his imagination of her body within the folds of her garments.

Derash

*2. **How lovely are your feet*** In response to Israel's retort—*mah* ("wherefore?")—to the nations, God begins His praise with the very word that marked her speech, *mah* ("how?"), while lauding her beauty in religious and cultural terms. If the nations appeal to the Shulammite to turn, that they might gaze "upon" her, the Beloved now casts His eye over her form

and celebrates her embodied virtues. The catalogue of features is a celebration of the *mitzvot*.

The praise begins with the Shulammite's feet (*pe'amayikh*). This is no mere physical reference, says R. Yudan (SongsR 7.ii.1), but an allusion to Israel's ascension to Jerusalem on the three annual pilgrimage festivals (called *regalim*, "feet," in Exod. 23:14, but *pe'amim* in 34:24 and Deut. 16:16).[59] The cycle of seasons is earthbound; it displays divine sustenance through the fruits of the land. Correspondingly, the celebrants walk on foot to the Temple, conscious of the divine gifts they shall acknowledge. Feet thus mark one's connection to the earth, and the divine beneficence received there. Other mitzvot highlight other limbs. Rituals thus embody tradition, and tradition raises the natural body to a spiritual state.

in sandals This reference to sandals (*ne'alim*) alludes to the virtue of the pilgrims, which was said to "protect [or: guard] them" (*no'alam*) against difficulties that might occur to their persons or their homes while on the journey (a concern first addressed in Exod. 34:24, and developed in B. Pes. 8b and YalSh, *'Eikev*, #875; cf. SongsR, ibid.). The feet of the pilgrims thus provide protective merit for those who undertake this commandment.[60]

daughter of nobles Israel is the daughter of the "noble [or: devoted] one" (*nadiv*), namely Abraham; "as Scripture says, 'The nation of devotees (*nedivei 'ammim*) gathered' (Ps. 47:10)—[these being] the nation of the God of Abraham" (SongsR 7.ii.3). And why is he so designated? Because he was the first to devote himself to God, his Creator (see Rabbi Shlomoh at B. Suk. 49a); the first to devote his body to God, when he circumcised himself (Gen. 17:24); and the first to ascend Mount Moriah (Gen. 22:2; later called Jerusalem [2 Chron. 3:1]) and offer a sacrifice to God, where his descendants now ascend with their own offerings (Maharsha on B. Suk., ibid.). The merits of the pilgrims thus derive from Abraham. Like him, they are devoted to God and offer spiritual and material gifts. (The merit of circumcision is considered separately, below.)

Your rounded thighs According to R. Yoḥanan, "all" sacrificial "purification" and divine "beneficence" come to Israel "by merit of the circumcision between their thighs." Indeed, their thighs are "like jewels" (*kemo ḥala'im*) of religious devotion on account of "so many illnesses" (*kammah ḥalayim*) that have been endured in fulfillment of this mitzvah (SongsR, ibid.)—in spiritual devotion to the "Artisan" (*'amman*) of the universe.[61]

The movement from feet to circumcision shifts the focus from devotion to God in space and ritual time (pilgrimage), to a physical act that ensures spiritual continuity. The first rite focuses on the Temple, a locus of communal celebration; the second on the sanctuary of the body, a sphere of personal commitment. Whereas pilgrimage festivals express gratitude for natural sustenance, circumcision signifies allegiance to generations past and one's spiritual heritage.

Remez

2. *How lovely are your feet* The gaze moves upward in its praise, beginning with the feet—symbolic of the spiritual pilgrimage of the soul (Malbim).[62] Indicative of this movement toward transcendence, the seeker is called a "daughter of nobles" (*nadiv*), this being an allusion to the just-mentioned conjunction of the human soul with its Beloved ideal, designated Ammi-nadib (6:12; cf. Immanuel).[63] Both her personal name (*Shulamit*) and epithet (*nadiv*) suggest this transformation, being hints of her appropriation of the qualities of *Shelomoh* (Solomon) and *Ammi-nadiv*.[64] She is on the path of perfection (*sheleimut*) by cultivating the gracious gift (*nedavah*) of Heaven. The names suggest that the human quest is an *imitatio dei*. As the self attains its spiritual potential (perfection), it becomes an earthly image (or recipient) of the divine ideal. Is this a hint of the sought-for resolution?

Your rounded thighs From the readily visible feet, the gaze shifts toward more hidden features. First mentioned are the thighs, perceived as "the work of a master's hand." The spiritual self is thus deemed to be finely tooled—gemlike within (though palpable to ex-

ternal sight). Like a jewel, the developed soul crystallizes our earthly nature.

Sod

2. ***How lovely are your feet*** From somewhere a voice gives assurance, by specifying those qualities that the self has already perfected. The body is a prism for this praise. Moving in ascending order, the initial praise is for the feet (*pe'amayikh*), which ground the self in all the "occasions" (*pe'amim*) of life—secular and sacred (Exod. 23:17). Feet provide a "foundation" in this world for the self, as it seeks to cultivate a spiritual discipline aimed at transcendent truths (Z. 3:180a).

Your rounded thighs The "hidden" turns of the thigh (cf. Peshat) intimate the realization that the clarity of things is often concealed. The spiritual task is to bring such matters to light (Z. 1:42a), and to hold them in mind as two aspects of one reality (Z. 1:45a; 2:247a). Praise of the Shulammite indicates that this achievement (crafted with artful precision, as if by "a master's hand") is a visible expression of her spiritual being.

3 Your navel is like a round goblet—
Let mixed wine not be lacking!—
Your belly like a heap of wheat
Hedged about with lilies.

3 שָׁרְרֵךְ֙ אַגַּ֣ן הַסַּ֔הַר
אַל־יֶחְסַ֖ר הַמָּ֑זֶג
בִּטְנֵךְ֙ עֲרֵמַ֣ת חִטִּ֔ים
סוּגָ֖ה בַּשּׁוֹשַׁנִּֽים׃

Peshat

3. The image of a mound of wheat set in a lily field is a sensual figure of femininity; the figure of a bowl of flowing liquid is a suggestive allusion to male fertility.

Your navel . . . Your belly This twofold depiction focuses on the same region of the body—the moon-shaped indentation on her belly, which appears to his eye as a protruding mound. The comparative particle is absent in this case, which presumably relies upon the one used in the previous verse (thus: "your navel/belly *is like*"). Alternatively, the images are metaphors ("your navel/belly *is*"), which has a more evocative effect.

round goblet That is, a "fully rounded [or: moonlike] bowl" (*'agan ha-sahar*). The first term refers to a bowl of some type (cf. Exod. 24:6; bowls inscribed with the word *'gn* have been unearthed at Palmyra and Petra).[65] The word *sahar* is unique to this passage, although *sihara'* is a common Aramaic word for "moon."

Let mixed wine not be lacking Alternatively: "may its libation-flow never cease." The unique noun *mezeg* (common in mishnaic Hebrew) may be a dialectal variant of *mesekh* (Ps. 75:9).[66]

like a heap of wheat Or "pile of wheat." Rashbam also adduces the suggestive angle of the woman's belly.

hedged about with lilies The passive participle *sugah* is another unique word. It may be a dialectical variant of the verb *sagah*, "to grow," found in Ps. 92:13; cf. the reduplicated form *sagseg*, "to sprout," in Isa. 17:11.

Derash

*3. **Your navel*** As the conduit of intergenerational sustenance (parent for child), this body part symbolizes ongoing responsibility (present and future). Ensuring justice is a major expression of cultural responsibility. Hence the sages link the expression "your navel" (*shorereikh*) to the Sanhedrin, whose court sustains the nation like an umbilical cord (SongsR 7.iii.1), providing the people with proper guidance and rule (*serarah*).

As a judicial forum, the seats of the Sanhedrin are arranged "like a rounded goblet" (*'agan ha-sahar*, literally a "moon-shaped threshing floor")—crescent-shaped "so that the members might view one another" during their deliberations; B. Sanh. 36b). Punning on a dialectical variant of Aramaic *sihara* (moon), *zihara*, some interpreters explained the *'agan ha-sahar* as an *'idra' de-'azhara'*, "place of warning"[67]—since it was from this center that witnesses were adjured and that judicial counsel "gave light" (a pun on Hebrew *zohar*) to the nation.[68] Israel is thus guided from the core of its body politic—the cord of nurture being the lifeblood of both justice and the values of *halakhah* that flow from this matrix.

Let mixed wine not be lacking Continuing the judicial theme, this clause exhorts the people to ensure that a Sanhedrin "never lack" (*lo' yeḥsar*) a composite (*mezeg*, "mixture") of twenty-three judges, with experts to lead them (B. Sanh. 86b–88a) and judiciously deliberate matters from the mixture of details and opinions at hand (SongsR, ibid.). From a personal perspective, this phrase points to more transcendent considerations: it alludes to the theological assertion that "The LORD is my shepherd, I lack nothing (*lo' 'eḥsar*)" (Ps. 23:1)—the

LORD being ***mizga' de-'alma'***, "Provider of the Universe" (SongsR, ibid.; PesiqR 10).[69]

Thus God praises the people Israel for their courts, exhorting that they be maintained in perpetuity. They are also admonished to focus on the divine source of their Good—physical, cultural, and spiritual. As a theological assertion, our clause is both a promise ("God, the Provider, will not be lacking") and an exhortation ("Let God, the World-Giver, not be lacking"—as you make legal decisions). Readers of this passage thus receive counsel to look to their body politic and determine whether it serves God and spiritual ends, or is only a means to social privilege and power.

Your belly The theme of legal decision continues with notes of caution and restraint. Just as Leviticus is the middle book of the Pentateuch, and just as it is filled like "heaps of wheat" (*ḥiṭṭim*) with laws concerning "sin offerings (*haṭṭa'ot*) and guilt offerings," so Israel's midsection is also compared to a heap of wheat. That is, concerns for religious purity are central to its ritual life (Tan., *Ki Tissa'* 2).[70] Interpreting these matters is thus of major importance. Just as a field of wheat is "hedged (*sugah*) about with lilies (*shoshanim*)," so is Israel circumscribed by "the words of Torah"—which protects her from sin (SongsR 7.iii.1) and provides a legal "hedge" (*siyyag*), through the teachings of those "who study" (*she-shonim*)[71] and apply its words in the traditional manner.[72] "Have you ever heard of a person who hedges his field with lilies [rather than with] thorns and thistles?" (PesiqR 10, 35b–36a). But such is the virtue of Israel. For though the words of Torah are pliable and can be trampled like lilies, they nevertheless provide Israel with hedges (protective formulations) in their quest for a life of piety and spiritual excellence.

Remez

3. ***Your navel*** Like this feature imagined beneath her garment's folds, the self is full and replete within, while evoking the gift of satiation and inner balance ("mixed wine") without. This is the soul's dual maturation, marked by an inner sustenance (received from higher sources) and an outer bounty (perceived by others). Comparable to the fruit of the vine, the developed soul is the cultivation of one's nature.

Your belly The perfected self seems bountiful, stacked with the grain of life—ready for further processing and sustenance. Comparable to the fruit of the earth (wheat), the developed soul is an offshoot of one's higher potential,[73] which can sustain the self and others in turn.

lilies A repeated emblem of the self.

Sod

3. ***Your navel*** The focus turns to the umbilical core of the self—bearing the sign of birth and physical origins, but symbolizing one's spiritual axis as well. As a physical and spiritual balance point, the navel is the bodily place to speak of harmonies—hence the blessing that "*mixed* wine not be lacking." The self is challenged to face the multiple aspects of reality (Z. 2:251a), and to link human knowledge to an encompassing Divine Wisdom (Ibn Sahula). The Jewish self is further challenged to integrate this cosmic wisdom with the truth of Torah, so that it may flow through the self (and its tasks) into the world (AhavD 189b). Encircling oneself with Torah wisdom is symbolized here by the image of surrounding oneself "with lilies," a spiritual "nourishment" of true life (ZḤ 87b).

4 Your breasts are like two fawns,
Twins of a gazelle.

4 שְׁנֵי שָׁדַיִךְ כִּשְׁנֵי עֳפָרִים
תָּאֳמֵי צְבִיָּה׃

Peshat

4. *Your breasts* Literally, "your two paired breasts."

like two fawns This figure repeats the one in 4:5 (the earlier formulation depicting the fawns as "browsing among the lilies"). This is again a sensuous image, evoking shapely movements. As with the belly and navel, the figures are male fantasies of the female body beneath her clothes.

Derash

4. *Your breasts* The praise of Israel's devotion to study culminates with this image of two breasts, symbolizing the dual Torah (written and oral) and its bounty of legal and spiritual gifts that nurture the people. On the human plane, the pair is exemplified by Moses and Aaron—teachers of law and ritual, and guardians of the civic and sacral spheres of religious life. The two are conjoined. Similarly, Scripture and Tradition are dual sources of sustenance that may not be separated. This is a fundamental axiom of Judaism. For this imagery, see Song 4:5.

Remez

4. *Your breasts* Suggesting the soul-self entire. The self has become both graceful and nubile, filled with the milk of life by which others may be sustained. Comparable to fawns, the developed soul is nurtured by higher powers—even as it is gently at home in nature.

Sod

4. *Your breasts* The breasts symbolize an integration of the emotions: a coordination (or balancing) of judgment and mercy, firmness and flexibility, and impulse and restraint in one's heart. This virtue is formulated as a twinning of forms. Breasts also evoke the sustenance that we may provide others, a nurture drawn from higher truths. Like the two tablets of Torah (Exod. 24:12; 34:29), such dual wisdom embodies divine truth in worldly forms (cf. TiqZ 14a), sustaining the self at its core (AhavD 190a).

5 Your neck is like a tower of ivory,
Your eyes like pools in Heshbon
By the gate of Bath-rabbim,
Your nose like the Lebanon tower
That faces toward Damascus.

5 צַוָּארֵךְ כְּמִגְדַּל הַשֵּׁן
עֵינַיִךְ בְּרֵכוֹת בְּחֶשְׁבּוֹן
עַל־שַׁעַר בַּת־רַבִּים
אַפֵּךְ כְּמִגְדַּל הַלְּבָנוֹן
צוֹפֶה פְּנֵי דַמָּשֶׂק׃

Peshat

5. Your neck is like a tower of ivory This figure evokes vertical stateliness and smooth whiteness (cf. 4:4).

Your eyes like pools This figure denotes a watery and shimmering quality, reminiscent of the girl's depiction of his eyes as doves—"by watercourses . . . Set by a brimming pool" (5:12).

Heshbon A town east of the Jordan River; see Josh. 13:15–28.

Bath-rabbim Mentioned only in this passage.

Lebanon tower Another architectural evocation. The youth surely intends a structure of exquisite prominence, Rashi's famous puzzlement [anent this simile] notwithstanding.

Derash

5. Your neck is . . . ivory This figure invites reflections on Jewish resistance to the "other," via a midrashic tradition (GenR 78.9) on the reunion of Jacob and Esau (Genesis 33). In that account, Esau "fell upon" Israel's "neck" and "kissed him" (*va-yishaqeihu*, v. 4); but the midrash says: rather, *va-yishakheihu*—he "bit him."[74] By rabbinic times, Esau had become an epithet for Rome and Christianity, and thus a symbol of political and religious dominance.[75] To protect against threats to their heritage, Jews had to develop modes of resistance. Thus SongsR 7.iv.1 transforms Israel's "neck" into "ivory." Jews needed external toughness to sustain a commitment to Torah in a hostile world, characterized by physical aggression (against its body) and cultural assault (against its soul).

Your eyes like pools in Heshbon As earlier, "eyes" are praised as a key bodily feature, a symbol for the orientation and direction of the community (especially through its legal institutions; see at 4:1). Thus scholars and judges deliberate (*meḥashevin*) legal topics as murky as dark pools (YalSh, Song, #992) and determine acquittal or guilt based on the majority number (*ḥushban*; Hebrew, *ḥeshbon*; B. Sanh. 40a). In daily life, the virtue of deliberation reckons (*meḥashevin*) the proper performance of the commandments (Leqaḥ Ṭov).

Sobriety of judgment is a core value. Whereas Scripture stressed only that "One must not incline [favorably] to the mighty (*rabbim*)" in judgment (Exod. 23:2), the sages reinterpreted it to mean that verdicts could be rendered only by "majority" (*rabbim*) decision (MdRI, *Mishpaṭim* 2).[76] This rule guided the Sanhedrin as well, and through it the *halakhah* and other decisions went forth from "the gate of Bath-rabbim"—the central "gate" of judgment (of the Sanhedrin), the judicial "seat" (*beiyt*) of the nation,[77] to the "populace" (*rabbim*)[78] at large (SongsR 7.iv.2). Justice by a majority (*rabbim*) for the multitude (*rabbim*) beyond its gates was the ideal, produced by clear-minded and morally fair deliberation. Religious love is thus expressed also through judicial care and due process for all.

Your nose The nose's prominence on the head is like the Temple at the apex of sacred space (SongsR, ibid.). The latter is "like the Lebanon tower," both for its spiritual preeminence and as a site for ritual purification. In "Lebanon" (*levanon*), sin could be "rendered pure" (*malbin*, "made white"; LevR 1.2; SifDeut, *Devarim* 6),[79] through repentance and sacrificial devotion of the self. The tower of Lebanon thus evokes the restoration of one's human stature.

The people Israel are thus depicted as faithful and pure from feet to face, as they move toward the Sacred Site (*Levanon*, the Place of

Purity), guided by reason and insight of the heart (*levavot*).[80] Through devotion, the sphere of the sacred—the "tower" that "faces... Damascus"—may cast its spiritual light farther afield, granting all exiles a place of "rest" (Ps. 132:14; Zech. 9:1).[81] At such a time, the site where God always has His eyes and heart focused (1 Kings 9:3) will radiate this gracious gaze; and the hearts and eyes of all will be infused by the godly light of beneficent love.[82]

Remez

5. ***Your neck*** Moving beyond the obscuring folds of the garment, the body's features become visible from the neck up. This landscape of upper features is dominated by cultural constructions. And rightly so, for the self is both its raw (inherent) nature and its achieved (spiritual) qualities. The face of the self appears as the manifestation of inner virtues. It is a shining spectacle from without, because it has been cultivated from within (Malbim).[83] This is the double realm mentioned in verse 1—a holy conjunction of spiritual and worldly perfections.

Sod

5. ***Your neck*** As the legs are foundations for the torso, the neck is foundation for the head—the locus of perception and conception. The neck anchors the twists of perspective and the height of one's gaze. Firmness of the neck also symbolizes sturdiness of bearing and rectitude.

Your eyes Atop the neck, eyes look out toward the world. Here, the eyes are compared to "pools in Heshbon"—reflecting orbs that "evaluate" the reality at hand, for "Heshbon" underscores the importance of our making a "reckoning" (*ḥeshbon*) of our actions and their impact (B. B.B. 78b).[84] Thereby we will be attentive to life's details and live with heightened awareness.[85] Correspondingly, "Bath-Rabbim" suggests the "multiplicity" (*rabbim*) of elements that confronts the self at every moment. The reckonings that we make within this swirl affect our spiritual character and virtue.

6 The head upon you is like crimson wool,
The locks of your head are like purple—
A king is held captive in the tresses.

6 רֹאשֵׁךְ עָלַיִךְ כַּכַּרְמֶל
וְדַלַּת רֹאשֵׁךְ כָּאַרְגָּמָן
מֶלֶךְ אָסוּר בָּרְהָטִים׃

Peshat

6. The head upon you... The locks of your head Both images refer to the hair, though this is only specified in the second phrase. The sequence of presentation is thus progressive; hence the present rendition of the initial phrase, *ro'sheikh 'alayikh*, is overly literal.

like crimson wool Following the prior toponyms, one might suppose that the depiction of the head hair "as *karmel*" alludes to Mount Carmel or to that region. But this designation must be qualified. Since the parallel phrase refers to "purple" or "scarlet locks," there is little doubt that the color crimson (*karmil*) is also intended (cf. 2 Chron. 2:6, 13; 3:14; Ibn Janaḥ; Ibn Ezra; Transl.). The poet has thus produced a striking double entendre.

locks The unique word *dallah* implies strands hanging down like the threads or thrum of a loom (cf. Isa. 38:12). This style or feature was presumably evocative. (Thus in Judges 16, there may be more to the Philistine name Delilah than the modern eye tends to perceive.)

king is held captive in the tresses By their captivating beauty. Her hair has a royal charm by which he (her king) is "bound" (*'asur*)—her colorful and abundant hair have put him in thrall.

tresses Indicating the "flowing" character of the hair. The rare noun *rehaṭim* evokes water running in troughs, as in Gen. 30:38. The noun is likely related to the Aramaic verb *r-w-t* (or *r-h-t*), "run," a dialectal variant of Hebrew *r-w-tz*; Aramaic *rahṭa'* refers to a "stream."[86] This term also evokes the "rafters" or "runners" of a building (*rahiṭeinu* refers to "beams" in 1:17)—and thus figuratively denotes that the youth feels bound in the clasps that run through her hair and lock it in place (Rashbam).

The shift from direct speech ("your hair") to an indirect reference ("a king") is abrupt, and the disjunction may be due to an ancient misreading. Following the two preceding pronoun suffixes (*ro'sheikh 'alayikh*; "your hair upon you"), it is possible that the consonants *m-l-kh* do not mark *melekh* ("a king") but *malakh*, "your (flowing) hair." Ben Yehudah suggested this construction;[87] and Reich identified the Akkadian cognate (*malû*).[88] The result would be a triad of terms referring to the hair of the maiden's head, with the final one referring to its being bound in a clasp.

Stylistics. The diverse figures for the lass utilize similes and metaphors. There are two patterns.

1. "your *x* is like (*kemo/ke-*) *y* + DESCRIPTIVE COMPLEMENT" (vv. 2b, 4, 5c)
   "your *x* is like *y*" without the descriptive complement (vv. 5a, 6a)
2. "your *x* is *y* + DESCRIPTIVE COMPLEMENT" (vv. 3a/b, 5b)

These variations, sometimes found in successive verses (vv. 2b–3) and sometimes in the same verse (v. 5), give the presentation of beauty arresting vitality and alternating rhythms.

Derash

6. The head upon you The praise extends to the "head" (*ro'sh*), compared first to "crimson wool" (*karmel*); then "the locks of your head" (*dallat ro'sheikh*) are likened to "purple."[89] This color conveys royalty,[90] so that the "tresses" are like a diadem in the sight of the male—the "king... held captive" by them. This figure depicts queenly beauty, refracted by the enthrallments of love. Furthermore, surely *ro'sh* and *dallah* evoke the similar-sounding words *rash* (also spelled *ra'sh* in 2 Sam. 12:1, 4) and *dal*, both of which connote "poor" or "indigent" persons.[91] Thus although the people be poor (in merit), they are regarded by God as Elijah on Mount Carmel (*karmel*), who successfully pleaded for divine mercy (1 Kings 18:37);[92] and though they be destitute (in means) they are deemed "precious as David" (Zech. 12:8),[93] who

wore the cloak of royalty (SongsR 7.vi.1; cf. LevR 31.4).[94]

In short, God is willing to overlook Israel's spiritual and physical impoverishment, while evoking memories of her meritorious ancestors. Such a re-vision asserts a new theological element: God's present and ongoing commitment to Israel. It transforms descriptive praise into a homily of consolation.

A king . . . held captive This refers to God, the King of kings, "bound" (*'asur*) to Israel's *rehaṭim*. Divine commitment to Israel (see previous phrase) even leads to the king's "enchantment" (*'asur* as "spellbound") with the woman's "tresses" (*rehaṭim*; the "flowing waves" of her hair; see Peshat).[95] This figure is interpreted to indicate God's "oath" (cf. *'asar* in Num. 30:3) to cause His presence (*Shekhinah*) to dwell among the "runners [or rafters]" (*rahiṭim*) of the Temple[96]—because of the merit of Abraham, who "ran" (*va-yarotz*) to greet strangers and provide them with food (Gen. 18:2, 7). (In the Targum, this verb is rendered *rehaṭ*; cf. SongsR and LevR, ibid.)[97] Interpersonal merits thus have intergenerational consequences.

Remez

6. The locks of your head The phrase *dallat ro'sheikh* alludes to the spiritual poverty (*dallut*) achieved by the soul, through which one may attach oneself to God (the Source; Head; *ro'sheikh*) (Sefas Emes).[98]

A king is held captive in the tresses The hair enchants its beholders.[99] The noble soul is like a Beloved king's beautiful consort. It draws others toward it and binds them in the weft of its being. The radiant soul evokes every ecstasy of love (vv. 7–10a).

Sod

6. The head The head's height symbolizes the supernal heights (*reiysha' 'ila'ah*) upon which the seeker is focused (Z. 1:13b). All the preceding virtues depend upon this direction of attention and the resulting influences that may flow to the self from on High. The corresponding reference to "the locks of your head" (*dallat ro'sheikh*) indicates the human head—seat of consciousness, which is spiritually "poor" (*dallah*) in relation to its munificent divine source. These two poles (Divine and human) are symbolized by the pair of phylacteries: the one put on the head symbolizes the supernal Divine, whereas that put on the arm symbolizes human receptivity (Z. 1:14a). The spiritual task is to join them mentally (one's mind to a higher reality), even as they are doubly fixed on one's body.

A king is held captive The ways that God is imagined (or spiritual consciousness cultivated) affect one's religious life. Thoughts of God, King of the Universe, are thus "held captive" by a person's "flow of mind" (*rehiṭei moḥin*) or thoughts.[100] Theological capacity is thus affected by the modes of thinking and conceptualization employed—be they exalted or trivial, crude or refined (TiqZ 6; Maggid, #1, 11–12).[101] Given human limitations, traditional teachings may even occasionally help break the barrier of immaturity or pettiness, opening the mind to greater possibilities.

7 How fair you are, how beautiful!
O Love, with all its rapture!

7 מַה־יָּפִית וּמַה־נָּעַמְתְּ
אַהֲבָה בַּתַּעֲנוּגִים׃

Peshat

7. ***How fair you are . . . O Love*** The youth is ecstatic. The evocation *mah yafit u-mah na'amt* is directed to *'ahavah*. The latter is a vocative addressed to the girl, first and foremost, since she is the focus of his praises and the source of his joy. This is how the Septuagint understood the passage. The present translation prefers the possibility that Love personified is (also)[102] invoked (Ibn Aqnin), thus echoing the maiden's repeated references to it (2:7; 3:5; 5:8).

with all its rapture Ibn Ezra seems to have construed *ba-ta'anugim* to indicate that love is the greatest earthly delight: "The soul has no greater pleasure (*ta'anug*) in the world, nor anything so fair and lovely, as [erotic] desire (*ḥeisheq*)."[103] This reads the prefixed preposition *ba-* as indicating something superlative within a class (as in "fairest of women," 1:8; 5:9; 6:1). The lass similarly referred to her Beloved's exemplary nature, saying that he was unique *ba-*, "among," the forest's trees (2:3).[104]

Derash

7. ***How fair are you*** The twofold expression of physical loveliness—"fair" and "beautiful"—evokes doubled forms of cultural praise (for performance of the mitzvot), similar to that in 4:1 (SongsR 7.vii.1). Here, too, the nation's external (physical) features are transformed by their religious deeds and spiritual comportment. Beauty is soul-deep.

O love, with all its rapture God expresses joy while praising Abraham (a personified aspect of Israel) for his consummate "love" of God—because of which he foreswore recompense from the King of Sodom after his military victory (Gen. 14:22–23).[105] Thus *ba-ta'anugim* refers both to the reason for Abraham's act ("his spiritual bliss" in God alone) and to its effect (he "relinquished" any material recompense).[106] He exemplified spiritual virtue and cleaving to God—not to worldly pleasure or gain (Ibn Yaḥye).

Remez

7. ***How fair you are*** An exultation of pure delight. It extends to the supreme object of all praise: *'ahavah ba-ta'anugim* ("Love, with all its rapture").[107] The self (soul), its ideal (Beloved), and the quality of longing (desire) are conjoined in the expression "Love" (loved one, Beloved, love quality). This entwinement transports all those who are transfixed by its power (Anatolo).[108] Love reveals love. Love of the Beloved emanates its qualities through the seeking self—outward to the world. Love is a rapturous wonder, in all its forms.

Sod

7. ***How fair you are*** The praise begun in verse 1, with reference to the beauty of one's movements (*mah yafu phe'amayikh*, "how beautiful are your feet"), continues with a celebration of total loveliness (*mah yafit*). The developed human qualities are validated and praised as most beautiful (Ibn Sahula). The sequence of terms even suggests a hierarchy. The initial level includes a spatial or physical beauty (*yafit*); a higher level includes mental or intellectual beauty (*na'amt*); and even higher is the state of transcendent rapture (*'ahavah ba-ta'anugim*)—whereby the Love of God, infixed in consciousness, emanates a sublime vision toward the world (Alkabetz).

8 Your stately form is like the palm,
Your breasts are like clusters.

8 זֹ֤את קוֹמָתֵךְ֙ דָּֽמְתָ֣ה לְתָמָ֔ר
וְשָׁדַ֖יִךְ לְאַשְׁכֹּלֽוֹת׃

Peshat

8. Having just depicted her figure part by part, the youth makes a comprehensive statement: the whole of it deserves praise. In so doing, he adds a new comparison. The figure is graphic and bold, even among the Song's suggestive imagery.

Your stately form The demonstrative pronoun *zo't* has an emphatic and deictic force (i.e., "this here—your bodily form!").

is like Once again, the lad uses the verb of comparison, *dametah* (see 1:9).

palm A tree of stature.

clusters Of fruit.

Derash

8. ***Your stately form*** Here, *qomah* ("form") emphasizes height, eminence, and stature. In the prior passage, Israel's physical beauty was reinterpreted in spiritual and cultural terms (vv. 2–7). Now the image is botanic, and she is compared (*dametah*) to a "palm" tree (*tamar*).[109] And just as that tree is upright and resistant to natural forces, so does the people Israel maintain its integrity (upright ways) and resist assaults on its spiritual welfare, namely false worship (idolatry) and venality (harlotry). The ancestress Tamar is exemplary—both in her own right, having overcome the accusations of harlotry by Judah (Gen. 38:24), and as a forebear of the martyrs who resisted idolatry in the time of Nebuchadnezzar (Daniel 3).[110] "Just as Tamar was sentenced to death by fire, but not burnt [by virtue of acquittal; cf. Gen. 38:26], so were these martyrs condemned to fire but not burnt [by grace of a miracle; Dan. 3:27]."[111] This history of righteousness is singled out and lauded in SongsR 7.viii.1. Through a striking interpretation of the *tamar* tree, the martyrs of Israel are personifications of Tamar, a person of upright and determined character.[112]

Remez

8. ***Your stately form*** After the public proclamation, a more personal voice ensues—one that views the inner self from without. This voice is perhaps a renewal of a dialogue between the soul (within) and its highest element (the Beloved, beyond). If the Beloved had earlier "likened (*dimmitikh*)" the seeking soul to a mare among the chariots of Pharaoh (1:9); now, in the thrall of Love, this voice proclaims that her entire being (form) "is like" (*dametah*) "a palm." As compared to the prior specification of separate features, the totality of her body is now lauded. This voice of praise (as if from one's higher self) induces the self to ascend further.[113] (The inner dialogue continues in the next verse.)

Sod

8. ***Your stately form*** The self is confirmed in its spiritual "form." It has stature and height, ascending like a "palm" tree from the divine sources that nourish it. Liturgical memory leaps to images of the righteous person, compared to a palm flourishing in the Temple (Ps. 92:13–15). Why this identification? Perhaps this is because the palm integrates male and female qualities. In like manner, the soul must seek a harmonious integration (Z. 2:126a) of virtues (Ibn Sahula; Alkabetz)—giving and receiving in a ceaseless flow; generating and nourishing in the proper balance.

9 I say: Let me climb the palm,
Let me take hold of its branches;
Let your breasts be like clusters of grapes,
Your breath like the fragrance of apples,
10 And your mouth like choicest wine.
"Let it flow to my beloved as new wine
Gliding over the lips of sleepers."

9 אָמַ֙רְתִּי֙ אֶעֱלֶ֣ה בְתָמָ֔ר
אֹחֲזָ֖ה בְּסַנְסִנָּ֑יו
וְיִֽהְיוּ־נָ֤א שָׁדַ֙יִךְ֙ כְּאֶשְׁכְּל֣וֹת הַגֶּ֔פֶן
וְרֵ֥יחַ אַפֵּ֖ךְ כַּתַּפּוּחִֽים׃
10 וְחִכֵּ֕ךְ כְּיֵ֥ין הַטּ֛וֹב
הוֹלֵ֥ךְ לְדוֹדִ֖י לְמֵישָׁרִ֑ים
דּוֹבֵ֖ב שִׂפְתֵ֥י יְשֵׁנִֽים׃

Peshat

9. I say Or "I thought" (*'amarti*; Gen. 20:11; Num. 24:11).

Let me climb . . . Let me take hold Abandoning propriety, the youth starkly divulges his fantasies to her. The cohortative verbal form of *'oḥazah* ("let me take hold") indicates desire (cf. *'okhelah*, "I would like to eat," in Deut. 12:20). The expression *ve-yihyu-na'* ("O let") that follows (v. 9b) introduces a further series of erotic desires about her breasts, breath, and mouth (MsP). With uncommon starkness, he imagines himself upon her, body to body and face to face, inhaling the aroma of her exhalation as fresh fruit (apricots; see at 2:3) and imbibing her mouth's moisture (v. 10a). These similes do not displace desire, they activate and inscribe it.

10. like choicest wine Or "like sweet wine" (cf. 1:2). The construction *ke-yeiyn ha-ṭov* is difficult—not the normal apposition of two nouns (*yeiyn ṭov*). The formulation seems to be elliptical for something like *ke-yeiyn ha-kerem ha-ṭov* ("like the good wine of the vineyard"; so Sforno and an earlier medieval commentator).[114] Comment on v. 10b below.

Derash

9. Let me climb the palm Literally, "I shall ascend" (*'e'eleh*). According to tradition, God says that He will be exalted (*mit'aleh*) through Israel's deeds (SongsR 7.ix.1) by virtue of the martyrs—who are "branches" of the palm, devoting their lives in sanctification of His Name (see Sifra, *'Aḥarei*, 13.13;[115] B. Sanh. 93a). Cf. Rabbi Shlomoh. The glory of Israel is her devotion to God, expressed in life through the commandments and in noble death through martyrdom. "As the heart of the palm is one, so is Israel's heart one for their God in heaven" (Gershuni).

the fragrance of apples By virtue of their devotion, the holy martyrs will ascend to heavenly glory; for Scripture does not say *ke-tappuḥim*, "like apples," but *ka-tappuḥim*, "like *the* apples"—that is, they shall merit the fragrant rapture of the heavenly Garden of Eden (Targum; cf. SongsR, ibid.). The Song thus conveys God's promise of ultimate beatitude. Israel's love of God will transfigure them with a heavenly aroma (*reiaḥ*), an intangible spiritual fragrance that intoxicated her from the outset (Song 1:3).

10. And your mouth The praise of martyrdom continues, extending into the past. In the words of R. Yoḥanan: "When" the martyrs (of yore) died for God's sake,[116] the Holy One called upon the angels to "descend and kiss the lips of their ancestors" (the patriarchs)—"the lips of sleepers" (i.e., long dead)[117]—for just as these persons "served Me with fire, so do their descendants similarly serve" (SongsR 7.x.1). Abraham was cast into the fiery furnace by Nimrod for not worshiping idols (GenR 38.13), and Isaac was bound upon the altar[118] until he appeared like burnt ash (LevR 36.5).[119] For such acts of devotion, Israel is called *qedoshim benei qedoshim*, "holy martyrs descended from holy martyrs." This is their spiritual genealogy.

Remez

9. I say The "I" voice marks two aspects of the developing self: the lower, upwardly

striving ego; and the higher, more perfected soul (see v. 8). Both express the desire to "climb the palm" and take "hold of its branches"—to ascend the ladder of spiritual growth in all its forms. The chariot of love (first as physical desire, later as spiritual longing) inspires this growth and transformation (Immanuel).[120] Ideally the "lower self" will purify its purposes and achieve its desired ends, guided by the "higher self" as it increasingly envisions the true Beloved.

your breasts The lower self compares Love's breasts to "a cluster of grapes," and its savory "breath" to "the fragrance of apples." One image moves from touch to taste—from the external to the internal; the other, from shape to spirit—from the otherness of feeling to the inwardness of breath. This is a further step toward the transformation of desire and its purification. The Beloved responds to what the self has become—and now proceeds to confirm this development.

10. And your mouth like choicest wine This phrase echoes an earlier statement of the self (2:3). Long before, under the Beloved's shade, the self said that "his fruit is sweet to my mouth (*ḥikki*)." These words return as the Beloved affirms that "your mouth (*ḥikkeikh*) is choicest wine (*yeiyn ha-ṭov*)." The self's higher part (the soul) realizes that it has attained spiritual maturity, and that its "mouth" (the channel of reception and giving) has become like the ideal. All this hints again at the spiritual goal of *imitatio dei* (see v. 2). Hearing this, the soul responds.

Sod

9. I say: Let me climb the palm The self internalizes the divine qualities that it seeks to attain. As if splitting into a voice that perceives and assesses itself from without, these qualities evaluate the self's achievements. Thus the soul says: "Let me" ascend the inner structure of my being—the qualities just praised—and be suffused by their divine-like aspects (their fragrance). Distinct from the daily practice of self-judgment, this is a moment of deep self-evaluation. It is the spiritual quest itself that is assessed. Ascending through the self with spiritual intent is like an ascent toward the mystery of God—the hidden summit (Ibn Sahula; Alkabetz).

10. And your mouth like . . . wine The confirmation of spiritual beauty culminates with the mouth, which speaks with a tasteful sweetness like "new wine" (*meisharim*)—symbolizing a quest for the Beloved that is marked by "uprightness" or "honesty" (*meisharim*). These virtues revive the mute soul from its somnolence.[121] The flowing wine is like an elixir that resuscitates the spirit and "properly" (*meisharim*) integrates the self's polar aspects (Z. 3:39a).[122]

[11] I am my beloved's,
And his desire is for me.

11 אֲנִי לְדוֹדִי
וְעָלַי תְּשׁוּקָתוֹ׃ ס

Peshat

4. HER LOVING RESPONSE (vv. 10b–11)

10b. Let it flow The verb *holeikh* is a participle, suggesting continued action.

my beloved Since the speaker calls the addressee the masculine form *dodi*, one may assume (with most commentators) that the lass now interrupts the beloved's ecstatic formulations and completes his thought—harking back to her own earlier words (1:2–4).[123]

as new wine Better, "truly"; see at 1:4. She concurs that her mouth's fluids should fill him "like choicest wine" (as he put it) flowing rightly. The image not only responds to the lad's fantasy of grabbing her breasts like a bunch of grapes (v. 9), but also alludes to his wishful comment that her bowl-like belly never lack poured wine (v. 3). Reciprocally enthused, she likewise evokes the intoxications of love.

Gliding over The verb *dobheibh* (common in mishnaic Hebrew) means to "flow" or "drip"; it is a *polel* participle derived from the middle-weak stem *d-w-b* (a dialectal variant of *z-w-b*).[124] The stem *d-b-b*, which is used for speaking in Num. 14:36, may also be alluded to (Ibn Ezra).

the lips of sleepers That is, the maiden's kisses will glide into her beloved's mouth like an elixir of love—and (by double entendre) even cause him to "babble" in his love-besotted stupor.

11. The maiden concludes on her own terms, with a strong proclamation of love for her beloved and his passion for her.

I am my beloved's An ecstatic response to all his verbal advances.

his desire is for me As she knows from his erotic exclamations. These words (*ve-'alay teshuqato*) convey her twofold conviction. His passion is not only "for" her—and consumes him utterly—but also his expressions of passion have seized her as well: they are "on [or: upon] me" (*'alay*). The phrase echoes Gen. 3:16, but inverted. Deftly but unmistakably, some fundamental transformation is intimated. The reciprocal expressions of love between male and female have an Edenic dimension, overcoming social hierarchies.

Derash

11. I am my beloved's Israel responds to the preceding praise. She reasserts her commitment to God (echoing 6:3)

And his desire is for me Taking the prepositional phrase *'alay* as "for me," this clause expresses God's love for Israel, and it comports with the preceding (divine) praise. Alternatively, construing *'alay* as "upon me," it is a statement of her passion for God, and it introduces her impassioned response to the song of love, which follows.

desire The noun *teshuqah* occurs three times in Scripture and connotes three types of love. The first (specified by our verse) indicates Israel's "desire" for God. It is a theological love grounded in spiritual (and covenant) considerations—and thus the basis of a religious heritage. The second (alluding to Gen. 3:16) indicates a married woman's "desire" for her husband. It is an eros grounded in physical and partnership considerations—and thus the basis for a family heritage. The third usage (found in Gen. 4:7) marks the "desire" of the evil inclination. It is an instinctual urge grounded in raw, natural passion. The human is a creature with all three characteristics: spiritual goals; social culture; and animal nature. For the sages, religious love is the uppermost of this hierarchy—the guide to the virtues of the second level, and the regulative principle channeling the third.[125]

Remez

10b. Let it flow to my beloved The inner dialogue shifts. The self that articulated its

desire in terms of "clusters of grapes" now wishes to bestow this beneficence upon the Beloved. The soul desires to offer the gift of Love of its own nature, transformed by dedication to higher ends. That is why it adds "as new wine" (*le-meisharim*). The love for the Beloved was deemed at the outset to exceed *meisharim*, "new wine" (1:4)—so transcendent was it believed to be over all natural elements. Wiser now, the self realizes that its spiritual love is an outgrowth (transfigured) of its natural desire; and so it wishes to bring just that (in Love) to the Beloved. Received "rightly" (*le-meisharim*), the energy of desire may be "properly" given.[126] The upper and lower realms need not be divided. Self and soul can live in spiritual harmony.

Gliding over the lips of sleepers The flowing wine, indicative of spiritual renewal, has aroused the self from the perplexity that had immobilized it in times past (see 3:1; 5:2). The self is renewed and revived—a spiritual dancer of the *maḥanayim*, easily moving between the realms of existence.

11. The self again proclaims its spiritual achievement. It knows itself as wholly devoted to the Beloved.[127] Furthermore, it realizes that its spiritual labor is confirmed by Him ("his desire is for me"). The relationship is characterized by reciprocity. But it may have a deeper, ontological resonance. For in these words one can hear a certain reversal of the curse of Eden and restoration of a primal harmony (see Peshat). No longer is desire a base passion, subservient to one's animal nature. In this reformulation, desire is rather deemed a vital current of Love—one that may be transformed, redirected, and transfigured.

Sod

11. I am my beloved's With these words, the soul feels reborn. It recommits itself in loving devotion to God and the spiritual virtues. Feeling this loving confirmation from without (a "desire" that descends "upon" the self), the individual ("I") is inspired to a fuller expression of this love (both within the world and within our soul). This conjunction is like a spiritual marriage of profound reciprocity: the soul is drawn toward God, through the divine love that intimates itself (Z. 3:132b). Suddenly the soul is joined to Divinity (*be-ḥad qeṭira' itqaṭarna beih*; Z. 3:228a).[128] This is a spiritual miracle.

CONCLUSION

In this most passion-filled and suggestive group of songs, the effects of beauty and love transform the individuals. The emotions range from private statements about the bewilderments of love (6:11–12) to dialogues about its intoxicating effects. Sight and feeling are transformed. Sight sprung from the buds of the vale or chariots on the road is filled with emotional innuendos and euphemisms; the reality of beauty can variously induce a leering gaze among bystanders (7:1) or thoughtful (but erotically charged) images in the wooing partner (7:2–11). As physical and emotional proximity increase (through the power of the imagery and the boldness of the dialogues), they drop the emotional veils provided by similes and metaphors; their passions become ever more transparent and reciprocal. From the interior psychological state at the outset, this cycle gradually moves through cautious discourse to reach the explicit emotions of a pair who share intimacies. With stylistic skill, the poet conveys the deepest interiority and the most pungent worldly images. Love is transformative: through its energies and passions, the outer world is internalized and fills the self with fantasies; meanwhile the self forcefully projects inner feelings outward, so that the public landscape reflects private desires. Subjectivity and objectivity meld in the heat of love. In both explicit and implicit ways, the poet adds to our experience of human beauty and desire, deepening the meaning of the Song's great subject, *'ahavah*.

CHAPTER 7:12–8:14

Longing, Love, and Loss

The final group of discourses is composed of four units, according to Masoretic tradition.[1] Each is distinct in style, topic, and focus. Internal subsections increase the diversity. Overall, these elements arouse a crescendo in the relationship between the maiden and her beloved, demonstrating the maiden's worthiness and appeal. The editorial collation is one of interlocking perspectives rather than compositional coherence. The cycle concludes with the beloved's abrupt departure. It deprives the Song of closure, which leaves the passions of love incomplete.

Unit 1 (7:12–8:4) has two parts. In the first, the maiden invites her beloved to go with her into the fields, where she will give her love to him (7:12–14). The second sequence (8:1–4) is composite. At the outset, the maiden speaks to her beloved and expresses her wish that they were siblings, explaining why—with erotic innuendo (vv. 1–2). This is followed by the maiden's reference to their intimacy, entwined in embrace, and an adjuration to her friends regarding love's proper timing (vv. 3–4). An abrupt shift divides these two dialogues. The first discourse is spoken to him directly (in the second person), whereas in the second she speaks to her friends about him (in the third person).

Unit 2 (8:5–7) also has two parts. In the first (v. 5a), an unnamed speaker sees a woman ascend from the steppe and asks: "Who is this?!" Nothing is explained. In the scene that follows (vv. 5b–7a) the maiden woos her beloved with memories of an earlier arousal and implores him to set her as a seal upon his body. She concludes by exclaiming the overwhelming power of love (v. 7b).

Unit 3 (8:8–10) has two parts. In the first (vv. 8–9) the maiden's brothers say that she is young and physically undeveloped; but the maiden overhears this and proclaims her nubile maturity (v. 10).

Unit 4 (8:11–14) has several parts. In the first (vv. 11–12), the beloved contrasts a great vineyard of Solomon, requiring hired workers and fees, with his own—this being (allegorically) his invaluable maiden. Suddenly someone tells the maiden that while "friends" seek her voice, she should let "him" hear it (v. 13). This speaker is presumably the beloved. The maiden's response is unexpected: she implores him to flee to the mountains (v. 14). With this the Song ends.

Several elements connect this final unit to the book's first. The Song begins and ends with references to kisses and the elixir of wine (1:2, 4 and 8:1–2); the intimacy of love and its proper timing appear near the beginning and conclusion (2:6–7 and 8:3–4); the intensity of love and its passions is repeated from first to last (2:5 and 8:6); references to the beloved's companions occur at the outset and the end (1:7 and 8:13); and the themes of the brothers and a vineyard frame the Song as well (1:6 and 8:8–9 + 11–12). Tamakh finely observed that great works of art conclude with references to earlier themes—a comment most apropos here.[2]

12 Come, my beloved,
Let us go into the open;
Let us lodge among the henna shrubs.

12 לְכָ֤ה דוֹדִי֙
נֵצֵ֣א הַשָּׂדֶ֔ה
נָלִ֖ינָה בַּכְּפָרִֽים׃

Peshat

1. THE MAIDEN'S WORDS AND WISHES (7:12–8:4)

The maiden invites her beloved into the fields, whose budding fruit and plants evoke the ripening pleasures of love (7:12–14). She then expresses the wish that they were like siblings, so that they could kiss in public and she could bring him home to enjoy the bounty of love (8:1–2). These words evoke references to the couple's embrace, with the oft-repeated adjuration of restraint (vv. 3–4; 2:6–7; 3:5).[3]

12. Come.../ Let us go out... Let us lodge The maiden's invitation (*lekhah*) is in the cohortative mood ("*let us* go"), expressing volition and desire. It is a charged evocation (Immanuel) that initiates a series of verbs denoting shared activity. She then says *neitzei'* then *naliynah* ("*let us* go out... *let us* lodge"); and subsequently adds *nashkimah* ("*let us* go early"; v. 13). Most of these modal verbs add the optional yet inclusive *-ah* ending.[4] The successive actions follow without interruption. The effect is a rapid-fire series of invitations for shared behavior.[5] The maiden's enthusiastic appeal echoes her beloved's earlier invitation to her in 2:10b, 13b.

into the open... The noun *sadeh* denotes a "field," in the sense of an open area.

among the henna shrubs Or "in the villages" (Transl.). The noun *kefarim* is the plural both of *kofer* ("henna bush") and of *kefar* ("village"). The poet presumably wished to convey both meanings. His bivalent form turns in two directions: following the word "field," *kefarim* indicates "villages"; but preceding "vineyards," it suggests "henna shrubs."[6]

Derash

12. Come, my beloved Ostensibly, Israel speaks this invocation to her Beloved LORD. But tradition has introduced a third element, deeming it to be the Holy Spirit calling to God—through, or on behalf of, Israel—to "come" see the virtues of this people, and to "lodge among the henna shrubs" (*kefarim*), where He may view the idolaters who "reject" (*koferim*) God (SongsR 7.xii.1). In this way, the faith of Israel will be fully appreciated (below).

Remez

12. Come, my beloved The self takes a further initiative. Earlier, the Beloved beseeched it to "come away" to the fields that were budding with incipient possibilities (2:10–13). On this occasion, the self reciprocates and invites the Beloved to "go into the open" field and "lodge among the henna shrubs."[7] This event is a milestone in their relationship. It reflects a deepening of the ways that the self and Beloved join together in the world (Immanuel).[8]

Sod

12. Come... Let us go As seekers, we are pulled in opposite directions. On one side: to bring our God-consciousness into the world—to "go into the open" and try to actualize our qualities in the medley of existence (Z. 1:121a).[9] On the other side: to withdraw with God in meditative isolation (Ibn Sahula; Alkabetz)—to perfect our traits or qualities.[10] Different situations will influence the self as it swings between these poles.

The key concern is that the ostensibly opposing impulses nourish one another and provide the right balance. The seeker knows that social ethics require an inner cultivation, and that an interior ethos withers without the tests of existence. Nonseekers do not always appreciate this tension, while seekers do not readily communicate this dialectic between an interior and exterior focus.

¹³ Let us go early to the vineyards;
Let us see if the vine has flowered,
If its blossoms have opened,
If the pomegranates are in bloom.
There I will give my love to you.

נַשְׁכִּ֙ימָה֙ לַכְּרָמִ֔ים 13
נִרְאֶ֞ה אִם־פָּֽרְחָ֤ה הַגֶּ֙פֶן֙
פִּתַּ֣ח הַסְּמָדַ֔ר
הֵנֵ֖צוּ הָרִמּוֹנִ֑ים
שָׁ֛ם אֶתֵּ֥ן אֶת־דֹּדַ֖י לָֽךְ׃

Peshat

13. **Let us see** This (implied) cohortative governs the succeeding three activities: "if" (*'im*) the "vine has flowered," *if* its "blossoms have opened," and *if* "the pomegranates are in bloom." The first and third botanic events echo the beloved's musings while walking in the wadi (6:11). The second event, *pittah ha-semadar*, continues the first and echoes his earlier invocation to the maiden, when he called her to "come" (*lekhi*) with him to the fields since "the vines [are] in bloom (*ha-gefanim semadar*)" (2:10, 13). The poet thus alludes to prior discourse via stylistic variation. These cross-references thicken the interpersonal dialogues.

There I will give my love to you The romantic enticement is explicit. She begins her invitation by calling him "my beloved" (*dodi*) and concludes by saying "I will give my love (*dodi*) to you." The renewal of nature and the arousal of human love are correlated. The boldness of this figure casts a suggestive light on the related images in 2:10–13 and 6:11. The same goes for the ensuing imagery in verses 14 and 8:2b (see below).

Derash

13. The religious practices of Israel are now portrayed. The Holy Spirit invites God to behold Israel, His own "vineyard" (Isa. 5:20), and see "if the vine has flowered"—this being the morning recitation of the *Shema*; "if its blossoms have opened"—this being the opening of the synagogues for prayer and study; and "if the pomegranates are in bloom"—this being the children devoted to Torah. For truly, just "there," in these holy habitations (synagogue, study hall, and home), does Israel "give" her "love to" God. Here, Israel refers specifically to all the pious people "who have come forth from me" (SongsR 7.xiii.1).

Remez

13. **Let us go** The repeated invitation "let us" underscores the shared action that is anticipated. They will soon visit the "vineyards" to "see if the vine has flowered"—symbolic of the spiritual possibilities and developments now blossoming (Ralbag).[11] And if the time is ripe, says the soul to her Beloved, "I will give my love to you," wholeheartedly (Malbim).[12] This going forth is a spiritual elevation, a further transcendence of one's natural state (Al-Fawwāl).[13] Only time and the grace of love could make this possible.

Sod

13. **Let us go...Let us see if** This is the twofold speech, directed to God and to the self. Addressed to God, the soul desires deeper development and self-examination—to see *if* there is an inner flowering of the spirit (Ibn Sahula); and if this is happening—"there I will give my love to you." That is, the self will devote itself unstintingly to God and spiritual perfection (Z. 1:44b). And when addressed to the self, these words mark an inner exhortation to go outward to the world—to see *if* our inner work has borne fruit and can respond to life's challenges; and if so—just "there" (in the world) "I will give my love to you" through acts of loving-kindness toward others. In both cases, the seeker is seeking.

14 The mandrakes yield their fragrance,
At our doors are all choice fruits;
Both freshly picked and long-stored
Have I kept, my beloved, for you.

14 הַדּוּדָאִים נָתְנוּ־רֵיחַ
וְעַל־פְּתָחֵינוּ כָּל־מְגָדִים
חֲדָשִׁים גַּם־יְשָׁנִים
דּוֹדִי צָפַנְתִּי לָךְ׃

Peshat

14. This verse concludes the maiden's initial speech and adds a second climax to her solicitation.

mandrakes yield their fragrance She evokes the aromatics of love, since the mandrake was a well-known erotic charm in antiquity (cf. Gen. 30:14–15; and Egyptian love poems).[14] Possibly she goes to see *if* these plants have begun to emit their fragrance (Rid), thereby carrying over the mood in verse 13. The giving off of a fragrance is an evocative theme in the Song (1:12; 2:13; similarly 7:9).

At our doors are all choice fruits The location *'al petaḥeiynu* refers to their "home" in the fields; thus the "choice fruit" (*megadim*) are decked around them.[15] This bounty was mentioned earlier by the youth in reference to the garden, to which he compared the maiden (4:13, 16). In this way, the girl mirrors her Beloved's depiction of her. The word *meged* connotes various kinds of natural "bounty" in Deut. 33:13–16.

Both freshly picked and long-stored Literally, "both new and old." The phrase *ḥadashim gam yeshanim* refers to "new" and "past" produce (the yield of successive years). See Lev. 26:10. The maiden hints that she is herself the ripened bounty and fruit of love. She is more explicit in the next phrase.[16]

Have I kept...for you Literally, "I have stored away...for you." She has taken the mandrakes and the choicest fruits from early and late reapings and stored them for her Beloved. She and her body are thus correlated with the fertile earth and its growth. This cornucopia of fruitfulness is for him alone; all her virginal freshness shall be his. She speaks of the fields, but her verbiage suggests otherwise. Her speech is bold and direct. Coy correlatives recede and are replaced by erotic evocations.

Stylistics. The maiden's speech opens with a call to her beloved, *lekhah dodi* ("come, my Beloved"); and these words are echoed at the end, *dodi... lakh* ("my beloved [I have stored them] for you"). Her solicitation is enunciated within this frame. The *duda'im* ("mandrakes") evoke and embody *dodi*.

Derash

14. Exemplary among the righteous (see previous comment) are the (male) "youths" without blemish, who are like mandrakes (*duda'im*; or "Beloved ones," *dodim*) in fragrance, and the (female) "daughters of Israel," who "cleave to their husbands" and merit being deemed "choice fruit" (SongsR 7.xiv.1).[17] Through such devotion, Israel is committed to God, ever harvesting her bounty and offering it for divine glory. Hence she says: "both freshly picked and long-stored have I kept, my Beloved, for you." Israel combines both "new" (*ḥadashim*; "freshly picked") practices and interpretations,[18] and older ones of "past times" (*yeshanim*, "long-stored"). Culling from all generations, the best is "stored away" (*tzafanti*) for God alone. Then God responds in kind: "Just as you [Israel] have stored things for me, so I have done for you. You have stored up merit through *mitzvot* and good deeds, and I have stored [for you] a bounty exceeding all the storehouses of this world" (SongsR ibid., end).[19]

Remez

14. The mandrakes yield their fragrance Reference to the budding mandrakes (*duda'im*) suggests the co-presence of the Beloved (*dodi*), to whom she has just promised to give her love (*dodai*). His being and her passion are magically infixed in this plant of desire, an objective correlative of their eros. More than mere meta-

phor, this plant is an embodiment of her love—arising from the earth and inscribed with godly desire.

At our doors In the hearts (doors) of self and Beloved lie "all the choice fruits" that have been gathered. This is the harvest of their love, brought from the fields (outer world) and given as an offering to one another. The two doors (*petaḥeinu*) mark the passageways between them. They are "open" to one another (the inner self to the transcendent Beloved, and the supernal to the soul). No longer is the Beloved on the outside, beseeching the self for entry ("Let me in," *pitḥi li*; 5:2). Now the self speaks of its preparations and gifts—"freshly picked" (because of the revived bounty of love) "and long-stored" (because cultivated over time).[20] Both have been "kept" for the Beloved. What has been "hidden" (*tzafanti*) away (discreetly; Ibn Tibbon)[21] is for this very moment. The treasures of love (new and old fruits) are bestowed: not for anyone, says the soul, but "for you" (my Beloved) alone (Immanuel; Malbim).[22] The "long-stored" and the newly grown are the bouquet of personal love: a gift of the spirit.

Sod

14. The mandrakes yield . . . fragrance The mandrakes (*duda'im*) symbolize the many modes whereby love for the Beloved (*dod*) may be expressed. The seeker asserts a blossoming of love—a spiritual realization of sorts. The soul avers (to God and itself) that it is prepared to lay this loving spirit at the "doors" of existence—these being the "openings" (*petaḥeiynu*) of possibility that lie ahead. Some features of inner cultivation have been worked on in the past, and these are "long-stored" in the heart and waiting to be activated in love. Other qualities are of a more recent vintage, "newly picked," as it were, and only now ready for challenges unseen.[23] The self concludes with a confession: all this work is not an act of self-centeredness—rooted in the ego—but is "kept, my Beloved, for you."[24] That is, our spiritual path is a form of divine service, whereby our soul is devoted to God. These practices of self-cultivation are thus not pragmatic tasks of self-improvement, but acts of worship. They seek to open spaces of human selflessness where Love may blossom.

8 If only it could be as with a brother,
As if you had nursed at my mother's breast:
Then I could kiss you
When I met you in the street,
And no one would despise me.

ח מִי יִתֶּנְךָ֙ כְּאָ֣ח לִ֔י
יוֹנֵ֖ק שְׁדֵ֣י אִמִּ֑י
אֶֽמְצָאֲךָ֤ בַחוּץ֙
אֶשָּׁ֣קְךָ֔
גַּ֥ם לֹא־יָבֻ֖זוּ לִֽי׃

Peshat

8:1–4. The maiden muses about her relationship, expressing the wish that she was like his sister—and could kiss him unabashedly in public (v. 1) and bring him to her mother's home (v. 2). A series of five verbs dramatize the maiden's desires. Is it actuality or intense longing that is next reported, when she says that "his left hand" was beneath her head in loving embrace (v. 3)? The reader will ponder the alternatives, given the context. Verbal considerations add to the ambiguity (see below). Has the longed-for time of true arousal arrived?

1. If only it could be More precisely, the idiom *mi yittenkha* expresses the wish "would that *you* could be." This is a standard formulation (cf. Exod. 16:3; Num. 11:29; Jer. 8:23). The emphasis on "you" here becomes apparent by contrasting this expression with promises and imprecations that are formulated solely with *yittein* ("let [or: may]" such-and-such happen; cf. Num. 5:21; Deut. 28:7; Isa. 41:2). The maiden's wish is conditioned by a simile ("like a brother of mine"), which opens a space between desire and reality.

As if you had nursed Hebrew *yoneiq* is a present participle that conveys the girl's active fantasy about her beloved "nursing" at her mother's breast. The tone is dramatic and realistic, without hypothetical qualification ("as if"). Having suckled at the same breast, they could be unabashedly bold in their public affection (see next comment).

Then I could kiss you / When I met you This is not expressed in the Hebrew as a consequence ("then"). Rather, the verbs continue the wish: "I would meet [or: find] you ... I would kiss you." The sequence emphasizes the two desired actions; for this is how the maiden

experiences her hope. Her wishes continue in the next verse.

Derash

8:1. If only it could be Keneset Yisra'el speaks. Having proclaimed her devotion to God (7:11), she now wishes to express this in public. The counterpoint is significant. Formerly, she had kept her religious service "hidden" or "set apart for you" (*tzafanti lakh*; 7:14); presently she is ready to display her feelings "in the street" (*ba-hutz*). Love's inwardness is ready for worldly expression. Hope and desire conjoin: "Would that *You* be given (*yittenkha*) ... to *me*." She beseeches God's immediacy in personal terms (You-me) so that she might witness it in all its ardor. At the beginning of her quest, she longed for God's kiss, as she sensed Divinity both transcendent and removed ("May *He* kiss me," *yishaqeini*; 1:2); she now longs to express this love directly ("I would kiss *You*"; *'eshaqekha*). Inaugurating this climax of courtship and praise, the kiss is once again a consummate act. It reinforces Israel's enduring desire for divine presence.

as with a brother This comparative evokes a query: *be-'eizah 'ah*—"what kind of brother" is spoken of here (SongsR 8.i.1)?[25] The "heartfelt love" of Joseph for Benjamin is one model—though custodial and beneficent. Another is the reciprocal love of Moses and Aaron. Having been nursed at the same mother's breast, these siblings had no compunction about kissing one another in public ("outside"[26] the settled areas, in the wilderness,[27] when Moses returned to Egypt from Midian; Exod. 4:27). These brothers thus provide a rabbinic paradigm for the spiritual relationship desired here (Tan., *Shemot* 27; ExodR 1.1 and 3). In

national terms, this longing expresses the people's desire to be restored from the burdens of exile (where restraint and privacy are operative) to the bounty of a renewed covenant community (where spiritual devotion may be freely expressed; Ibn Aqnin and Netziv). Israel yearns for an intimate relationship with God.

no one would despise me Having cultivated her religious service, Israel is ready to display it without shame. The sense of covenant has come to maturity.

seeker wishes for the kiss of bonding (*ḥibbur*) and spiritual conjunction (*deveiqut*) (Immanuel), so as to transform the world in the light of a higher mindfulness (Ibn Aqnin).[29] The desire is not to remain in the fields in contemplative isolation, but to return to the social world with the gifts of God—and to kiss the Beloved in all the manifestations of life found "in the street." Then all one's encounters in the outside world (*ḥutz*) would express one's loving devotion (*mei-'ahavah*) to God (Sforno).[30]

Remez

8:1. If only it could be A new longing fills the soul. The offerings of olden love were conveyed with deep passion; but the soul realized that this had to be expressed privately, in the fields (7:12–14). The present speech reveals the soul's self-consciousness about the public expression of intimate love. In the glare of the everyday, the heart fears the ridicule of worldly spectators (Malbim).[28] In the byways of daily life, the intensity of spiritual love could be misjudged; it would surely seem strange to those who have not cultivated it. But were the Beloved like a "brother," recognizable and somehow worldly . . .

Then I could kiss you . . . in the street The self has a great desire to express its intimacy with God openly, such that "no one would despise" her. But among those who do not understand, the intense desire for spiritual realization is mocked as a flight from the everyday. The

Sod

8:1. If only it could be The soul yearns for intimacy with God. But this is difficult. Divinity is elusive and transcendent—ever escaping human knowledge and experience. Nevertheless the soul has felt God's presence (7:11)—and so dares address Divinity in personal terms. Hope pushes the heart forward: "if only." If only this intimate feeling could be confirmed, the soul would proclaim God's reality in public and not fear derision. The soul waits and hopes; but the answer is stirring in the depths. Hidden in the soul's expression of hope is the gift of God's confirming reality—for the word of hope, *mi* ("if only"), hides a hint of spiritual wonder (*mi* as "Who?"—a mystical epithet of God as the most transcendent Mystery; Ibn Sahula; Z. 1:1b). Surpassing understanding, this awakened wonder *is itself* an opening toward the Ineffable. Loving desire has prepared the heart to receive.

2 I would lead you, I would bring you
To the house of my mother,
Of her who taught me—
I would let you drink of the spiced wine,
Of my pomegranate juice.

2 אֶנְהָגְךָ֗ אֲבִיאֲךָ֛
אֶל־בֵּ֥ית אִמִּ֖י
תְּלַמְּדֵ֑נִי
אַשְׁקְךָ֙ מִיַּ֣יִן הָרֶ֔קַח
מֵעֲסִ֖יס רִמֹּנִֽי׃

Peshat

2. ***I would lead you, I would bring you... I would let you drink*** This sequence of verbs stresses her desire to bring the beloved home to the elixir of love. These actions are correlated by a pun. The list begins with *'eshaqekha* ("I would kiss you," v. 1) and ends with *'ashqekha* ("I would let you drink"; literally, "I would slake you"—a *hif'il*-causative). Both verbs emphasize oral intimacy: the first refers to kisses; the second to the incorporation of delicacies (see below).

Of her who taught me The verbal phrase *telammedeini* is difficult. The present translation seems to construe a double genitive ("of my mother... of her who taught"), presumably due to the preceding phrase *'el beiyt 'immi* ("to my mother's house"). However, the verb is present-future; and thus, if it refers to the mother, would mean something like "she who will instruct me" (Ibn Ezra), or "she shall teach me" (Targum; Rashbam). Yet this action is perplexing in light of the earlier reference to the maiden bringing her beloved home (3:4b). In that instance, the parallel to *'el beiyt 'immi* ("to my mother's house") is *'el ḥeider horati* ("to the room of she who bore me"). Hence the verb in 8:2 may be a scribal error for *teiladni* ("she who bore me"). But this reformulation is problematic. Grammatically more preferable is *yeladetani*, "who bore me"; cf. 8:5).[31] One may thus suppose that the formulation *telammedeini* is a misinterpretation of (the earlier word) *horati*, construed as "she who instructs me" (that is, a causative form of *yarah*, "teach," rather than as the participle of *harah*, "conceive").[32]

Alternatively, it is a deliberate transformation of this verb and its import. Thus Immanuel proposed that our verb expresses the maiden's desire that the beloved ("you") teach her the ways of love in her parental home.

spiced wine MT vocalizes this construction with the absolute form, *yayin ha-reqaḥ*, rather than the expected construct form, *yeiyn ha-reqaḥ*. Such a formulation is unique, as is the use of the singular collective *reqaḥ* for "choice spices" (instead of *merqaḥim* in the plural).

pomegranate juice This second drink is more evocative. She presumably hopes to offer him the sweet juice of her love. The preceding context (7:13–14) supports this understanding, as also the striking self-reference ("*my* pomegranate") in the context of love talk.

Stylistics. The phraseology of finding and taking (a male homeward) is a type-scene, modified in each setting for rhetorical effect. Note the following instances. The first two occur in the Song and they feature encounters with the beloved male; the third occurs in Proverbs and deals with a man importuned by a wayward woman.

1. Song 3:4—(i) Seeking [the beloved] outside, "in the streets... and squares, *reḥovot*"; (ii) "I found, *matza'ti*, the one I love" ; (iii) "I held him fast, *'aḥaztiv*"; (iv) "I brought him, *havei'tiv*"; (v) "to my mother's house, *'el beiyt 'immi*."

2. Song 8:2–3—(i) Seeking [the beloved] "outside, *ba-ḥutz*"; (ii) "I would find you, *'emtza'akha*, and "kiss you, *'eshaqekha*"; (iii) "I would bring you, *'aviy'akha*"; (iv) "to my mother's house, *'el beiyt 'immi*."

3. Prov. 7:10–18—(i) A woman solicits [a man] "outside, *ba-ḥutz*... in the squares, *ba-reḥovot*"; (ii) she goes out and tells him, "I have found you, *'amtza'aka*"; (iii) she "held him fast, *ve-heḥeziqah bo*" and "kissed him, *ve-nasheqah lo*"; (iv) she prepared her "house," *bayit*, for him and enticed him to join her in "lovemaking, *dodim* and *ba-'ahavim*."

Derash

2. ***I would lead you*** This expresses Israel's desire to bring God down "from the upper realms to the lower ones"—to worldly immanence, presented here through the figure of "my mother's house" (LevR 1.10; SongsR 8.ii.1).[33] Formerly, this "house" was Sinai, the initial locus of spiritual intimacy, where Israel was formed and nurtured. And now it betokens all the social spaces of religiosity—synagogue, study hall, and home. The subjunctive mood ("if," "would") underscores the present longing for renewal.

The maternal images present an exegetical challenge and opportunity. At one level, the figure *beiyt 'immi*, "my mother's house," can mark the founding locus of "my people" (*'ummi*)—this being Sinai (cf. Derash at 3:11). In this sense, Sinai is the cultural "mother" of the nation. This is a striking but not daring image, typologically linked to the religious institutions that continue its tasks (synagogue or home). But at another level, the maternal imagery connotes God, at whose earthly home (namely Sinai) Israel derived her formative spiritual initiation. This more daring theological expression draws on primordial emotional sensibilities. Images of (divine) transcendence may thus arise from experiences of primary (human) sustenance. Such theological expressions appear already in Isa. 49:14–15.

who taught me Viewed as the font of intergenerational instruction, Sinai-as-Mother involves the reception of past traditions and their guidance for the future. This dual dimension (of past and present) is encoded in the verb *telammedeini*—which suggests both the past-perfect ("she who taught me") and the present-imperative ("instruct me!" now). Religious instruction is deemed formative and ever transforming.[34] Viewed as a bestowal from God-as-Mother, Torah and Tradition together form a life-giving fluid. The convergence of the images deepens their theological power.

I would let you drink This subjunctive expression ("would") expresses Israel's readiness for reciprocity. What she has received from God ("commandments and good deeds"; SongsR 8.ii.1), she promises to augment through study and practice—this being a return of the spiritual gifts to the Source of beneficence through their worldly enactment. Thus *Keneset Yisra'el* desires to provide "drink" to God (*'ashqekha*; a verb that echoes the verb "kiss," *'eshaqekha*, in the prior clause). This drink is Torah culture: "spiced wine" refers to the study of Mishnah (and legal midrash);[35] "pomegranate juice," to the study of *aggadah* (homiletic midrash), "whose taste" (*ṭa'aman*) gives new sense and meaning to Scripture[36] (SongsR, ibid.).[37] The kisses of Israel thus symbolize the activity of Oral Torah; they are like a spiritual libation offered to God for the glorification of Torah and its values.

Remez

2. ***I would lead you . . . To the house*** The seeker desires to express spiritual inwardness in a manifest way. But the true course of this relationship must transpire in hidden spaces. The self knows this from earlier experience, having previously sought the lost Beloved (in the streets) and brought him home to "my mother's house" (3:4). Once again the space of intimacy is "the house of my mother." And as earlier, the mother "who taught me" is the interior realm (or womb) of one's being, where the Beloved guides the soul. To enter this place is to deepen the instruction that has begun to mature (Ibn Aqnin)—an inner wisdom marked by love for the Beloved. The hope expressed by the word *'enhagakha* ("I would lead you") is the longing to draw the Beloved into one's heart, and to transform this presence into a spiritual practice (*hanhagah*).[38]

I would let you drink The self is filled with an overflowing love; it wishes to bestow this gift upon the Beloved. It has received truth and beneficence from this Beloved ("the spiced wine") and now hopes to give of it in a personally integrated way ("my pomegranate juice"). This act of gratitude makes use of the gift in new forms.

Sod

2. ***I would lead you*** The expressions of desire continue, with a yearning to draw God close through spiritual practices. This must be done in private contemplation, which differs from a public proclamation of faith (v. 1). The figure "house of my mother" refers to the two foci of meditative consciousness that must be cultivated: God as most intimate Immanence, in the inner space of the heart; and Divinity as most ultimate Transcendence, beyond all Being. As the space of the heart, the maternal figure suggests an interior realm where insight births spiritual wisdom (AhavD 207b); and as the hidden height of heaven, this figure suggests the infinite Womb of Being, which mysteriously gestates human thought, including the imagining of God (Z. 2:258a).[39] It is to these holy spaces—as to a mother's home—that the soul goes for spiritual regeneration. The desire to kiss God (*'eshaqekha*; v. 1) expresses the gift of selfhood—a spiritual libation (*'ashqekha*, v. 2) offered in sacred gratitude. The religious life involves such giving and receiving: a giving back to God (in human terms) what one has received from the House of Divine Nurture.

3 His left hand was under my head,
His right hand caressed me.

3 שְׂמֹאלוֹ֙ תַּ֣חַת רֹאשִׁ֔י
וִימִינ֖וֹ תְּחַבְּקֵֽנִי׃

Peshat

3. An image of physical entwinement, repeating 2:6 exactly. Either this scene depicts their recent encounter in the present ("his left hand under . . . his right embracing me"), or it envisions a future enactment ("will embrace me"). The phrase lends itself to such a bi-temporal aspect. The present rendering as a past event ("was") does not preserve the poignant ambiguity.[40]

As in 2:6, this image is followed by an adjuration.

Derash

*3. **His left hand*** This figure recurs in contexts of intimacy. It is found at 2:6, after the woman states that she was brought (*hevi'ani*) to the "house of wine" (2:4); and it occurs here, after she states her desire to bring her Beloved (*'avi'akha*) to her "mother's house" (8:2). In both cases the image of embrace is followed by an adjuration to heed the pace of love (2:7 and 8:4). For the cultivation of true religious love requires discipline and practice. Crucial in this regard is the decision to surround oneself with ritual forms—like the wearing of fringes (tzitzit), which are compared to the support of the right hand, and donning phylacteries (tefillin), which are like the embrace of the left. Conscious of God at all times, the Jew grows through the practice of mitzvot in the pure love of God (cf. SongsR 2.vi.1).

Remez

3. Spiritually matured, an old memory returns to the soul. Earlier, the soul felt entwined in the embrace of love, adjuring itself (via the maidens, her emotional "parts") to restrain this overwhelming emotion and let it arise in a suitable and timely fashion (2:4–6, 7). Now feeling more secure in its love, the soul desires to lead her Beloved more deeply inward and to be fully enfolded in His embrace. This is a vision of love realized in the imagination. The soul projects this desired conjunction as something that has seemingly occurred. Reaching into the depths of the soul, one hand of the Beloved gives it strength, while the other provides inspiration (Immanuel). The soul experiences both.

Sod

3. The magnitude of all-encompassing Divinity is given intimate expression through this figure of entwinement. The embrace suggests a providential care that sustains and nurtures the self (Ibn Sahula). It also intimates the interconnectedness of the Whole, a mysterious integrality that the soul seeks (ZḤ 45c).[41]

4 I adjure you, O maidens of Jerusalem:
Do not wake or rouse
Love until it please!

4 הִשְׁבַּעְתִּי אֶתְכֶם בְּנוֹת יְרוּשָׁלָ‍ִם
מַה־תָּעִירוּ | וּמַה־תְּעֹרְרוּ
אֶת־הָאַהֲבָה עַד שֶׁתֶּחְפָּץ׃ ס

Peshat

4. *Do not wake or rouse* The adjuration formula used here is *mah–mah*, not *'im–'im* as in 2:7 and 3:5. The negative import is the same. (For the use of *mah* in a series of negations, see Prov. 31:2). In the context of physical encounter with the beloved, the stylistic variation may be giving a double entendre to the maiden's words: she not only enjoins her friends from arousing love prematurely, as before, but also asks them (coyly) "for *what* [reason]" would you awaken or arouse love now?![42] For it is no longer needed; love has been quickened and is near fulfillment. Such a rhetorical ploy by the poet fits the scene's mood.

Derash

4. This adjuration counsels messianic restraint[43]—for historical, theological, and spiritual timing is crucial. More broadly, it advises maturation in one's religious life, so that each personal quality can mature incrementally. The student of the Song is called to heed this admonition. See also at 2:7 and 3:5.

Remez

4. *I adjure you, O maidens* This old-new adjuration is transformed as well. No longer an admonition of restraint, it projects a desire that this state endure until its intensity subsides. To mark this shift, the speaker alters the terms of adjuration. The negative command now includes a positive overtone—"how" or for "what" purpose would you restrain love, for its time of realization has come?![44] (see Peshat).

Sod

4. *Do not . . . rouse / Love until it please!* Sensing both (see v. 3), the soul proclaims the truth of timeliness: spiritual arousal must be cultivated; for only then, with proper ripening, will it find purified expression and expansion (cf. TiqZ 68a).[45] True and proper love—the right arousing to the right occasion—cannot be forced.

5 Who is she that comes up from the desert,
Leaning upon her beloved?
Under the apple tree I roused you;
It was there your mother conceived you,
There she who bore you conceived you.

5 מִ֣י זֹ֗את עֹלָה֙ מִן־הַמִּדְבָּ֔ר
מִתְרַפֶּ֖קֶת עַל־דּוֹדָ֑הּ
תַּ֚חַת הַתַּפּ֙וּחַ֙ עוֹרַרְתִּ֔יךְ
שָׁ֚מָּה חִבְּלַ֣תְךְ אִמֶּ֔ךְ
שָׁ֖מָּה חִבְּלָ֥ה יְלָדַֽתְךְ׃

Peshat

2. PAST MEMORIES, PRESENT PASSIONS (vv. 5–7)

Two voices and settings occur. In the first (v. 5a), someone perceives a female figure and asks about her. In the second (v. 5b), we hear the maiden speaking to her beloved, reminding him how she had aroused his love under a tree (v. 6), then imploring him to bind her as a seal upon his body—so mighty is her love (v. 7).

Verses 6–7 are redolent with mythic vibrations; but this is not myth. The poet has transformed older figures into metaphors saturated by personification and an aura of the other. They convey a mythic aura without narrating or inferring a mythic reality as such.

5. ***Who is she that comes up?*** The speaker's identity is unmarked. The query is rhetorical and calls attention to the maiden's appearance in her beloved's company, bound to him in love.[46] Similar formulations occur in 3:6 and 6:10. Such queries serve as choral interventions that introduce the maiden's sudden advent or glorious appearance.

Leaning upon her beloved The verb *mitrappeqet* is unique. Rashi and Ibn Ezra adduced an Arabic cognate that suggests that the maiden was "joined" or "bound" to her beloved.[47] The Septuagint already conveyed this sense of attachment. Use of the *hitpa'el* form connotes repeated or continuous activity (cf. *mithalleikh*, "walk about; go back and forth," in Gen. 3:8 and Job 1:7).[48] The verb also occurs in GenR 45.4, where it conveys the desire of women to be joined to their husbands; but this usage may derive from our Song passage.[49]

apple tree For *tappuaḥ* as a species of apricot, see at 2:3. The maiden seems to allude to that earlier dialogue.

I roused you The verb *'orartikha* is redolent, conveying the arousal of desire with the verb used in the adjuration formulas (2:7; 3:5; 8:4), where it suggests the stimulations of love.[50]

there . . . There The locative *shammah* alludes to the place of conception—explicitly for the beloved's mother, but implicitly of the pair's present love. This adverb echoes the use of *sham* in 7:13, when the maiden promised to "give" her "love" to her beloved ("there" in the vineyards) at the time of nature's rebirth. She has increased the intensity of her love language.

your mother conceived you Or ". . . had the pangs of child-birth"; cf. Rashi, Rid.[51] This image brims suggestion.

Derash

5. ***Who is she that comes up*** The phrase refers to Israel's ascension (physically and spiritually) from the desert. The figure also evokes the people's attachment to God. From a historical perspective, the phrase "leaning upon her Beloved" suggests national loyalty during times of wandering and exile (SongsR 8.v.1). In the present context (following Israel's expressed readiness to be with God in public), the passage affirms the people's spiritual maturation. It is visible to all.

Leaning upon The verb *mitrapeqet* elicits midrashic reflections concerning Israel's life in the travail of history. The dual topics of Torah and the dominion of the nations (the positive and negative dimensions of Israel's existence) underpin R. Yoḥanan's teaching that this verse points to a future time when "the difficult periods (*pirqei*) of Torah and [foreign] dominion" will end (SongsR 8.v.1). On his understanding, the verb *mitrapeqet* encodes the divine promise

that Israel will "unloose (*mattir*) textual confusions" (i.e., achieve Torah mastery) and break free (*maphqir*) of foreign rule. Alternatively, when read as evoking *mitpareqet*, the verb denotes the "dissolution" of textual difficulties and the nation's "redemption."[52] More darkly, Ibn Sahula states that Israel will be glorified for having been "broken apart" (*mitpareqet*) on the rack of suffering on behalf of her Beloved God.[53]

Under the apple tree The people of Israel appeals to divine favor by recalling its commitment to the covenant at Sinai in the month of Sivan. It was then that God was "roused" in love for this people—who came to dwell under His bower and imbibe His teachings (cf. 2:3). Why an "apple tree"? Because its flowers bud in this month prior to its leaves' appearance, just as Israel received the Torah at this time and avowed covenant commitment before its full comprehension of the Law—saying "We shall do" first, "and we shall hear" second (Exod. 24:7) (cf. SongsR ibid.).[54] The bower image marks divine sovereignty and Israel's decision to live "under" the guidance of God's instruction (ibid.).

there your mother conceived you Now *sham ḥibbelatekha* continues the maternal imagery from verse 2, since at Sinai ("there") the nation was "conceived" and born;[55] and there God announced His formative role as the one "who took you out of Egypt." But Sinai also evokes a negative feature, since the people were there "put in distraint" (*ḥubbelah*), and her merits held in surety (Exod. 22:25), when she disavowed God for images of gold (sin of the calf). This situation induced R. Levi to perceive in this verb a poignant hint of divine mourning (*mit'abbeil*) for Israel's spiritual death (SongsR, ibid.).[56] Thus for the sages, Sinai was a bivalent event, reciprocally affecting God and Israel. It was both a time of covenant union and idolatrous rupture; of divine gift and human rejection. Scriptural language again provides the prism for theological reflection.

Remez

5. Who is she that comes up Is this the voice of the maiden's friends, now witnessing an intimate moment between the soul and her Beloved (she ascending, "coming up from the desert," and bound to Him, "leaning upon her Beloved?"). Or is this the soul imagining its conjunction with the Beloved? If so, the soul attests to its spiritual ascendance—envisioned within (Immanuel). The two alternatives conjoin.

Under the apple tree Suddenly, an old figure of intimacy (2:3) is recalled and reformulated. The seeker states how her desire for fulfillment had "roused" her Beloved under such a tree, adding that it was just "there" that the supernal reality of the Beloved ("*Your* mother") "conceived" and "bore" Him into the human soul. The images of birth express the self's feeling that its desire for spiritual fulfillment stimulated the Beloved's occurrence in its soul—as if the soul's site was nurtured by the "womb of Being."

Thinking objectively, the soul may worry whether such imagery is spiritually appropriate. But feeling subjectively, it trusts its capacity to convey inner truth with human images. The Song is a song of such images.

Sod

5. Who . . . comes up Longing evokes memory. Awaiting the right time, the soul pauses in reflection. As if speaking to itself—but hearing the truth from afar—a voice proclaims wonder at the soul's achievements: "Who (*mi*) is this?!" Can one really recognize this transcendent self, which has arisen from material existence (symbolized by the "desert") and ascended toward its Beloved?[57] This question is also an exclamation. For truly this soul has progressed and ascended toward God!

Under the apple tree The soul recalls an earlier moment, when it first compared the Beloved to a similar tree and desired sustenance

in its shade (2:3; AhavD 217b). Now, with an enlarged spiritual vision, this arbor is like a cosmic tree—rising from the natural world and extending throughout Being; or, as if rooted in heaven, descends inversely into the natural order, giving heavenly nurture to all beings.[58] Recalling its spiritual efforts, and the benefits received, the soul feels that its own acts have aroused the bounty that enriches its spirit (Ibn Sahula).[59] The tree is like a cosmic configuration, with infinite filters streaming from the origins of things (the birthing mother of the passage);[60] and its fruit is like the buds of spiritual insight, fertilizing upon its branches. Through such wondrous images, the soul dreams theologically.

6 Let me be a seal upon your heart,
Like the seal upon your hand.
For love is fierce as death,
Passion is mighty as Sheol;
Its darts are darts of fire,
A blazing flame.

6 שִׂימֵנִי כַחוֹתָם עַל־לִבֶּךָ
כַּחוֹתָם עַל־זְרוֹעֶךָ
כִּי־עַזָּה כַמָּוֶת אַהֲבָה
קָשָׁה כִשְׁאוֹל קִנְאָה
רְשָׁפֶיהָ רִשְׁפֵּי אֵשׁ
שַׁלְהֶבֶתְיָה*׃

v. 6. ה׳ רפה

Peshat

6. This is one of the great expressions of love in the Song. The formulations progress in severity: the qualities of *'ahavah // qin'ah* (love and zealous passion) are *'azzah // qashah* (fierce and harsh) as *mavet // she'ol* (death and the netherworld).

Let me be a seal The present translation conveys wish or desire. More precisely, the verb is an imperative (*siymeini*, "set me") that governs the two ensuing similes (*kh/ka-ḥotam*, "as a seal") and the two areas of placement ("upon your heart . . . upon your arm").[61] The first such place is emotional and internal; the second physical and external. Together they convey her desire to be an insignia both upon and within him, body and soul.

seal In biblical sources, a seal denoted affiliation, and it was an object of identity or stature. Thus Judah could be identified by his "seal" (Gen. 38:18, 25); and when God promises Zerubbabel that he shall be the future leader of Judaea, the language used is "I have set you as a seal (*samtikha ka-ḥotam*); for I have chosen you—says the Lord of Hosts" (Hag. 2:23). Rashbam understood the seal as a sign of remembrance—symbolizing the maiden's desire to be ever present to her beloved (in mind and heart).[62]

For The maiden explains her request.

love is fierce as death The figure *'azzah kha-mavet 'ahavah* evokes the overwhelming intensity of "love" (*'ahavah*), comparable to "death" (*mavet*) itself; and the point is enforced by adding that love's "passion is mighty as Sheol" (*qashah khi-sh'ol qin'ah*). Pounding in the maiden's heart, love is all-consuming—vanquishing its victims like death. And like death, love is a rupture.

Love is also like death because it (too) sharpens awareness of the finitudes and fortunes of existence. The marvel of love can be lost; but the fear of death can also be transcended through love. This point is evoked in SongsR 8.vii.4, which cites Eccles. 9:9: "Enjoy life with the woman you love—all your fleeting days."

Its darts are darts of fire, / A blazing flame The maiden further clarifies her similes: the flames of passion are like fiery "darts" (or "sparks"), flaring in many directions. The first reference to fire, *reshafeyha*, is intensified by the sequel, *rishpei 'eish* ("darts of fire");[63] and this designation is itself modified by the figure *shalhevetyah*, "a blazing flame" (also Immanuel).[64] This term is formed from the noun *lahav*, "flame"—intensified at the beginning by the *sh*-causative prefix,[65] and at the end by the divine complement *-yah* (cf. Jer. 2:31, where *ma'pelyah* means a "dense darkness").[66] See Rid (ad loc.) and Radak (on Gen. 1:2).

The power of this depiction derives from a cluster of old mythic figures. A similar argot occurs in Ugaritic mythology with dim reflexes in Scripture.[67] Regarding *mavet*: In Ugaritic poetry, death is personified as the divine figure Mot; while in Ps. 49:15, the being who shepherds Sheol's inhabitants is called Mavet (the name Azmavet in 2 Sam. 23:31 conjoins the two elements of our simile; and Mot is also called *'z*, "mighty").[68] As for *reshef*: In Ugaritic texts, Reshef appears as a god or agent of plague; and in Deut. 32:24, a divine agent of doom is called Reshef (also a member of the retinue around the heavenly war chariot in Hab. 3:5).[69] These

various images with a mythic valence further convey the otherworldly and death-defying power of *ʾahavah*.

Derash

6. Let me be a seal The mood of longing resumes (see v. 1). For some sages, the Song's phrase conveys the people's wish to be restored to God after the dislocations of exile. Uprooted physically and spiritually, the people yearn to be a seal affixed to their Beloved. Rabbi Meir perceived in these words a prayer of supplication that counterpoints the prophecy in which God threatened to remove the monarchy from King Jehoiakim—like a seal (Jer. 22:24).[70] And in the words "Let me be (*siymeini*) a seal (*ḥotam*) upon your heart," he heard Israel ask God: "[Re-]establish me (*siymeini*) as you planned (*ḥashavta*) in your heart" (SongsR 8.vi.1–2).[71] This is both a plea for forgiveness and a prayer for redemption.[72] Such a renewal would yield a transformed religious consciousness.

For R. Berekhiah, the "seal" refers to the phylactery bound on the arm and facing the heart as a symbol of this new awareness (SongsR 8.vi.i.). On this view, the Song passage was God's injunction to Israel: "Set Me—My teachings—as a seal upon your heart" for your spiritual direction! (Rashbam). Two ideals are projected: connection to God through spiritual love and through the divine teachings. In the first, the people long to be attached to God, with all their heart; in the second, God enjoins the people to attach His teachings to them, near their heart. The two voices reflect a religious dialogue. The human voice wants unmediated connection; the divine voice cautions the seeker to mediate religious love with thoughtful action—for the sake of heaven and human beings.

For love is fierce Rabbinic tradition distinguished this phrase from the next ("passion is mighty as Sheol"), in order to juxtapose two divine attitudes toward Israel: *ʾahavah* ("love") and *qinʾah* ("anger, passion")—classically formulated as "I have loved you" (Mal. 1:2) and "They angered Me by [worshiping] false gods" (Deut. 32:16) (SongsR 8.vi.4). On this basis, the sages contrasted the piety of Israel with the challenge posed by the nations. When interpreting the speaker as Israel, the sages heard the people swear loyalty to God—both for His gracious love (when they obey) ***and*** for His terrible wrath (when they do not).[73] But when interpreting the speaker as the nations, they have them mock Israel's piety—"What good is [divine] love alongside [such] anger?"[74] The two paired clauses palpably express a deep theological perplexity in the nation's soul.

Theological emotions are not abstract, but often reflect deep human experiences and analogies. Knowing this, the sages exemplified our religious polarity in terms of parental love, friendship, and marriage. First, with respect to parental love, preferential treatment can produce anger and enmity among siblings, as evidenced by Isaac's "love" for Esau (Gen. 25:28), which induced family machinations resulting in the latter's hatred of his brother Jacob (ibid. 27:41); similarly, Jacob's "love" for Joseph (ibid. 37:3) elicited his brothers' jealous hatred toward him (v. 4). Second, with respect to friendship, David's loyal "love" for Jonathan (1 Sam. 18:1) undermined Saul's benevolence toward David (v. 9) and led to a family rupture. And finally, with respect to marriage, a husband's love for his wife (Eccles. 9:9) may be ruined by a "jealous" suspicion of her disloyalty (Num. 5:14), with dire consequences. Love and jealousy are interrelated valences, locking people in complicated dynamics and consequences (see SongsR ibid.).[75]

Remez

6. Let me be a seal The seeker desires ("let me") to be sealed upon the Beloved ("upon your heart" and "hand"—the twin sources of inner and outer expression), and states this with an imperative urgency (see Peshat). The self yearns to be conjoined to the Beloved, the divine reality to which it is subject.[76] But however much it may desire this, the soul cannot bring it to realization. This requires an act by the Beloved; and thus the soul beseeches Him to raise her (through this attach-

ment) to a higher level of mind (heart) and deed (hand).[77] The request oscillates between supplication and bold petition. Its sole justification is the intensity of its love—which is now expressed.

For love is fierce as death True love consumes our entire being. This great, flaming "passion" annihilates all other interests through its fiery force. The all-consuming finitude of death symbolizes the way that the passions of love burn away a sense of independent selfhood. In different ways, every lover knows this. One must give oneself (in order) to Love, be it human or divine.

Sod

6. ***Let me be... the seal*** The soul longs to be imprinted in the heart of God, whose vitality extends throughout Being. Human images of "heart" and "arm" come forcefully to mind; for the soul is aware of its yearning heart and how it strives to reach God through God's worldly creations. The soul desires a permanent presence with God, an enduring spiritual awareness. It prays that the "impressions" that Divinity has made upon its soul (TiqZ 65a)[78] will leave some effect or trace on the heart of Being (Z. 1:244b). It fears that its spiritual experiences will dissipate, and be of no ultimate consequence.

Like the seal upon your hand How can the soul impress itself upon Being? Perhaps through the very mystery of the seal. Older spiritual masters noted that the consonants of *ke-ḥotam* ("as a seal") may be recombined as *koaḥ tam*—suggesting that one should receive the transcendent "Might" (*koaḥ*) of Divinity with a "pure" (*tam*) and focused integrity (TiqZ 68a). This is a beginning. It requires a transformed and receptive self.

For love is fierce as death The soul confesses its consuming passion for God. This is a dying to everything other than the quest for pure love—even a dying to the self and its ego needs (Ibn Sahula). Love of God is the core desire. It is a centering point that gives stability and worth to all moments and beings (*ve-khola' bi-rḥimuta' qayyema'*; Z. 3:267b).[79]

7 Vast floods cannot quench love,
Nor rivers drown it.
If a man offered all his wealth for love,
He would be laughed to scorn.

7 מַ֣יִם רַבִּ֗ים לֹ֤א יֽוּכְלוּ֙ לְכַבּ֣וֹת אֶת־הָֽאַהֲבָ֔ה
וּנְהָר֖וֹת לֹ֣א יִשְׁטְפ֑וּהָ
אִם־יִתֵּ֨ן אִ֜ישׁ אֶת־כָּל־ה֤וֹן בֵּיתוֹ֙ בָּאַ֣הֲבָ֔ה
בּ֖וֹז יָב֥וּזוּ לֽוֹ׃ ס

Peshat

7. Vast floods . . . rivers Having introduced the theme of destructive fire, the maiden adds that this blaze cannot be extinguished—either by *mayim rabbim*, "vast floods" (or "mighty torrents"), or *neharot*, "rivers." Both water elements have semimythic valences in Scripture and Ugaritic literature. In Ps. 93:3–4, the cosmic waters are called *mayim rabbim*;[80] and in Hab. 3:8, 15, *mayim rabbim* and *neharim*—the masculine counterpart of *neharot*—figure in a scene portraying a theomachy (divine battle) against mythic waters.[81] In Ugarit, the river of the Canaanite god El was called *rbm*.[82]

If a man offered This sentence adds a new element: love cannot be purchased; it is not a commodity for exchange. The maiden formulates this in hypothetical terms, to highlight the absurdity of such an assumption. Literally, she states: "Were a person to give (*'im yittein*; viz., in payment) all the wealth of his household, he would be mocked (*boz yabhuzu lo*)." Indirectly, these words echo her earlier thoughts about the beloved. She had then opined, "Would that (*mi yittein*) you were like a brother to me" (8:1)—in which case she could kiss him in broad daylight "and no one would despise me (*lo' yabhuzu li*)." Hearing both, the reader perceives two salient modalities of love in the Song: its public sanctions and controls, and its inestimable value and worth. Through this intertextual nexus, the poet reveals two aspects of the maiden's psychological tenor.[83]

Derash

7. Vast floods cannot quench love Israel's love for God is unquenchable, a bulwark against the challenges (spiritual and material) posed by the nations (SongsR 8.vii.1; ExodR 49.1).[84] Stubborn resistance has kept *Keneset Yisra'el* faithful to its divine sources of sustenance. Love of Torah—like "a blazing flame" (*shalhevet-yah*) cast from heaven (SongsR 8.vii.4)—has served as an eternal fire on Tradition's altar. And divine love (constantly expressed through Torah and Tradition) has provided a spiritual polestar, orienting the people amidst the confusions and challenges of secular culture.[85]

If a man offered . . . wealth Love of God is an unquenchable fire, incommensurate with earthly entities. It has no natural measure, being a supernatural grace to be cherished and cultivated. Culturally, this love is expressed through commitment to Torah, itself a heavenly fire (Deut. 33:2)—and thus utterly different from Promethean productions ignited by self-serving goals. Israel's love of God (through Torah) is a spiritual service; it cannot to be acquired by any kind of self-aggrandizement (cf. SongsR, ibid.).

laughed to scorn The deserved treatment (*boz yabhuzu lo*; cf. v. 1) of spiritual hucksters.[86] Inflamed inwardly, Israel proclaims before God: "How greatly do I love Your Torah; it fills my speech all day long" (Ps. 119:97;[87] cf. NumR 2.16). Devoted to a life of the spirit, true students of Tradition relinquish worldly rewards. Rabbi Oshaya was an exemplar of this virtue, and so his companions memorialized him with this verse (SongsR, ibid., end).

Remez

7. Vast floods cannot quench love This says it all. There is no antidote for love save its own realization. The yearning of love and the

desire for spiritual fulfillment transcend natural feelings. Hence, nothing natural can quench it.

If a man offered all his wealth One cannot procure "love" as if it were a quantifiable entity. It is not. It is incommensurable. It flares up from one's inmost depth. To think otherwise invites "scorn"—an even greater derision than that expressed by those who (without sympathy or knowledge) mock love's visible reality, spiritual or otherwise (v. 2). The reuse of the verb *yavuzu* (in vv. 2 and 7; see Peshat) sharpens this point.[88] Love exceeds all bounds. Lovers want their Beloved ones, nothing else; and seekers desire spiritual fulfillment, totally.

Sod

7. ***Vast floods*** The fire of divine love is an ineffable force; nothing in the "flood" of experience can overwhelm it (Ibn Sahula).[89] Spiritual longing transcends ordinary experience. As such, it can endure the riptide of the commonplace. Beyond worldly value, no amount of natural desire is its equivalent. Anyone who thinks otherwise deserves "scorn." Loving God, the soul expands its borders; what returns to it as worldly experience is transfigured by a sense of the Absolute. Only the true seeker understands this. If a person would "offer" their "all" to God—"for" God's "love" (REzra)[90]—onlookers might mock this as excessive. But the devoted self will be inured.

8 "We have a little sister,
Whose breasts are not yet formed.
What shall we do for our sister
When she is spoken for?

8 אָח֖וֹת לָ֣נוּ קְטַנָּ֔ה
וְשָׁדַ֖יִם אֵ֣ין לָ֑הּ
מַֽה־נַּעֲשֶׂה֙ לַאֲחֹתֵ֔נוּ
בַּיּ֖וֹם שֶׁיְּדֻבַּר־בָּֽהּ׃

Peshat

3. A FRATERNAL SPECULATION (vv. 8–10)

This unit features a dialogue involving the
maiden and her brothers. The latter state that
their sister is young and undeveloped, and
wonder what to do should a suitor appear.
They speak in metaphorical terms, and the
images are ambiguous. At any rate, she intervenes with an answer: she is already suitable for
marriage.

The occurrence of this unit here is puzzling.
It presumably provides an ironic counterpoint
to the maiden's own last words (v. 7), when she
said that anyone who would put a price on love
is worthy of derision.

**8. *We have a little sister, / Whose breasts
are not yet formed*** The brothers speculate
about her marriage value, given her present
physical condition (their say over her future recalls 1:6). They say that their sister is *qetannah*,
"young" and immature, as suggested by her
"lack" (*'ein lah*) of breasts. In Ezek. 16:7–8, the
maturity of a girl for "sexual activity" (*dodim*) is
marked by "firm breasts and [pubic] hair."

What shall we do for our sister This is
their worry. How could they make her appear
more desirable?

When she is spoken for The idiom *ba-yom
she-yedubbar bah* means "on the day that she is
spoken about [for marriage]."[91] Cf. 1 Sam.
25:39, where it is stated that after Nabal's death,
David "sent" messengers to "speak for her"
(Nabal's widow, Abigail) on his behalf (*va-
ydabber be-*) regarding "marriage" (*le-qahtah lo
le-'ishah*; literally, "to procure her for him[self]
as a wife").[92] Cf. B. B.M. 84b. The brothers'
concern to get the best return for her explains
their ensuing deliberations.

Derash

8–10. This cluster of verses reflects a puzzling dialogue (see Peshat). The sages tried to
explicate the unit by interpreting it in terms of
historical events and scriptural episodes. The
result is a series of discourses on exemplary
values, further presenting the Song as a thesaurus of cultural ideals. As elsewhere, martyrdom
is given a special status, and Abraham deemed
its prototypical devotee (SongsR 8.viii–x; Tan.,
Lekh-lekha 2).[93] The spiritual drama of his trial
is elevated to the nation's founding, for his devotion resulted in a spiritual patrimony.

Other sages projected other scenes of trial
and endurance (SongsR 8.ix.2 and passim).
Surely love unto death—spiritual resistance at
all costs—was a weighty ideal. The affirmation
that "Love is strong as death" was no empty
phrase. It was therefore a balm to hear the interpretation of the assertion "I am a wall" as
God's personal guarantee to protect Israel from
the torment of the nations (ibid.). (Years earlier, a similar promise was offered to Jeremiah;
Jer. 1:18–19.) Such exegesis offered a promise of
divine hope.

8. *We have a little sister* Various sages
refigured this discourse in terms of Abraham's
virtues. According to R. Berekhiah, the little
"sister" (*'ahot*) is Abraham because he "gathered" (*'ihah*) the nations to God's service
(SongsR 8.viii.2), whereas according to Bar
Kappara, Abraham was devoted to the commandments and good deeds while still "little"
in age.[94] Like a girl whose "breasts" (*shadayim*)
"were not yet formed," he was one who had
"not yet" (*she-'adayin*) come to full knowledge
of the commandments (SongsR, ibid.). Given
all this, it was wondered whether he could withstand the test of martyrdom: "what shall we do
for our sister on the day she is spoken for

(*yedubbar bah*)?"—read this as "... the day she is spoken against," this being the day when King Nimrod decreed that Abraham be cast into a furnace as a test of his loyalty to his God.[95] The model of the patriarch thus provided a prism for deep cultural reflections.

Remez

8. We have a little sister Who speaks? Ostensibly, the brothers; but perhaps the self is overheard musing in private monologue. Having wished the Beloved to be like her "brother" (v. 1), she feels like a "little sister" growing in love and full of potential ("whose breasts have not yet formed"). Without further spiritual guidance, the self feels arrested in its development. Thus the self turns inward and asks: "What shall we do for our sister when she is spoken for?" Each moment has its challenges, and the self wants to respond appropriately (Ibn Aqnin). Despite prior achievements, doubts about worthiness and readiness linger. One must turn to the guides and engage in proper preparation (*hakhanah*) (Al-Fawwāl).[96] The phrase *yedubbar bah* ("spoken for") also indicates speech "spoken within" one's soul.

Sod

8. We have a little sister Self-doubt again seizes the mind and challenges the soul's achievements. The ordinary suddenly intervenes. The brothers' voice (ordinariness) recalls an earlier time when they insinuated themselves into the soul's will and directed it toward worldly labors—not its true spiritual tasks (1:6). Now the soul must overcome a sense of doubt, misdirection, and hesitation. Suggestions of unworthiness (being "little" and undeveloped) leave the soul vulnerable before this precious moment "when" it was "spoken for"—for has not God just called her "to turn" to Him, and praised her beauty (and development; 7:1, 2–7)? Has she not matured and achieved a measure of wisdom (Z. 3:296a),[97] that she might devote herself to spiritual service?

9 If she be a wall,
We will build upon it a silver battlement;
If she be a door,
We will panel it in cedar."

9 אִם־חוֹמָה הִיא
נִבְנֶה עָלֶיהָ טִירַת כָּסֶף
וְאִם־דֶּלֶת הִיא
נָצוּר עָלֶיהָ לוּחַ אָרֶז׃

Peshat

9. ***If she be a wall... If she be a door*** These two figures are indeterminate. If interpreted as juxtaposed and symbolic opposites, the "wall" suggests intact chastity and the "door" open profligacy (so Ibn Ezra).[98] Alternatively, the images are complements, symbolizing parts of her body. The brothers' language remains indirect and implicit; but their direct and explicit concern is to preserve the presumptions of appearance and propriety.[99] Hence they weigh their options.

They decide either to build up her appearance with fancy accoutrements (symbolized by the silver turret "built" upon her) or to guard her virtue with a protective shield (symbolized by the cedar paneling "affixed" or "bound up" upon her for safekeeping—taking *natzur* in this multiform sense).[100]

Derash

9. ***If she be a wall*** Projected as a discourse in heaven, the sages ponder the preceding case. If Abraham stands resolute as "a wall,"[101] and offers himself a martyr for God (Tan., *Lekh-lekha* 2),[102] he will be divinely rescued. Furthermore, "a silver battlement" (*ṭirat kesef*) will be built upon him—namely the future people Israel, who are likened to silver (Tan., ibid., interpreting Ps. 64:14). But if he shows himself to "be a door" (*delet*), "poor" (*dal*) in devotion (Tan., ibid.) and inconstant in observance (SongsR 8.ix–x.1), "we will panel (*natzur*) [him] in cedar"—deeming him a "figure" (*tzurah*) easily breeched and not deserving a spiritual patrimony.[103] These figures (wall and door) thus juxtapose the virtue of resilience (before spiritual threat)[104] to a poverty (*dallat*) of personal resources (Netziv).

Remez

9. ***If she be a wall*** The self reflects on its character. How sturdy has it become? If it is like a wall, fixed and embracing, then just that should be enhanced by "silver battlements"; that is, its own resources should be developed for appropriate use. Alternatively, if the self feels like "a door," or a portal that does not firmly limit external elements, then just that should be rectified by a "cedar panel"; that is, the gateway to one's spirit must be protected. The self must determine its central traits and develop them. Otherwise, the powerful expressions of love—and the path to fulfillment—will be undermined.

Sod

9. ***If she be a wall*** The soul struggles with self-doubt and ponders defensive solutions. But these proposals arise from a false consciousness. What would be gained by such a response, demeaning desire (*kesef*)[105] and coating it with a "silver" (*kesef*) veneer? What benefit would accrue by laying siege to the heart[106]—sealing shut the "door" (*delet*) of the spirit? Confusion leaves the soul perplexed.

10 I am a wall,
My breasts are like towers.
So I became in his eyes
As one who finds favor.

10 אֲנִי חוֹמָה
וְשָׁדַי כַּמִּגְדָּלוֹת
אָז הָיִיתִי בְעֵינָיו
כְּמוֹצְאֵת שָׁלוֹם׃ פ

Peshat

10. The maiden disrupts their musings with her response. With this retort, she co-opts one part of her brothers' double figure (the wall).

like towers The phrase *ke-migdalot* refers to her full breasts. She thus asserts her physical development and readiness for marriage (contra their critique). Her comment evokes the youth's earlier depiction of her neck as "like the tower (*ke-migdal*) of David," built in splendor and decked with ornaments (4:4).

So I became in his eyes / As one who finds favor This part of her response is obscure. She presumably underscores to her brothers that she is ready for betrothal. The expression *motze'eit shalom* suggests the peace of mind that marriage brings, as when Ruth blessed her daughters-in-law by saying: "May the Lord grant that each of you find (*metze'na*) security (*menuḥah*) in the house of a husband!" (Ruth 1:9).[107]

The plot to outfit the maiden for public appearance highlights the brother's regard for her financial worth. The episode seems out of joint at this juncture. Occurring just after the maiden's celebration of love and its incommensurable value, the brothers' attitude ostensibly exemplifies those procurers of love whom—she said authoritatively—are to be "laughed to scorn" (v. 7).

Derash

10. ***I am a wall*** Pondering these alternatives, Abraham responds point by point (SongsR, ibid.). He first proclaims his religious devotion, professing himself steadfast as a wall; and then he says "my breasts are like towers," thus asserting that his descendants will also be tzaddikim—"righteous" martyrs like Hananiah, Mishael, and Azariah (persecuted by Nebuchadnezzar), or like R. Hananiah and his pious companions (slain during the reign of the Roman emperor Hadrian).[108]

As one who finds favor Upon hearing Abraham's testimony, God promises to deliver (*motzi'*) him "safely" (*be-shalom*) from his trial,[109] after which the devotee declares: "So I became in [God's] eyes as one who finds favor (*motzei't shalom*)"—having emerged "whole" (*be-shalom*), physically and spiritually, from the trial.[110]

Remez

10. ***I am a wall, / My breasts are like towers*** The soul's response, after pondering the above matters. She avers that her inner character has developed and serves as visible adornments. She knows this with an inner knowledge. And she knows something more: that "I became in his eyes as one who finds favor." The sense of self and its qualities have been stimulated by the desire for the Beloved, and nurtured through His loving favor. The Beloved's gaze has cultivated her beauty, as His presence has stimulated its refinement. These words mark a higher self-realization.[111]

Sod

10. ***I am a wall*** The soul regains its balance and transforms doubt into virtue. Speaking in the first person, the self speaks with confidence. Owning the images, the adept says: the wall is not a defense against anxiety, but a structure of spiritual resilience; and the breasts are not signs of immaturity, but sources of sustenance. When the self speaks of "my breasts," it refers both to the supreme Source of spiritual nurture and to the self's personal

resources—that is, to Divine Wisdom in the fullest sense (Z. 3:296a) and to this Wisdom's beneficiaries (Ibn Sahula).

So I became . . . finds favor The soul asserts its connection to the supernal heights above, and to the human actuality below. This dual covenant results in a spiritual harmony or "peace" (*shalom*)[112]—a joining of the transcendent to the immanent in a spiritual bond (*le-qashra' qishrin di-mheimanuta' bi-r'uta' de-libba'*; Z. 1:256b).[113] If the perception of Divinity marks an inward, contemplative element, the gifts offered others are more active and worldly. This conjunction of a *vita contemplativa* with a *vita activa* constitutes a deep spiritual integration (Alkabetz): a balance of mind and body.

11 Solomon had a vineyard
In Baal-hamon.
He had to post guards in the vineyard:
A man would give for its fruit
A thousand pieces of silver.

11 כֶּ֣רֶם הָיָ֤ה לִשְׁלֹמֹה֙
בְּבַ֣עַל הָמ֔וֹן
נָתַ֥ן אֶת־הַכֶּ֖רֶם לַנֹּטְרִ֑ים
אִ֛ישׁ יָבִ֥א בְּפִרְי֖וֹ
אֶ֥לֶף כָּֽסֶף׃

Peshat

4. CONCLUDING CODA AND FINAL FLIGHT (vv. 11–14)

Like the previous discourse, the first one in this unit (vv. 11–12) is puzzling at this juncture. The speaker says that Solomon had a vineyard that he gave to watchmen, who reaped one thousand talents of silver for its produce and received one-fifth of this as wages; but he, by contrast, has his own (precious) vineyard. In context, it seems that this vignette is both symbolic and ironic: symbolic, insofar as the reference to Solomon's thousand talents hints at his harem (see below); and ironic, insofar as such an episode would again mock those who buy love (see v. 7).

Two pieces conclude the cycle. In verse 13, someone tells the maiden that "friends" seek her voice, adding: "let me hear [you/it]!" The speaker is presumably her beloved; and she presumably fears these "others," for she answers his plea with an exhortation to flee (v. 14)—leaving her alone to preserve their pact of love in her heart.

11. *Solomon had a vineyard* The clause *kerem hayah li-shlomoh* does double-duty, marking a vineyard "belonging to" Solomon in Baal-hamon, an otherwise unknown place. Its form is like the introduction to a parable (as in Isa. 5:1, *kerem hayah li-ydidi*, "My beloved had a vineyard"),[114] introducing the subject and figure to be discussed. However (in contrast to Isa. 5:1–7), because this figure's meaning is not spelled out, it remains suggestive at best (see below).

He had to post...in the vineyard Rather, "he leased the vineyard." Here the verb *natan* has a financial sense: "he rented" or "sold it for hire," as in 1 Kings 21:1–2, where this verb is used to specify the proposed lease of a vineyard.[115]

guards The noun *noṭerim*, literally "watchmen," here refers to tenant farmers.[116]

A man would give for his fruit / A thousand pieces of silver The terms of the lease agreement are now stated. Each watchman, or vintner, would harvest (*yavi'*, literally "bring") the worth of a thousand silver pieces to benefit from "its fruit" (*be-firyo*)—the profit or remaining percentage of the overall "produce" they could earn. As formulated, this is merely a summary of a crop-rental agreement. Its significance for the Song is suggested in the next verse.

Derash

11–12. These verses comprise a unit of discourse whose complexities are legion (see Peshat). From this dialogue, the sages wrested a theology of exile, emphasizing the consequences of sin and the hope in divine providence. Various interpretations in SongsR 8.xi.1 (beginning) and xii.1 (end) propose an integral teaching on exile and restoration.

11. Solomon had a vineyard The past tense indicates loss. Taken as a cultural allegory, Solomon (*Shelomoh*) refers to God, who once had a vineyard (Israel) "in Baal-hamon"—this phrase marking the people's "idolatrous worship of" or "yearning for" (*hamu*) Baal, and the resulting invasion of pagan "hordes" (*hamonot*) in punishment—measure for measure. Hence God delivered the people and land to the "guards" or "practitioners"[117] of idolatry (Mat-Keh), led by Nebuchadnezzar,[118] the "man" (representative leader) of Babylon, who gave (*yavi'*) "a thousand pieces of silver" for its "fruit"—this figure hinting at the one thousand "righteous" persons (namely, artisans) that he deported (*yavi'*, "brought") to captivity (cf. 2 Kings 24:16)[119] (SongsR 8.xi.1).

Remez

11. Solomon had a vineyard The self reflects further. The ideal Beloved (the perfected One, *Shelomoh*) is the source of the soul's possibilities. Spiritual growth is a possibility that must be cultivated and protected. It begins as a potential, with turmoil and confusion—"Baal-hamon" signifying that the self is the "owner," or *baʿal*, of its own "confusion," *hamon*. The onset may feel forbidding, with inner defenses (or "guards") posted roundabout. Thus one may have to pay a high price ("a thousand pieces of silver") to acquire spiritual "fruit." This is not the price of love, maligned in verse 7, but the cost of self-care (Immanuel). When love is born in the soul, it comes as a grace; what must be acquired is the appropriate development. The soul had long since determined to initiate this process, saying "My own vineyard I did not guard" (1:6)—a vital turning point. The quest is now coming to fruition.

Sod

11. Solomon had a vineyard Having recovered its spiritual fortitude, the soul reflects on this achievement of *shalom* (v. 10). Her attainment of "supernatural" love is contrasted with "natural" love, symbolized by the earthly dominion of Solomon (*Shelomoh*). Worldly desires are marked by accumulation, fear of loss, and the calculation of percentages. One sees the world in terms of aggrandizement or gain—external factors only. The soul reflects that once it too was trapped by the vagaries of appropriation. Its own soul-truth, or vineyard, was not its own. With these words, the soul utters a confession. And in the same breath, it reaffirms its bond with God, the King of True Harmony (*ha-melekh she-ha-shalom shelo*)—who has given her resources to achieve a higher reality, even within the natural world. Torah is the heavenly gift for this purpose (ZḤ 21b–22a); the "guards" (*noṭerim*) are those persons who cultivate and protect their spiritual resources (Ibn Sahula).

12 I have my very own vineyard:
You may have the thousand, O Solomon,
And the guards of the fruit two hundred!

12 כַּרְמִ֥י שֶׁלִּ֖י לְפָנָ֑י
הָאֶ֤לֶף לְךָ֙ שְׁלֹמֹ֔ה
וּמָאתַ֖יִם לְנֹטְרִ֥ים אֶת־פִּרְיֽוֹ׃

Peshat

12. ***I have my very own vineyard*** The clause *karmi sheli le-fanai* literally means "My own vineyard is before me." (On the syntactic construction *karmi sheli*, see at 3:7.) The speaker juxtaposes the large vineyard of Solomon with his own.

You may have the thousand, O Solomon The speaker dismisses the big profits: Solomon can keep the thousand silver pieces he has gained, and the watchmen can enjoy the two hundred they receive for their work as renters—for all he cares![120]

Viewed straightforwardly, the episode contrasts the vineyard of Solomon with one belonging to the speaker. But as suggested, the discourse has the form of a parable. From a contextual viewpoint, it may be construed as follows: The speaker is (impliedly) the youth who juxtaposes the king's vineyard estate—tended by many for a price—with his own single holding. With gusto he says that Solomon can keep his vineyard (and its profits), for he has his very own, right "before" him. This response suggests a symbolic tenor. If the speaker's own vineyard (*karmi sheli*) is his darling maiden (who had referred to herself as *karmi sheli*; 1:6), might not the reference to Solomon and his thousand talents hint at the "one thousand" women in his harem (1 Kings 11:3)?! And if so, might not this vineyard in "Baal-hamon" hint that the king was not only the "master of much wealth (*hamon*)" (1 Chron. 29:16), but also the "lord of a bevy (*hamon*)" of women (2 Chron. 11:23)?[121] On this understanding, the discourse has the youth proclaim his disregard for procured women and wealth (Immanuel). Once again, we have an ironic vignette deriding the notion that true love could be bought.

Derash

12. ***I have my . . . vineyard*** Continuing the allegory (v. 11), the wicked king boasts of his success before God (*Shelomoh*): "O Solomon," your "thousand" (exiles) is now diminished to the sum ("fruit") of "two hundred" souls. However, God answers: to the contrary—the first thousand has waxed strong, and each one has produced two hundred more (Radal)—the fruit of their piety, and a token of their restoration. If the remnant retains its spiritual character during times of dispersion, the transplanted seed will yield new fruit.

Remez

12. ***I have my very own vineyard*** The self speaks of itself with spiritual self-assurance, while offering acknowledgment to Solomon for the price paid ("you may have the thousand, O Solomon"). Even the guards are thanked for their protective custody; for they kept the "fruit" ripe until the soul could acquire it. They too must be acknowledged at this moment.

Sod

12. ***I have my . . . own vineyard*** The preceding reflections are restated. The self affirms its spiritual nature. Having its own soul, it is not affected by the hoopla of the world. The soul sees the world of vanity for what it is and rejects that path. Within the vast universe of Divinity, the single soul makes a statement. It is an assertion of spiritual courage and commitment. We possess no outside assurance or internal guarantee that the soul will maintain its integrity. To ask for such validations would be to fall into the trap of worldly speculations. The spiritual self must proceed differently. It must stand firm in silent conviction, determined to distinguish the sacred (godly) from the profane (merely natural)—as best as possible (Z. 2:227a–b).

13 O you who linger in the garden,
A lover is listening;
Let me hear your voice.

13 הַיּוֹשֶׁבֶת בַּגַּנִּים
חֲבֵרִים מַקְשִׁיבִים
לְקוֹלֵךְ הַשְׁמִיעִנִי׃

Peshat

13. O you who linger in the garden Literally, "O you who dwell in the gardens." The youth speaks further to his darling, calling her *ha-yoshevet ba-gannim*, "dweller of gardens."

A lover is listening; / Let me hear your voice The Hebrew syntax is somewhat ambiguous: an indirect object ("your voice") is placed between two verbs. The present translation construes that object as being governed by the second verb. (The Hebrew lineation shown above reflects this translation's reading.) However, this is forced;[122] normal syntax and the Masoretic punctuation associate the indirect object with the first verb. This yields a different meaning, as explained below.

A lover is listening Literally, "friends are listening." The present translation notes that the plural construction yet renders in the singular, perhaps because only one male "friend" has appeared in the book up to this point—namely, the beloved. More likely, the plurals in *ḥaveirim maqshivim* suggest that a group of companions (his?) are nearby—and listening "to [or: for] your voice (*le-qoleikh*)."

Let me hear your voice This translation has the beloved himself ask to hear the maiden's voice (as in 2:14). More likely, the verbal imperative *hashmi'ini* ("Let me hear") has only an implied object ("it").

Overall, the speaker points to the attentive presence of the "friends," while emphasizing his desire that she speak to him alone (or quietly; Immanuel). Thus: "*Friends* want to hear your voice; [but] let *me* hear it."

Derash

13. O you who linger The dialogue of love between the Beloved and Israel nears its end with this evocation of pathos and longing.[123] Confessing her love of God beyond the threat of death, and her unquenchable thirst for Torah, the nation gathers in its sacred habitations (the synagogue and study hall) for prayer and learning. These locations constitute "the garden" of God where the people's voice seeks heaven with a common longing and intent.[124] The sages seal this dual recitation—the people's "voice" in prayer and study—with a divine response. For them, God and His angels resonate to this human piety. They are the "fellowship" (*ḥaveirim*; see Peshat) that "is listening" (SongsR 8.xi.1–2).

Remez

13. O you who linger in the garden The climactic confirmation is now stated. First, the Beloved acknowledges the self's attainment: she "sits [or: dwells]" in the garden of Love, as an embodiment of the Beloved's love (see 4:12, 15, and 5:1). He then adds that "the companions" (the self's highest qualities) "attend" with it (the Beloved; "me") to "hear your voice." Did not the Beloved request this long ago (2:14), when the self was making progress (though hesitant and "hidden" from view)? He again asks to hear the soul's voice.

Sod

13. O you who linger And then it comes: a confirmation. A divine voice beckons to the soul: You speak truly from within your "garden" of spiritual desire (your inward place: *beseiter ha-madreigah penima'ah*; ZḤ 56a). But other seekers await your help. So go forth and "let Me hear your voice," guiding others to a holy life. Just this is an act of love devoted to Me. It is a way of finding Me in the world. You have asserted your soul; now develop it through love of your companions, fellow travelers on the spiritual path (Ibn Sahula).

The adept hears this with bated breath. It is the gift of destiny; a charge to build up the world's spiritual resources.

14 "Hurry, my beloved,
Swift as a gazelle or a young stag,
To the hills of spices!"

14 בְּרַ֣ח ׀ דּוֹדִ֗י
וּֽדְמֵה־לְךָ֤ לִצְבִי֙ א֣וֹ לְעֹ֣פֶר הָֽאַיָּלִ֔ים
עַ֖ל הָרֵ֥י בְשָׂמִֽים׃*

v. 14. סכום הפסוקים של הספר 117 וחציו 4.14

תם ונשלם תהילה לאל בורא עולם

Peshat

14. Hurry, my beloved The youth now receives an answer—but not the one he hoped for: *beraḥ dodi*, literally "Flee, my beloved." Having been alerted to the friends' nearness, the maiden (apparently disconcerted) tells her beloved to run away "like a deer" among "the hills of spices." Her words echo an earlier exhortation (2:17), when she urged him to depart ("turn") and bound "like a deer" upon the "hills of spices" (or "cloven hills"; see comment there).

The aromas of spring evoke their blossoming love, but the pathos of separation hangs in the air. Unstated and indeterminate is their reunion. Such is the great rhythm of the Song—filled with songs of love, sometimes requited and other times silenced in midsentence.

Derash

14. Hurry, my beloved In response to God's address (v. 13), the people answer: Hasten, LORD, as "a gazelle" (*tzvi*), and hear the longing (*tzivyon*) of our souls in prayer (SongsR 8.xiv.1). May it be as acceptable before You as the "spices" of good deeds, and may You keep Your watchful eye upon Israel—be she worthy or not—like a gazelle that sleeps with one eye open and alert at all times (SongsR, ibid.; Targum).[125] The darkness of the world would then be illumined by this heavenly gaze; as Scripture says, "Truly the eye of the LORD is on those who fear Him, [for those] who wait for His faithful care" (Ps. 33:18).[126] A heartfelt longing thus concludes the Song. It is a prayer for God's imminent advent, at the right time (SongsR, ibid., end).

Remez

14. Hurry, my beloved The soul's voice indeed comes—seeking further bliss. What more could it say to the Beloved One than this: "hurry" . . . "to the hills of spices"? For is not the soul, like a garden of love, resplendent with "spices" (4:14)? And what more could the soul desire than the Beloved's presence? Love wants more love; and the self wants its fulfillment as soon as possible. "Hurry, my Beloved" is the passionate appeal that only the inner heart can speak.

Sod

14. Hurry, my beloved What can the soul answer? What response is appropriate? Perhaps this: Please, God, come swiftly as before. Be again like a "gazelle" and come to the "hills of spices"—the space of love in the heart, where those who love You await Your kiss of spiritual strength.

There is no answer or guarantee. Risks and rewards are mysteriously interfolded. The spiritual life is open-ended.

CONCLUSION

The final cluster includes a variety of topics, moods, and genres. Despite this variety, there are also continuities of voice and theme that integrate the portrayals of love found in the Song. I annotate them here, since they allow us to review the languages of love occurring in this unit and elsewhere in the Song. Six features are notable. First and foremost is the solicitation of love, expressing erotic desire in harmony with the natural world (here, 7:12–14;

elsewhere, 2:10–13). Second is the phenomenon of private desire and hope, and the longing for love's unabashed fulfillment (here, 8:1–3; elsewhere, 3:4). Third is the memory of love's onset and its natural setting (here, 8:5b; elsewhere, 2:3). Fourth is the desire for a physical connection, by placing tokens of love upon one's body for the sake of intimate nearness and evidence of love's concrete character (here, 8:6–7; elsewhere, 1:13). Fifth are the attempts to quantify the value of love or estimate its value (here, 8:8–9, 11–12; elsewhere, 7:7). And sixth are the many portraits of love in natural and supernatural terms, via metaphors and similes. The last point is emphatically marked in this cycle by the great image at its center, wherein the maiden exults that *love* is as mighty and fierce "as death" (8:6–7). These similes are the climactic attempt of the poet's own desire to measure or qualify the power of love. They thus serve as an expression of the Song itself and of its attempts to emblazon the mystery and power of love on the sensibility of its readers.

The oscillations of love are also given renewed expression in this cycle. The Song began with the maiden's desire for presence and intimacy, but concludes with her wish for absence and separation. The compelling force of these shifts cannot be denied. Repeatedly, there is longing for personal presence, though this often ends in loss or withdrawal. Such paradoxes are the inexplicable heartbeat of love. The Song of Songs gives them voice.

NOTES TO THE COMMENTARY

1:1–17

1. The first two units are marked off by major paragraph breaks, and the third by a minor paragraph break. The fourth unit, 1:15–17, continues through 2:7, possibly because 2:1–3 could be understood to continue the conversation at the end of chapter 1. (However, construing such a continuity adds other extraneous factors; see discussion at 1:15–17 and in chapter 2.)

2. The translators note that the Hebrew literally reads, "Let him give me of the kisses," but this rendering drops the strong wish element; their translation, "Oh, give me of the kisses" retains that wish element but it transforms the entire statement into a direct address against the explicit third-person verbal form (see the commentary).

3. The Hebrew in both cases is *ḥaverim*, "friends." NJPS renders contextually, which obscures this link; see at 8:13.

4. Cf. Songs Rabbah: "The best (*meiṭav*) song."

5. Cf. the list of exemplary songs that spans ancient Israelite history—from Egypt to the final redemption—in MdRI, *Beshallaḥ* 1 (Horowitz-Rabin, ed.), pp. 116–18.

6. Isaiah's prophetic trope, which is clearly allegorical in its use of key terms (*dod*, "beloved"; and *kerem*, "vineyard"), presumably influenced rabbinic readings of the Song.

7. The medieval commentator Mosheh ben Sheshet (12th century?) construed this passage to mean that the people transposed the prophet's divine words into mere erotic songs. See *A Commentary on the Books of Jeremiah and Ezeqiel by Mosheh ben Shesheth*, edited by S. Driver (London: Williams and Norgate, 1871), ad loc. His contemporary R. Eliezer of Beaugency referred to these songs as *shir dodim*, "love songs." See his *Kommentar zu Ezechiel und den XII kleinen Propheten*, edited by S. Poznanski (Warshau: Mekize Nirdamim, 1909), Lieferung I, ad loc.

8. Centuries later, R. Akiva lambasted those who chanted the Song of Songs in such a manner (T. Sanh. 12:10; cf. B. Sanh. 101a). For details, see the introduction.

9. This point was articulated in the Middle Ages by Anon. 2.

10. Similarly ambiguous are the more contracted formulas "Prayer of/about (*le-*) Moses" (Ps. 90:1) and "Praise of/about (*le-*) David" (Ps. 145:1). Rashbam adduces the latter. They serve as semantic cognates only; they do not offer a clear explication.

11. MsP states that "the author tells us (*ha-sofer magid lanu*)" merely that Solomon recited the Song. He adds that the actual composition begins only at v. 2.

12. This tradition was influenced by the report in Prov. 25:1, that the "men of Hezekiah" copied or transmitted proverbs. Perceptively, Anon. 2 suggested that this group also selected our songs from all the songs of Solomon (aided by divine inspiration)—thus giving the Talmudic claim a historical-theological interpretation.

13. Songs Rabbah (ibid.) adds *me'ulleh* ("superior") to this list. Some have regarded the totality of songs noted here as referring to the traditional number of songs sung by Solomon (1005, according to 1 Kings 5:15). Rabbi Eleazar understood the passage to indicate that there were 1,005 cantillation notes for each word (*davar*) in the song (taking the singular "his song" in 1 Kings 5:15 to refer to "its song [notes])" or cantillation; cf. Maharzu, though he qualifies the assertion). Other sages said that this multitude of intonations was for each "parable" (*mashal*). Alternatively, the "songs" refer to the diverse songs of Scripture (variously listed at this point in the Targum and SongsZ; and cf. also in the MdRI, *Beshallaḥ, Shirta* 1).

14. The dedication of the superscription, *li-Shlomoh*, was midrashically interpreted as "to" or "for God"—"whose is peace," *she-ha-shalom shelo*; that is, the name *Shelomoh* was deduced as if from the noun *shalom* ("peace") plus the archaic pronominal suffix *-oh* ("his"; cf. *'ohaloh*, "his tent," in Gen. 9:21; 12:12:8). The phrase is notoriously difficult to translate. The full epithet referring to the King or One "whose is peace" conveys the sense of God as master or owner of peace, this being deemed a central attribute (thus the word "master" in the textual comment is a circumlocution). (The pronominal form is common in old northwest Semitic, and well attested in Aramaic and Moabite inscriptions and in Ugaritic texts.)

15. Aggadat Shir Ha-Shirim (S. Buber edition, p. 17) reads, "If (*'ilu*) the Song of Songs had not been given in the Torah" (*lo' nitnah ba-Torah*). But this makes no sense; it seems to be a hypercorrection for the more radical reading, "If the Torah had not been given" (*lo' nitnah Torah*), the Song would have been sufficient to guide the world. Songs Zuta offers a variant: if the Song had not been given "in Scripture . . . etc." In this spirit, Ibn Sahula states that had the Song of Songs not been given in Scripture, it, "would have been sufficient (*dayyam hayah*) for Israel and worthy (*u-khda'i*) for guiding." More recently, S. Lieberman (*Midreshei Teiman* [Jerusalem: Wahrmann, 1970], 14 n. 1) suggests the reading "(*'ilu lo' nitnah ba-Torah 'elah*), If only the Song of Songs had been given in the Torah." There, this tradition is reported in the name of R. Akiva.

16. Al-Fawwāl renders *shir ha-shirim* as *dimyon ha-dimyonim*, meaning that the Song uses many images that replace and overlap one another. His conception also draws on medieval poetic theory; cf. Marciano (2), ad loc.

17. Cf. R. Avraham Y. Kook, *'Orot Ha-Qodesh* (Jerusalem: Mossad HaRav Kook, 1978), 2, 444–45.

18. The ideal of moving toward Divine unity (through multiplicity) is also expressed in ZḤ 61b, where the title's four words are identified with the four letters of the tetragrammaton, marking the mystery of the *Shema*-proclamation (Deut. 6:4).

19. The literal rendering lacks the strong wish element; the translators' idiomatic rendering includes the wish element but transforms the entire statement into a direct address, against the explicit verbal inflection.

20. Technically, this is a jussive verb inflection. See the discussion in GKC §109 *b*.

21. Cf. the formulation of C. D. Ginsburg, "O for a kiss," ad loc.

22. Among moderns, Zakovitch, 46, suggests that the maiden's words are a "daydream" (*ḥalom be-haqitz*). This seems unlikely, given the context; in contrast, the semi-dream states in 3:1 and 5:2 are more explicit and contextually integrated.

23. This shift of voice is more a shift of mood and imaginative reference than a rhetorical variant (so Ginsburg, comparing Deut. 32:15). Such a rhetorical feature was also recognized by Ibn Aqnin, ad loc., who adduces Ruth 4:4, among other citations.

24. This possibility was noted by Anon. 1 and Anon. 2. The interpretation of *dodekha* as *'ohavekha* ("your love") is also stressed by Immanuel.

25. UT 1084:1–2; published in C. H. Gordon, *Ugaritic Textbook* (Rome: Pontifical Biblical Institute, 1965); see text listing and index. Cf. the discussion by Albright (1963).

26. In SongsR and many earlier sources, rabbis speculated as to when and where the Song was revealed to Israel (e.g., at the Sea, at Sinai, in the Tabernacle, at the Temple's dedication).

See the citations and discussions adduced by S. Lieberman, "*Mishnat Shir-Hashirim*," in G. Scholem, *Jewish Gnosticism, Merkabah Mysticism*, 118–23.

27. For an influential expression of the notion that all laws of the oral tradition are embedded in the decalogue, see Saadia Gaon's so-called *'Azharot* for Shavuot, found in *Siddur Rav Sa'adiah Ga'on*, ed. I. Davidson, S. Asaf, B. I. Joel (5th edition, Mekize Nirdamim; Jerusalem: R. Maas, 1985) pp. 191–216. For an extended discussion, see R. M. Kasher, *Torah Sheleimah* (new edition; Jerusalem: Bet Hotza'at Torah Sheleimah, 1992), volume 16, in the addenda.

28. This portion of the midrash is achieved by several puns. The association of the *neshiqot*, "kisses," of Torah study with weaponry is connected to 1 Chron. 12:2, which refers to soldiers who are *noshqei qeshet*, "archers"; *mashaq*, "noise," in Isa. 33:34 is reinterpreted as the "conjoining" (*mashiq*) of ritual pools discussed in the Mishnah (Miqva'ot 6:8); and the ultimate cleaving to God is connected to Ezek. 3:13, which refers to the "touching" of the wings of the heavenly beings as *mashiqot*. All these terms are the spiritual benefits of the "kisses," *neshiqot*.

29. Cf. Exod. 24:7. The theme of commitment in SongsR is conveyed by the people's proclaiming, "Yes, yes!" to each Word of the decalogue—signaling their readiness to accept all tasks of Torah and Tradition. In other sources, the people aver or "promise" their commitment. Cf. LevR 86.5. See also the discussion of M. Hirschman, *A Rivalry of Genius*, pp. 192–93.

30. The comment accounts for the fact that *dodim*, "love," here is written without the *vav*, hence it looks like *dadim* (breasts); cf. Prov. 5:19. See the Septuagint on this lemma.

31. See the discussion of Maharzu, ad loc.

32. For a similar point, see *Midrash Rabbah Ha-Mevo'ar, Shir Ha-Shirim*), 1, 73.

33. Cf. MatKeh: the sages are the *dodim* or beloved of God.

34. Cf. DeutR 7.3.

35. According to Leqaḥ Ṭov, *ṭovim* refers to all the "good things" (*ha-ṭovot*) or godly gifts bestowed upon Israel.

36. See *Guide of the Perplexed* 3:51. On this image, see my *Kiss of God*, pp. 17–18, 24–30.

37. Al-Fawwāl suggests this possibility. But most philosophers were dubious of such a contact, even with respect to the angelic Active Intellect (the tenth sphere from on High). Maimonides' formulation (in *Guide* 3:51) is ambiguous and subject to both possibilities (viz., Moses died *bi-nshiqah*—with [or: in the state of] a divine "kiss").

38. On the effects and uses of scent, see D. Green, *The Aroma of Righteousness*.

39. On this grammatical point, see GKC §143 *e*.

40. Similarly, Zakovitch, 47. He adduces Gen. 17:20 (referring to the Ishmaelites).

41. So also Rashbam.

42. See Leqaḥ Ṭov and Rid.

43. And cf. Leqaḥ Ṭov, which notes the lack of correspondence between noun and verb (and see below).

44. And among modern critics, see also H. Graetz, 109, 126.

45. This is the descriptive sense given by Rid, who is aware of the grammatical issue but does not emend the text.

46. See M. Baillet, J. Milik, R. De Vaux, ed., *Les Petites Grottes de Qumrân*. Discoveries in the Judaean Desert of Jordan, 3 (Oxford: Clarendon Press, 1962), 113. The editors emend this form to *mrqḥat*, thus yielding some ointment-like oil.

47. Regarding Deut. 33:3, Ramban says that the form *tukku* is like *ḥukku*; see also Ibn Ezra and Tamakh. Already Anon. 2 saw a link to *tirgalti* in Hos. 11:3. Beside the *ti-* prefix, old causatives with the *š* prefix are preserved in biblical Hebrew (and biblical Aramaic). Overall, see J. A. Soggin, "Traces of Ancient Causatives in *š*- Realized as Autonomous Roots in Biblical Hebrew," in his *Old Testament and Oriental Studies* (Rome: Pontifical Biblical Institute, 1975), 188–202. See also below at 8:6.

48. For such effects more conceptually presented, see R. Jakobson, *Language in Literature*, chapters 11–12 especially.

49. The language refers to conversion: *megayyeran u-makhnisan taḥat kanfei ha-Shekhinah*: "(he) converted them and brought them under the wings of the divine presence."

50. Also MatKeh.

51. Rashi picks up on the matter of all peoples of the earth receiving this beneficent fragrance.

52. According to AgShir, the "oils" are "the words of Torah"; and Ibn Aqnin interpreted them as the "kindnesses of God"—His acts of beneficence.

53. For this sense of *ṭuraq*, see the peshat. Midrashic comments abound regarding the pouring of oil from container to container as an analogue to the development of religious consciousness.

54. This confusion may be deliberate. The word *'aḥarekha* fits in two directions: either "draw me *after you*; let us run" or "draw me; *after you* we shall run" (this bi-modal possibility was already noted in SongsR, ad loc.)

55. See especially the influential note on the stem *z-k-r* by Ibn Janaḥ, *Sefer Ha-Shorashim*, 175. Among moderns, see Gordis, p. 78.

56. Alternatively, Ginsburg proposed that it refers to the upright youth, thus paralleling the young lasses. But the context and emphasis on wine makes this less likely.

57. Rashbam interpreted this call to be that of the people's supplication that God draw them out of exile—thus a historical focus.

58. For its part, MidShir speaks about more hidden, spiritual things.

59. Rabbi Yitzḥak further specified this intimacy: to say *bakh* to God is to speak to God through the language of Torah—for the Torah is composed of combinations of the twenty-two letters of the alphabet (the numerical value of *bakh* being 22 = 2 + 20); cf. SongsR ibid.; Tan., Lekh Lekha 9; PdRK 22.30.

60. Also see Maharzu, noting that love and fear are the two fundamental paths of divine worship.

61. Ginsburg already intuited the poetic structure and double sense of the passage. See ad loc.

62. For its part, MShir speaks of religious merits.

63. Rashi states: *ve-ha'i lashon "ra'u" bizzayon kemo "'al tir'uni she-'ani sheḥarḥoret."*

64. See in his *Sefer Ha-Riqmah*, 2, 142.

65. Similarly Rashbam, invoking *'adamdam* ("light red").

66. Rashbam pointedly takes this reference to "my vineyard" in the straightforward sense (*ke-mashma'o*).

67. See the Sefas Emes, in a discourse for *Tazri'a* (1892).

68. In the *Liqquṭim*, s.v. *sheḥorah* (also printed in his Prayer Book, *Siddur 'Avodat 'Elimelekh*, p. 273), R. Elimelekh speaks of a loss of *qedushah* (holiness).

69. The noun *nefesh* as "appetite," "desire," or "wish" (e.g., Exod. 15:9; Jer. 50:19; Prov. 6:30; Isa. 56:11) may also be evoked in the Song.

70. Rashbam perceives here the maiden's sense of herself as the beloved's flock; hence he supplements the verb—as if she said, "Where do you shepherd me?"

71. Ibn Ezra deems *'eiphoh* to be a blend of *'ei* ("where") + *poh* ("here"). It thus highlights the desire for "place." Cf. *'eikhoh* in 2 Kings 6:13.

72. An old rabbinic tradition links the "covering" with the practice of concealing the lip during mourning (see Rashi).

73. For Ha-Shoshani, see Grossman, "Haggahot R. Shema'yah" (1991): 44. The Gaon's son, R. Abraham, follows suit (without citing parallel texts; he simply glosses *'otyah* as *to'yah*).

74. Also note MShir: what will be the nation's future; cf. Ibn Aqnin.

75. For these valences (in the two queries), see Peshat.

76. NJPS renders "tents" (see Peshat) for *mishkenot* ("dwellings"), which is not to be confused with *'ohalim* ("tents") in v. 5.

77. Pope, 338, refers to the famous episode recorded on the tomb of Tutmose III, recording how, during a campaign against Kadesh, the enemy sent out a mare in heat to incite the male stallions of the Egyptians—and how the danger was averted; see J. Breasted, *Ancient Records of Egypt* (Chicago: University of Chicago Press, 1906), II:233; no. 589. This ruse must have been quite common, for Songs Rabba (ad loc.) also records a tradition that the Israelites appeared to the Egyptians as mares, and the latter pursued them into the sea. And there are other variations.

78. The supplemental use of the *yod* was noted also by Immanuel.

79. This Sod section construes *susati* here in personal terms (cf. the Peshat).

80. See the discussion of such strings of stones as amulets in E. Reiner, *Astral Magic in Babylonia*, Transactions of the American Philosophical Society 85.4 (1995), 125.

81. In addition to sages and students, MShir emphasizes those who devote themselves to the needs of the community.

82. Cf. Ibn Aqnin, *yoshevin ve-ḥorezin*, "who sit and study" with devotion.

83. The Vilna edition reads *msymh* (rendered *mesayemah*); but I have emended this to *mesuyamah* to conform to the previous passive participle. A similar silent emendation occurs in MatKeh, who justly explains the verb as meaning "a word that is specified and established very well."

84. Ibn Aqnin: the *torot* and the vowel points (*nequdot*).

85. NJPS renders *na'aseh* as "we will add." But this does not capture the tooled nature of the making; I have added another spiritual level.

86. Rashbam; see also Immanuel.

87. See his comment s.v. *be-meisav raḥav*.

88. Per MShir, this was the odor of the incense offered to the calf; according to Piyyuṭ 1 (p. 61), it indicates the "stench" of idolatry (*reiaḥ gas*).

89. Rashi remarkably is able to blend the positions of R. Meir and R. Yehudah, by treating the noun *reiaḥ* as a euphemism for divine love.

90. Heb. *yalin* is in the continuous present mood (with future prefix). Rashbam identifies the clause's implied subject as the male, not the sachet (contra R. Ḥanina in SongsR).

91. Construing *tzeror ha-mor* as like *tzeror shel mor*.

92. E.g., B. Shab. 26a; Pliny, *Historia Naturalis* xii, 14 and 24.

93. Cf. D. Green, *The Aroma of Righteousness*, pp. 178–81; and Ch. 5 overall, for the larger thematic involved.

94. See also Rabbi Shlomoh.

95. AhavD conjoins both processes (the initial expansion of religious experience, initiated by God; and the secondary human act, in response) to v. 12. This insight, I think, makes more forceful sense by conjoining vv. 12 and 13.

96. REzra developed these (and related) verbal associations in his theosophical comments about the shapes of the Divine Glory and the place of the transcendent souls hidden under the heavenly Throne. My comment is a more metaphoric adaptation, inspired by his remarks.

97. Rashi sees here a continuation of the theme of atonement, with God's statement of forgiveness to Israel.

98. Cf. in the Keret Epic, Krt: 96–98; text in Gordon, *Ugaritic Textbook*, ad loc.

99. See Nissinen: 589, l. 9b.

100. According to R. Yehudah, the Ark's extended staves (1 Kings 8:8) were like the protruding breasts of a woman, awaiting the presence of the Divine; in this context, Song 1:13 was adduced! See my discussion in *Biblical Myth and Rabbinic Mythmaking*, pp. 173–77.

101. On "our rafters" (*rahiṭeinu*), see the Peshat.

102. In the words of REzra: *ve-khol zeh mashal le-'inyan ha-ḥibbur ve-ha-qiruv* ("and all this is an allegorical figure for the spiritual event of conjunction and intimacy")!

2:1–17

103. The first Masoretic unit ends at 2:7, having begun with 1:15—presumably because of a sense that chapter 2 continues the intimacy in nature depicted in 1:15–16. In my commentary to the previous chapter, I explained why I prefer the medieval chapter division in this case.

104. See the preceding note and the ensuing discussion.

105. Both use the phrase "(she) praises herself" (*meshabba-ḥat 'atzmah*).

106. E.g., Transl.; and Fox, ad loc.

107. Also proposed by Zakovitch, ad loc.

108. See Feliks' discussions in *'Olam*, pp. 234–40, 242–43; and *Shir Ha-Shirim. Teva'*, 28–30; see also Zohary, *Plants*, 176–77.

109. So also Exum, 113; cf. Bloch and Bloch, 148–49. Regarding the trait of modesty, cf. Fox, 107.

110. Tamakh also rightly notes that this language has a rhetorical appeal to the beloved.

111. Cf. Ibn Aqnin: *ḥibbevani*, "loved me."

112. The Midrash (SongsR 2.i.1) cites Isa. 30:29 as a proof text—referring to the once and future song.

113. And see the discussion below, at v. 14.

114. Ibn Tibbon regards the *ḥavatzelet* (lily) as an aspect of the intellect; the *ḥoḥim* (thorns) as powers of the soul (also Ibn Aqnin). By contrast, Ralbag stated that these thorns denote the impediments of intellectual growth or development.

115. That is, for Immanuel, the self/soul is a beautiful flower and worthy of knowledge of the "valleys" (*'amaqim*)—these being the hidden (degrees of) esoteric wisdom (*ha-sodot ha-tzefunot*).

116. For REzra and other mystical commentators (based on midrashic teachings) the hues of the lily signify shifts of divine sefirotic valences. According to Z. 3:107a, the lily has two colors, white and red, symbolizing the divine attributes of mercy and judgment.

117. Specifically noted are the blessings of consolation in a house of mourning; the blessing for a bridegroom at a wedding feast; and the ability to lead a quorum in the statutory prayers before the Shema (cf. B. Meg. 23b).

118. According to AgShir, the danger comes from idolaters.

119. Cf. A. Heschel, *God in Search of Man* (New York: Farrar, Straus, Cudahy, 1955), 416.

120. Rashbam notes a grammatical complementarity in the imagery: she is a *shoshannah* (feminine noun), while he is a *tap-puaḥ* (masculine noun).

121. In ancient Near Eastern love lyrics, the male is frequently identified with an apple tree; see in Westenholz, "Love Lyrics," 4:2482; and also in Sefati, *Love Songs*, 320–23.

122. Moldenke, *Plants of the Bible*, 184–88.

123. In its plain sense, the masculine pronoun refers back to the tree; cf. Riq (*musav 'al "ke-tappuaḥ"*).

124. In an Assyrian love lyric, the female also desires to sit "in the shade of the cedar/cypress"—her lover's protective and physical presence. See Nissinen: 589, ll. 9a–b, 10.

125. Although literally "I delight and I sit," the second verb is subordinate to the first, yielding the fuller sense of "delight to sit"; so Ginsburg, 142.

126. The first verb, *ḥimmadti*, expresses intense desire. It is the so-called frequentative *pi'el*. See IBHS §24.5; noted also by Bloch and Bloch.

127. See also Rashi and Ibn Aqnin (shade of the commandments).

128. The noun *peri* connotes the "fruit" or result of an action in biblical and rabbinic Hebrew.

129. According to Ibn Aqnin, the "apple" indicates the benefits (*maʿalot*) of the divine qualities.

130. Malbim also regards "his fruit" as connoting divine care or providence; viz., the "apple" is the separate intellect which gives benefits to the human soul. Immanuel regards the "shade" to be the inner aspect or spiritual dimension of this divine element (though not the essence).

131. For Al-Fawwāl, the "fruit" symbolizes the actualization of the self via the soul's perfection (that is, its proper nourishment and development from the higher powers).

132. Ibn Sahula and other kabbalistic commentators perceive in the tree the flow of sefirotic vitality—from highest sources to the Shekhinah below. See Z. 1:85a–b.

133. Thus MsP, Rid, and Tamakh, among medieval commentators; Murphy, 137 and Exum, 118, among moderns.

134. So also Rashbam.

135. So also Immanuel, referring to it as a "banner/standard of the camp" (*degel maḥaneh*), as commonly in the account of the tribal wanderings in the desert; cf. Num. 2:3, 10, 18, 25. For the phrase "each [household] (*ʾish*) under its standard (*diglo*)," see Num. 1:52. NJPS, "man." For other instances where *ʾish* refers to households, see Exod. 12:4, 16:16; Num. 2:2, 34.

136. See already Gordis, "The Root D-G-L," 204.

137. For another proposal, see Riq's interpretation of the verbal noun in terms of *digulo*, meaning his splendor or majestic bearing.

138. In the text, the exemplary slip of the tongue is *ʾahavta* (as in the Shema, to "love" God) vs. *ʾayavta* ("hate").

139. Immanuel observes that due to the imbibing of the wine (the virtues of wisdom), the soul has become attractive to the divine powers—and attracted toward the divine, as well. (On "wine" here, see the peshat.)

140. See the fundamental study by H. Lewy, *Sobria Ebrietas. Untersuchungen zur Geshichte der Antiken Mystik* (Giessen: A. Töpelmann, 1929).

141. Also noted by Anon. 2 and Immanuel.

142. Cf. Ibn Aqnin: the terms denotes intensification or strengthening (*ḥizzuq*).

143. So also Fox, who stresses illness; but the context argues the contrary. See below.

144. Cf. Ps. 109:22 and comments of Radak and R. Menaḥem Ha-Meiri, ad loc.

145. This understanding is also found in Maharzu, and in YefQol at greater length.

146. See *Mishneh Torah, Hilkhot Teshuvah* 10:3.

147. See Samuel Kramer, *The Sacred Marriage Rite: Aspects of Faith, Myth, and Ritual in Ancient Sumer* (Bloomington: Indiana University Press, 1969), 105. Cited by Bloch & Bloch.

148. Also noted by Bloch & Bloch. For the image, see Keel, 90 (no. 44).

149. It is referred to by Semitists as an *iprus* form. A classic example is *ʾaz yashir* in Exod. 15:1, meaning "then (Moses and Israel) *sang*." For the grammatical issue, see IBHS §31.1.1.

150. Ginsburg renders this "Let his left hand" and also gives it a present-future aspect.

151. Ibn Aqnin interprets this passage to indicate that the soul needs ongoing "support" in order to acquire the proper intellectual perfection.

152. In the Assyrian love lyric noted above (n. 10), the woman's thigh is compared to a "gazelle in the field"; see Nissinen, 589, l. 5. The animals' energy or power presumably inspired the Septuagint reading of *ʾayelet* as *dunameisin* presumably reading the noun as the abstract *ʾayalut*, despite the parallel term.

153. This echo of the powers above and below is already suggested by the comment of R. Eleazar in SongsR 2.ii.18.

154. Note the incantation invoking *belit ṣeri* ("goddess of the field") in Šurpu 7 67–68. See E. Reiner, *Šurpu—A Collection of Sumerian and Akkadian Incantations* (Archiv für Orientforschung, Beiheft 11; Graz, 1958).

155. For this spell, see Robert D. Biggs, *Šà.Zi.Ga: Mesopotamian Potency Incantations* (Locust Valley, N Y: J. J. Augustin, 1967), 26. It is noted also by Fox, who rejects it in favor of taking the gazelles and other animals as euphemisms for God. My suggestion is that the author plays on a series of divine terms, yet without contradicting their vivid erotic and earthy quality—something the Mesopotamian incantations make clear. According to Ibn Ezra and Rid, the animals are metaphors for the women, whom she is adjuring by their lives. This seems unlikely, as is the assumption that the animals are connected to goddesses of love, proposed by T. K. Cheyne, "New God Names," 104–5.

156. The reason for this may be Late Hebrew blending of pronouns; cf. Ruth 1:11 (mentioned orally by C. H. Gordon decades ago). For late linguistic features in the Song, see the introduction.

157. Rashbam suggests that the verb *taʿiru* has the sense of *tasiru*; i.e., the maiden requests that the maidens/nations not try to "remove" or dissuade her of her love. Rashbam follows the tradition in Rashi—and uses this to indicate Christian attempts to convert Jews. His etymology is odd but reflects a recurring interpretation in Ashkenaz at that time. On this matter, see Japhet, *Rashbam*, 174 n. 22.

158. In AgShir, *ʿad she-teḥpatz* refers to the advent of redemption; cf. Piyyuṭ 14 (e) (p. 143), where the phrase means *ʿad qeitz pelaʾot*—"until the end of the wondrous (events)."

159. SongsR reads *yaʿalu ḥomah*, "they went up [like a] wall"; the version in B. Ket. 111a (see the ensuing reference) has *yaʿalu be-ḥomah*, "they went up in [the formation of] a wall." Based on the latter, my conjectural emendation is a slight orthographic correction of *ke-* for *be-*; hence the reading "like [or: as] a wall."

160. The precise meaning is uncertain. Some have suggested esoteric teachings in general; others suggest that the secret of Jewish calendar calculations (lunar–solar adjustments) is involved.

161. This interpretation trades on a pun between the adjuration of "hinds" (*tzevaʾot*) and the divine promise to make Israel as numerous as the "hosts" (*tzevaʾot*) of heaven.

162. Immanuel understands the maiden's address to the daughters of *Yerushalayim* (Jerusalem) to indicate that the soul is ready for *sheleimut* (perfection).

163. Malbim interprets the passage to indicate that the elements of the body are aroused from sleep and seek to disrupt the conjunction, but the soul doesn't want this conjunction to be disturbed.

164. Thus Ibn Tibbon understands the phrase *ʿad she-teḥpatz* (until it please) to indicate a process, and that one must learn the proper "order" of love (that is, *ʿal ha-seider*).

165. See the peshat for such meanings for *taʿiru*, *teʿoreru*, and *teḥpatz*. Regardless, the mystical layer requires its own assessment of the phrases. Since diverse sensibilities are involved, different meanings may be discovered in the same words. I thus give two different meanings to the verbs and take the adverb *ʿad* to mean "while" and not "until." The goal is to render a coherent spiritual sense to the sod.

166. Offering supernal referents, many mystical commentators regard the "gazelles" and "hinds" as transcendental qualities. Cf. REzra, ad loc.

167. The Masoretic punctuation denotes a conjunction between *qol* and *dodi*, and a disjunction between them and the next phrase.

168. See the discussion in GKC §136*d*. In other cases, *hinneih* may convey surprise; see C. L. Miller-Naudé and C. H. J.

van der Merwe, "*Hinneh* and Mirativity in Biblical Hebrew," *Hebrew Studies* 52 (2011), 53–81.

169. Cf. the similar topos in an Egyptian love lyric, where the girl awaiting the sound of her lover ecstatically says, "my brother is coming to me" (P. Harris 500 Group B, 15:A; see in Fox, 24).

170. Alternatively, it can be construed as a perfect verb, indicating time past—as Ibn Aqnin suggests.

171. The sages interpreted the beloved's "leaping" (*medalleg*) as God's "skipping" (*dillug*) over the fixed calculations. This act of love echoes the earlier statement that God's "banner" (*degel*) of love was over Israel (see above).

172. S. Lieberman suggests a derivation from Greek *deuro* ("come"); cf. PdRK, Mandelbaum edition, 1.90 (at note 4; and note text variants adduced in the apparatus). MatKeh understood *deo* as the Latin (vocative) "God!" YefQol treated it as Hebrew, a kind of "love expression"; viz., "dear one."

173. For the different senses for *qol* alluded to here, see the peshat.

174. This preposition is compared to the usage in Gen. 26:8 and Judg. 5:28 by MsP.

175. For Ibn Aqnin, the images of this passage suggest God's call to the people to repent. For Leqaḥ Ṭov, the images indicate divine providence; for the Netziv, hidden providence.

176. For Ralbag, this passage suggests that the soul-intellect is still obstructed in its perception of the higher elements.

177. Sforno offers the perceptive comment that one does not sense God's reality until one is aroused to search for it.

178. This Aramaic form occurs in the Vilna edition; Rabbi Shlomoh either had a Hebrew version or translated the Aramaic as *zarzi ʿatzmeikh*.

179. According to Immanuel, this is a call to achieve a new spiritual level on the way towards perfection.

180. REzra states that these figures are "all a parable" (*mashal*) for supernal events.

181. On a similar bivalent wordplay, see at 7:12 regarding *kefarim*.

182. The usage of the time designation *zmr* in the tenth-century B.C.E. Gezer Calendar does not apply to the song's situation—which is early spring, not June-July (the time of pruning indicated in that seasonal schedule). See Lemaire, "Zâmîr dans la Tablette," 22–24.

183. Specifically, Ibn Ezra emphasizes the singing of the birds (in springtime).

184. This adverbial usage is followed by many moderns. Cf. Fox, Zakovitch, and Bloch and Bloch.

185. In the Targum, the related word renders the Hebrew noun *nitzah*, "blossom," as commonly in Aramaic. For a discussion of the uses of the word *semadar*, see Aḥituv 37–40. The term is found on a jar inscription from the eighth century B.C.E. (5th level at Hazor). See A. R. Millard, "Recently Discovered Hebrew Inscriptions," *The Tyndale House Bulletin* 11 (1962), 9.

186. For Leqaḥ Ṭov and Ibn Aqnin, the "winter" refers to the exile.

187. So also Rashi.

188. This plural form is based on the nominal form *qāṭūl*; see M. H. Segal, *A Grammar of Mishnaic Hebrew* (Oxford: Clarendon Press, 1927), pp. 106–7, #235. It has a similar occurrence in other verbs of the same type (e.g., *laqoḥot*, "purchases," in M. Ket. 8:1; and *mashoḥot*, "measures," in M. Eruv. 4:11; this is also the punctuation of Ḥ. Yalon in Ḥ. Albeck, *Shishah Sidrei Mishnah* [Jerusalem-Tel-Aviv: Mosad Bialik, 1952], ad loc.). For a midrash similar to the one found here, see B. Ḥul. 83a.

189. That is, the time of arousal has arrived (Ibn Aqnin)—here and in the images that follow.

190. Cf. Malbim, for whom the "winter" signifies nature as ground of change and renewal. For Al-Fawwāl, this barren state refers to the soul's childhood or adolescence—which has passed.

191. This interpretation takes *ba-ʾaretz*, "in the land," as a figure for a person's naturalness or earthiness (*ʾartziyut*)—this being a common trope in Hasidic discourses.

192. According to Ibn Tibbon, this is a divine call to the soul, admonishing it: "Arise" (*hitʿoreri*), why hide?

193. The plain sense of *seiter ha-madreigah* is the "hiddenness of the cliff" (its ascending crags); this reuse plays on each of the words, taking the first to be a turning away, or self-concealment, and the second to allude to spiritual gradations (*dargin*, a term that is used frequently in the Zohar).

194. So also Ibn Ezra; but Rashbam suggests a perfect verb (of the *paʿlu* type; cf. *ʾaḥeru* in Judg. 5:28), interpreting the event as the killing of foxes while the lovers are strolling.

195. Ibn Ezra also notes the imperative, adducing Job 6:22.

196. According to Lys, "Notes sur le Cantique," 171, the verb *meḥabbelim* ("ruin") conveys the added sense of defloration.

197. Rabbi Berekhiah noted that the first noun is written *plene*, with a *vav*; the second is without it. This variant leads to an association of the noun with the formulation found in Isa. 40:12 (which states that only God can determine *shaʿalo mayim*—the "handbreadth [or: measure] of the sea." According to others, it refers to the "paths" of the sea (cf. Maharzu, second opinion). Cf. the version of this midrash in TanB, *Boʾ*, 27a (and S. Buber's note 137).

198. See Isa. 5:1–7. In v. 1, this is called "The song of my beloved [viz., God] for his vineyard [Israel]."

199. For Immanuel, the "foxes" symbolize impediments to growth and perfection.

200. Ibn Aqnin stresses the "mutuality" (*ha-hatʾamah ve-ha-shivyon*) "between" them.

201. For strong erotic innuendos connected with the garden, see below at 4:17–5:1 and 6:11, with parallels from assorted Assyrian love lyrics.

202. The first midrashic image, of divinely caused suffering, may read *roʿeh* as *roʿeʿa*, "causes suffering." I have readapted the second image; the midrashic source speaks of those who are able to withstand suffering, and to endure it as a spiritual challenge, as against those deemed "broken vessels" (*qanqanim meroʿaʿim*)—those of little faith, who cannot withstand the test.

203. Fox argues that were the late afternoon meant, we could have expected the verb *naṭah* to indicate the spreading of the shadows (cf. Jer. 6:4). Rashi regards this as the heat of midday; Tamakh adopts this view and makes a philological case (taking *yafuaḥ*, the blowing breeze, to be related to the blast of hot air, as in the use of *piaḥ* to indicate the "blast" of a furnace; but this is unlikely). He may have known Rashbam's similar comment.

204. See also Rashi.

205. Also cf. AgShir and Ibn Aqnin.

206. See J. Taʿan. 4:5, where Hebrew *beter* is interpreted as *beitar* (written: *beiyt tar*). This observation is also made by MatKeh.

207. For Ibn Aqnin, the image of the passing of the morning haze ("the shadows flee") indicates the need for constancy while the spiritual qualities are in the body. In like manner, Al-Fawwāl suggests that this passage refers to the need to engage in intellectual pursuits until the light of day—this symbolizing enlightenment.

208. Cf. Al-Fawwāl, who perceives here a final counsel to the soul to achieve wisdom ("turn" [higher]; that is, make further progress) and "leap" from wisdom to wisdom.

209. This construal of the clause accords best with the mystic interpretation that follows.

210. NJPS "set out"; see the peshat. Rendering as "turn" accords best with the spiritual dynamics depicted in the sod.

211. NJPS "hills of spices"; see the peshat. Rendering as "break-back hills" accords best with the spiritual dynamics depicted in the sod.

212. Ibn Sahula notes that this withdrawal refers to the need to crush false desire.

3:1–11

1. My subdivision differs from the Masoretic arrangement, whose three units are 3:1–5, 6–8, and 9–11. That arrangement deems the reference to Solomon's bed (v. 7) to be linked to the reference to a maiden ascending from the steppes (v. 6). But there is no necessary reason to join these two features. More reasonably, v. 7 suddenly introduces (via the word *hinneih*) a new image—the "couch"—and this marital feature is naturally conjoined to v. 8 and its (and subsequent) marital imagery. Moreover, as will be observed below, such units 1 and 3 are linked by numerous terms and images, forming a literary diptych around v. 6.

2. Psalm 45 has traces of a royal wedding song, composed for a king and his bride.

3. Keel, 120–21, also notes the deep yearning expressed here. The dream image depicts the maiden's inner state of recurrent fantasy (cf. Levinger, 41; also Fox, 118, though he considers the wandering to be a real action; and Exum, 133). According to J. T. Willis, "On the Text of Micah," 538, the phrase "upon my bed" means "in my dreams" (he compares Job 7:13–14, 33:14–15; and Dan. 4:2–10).

4. Ginsburg's attempt to find here a reference to the maiden's nighttime couch is not convincing.

5. Ibn Aqnin regards the isolation upon the bed as symbolic of the exile.

6. This follows the abbreviated teaching of R. Alexandrai. MatKeh deemed *ba'u leiylot* as implied in *ba-leiylot* (the latter regarded as a crasis—a contraction of the fuller form).

7. The "dark" is also a symbol of the absence of "illumination," or divine presence (Al-Fawwāl).

8. For a philological discussion on the iterative aspect of *ba-leiylot*, see the peshat.

9. Alternatively, the situation on the bed implies indolence and laxity (Ibn Tibbon), or a state prior to death (taking the reference to *mishkavi*, "my couch," to hint at a deathbed situation, when one is *shekhiv mei-ra'*—rabbinic parlance for a fatal illness [cf. T. B.B. 8–9; B. B.B. 151a]; Ibn Tibbon). My reading builds on these features, while regarding the soul's situation as a "sickness unto death."

10. If the verb is interpreted as an old preterite, with the sense "so I arose," the emotional force is lost; but this is crucial to the speaker's mood.

11. Rid says *ha-kol le-phi pheshuto*, "the entire [episode must be understood] according to its plain sense." But this need not preclude the concrete reality of a dream.

12. For both, a key factor in their interpretation is the image of getting up "off" the bed.

13. Ibn Aqnin speaks here of the desire of the intellectual soul for "direction" (*kavvanah*) and "good counsel" (*'eitzah ṭovah*).

14. For Al-Fawwāl, these guardians were protectors of the body and its passions, while one went forth on a spiritual quest.

15. According to the Hebrew, the watchmen are the subject of the action; see the peshat.

16. Saadia glosses *ki-m'at* by *'akh me'at aḥar*, "just a bit after."

17. Cf. Immanuel. Carol Meyers has taken special note of the first locution ("mother's house") and highlighted its female "features"; see her "'To Her Mother's House': Considering a Counterpart to the Israelite *Bêt 'āb*," in *The Bible and the Politics of Exegesis: Essays in Honor of Norman K. Gottwald*, edited by D. Jobling et al. (Cleveland, OH: Pilgrim Press, 1991), especially pp. 46 and 49.

18. MsP comments on this ensconcing as highlighting a love tryst. He states that the couple are secluded: *leravvot 'immo dodim beli boshet*, "to enjoy lovemaking with him without shame." Rashbam is more circumspect: *ve-sham nitḥabbevah be-'ahavat ne'urim* ("there we shall join together in youthful love"); see also Anon. 1, 170. There is no reason to suppose any trace of a matrilocal custom whereby a bridegroom was brought to the bride's home.

19. So YefQol; this pun (*benei 'immi*, "my mother's sons," taken as *benei 'ummati*, "the people of my nation") recurs at v. 11.

20. The sages based their interpretation on a pun (taking the verb *horah*, "bear," as if from the noun *hora'ah*, "instruction"). See MatKeh.

21. LevR 1.10 cites Song 3:4 in connection with an exegesis of the words "Tent of Meeting" (Lev. 1:1). LevR adds the analogy: Israel was not liable for the Torah until it was proclaimed like a government "decree" (*diatagma*). On this point, see S. Lieberman, *Hellenism in Jewish Palestine*, 200–201, citing SongsR on 2:3, where a variant occurs.

22. Immanuel understands the seizing or holding the Beloved as a spiritual cleaving; it thus serves as a spiritual symbol for "ongoing, perpetual conjunction": *deveiqut ratzuf nitzḥi*.

23. For Ibn Tibbon, this denotes a movement from the attempted attainment of perfection of the body (the "mother's house") to deeper mysteries of Torah (the room of "she who conceived me").

24. Reading *horati* as "her who instructs me" rather than as "her who conceived me." The pun is striking. The present comment utilizes its force.

25. See the account of interpretative possibilities in Immanuel.

26. Ibn Aqnin speaks of the nation aroused to a faithful repentance.

27. Immanuel speaks of a self-adjuration of caution, for although the soul has begun to enter the divine dimension, it is conscious of its distinction or separateness from the divine, and of the need for ongoing readiness for perfection (*sheleimut*)—this being its speech to the "daughters of Jerusalem/*yerushalayim*).

28. The use of this pronoun (with and without the question) in Scripture always means a person or a group of people, not an inanimate object (such as the couch in the next verse). Cf. Fox, 119. According to Rashbam, the male speaks; according to Riq, it is Solomon. Rid rightly notes, "All this is part of the narrative of love told by her."

29. Not "what is this?" namely the couch (so Ginsburg); and also not assuming that the couch is a euphemism for the "bride" (Dirksen: 222). In the Song, *mi* is always a query regarding a person (see also 6:10 and 8:5, and the comments there).

30. According to Rashbam and MsP, this is the Beloved's praise; according to Rid, the maiden is reporting his response to finding her.

31. Characteristic are the speculations and suggestions of Gordis.

32. See *Maḥberet Menaḥem*, s.v. *'avaq*, *18. Rashbam reads: *daqat ve-shaḥaqei merqaḥat*; Japhet, *Rashbam*, 62, proposes the supplement: *daqat [samim] ve-shaḥaqei merqaḥat*.

33. The midrash plays on the Aramaic renderings of *'alah* as *salaq*, meaning both "go up" (Targum, ad loc.) and "die" (see Targum Neofiti at Num. 21:1). SongsR glosses this sense by noting Israel's "death" (*mitatah*) in the desert, and citing Num. 14:35, which states that the people "died" (*yittammu*) in the desert.

34. For the Netziv, this includes communal charity that is aroused by renewed Torah study.

35. According to these Tannaitic sources, it was the divine cloud that smote the snakes, not the smoke and fire from the Ark. For the two older sources, see MdRI, edited by Horowitz-Rabin, 81; and *Siphre D'Be Rab*, edited by H. S. Horowitz (Jerusalem: Wahrmann Books, 1966), 79.

36. Based on Exod. 15:16. With respect to the fear that fell upon the Canaanites, the verb *tippol* (an old preterite with the sense "fell") was construed there to indicate the present and future (viz., Israel would continue to strike fear in their enemies).

37. Gen. 49:1–2 provided a classic textual site for this event, it being the occasion when Jacob gathered his sons around him for a final blessing. See the reference to the blemish in Targum Jonathan 2 at v. 2; and in the so-called Fragmentary Targum at v. 1, in Ginsburger, *Das Fragmententhargum*, 24. The tradition and terminology was ancient. See already the comment on the Shema in SifDeut 31 (Finkelstein, ed.), 49. Also cf. Targum Jonathan 1 at Gen. 35:22; and PesiqR 39 (165b).

38. Technically, the Hebrew interrogative *mi* functions here as a predicate in a verbless clause (a so-called animate pronoun); i.e., "*who* is"; and the demonstrative *zo't* functions here as giving specification to a female; i.e., "*this* one" [or: she]. On these matters, cf. IBHS §§18.2b and 17.3b.

39. This construction (noun + anticipatory suffix + relative pronoun + subject) is like that found in biblical Aramaic (cf. Dan. 2:20, *shemeih di-eloha'*, "the Name of God") and commonly in mishnaic Hebrew (cf. M. Shab. 1:1, *yado shel 'ani*, "the hand of the poor"); see M. H. Segal, *A Grammar of Mishnaic Hebrew* (Oxford: Clarendon Press, 1927), 191–92 (para. 387–89). The syntactic feature is late; earlier biblical Hebrew normally employs the construct chain to indicate belonging (i.e., *miṭṭat X*).

40. See also 1:5, 3:9, 3:11; 8:11–12.

41. Ibn Sahula (at vv. 7–8) refers to the three stages of life (childhood, maturity, old age) and the spiritual tasks and impediments of each one (the need to cultivate theological wisdom about divine providence; to sustain integrity during one's business and material life; and to attain a level of physical and spiritual purity as one becomes an elder).

42. Cf. *'ḥd ḥrth*, "skilled in plowing." See Jonas Greenfield, "Ugaritic *mdl* and Its Cognates," *Biblica* 45 (1983), 532–33. Noted also by Fox.

43. The translators cite the Akkadian verb *aḫāzu*, "to learn." Cf. Felix Perles, *Analekten zur Textkritik des Alten Testaments (neue folge)* (Leipzig: Gustav Engel, 1922), 52–53. Noted also by Fox.

44. Both verbal forms are passive participles treated like adjectives. This is another feature of mishnaic Hebrew; Segal, op. cit., pp. 57–58 (simple stem; paragraph 113), and 62 (intensive stem; paragraph 127). By contrast, biblical Hebrew regularly uses the active participle form (cf. 2 Chron. 25:5 for *'oḥez*; and 2 Sam. 22:35 for *melammed*). On this stylistic feature, see the comments of Saadia and Ibn Ezra.

45. The Hebrew phrase *paḥad ba-leiylot* (literally, "terror during the nights") has an exact parallel (*puluḫtu ša lilāti*, "terror of the nights") in an Akkadian incantation. It describes Zaqar, god of dreams. See T. H. Gaster, *Myth, Legend and Custom in the Old Testament: A Comparative Study with Chapters from Sir James G. Frazer's Folklore in the Old Testament* (New York: Harper & Row, 1969), p. 813, no. 335. Gaster also links this to terrors during the wedding night. On such matters, see G. Dalman, *Arbeit und Sitte in Palästina* (Güttersloh: C. Bertelsmann, 1928), 1, p. 639.

46. According to R. Azariah, the "warriors" symbolize the blessing of the people "with *gevurah*"—the power of the divine name (the sixty letters overall).

47. A unique occurrence; cf. Ibn Ezra: *'ein lo domeh* ("nothing resembles it").

48. Anon. 1 catches the erotic character of the phrase, glossing *ratzuf* with *davuq* (i.e., "bound," "layered" with love), adding that it has been embossed by Solomon and his beloved.

49. Noted by Exum: 2005, 139, as an emendation. Less likely is the suggestion of Driver, "Supposed Arabisms in the Old Testament," *Journal of Biblical Literature* 55 (1936), 111, that *'ahavah* derives from an Arabic word for "leather."

50. Regarding the *'apiryon*, Ibn Aqnin unabashedly states: *she-'alav ha-mishgal 'asher hu' sibbat ha-periyah* ("Upon it was the act of cohabitation, which is the cause of fertility").

51. This sense was noted in B. Ket. 10b, with the observation that calling a bed *purya'* reflects the fact that people "are fruitful (*parin*) and multiply upon it." Cf. Ibn Aqnin, who stresses the erotic aspect.

52. Ibn Tibbon speaks here of the spiritual labor of *tiqqun ha-nefesh* (repair or perfection of the soul-intellect).

53. Thus *'asah lo* (NJPS "made him") is construed as "made *for himself*"—for spiritual ends (*le-tzorekh 'atzmo*). If this King Solomon is the ideal subject of human perfection, the phrase speaks of his spiritual labor for his soul's development. If, however, this king is but another aspect of the perfected Divine Majesty, the phrase speaks of the imparting of these qualities to the questing soul—i.e., a gift for the soul's development or self-"making."

54. The name *lebhanon* ("Lebanon") means roughly "White Mountains," after the high peaks that are often covered with snow in winter; it is derived from the word *labhan* ("white").

55. So also Ginsburg. In the Aleppo Codex, the *yod* in *tze'eynah* is absent; and in the margin is a Masorah Parva note affirming the *ḥaser* spelling. (See archive.org/stream/Aleppo_Codex.)

56. See Y. Muffs, *Love and Joy*, chapters 7–8. Muffs gives voluminous documentation of Mesopotamian, biblical, and rabbinic sources, but this reference seems unnoted.

57. The present translation reads, "Solomon's couch," for the sake of English idiom, but the Hebrew construction actually highlights the anticipatory pronoun. See the comment at v. 7 and the evidence adduced there and attached notes.

58. The text switches genders, specifying the males who are marked by special hairstyles, circumcision, and ritual fringes (SongsR 3.xi.1; and parallels in PdRK 1.3 [Mandelbaum ed., p. 5]).

59. E.g., the claim that the heavens are composed of both fire and water—coexisting there although they are incompatible on earth; this derives from a midrashic wordplay, interpreting *shamayim* ("heavens") as if from *('ei)sh* ("fire") + *mayim* ("water").

60. The verbal play between *Tziyyon* ("Zion") and *metzuyyanim* occurs in the oldest midrashic strata.

61. Al-Fawwāl emphasizes the latter point, especially the importance of modesty with respect to one's material or earthly being (*ha-tzenu'im be-golmam*).

62. Immanuel takes "go forth" as a movement of realization, from potentiality to actuality.

63. For uses of the stem *'-t-r* as referring to encirclement, see 1 Sam. 23:26 and Ps. 5:13.

64. See the derash for similar plays on the word *tziyyon* ("Zion").

4:1–5:1

1. Cf. Rashbam, who indicates that the verbal doubling (*kefel lashon*) is "to strengthen and certify" (*le-haḥaziq u-le-ha'amet*) the speech.

2. Riq has *mi-tokh*.

3. Cf. Septuagint; also Targum Yerushalmi, which renders *vatitkas* ("she covered herself") in Gen. 24:65 as *ve-'ittzamtzemat*.

4. See *tze'if* in Gen. 24:65 and 38:19.

5. The parallel noun is *shovel*, apparently a "train" or "robe." The ensuing image in v. 2, and its parallel in v. 3, suggest a partial exposure of the body. See next note.

6. Bloch and Bloch argue that the prophetic language refers to the shameful uncovering of hair, along with exposure of the thighs. In their view, verse 3 adds to the disgrace and indicates the woman's nakedness or "sex."

7. In Job 6:17, the verb has the sense of contraction (Immanuel), with the force of drying up or evaporating (cf. NJPS).

8. See Tuell, "A Riddle Resolved," who provides documentation and discussion.

9. In the Talmud, the phrase for watery turbulence is *meiy gelashim*. Rashbam similarly follows Menaḥem b. Saruq (*Maḥberet*, s.v. *galash*; p. 107*) and the earlier Targum tradition (where an Aramaic noun derived from *g-l-sh* renders the Hebrew noun *gabaḥat* in Lev. 13:42–43). And on this basis, Rid suggests a downward movement, as from a height.

10. The short version of Ibn Ezra's commentary follows suit.

11. In Tan., *Tetzavveh* 5, we have another version in the name of R. Shimon b. Pazzi. He taught that God praises Israel here *belashon kaful* (by "doubling" or "linguistic repetition"). See also the comment by Maharzu, who notes that the midrash in SongsR has presented the material in "pairs" (*zugot zugot*), highlighting their similarities and correlations.

12. This is based on the parallel use of the noun *ʿorlah* in Leviticus to denote both the fruit of a tree "forbidden" during the first four years of its planting, and the male foreskin. According to Lev. 19:23–25, during the first three years the fruit is not to be eaten; on the fourth year it is set aside as a "jubilation before the LORD," and only on the fifth year may the produce be consumed. And according to Lev. 12:3, the male foreskin must be removed on the eighth day after birth. (On the planting of fruit trees and eating the produce, see the references in *Torah Temimah*, and the technical discussions appended thereto. The fourth year of fruit produce is called in rabbinic literature *neṭaʿ revaʿi*; it is cited alongside those references.)

13. M. Ohal. 1:9 refers to the capacity of all 248 limbs to contract impurity, and the importance of the eyes to direct the self toward purity.

14. Ibn Tibbon notes ten types of praise, descriptive of the soul in its various modes or aspects; Malbim states that the several parts of the body refer to various spiritual virtues (like speech and thought). For Ibn Aqnin, v. 1 denotes the powers of the intellectual soul (like thought and memory); whereas vv. 2ff. refer to aspects of the sensual part of the soul. All these are integrated in her (cf. v. 7).

15. Cf. Al-Fawwāl, who perceives here an allusion to esoteric dimensions of the soul; specifically, the mysterious conjunction of form with matter.

16. REzra remarks that these features of the body are "images and parables known to the mystical illuminati (*ha-maskilim ha-mequbbalim*)." He does not elaborate, leaving his commentary esoteric on this point. (In his introduction, he notes that some symbols should not be specified in detail and that one should be circumspect about them.)

17. Cf. Rashbam and MsP.

18. See Rid, who glosses with *ḥaruzot*, "in orderly array."

19. See also Maharzu, ad loc.

20. In the Midrash, this is proved retrospectively from phrases about sin occurring just before and after the Song of Hannah in 1 Samuel 2 (also see Maharzu). For the Netziv, the image stands for the purification prompted by repentance.

21. Literally, "twins"; more figuratively, "similar" or "related."

22. Literally, a "miscarriage" or "loss" at birth; my use of "rupture" here is intended to evoke the term's literalness.

23. This Zoharic passage links up with the first verse—indicating that through a supernal and perfected vision, all becomes one; all distinctions are erased. This mystic vision is unitive.

24. Ibn Sahula emphasizes the transforming power of the rituals of food and *mitzvot*.

25. That is, those who are "bound" or "attached" to God.

26. Commentators like Immanuel and Malbim speak here of the quality of speech.

27. For Immanuel, the "veil" is an enclosure that discloses—a fitting image for the indirect revelation of spiritual matters.

28. Blending the two comments: the first notes the initial silence of speech; the second its gifts.

29. Alkabetz focuses on the sense of *ḥuṭ*, "thread [or: cord]," as a device for measuring length.

30. This supposition was first advanced by Delitzsch; the philological evidence has been supplied by A. M. Honeyman, "Two Contributions," 51–52.

31. See Krauss, 1941:127; he renders the phrase "built in terraces" (p. 128).

32. For the Tyrian custom of decking warships and city walls with shields, see the illustration in Harden, *The Phoenicians* (New York: Penguin, 1980), plate 50. Assyrian art also portrays cities with shields on the turrets, as in the relief depicting their siege of the Israelite town of Lachish; for which see Pritchard, *The Ancient Near East: Supplementary Texts and Pictures Relating to the Old Testament*, 2nd ed. (Princeton: Princeton University Press, 1969), #373.

33. This follows Maharzu; he interprets this transposition as a *notariqon*, "acronym," and was guided by the Midrash explication.

34. Other examples cited in SongsR: the battles against Sihon and Og, and inheritance of their lands, as mentioned in Psalm 136 (ibid.); the account of the Exodus in Psalm 68 (ibid., 2).

35. Alternatively, this indicates the mouth of "prayer." See LṬov and MShir.

36. See B. B.B. 14a; LevR 7.1. For variations, see SongsR (ibid.). MatKeh notes variations found in medieval discussions (cf. *ʾOt ʿEmet*). See also the cross-references in Maharzu, ad loc. These ten authors are deemed to be "ten righteous persons," all worthy to give praise to God. David incorporated their works into his own, and the whole book of Psalms was attributed to him since he authored the majority of its prayers—he being the true "sweet singer of Israel" (2 Sam. 23:1). See the comment of R. Huna (SongsR, ibid.).

37. See the comment of R. Berekhiah, at the end of the section.

38. Cf. LṬov: "Master of all the Worlds," protector of Israel.

39. See Mishneh Torah, *Sefer Ha-Madaʿ*, *Hilkhot Deiʿot* 2–4.

40. See Rashi, ad loc. (glossing the reference to food with "all kinds of tasty morsels").

41. Cf. in MShir the image of the breasts expressing (literally, "flowing with") wisdom.

42. Punning on the "browsing" (*roʿim*) gazelles.

43. In a striking comment on the tower's nature, Immanuel interprets *banuy le-talpiyyot* as "built [for the striving] for learning" (following an old rabbinic interpretation of the noun *talpiyyot* as indicating *ʾaluph*, "learning") and for spiritual growth; and the ornaments described as *taluy ʿalav* point to the need to bring the self under proper discipline and humility. Ibn Aqnin also employs the same figure of learning.

44. See the previous note.

45. Relatedly, Al-Fawwāl perceives here the structure of the self in the proper order (a hint derived from the tower's being a symbol of the fourfold structure of nature—namely, animal, vegetable, mineral, and human (or rational/intellectual).

46. Ibn Aqnin takes the image of browsing among the lilies as indicative of the soul's quest or search.

47. Maharzu notes this overall midrashic link. Radal notes the verbal link between the *givʿah* ("hill") of frankincense in Song 4:6 and the *givʿah* ("hill") of foreskins in Josh. 5:3.

48. Maharzu also makes this association.

49. For the larger issue of self-sacrifice in devotion to God, see MShir.

50. The word used by Malbim is *deveikut* (bond or union).

51. From a different perspective, Al-Fawwāl understands the speaker to be Solomon and his words to indicate his quest

for the perfection of his soul (that is, he will continue his search for wisdom and turn his soul toward it until its complete actualization).

52. See also NumR 7; and especially 13.8 (noted by MatKeh). Note also PesiqR 7 (Ish Shalom ed.), 28a, citing this song verse.

53. Ibn Tibbon denotes the soul as *sheleimah*, "whole" and "integrated."

54. For this, see also Zakovitch, 94.

55. The Hosea passage likewise refers to a "leopard." (NJPS construes the verb there as "lurk" rather than "leap.") Alternatively, the verb *tashuri* continues the theme of "coming." This sense is conveyed by Septuagint *deuro* ("come"; cf. Syriac *'eti*).

56. Radak lists this verb under the stem *sh-w-r* (*Sefer Ha-Shorashim*, Berlin: J. Biesenthal & F. Lebrecht, 1847; 195). Cf. Immanuel.

57. This follows the analysis of Cogan. Cf. Rashi re *'amanus*.

58. Horovitz-Rabin ed., p. 52.

59. For the MdRI passages, see Horovitz-Rabin ed., p. 51. This text and others are discussed in my *Biblical Myth and Rabbinic Mythmaking*, 134–44.

60. See in J. Charlesworth, ed., *The Old Testament Pseudepigrapha* (Garden City, NY: Doubleday, 1983), 1, 300–302.

61. See, for example, his words in *Sefer Eish Qodesh* (Jerusalem, 1960), 159–64, 178f, 191. The English reader may consult N. Polen, *The Holy Fire: The Teachings of Rabbi Kalonymus Kalman Shapira* (Lanham, MD: Aronson Books, 1999), especially chapter 6 ("The Mystical Vision of Divine Weeping").

62. See also the comment of MatKeh.

63. For uses of this term as "gift," see SongsR and YalSh. (This interpretation probably underlies the Targum's use of *doron*.)

64. The image refers to being a "tough ground," resistant to plowing (for *nir* as ploughed land, cf. T. B.M. 9:24 and Men. 9:3).

65. The midrashic link to Hermon is forced: just as the fertility of this mountain is in its lowlands, so is the priesthood and kingship descended from the last of the patriarchs (viz., Jacob—and not Abraham or Isaac, who produced the lineages of Ishmael and Esau, respectively; see YefQol).

66. According to Sefas Emes (in his teaching for Passover 1884), this is an allusion to higher states of faith (*'emunah gevohah*).

67. Ibn Tibbon speaks of the "Lebanon" (whiteness) as the soul's pure qualities (*ha-middot ha-neqiyyot*) and the animals' dens as the inner hiding places of the body's powers (*me'onot koḥot ha-guf*). Immanuel here hears a call to overcome the powers of the body, the impediments to spiritual fulfillment.

68. Taking the verb *tashuri* in the sense of "see"; cf. the next note.

69. Taking *tashuri* in the sense of "bound forth" (NJPS "trip down") or "venture forth." For these alternatives, and the pun involved, see the peshat.

70. Cf. Z. 2:2b–3a, where the focus is historical, referring to when the people in faith said "we shall do" at Sinai (Exod. 24:7). The perspective above suggests a more universal spiritual consciousness.

71. That is, *mashakht 'et libbi*, "you attracted [or: drew away] my heart"; see B. Shab. 53b and Rashi's comment s.v. *libbavtini*.

72. See the discussion in IBHS §24.4, especially §§f.

73. See in his *Sefer Ha-Shorashim* (edition of W. Bacher), 238.

74. Ibid.

75. Calling one's beloved girlfriend a "sister" is a frequent expression of intimacy and affection in Egyptian love lyrics. Cf. P. Harris 500, Group A: 7 (A); P. Chester Beatty 1, Group A: 31 (A); and Group B: 38 (A, C), where the girl speaks thus of herself to her male friend (see texts in Fox: 14, 52, 66, respectively).

76. The figural rendition in NJPS may be in deference to the biblical laws of consanguinity (cf. Leviticus 18).

77. So according to both the Leningrad Codex and the printed Masoretic Bible of 1521–22, edited by Jacob ben Ḥayyim ibn Adoniyah of Tunis (Venice: Bomberg, 1524–1525).

78. See SifDeut 32, where the double bet is construed in terms of the need to devote both inclinations (the good and evil ones) to God. This gives a midrashic explanation to the point made in M. Ber. 9:5. For a full discussion, see Fishbane, *The Kiss of God*, pp. 4–5.

79. See Ezek. 20:7–8, and midrashic references in SongsR 2.ii.2 and ExodR 16.2.

80. Ibn Yaḥye taught that the *bet* of *be-'aḥat* means "because of" or "on account of" (*ba'avur*); for him this singular "eye" was Abraham.

81. MatKeh notes a different enumeration in DeutR, *Va-'etḥannan*, 2 (end). See also Maharzu.

82. See the elaboration of this theological point by YefQol.

83. Also P. 5 (p. 85), "in prayer and holiness."

84. On *ṭov*, see the peshat at 1:2.

85. Ibn Sahula refers to this integral, supernal wisdom by the term *he-ḥokhmah ha-kelulah*.

86. On various considerations, see overall Nahum N. Glatzer, "A Study of Talmudic-Midrashic Interpretation of Prophecy," in his *Essays in Jewish Thought* (Tuscaloosa: University of Alabama Press, 1978), chap. 2.

87. See the discussion of E. E. Urbach, *Me-'Olamam shel Ḥakhamim* (Jerusalem: Magnes Press, 1988), "*Matai Paseqah Nevu'ah?*," 9–20. Also see the next note.

88. See ibid., "*Halakhah ve-Nevu'ah*," 21–49, with extensive references.

89. On this topic, see *She'eilot U-Tshuvot Min Ha-Shamayim le-Rabbeinu Ya'aqov Mi-Marveish*, edited by R. Margulies (Jerusalem: Mosad Ha-Rav Kook, n.d.). Cf. the instructive (Mishnah) mediation of an angelic *maggid* in Joseph Karo's *Maggid Meisharim*.

90. See *Guide for the Perplexed* 3:51.

91. See also Radal, who develops the image of bitter matters that set one on edge, and their sweetening through meaningful interpretation.

92. According to Al-Fawwāl, this image refers to the deeper mysteries that should be safeguarded as esoteric matters, in contrast with those mysteries of nature that may be disclosed. (The true mysteries are called *ha-sodot be-'emet*.)

93. See, for example, in Nissinen, 590, lines r.17–18, where the female (who has adorned herself for this purpose, ll. 15–16) says that she wishes to "go to the garden" (*ana kiri tallikamma*), implying consort with her beloved. In lines 20, 30e, the female and male wish to see "the plucking" of their "fruit" (cf. Song 5:1); and in Lambert 1975:110, line 35, we have the phrase "with the plucking of a bird I will pluck you (f.)." Nissinen, 616, also mentions KAR 158 vii 26: "She seeks out the beautiful garden of your abundance." See the other garden imagery in the love charm edited by Westenholz, cited below at 6:11, where other images will be added.

94. Cf. his phrases such as: *remez 'el hitḥabberut*; *tzimḥat ha-ḥesheq*; *le-hit'alles be-'ahavah*. And regarding the gathering of spices and honey, he proposes that this "hints at *leqiḥat mi-besarah*"!

95. Cf. the figure in Ps. 147:18b, "He [God] breathes [literally, "causes His wind to blow"] [and] the waters flow [*yizzelu*]."

96. Cf. Rashbam.

97. See the full discussion by S. Paul, "A Lover's Garden of Verse," 99–110. This rich evidence is discussed in the Introduction. See p. 15 above and nn. 35–40.

98. In his long version, Ibn Ezra uses the noun *se'if* (thus indicating branches or some sort); but in the shorter version he uses *nata'* (and thus suggests some kind of planting or plantation). Many traditional commentators (such as Rabbi Shlomoh,

Tamakh, and Sforno) see here a reference to an arid plot that then is fructified as a *pardes*. They are influenced by the term *beiyt sheluhin* in the Mishnah (cf. M. M.Q. 1:1), which indicates a dry bed needing irrigation. But this is unlikely here, where the focus is on plants or branches producing abundance. Perhaps that is why the Gra, while adducing the rabbinic phrase, opts for a broader paraphrase, *sedotayikh* ("your fields").

99. See Anon. 1.

100. Literally: "When you are disrobed [*peshutah mi-begadim*] and naked, you are like an orchard filled with pomegranates and sweet fruits." For the dictionary entry, see Ibn Parḥon, 69b. He presumably construed the verbal stem *shalaḥ* to mean "cast off" (thus, "disrobe") in this context.

101. Understanding this dimension, Malbim suggests that the "lips" refer to external speech and the "tongue" to internal speech (involving a purification of intention or thought).

102. For Ibn Aqnin, the garden is a fullness that evokes the redemption or perfection of the soul. See, overall, R. P. Harrison, *Gardens*, especially the first chapter.

103. The Zohar does not spell out how it arrives at its claim that v. 14 lists thirteen spices. As for *Yishtabbaḥ*, it features a list of twelve types of praise, culminating—as the Zohar understands it—with a thirteenth reference to the Kingdom of God, *Malkhut*, a cognomen of the Shekhinah.

104. The terms "acquired" (*niqneit*) and "48 ways" follow the mishnah. In rabbinic tradition, chapter 6 of Pirqei Avot is called *Pereq Qinyan Torah*, "The Chapter [Dealing with] Acquisition of the Torah." (It is a supplement to Mishnah Avot.) For this teaching, see also NumR 18.21. The link to Pirqei Avot was noted also by MatKeh and adduced by Maharzu.

105. Regarding the spiritual levels of Torah, cf. Ibn Aqnin.

106. Malbim speaks here of the flow of spiritual essences.

107. The passage depicts the flow of blessing and light from "Lebanon" = (the *sefirah* of) *Binah*, through the "stream" = *Tif-eret*, into the "fountain" = *Yesod*, and thence to the "well" = *Malkhut*. That is, the verse points to the emanating flow of divine bounty from the supernal feminine (mother) above to her daughter below, by way of two masculine symbols of progeneration. This is thus both an account of cosmic creation and the flow of understanding and all divine gifts from the primordial realms into the lower, worldly dimensions.

108. According to Rashbam, the girl is the speaker and wishes the winds to blow fragrances upon her lover, to arouse him to her.

109. See also the Netziv: this passage indicates the words of Jews who come to the Temple in thanksgiving and piety.

110. For Al-Fawwāl, what is unlocked is the hidden wisdom that now flows into the garden of the intellectual soul.

111. For Malbim this is captured midrashically, since he perceived in *tzafon* ("north") a hint of *tzafun* ("hidden"). Immanuel had earlier spoken of an allusion here to knowledge of the hidden.

112. The Zohar passage focuses on the hidden matters or thoughts of the heart (*tzefonei libba'*) that must be dealt with and transformed.

113. REzra understands this as the flowing of wisdom, wafting downward; the spreading of "perfume" (*besamim*, a plural in the Hebrew) alludes to an emanation of the radiance of wisdom.

114. The verb *ba'* is commonly used in biblical Hebrew to connote sexual relations (cf. Gen. 38:2–3, 8, 16); the derived noun *bi'ah* is a technical term for this in rabbinic Hebrew (cf. M. Git. 1:1).

115. In order to indicate that the Shekhinah is in the people's midst (Ibn Aqnin).

116. The word derives from Greek. The Aramaic derivative *ginuna'* renders *ḥuppah* ("wedding canopy") in the Targum to Ps. 19:6.

117. The distinction between the restorative and the utopian modes of messianism was presented and elaborated by G. Scholem, in "Toward an Understanding of the Messianic Idea in Judaism," the opening chapter in his *The Messianic Idea in Judaism, And Other Essays on Jewish Spirituality* (New York: Schocken Books, 1971).

118. Immanuel comments that the perfections prepare the soul for spiritual conjunction. For Al-Fawwāl, the passage alludes to the importance of the proper developmental sequence in the attainment of wisdom. According to Ralbag, the proper curriculum for intellectual adepts is one of the song's core teachings (see the introduction).

119. Ibn Aqnin stresses that the Beloved's coming (or invocation) is for the soul's further instruction, so as to protect it from its natural bent (viz., the hylic forces of nature).

120. The emphasis in this Zohar passage is on the giving of God's sustenance to others. I have extended the meaning to spiritual gifts. Literally, *le-qayyema nafsha'* means "to sustain a life."

5:2–6:3

1. In Tamakh's words, "In a dream she speaks of him."

2. According to Riq, she is in a disconsolate state of yearning (*mit'annah*).

3. Noted also by Zakovitch, ad loc.

4. See GKC §§22 *q*, *s*.

5. Ibn Ezra notes that in this case the letter *vav* has been transposed, now preceding the *tzade*. Rid also indicates that it refers to hair.

6. LṬov stresses that the subject of "I am awake" is God, concerning whom the psalmist states: "God is the Rock of my heart, my eternal portion" (Ps. 73:26)—namely, that God is the part of the soul-self that ever remains spiritually vigilant.

7. See *Me'or 'Einayim* by R. Menaḥem Naḥum of Chernobyl (Jerusalem: Machon Me'or Ha-Torah, 2006), 1, *Vayeitzei'*, 109a–110b. For the prophet Elijah as the exemplary harbinger, see Malachi 3:23–24.

8. The version in PdRK 5.6 (*Ha-Ḥodesh*; Mandelbaum, ed., 1, 87), reads: a space wide enough for "tents and siege engines [that is, an entire army and its battlements] to enter"; also the term for "eye" of a needle is *ḥarirah* (see *Arukh*, s.v. *ḥrr*), not *ḥuddah* (SongsR).

9. This may be a play on *'aḥuy* ("joined [or: made akin]"). By contrast, Radal takes the verb as indicating the "conjoining" or "stitching together" of God and Israel (through Israel's performance of the two commandments of paschal offering and of circumcision—two being a notion of completeness in rabbinic terms, insofar as two stitches make a complete act of sewing, when defined as one of the forbidden labors on the Sabbath; see M. Shab. 13:1).

10. Probably read *nitre'u*, as in PdRK; this is the verbal form for the other verbs in the sequence.

11. Ralbag stresses the difficulty of intellectual growth and its natural-material impediments. On the complexity of the spiritual dynamic of longing coupled with sudden withdrawal (expressive of inner-spiritual turmoil), see R. Joseph Soloveitchik, *And From There You Shall Seek*, chapter 1 and passim.

12. For Al-Fawwāl, this depicts the soul's preparation for perfection.

13. For Ibn Aqnin, the soul speaks to the agent intellect, saying that it is ready for contact with the Beloved. Cf. the Sefas Emes, sermon for *Terumah* (1882), where the emphasis is the inner arousal of a spiritual dimension of the self/soul. In a teaching

for *Shemot* (1885), the emphasis is on the needs for inwardness and for this spirituality to be transferred to all our limbs.

14. See *Guide* 3:51. Maimonides interprets this verse in terms of a meditative focus on God at night, during our withdrawal from worldly activities. Malbim sees this section as part of the fall of the self into indolence (beginning at 5:1). In his view, the soul (of Solomon), which had enjoyed spiritual conjunction, fell asleep and forgot the Beloved.

15. Thus Malbim stresses the ongoing separation of the soul from its source.

16. Ralbag stresses the beginning of the emanation of higher Divine Intellect, whereas the soul attests that it still needs assistance in this process.

17. For Ibn Aqnin, the soul is ready for this transformation; it does not want a return to being subject to the body.

18. Night was the occasion for the spiritual exercise practiced by Maimonides in the seclusion of his room, when he recited the bedtime *Shema* and focused on God's Unity and the injunction of love that derives therefrom (cf. Deut. 6:4–5). The exercise is described near the conclusion of *The Guide of the Perplexed* (3:51).

19. The "head" is here understood as the height of Divinity, contemplated as a spatial figure, and the "locks" (*kevutzotav*) as its infinite "extensions" (the latter term construed in kabbalistic fashion as *kitzvotav*—a verbal play in ZḤ 24b and elsewhere). Use of this term to indicate the six spatial dimensions of the divine pleroma is first found in *Sefer Yetzirah* 1.13.

20. So also in Fox and in Bloch and Bloch.

21. Also in Exum, 192.

22. The biblical Hebrew verb is written with an *'alef* (cf. Mal. 1:7, 12); in rabbinic Hebrew it is spelled with an *'ayin*. The Aramaic evidence is also adduced by Zakovitch. The ambivalence of both actions is conveyed by rhetorical questions introduced by the formulation *'eikhakhah* ("was I to?"; or "how then could I?"). Cf. the similar double usage in Est. 8:6.

23. For example, in P. Chester Beatty 1, Group C, no. 46; adduced and cited by Fox, 182–83.

24. Typical is Ibn Sahula's characterization of this hesitation as an indolence. AhavD (151a) refers to this hesitation as a *tirḥah qeṭanah*; viz., an indolence induced by the sense that the act is a "bit of a bother."

25. The verb is taken in its standard spiritual trope, implying a "stripping" of false theological ideas or epithets (*kinuyyim*; used in ZḤ 4b). The Zohar passage is from the divine perspective, focused on God's descent through layers and garments of concealment. I have transferred this to the consciousness of the human person.

26. Alkabetz focuses on the struggle with the physicality of existence. In this spirit, I interpret *raglay*, "my feet," as a midrashic trope for *hergeilay*, "my habits"—an oft-repeated Hasidic trope.

27. REzra says that the *Shekhinah* has entered the self, yet she may depart if we do not act in the proper spiritual manner.

28. Following the strong and evocative formulation of Bloch and Bloch, who render as "reached in."

29. See Peshat. For the sages, the preposition *min* here means "through," rather than an expression of withdrawal "from."

30. Cf. Peshat. NJPS "my heart," offers a less concrete rendering.

31. "My passions [literally: innards] were aroused." See Metzudat Tziyyon.

32. Alternatively, via reading this passage as the Beloved's putting his hand through the door (cf. peshat), Ibn Tibbon stresses divine initiative in the process.

33. According to Malbim, this points to the penitent's transformation of mind-spirit, and the desire for holiness and contact with Divinity.

34. By contrast, Al-Fawwāl refers all this to the positive emanation of the higher divine wisdom.

35. See the peshat for the ambiguities of the formulation, understood here in spiritual terms.

36. See the peshat regarding the preposition *min*.

37. In the sense of becoming hidden; cf. Rid.

38. Ibn Ezra also adduces Jer. 31:21 as a parallel use of the verb in the sense of "departing."

39. This penetrating insight of the AhavD considers the spiritual task as performing acts *mei-'atzmo* ("from one's [inner-]self"), i.e., the self must come to the awareness that the absence must induce an inner self-strengthening (*she-'aḥazeq 'et 'atzmi*).

40. See Immanuel. Based on this passage in Isaiah, Rashbam suggests that what the watchmen stripped away was her jewelry. But this reading softens the event, which more naturally counterpoints her having stripped and dressed earlier.

41. For the initial citation, see *The Fragment Targums of the Pentateuch*, edited by M. Klein (Rome: Biblical Institute Press, 1980), ad loc.; for the second, see *The Neofyti Targum of the Pentateuch*, edited by A. Díez-Macho (Madrid-Barcelona: Consejo Superior de Investigaciones Científicas, 1968–78), ad loc.

42. For Ibn Aqnin and Al-Fawwāl, the guardians are the powers of the body (feelings and sensibilities) that interfere with the spiritual search. According to Ralbag, the senses have again been engaged—which impedes the search (as symbolized by the beatings).

43. Read differently, Ibn Tibbon interprets the mantle's removal as the removal of constraints (*meni'ot*) that prevent the fulfillment of one's intentions.

44. For the range of interpretative possibilities, and Immanuel's discussion, see the reference at 2:7.

45. For this literary phenomenon, and various examples, see R. Culley, *Studies in the Structure of Hebrew Narrative* (Philadelphia: Fortress Press, 1976); for a treatment of the variations of the applicable motif of the "Matriarch of Israel in Danger," see already K. Koch, *The Growth of the Biblical Tradition* (London: Black, 1969), passim.

46. Rashbam speaks of Israel's suffering in exile (*me'uneh ba-galut*).

47. By contrast, Immanuel adds that this "sickness" is the endurance of ascetic practices to suppress natural human desires.

48. In this Zohar passage, the "maidens" are the higher, heavenly souls. I take them as a human reflex of this higher awareness. The higher self is enflamed with love, and proclaims the unity of God with mouth, heart, and soul (cf. 1:142a).

49. In the midrashic colloquy, the nations say: "You are handsome (*na'eh*) and you are mighty, come and intermingle (*hit'arevu*) with us." Since the time of Ezra (9:2), the latter term has connoted intermarriage and assimilation. The term *na'eh* picks up on Rabbi Akiva's statement that he will speak of the "glories" or "beauty" of God (reading *ne'otav* with MdRS and Eifat Tzedeq, and especially Mss. Marshall Or. 24 and Munich Cod. Hebr. 117—these sources being the basis of MdRI, Horovitz-Rabin, ed., p. 127, l. 10). On this reading, the noun interprets *'anveihu* ("I shall glorify him") of the lemma (Exod. 15:2) as if from the stem *n-v-y* ("be beautiful"). Alternatively, the reading in the midrash is *navotav* (per Geniza fragments; see Rabbinowitz, *Ginzei Midrash*, 13). The latter version is to be preferred. See also the excursus.

50. In Malbim's terms, the query ponders the difference between spiritual desire (*teshuqah*) and physical love (*'ahavah*).

51. Al-Fawwāl asks whether the spiritual search can proceed without divine images, and if not, which ones are appropriate (see at vv. 8–9). The ensuing depiction conveys (for Al-Fawwāl) the search for intellectual perfection through the use of proper imagery and terms.

52. Ibn Sahula understands this verse in such a manner, i.e.,

as a query about the scale of achievement of spiritual wisdom attained by the seeking soul. The Alkabetz follows suit, understanding the question to be posed by the soul's powers regarding the virtuous person.

53. See the discussion in the derash section, where theological issues are involved.

54. A full account of the traces of this theology is provided by S. Lieberman, in his appendix ("D") to Gershom Scholem's *Jewish Gnosticism*, 118–26.

55. See my discussion in *The Kiss of God*, 60–71.

56. Ibn Tibbon emphasizes the ten statements of praise (*shevaḥim*) used here.

57. On this topic, see W. Kandinsky, *Concerning the Spiritual in Art* (New York: Dover, 1977), especially chapters 5 ("The Psychological Working of Colour") and 6 ("The Language of Form and Colour").

13. REzra took the colors to refer to the rainbow, this being the color spectrum refracting Divinity; and thus related to the throne image seen by R. Akiva when he ascended mystically on High. Rabbi Joshua ibn Shu'aib, *Derashot*, 42, evoked the supernal aspect of the anthropomorphic configuration depicted, referring it to the supernal gradations beyond the throne and also "esoteric matters forbidden to [all human] thought" (*devarim ne'lamim she-'afilu ha-maḥashavah 'asurah bo*).

59. Alkabetz notes that the Beloved integrates the traits of mercy and judgment—and also integrates all things in all manner of perfection (*sheleimut*).

60. This last point was noted also by Zakovitch. It may be further noted that the phrase *zahav muphaz* ("pure gold") occurs in 1 Kings 10:18, which was clarified or reformulated as *zahav ṭahor* in the later 2 Chron. 9:17. On this, see Fishbane, *Biblical Interpretation*, 57.

61. See n. 12 above; and also the esoteric traditions collected and presented by M. Cohen, in *The Shi'ur Komah: Liturgy and Theurgy in Pre-Kabbalistic Jewish Mysticism* (Lanham, MD: University Press of America, 1983); and *The Shi'ur Qomah: Texts and Recensions* (Tübingen: J. C. B. Mohr, 1985).

62. For a collection of these notions of Torah, in fragmentary and full formulations over many generations, see the study by M. Idel, "The Concept of the Torah in Heikhalot Literature and its Metamorphoses in Kabbalah," *Jerusalem Studies in Jewish Thought* 1 (1981): 23–84 (Hebrew). Indicative of the continuity of this bold form is the medieval commentary of a *piyyuṭ* by R. Eliezer Kallir dealing with the cosmic size and anthropomorphic form of the Torah—itself a divine manifestation; see the study by E. E. Urbach, "Peirush le-Silluq Ha-Qalliri le-Pharashat Sheqalim 'Az Ra'ita ve-Safarta'," in *Sefer Ḥayyim Shirmann*, A. Abramson and A. Mirsky, ed. (Jerusalem: Schocken Institute, 1970), 1–25.

63. On the origin and variations of this formula, see I. Tishby, *Ḥiqrei Qabbalah ve-Shluḥoteyha* (Jerusalem: Magnes Press, 1992), 3, 941–60.

64. See *Me'or 'Einayim*, 2a.

65. See *Aruch*, s.v. *kotz* 4. On interpreting flourishes, see B. Eruv. 21b and B. Men. 29b).

66. This reading of LevR integrates it with the formulation in SongsR. The transmission is garbled in the various renditions.

67. The text in SongsR, ibid., is ambiguous, but most likely the intent is "thorns." The reading in LevR, ibid., is totally garbled.

68. Cf. Targum, *mafqanot maya'*.

69. Maharzu interprets this idiom in terms of Torah's "fullness" (*malei' davar*).

70. This verse is adduced by SongsR, ibid., 2, with reference to Jerusalem.

71. According to Malbim, the head is the seat of thought (*maḥashavah*) and will (*ratzon*)—though for Malbim (following the standard theological allegory of the passage), this refers to the supernal Godhead. This view is also found in Ibn Aqnin. For Al-Fawwāl (cf. n. 51) the symbolism of the head refers to the *matzui ha-na'aleh* (most "supernal Reality"), which is without *'erekh ve-dimyon* ("comparison or image").

72. See R. Menaḥem Naḥum of Chernobyl, *Me'or 'Einayim* (first torah).

73. Cf. AhavD 161a.

74. Literally, *razin de-ḥokhmeta ila'ah* ("mysteries of supernal Wisdom"). The sense of infinities of meaning is conveyed in this passage by the word *taltallim* ("locks")—understood via its old rabbinic interpretation as *tillei tillim* ("piles and piles"; see peshat).

75. According to Ibn Sahula, the "head" signifies the highest, most supernal elements, while the "locks" (*taltallim*) indicate that all the worlds "descend from [or: are dependent upon]" (*teluyim*) the supernal Torah.

76. Presumably, a weakened pronunciation of the guttural letter *ḥet* in the noun *leḥayav* evoked the Aramaic verb *la'ah*, "to labor," and thus this interpretation.

77. Along with the evocation of "taste," the noun *ṭa'am* variously denotes "meaning; sense; scriptural proof" in rabbinic Hebrew; its range of meanings in biblical Hebrew is broad, as well (cf. "taste" in Exod. 16:31; Num. 11:8; "meaning [or: sense]" in Ps. 119:66). The same noun in Aramaic means "interpretative sense; explanation" in Daniel and Ezra, as also attested in Akkadian. This range of meanings is in play in the midrash.

78. In the old rabbinic sources, *talmud* refers to legal midrash (i.e., clarifications of the law based on scriptural proofs and analysis, as against the formulations of the Mishnah). More generally, it can refer to one's studies (as in SongsR 5.xiii.1, where one studiously repeats one's *talmud*).

79. See also Maharzu.

80. See the comment of R. Joshua in SongsR 5.xiv.2. In ExodR 47:7, it is "the Talmud" that is "studded with beryl" (i.e., filled with many meanings).

81. For Immanuel, the emphasis on the cheeks focuses on the importance of speech and verbal restraint.

82. NJPS "an excellent young man." However, there the scope of *baḥur* actually includes the final detail in that verse, which emphasizes his height as a distinguishing trait.

83. So also Zakovitch; the puns are noted also by Bloch and Bloch.

84. Cf. P. 19 (p. 317: *shoqav yesod 'olam le-hit'oshesh*).

85. The teaching of God's "desire" is found only in NumR. Reference to the "words of Torah" (in LevR) was deleted in SongsR (which is derived from it). The latter version is the most truncated.

86. See also at 4:8 and 11.

87. Zohar 3:16a links this passage to the cedar imagery of Psalm 92.

88. Ibn Aqnin stresses that the intellectual soul recounts the agent intellect's instruction as "sweet"; and that all its emanations are "pleasing." See also Al-Fawwāl.

89. This passage focuses on the mystery of the King as residing in his mouth, linking all this to 2:3. Similarly, Ibn Sahula stresses the descent of the supernal quality of Understanding (*Binah*) via speech (*dibbur*). Alkabetz transfers the taste of perfected speech to the adept, the *dod* ("Beloved") who seeks the truth of Torah and Divinity.

90. NJPS "every part of you."

91. Cf. the formulations in Leqaḥ Ṭov and MShir; P. 8 (p. 94); and also Ibn Aqnin.

92. MatKeh emphasizes that God will come to Israel "and not to another."

93. Al-Fawwāl understands these two queries as the search for the most appropriate images, as one embarks on their spiritual and intellectual quest.

94. See peshat.

95. A longing expressed through "sundry prayers and requests" (*kammah tzelotin u-v'otin*).

96. See the references in Paul, "Garden of Delight," 107, referring to "the plucking of your [Nabu's] fruit (*katapu ša inbika*)"; citing Livingston, *Court Poetry*, 37.

97. The Zohar understands this to be a complex integration of the divine structure with the soul's structure (the *shoshanim* suggesting the six, *sheish*, lower "limbs" of these parallel forms)—an act of integration performed during worship, as the liturgy expresses Divine Unity.

98. According to REzra, the descent of the most recondite Divinity into the gradation of knowledge channels its flow to the structurer's six lower formations (see previous note). The spiritual self participates in this process, at this exalted level of spiritual reception.

99. According to Ibn Aqnin, the intellectual aspect of the soul speaks to its assistants regarding the light of intellect it receives from the agent intellect.

100. The name of the month of Elul (*'elul*) has long been considered an acronym of the initial letters of this phrase (*', l, v, l*). Thus during Elul the soul devotes itself to God, with the desire that this religious love will be reciprocally confirmed (and affirmed). See the Sefas Emes for Rosh Ḥodesh Elul (1887 and 1888); and on the determination to annul natural desires as one dedicates oneself to God alone, see his *parashat Shofeṭim* (1898).

6:4–10

1. Rashbam continues this pericope through 7:11.

2. This is also the force of the Targum's midrash here ("when you desire to do my will," *de-tzevotakh . . . re'uti*); it is, in fact, a double exposition of the Hebrew.

3. Hence Rashbam: *ka-ḥayyalot*, "like military camps."

4. See Goitein, "Ayummah Kannidgalot," 220–21; his interpretation of the verse was influenced by the imagery of v. 10, where the phrase recurs. See below.

5. Rashi: "When you are pleasing [or: favorable] (*retzuyah*) to me"; and cf. P. 8 (p. 94: *na'avah ve-retzuyah*, "beautiful and desirable").

6. This refers to the so-called lesser holy gifts (*qodashim qalim*), like festival offerings and tithes and thanksgiving beneficence (cf. B. Pes. 7a). See also Maharzu.

7. See Finkelstein edition, p. 69.

8. That is, desirable due to the quest's effort (Immanuel).

9. My comment deals with the spiritual self. The Zohar passage adapted here focuses more on Israel's beauty despite the ravages of exile (as the Holy One confirms: *shapirta ihi 'al kol dargin*). The passage assembles interpretations based on the Song. REzra considers this beauty to be a depiction of Wisdom (noted at the outset of his commentary).

10. See the metaphoric and symbolic interpretations in derash (based on SongsR). Ibn Sahula indicates that the soul has become favorable for arousing herself from spiritual indolence. The other references (Jerusalem and towers) are likewise treated figuratively in the Midrash.

11. On *nidgalot*, see peshat. Whatever the astral or celestial background (see peshat here and at v. 10 below), the image appears somewhat terrestrial in this sequence.

12. See the philological discussion at 4:9.

13. Rid has the youth request the maiden to turn toward him (*le-negdi*), but this seems unlikely.

14. See Fox, who adduces *'arheb*, which is the Syriac equivalent of our Hebrew causative form *hirhibh*.

15. Also, the first instance has a reference to the shorn flock, whereas here the term "ewes" is used (see at 4:2).

16. As in 4:2, use of the relative pronoun in 6:6 (*she-kullam*, "all of them") is followed by a pun (*shakkulah*, "miscarriage").

17. This is an allusion to B. Ta'an. 10a. Persons of exemplary piety, called *yeḥidim* were the first to fast if a drought threatened (see 6a, developing M. Ta'an. 1:4; and 12a). MatKeh interprets *yeḥidim* as the "middle group" between the children and elders; but this is unlikely given the fundamental worth of their fasting in times of drought (irrespective of when various sages fixed the onset of special fasts by these special persons). Subsequently, if such penitence fails, the entire community fasts.

18. An allusion to ibid., 14a: "When a court [*beit din*] proclaims [*gozerim*] fasts and children afflict themselves [*mit'annim*]." This refers to the "children" [*tiynoqot*; literally, "sucklings]." In extreme circumstances, both they and pregnant women must fast.

19. Cf. Maharzu, who interprets the idiom *lifshoṭ yadi be-'olami* to mean that God will extend his might "to rule the world and proclaim [His] kingship."

20. In a striking inversion of these themes, the Netziv has God tell Israel not to be so consumed by divine love that the people abandon the commandments, so greatly desired by God.

21. Noted also by Zakovitch. Cf. Amos 1:3, 6, 9, 11, 13; 2:1, 4, 6. The pattern "3 + 1" recurs in the oracles of Balaam and in the account of the catastrophes of Job.

22. And see Rashi and Ibn Ezra.

23. For Ibn Tibbon, the soul is *meyuḥedet le-hishtaddeil*, bearing a "singular" and unique capacity to "strive for" the intellect's perfection. Cf. Immanuel, *meyuḥedet le-dodi* ("singular [or: special] to my Beloved"). According to Ralbag, the soul is whole and one, without multiplicity; and it is thus the choice one—capable of perfection.

24. According to Immanuel, the incomparability is conveyed by the praise of women "beyond [or: without] number."

25. AhavD 175a speaks of a spiritual purity of vision and intention.

26. On the literal mention of radiance here, see peshat, s.v. "delight"; cf. vv. 4 and 10.

27. See the article by Goitein cited above, note 4.

28. According to Ibn Aqnin, Israel is praised for its alacrity in performing the commandments.

29. For Ibn Tibbon, being pure (*barah*) suggests a perfection of the speculative soul (*ha-nefesh ha-'iyyunit*). For Immanuel, self is transfigured via the divine light or intellect—which radiates from and through the soul.

30. So Immanuel, taking *'ayummah* in the sense of an "awesome" spiritual magnitude.

31. The first Zohar passage cited links our verse with images of the dawn and their role in proclaiming the promise of national redemption; the second passage focuses on the two supernal feminine gradations: *mi* ("who") and *zo't* ("this one [or: she]"], namely Binah and Malkhut, respectively. See further Y. Liebes, *Pulḥan ha-Shaḥar*, ch. 16, especially 156–59. I have adapted these mystical perceptions of the transcendental realms to the human quest.

6:11–7:11

1. Rashbam begins the pericope at 6:4 and continues it through 7:11.

2. See Exum, Fox, Zakovitch.

3. This is the chariot of her beloved, given the epithet *'ammi-nadiv* (see below); so also Ḥakham. Alternatively, they are chariots of a certain type or belong to a certain type of person (see below).

4. Thus Rashbam, who resorts to various paraphrases and fillers to produce this sense. Among moderns, Zakovitch presumes that she has somehow gone off or "disappeared" (his term) in a chariot. Keel suggests that she was overcome with desire and fled the scene.

5. For a little garden in a *bitan* (Esther 1:5), see Oppenheim, 331, who refers to small houses in parks or "a kiosk in a garden."

6. So Moldenke, *Plants of the Bible*, 119.

7. Cf. Keel.

8. See also Bloch and Bloch.

9. See the Assyrian evidence adduced at 5:1; and add the evidence and discussions found in Westenholz, pp. 202–3 (ll. 6–11), where the magician says, "Blooming are you, to the garden you go down [*kirišum turda*]"); see also pp. 212–13. Also note the incipit to a late love lyric: "As I [went down] to the garden of your (feminine) love"; see in W. G. Lambert, "The Problem of the Love Lyrics," in *Unity and Diversity*, 104, ii 9.

10. The ocular aspect links back to 6:9 as well.

11. The formulation found in Job 8:12 is *be-'ibbo*, "in its bud" (NJPS, "still tender").

12. The Hebrew stem is *'-b-b*.

13. Rashbam links the Aramaic noun to our verse.

14. See Nissinen: 619, citing G. Leick, *Sex and Eroticism in Mesopotamian Literature*, 74. Regarding *inbu*, see Nissinen: 609, with text references; and also Lambert: 1987, 28–29.

15. According to the peshat one could sustain a reading whereby v. 11 shifts to the maiden, who is also the speaker of v. 12 (see peshat).

16. According to Ibn Tibbon, the woman (the human intellect) is compared to a nut grove because these nuts have an external husk of materiality.

17. For Immanuel, the self descends via the intellect to understand the powers of the soul; and the soul is compared to a nut (*'egoz*) because of its several compartments. (This is a widespread medieval trope, found among the pietists of Ashkenaz and in spanish Kabbalah.) Cf. Abrams, *Sexual Symbolism*.

18. These Zoharic passages stress that the soul went down "to" (*el*) the garden—but did not enter it; and it only attempted "to see" (*lir'ot*), since for humans there is no divine seeing (*ra'iti*). See the penetrating analysis by Sh. Asulin-Regev in her *Ha-Parshanut ha-Mystit le-Sefer ha-Zohar*, 83–84.

19. Cf. AhavD 179.

20. Rashbam is a bit more restrained. He glosses: *'alah be-nafshi*, "I [suddenly] thought."

21. Alternatively, with Rashbam, the person decided to ride in the chariots.

22. NJPS renders this phrase as "I was distraught." Cf. the formulation *lo' da'at nefesh* in Prov. 19:2.

23. This presumption is supported by the cognate expression in Akkadian, *ramanšu la ide* ("he did not know himself"). For the identification of this medical idiom and its relation to our verse, see Paul, "An Unrecognized Medical Idiom," 54–57.

24. The double-duty usage was noted also by Zakovitch, 117, but without explication.

25. This last point is well noted by Bloch and Bloch.

26. Many medieval commentators (like Tamakh) regard the maiden as the speaker—suddenly snatched back by the court's women and placed in the royal coach, where she unwittingly finds herself. Among moderns who also see her as the speaker, Ginsburg notes that the maiden says that her soul's great desire brought her to these chariots. He thus follows the rabbinic phrasing but with a psychological nuance. The euphemistic suggestiveness of the verse was perceived by Levinger, 73, who says that the lass felt like a "chariot" for her beloved.

27. An elaborate emendation by N. Tur-Sinai, "Shir Ha-shirim" (ad loc.), yields the same sense. Retaining the initial idiom *lo' yada'ti nafshi*, he reconstructs the remainder of the verse by re-dividing the letters and adding new vowels. Instead of the received consonants *s-m-t-n-y m-r-k-b-t '-m-y n-d-b*, he reads *sh-m t-n-y m-r-k b-t '-m-y n-d-b*. He thus emends MT to: *sham teni morakh bat 'ammi nadiv*, with the meaning: "I am beside myself [with joy], [for] there [viz., in the garden; v. 11] you will give me your myrrh, O nobleman's daughter." That English rendition basically follows Gordis (pp. 67, 92), who adopts Tur-Sinai's emendation. The latter was perhaps inspired by the older suggestion of Graetz, who proposed *samtini morakh*, "You have made me fearful, [O nobleman's daughter]."

28. For a similar inversion of the construct form, see Jer. 17:3, with the formulation *bamoteykha be-ḥaṭṭ'at* instead of *ḥaṭṭ'at bamoteykha* ("the sin of your high places"); and cf. *berit 'am* in Isa. 42:6, usually construed as if it were *'am berit* ("a covenant people").

29. So also Zakovitch. Rashbam, however, says that she determined to return to "my people [that is] noble" (thus interpreting the formulation as gapped).

30. Bloch and Bloch argue for the construction being superlative in force (p. 195), and thus they render: "the most lavish of chariots." Less likely is Fox and Exum, "chariot with a nobleman."

31. According to the Netziv, Israel expresses incomprehension as to why God has cast her among the nations, to suffer at their hands.

32. This view derives the verb *nadiv* as from the stem *nadav* ("to give freely; to donate").

33. Al-Fawwāl understands the name as indicating that the intellect is filled with *shefa'* ("efflux") and *nedivut* ("beneficent giving"). For Malbim, this passage suggests an ecstasy for the soul that takes it beyond awareness or thoughts of this world. In other words, *lo' yada'ti* means "not-knowing," an individual loss of awareness.

34. Ibn Tibbon understands the chariot to symbolize the perfected human intellect's receptivity.

35. On *nefesh* and desire, see peshat.

36. On this nomenclature, see peshat.

37. Ibn Sahula reads the words of the soul as a complaint, wondering why God has given it such a physical constitution and structure, the cause of sin and weakness. This is a puzzling turn, and understandable only from the perspective that under the impact of this moment of looking, we flee in fear (a reading with medieval precedents). See also AhavD 180b, "I didn't know how [or: was unable] to protect myself from sin" (*lo' yada'ti le-hizzaher mei-ha-ḥeit'*).

38. So also Bloch and Bloch.

39. So also Anon. 1.

40. The noun *maḥol* (dance) literally indicates a circling or whirling motion. Cf. M. Gruber, *The Motherhood of God*, 170–71. It may be noted that what the dual occasionally does is to *regard a set of items as a functional unit*. That is, the number of elements can be more than two, so long as they are viewed as working together in concert. Hence *shinayim*, "teeth"; *me'ayim*, "internal organs"; *kera'ayim*, "[four] legs [of cattle]"; *shiv'atayim*, "sevenfold." (See Yishai Tobin, "The Dual Number in Hebrew: Grammar or Lexicon, or Both?" in Ellen Contini-Morava, ed., *Between Grammar and Lexicon* [Phila.: John Benjamins, 2000]: 87–116.)

41. Research since the original publication of NJPS in 1969 has shown that the Tiberian Masoretes of the Aaron Ben-Asher school promulgated a more uniform text than the NJPS translators had believed. The minority reading that the latter adopted can no longer be called "the Masoretic text" per se.

42. There are two versions of the tradition. The account in GenR is stylistically more simple (see in the edition of Theodor-Albeck, 2, p. 745, formulated as a proem by R. Berekhiah); that in SongsR is transmitted in the name of R. Samuel b. Ḥiyya in the name of R. Ḥanina.

43. According to Rashbam, the call to return is voiced by prophets who exhort the people to repent and obey the Torah. The Netziv understands the call as the voice of the nations, who supplicate Israel to return, having let them depart at one time or another.

44. Ibn Aqnin interprets the name *Shulammit* as *sheleimah be-dat*, "perfected in [the practice of her] religion."

45. "Dwells" (*dar*) in GenR (ibid.); "accompanies [or: guides]" (*mitnaheig*) in SongsR (ibid.); the former is supported by Exod. 25:8; the latter by 2 Sam. 7:6. Cf. the linguistic correlation in MatKeh.

46. In GenR (Theodor-Albeck, ed.) and SongsR (Vilna ed.) the formulation is *msyymym* (traditionally *mesayyemim*, "who conclude" [the *Shemoneh 'Esrei* with this blessing]), spelled with a *samekh* and presumably a midrashic play on *va-yaseim* ("and grant you"), spelled with a *sin*. But several GenR manuscripts and the primary printed editions (of Venice and Constantinople) read *msymym* (i.e., *mesiymim* ("who grant [or: place]"). This is the simpler version and may be formed from the midrashic play just noted. Radal proposes emending to the latter formulation, in light of the scriptural word; he suggests that this is the primary version.

47. That is, God will spread or grant peace to Israel "like a river" (*ke-nahar*; perhaps meaning that the nations will flow to her with good will and peace [Radak].

48. This dependence of God's world-maintenance upon Israel's covenant commitment echoes SongsR 1.ix.1. The theme is famously rendered in B. Shab. 88a.

49. This follows the insight of MatKeh.

50. Genesis 32:2.

51. For the latter point, see S. Buber, ed., ShṬov, 138b–39a; cf. the variant in B. Ta'an. 31a.

52. See ShṬov, ad loc.; cf. SongsR at 5.9, and the allusion to MdRI noted there.

53. Ibn Tibbon perceptively understands the call to turn as the voice of the Beloved confirming the self's achievement and its readiness to receive perfection.

54. For Immanuel and Malbim, the body senses the ascension of the soul and beseeches it not to depart.

55. According to Ralbag, the soul is told to turn and prepare for a higher level of intellect; and also that the higher powers will continue to look upon it (with providential favor). Cf. Ibn Aqnin.

56. According to Ibn Aqnin, after the self is beset by dual inclinations and tensions, it says that it can resist these natural forces, due to divine help. Malbim similarly perceives here a tension between the call of the higher powers and inclinations, and lower worldly and physical desires. My comment follows in his spirit.

57. Cf. his comment on the description in 5:10–16, which descends from top to bottom. Rashbam also cites the rabbinic passage.

58. The acoustic effect of Judg. 5:28 is also noted by Bloch and Bloch. Zakovitch suggests a reference to a stepping movement.

59. See also AgShir.

60. For the Netziv, the sandals hint at the people's modesty: "locked" (*na'ul*) and "covered up" (*mekhuseh*).

61. The figure of God as world-craftsman is taken over from a subsequent teaching in SongsR, ibid., but used there for a different purpose. The topic occurs famously in the opening proem of GenR, where God is deemed the creator-craftsman of the world.

62. For Ralbag, this represents the ascension of intellect from the lower, posterior analytics to the higher ones.

63. For Immanuel, she is now called "daughter of Nadib" because of her capacity to receive the higher wisdom and perfection.

64. In Ralbag's view, the term *nadiv* (literally "noble one") indicates the incorporeal agent of the intellect; the term *bat nadiv* refers to the human imagination "effected" by the intellect.

65. See J. T. Milik, *Dédicaces faites par des dieux (Palmyre, Hatra, Tyr) et des thiases sémitiques à l'époque romaine* (Paris: Paul Guethner, 1972), 108; cited by Fox.

66. The noun *msk* also has this sense in Ugaritic texts; see UT 67:I: 21. Note also *mimsakh* in Isa. 65:11, and B. A.Z. 58b.

67. See the comment of R. Abun bar Ḥisdai in SongsR, ibid., and reinforced in MatKeh.

68. Noted also by Radal.

69. In PesiqR 10 (Ish Shalom, ed., 35a, top), *mazeg* in the Song is read as *mozeig*—referring to God "who pours" or provides for all, and does not allow His universe to "lack" anything. In ShṬov at Ps. 23:1 (in Buber edition, 99b), the citation is supported by the song passage, but without exegetical elaboration.

70. This is adduced in the name of R. Yoḥanan, who states that Leviticus deals "entirely with the atonement [effected by] sin offerings and guilt offerings (*kapparot haṭṭa'ot*)." SongsR 3.1 mentions the centrality of Leviticus in the Torah, but states only that it is comprised of a "heap of sins" (*haṭa'im*); Tan. has "heap of *haṭṭa'ot*)."

71. This follows the exegesis of *shoshanim* (2:2): as if *sheshonim*.

72. SongsR, ibid., interprets the lilies as the words of Torah; the "words of Torah are as soft [or pliable?] as lilies."

73. Ralbag regards the wheat as indicating the potentialities of the intellect.

74. I.e., "he came *le-nashekho*, to bite him" (not *le-nasheqo*, "to kiss him"). This follows the exegesis of R. Yannai, ad loc. (see edition of Theodor-Albeck, 2, p. 927). The basis of such exegesis was an interpretation of the super-consonantal dots. Historically, these dots indicate scribal notations concerning problematic words or diverse copying traditions (already in the Qumran scrolls). For a discussion of this rabbinic phenomenon, see S. Lieberman, *Hellenism in Jewish Palestine* ("The Ten Dotted Places in the Torah"), 43–46. See the materials in *Massekhet Soferim*, ch. 6.

In an older Tannaitic version of the foregoing exegetical tradition, in SifNum 69 (*Siphre D'Be Rav*, H. S. Horowitz, ed., p. 65), the dots are interpreted to mean that Esau did not kiss him "with sincerity" (literally "with his full heart"; *be-khol libbo*). The later version in GenR, attributed to R. Yannai (see above), reflects latter tensions with Rome and Christianity. The earlier formulation to which Yannai responds was that he did kiss him "with a full heart" (*mi-khol libbo*); a variant that reflects love and remorse (Tan. *Vayishlaḥ* 4 notes that this kiss was a "true" kiss, *shel 'emet*; and TanB has the variant kiss "of love," *shel 'ahavah*).

75. Overall, see G. Cohen, "Esau as a Symbol of Rome," 243–69.

76. See in the Horowitz-Rabin edition, p. 323. This is a remarkable reinterpretation of the lemma.

77. See also Radal. The phrase *sha'ar bat rabbim* could also be midrashically rendered as the "[judicial] seat (*bayit*), [where judgment was the] product [or: daughter] (*bat*) of the calculus-measure (*shi'ur*) of the majority (*rabbim*)."

78. That is, the "many."

79. Noted anonymously in SifDeut (Finkelstein edition, 15); whereas in LevR 1.2 it is attributed to R. Shim'on bar Yoḥai, and in SongsR, to R. Ṭavyomi. The identification of the Temple with Lebanon is an old symbolic figure, found in the Qumran scrolls and commonly in the Targum.

80. The various midrashic comments (see previous note) state that Lebanon (*Levanon*) is known as the Temple because "all hearts" (*levavot*) rejoice in it.

81. Adapting and transforming the traditions in SongsR, ibid., 2.

82. Building upon but transforming LevR 1.2; also interpreting Lebanon.

83. Malbim sees the emphasis on parts of the body that extol the soul's powers; but all this will pass with death (see his comments on vv. 3–5, especially).

84. The Talmudic homily in this passage builds off of Num. 21:27, as follows: *bo'u ḥeshbon* (NJPS "come to Heshbon") calls on persons to actively "reckon" their deeds, while *ha-moshelim* (NJPS "the bards") refers to those who "rule" their evil instinct.

85. See the Hasidic development of the rabbinic homily in *Netivot Shalom* by R. Shalom Barzofsky (Jerusalem: Yeshivat Beit Avraham Slonim), *Be-midbar*, *Ḥuqqat*, 127b–129b.

86. The latter identification was noted also by Bloch and Bloch; and earlier by Fox.

87. E. Ben-Yehudah, *Millon Ha-Lashon Ha-ʿIvrit: Ha-Yshanah Ve-ha-Ḥadashah* (Jerusalem; Berlin-Schöneberg: Langenscheidt, 1908–59), s.v. *ml*.

88. See Reich, "The Beauty and the King?" adducing the *Chicago Assyrian Dictionary* M/1, s.v. *malû* (A) ("uncombed hair").

89. The metonymy of the first half of the parallelism is supplemented by the explicit reference to hair in the second one.

90. See explicitly, Esther 8:15.

91. For *rash*, cf. 1 Sam. 18:23; for *dal*, cf. Lev. 14:21. Cf. AgShir.

92. According to the versions (cited in the commentary), Elijah appealed to God with the words "[Since] we have no merit, look to the covenant (*berit*)"—alluding to the thirteen attributes of divine mercy (Exod. 34:6–7).

93. Rereading the verse as "the feeblest of them shall be in that day like David."

94. Tan., *Tetzavveh* 6, is a later, much truncated formulation.

95. "Held captive" gives one of the usages in biblical Hebrew (i.e., "bound" in prison; cf. Gen. 39:20 and 40:5). But there are overtones of a "spell" of enchantment (following rabbinic usage of this verb in magical contexts; and the term is already attested in Akkadian with this sense).

96. See also the comment above at 1:17, with the midrashic sources provided.

97. SongsR and LevR stress running for food; Tan. denotes two acts of running (the first to extend welcome to strangers). This explanation is attributed to R. Abba b. Kahana.

98. See *parashat Tetzavveh* (1872).

99. For Ralbag, this king is the material intellect, held captive by the attributes prepared by the soul; an alternative possibility is that the agent intellect is held captive by the material intellect (upon which it emanates) if the latter is limited in its development.

100. See peshat regarding *rehaṭim* ("flow of hair") as being related to the flow of water in troughs. Various masters have suggested that this image indicates the flow of thoughts (see below).

101. The work *Maggid Devarav Le-Yaʿaqov* is also called *Liqquṭei ʾAmarim*.

102. Tamakh incorporates both possibilities into his paraphrase.

103. Aquila has Greek *thugatēr truphōn*, thus reading or construing Hebrew **bat ʿanugim*, "O daughter of pleasure."

104. For this last point, see Bloch and Bloch.

105. Maharzu stressed the divine beneficence outweighing any earthly compensation.

106. Biblical Hebrew *taʿanugim* ("pleasure") was explained in SongsR, ibid., in terms of Abraham's being *mitḥaṭṭeiʾ* with respect to the King of Sodom. This rabbinic explication is perplexing. MatKeh suggests that he "purified himself" by removing himself, i.e., he "foreswore" (*mitnaqqeih*) all benefit for his actions—following the early medieval lexicon *Arukh*, which provides this explanation on the basis of a contextual inference. See *Aruch Completum*, s.v. *ḥṭ*, 3, p. 367a.

107. Cf. Ibn Tibbon: "Who delights in pleasure" (*ʾohevet ha-taʿanugim*).

108. Anatolo interprets this passionate love as having intensity and endurance; see on *parashat Vaʾetḥannan* 161a–b (for the text, see bibliography).

109. Cf. Metzudat David; Gallico.

110. The descendants were Hananiah, Mishael, and Azariah (known as Shadrach, Mishakh, and Abednego; Dan. 1:6–7).

111. Variously explained in the sources—e.g., in SongsR 7.viii.1 by virtue of the illusion of fire cast by the radiance of heavenly bodies (see R. Eleazar and R. Samuel, for different versions); or in ix.1, by the miracles of the furnace either floating or bursting; or one or many angels intervening on their behalf.

112. Judah avers that she is more "righteous" (*tzadeqah*) than he, thus deserving acquittal (Gen. 38:26). See GenR, ad loc.

113. Ibn Aqnin nicely notes that here the agent intellect praises the human intellect for its inner balance of powers (*shivui ha-mishqal*).

114. See in *Sefer ʾArugat Ha-Bosem. Ḥibro R. ʾAvraham beR. ʾAzriel*, E. E. Urbach, ed. (Jerusalem: Mekize Nirdamim, 1939), 1, 196.

115. See s.v. *ve-ḥay ba-hem*.

116. Presumably specifying here the martyrs (Hananiah, Mishael, and Azariah) just lauded.

117. See also Maharzu.

118. Regarding Abraham and Isaac, see also Maharzu and YefQol. The inclusion of Jacob is not clear. Perhaps this was understood as a forecast of trials by fire (martyrdom) on the basis of Obadiah 18, which states that "the house of Jacob will be fire."

119. For this and related traditions, see S. Spiegel, *The Last Trial* (New York: Pantheon Books, 1967); originally published as *"Mei-ʾAggadot ha-ʿAqeidah"* in the A. Marx Jubilee Volume, 1950.

120. Immanuel understands the "I" voice to be the separate intellect, which wants to conjoin with the soul. Alternatively, Malbim perceives in the ego-I an attempt to impede the soul's departure.

121. AhavD (220b) refers to the regeneration of speech (giving it *ḥiyyut*, "vitality").

122. REzra interprets the figure to hint at the elicitation of a higher wisdom and hidden speech, which may flow into the spiritually cultivated soul.

123. Tamakh renders *le-dodim*, "for love," thereby obviating the textual issue.

124. Noted by Fox.

125. See succinctly SongsR 7.xi.1.

126. That is, given to God and to all others who desire (spiritual) wisdom (Immanuel).

127. For Malbim, this phrase expresses the soul's spiritual departure with a divine kiss. (It is now in a state of cleaving to its heavenly source.)

128. REzra expresses this theme in different terms.

7:12–8:14

1. These four units include three Masoretic paragraph breaks, and a final one distinguished by a section divider. The later unit, 8:11–14, is regarded by many moderns as (at least in part, vv. 11–12) an addendum; this is because of the sudden mention of Solomon's royal vineyard and its workers. Rabbinic tradition also had some qualms about this material, and judged 8:11 as one of the instances where the name Solomon is not a sobriquet for God (King of Peace), but for the king of flesh and blood; hence they considered this name not "holy" but common (see B. Shevu. 35b; the reference to Solomon's bed in 3:7 is proposed as another possibility—the discussion concerns sacred divine names and their use or misuse).

2. See the conclusion to his commentary, pp. 198–99 (at v. 14).

3. Cf. the fuller explanation, developed above. Unless one includes her musings in the context of her love-talk to the Beloved, one is constrained to see this as part of a fantasy or daydream; so Zakovitch (pp. 128, 130). Neither Fox nor Bloch and Bloch discuss the issue. Exum comes closer to my interpretation, it seems, when she construes the reformulated adjuration as a kind of rhetorical question (see below).

4. The absence of a cohortative *-ah* ending for *neitzei'* is presumably because the following word begins with *ha-* ; cf. v. 13 with *nir'eh*, "*let us* see."

5. Cf. the similar sequence without conjunctions (asyndetic construction) in Ps. 95:1, 6.

6. Fox has also caught this bivalent quality of the noun. Cf. at 2:12 regarding *zamir*.

7. Ibn Tibbon perceives and accentuates the erotic suggestiveness formulated here (*nit'alesah sham be-'ahavim—ke-derekh ha-hosheqim ve-ha-mena'afim*).

8. Immanuel regards this passage as a call to spiritual wandering, in order to determine whether the self's development is ripe (having moved through the various levels of wisdom—practical, physical, and metaphysical).

9. The passage in the Zohar uses our verse to teach the need to keep God in mind as one goes "on the way"—like an interior *tefillat ha-derekh*, "prayer for a journey."

10. Cf. also the discussion in Maggid, #22 (pp. 35–37).

11. For Ralbag, the call (understood allegorically) is to see if the senses have been sufficiently perfected (by the acquisition of proper knowledge); and if so, the higher intellect will bestow upon the self its love (intellectual powers) for its further benefit and development.

12. According to Malbim, this giving connotes a spiritual ecstasy, a total donation of self.

13. In more medieval terms, it is the transcending of the material sensibilities of existence (the *murgashot*); cf. Al-Fawwāl.

14. See in the texts translated by Fox; Group A, no. 20B (p. 31); Group B no. 21A (p. 37) and 21 E (p. 38). For a rabbinic reference to a love potion, see B. Git. 70a.

15. Following the interpretation of Bloch and Bloch; and cf. Fox, earlier.

16. Fox also catches the nuance that the fruits "stored up" are the fruits of and for love.

17. AgShir adds that in exile, even the wicked of Israel have a goodly fragrance.

18. According to Leqaḥ Ṭov, traditions are made, renewed, or innovated "from their own reasoning."

19. SongsR, ibid. (in the name of R. Abba b. Kahana), creates a striking new teaching from early traditions found in SifDeut, *Ha'azinu* 324; and *Vezo't Haberakhah* 356.

20. According to Al-Fawwāl, the new (*ḥadashim*) and old (*yeshanim*) indicate the knowledge of existing nature ("constantly renewed," *mitḥaddeshim tadir*), and of matters that are perpetual and unchanging.

21. According to Ibn Aqnin: within the soul.

22. In the view of Immanuel, all the acquired qualities have been set aside (used only for the highest spiritual purposes) for God alone (the highest intellect). In Malbim's view, this act of giving connotes a total devotion to God, with all one's love hidden away for this consummate moment.

23. Ibn Sahula adds that even "new" practices, not fully developed, have their own fragrance.

24. Thus the verb *tzafanti* is more than the prosaic "kept." It connotes a "hidden saving" or "laying in inwardness" for devoted acts of love (cf. Alkabetz, ad loc.).

25. The supplemental phrase "does Scripture speak about" is found in ExodR 5.1. See *Midrash Shemot Rabbah* (A. Shinan, ed.), ad loc., p. 19.

26. NJPS renders *ba-ḥutz* as "in the street," which is its usual meaning in Scripture. Here, however, the spatial locus is in contrast to the inside space of the maternal home, noted in v. 2. Better: "outside" or "in public."

27. This is how the Midrash (SongsR to 1.1 and ExodR) explains the external space of their meeting.

28. According to Malbim, the soul speaks thus to God. She is ready to abandon her body for a kiss, despite the natural world's scorn.

29. Ibn Aqnin understands the speaker to be the intellectual soul addressing the active intellect, and desiring that the latter not cease from being with her.

30. Al-Fawwāl desires intellectual conjunction *ba-ḥutz*, while engaged in philosophy (*'iyyun*), called *ḥokhmot ḥitzonot*.

31. The Septuagint reads *tēs sullabousēs me*, which means something like *'el ḥeider horati*; the verb is thus construed like the one in 3:4. Perhaps vocalize *yeladatni*, as in Jer. 20:14.

32. I have also found this suggestion in Gordis.

33. Also see SongsR 3.iv (cited at LevR loc. cit. and 5:2).

34. Ibn Aqnin emphasizes the issue of proper worship.

35. SongsR, ibid., refers to the "great Mishnahs"—like that of R. Ḥiyya Rabba, traditional compiler of the Tosefta; and those of R. Hoshaya and R. Kappara, which are incorporated into the present Mishnah through the editorial work of R. Akiva and, finally, by Rabbi Judah.

36. In rabbinic parlance, the "meaning" or even "support" of Scripture, as derived through rabbinic exegesis, is its *ta'am*, "sense [or: meaning]."

37. In SifDeut, *Ha'azinu*, 317, different aspects of the Oral Torah are compared to the different fruits and fluids in Deut. 32:14. The Haggadot (homiletic Midrash) are compared to fermented grape juice (NJPS: "foaming grape-blood"), "because they stimulate the heart like wine" (Finkelstein, ed.), p. 359.

38. Malbim refers to this as bodily practice, *'avodah she-ba-guf*. Immanuel indicates the need to transcend bodily desires through practice of the *mitzvot*.

39. Ibn Sahula proceeds in this spirit, understanding *'immi*, "my mother," as the cosmic Mother, and Wisdom (*Binah*) as the spiritual principle gifting transcendent knowledge.

40. Fox, Bloch and Bloch, and Exum all present this image in the present in both instances.

41. Literally, "integrating male and female" (*kalil dekhar venuqba'*).

42. I agree with Exum's translation and overall intent (248), though for different reasons. She sees this shifting rhetorical formulation in anticipation of "the climactic affirmation of love" in vv. 6–7. And see above pp. 9–10.

43. Cf. Ibn Aqnin: "One should not arouse the redemption until the proper [appointed] time."

44. According to Malbim, this is an oath against the powers that would separate the soul from Divinity. Others continue to see here a caution against impetuous development (Ibn Tibbon, Al-Fawwāl, and Immanuel).

45. "One must arouse [love] in the proper manner" (*tzerikhin le-'it'ara' lah ki-deqa' ye'ut*).

46. Rashbam regards the speaker as the woman, who tries to entice her Beloved by saying that "others" speak so exultantly about her!

47. Arabic *rafiqa*. This may be a later gloss in Rabbi Shlomoh, having derived from Radak's dictionary, who cited his father. See Eppenstein, "Les Compairisons," 56, who deems the source to be Ibn Janaḥ. Others suggest that the verb is a metastasis for *mitpareqet*, meaning that she has been or is "broken apart" by love (Immanuel; Ibn Sahula).

48. E. A. Speiser deemed this an iterative *t*-stem infix, homonymous with the regular *hitpa'el*, and with Akkadian cognate equivalents. See his "The Durative Hitpa'el: A *tan* Form," *Journal of the American Oriental Society* 75 (1955): 118–21.

49. A point noted also by Fox.

50. It is even harder here than in the accounts of the adjuration to go along with Fox's comment that the verb "means simply to wake one from sleep" (168).

51. So also Rashbam, who understood *ḥibbelatekha 'immeikh* as meaning *ḥibbelah 'immeikh* ("your mother writhed [with you]"). Cf. Ms. Hamburg 23; Ms. Budapest A384, which reads *ḥibbelah mi-mekha* ("writhed with you"). These readings are noted in the edition of Japhet, *Rashbam*, ad loc.

52. The verb *mitpareiq* is used to denote the "breaking apart" of "joints" (*peraqim*) or "limbs" (cf. B. Ber. 6b; also B. Nid. 9a); and Aramaic *'itpariq* renders "redemption" or "release" in the Targum to Lev. 19:20). MatKeh also intuited an exegesis based on the inversion of letters, suggestion that *mitpareqet* connotes *manaḥat peraqim*, the resolution of textual topics. Maharzu is more cautious, opining that R. Yoḥanan's exegesis "requires investigation."

53. Cf. Leqaḥ Ṭov, who emphasizes Israel's "suffering" in the pre-messianic age. A most poignant use of the theme of being broken and killed as a martyr, citing just our passage (and presumably based on Ibn Sahula's use of it) occurs in a fifteenth-century sermon by R. Abraham b. Eliezer Ha-Levi. The text was first published by G. Scholem in "Peraqim be-Toledot Sifrut Ha-Kabbalah," *Kiryat Sefer* 7 (1930–31): 152–55. It is found in Ms. Oxford 2295, folios 1–2. See my translation and extended discussion in *The Kiss of God*, pp. 55–60.

54. See derash at 2:3, as well.

55. So R. Berekhiah: *'itberit beriyah ḥadeta* (SongsR, ibid.).

56. I assume that this theological addition is based on a verbal pun, due to weakened vocalization of the letter *ḥet* in *ḥubbelah* (understood in a negative, destructive sense—not as legal distraint), so that it evoked the stem *'a-b-l* (mourning). The sense of divine wrath is stressed by R. Levi himself, when he says that at Sinai, Israel "angered" God (*hiqtzaftem*)—probably alluding to Deut. 9:7. A later addendum to his comments states in Aramaic that "there are places that call a house of mourning (*'abheilah*) a 'house of wrath (*qetzofah*).'"

57. On *mitrapeqet* as "longing" and not only "leaning" (NJPS), see peshat.

58. The image of an inverted cosmic tree is found in *Sefer Ha-Bahir*; see G. Scholem, *Origins of the Kabbalah* (Princeton: Princeton University Press, 1987), 71–80.

59. Ibn Sahula speaks of a supernal font of Wisdom.

60. Cf. Ibn Sahula, who reports that he heard a tradition that *shamah*, "there," refers to a "hidden place" (*maqom nistar*) in the depths of Supernal Being.

61. The NJPS translators note that the noun *zero'a* literally corresponds to "arm" rather than "hand."

62. Note also his comment regarding the figure of remembrance in his comment at Exod. 13:9, where he cites this song passage.

63. The meaning of *reshef* in Job 5:7 is uncertain.

64. He uses the verb *le-haflig*.

65. For this phenomenon, see J. A. Soggin, "Traces of Ancient Causatives in š- Realized as Autonomous Roots in Biblical Hebrew," in his *Old Testament and Oriental Studies* (Rome: Biblical Institute, 1975), 188–202.

66. Rashbam regards this as one word and neutralizes the divine complement.

67. See my discussion in *Biblical Myth and Rabbinic Mythmaking*, 91 (and notes). Apart from the mythic dimensions, it is quite striking that in a Ugaritic letter (CTA 53 = UT 54) the outbreak of a disease led the writer to say that, "death is very strong" (*kmtm / 'z. m'id*), ll. 12–13.

68. See *Die Keilalphabetischen Texte aus Ugarit*, edited by M. Dietrich, O. Loretz, J. Samartin: 1:6 vi. 17.

69. For ancient Near Eastern evidence regarding Reshef, see D. Conrad, "Der Gott Reschef," *Zeitschrift für die alttestamentlische Wissenschaft* 83 (1971): 157–83, and A. Caquot, "Sur quelques démons dans l'Ancient Testament (*Reshep, Qeteb, Deber*)," *Semitica* 6 (1956): 53–69.

70. Picking up on the second phrase, "like a seal on your arm," and its resonance in Jeremiah. The first clause refers to the seal near the heart.

71. A bit more elliptically, Maharzu paraphrases "set me as a seal" as "by a thought in the heart." MatKeh interprets *siymeini* as if *siym mi-menni*, "make of those who [descend] from me."

72. R. Nehemiah and the sages, respectively (SongsR, ibid.).

73. See the Targum on this verse.

74. See the similar use of this comment in TanB, *Vayeishev* 19, 1, 188; cf. *Midrash Rabbah Ha-Mevo'ar. Shir Hashirim*, 3, 355, where it is linked to mismanaged human love in the case of Jacob and his sons—not to divine–human love or a challenge by alien scoffers. On such misguided love and its consequence, see below.

75. Regarding Jacob's excessive love toward Joseph, and the consequences of jealous enmity, TanB adds: "For his father loved him too much."

76. Ibn Aqnin understands this to be spoken by the human intellect (*sikhlit*) to the agent intellect.

77. The Sefas Emes also interprets this request as a desire for divine dimensions to be imprinted on the soul. See his comment on *parashat Lekh-lekha* (1888).

78. TiqZ teaches here that whoever preserves a "trace" (*reshimu*) of Divinity preserves something of the mysterious Divine Name upon it. The figure derives from the impression of a seal.

79. "And all things are sustained by Love."

80. See H. Mays, "Some Cosmic Connections of *Mayim Rabbim*," *Journal of Biblical Literature* 74 (1955): 9–21.

81. For this battle, see my *Biblical Myth*, 55–56.

82. See in *Corpus des tablettes en cunéiformes alphabétiques à Ras Shamra-Ugarit de 1929 à 1939*, edited by A. Herdner: 3.3.39.

83. It has been suggested that Prov. 6:20–35 reworked Song 8:6; see Daiches and (apparently independently) Zakovitch.

84. See MatKeh (at both places), who also cites NumR 2.16, where the nations are identified with "kings and princes." He notes the stylistic differences in the first two sources.

85. Ibn Aqnin emphasizes Israel's love of God "despite the nations."

86. In a striking expression, it is taught that even were the nations to give all their wealth for Torah, *'eino mitkappeir be-yadam*, "it would hardly suffice"—perhaps hinting that they could never find atonement; and indeed this seems to be the force of the statement that even were they to offer all their wealth in recompense for "the blood of R. Akiva and his compatriots (martyrs)," *'ein mitkapper la-hem le-'olam*, "they would never achieve atonement." This is a most powerful explanation of *yabhuzu*, "they would be scorned," reflecting a deep injunction against the Romans and other perpetrators of tragedy and death.

87. NJPS: "O how I love Your Teaching! It is my study all day long." The noun *siḥati*, "my study," is contextually and culturally apt—connoting one's "preoccupation" with Torah via incessant Torah "conversation."

88. Also compare the phrase *mi yittein* there (v. 2) and *'im yittein* (here).

89. For Ibn Sahula, the fire of love is in contrast to mere existence, which is deemed worthless and futile.

90. REzra deftly inverts the passage to suggest that if persons devote themselves totally to God, it might seem ludicrous, yet it is truly a sanctification of God in public.

91. So also Gordis; Fox; Bloch and Bloch.

92. The Akkadian cognate verb (to Hebrew *laqaḥ*) is *aḫazu*, and it is likewise used to indicate the "purchase" or financial acquisition of a wife.

93. A teaching attributed to R. Berekhiah in both sources; also in GenR 39.2, though much truncated.

94. GenR 30.8 includes the tradition that he came to recognize God at the age of three years.

95. GenR 38.13. The phrase here refers to Abraham going "down" into the furnace, the term used in SongsR, ibid., and thus its source.

96. Al-Fawwāl speaks of the need to cultivate the soul, so that it would be prepared at the time of death for release from

the body ("on the day it is spoken for"—decreed on High). I have adapted his insight.

97. That is, she has developed from a lower to a higher spiritual wisdom. This Zoharic passage indicates two types of Wisdom. Another (3:77b–79a) articulates this further: there is both a higher, supernal wisdom (*Binah* = *ra'yah*), and a lower supernal one (*Shekhinah* or *Malkhut* = *'aḥot*). Thus the "sister" symbolizes a certain level of spiritual achievement, but not the highest. I have reformulated this insight with respect to human spiritual growth.

98. See similarly Anon. 1; among moderns, Pope, Zakovitch, Bloch and Bloch, and Exum.

99. Fox also perceived this, emphasizing the figure of the wall's flatness (indicative of her lack of breasts). He equivocates regarding the door imagery (172).

100. There is thus no reason to consider this an aggressive act of bolting her shut, unless one sees the image of the door as conveying sexual promiscuity (cf. Ibn Ezra; Bloch and Bloch). The verb can have a less warlike sense, meaning "to bind" or "to fasten," derived from either *tz-w-r* or *tz-r-r* (also Fox). Also cf. B. B.B. 49b (where *la-tzur* means "to seal" a jar).

101. With SongsR, ibid. (*devarim*, "matters").

102. In SongsR, ibid., he is to endure the matters as a wall; in Tan., he is to "give his soul" (*notein nafsho*) stalwartly as a wall—a phrase used to indicate devotion unto death (cf. SifDeut. 32, on Deut. 6:2 "all your soul"; and also M. Ber. 9:5), a matter confirmed by the subsequent phrase, "and devote himself to the sanctification of the [divine] Name" (*ve-yimsor 'atzmo 'al qiddush ha-Shem*).

103. Cf. Aqedat Yitzḥak.

104. Ibn Aqnin: "good deeds" will protect the people like a wall.

105. See remez at 1:11, "spangles of silver," for the word association.

106. For the verb *natzur* as "besieged," cf. Isa. 1:8 and Jer. 4:16; for other meanings, see peshat.

107. I follow the excellent suggestion of Zakovitch.

108. SongsR merely says "righteous ones like me"; GenR notes the first of the two historical examples; Tan. mentions both instances (the first is also the subject of an independent homily based on this verse, later in SongsR).

109. SongsR, ibid.

110. Tan., ibid. And GenR, ibid., has the full idiom of entering and departing safely.

111. Focusing on the comparative particle *ke-* in the phrase "as one who has found favor," Ibn Aqnin suggests that the intellect has not attained its full measure of achievements (*hassagot*).

112. For the term, see peshat; NJPS "favor" deals figuratively with the valuation denoted in the plain sense. In the present sod context, spiritual wholeness is suggested.

113. Literally, "to bind [together] with mindfulness the bonds of Faith." This symbolizes the entire structure of *sefirot*. The unit occurs among the textual deletions (*hashmaṭot*).

114. See also Fox.

115. Zakovitch notes this comparative point.

116. Our translators apparently construed *noṭerim* in light of 1:6, where it does mean "guard." This then prompted them to construe *natan* as the commissioning of agents. But the syntax argues against this reading; the verb's direct object is the vineyard—not the agents. Their translation would correspond with something like *natan noṭerim 'et-ha-kerem* (cf. 1:6), more than with *natan 'et-ha-kerem la-noṭerim*.

117. These guardians of idolatry are called *mishmarot*—translating and transforming the biblical word *noṭerim*, the "guards" or "protectors" of foreign worship. Cf. MatKeh.

118. Cf. AgShir and LṬov.

119. The sages interpreted *ve-khol he-ḥarash ve-ha-masgeir* to refer to a total of one thousand; other interpreters suggested that each group ("the craftsmen and smiths") comprised a thousand—but that would undermine this midrash. According to tradition, they were righteous scholars.

120. Per Rashbam, the new buyer pays 1,000 shekels to the owner and pays off the "guards" (workers) with a 200-shekel quittance fee (their normal 20 percent profit).

121. Regarding the likelihood of puns, see also Zakovitch. Ibn Ezra suggested that the reference was a toponym. Even so, that would not end the matter.

122. So also Fox, who emends the first phrase to yield *ḥaveiray maqshivim*, "my companions attend" (i.e., are listening). The syntax of the next clause must still be explained.

123. The Netziv regards this as "another song" (i.e., separate and self-contained).

124. Viz., reciting the *Shema* in focused unison—as noted in SongsR 8.xi.2: *be-khivvun ha-da'at, be-khol 'eḥad, be-dei'ah ve-ṭa'am 'eḥad*).

125. Leqaḥ Ṭov states that this is the people addressing God concerning the suffering of exile.

126. The first part of the verse is cited in SongsR, ibid.

EXCURSUS

A History of Jewish Interpretation of the Song of Songs

Peshat: The Exegetical Revolution and Its Exemplars

The emergence of the *Peshat*-type of commentary in northern Europe in the eleventh to twelfth centuries was a veritable revolution in Jewish intellectual culture. After a thousand years during which midrashic exegesis was the signature mode of rabbinic creativity, a radically new emphasis emerged on the primary sense of Scripture: its language, style, and context. To be sure, scholars in the traditional academies of learning also had studied the words and phrases of Scripture with great care (as is evident in the legal and homiletic sources from earliest times). But their chief concern was to resolve issues of terminology and syntax in a particular text in the light of terms and styles found elsewhere in the Torah (when dealing with legal matters) or to correlate similar words or figures throughout Scripture (when proposing theological themes). The focus on a given textual unit as the sole arbiter of its meaning—to study Scripture in its own right and on its own terms—was a new and distinctive concern. The ways that different commentators performed this exegetical task, and how they related it to rabbinic concerns, varied; and this variance often depended on personal proclivities or cultural ambience. For example, the rise of grammatical interests among Spanish Jews influenced Rashi, who had studied in Spain. Jews in northern France were challenged by Christians to produce a grammatically defensible reading of Scripture. Similarly, the distinctive culture of twelfth-century renaissance humanism affected contemporary Jewish commentators, Rashbam in particular.[1] (On these exegetes, see below.)

The Song of Songs required special attention and consideration. The often erotic and suggestive content of the *peshat* had long been a sticking point. What was one to do? How could one sustain a commitment to the plain sense under circumstances where *derash* interpretations of the Song had taken cultural predominance? The earliest proponents of *peshat* wrestled with their new, dual loyalties. They tried to present the plain sense of the words and passages without discrediting the authoritative rabbinic sense. They produced complex combinations of the two types, trying to maintain loyalty to the older rabbinic tradition while accentuating the newer grammatical and contextual approaches.

Medieval Exemplars

Eventually, an independent *peshat* commentary emerged without rabbinic (*derash*) layers or embellishments. Rashi, Rashbam, and R. Abraham ibn Ezra represent the first type of *peshat* commentary; two anonymous commentators from the same general region (Northern Europe) in subsequent centuries represent the second type.

TYPE ONE

1. Rashi (Rabbi Shlomoh ben Isaac; 1040–1105) characterized his new exegetical task (of *peshat* interpretation) in a decisive way. In a key comment on Gen. 3:8, he proclaimed: "There are many [kinds of] *midreshei aggadah* [midrashic expositions, dealing with this and other texts], . . . but I am only concerned with the plain sense (*peshuṭo*) of Scripture and those instances of *aggadah* that explain the text in a fitting manner."[2] With these words, Rashi threw down his gauntlet. His primary concern was the grammar and meaning of a scriptural passage in its context. (As he wrote to his disciple Shemaʿyah, each "word is fixed and set in its [linguistic] setting and foundation.")[3] Moreover, he would consider only those rabbinic comments that could also explain (and fit into) the given narrative setting. Put differently, Scripture (in its plain sense) was the matrix of exegetical attention, and thus rabbinic tradition functioned only insofar as its teachings were consistent with the biblical interpretation.

These considerations are the primary exegetical criteria articulated by Rashi in the introduction to his commentary on the Song. But his prologue extends beyond these principles, and he introduces other matters that have a bearing on the scriptural work being studied. The following points are pertinent. The Song's passages may be multivalent (i.e., "they can have diverse meanings"), but none of them can go beyond the primary contextual sense.[4] Hence, one must fit *all* "verbal explications" into this setting, and rabbinic expositions that seem to be related must likewise fit this contextual mold. Accordingly, the midrashic corpus (wide-ranging and diffuse) must be sifted for relevant material and arranged to fit both the Song's primary topics and its verbal sequences.

What are the topics and sequences of the Song (given that it does not have a clear narrative plot)? According to Rashi, Solomon (through divine inspiration) envisioned that in the future, Israel would be exiled. Eventually Israel would appeal to God's good graces, drawing on words that recalled its former glory as well as God's previous deeds and promises on its behalf. Rashi indicates that Solomon formulated this plot in terms of a young woman abandoned to "living widowhood," who pines for her husband and recalls their former love. Her husband, in turn, expresses his grief at their separation and tells her that this separation is not a divorce, that she is still his wife. A presumed correlation exists between Solomon's "vision" of Israel's future (in which the maiden recalls her past and requests reconciliation with God) and the Song's plot. And this reconstructed plot (the Song's plain sense, deemed an allegory of Israel's sacred history) is the basis for Rashi's reading of the verses and his choice of rabbinic sources, a reading

so deft that the reader (with the allegory of the prologue in mind) often senses hints of Israel's history in his exegetical explication of the verses.

Rashi's stunning achievement is his revelation of the masterly way that the Song's plain sense (*peshat*) discloses the various topics of biblical history (as deduced by generations of midrashic interpreters)! Whenever this is not fully evident, or whenever Rashi wants to supplement the textual hints with a more explicit statement, he ends his *peshat* commentary, and he then introduces the historical theme (alluded to in the initial portion of his comment) with the term *dugma'*. This word connotes that a complex of images in a given verse is a literary figure for a particular event in Israel's sacred history.[5]

Rashi's strategy with respect to the *peshat* is both subtle and canny. He reconstructs the plain sense of a passage on the basis of his assumption that the Song narrates historical allegories of Israel's sacred history as formulated in the *derash*. Thus the *peshat* is not freestanding. Rather it depends on a prior sense of the *derash,* hallowed by the sages. One starts with a focus on the Song's lexical or thematic sense.[6] Ostensibly, the plain sense (*peshat*) of the plot provides the terms for assessing the *dugma'* (allegorical figure) of biblical history. But in actuality, the opposite is the case. The reconstructed plain sense is, in fact, deemed by Rashi to be the primary one in the mind of the author (Solomon), who wrote about history through a drama of love and its various images. More paradoxically still, the intent of the author (Solomon) is actually the intent of the commentator (Rashi). Consider the following example that appears at the beginning of the commentary:

> "*Let him kiss me with the kisses of his mouth*. This is a song in her [the maiden's] mouth, in her exile and widowhood. [And it means:] Would that I be kissed by King Solomon with the kisses of his mouth, as of yore; for though there are places that [have the custom to] kiss on the hand or shoulder, I desire and yearn that he treats me as before, like a groom with a bride [who kiss one another] mouth to mouth. *For your love is* to me *better than* any *wine* banquet. Now all this is an explication of the [plain] sense (*bei'ur mashma'o*). It is formulated in figurative terms (*dugma'*) because God gave [the people] Israel His Torah and spoke with them face to face; and this love remains sweeter than any other enjoyment. They are [also] assured by Him that He will return and explicate its secret meanings and some of its deepest mysteries; and they supplicate him to fulfill His promise. This is [the deeper meaning of the phrase]: *May He kiss me with the kisses of His mouth*.

Rashi begins by explicating the *peshat*, following the plotline he enunciates in his introduction. We learn that the maiden is one of Solomon's wives who was abandoned by the king and longs to be kissed again as she was when she was a young bride. Since we know that the Song is a historical allegory, the request of the maiden is thus (figuratively) Israel's desire to be restored to God and kissed by Him as "in former times." It is thus evident that Rashi construes the verb *yishaqeini* as a verb conveying a future optative mood, meaning, "Would that he kiss me [again]." This is not the plain sense of the verb in context since the Song opens with a statement of desire for a kiss in the present ("Let him kiss me [now]"). But this sense is feasible, and Rashi chose it because it serves the plot of a longed-for renewal of love. Moreover, it subtly alludes to the original event of kisses at Sinai (when, according to the Midrash, God sealed his commandments with kisses on the mouth of those who accepted them; SongsR, ad loc.).

The ensuing discussion about different kinds of kisses also derives from the Midrash, skillfully woven into the narrative frame. The rabbinic comment merely compares two types of kisses (one on the hand, another on the mouth) whereas Rashi reformulates this topic and emphasizes the kisses on the mouth. An attentive reader, with Rashi's allegory in mind, by now might think of the event at Sinai. Because this historical moment is implied, to make an explicit reference Rashi adds a *dugma'* section to his commentary. He therefore states that the original bestowal of kisses was the revelation at Sinai, and he links the revelation to the phrase about the great sweetness of this love.

This leads to a further point. Rashi repeats the verb *yishaqeini* at the end, but he now interprets it as a request for a bestowal of new kisses in the future ("Let Him kiss me [in times to come]"). What might this mean? For Rashi the second sense of the verb refers to a future revelation of a deeper aspect of the original divine kisses (i.e., a request for a more esoteric dimension of the Law). Rashi also derives this point from the ancient midrash, albeit from a comment adduced with regard to the ensuing phrase ("for your love," etc.).[7] In Rashi's use of the midrash, attention shifts to an eschatological dimension of the renewal of the kisses. This event will be nothing less than a supplement to the revelation at Sinai. In this way, the hope for restoration joins with an expectation that God will disclose hitherto unknown meanings of the Torah. The initial verb is thus reinterpreted to convey this future hope: "May He [God] kiss me [in the future] with the kisses [new teachings] of His mouth."

Rashi's conclusion thus goes beyond the text's *peshat* sense and gives the passage a prophetic significance duly fitted to the Song's grammatical features. The overall result is a plain sense in the service of historical theology (past and future). Reworked, the Song's plain sense becomes a teaching of rabbinic tradition. Rashi thus integrates *peshat* and *derash* approaches in a complex and exemplary way, producing a sophisticated religious exegesis of the highest order. One cannot doubt that Rashi used the tools of his Song of Songs commentary to address his own historical community—longing for redemption and hoping for new understandings of the Law.

2. Rashi's grandson and disciple, Rashbam (R. Samuel ben Meir; 1080–1160), was inspired by his great teacher, but he charted an independent course in his interpretation. He follows his grandfather in his introduction where he states that he will focus on the "figural aspects of the composition" and that he will "teach and discuss its *peshat* according to its style and language (*be-shiṭato u-millato*)." He likewise wants to project a coherent plot onto the Song; in his view (different from Rashi), the text tells of the plaints of a "young virgin" abandoned by her beloved, who left on a journey; and she recalls for her friends his expressions of love. The entire Song of Songs is thus assumed to be a reprieve of this past relationship. To properly comprehend the literary formulation, Rashbam opined that the interpreter must be as "savvy" as Solomon (called Agur), who gathered wisdom (*'agar*) "from all the people of the east," and who composed "his song" in the manner of "worldly convention" (*nohag ba-'olam*) dealing with such matters.[8] This is precisely the kind of "wisdom" Rashbam employs throughout his

commentary. He even used the expression "worldly convention" (*minhag ha-ʿolam*) to refer to the troubadour love songs in his time and region ("and even today it is the practice of singers to sing a song of the songs of love that recounts an episode dealing with the couple according to worldly convention"; see his comment at 3:5). However, nothing is stated in the introduction about the text being a national allegory concerning God and Israel,[9] and no references to rabbinic traditions are ever adduced to supplement the textual analysis. The allegorical aspects are found only in units following his *peshat* analysis (but also without rabbinic references). This allegorical analogue is called a *dimyon*.

Rashbam thus takes Rashi's insights to a new level, producing a new kind of *peshat* commentary on the Song. The text's discourses are deemed complete unto themselves, and they must be understood solely in terms of their linguistic and stylistic features without any rabbinic supplement. The formulation of the plain sense sets forth the key terms and plot elements that serve as the template for the allegorical reformulations. For Rashbam the central focus is the text and its imagery; and on that basis, the interpreter may construe the allegorical meanings. To guide the reader, Rashbam articulates the *peshat* in a way that enables the allegorical analogues to emerge in the course of his commentary, even seeming part and parcel of this primary level. As an example, we consider his comments on 1:2. It is instructive both for the way it silently quotes Rashi and for its distinctive traits.

> *Let him kiss me*. Would only that my beloved come and kiss me with *the kisses of his mouth* upon my mouth, with all his dear love, as in earlier times; *for good* and sweet are his words of love to me—more than any drink or sweet savor. . . . *Your love*. Sometimes the bride sings as if she is talking with her beloved, and sometimes she speaks to her friends because he is not nearby. *Than wine*. Every sweet drink is called wine. And the *dimyon* for this [passage] is the Torah, which was spoken to Israel mouth to mouth (from the mouth of God).[10]

Rashbam's indebtedness to his grandfather, Rashi, is evident in the tone of the opening verb, the account of the kisses, and the topic of sweet wine. Equally notable is Rashbam's greater conciseness and his stylistic observations, particularly the care with which he accounts for the shifting pronouns (she first speaks of the beloved in the third person, "may *he*," and then seemingly speaks to him directly, saying "*your* love"). Also characteristic is the absence of rabbinic phrases and a reference to an allegorical code. The exposition of the speech stands on its own terms. The unit introduced by the word *dimyon* specifies that the kiss in the verse refers to the teachings of the Sinai revelation. Unlike Rashi, who stated in his prologue that the Song's narrative has a certain allegorical correlation, Rashbam makes no such remark. It is left to the reader to infer the analogy involved through a careful and savvy study of the text's style.[11] The *dimyon* comment makes this explicit. For Rashbam, the *peshat* is the Song's core, so one must read it carefully and perceptively.

Another feature of Rashbam's *peshat* commentary is his keen appreciation of style and language. This is evident in his interpretations of the dialogues and relations between the maiden and her beloved. Reading the Song with contemporary love lyrics in mind, Rashbam often highlights erotic situations and innuendos. For example, in his comment on 1:13 ("My *dod* is to me a bag of myrrh, lying between my breasts"), he

forthrightly states that: "Now they are lying on their bed, and speaking together words of enticement and inducement." This depiction of love-talk in bed is an attempt to make sense of the text. Even stronger is his remark at 2:14, in connection with the Beloved's desire to see his hidden dove. Commenting on the youth's request, Rashbam says: "Now the lover speaks to his loved one outside . . . and they went walking together in the orchard to express their love (*le-hitḥabbeiv*) there with one another." The exegetical concern to relate speech to setting has produced these comments.[12] Overall, one can note a far greater independence of the *peshat* commentary in Rashbam than in Rabbi Shlomoh (who integrates it with elements of *derash*). Other contemporaries develop this further.

3. Rabbi Abraham ibn Ezra (1089–1164) is a student of *peshat* whom we should consider carefully in this context. He produced two commentaries to the Song (long and short) and divided his remarks into three discrete parts. As he specifies in the introduction to his long version, the three divisions are (1) the explanation of difficult words; (2) the explanation of the text's plain sense (which he calls the *mashal*, "figure"); and (3) the explanation of the imagery in allegorical terms (which he calls the *nimshal*, "application of the figure"). When considering this structure, which moves from an explanation of the words of a verse to the verbal figures and their contextual sense, and then to the rabbinic interpretations, one may think that the *peshat* becomes subsumed by the *derash*. But first impressions are deceiving. It is true that Ibn Ezra opens his introduction by saying that Solomon composed the Song as an allegory about God and Israel, in the manner of prophets like Hosea and Ezekiel, and stridently declares that "Never, never (*ḥalilah ḥalilah*) should the Song of Songs be considered words of desire (*divrei ḥeisheq*) but solely in the manner of an allegory."[13] In stressing his point, he meant to caution his readers not to treat this work like a contemporary love lyric because the phrase *shirei ḥeisheq* ("love songs") was commonly used in Spanish Jewish culture to refer to secular love poetry composed in the Arab manner.[14] His negative comment thus seems to be diametrically opposed to Rashbam's positive evaluation of (French) love lyrics as a stylistic guide for understanding the Song. But as suggested, first impressions are deceiving. A careful reader will note that Ibn Ezra goes on to say that the second section of his commentary, dealing with the Song's literary allegory (the figures), "is [written] with words of desire" (*divrei ḥeisheq*); and the verb *ḥashaq* recurs repeatedly in his commentary (at 1:1; 2:9, 3:8; 4:1; 6:2, 6; 7:1).

How may one understand this? Of particular interest is Ibn Ezra's remark: "Words of desire (*ḥeisheq*) would not be proper in the city, in public; hence this is an allegory [about] a very young girl, without breasts, who was guarding her vineyard and saw a shepherd pass by—and intense desire (*ḥeisheq*) befell them both" (1:2). By using such terms, he accounts for the opening words of erotic passion, and he sets the scene for the maiden's repeated longing for her beloved. (This is especially poignant because according to his understanding she was one of the women of the king's entourage; see his comment at 1:6.) Even more remarkable is his comment at 6:2 when the beloved exults over the maiden's hair and says, "A king is bound in its tresses." Interpreting this, Ibn Ezra states that it may mean that "the king was desirous to be bound and caught in

[her] strands of hair; and just such a theme was mentioned by the kings of Araby (Kedar) when they were similarly impassioned by love (*ha-ḥosheqim*)." There can be little doubt that Ibn Ezra alludes here to contemporary love lyrics in Arabic, and he applies this insight to his interpretation of the Song.

We are thus led to the conclusion, according to Ibn Ezra, that Solomon wrote his Song as an allegory but adroitly employed the conventions of love lyrics. Presenting these songs in a unit *separate* from their allegorical application (the third section, which usually follows the rabbinic tradition) gives them an *independent* literary status, enabling the reader to appreciate the plain sense underlying the allegorical tropes. Our commentator can have it both ways. He can spell out the Song's erotic features—with their many suggestive nuances—and he can propose the presumed intended meaning of the work quite separately. Significantly, only his interpretations of the *divrei ḥeisheq* proceed according to the text's "[literary] context in accord with its plain sense." The second level of interpretation (the figures) has its own literary valences and considerations, and these must be evaluated in their own right. By not conflating the second and third parts of the commentary, Ibn Ezra could highlight the Song's erotic components without conflating them with rabbinic values or proprieties. This mode of presenting the *peshat* is not completely freestanding, yet nevertheless it has a clear and independent value.

Other contemporary commentators took the next bold step and presented *only* the Song's plain sense. In these commentaries the *peshat* stands alone without any rabbinic support or addition. This approach generated even more assertive explications. The following are two instances.

TYPE TWO

1. Two anonymous commentaries from sometime between the 11th and 14th centuries produced striking works (distinct in the history of medieval Jewish exegesis on the Song) are focused on the worldly love of the lass and her beloved. The first appears in a unique (Prague) manuscript (MsP). Initially attributed to Rabbi Joseph Kara from the school of Rashi (Einstein, *R. Josef Kara*, 30), this view has been debated; a recent evaluation has prompted the suggestion (Japhet, "Peirush Anonimi," 229) that it may derive from the circle of Rabbi Eliezer of Beaugency, the great disciple of Rashbam. At all events, MsP evidences a most innovative and independent spirit. For him, the work is a love lyric plain and simple, with much suggestive dialogue and imagery. Note the following:

> *Let him kiss me*. [The text] according to its plain sense deals with one of Solomon's wives, the most beloved of them all, and she loved him; and it is concerning her that he composed this Song. The full account of her endearment and the events that transpired are detailed below. And the verses [themselves] support this view; as it says later on, *There are sixty queens and eighty concubines* that he married, and *My dove is unique* (6:5), she being the most beloved of all; for this woman implores him that her request be granted. And what is that request? *Let him kiss me*—the king, my husband—*with the kisses of his mouth*, which is a true kiss, for some people kiss on his or her hand. *For your love is better* MI-YAYIN. Its precise linguistic sense is: *Your love* and lovemaking are best and *most pleasing* through (*MI-*) the drinking of wine (*YAYIN*).... This usage is compara-

> ble to [the phrase] *Let us carouse in love* (Prov. 7:18) . . . [and the interpretation can be confirmed] by the ensuing verse, *We shall savor love through wine* (MI-YAYIN) (v. 4). . . . Others interpret MI-YAYIN as "better than wine"; but this does not seem correct.

Our exegete has set the Song within Solomon's palace harem, deeming his feelings for the young woman and hers for him to be reciprocal. They loved one another in a special way, and he even composed this work to celebrate their relationship. For her part, she referred to him as her husband, boldly addressing him with intimate requests. The Song is thus a kind of lyrical novella composed by the regent Solomon, whose content reflects a real love relationship between him and his beloved maiden. This is emphasized from the outset since her opening request is presented as intimate love talk between the couple. The writer's sense of the erotic nuances at play is informed by his close reading of Scripture (noting similar words and phrases in other passages) and a realistic sense of the use of wine as an aphrodisiac. Thus the *peshat* commentary is not a literal but rather a studied assessment of the language of the verses within their literary settings. The commentator also applies this sensibility to figures of speech. This is evident from the assertion that the phrase "lying between my breasts" (1:13) is "a euphemism." Thus the *peshat* involves more than meets the eye; a careful exegete must read with eye and imagination together.

2. Another anonymous commentator from this same general period, is even more explicit on the same topics.[15] For example, the verb *ḥashaq* appears repeatedly to portray the Song's passions. Using this terminology, the writer not only speaks of "the cohabitation of lovers and desirers" (*mishkav dodim ve-ḥosheqim*; 2:6) but even has one lover say to the other: "*You* (*or she*) *will teach me* the conduct of lovers (*mishpaṭ ha-ḥosheqim*) and the manner of intimacy (*ʿinyan ha-ydidut*)—how I may do things that will please you?" (8:2). The commentator also treats 1:13 ("lying between my breasts") as "a euphemism," expounding on the relationship between kisses and passion: "This is why she compared his kisses to wine: Of all the drinks in the world . . . [wine] warms the body and inflames it . . . [Similarly,] kisses inflame his body more and more" (1:2). Beyond such matters, this work also specifies paraphrases and explications to bring out the inner consistency of passages in their contextual sense. As in the MsP commentary noted above, here, too, *peshat* has achieved an independent stature and eminence.

One final element in this commentary is of special note in light of issues considered above regarding the impact of contemporary love poetry on the Song's interpretation. It is the striking but implicit citation from a love poem by Yehuda Halevi (*ʾAt ʿOfrah Tziviyyat ʾArmon*).[16] Commenting on 4:1, where the woman's hair is compared to dark goats, our exegete extols the "blackness" of these animals and says:

> *Black hair is beautiful*, as [she] said [of his hair], *black as a raven* (5:11). It is similarly a beautiful [feature] for a woman; as the poet said: "For the nature and hair of your head I shall bless He who makes light and creates darkness."[17]

The poet quoted is not specified by name, but Halevi composed very similar lines in praise of a woman's beauty. And thus, if this poet did not actually combine the words "hair" and "your head" from 4:1 and 7:6 and adapt these descriptions to his own purpose (using a sacred song for his secular verse), one may at least appreciate that our commen-

tator cited these lines to produce a stylistic parallel to the Song from contemporary love poetry (just like Rashbam or Ibn Ezra; see above). Thus the Song's words might either inspire new love poetry (the first alternative), or their interpretation might be exegetically enhanced by reference to contemporary love poems (the second alternative).

Modern Exemplars

The history of interpretation sometimes continues in established tracks, and sometimes earlier forms return after periods of eclipse. This is particularly true of *peshat* interpretations of the Song of Songs, where one may observe a noticeable recurrence in the mid-nineteenth century of the two basic paradigms of exegesis evident in northern France five hundred years earlier. One type was a reading of the Song's plain sense as a prequel to an allegorical sense presumed to be the author's intended meaning. The other was a study of the Song and its language solely on its own terms. The two types represent two ends of the exegetical spectrum of Jewish interpreters in this period.

TYPE ONE

The first type is exemplified by R. Meir Loeb ben Yechiel Michel, known by the acronym Malbim (1809–79). Malbim was born in Volhynia (Ukraine). Renowned for his great Bible commentaries, he also served as the chief rabbi of Bucharest, Romania. His commentary on the Song of Songs, entitled *Shirei Ha-Nefesh* (Songs of the Soul), appeared in 1860. It was innovative in every respect—both in its *peshat* sense and in its allegorical dimensions. According to Malbim, the Song is a collection of five separate religious experiences in the life of Solomon (all recorded in the book of Kings). The first four were divine revelations (prophetic and visionary) of brief duration, whereas the fifth resulted in a mystical death in ecstasy. Deeming the Song to be based on the memory of these personal experiences, Malbim provided both historical accuracy and thematic coherence to the various songs that others (so he stresses) had deemed both fictive and disconnected compositions. Malbim developed his notion that the Song is built around five songs from 1 Kings 5:12, a verse that reports that Solomon composed 1,005 songs in his lifetime. In Malbim's interpretation of this account, the five songs mentioned referred to the king's religious experiences (which were incorporated in the Song), whereas the other thousand songs dealt with the king's vineyard in Baal Hamon (Song 8:11–12) and are not extant.

The five songs of Solomon are (1) 1:2–2:7, (2) 2:7–17, (3) 3:1–5:1, (4) 5:2–16, and (5) 6:1–8:7.[18] On the surface of the narrative, all five units recount the special relationship between King Solomon and the one he desires (*ḥashuqato*) or between a shepherd and a shepherdess—both relationships replete with words of desire (*divrei ḥeisheq*) and formulated in figurative terms. There is no doubt, states Malbim, that "the *peshat* is the key" to the interpretation of the Song (of five songs), and its songs must be studied carefully to decode the various spiritual events in the life of Solomon (recorded in the book of Kings). For example, we read in the first section (1) about a shepherdess longing for the kisses of her beloved, who suddenly appears near the walls of her home.

She asks him to tell her where she might find him after which she flees to the desert and joins him—"his banner of love" upon her and his arms entwined around her until she sees her companions running after her. She requests them not to disturb the event of love. But such was the result, and the boy and girl separate.

This is clearly no mere summary of 1:2–2:7 but Malbim's creative reconstruction of the contents, which yields both narrative and emotional coherence. In such reformulated terms, this *peshat* commentary serves as the key that unlocks the Song's parabolic dimensions and enables the commentator to connect them to the first of Solomon's spiritual experiences (recorded in 1 Kings 3). On that occasion Solomon went to Gibeon to offer sacrifices and his soul filled with divine love, whereupon God appeared to him and asked him what he would request. Solomon said that he wanted "knowledge of God." He was granted both a vision and a spiritual conjunction with God until the women of Jerusalem (worldly creatures) disturbed his spiritual reverie so that he returned to his bodily state, awakening from his vision. This is a remarkable interpretation of the parable (and one can see how the Song's meanings interact with the passage from Kings). However, for Malbim, this allegorical reconstruction is merely the first of two interpretations. The second is an explanation of the figures portraying Solomon's experience in terms of an allegory of the soul (the young maiden) that seeks spiritual wisdom and perfection (with her beloved one) despite the presence and interference of physical states (represented by the king of flesh and blood). Such an allegory has precursors in the medieval period as we see below (*remez*). I mention the allegory here because it indicates the final step in Malbim's interpretative enterprise. He begins with a study of a figural narrative (the Song) that (in his view) recasts the personal biography of Solomon; he then reinterprets these figures as the spiritual dynamic of the seeking soul (of every person) throughout the fivefold cycle of songs in the Song of Songs.

Malbim demonstrates remarkable acuity as a reader of the *peshat*. In his view, the *peshat* is the essential first step for penetrating the Song's other senses: one sense being autobiographical, the other of a more universal character. Paradoxically, the *peshat* does not stand entirely on its own terms because it is a *mashal* ("parable") that must be decoded in terms of the personal history of Solomon. Nevertheless, this level is formally independent of the so-called *melitzah* ("trope") meaning that transforms the Song's figures and gives them spiritual significance.

TYPE TWO

The second paradigmatic author of the early modern period is Heinrich Graetz (1817–91), whose commentary *Schir Ha-Schirim oder das Salamonische Hohelied* appeared in 1871 and presented the *peshat* in the critical-historical mode of the times. The author taught at the Breslau Jewish Theological Seminary, and he wrote commentaries on biblical books, as well as a renowned history of the Jews from antiquity to the modern era. His strong interests in philological and historical matters are fully evident in his work on the Song. He studies the text on its own terms: its literary style, narrative content, and textual features are the primary concerns. In addition, Graetz precedes his analyses with an extensive introduction that places the work within a new tradition of study—a comparative analysis of the book with other examples of love lyrics in antiquity.

In addition to his attempts to determine the extent or nature of the dialogical units (and to evaluate whether the text is best considered a drama or a collection of marriage songs), Graetz makes a detailed attempt to date the Song's language (and suggest thereby the date and strata of composition). In this regard, he analyzed the various Aramaic, Persian, and Greek linguistic elements in the book, the traces of Greek customs and attitudes, and the parallels with later Greek poets like Theocritus.[19] Recently, scholars have found grounds to doubt his late dating of the work. Similarly dubious is the suggestion that the Song's editor composed it to counter excessive Greek erotic poetry with a Jewish text (from the latter part of the third century B.C.E.) that is only apparently erotic in nature. Yet such evaluations should not prevent a careful consideration of other conspicuous similarities to Hellenistic erotic poetry[20] or preclude the possibility that this overall milieu was precisely what prompted some sages to consider the Song to be a historical allegory and to find prophetic tropes to support their position.[21]

Graetz's commentary, like other Jewish works of the period, drew from the works of earlier and contemporary Christian scholars like F. Delitzsch (1851) and F. Hitzig (1855), who also studied the Song as a freestanding cultural document, focusing on its philological, stylistic, and historical features. In subsequent periods, not all modern Jewish scholars interested in the *peshat* used these books or saw their work as continuing in the style of medieval commentary. Notable among these traditional exegetes are R. Breuer (1912) and A. Ḥakham (1973). Almost all other commentators (traditional and otherwise) considered their scholarship as part of a broad international and academic framework, exchanging critical evaluations back and forth. Noteworthy among these Jewish scholars are M. Jastrow (1921), R. Gordis (1954; 1974), M. Fox (1985), Y. Zakovitch (1992), and A. and Ch. Bloch (1995). Concerned with literary style and form, with determining dialogue units and subgenres, with philological analysis and textual versions (Syriac, Greek, and Hebrew fragments from the Dead Sea Scrolls), with ancient Near Eastern (or other) love lyrics, and with studies of flora and fauna mentioned in the Song, there is a broad overlap and shared enterprise between these Bible scholars and contemporary Christian commentators like R. Murphy (1990), O. Keel (1994), and C. Exum (2005). In addition, the modern critical and literary approach to the Song has produced a vast array of detailed monographs and shorter studies in many languages. All these have contributed to some of the observations made in the introduction with regard to love lyrics in the Bible and its ancient environs and regarding the poetics of the *peshat*. All have been taken into consideration in the running commentary.

Derash: The Forms and Formulations of Covenant Love

The preeminent concern of the classical rabbinic tradition was to explain and expand the covenant traditions of the Hebrew Bible. Since the sages considered the Song of Songs to be the paradigm expression of covenant love between God and Israel, they interpreted its dialogues and images in this vein. In so doing, they continued the allegorical expressions of this relationship recorded in Scripture. The prophet Hosea

spoke of the covenant and its restoration in terms of bridal espousals: "I shall espouse you to Me," says the LORD, "with a gracious and merciful love" (Hos. 2:21).[22] Later prophecies of hope and restoration reflect similar marriage figures. Particularly powerful is the use of these themes in Isa. 54:1–8. In this passage, Isaiah tells the people that the shame of their youth and widowhood would be forgotten, "For your Maker is your Espouser." Indeed, "as a forsaken wife," God will "take" Israel "back" because "I have loved you with everlasting kindness" (vv. 5–8).[23] The conjunction of divine love and marital renewal in these prophecies is evident.

According to the sages, the Song sings of the mutual love between God and the people Israel. In fact, they suggest it was called "Song of Songs" to indicate that it is a collection of songs that respond to one other. "In all other songs [in the Bible] either God sings the praises of Israel or Israel sings the praises of God. . . . Only in the Song of Songs is their praise of Him answered by His praise of them. Thus God praises Israel, saying: 'Behold, you are fair, my darling; behold you are fair' (1:15); and Israel responds accordingly (with the words of the next verse): 'Behold, You are fair, my beloved, so handsome.' (SongsR 1.i.11)[24]

Midrashic comments from earliest times detail the historical expressions of that love: God's gracious deeds for Israel over the generations, and Israel's fidelity to God through its steadfast devotion and study. Overall, references to sin were minimized or complemented by positive traits. In one instance, after R. Meir interpreted 1:12 negatively (taking the phrase "While the king was on his couch, my nard gave forth its fragrance" as a reference to the odor of sin when Israel built the Golden Calf while at Sinai), R. Yehudah rebuked him and said: "Enough, Meir! One may not expound the Song of Songs for shame, but only for praise—for the Song of Songs was only given for the praise of Israel" (SongsR 1.xii.1). R. Yehudah was a student of R. Akiva, who also noted that the Song was "given" to Israel (M. Yad. 3:5), using a term that connotes divine revelation.[25]

The Song and the Torah: Ancient Examples

EXEGESIS AND EXPLANATION

The shift from the few allegories about Israel and God in prophetic literature to the extensive allegories of God and Israel in rabbinic literature is significant. As noted earlier, M. Ta'an. 4:8 preserves an early record (by the third century C.E.) of such a reading. In it, a popular recitation of Song 3:11 was allegorically historicized: the joyous "wedding day" of Solomon mentioned in the verse was said to refer to the giving of the Torah at Sinai; and the "day of bliss" was identified with the building of the Temple. In this way the two synonymous expressions of a time of marital joy were differentiated and applied to distinct events in the history of Israel. Implied overall is the identification of the masculine subject with God, and of his female counterpart with the people Israel. The conciseness of the formulation suggests that this is a fragment of a fuller tradition. This suspicion proves correct.

1. A contemporary legal midrash dealing with the dedication of the Tabernacle in Leviticus 9 spells out all the attributions implied in Mishnah Ta'anit. And its expository style suggests that we have a version of an old homily that connected the day of the dedication of the Tabernacle with the event celebrated in Song 3:11, phrase by phrase.[26] This explication emphasizes the following thematic correlations: the "daughters of Zion" (*Tziyyon*) refer to those people who "distinguished" themselves (*metzuyyanim*) by giving "King Solomon" (*Shelomoh*), who is God and Master of "Peace" (*shalom*), a "diadem," which is the Tabernacle, embroidered in crimson. The people Israel are also called "his mother" (*'immo*), as hinted at in Isa. 51:4, "Listen to Me, My people (*'ummi*)"; and "his wedding day" and "the day of his bliss" refer to the descent of the *Shekhinah* to the Shrine and a new heavenly fire to the altar, respectively (Lev. 9:23–24) (Sifra, *Shemini* 1.15–16).

This ancient sermon offers a remarkable allegorical explication of Song 3:11, presenting multiple epithets for God and Israel. It produces the significance of the names Solomon and Zion via plays on the two terms. It supports the bold identification of Israel as mother by a punning reference to another text—without any qualification or explanation. But this striking issue warranted justification, as evidenced by another tradition from the same period. There we find R. Shim'on bar Yoḥai in a quandary about the designation of Israel as God's mother. He turned to R. Eleazar and asked if his father (R. Yose) had passed on any explanation. The subsequent discussion preserves an attempt by early sages to account for the various family terms used (allegorically) in the Song and also to give them a certain sequence. Thus we are informed that God so loved Israel that He first called her "my daughter, then "my sister" (5:2), and finally "my mother" (3:11). The latter point is proved again by citing Isa. 51:4, but the hint is now explained on the basis of the spelling *'mmy*, which could be pronounced *'immiy* ("my mother") rather than *'ummiy* ("my people"). Hearing this explanation, R. Shim'on kissed R. Eleazar and said: "If I had only come into the world to hear this teaching, it would be sufficient!"[27]

The foregoing examples disclose some of the rich allegorical tropes in circulation among the early rabbis, and their attempts to find explanations for the more difficult ones. The two cases point to two distinct settings for the study of the Song. The first was Torah study and attempts to correlate its verses with others from the Prophets or Writings (whether for purely academic or also homiletic reasons). The second was scholarly deliberations on the meaning of certain terms in the Song (mostly for theological reasons). I note other instances of both phenomena below.

2. The next example (from the same period) brings the preceding comment into focus.

> "And they stood (*va-yityatzevu*) at the base of the mountain" (Exod. 19:17) [means]: they were gathered compactly. And their [physical] situation is referred to explicitly (*meforash*) in the Writings, "My dove in the clefts of the rock, hidden in the cliff" (Song 2:14). [But] R. Eleazar [disagreed and] said that this [Song passage] refers to [the event at] the Sea [since that verse] continues, "Let me see (*har'ini*) your face" (ibid.), which is like what is stated [in the Torah when the people were at the Sea]: "Stand (*hityatzevu*) and see (*u-r'u*) the salvation of the LORD" (Exod. 14:13). [Moreover, the Song passage continues:] "Let me hear your voice," which is like

> [the adjacent Torah verse:] "And Pharaoh drew close... and the Israelites cried out to the LORD" (Exod. 14:10). [And further, the Song adds:] "For your voice (*qol*) is sweet," [which is like the passage:] "And their cry (*qol*) ascended to the LORD" (Exod. 2:23); [and the Song also says:] "And your face is comely," [which corresponds to] "And the nation had faith" (Exod. 14:31). (*Mekhilta de-Rabbi Shim'on bar Yoḥai*, *Yitro*, on Exod. 19:17).[28]

Much can be gleaned from this passage. As is evident, the sages were studying a passage of Torah. First they commented on the meaning of the verb used; then they added an explication of the people's physical situation based on a figure in the Song. The latter was allegorically correlated with the Torah verse through an identity of the dove with the people Israel, the rock with Sinai, and the clefts with the base of the mountain. Although these relations are not specified as such, the correlation presumes as much in order to produce this intrascriptural explication. Moreover, the correlation is introduced by the technical term *meforash,* thereby showing that the citation from the Song is not a casual textual association but executed as part of an established exegetical practice. In the background is an understanding of the Song as a work containing figures that explicate events recorded in the Torah; however, the precise correlation was a matter of interpretation. The text presents two different opinions, one is anonymous, the other offered by R. Eleazar. According to R. Eleazar, the Song passage should be correlated with the crossing of the Sea, and he suggests links between it and the Torah passage to prove his point. We note that although this sage's comments rely on text from the Song, his concern was to explicate Exod. 19:17, which begins with the verb *vayityatzevu*; hence, the link between the Song and Exod. 14:13, which uses the same verb, is a compelling observation.

The allegorical study of the Song was thus not an abstract exercise; it had a practical end: to correlate topics in the Song with the major "narrative code"—the Torah. Understanding the Torah and connecting its verses or events to other parts of Scripture was the major focus of rabbinic study. The use of a technical exegetical term (*meforash*, "explication" or "elucidation") indicates the seriousness of the process;[29] however, the Song's figural density enables the explication to result in diverse interpretations. A late midrashic source refers to the Song's compact style as a factor in understanding its allegorical purposes (see Yalquṭ Shim'oni, Song, #980, end).[30]

3. We now consider another instance where a sage was perplexed by the meaning of a verse in the Song—not in the course of Torah study, but in its own right. We read:

> Once R. Yoḥanan ben Zakkai was going up to Emmaus in Judea, and he saw a girl picking barley corns from the excrement of a horse. He said to his disciples: "You see this girl—what is she?" They answered: "She is a Jewish girl." "And to whom does this horse belong?" "To [a foreign] horseman," they answered. Then R. Yoḥanan said to his disciples: "All my life I have been bothered by the verse *If you do not know, O fairest of women, go follow the tracks of the sheep* (Song 1:8). I would read it but not know what it meant [until now:] *If you do not know* [means:] you were unwilling to be subject to God, therefore you are now subjugated to the most abased of the nations." (*Mekhilta de-Rabbi Ishmael*, *Baḥodesh*, 1).[31]

This episode attests to the economic suffering of Jews after the destruction of the second Temple (in 70 C.E.). We find one of the great masters of the period traveling the roads with his disciples and stopping before a sorrowful sight, which illumines for him

a passage in the Song. He even perceives in it a prophetic dimension when read allegorically. Interpreted in light of the woman in distress, R. Yoḥanan understands the verse as warning the people (the "fairest among women") that if they do not serve their God ("do not know" Him), they shall walk among dung pellets and be subjugated to lowly masters (tent dwellers). He admits that he had often read that passage without understanding its significance—until now. For this sage, the Song was more than a historical allegory keyed to verses in the Torah. It also contained prophecies, forecasting Israel's doom for her disloyalty ("If you do not know" God, you will "go out among the tracks of the sheep"!).[32]

SPIRITUAL PEDAGOGY

In addition to the preceding cases, where passages in the Song help illumine texts in the Torah or contemporary circumstances, the following example shows how the Song was used to articulate spiritual ideals for Jews in times of persecution. I alluded to this passage in the introduction, when referring to R. Akiva's belief in the Song's sanctity. I now consider it in greater detail.

In the course of the Song narrative, the maiden bolts about in search of her beloved and enlists the help of her friends. She tells them that if they find him first, they should tell him of her heartsick love (5:8). Intrigued by her anguish, the women want to know what makes him special to her (v. 9). She then provides a detailed account of his eminence and beauty (vv. 1–16). Duly impressed, they offer to join her in the quest (6:1). But the maiden rebuffs this solicitation, proclaiming that she and her beloved are exclusively devoted to one another (v. 3)—period.

All this undergoes a remarkable allegorical transformation in a homily by R. Akiva in *Mekhilta de-Rabbi Ishmael* (*Beshallaḥ*, 3).[33] In this source, the companions represent the nations of the world who ask Israel: "How is your beloved different from other beloveds that you have so adjured us?" (Song 5:9). They wish to know why Jews are willing to die and suffer martyrdom for their Beloved (even citing 1:3, "Therefore the maidens, *ʿalamot*, love you," which is understood to mean that Israel loves God even *ʿad mavet*, unto death!), and they propose assimilation instead. Since R. Akiva was put to death as a martyr during the Hadrianic persecutions (132–35 C.E.), the issue has contemporary bite. The sage uses the Song to help Jews frame a response. R. Akiva answers the nations by saying that he will give them only a small sense of God's praiseworthiness. Therefore, he cites only the opening verse of the depiction of the Beloved, without explication, saying: "My beloved is white and ruddy, exalted among the myriads" (5:10). But even this small bit of praise is sufficient to stimulate the nations' desire to convert, and the verse that follows is now put into their mouths: "Whither has your beloved gone, O fairest of women? Whither has your beloved turned? Let us seek him with you" (6:1). But Israel rejects this suggestion, asserting "I am my beloved's and my beloved is mine" (6:3). Israel deems its relationship with God to be exclusive; there can be no partnership: "You can have no part of Him."

Much can be said about the use of the Song here. First, the entire unit (5:9–6:3) has been allegorically recast as a debate between Israel and the nations about the reasons for

serving God and about loyalty in the face of persecution. It is a formulation that would have made a powerful impact on a community facing martyrdom for faithfulness. But it is the specific argument that R. Akiva uses that must be emphasized. The nations want to know what makes the Jewish God special, and the sage answers with just a "bit" of praise for the Divine. Perhaps the nations are enthralled by an account of divine beauty that exceeds the beauty of their gods as represented by statues found in public and sacred places, which the Jews of Judea might have seen. Because the sage holds back and does not elaborate, one could suspect that he is merely giving a fraction of praise of God's supernal form as known in esoteric circles. The notion of a heavenly Divine Body was referred to as the *Shi'ur Qomah* (Measure of the [Divine] Stature),[34] and many hints (and accounts) of this topic appear in homilies of the same period.[35] Moreover, the very words used by R. Akiva with respect to God's "beauty and praise" are themselves technical terms used to laud this Stature of Divinity in many mystical sources.[36] Hence R. Akiva probably hints here (to Jews, whom he addresses in this dialogue) of esoteric matters about God so that they might remain loyal. In providing the hint, R. Akiva has certainly drawn from his own mystical proclivities (and from a mystical reading of the Song).

This passage returns us to a point made earlier: verses from the Song were quoted in relationship to passages in the Torah, which were studied in diverse settings. This is the situation here. The dialogue with the nations is but one exegetical unit among several adduced to explain Exod. 15:2, "This is my God and I shall exalt Him." For his part, R. Akiva explicates both phrases of the passage. The phrase "And I shall exalt Him" (*ve-'anveihu*) is the jumping off point for the sage's homily, which begins: "I shall speak of the beauty (*ne'otav*) and praise of 'He who spoke and the world came to exist' before the nations of the world; for behold the nations of the world ask Israel," etc.). R. Akiva's teaching is thus inaugurated by a wordplay on *'anveihu* (especially since in that era, *ne'otav* may have been pronounced *na'votav*).[37] In addition, the second half of the verse in the Song of Moses (the Torah passage studied), "This is *my God*," was correlated with Israel's rejection of the nation's interest in their God when they asserted: "*My beloved* is mine."

The homilist thus understood the proclamation in Exod. 15:2 as a statement of exclusive relationship, and he used it to climax his sermon dealing with the praise of God. The result is that one song (the Song of Songs) is correlated with another (the Song of Moses) in a deft, midrashic fashion. Such a connection would have made a strong theological point to the listeners: the affirmation of loyalty by Israel at the Sea presages religious loyalty in the present. The two events were connected. The proclamation of Moses and Israel at the Sea was thus a typological harbinger of spiritual loyalty in times of danger. R. Akiva perceived the verbal and theological links between Moses's words and those of the Song, and he produced this sermon for his people.[38]

The Song of Torah: Comprehensive Cases

TORAH-CENTERED TEACHINGS

As noted, the earliest allegorical uses of the Song linked it to the study and explication of the Torah because the Torah was at the core of intellectual and religious life. The Song offered a rich resource for homilies that supplemented the meaning of the Torah portion on the Sabbath and other occasions. Among such occasions were the Festivals which included homilies built around the special Torah passages recited on these holidays. Students of Scripture would thus assess the Song's verses for their possible links to the Torah and other scriptural passages. These correlations often included chains of passages that used verses from all three parts of the canon (the Torah, Prophets, and Writings), thereby demonstrating the canon's theological and thematic unity. The practice of conjoining passages was developed in various homiletic circles, and different sources report how sages "would enchain (*ḥorezim*) the words of Torah—moving from words of Torah to [those of] the Prophets, and from the Prophets to [passages in] the Writings." This procedure was even linked to Song 1:10, "How lovely . . . is your neck in chains (*ḥaruzim*)" (SongsR 1.i.10). Midrashically inflected, the people Israel (the maiden) were praised for their Torah study, which decorated them like fine jewelry.

A collection of homilies for the Sabbaths preceding the Festival of Passover (to which the Song was linked from ancient times; see "The Song of Songs and Jewish Religious Practice" in the Introduction) includes a good example of the use of a sequence of verses from the Song in conjunction with a Torah passage. One such Sabbath is Shabbat Ha-Ḥodesh, the Sabbath preceding the New Moon of Nisan, when the Torah lection began with Exod. 12:1–2, "The Lord said to Moses and Aaron: This month (*ha-ḥodesh*) shall mark the beginning (*ro'sh*) of months." Sermons for this Sabbath day were customarily tied to this passage—interpreted so as to teach something about "this month"—whose significance is twofold. It is the time that heralded the onset of time reckoning (Nisan marks the first month of the calendar year), and it is a proclamation of religious significance. Understood in the latter sense, the Torah verse means that "this month" of Nisan "shall" be (both now and in the future) the "foremost (*ro'sh*) of months"—precisely because the fifteenth of Nisan commemorates the Exodus from Egypt, which served as the predominant paradigm for the redemption to come.[39] A major anthology of such sermons is found in Pesiqta de-Rav Kahana (ch. 5), a collection of festival homilies arranged around the fifth century C.E. Within this ensemble (that is, within the chapter's eighteen sections), a group of sermons contemplate Song 2:8–13 (sections 7–9).[40] These sermons attest to the key role the Song played in homilies for this period.[41]

The first unit of this group (section 7) opens with a citation from 2:8, "Hark! My beloved . . . comes, leaping over mountains, bounding over hills." A succession of interpretations of this verse follows (deriving from different sages and different periods). These interpretations speak of both the Exodus from Egypt and the future redemption as occurring in "this month"—"the foremost of months." In one case, this "beloved" is identified with Moses, who tells the people that because God desires their salvation, He

will "leap" or skip over the servitude of four hundred years (forecast in Gen. 15:13) to hasten the redemption from servitude. In another we are told that God will "leap over" (ignore) the mounds of false worship practiced by the people to quicken the final redemption. All these homilies reflect numerous allegorical readings of Song 2:8 from generation to generation, as preachers addressed their audiences on Shabbat Ha-Ḥodesh. The sermons in sections 8–9 are linked to Song 2:9–13 (whose verses are also read phrase by phrase) and to the opening sermon. All the sections also have multiple homilies and expand the themes of the initial homily (linking Exod. 12:1–2 and Song 2:8). In the conclusion of this collection, the editor returns to the main format and cites various other verses from the Prophets and Writings, which serve as prequels to different sermons on Exod. 12:2 (sections 10–19).[42]

SONG-CENTERED TEACHINGS

Throughout the centuries, preachers brought numerous verses from the Song to supplement the central Torah passages and, especially, to extend their meaning in new theological directions. These Torah-centered teachings (based on daily, Sabbath, and festival study) appear in the major midrashic anthologies. Because of the key importance of the Song of Songs in the Jewish religious imagination, collectors eventually assembled and presented ensembles of these teachings as the meaning of the Song's verses in their own right. Scholars and anthologists combed the older collections for all prior uses of the Song, reformulating them in a significantly new way. The earlier homilies were turned on their heads. Instead of the Torah passages providing the citations for study with verses from the Song tacked on, the verses from the Song provide the exegetical starting point with the Torah passages invoked to develop the teaching. The content is often the same; however, beginning with verses from the Song made a fundamental difference. Readers of the new collections would now start with a phrase from the Song, whose language would then be unpacked as figurative allegories for events in the Torah. This shift gave the Song's images a new cultural primacy. Collections like Song of Songs Rabbah (SongsR) are thus literary works of major significance—transforming the original living homilies into a written anthology. The Song's scattered uses are now also regrouped, presented in a verse sequence from 1:1 to 8:14.

An instructive example of this shift—from Torah homilies that cite the Song, to Song citations that cite the Torah—occurs in Midrash GenR 63.4. The teaching begins with the following (Torah) citation and comment:

> "Isaac was forty years old (when he took to wife Rebekah, daughter of Bethuel the Aramean of Paddan-Aram, sister of Laban the Aramean)" (Gen. 25:20). Rabbi Isaac said: If the intent of the passage is to teach us that [Bethuel] was from Paddan-Aram, why does Scripture add "sister of Laban the Aramean"? To inform you that her father was a cheat, her brother was a cheat, and that the people of that place were cheats. And that righteous person [Rebekah] dwelling among them, to what may she be compared? To "a lily among thorns" (Song 2:2)![43]

Two details stand out. The first is that the sages paid close attention to the language of the Torah passage, noticing an apparent redundancy in the formulation. If the text specifies that Bethuel is an Aramean, *'arami*, from Paddan-Aram, why add that Rebekah was also the sister of an Aramean? This observation provides the pretext to

indicate that Scripture does not use words frivolously but for specific purposes. In the present instance, the ethnic attribution is repeated to underscore the immoral character of the family (by scrambling the letters of *ʾarami* one gets *rama'i*, cheat), and Song 2:2 is cited to underscore the unique moral attributes of Rebekah within this environment. The homilist has scored a rhetorical point by means of this concluding analogy, and there is no reason to think that he understood the final simile as an allegorical reference to Rebekah. But whatever R. Isaac's thoughts were on this matter, the compiler of SongsR produced a different result. Since he collected citations of the Song from various sources, arranging them in their proper verse sequence, it is now 2:2 that opens the discussion and introduces the presentation of R. Isaac's teaching (almost verbatim). In its new format, there is no doubt that the phrase "lily among thorns"—which answers the question "to whom may she be compared?"—*is now* an allegory for Rebekah among her deceitful brethren. This example speaks volumes for how these scholars and anthologists reformulated and reinterpreted the Song's figures.

SELECTED THEMES FROM SONG OF SONGS RABBAH

Among the many collections of midrashic teachings on the Song (e.g., Aggadat Shir Ha-Shirim, Midrash Shir Ha-Shirim, and Leqaḥ Ṭov), Song of Songs Rabbah is culturally preeminent, and therefore it is the basis for the observations to follow. (The commentary cites the other anthologies as well.) It displays stylistic structure in its comprehensive form and in the arrangement of the smaller units. In both respects, theological and religious themes are central. Particularly notable are the themes of Torah (and study), martyrdom (and suffering), and messianism (and memory). The Song's verses anchor all these themes with other passages from Scripture providing support. I use these categories to provide a brief overview of the concerns of the collectors and the topics they wished to emphasize.

Torah. Of major importance is the phrase "Let him kiss me with the kisses of his mouth" (1:2). The editors of SongsR use this passage as the verbal matrix to present various teachings about the Sinai revelation and the culture of study in Judaism. For example, an angel or the Divine Word sealed each of the Ten Commandments with a "kiss" when the people accepted the commandments and the laws that would be derived from them (SongsR 1.ii.2). The study of Torah was also sealed with "kisses" (*neshiqot*) of praise for students whose utmost desire (*shuqiyuton*) was to know the Word of God (1.v.2). This key verse also provided the terms for articulating the various spiritual benefits that could be attained from devotion to Torah, which is like a "weapon" (*nesheq*) that protects the student, a "conduit" (*mashaq*) that purifies, and a means for coming into mystical "contact" (*mashiq*) with God (ibid.). Given the variety and range of materials presented, and their position at the head of the anthology, there is little doubt that the anthologists deemed them of major importance.[44]

All these issues assert themselves through savvy and strategic wordplays. Particularly noteworthy are the teachings based on the ensuing phrase, "for your love (*dodekha*) is better (*ṭovim*) than wine." This clause becomes the exegetical springboard

for stressing the great importance of the Written and Oral Torahs for Judaism. To highlight the value of Torah over wine or other earthly substances, in one instance we learn that "the words of Torah" are "similar" to one another, like close relations—who are called *dodim* (Lev. 25:49), and thus they lend themselves to new and productive intertextual relations and correlations. We then receive another tradition that transforms this interpretation and emphasizes the importance of the Oral Torah. According to R. Yoḥanan, the passage in the Song means that the "words of the Scribes" (the sages who taught the Oral Torah) are "more precious" (better) than the "words of Torah," on the basis of another verse from the Song, "your mouth is like the best (*ha-ṭov*) wine" (7:10), which came to mean that matters of the "mouth" (the Oral Torah) are better than wine! And why is this so? Because the oral tradition supplements the written Torah and even protects it (taught R. Tanḥum) through its many legal stringencies that circumscribe the written rulings of the Torah like a fence (SongsR, ibid.).

Other teachings highlight other values central to a religious life built around the study and practice of Torah. For example, when the Song states (in 1:10) that "your cheeks are comely in plaited wreaths (*ba-torim*)," we learn (by virtue of a pun) that the people Israel beautifies itself by constantly moving its mouth (cheeks) while engaged in their study of *Torah*—the Written and the Oral, and in their devotion to learning the many laws related to the sacrifices, which are each called *torah* teachings (*torim*; cf. Lev. 6:2, 7, 18; 7:1, 11). With regard to another matter, we read that Israel is particularly distinguished when they "read the words of *Torah* in [their seasonal] order (*toreihem*): the laws of Passover on Passover, the laws of Shavuot [Festival of Weeks] on Shavuot, and the laws of Sukkot [Festival of Tabernacles] on Sukkot." Such endeavors transform the people through their learning and also demonstrate their devotion to God. The teachings in SongsR thus offer religious instruction of the highest significance.

Martyrdom. As noted earlier, the issue of devotion to God through martyrdom was very much a live issue in antiquity, and R. Akiva paid specific attention to it in one of his homilies. Dying in loyalty to God was thus an issue to be considered by the teachers, and precedents were also sought. Taking up a verbal sequence in Songs Rabbah, the patriarchs were presented as models of devotion in their readiness to suffer as Jews and remain loyal to their faith. Two phrases in the Song, "My beloved to me is [like] a bag of myrrh" and "My beloved is to me a spray of henna blooms in the vineyards of Ein Gedi" (1:13–14) thus take an unexpected exegetical turn in the midrashic corpus (SongsR 1.i.13–14).

The midrash links the first sentence to Abraham, and the reference to the myrrh is a connection to his act of spiritual courage. Just as myrrh gives off scent only when heated by fire (*'ur*), so was the merit of Abraham palpable when he was thrown in the furnace in *Ur* of the Chaldeans as a test of his religious faith (according to a legend in GenR 38.13), and he remained loyal to God in the heated flames. Despite this suffering, Abraham proclaimed that "Nevertheless, He [God] lies between my breasts"—in my faithful heart. In another version of this topic, we read the following interpretation: just as one who gathers myrrh (*mor*) smarts (*mitmarmerot*) from its burning qualities, so did Abraham suffer (*memareir*) torture for God's sake—yet he remained faithful. The

midrash then connects the first phrase of the next sentence (referring to a "spray of henna") to Isaac, insofar as he "was bound" upon the altar (Genesis 22) like henna (*kopher*), and for this act Isaac "atones" (*mekhappeir*)—for all time—for the sins of Israel (according to a tradition in GenR 56.10). Finally, the midrash associates the last clause, "in the vineyards of *Ein Gedi*," with Jacob since these *karmei* (vineyards of) *'ein gedi* evoke how he came before his father Isaac with a "disfigured" (*kerum*) countenance—utterly shamefaced for his act of deception when he wore a garment of "goat (*gedi*) skins" to receive the divine blessing, whose rich bounty was a "font" (*'ein*) of beneficence for the world. Jacob thus endured inner suffering (or remorse) out of loyalty to the spiritual and material benefits that would ensue through him.

This collection of midrashic interpretations is clearly no mere anthology. Major themes of ancestral suffering and loyalty stand out. Abraham is the exemplary model of enduring a trial for monotheistic belief; Isaac is the one whose near sacrifice perpetually atones for the people (his act and the sound of the ram's horn evoke divine mercy on Rosh Hashanah; GenR 56:9–10); and Jacob demonstrates filial loyalty, obeying his mother but cringing in shame before his father so that the divine blessing may follow his lineage. Cultures teach by example, and these were ancestral models to remember—their ancient deeds concealed within the Song's language but revealed anew through exegesis.[45]

Messianism. The messianic hope for national restoration and spiritual renewal recurs in many units of SongsR. We observed earlier how teachings based on the phrase "like a lily among thorns" offered different examples of redemption, concluding with homilies on the redemption to come. Other verses in the Song were adduced to tamp down the messianic drive through interpretations of the phrase "Do not arouse or awaken love before its time" (2:7; 3:5; 5:8; 8:4).[46] The four instances of this adjuration refer to four oaths that God had foresworn Israel. The people were not to rebel against the kingdoms (e.g., Rome), to press (or calculate) the messianic time, to reveal the mysteries (or the secrets) of the lunar cycles, or to rise up en masse from the exile (SongsR 2.i.7; cf. B. Sanh. 111b).[47]

But as the teachings in SongsR derive from various times and teachers, there is no one perspective on the messianic impulse. Indeed, a strong longing for the messianic age and redemption remained, and discussions abound regarding the merits required for redemption to occur. Some homilies on 4:8, "Trip down (*tashuri*) from Amana's (*'amanah*) peak," reveal the spiritual mentality of those who awaited the redemption. For example, focusing on the opening verb, some proposed that Israel merits redemption for the song (*shirah*) the people sang to God at the Sea (Exodus 15); others suggested that the people's crowning merit was the sacrificial offerings that they brought to the Temple (*tashuri* suggested the noun *teshurah*, used for a "gift" in 1 Sam. 9:7). Focusing on the words of the passage, *ro'sh 'amanah* ("Amana's peak"), some perceptive teachers suggested that Israel would be redeemed because of the merit of Abraham, who was the "first" or "foremost" (*ro'sh*) person of monotheistic faith.

Such tokens of hope salved the spirit of some; others awaited the end in faith. Hope and faith combine in the teaching of one homilist, based on the Song's paradoxi-

cal conclusion, "Flee, my beloved, and be like a gazelle or young stag, upon the hills of spices" (8:14).[48] In prayerful hope, the speaker beseeches God to "flee" from the nations and come to Israel, who so awaits this advent in its exile. But then the second plea ("be like a gazelle") takes over, and the homilist speaks of the mystery of divine providence and the need to abide in deep faith until the nation merits redemption. Listen to the preacher:

> "Be like a gazelle": [Why this comparison?] Just as a gazelle when asleep keeps one eye open and the other shut, so when Israel does the will of God He looks upon them with His two eyes—as it says: "The eyes of the LORD are upon the righteous" (Ps. 34:16); but when they do not do the will of God, He looks upon them with one eye—as it says: "The eye of the LORD is upon those who fear Him" (Ps. 33:18).

For the homilist, the people are not wholly righteous and merit only a portion of divine providence, but it is still the eye of God that keeps Israel in mind. SongsR thus ends on a teaching of faith in God's abiding care and the challenge to obey the will of God. This teaching shows how the Song provided a voice for theological hope—for those who were initially addressed and for the many generations that inherited the Song and its rabbinic interpretations.

Midrashic Paraphrases and Sacred History

THE TARGUM

The midrashic compilations on the Song are robust anthologies of rabbinic teachings, featuring the insights of different sages and derived from sermons or study. They comprise a vast encyclopedia of cultural and religious information. But we may assume that its popular dissemination would have been primarily through public homilies and teachings by the sages and that only select scholars would have had access to its written content—at least until the incorporation of this material into the popular Yalquṭ Shimʿoni compendium of thirteenth-century Ashkenaz or the Midrash Rabbah collections of the sixteenth century (1514).[49] Nevertheless, another form of public instruction conveyed the Song's traditional interpretations to laypersons in the synagogue. This was the Targum.

From early antiquity, we have running Aramaic renderings of the Torah (called Targum), designed to provide vernacular translations and paraphrases to Jews listening to weekly lections in the land of Israel. Some of them (like Targum Jonathan) even included rabbinic traditions at different points. This educational enterprise had a particularly significant impact on the way the public came to understand the Song of Songs. The Targum to the Song presents renderings verse by verse, fully infused with a plethora of rabbinic themes and traditions. Over sixty complete manuscripts attest to this work's wide distribution. (By contrast, only four extant manuscripts of Songs Rabbah circulated in the Middle Ages.) These Aramaic paraphrases even sponsored spin-off translations (into such languages as Judeo-Arabic, Judeo-Persian, and Yiddish) as local vernaculars replaced Aramaic. Given its diffusion in many cultures and lan-

guages, it may even be claimed that the Targum on the Song of Songs was one of the most beloved works of the popular Jewish library for over a millennium. The standard Targum to the Song was composed around the seventh or eighth century C.E.[50]

Several factors give this composition a distinctive character, even among other Targum paraphrases that incorporate rabbinic traditions. Like them, the Targum on the Song presents its comments without citations of earlier sources or references to rabbinic teachers. Hence, the verse-by-verse explanations are presented as *the* traditional meanings of the Song in a straightforward manner, with one notable difference. Unlike the other Targums, the Targum to the Song specifies the speakers of the dialogues (these being primarily God and Israel in accordance with the traditional rabbinic interpretation), and it provides symbolic meanings to topics and items mentioned in the text (these also follow traditional understandings). However, unlike the midrashic sources that inspire it, this Targum rarely offers multiple views on a given verse or topic, splicing several into one integral narrative. Hearing such voluminous paraphrases, a traditional audience would thus hear the Song's recitation and simultaneously learn rabbinic traditions and values. Finally, and significantly, the Targum presents the Song as *a coherent work of sacred history* from the Exodus to the coming of the Messiah. This is an original and influential achievement of the Targum on the Song because it culled its materials from the panoply of rabbinic traditions found in the Midrash, giving them narrative cohesion. The result was a new midrashic form of religious historiography, emphasizing patterns of salvation and sin.

This historiographical feature of the Targum on the Song deserves further specification as it is within its framework that the teacher stresses certain topics or selects others from past interpretations. Three major historical periods can be noted in the Targum's presentation of biblical and Jewish history through the Song. A sermonic and liturgical frame encases these three periods.

1. *The Preamble*, composed of an ensemble of ten songs (from the Sabbath Song of Adam to the Song of the Passover of Redemption—the ninth being the Song of Songs; Song 1:1) and an opening benediction (1:2).
2. *Part 1* covers the period from the Exodus from Egypt to the Reign of Solomon (including the Exodus, the Desert Wandering, the Conquest, and the Temple; Song 1:3–5:1). *Part 2* covers the period from the Exile in Babylonia to the Hasmonean Age (including the fall of Jerusalem, the exile and return, and the restoration of the kingdom; 5:2–7:11). *Part 3* covers the period from the Exile in Edom (Rome) to the Messianic Age (including the dispersion and ingathering of exiles, as well as the restoration of the Solomonic kingdom; 7:12–8:12).
3. *The Conclusion*, composed of (A) a prophetic plea by Solomon to Israel at the "end of days" (Song 8:13) followed by (B) a final prayer (8:14). Recurrent topics include exile and redemption, Torah study, and the building and rebuilding of the Temple. In many instances, some topics are combined.

The following two examples demonstrate the work's exegetical methods and thematic concerns. I italicize citations from the Song to highlight the Targum's style of integral narrative.

> *I have come into my garden, my sister and bride; I have gathered my myrrh.... Eat... lovers* (5:1). TARGUM: The Holy One, blessed be He, said to His people, the House of Israel, *I have come into My* Temple, which you have built for Me, *My Sister*, Assembly of Israel, who is likened to a chaste *bride.... I have* received... the incense of your spices.... Now come, priests, *lovers* of My precepts, and *eat*... of the offerings.

It is evident that this commentary is a running narrative attributed to God and addressed to Israel. The midrash (SongsR 5.i.1) includes the various identifications that characterize the meaning of the figures and integrates them into this unit. Ordinary listeners would not necessarily know that there were other traditions of a different sort (e.g., that this divine advent to the Tabernacle comes after a period of heavenly withdrawal; or that the obedient priests were elsewhere identified with Nadab and Abihu, said to have sinned by serving God while in a state of inebriation).[51] They would merely hear this explanation as the authoritative meaning of God's entry into the Temple, along with God's invitation to the precept-loving priests to enter and perform their sacred service. Everything has been historicized and refigured. The Song verse is revealed as a condensed allegorical narrative.

In a second example, the act of faithful service is extended to the people as a whole, praised by God for enduring punishments with love.

> *How fair and how pleasant are you, Love, in delights* (7:7).[52] TARGUM: "King Solomon said: *How fair are you*, Community of Israel, when you take upon yourselves the yoke of My kingdom [and] when I reprove you with chastisements for your sins, and you accept them with *love*, and they seem in your eyes like *delights*."

Here again is a transformation of the Song, now focused on two expressions of the love of God. The first alludes to Israel's acceptance of God's Lordship twice daily, through their recitation of the *Shema* (Deut. 6:4–6). The second refers to the spiritual act of accepting suffering in love (being deemed an expression of God's love, whereby the people are induced to reflect upon their sins and repent; B. Ber. 5a). Both expressions are read into the Song's verse, which is simultaneously a teaching of this virtue and a divine valorization of it. For the Targumist, love of God is a fundamental religious trait to be publicly recited in the daily liturgy and privately expressed through a humble acceptance of divine sovereignty—even in travail.

The Targum is a remarkable reprise of rabbinic interpretations in the service of the biblical text. Through it, rabbinic values—*derash* in every sense—extend beyond the study hall to the entire community.[53] One may surmise that the Targumic culling of older traditions and the Song's presentation as a historical narrative influenced Rabbi Shlomoh's view (see above).

LATER IMPACT OF *DERASH*

Midrashic interpretations of the Song continued to influence Jewish life through many other cultural channels.[54] In addition to the continuous and broad influence of diverse collections of Midrash, like the Yalquṭ Shimʿoni and the Midrash Rabbah volumes, this rabbinic material was repeatedly cited, reworked, and taught in commentaries across the historical spectrum. Among those that had broad and influential appeal are the

works of R. Ovadia Sforno of Italy (ca. 1475–1550) and R. Moshe Alsheikh of Turkey and Eretz Israel (born ca. 1520); R. Elijah b. Solomon, the Gaon of Vilna (1720–1797), along with the clarifications of his nephew R. Gershon (entitled *'Avodat Ha-Gershuni*)—both of the eighteenth century; R. Naftali Tzvi Berlin (Netziv, 1816–93), head of the Volozhin Yeshiva (Lithuania), whose commentary *Rinnah Shel Torah* is rich in rabbinic sources and spiritual nuance; and Berlin's nephew and student, R. Baruch Halevi Epstein (1860–1941), whose popular *Torah Temimah* commentary (1902) included an annotated midrashic commentary on the Song—a handbook that had wide traditional appeal in the nineteenth and twentieth centuries in Russia.

Sermons and homilies constituted a third channel that diffused the Song's *derash* interpretations. Here, too, the spectrum was wide and diverse. Among the most celebrated authors of *derashot* (sermons or homiletic commentaries) were R. Eleazar of Worms (thirteenth century) and R. Joshua ibn Shu'aib of Spain (fourteenth century), whose Passover sermons (the first sermon for the Sabbath prior to the holiday [the great Sabbath], the second one for the last day of Passover) are replete with teachings on the Song, based on the Midrash.[55] Subsequently, Hasidic masters delivered numerous oral teachings on this festival. The Passover teachings of R. Yehudah 'Aryeh Leib, the Rebbe of Gur (1847–1905), collected in his work *Sefas Emes* and supplemented by the annotations of his dynastic followers during several generations, emphasize the Song's midrashic components in a notable way.[56] It is important to bear in mind that such sermons were delivered orally to the public before their transcription or publication. This fact highlights the living and communal character of such pedagogy and its impact on diverse members of the population (not just the scholarly class). In the mouth of these orators or preachers, the Song was a living book and its words had an immediate and direct impact upon its listeners. (For more on these Hasidic commentaries, see Sod.)

A fourth major channel for the diffusion of the rabbinic commentaries on the Song must be mentioned: the *liturgical poetry* (called *piyyuṭ*) composed for the festivals, in particular the scholarly poems woven into the *Yotzeir and Musaf 'Amidah* prayers recited on the holidays. For example, on the key days of Passover—the initial and final days (and the intermediate Sabbath)—the Song and its midrashic meanings were given a special place of importance in communal worship. From the mid-tenth century on, in Ashkenaz (Franco-Germany) and elsewhere, these poems were a staple part of the synagogue rite, with long compositions citing and commenting on every verse, offering poetic renditions of rabbinic teachings on the Song. Particularly famous among the liturgical poets of this time, whose works on the Song became celebrated and copied and varied over the centuries, were poets and scholars like R. Shelomoh Ha-Bavli, R. Shim'on bar Yitzḥak, and R. Meshullam bar Kalonymos (Italy and Ashkenaz, of the tenth centuries).[57] The festival prayer book (called *Maḥazor*) of different regions canonized these and other compositions (according to regional preference and custom), and new editions swelled with further recitations. In the mouth of the *ḥazzan* (cantor), the Song's words and the many traditions of the sages found a melodious tone and integrated form for the congregation.

By way of example, I cite here a stanza from a poem recited in the city of Mainz on the first day of Passover (for another snippet, see the introduction). It offers the con-

gregation a poetic version of the anthology of opinions found in SongsR regarding who originally recited the Song and where. Rather than a catalogue of diverse views, the opinions are now melded into one cultural overview. According to the rendition presented here, the Song had been repeatedly recited from ancient times until it was studied and sanctified as a special work of sacred Scripture.

Shir Ha-Shirim (Song of Songs)
  and Song of the Upright (*yesharim*),
[Whose] songs are sung (*meshorerim*)
  to the Lord of Lords (*sar ha-sarim*);
A song sung (*shoreruha*) at the Sea by those who crossed [over],
  and a song, which the holy ones (Israel) recited at Sinai;
A song that at the Tabernacle the noble chiefs [of the tribes] declared,
  and a song that in the Temple was composed into prayer;
A song that the angels of attendance (*shareit*) said on High,
  and with which those [saintly ones] who justify the many (Israel) penetrated
    [the heavens with their divine-like praise];
And expounded and examined it,
  and explicated and decoded it (*pishruha*)—
And which her children (the sages of Israel) duly ratified (*va-yei'asheruha*),
  and sanctified above all [other] books (the Writings).[58]

Remez: Personal Love of God— With All One's Heart, Soul, and Mind

The Torah charges every member of the covenant community with the religious duty to "Love the LORD your God with all your heart, with all your soul, and with all your might" (Deut. 6:4). This ideal was meant for all (Deut. 10:12). But what were the spiritual components of this love? Rabbinic interpretation pondered the matter from early times. A teaching recorded in Midrash Sifrei Deut. (32) achieved paradigmatic status in later generations.[59] It emphasizes total commitment. "All one's heart" means the redirection of all one's desires to God; "all one's soul" means a readiness to commit oneself totally to God (mentally and physically, if necessary); and "all one's might" means the devotion of all one's resources to God. This threefold ideal tallies with the Song's many traditional interpretations (see above, *derash*), whereby love of God is *the* spiritual virtue: engaging the entire self; exceeding personal desires; and transcending all earthly goods and concerns. In light of such individual spirituality, the love quest of the maiden for her beloved could be seen as an allegorical expression of a personal longing for God. Her desire for a kiss from "the one my soul loves" suggests the wholehearted desire of the human seeker for God, the true Beloved. To her, the voice of her beloved suggests a divine call to the human seeker to "return" to God, the ultimate spiritual source. If Torah addresses the nation, the Song also speaks to the trembling heart—to those who long for God with all their being.

Reading the Song as an individual quest for God required an allegorical interpretation of its contents. At the plain-sense level, the Song reveals particular characters in the real world, whose dialogues of desire and love have a concrete and physical directness. But allegory presumes that something else hides within or behind this surface sense. In this case, the Song's physical sensuality is deemed the outer form of a spiritual ardor; its external sense is the lure of natural love but not the text's innermost truth. The interpretative task was to penetrate the literary veil and disclose its inherent core. Jews in the Middle Ages referred to the external formulation as a parable (*mashal*), combing its features to discern any allusion or hint (*remez*) of the intellectual content concealed therein.

Allegory is never self-evident but presupposes an art of concealment whereby an author uses a series of literary figures to hide something else. Discerning the correspondences between the outer expression and the inner sense of a passage requires prior knowledge of its thematic template. Only on this basis can the various figures and personalities of a text make intellectual sense; otherwise the meaning is utterly fanciful and cannot be sustained over the long haul. Accordingly, one must read the text's words with something else in mind.[60]

If this something else in mind is a philosophical program whose intellectual or spiritual ideal is to cultivate one's (inherently divine) intellect or soul and direct it toward God or the Divine Intellect (as in programs derived from Greek thought), then the Song's content undergoes a radical rereading. The maiden may then be deemed a figure for that soul, and her desire for the beloved's kisses symbolize her quest for ultimate bliss and union with Divinity.[61] Under this allegorical sun, the maiden's ongoing turmoil (i.e., her desires for fulfillment, her sense of loss, and her ongoing search) represents the turmoil of all human seekers, bound to the physical world and its attractions (for she is an embodied soul) yet seeking higher goals. Reciprocally, the beloved's words to the maiden represent divine praise for perfections achieved or encouragement for the sustained acquisition of certain traits. The savvy interpreter fills in the details of these matters through the text's imagery (e.g., the budding plants may hint at intellectual development, and sleep may represent spiritual sloth or lethargy). In this vein, the many oscillations and repetitions found in the Song are deemed textual evidence for the arduous task of spiritual development, requiring emotional patience and intellectual fortitude.

The path to a full reading of the Song of Songs as a philosophical allegory can be traced through a series of precursors. Through a close look at several love poems and philosophical discourses beginning in the tenth century C.E., it is possible to discern varied uses of the Song's imagery and phrases to express new spiritual or intellectual content. These attest to an ongoing revision of the Song's content, and to a transformation of its uses and significance. Over time, small droplets became the waves of a spiritual current that would crest in the twelfth to thirteenth centuries with the appearance of full-scale allegorical commentaries that transformed the Song into sustained teachings about the individual's quest for personal perfection through intellectual (or spiritual) love of God. We now turn to this important phenomenon.

The Song of Songs and Medieval Love Poetry

THE SONG AND THE VOICE OF THE POET

In the Middle Ages, Jewish secular and religious love poetry was embedded in the culture and styles of Arabic poetry, which had developed from pre-Islamic verse to the more developed forms found in Muslim Spain. The two streams are distinct but dovetail. From the tenth century, clear evidence exists of earthly love lyrics composed by poets such as Yitzḥaq ibn Khalfon and Yitzḥaq bar Mar Shaul. Their works not only display the wine and nature motifs of contemporary Arabic poems, but the poems also frequently address a young boy called a *tzevi* ("gazelle").[62] Samuel ibn Nagrillah (known as the Nagid) was a master of these tropes, and he laced his secular lyrics with language drawn from the Song of Songs. The following are two examples: In the first we are told that the "winter" has "passed," / and "the turtledoves are seen in our land / . . . therefore, friends . . . / . . . come to my garden, where lilies, / their fragrance like myrrh, you may gather; / and drink wine, friends."[63] The use of the language of 2:11–12 and 4:16–5:1 boldly concretizes the invitation of loving fellowship extended here. In the second case, the same poet proclaims, using the Song's words (4:9; 8:6–7, 2; and 5:14, respectively), how "The eyes of my gazelle have pierced my heart . . . / [so that] even if waters could quench the love of lovers— / [love] for you would burn in the depth of my heart like fire! / So arise, my beloved one . . . and take the cup of the juice of my pomegranate . . . / from hands [like] golden rods studded with beryl."[64]

Some compatriots felt that such expressions pushed the envelope of propriety. The Nagid parried this criticism and said that his erotic lines were merely allegorical images and should be construed as figures of divine-human love similar to "the interpretation of the Song of Solomon / in [such phrases as] 'My beloved is white' and [the maiden's] 'eye is a pool.'"[65] Not everyone was convinced, and the issue remained controversial. Even two centuries later such uses of the Song were condemned, as is evidenced by Maimonides's admonitions in his commentary to the Mishnah, where he censored such offenders and said that those who apply the Song to base ends engage in licentiousness and traduce sacred Scripture as well.[66] One must remain prudent and use the sacred language for holy purposes only. In reply to a letter, he added that one must not listen to bawdy ditties, even ones composed in Arabic (and even if recited in prose).[67] Such frivolity is likewise prohibited. In all this, Maimonides caps a spate of censorious comments by rabbinic authorities. Among the earliest is a responsum by Rav Ḥai Gaon (939–1038), who issued a ruling against Arabic love songs[68] and their Hebrew uses or variations.[69]

Nevertheless, such "gazelle poetry" (filled with motifs of loss and longing) struck a sacred chord. Thematic harmonies with the Song forged a crossover that gave the forms and language of this secular lyric a new spiritual setting. The following two examples highlight this transformation: The first is a poem by Dunash ibn Labrat (the first known Hebrew poet of medieval Spain; 920–990 C.E.).[70] In it the speaker bemoans the loss of his "beloved" who has "fled like a gazelle," leaving him to "seek" endlessly for his "loved one" and pine for him "sick of heart . . . upon (his) bed." These motifs are

part of the stock Arabic poetic repertoire but now studded with phrases from the Song. The reader is struck by the pathos of human love expressed here until a response arrives that turns it all upside down. Unexpectedly the poet addresses the speaker at the end as the "Shulammite"—the epithet of the maiden in 7:1—and promises a day of comfort. The bereft speaker (now evidently the people Israel) takes heart and proclaims that her redeemer's "banner of love is upon me" (2:4).

This shift of voice in the poem is significant for it formulates the language of national-religious love in personal terms. In doing so, it goes beyond older midrashic uses of this theme and reconnects with the individual voice in the Song. The result is a deft integration of the personal dialogues of the *peshat* with the national spirit of the *derash*. It suggests the beginning of a transformed use of the Song—one that lets the *personal eros* of the older love lyric come to the fore while keeping it (simultaneously) in allegorical check.

The second example is a poem by Solomon ibn Gabirol (1021/22–1057/58), which expresses a similar combination of the personal and the national pathos.[71] I italicize the phrases drawn from the Song of Songs in the example below to highlight its rich mosaic of allusions.

> The gate, which has been shut, *arise* and *open*;
> and *the gazelle, who has fled,* send to me.
> From the day you came to *lie upon my breast*,
> there you left *your sweet scent upon me*.
> *Who is* this image of *your beloved*, *beautiful bride*,
> that you say "Send and fetch him"?
> He is lovely of eye, ruddy and of goodly appearance?
> *This is my beloved and my friend*: arise and anoint him!

It is evident that this poem is saturated with language and themes derived from the Song of Songs: the fifth cycle (especially 5:2, 5, 9–10, 12, 15–16) but also key uses of 1:12–13 and 8:14. This affects the concreteness and tone of its religious expression. In a bold manner, the poem's voice is the maiden in the Song, which is now (allegorically) the personal voice of Israel, bereft of God, her "gazelle," who has fled. The entire poem is thus a personal quest for this lost love. Building on the Song's language, the (divine) youth had come calling and appealed to the maiden (Israel) to arise and open her door to him. But her reaction was hesitant, and when she finally sought to let him in he had long departed. Now the speaker beseeches her companions for help. Before they can respond, with a request for a full depiction of her beloved, she addresses God directly, recalling the intimacy of their love and the scent that still remains. The full force of the national allegory is exacerbated by this poetic reprise of the personal love language from 1:12–13. Indeed, its bold formulation gives no hint of allegory but allows the personal feelings of human love to infuse the religious content in the most palpable of ways. This use of concrete language continues with the maiden's depiction of the Beloved—but with a twist. Instead of the expected depiction of the Divine Beloved as one of "ruddy" complexion, based on 5:10, we read instead a phrase from 1 Sam. 16:11, where young David is described in these very terms. This is followed by the maiden's appeal to her friends to anoint the beloved, using words from the next verse (ibid., v. 12).

With this shift, the original scene of a longed-for spiritual love takes an unexpected turn. Now the longed-for beloved is none other than the long-awaited Messiah—King David—the once and future messianic king! The personal longing for God is transformed into an allegory of national promise; the divine gazelle awaited by the poet is portrayed as a messianic figure. Like in the previous example, the charged language of the Song fills the speaker's longing with concrete pathos, giving the messianic expectation great poignancy. The renewal of the Song's personal voice (through a spiritual transformation of the gazelle genre) enables new individual religious feelings to be expressed. It takes to the very brink the use of the Song of Songs to express national longings *in personal terms*.

THE SONG AND THE SOUL OF THE POET

We turn now to the first evidence for the allegorical use of the Song to depict the theme of the redemption of the soul—a major topic of medieval Jewish intellectual culture, deriving from Greek philosophy (as mediated by Arabic translations). While this legacy was not unknown,[72] its reformulation through the Song's language is new and striking. A poem by Judah Halevi provides vital testimony.[73] In it the speaker praises God, expressing hopeful confidence in divine salvation from personal difficulties. The opening language is drawn from Ps. 116:7, "Be at rest (*shuvi*)... O my soul (*nafshi*), / for the LORD has been good to you." The focus of this biblical prayer has a concrete this-worldly character; its subject (the "soul") is a human being. Halevi's adaptation is totally transformative. His focus is solely on the soul—referred to as the "precious one, from the precious [heavenly treasury] of your Creator derived"—which is invited to find solace with God. With this call, the poem stresses the worldly wandering of the soul and its yearning for a peaceful restoration (or return) to its divine source. The prayer closes thus:

> Have you thirsted to behold the splendor of God, / and serve Him eternally?
> Return, return, O Shulammite, / —to your Father's Shrine, as in your youth!

This conclusion, which speaks of the spiritual fulfillment of the soul before the Throne of God, climaxes with a citation of Song 7:1 ("Turn back, Turn back, O maid of Shulem"; *shuvi, shuvi, ha-shulamit*). In this poetic context, the final appeal addresses the individual soul as the "Shulammite," according it a distinct allegorical persona. So personified, the human soul is invited to return to her primordial abode and her Divine Father in heaven. This conclusion also clarifies (retrospectively) the initial exhortation, which now also can be understood as an appeal to the soul to "return" to God and receive her heavenly reward. Emanated from her supernal Source, the soul has remained true to her spiritual nature during her worldly existence and thus is offered (in recompense) eternal bliss on High. But who calls her? It is surely God, the Song's Beloved, who now speaks to the soul so lovingly and personally as "*My* soul"! The self-address of the biblical psalm has thus been totally transfigured under the impact of this allegorical reading of the Song. For if the soul is now personified as the maid of Shulem

(i.e., "perfection" or "integrality"), who else may claim her other than God, her own Beloved Father? Halevi's prayer thus implies a spiritual dialogue between the human soul and God, presupposing (or forging) a reading of the Song as an allegory of the soul—cast into the lower world but seeking her Beloved who, ultimately, invites her to return to His Abode.

We thus stand before a trace of an exegetical revolution: the reading of the Song of Songs as an *allegory of the soul in dialogue with God*—striving for perfection in this lower world as a prelude to eternal bliss in heaven. Somehow Halevi could presume that his prayer would make sense to his readers and that his use of the Song to portray the soul's redemption would fall on educated ears. It thus seems that his interpretative transformation has deeper roots.

The Song, the Soul, and Philosophical Discourse

The earliest evidence of reading the Song of Songs in terms of a philosophical allegory about the destiny and fulfillment of the soul occurs in the Spanish west around the early twelfth century. Although the content is both limited and indirect, it offers intriguing hints of a cultural prehistory. Famously, in the introduction to his commentary on the Song, Abraham ibn Ezra starkly rejects "the philosophers who began to explain the book in terms of the secret of the universe and the conjunction of the supernal soul with the body on a lower level" (thereby implying earlier attempts to interpret the maiden in terms of the corporeal self that had received a divine soul and longed to be conjoined to it without bodily encumbrances). One might think that this was his decisive word on the subject. But this is not the case. Ibn Ezra actually composed a philosophical tract that followed an exegetical strategy similar to the one he condemns. That work is known as *Ḥay ben Meiqitz*, and it is his Jewish revision of a celebrated composition by the Muslim philosopher Ibn Sina (Avicenna). It depicts its hero as a person who strives to be awakened to eternal life by conjoining his soul to the upper spheres. Musing on his spiritual journey, the seeker initially says that "The sons of my mother set me as a guard of another's vineyard;" then he calls upon the Divine Active Intellect (his own cosmic mentor) to "Draw me after you, let us run together, [so that] I may rejoice in you."[74] One can hardly miss the allusions to the Song here (1:6 and 4, respectively), now used to present the unredeemed self as encumbered by false vineyards—these being its nonspiritual pursuits in the physical world and longing to be graced by divine favor and aid—this being the restoration of the soul to its heavenly Source.

The preceding uses of the Song do not mean that there was anything like a systematic Jewish philosophical allegory at this time. Thinkers like Ibn Ezra may have used its personae and figures (and its dialogues) merely to make isolated allusions to the entrapment of the soul in the body and to the longing for its release to Divinity (a theme with Neoplatonic resonances). Other similar uses are suggested by a contemporary Jewish treatise on the soul, a work of unknown authorship, later entitled *Kitâb Ma'âni al Nafs* (Book of the Meanings of the Soul).[75] It adduces (among others) two epithets for the soul based on terms in the Song.[76] One of these is "Shulammite"—so

called because she is bidden from on High to "turn back" or "return" to her divine origin "in peace" (*be-shalom*). This certain allusion to 7:1 is complemented by another that refers to the soul as the "Dance of the Two Camps" (from the same verse) because she knows her dual nature, it being divine in substance but also imprisoned in an earthly body. There is no further elaboration here. But one senses another instance of an emergent spiritual mentality that turned to the Song as an allegory of the worldly wandering and spiritual quest of the human soul. And then, seemingly without precedent, a full-scale commentary tradition emerged around the Song in the late twelfth century. The phenomenon was catalytic. Philosophical interpretations became a robust mode of intellectual expression for several centuries.

Philosophical Commentaries in the West (12th through 14th centuries)

The emergence of philosophical commentaries on the Song occurred at a transitional point in Jewish intellectual history, marked by a shift of influence from the Islamic world to Christian Europe and by a new interest in Aristotelianism (in its Averroean and Maimonidean forms). Possibly the earliest expression of this change is the long-forgotten work of Joseph Al-Fawwāl (Aragon, thirteenth century). He produced a very sophisticated philosophical commentary, which was influenced by Arabic translations of Greek philosophical terms; however, he was unaware of the Hebrew terminology then being developed by the Tibbonide family in southern France.[77] The Song of Songs also elicited philosophical interest for this family as one can see from the brief but programmatic comments made by Samuel ibn Tibbon (ca. 1165–1232),[78] the full-scale commentary of his son Moses (fl. 1244–83), and the sermons of his son-in-law and disciple, Jacob Anatoli (ca. 1194–1256). The commentary of Gersonides (Levi ben Gershon, 1288–1344; also known as Ralbag) also emerged in this cultural environment though this author claimed ignorance of any other treatments.[79] The work of Immanuel of Rome (1265–1335?) shows the broad reach of this intellectual trend (he quotes or copies Moses ibn Tibbon at great length). It is also evident somewhat earlier, and apparently independently,[80] in the Judeo-Arabic commentary written by Joseph ibn Aqnin (in Fez sometime after 1185)[81] and in that produced by Shemariah Alqriti (Negroponte, thirteenth century).

What characterizes these works? I note three features, which set the terms for the ensuing discussion:

1. The first consideration is the transformation of the concrete dialogues of love and longing in the Song into *a spiritual dialogue between the rational human soul* (the maiden) *and the Divine Intellect* (the male). Such an allegorical personification of the main characters of the work recasts the primary dialogue into medieval philosophical terms. Thus understood, the task of the self was to develop one's "rational soul" or intellect, bestowed by Divinity, so that it might make contact with the Divine Intellect in this life and conjoin with it after death. The human body and its "natural soul" constitute the baser parts of the self, which could impede one's spiritual or intellectual development unless brought

under control. The Song's different choruses are thus employed by the commentators to express both the negative (bodily) or positive (spiritual) components of the soul. The Song of Songs thus speaks of the quest of the person for Divinity, the travails and triumphs on the way, and the exhortations or praise offered by Divinity to prod the soul on its pilgrimage of inner perfection. A philosophical matrix and ideal thus constitute the Song's meaning. It is now an instruction in spiritual wisdom.

2. The second consideration follows from this point. The Song *conceals its meaning in literary figures, in order to prevent easy access* to the work's philosophical meaning. Only the discerning eye might perceive the "apples of gold" (the philosophical truth) "within the settings of silver" (the literary configurations) as Maimonides famously characterized allegory on the basis of Prov. 25:11.[82] One cannot rush the process. And for medieval Jewish thinkers, philosophical truth stands on a firm cultural curriculum. That foundation is the study and practice of tradition as formulated by rabbinic law and religiosity. Only gradually, on the basis of a carefully acquired philosophical wisdom, can one hope to refine the body and mind and progress on the (elite) path of personal perfection. The commentators detail the difficulties and drama of the spiritual quest through their interpretations of the Song, which is deemed *a work of deliberate pedagogy* for the philosophical adept. The text is thus *an esoteric teaching for the few*—the public Torah and rabbinic readings of the Song being exoteric instructions for the masses. Slowly, the philosophical seeker may learn to love God in an appropriate manner—not with the feelings of the heart, which are variable and physical, and not solely with religious devotion or selfless service—but with the mind alone: one's unique godly quality within.

3. The third consideration is that the Song's eros is now *transformed* and wholly spiritualized. *The philosopher loves God with a refined intellectual love*. All dross has been smelted in the fire of a focused intellectual discipline. Bodily passions are sublimated utterly though they offer a human analogy. Rabbeinu Saadia suggested as much when he said that one must love God with the same intense passion that one might have for a woman who consumes one's thoughts to utter distraction.[83] This figure was developed further by Maimonides in the *Mishneh Torah* (*Hilkhot Teshuvah* 10.3) when he stated that the truly "appropriate love" for God was one that was so "fierce" and focused that one was "crazed" with an all-consuming "love-sickness." And he adds, "And all this is what Solomon said in parable, 'for I am love-sick'—*and all of the Song of Songs is a parable of this matter*." Such a love is even designated *'ishq* in the *Guide* (III:51)—an Arabic term for an all-consuming passion—where it qualifies the highest degree of contemplative focus ("perpetual mindfulness") on God, itself represented figuratively by Song 5:2, "I am asleep and my heart is awake; the voice of my Beloved knocks." This is a transfiguration of passionate love into a state of meditative attentiveness to divine matters. The true philosophical contemplative may even hope to transcend all bodily constraints and die with the kiss of God, this latter

symbolizing a conjunction between the human soul and Divinity.[84] Inspired by the great Maimonides, commentators on the Song annotated the spiritual journey and goal in detail. Joseph Anatoli made the same point with notable conciseness: "The [Song] is oriented to the perfected passion (*ha-ḥeisheq ha-shalem*) known to all cognoscenti... and which [this passion] should only be applied with respect to the attainment of the knowledge of God and love of Him."[85]

COMMENTARY AS A FORM OF PHILOSOPHICAL INSTRUCTION

The burgeoning of Jewish philosophical commentaries on the Song produced a new mode of intellectual discourse, supplementing the treatise form for a century and a half. The treatise type is marked by the systematic presentation of philosophical themes, using rhetoric and logical argument, and citing scriptural prooftexts in the process. In this form, philosophy incorporates the scriptural sources into its pedagogy. By contrast, the commentary type is not a systematic presentation of ideas, since it follows the sequence of the biblical verses and their content. Exegetical in style and format, it does not purport to present ideas in the form of logical reason. In this regard, the particular insights and emphases of the specific interpreter stand out. The commentator of allegorical meanings thus discloses through exegesis what the philosopher demonstrates through syllogisms. In this way, Scripture is shown to reflect philosophical truth.

The interpreter's belief in an esoteric core to the Song is a fundamental presupposition of the entire enterprise and conditions the search for philosophical gold. In this regard, Al-Fawwāl noted (at 8:7) that the Song is virtually a "locked and impenetrable" work, which makes it subject to many interpretations. The task is to penetrate Solomon's mind, seeking to fathom his divine wisdom through a wisdom-seeking spirit. In this same regard, Samuel ibn Tibbon stated that a first task is to appreciate that Solomon chose his rhetoric with great care. Indeed, for each of the three books tradition ascribes to Solomon (Proverbs, Ecclesiastes, and the Song of Songs), he employed distinct stylistic forms to convey their philosophical truth. He composed the adages in the book of Proverbs by means of parables (*meshalim*)—hence the title "The parables (*mishlei*) of Solomon," and he formulated his reflections in the book of Ecclesiastes by means of discourses (*devarim*)—hence the title "The words (*divrei*) of Solomon." He expressed the Song's truths through songs (*shirim*)—hence the title "The Song of Songs (*shir ha-shirim*) of Solomon." We should thus expect that the medium fits the message. And so it does. Regarding the Song, the choice of songs to teach the inherent wisdom is because this kind of language elicits a deep yearning most appropriate to the desire of the soul for intellectual perfection.[86] But it does more: it adroitly reveals the esoteric truth of Scripture.

According to Samuel ibn Tibbon, the search for divine wisdom is the Song's allegorical core. He contended that Solomon, following an ancient esoteric precedent, believed that the task of the philosophical interpreter was to locate the hints of hidden wisdom in Scripture and, by "widening the holes" of the "setting of silver" (properly interpreting the literary figure), disclose the "golden apples" (the deeper allegorical sense) within. The Song was deemed a preeminent expression of such an esoteric prac-

tice—composing an allegorical work about the quest for divine wisdom that simultaneously revealed (through subtle hints) some of the deepest truths of Scripture.

Ongoing interpreters had to continue this task of recovering the hidden secrets of Scripture encased in the Song, but this required the most astute interpretative attention to the text's language and figure. Nevertheless, if one read the Song in a discerning spirit, it was possible to find the magic key. For Samuel ibn Tibbon, the major intertextual clue was hiding in the allegorical narrative of the Garden of Eden (long believed to contain esoteric mysteries). In his view, the "open sesame" to this text lay in the fact that immortality was not explicitly prohibited in the Garden.[87] That is to say, the interpreter first must recognize that the fruit of the tree of life was not precisely forbidden in Gen. 2:16–17 (by noting the precise formulation: "of every tree of the garden you are free to eat; but as for the tree of the knowledge of good and bad, you must not eat of it"). Unfortunately, Adam and Eve did not attend to the divine words carefully enough. They took fruit from the forbidden tree, and so they were exiled from Eden—with angelic beings appointed "to guard" (*li-shmor*) the way back to the Source of immortal life (Gen. 3:24).

King Solomon, however, grasped this esoteric hint. He wrote the Song of Songs as a kind of commentary to "open" up this matter in the Torah for persons who were both allegorically skillful and philosophically worthy. Consequently, those who had eyes to see and a mind to know might grasp that the Song itself discloses the significance of the guarding of the Garden—for there the seeker engages certain "guardians" (*shomerim*) in her search for divine wisdom until she finds "him" and holds him close (3:3–4). Later, the seeker engages these guardians again, though on this occasion she is bruised in the process (5:6–7). If the first encounter hinted at the fact that a person must pass the muster of the guardians of the garden of wisdom to gain access to the tree of life, the second encounter underscores the difficulty of this intellectual quest. For Samuel ibn Tibbon, these textual hints suggest the secret truth of Scripture. Namely, that from the outset eternal life was offered to humankind in Eden, and that despite the sin and banishment from this Source, immortality remains a possibility for those who strive for it appropriately and heed the counsel (and chastisements) of its divine guardians.[88]

Such then is the way of a philosopher who revealed and concealed what Scripture (in Genesis and in the Song of Songs) had revealed and concealed.

Moses ibn Tibbon followed his father's insight about the possibility of immortality in Eden, decoding other details throughout his full commentary on the Song. Thus he regarded the Song to be a commentary on the Torah's esoteric wisdom. Accordingly, the commentator on the Song was a supercommentator—if he could attain some sense of Solomon's wisdom.

THE STAGES OF WISDOM

As a work of philosophical instruction, the Song was deemed to specify proper sequences of intellectual development. These sequences reveal stages of considerable pedagogical interest, sometimes through patterns of literary figures but also through the Song's overall sequence. For such interpreters, the text is no rough hodgepodge of

images and dialogues but a carefully designed structure of philosophical instruction. Guided by the savvy commentator, the reader (or initiate) can learn the intellectual curriculum and the order of its acquisition. The commentator is thus not solely an exegete, adept at allegorical disclosure, but a philosophic master cultivating his disciples.

Immanuel of Rome and Joseph Al-Fawwāl offer instances of how certain verses specify the stages. For Immanuel, Song 1:11 is exemplary. On the surface it depicts the golden and silver ornaments to be made for the maiden, but through allegory it alludes to the acquisition of intellectual beauty. Thus the "spangles of silver" (*kesef*) mark the primary impulse whereby the human soul "desires" (*nikhsefah*) wisdom and begins the process of education, beginning in youth with traditional learning and practice when topics are received without proof (these being the "wreaths of gold"). The path continues with the natural and divine (metaphysical) sciences, whose topics are now inculcated through logical demonstration and reflective thought. These thinkers, like Maimonides, emphasized that philosophy must be built upon the firm foundation of tradition, which is neither subversion nor displacement.[89]

Al-Fawwāl marks the developmental stages in his comments on 2:10–13. After childhood and adolescence (when the "wintertime" has passed), there is an onset of intellectual development (the "rain"). When properly cultivated, wisdom can "bud" and flourish in old age—this being the "time" for pruning one's material intellect of its products and realizing its fruition. The result is the acquisition of a Divine Intellect by the human soul and full control of the animal soul. But one must be vigilant. In 2:15, Solomon warns young seekers to proceed with caution and not imprudently "ruin" their "vineyard" (soul) by letting the "foxes" of their hidden desires run havoc over what they have so ardently cultivated. Solomon and the commentator thus give counsel to the adept.[90]

Joseph ibn Kaspi (1280–post 1332) and Gersonides offer cases whereby the Song's very structure marks the stages of intellectual development. According to Ibn Kaspi, the progress of the soul's four periods corresponds to the Song's four units, each marked by the verse "I adjure you, O maidens of Jerusalem" (2:7; 3:5; 5:8; 8:4). "Part 1 marks when the body is in a state of beauty and pleasure, from the onset of education until the age of twenty; part 2 is during its time of strength, vigor and desire, until the age of forty; part 3 is a time of wisdom, reason, and thought, until the age of sixty; [and] part 4 is when one is a graybeard and an elder without any desire, until age eighty." The recurrence of the adjuration formula thus marks fixed periods of intellectual and spiritual development.[91] Moses ibn Tibbon used the same phrase to stress that one must develop one's intellectual capacities "in proper order." Each life stage requires its own comportment and study. One should not try to "break down barriers" and speculate about metaphysical matters in an untimely way. According to most philosophical commentators, the Song warns against such folly.

Among all the commentators to the Song, Gersonides provides the most detailed account of a strict philosophical program. He regards the work as a composition designed solely for the intellectual elite, comprising a precise curriculum of study so that the worthy adept might overcome the various difficulties in achieving philosophical perfection and can proceed in an orderly manner toward the goal. Reading Gersonides's

discussions, there seems little warrant for the various categories that he presumed latent in the text, let alone the specific details. But they are presented with much assurance as he asserts his belief that the Song of Songs provides a curriculum for the philosophical life, whose ultimate end is a blessed felicity (*hatzlaḥah*)—the state of knowing God to the highest (human) degree possible.

In Gersonides' view, the Song is a dialogue between the human material intellect and the Divine Agent Intellect. Its overall structure comprises an opening introduction followed by five major units, which present the agenda of the intellectual life in topics of increasing abstraction. These break down as follows: (1) 1:2–8, the general introduction; (2) 1:9–2:7, on the effort required to overcome the impediments of one's moral nature; (3) 2:8–17, on the effort required to overcome the impediments imposed by one's imagination; (4) 3:1–4:7, on the acquisition of practical skills of various kinds; (5) 4:8–8:6, on the acquisition of a knowledge of physics; and (6) 8:7–14, on the attainment of metaphysical knowledge. The adept thus progresses from moral issues to those of the imagination and then acquires a succession of disciplinary skills involving increasing modes of abstraction. Thus knowledge begins with experience, on the basis of which one makes ethical and other judgments; and then gradually the student learns types of reasoning that lead the mind to the plane of physics and the celestial realm; and from there to the abstract qualities of Divinity. One cannot skip any step or disregard the process. The God-given world is ordered hierarchically, and the process of study must go from the ground up, back to God. Since all is ordered, the student must also proceed according to "the proper order" (*ba-seider ha-ra'ui*) as well.[92] The Song stakes out this process and the philosophical gold to be found at each point.

TOPICS OF PHILOSOPHICAL THEOLOGY

Nowhere in the philosophical commentaries does theological reflection develop by logical abstraction or analytic argument. Rather, the topics are generated by the Song's concrete figures and stylistic patterns. And because the text provides no inherent standard to evaluate the theological assertions of the interpreter, different commentators find different topics in the same verses and sometimes more than one as well. The result is a lack of similarity or unanimity across the entire exegetical field. The following three instances are offered as exemplary cases of how philosophical allegorists use the Song to think about certain religious issues: (1) the transcendent and immanent God, (2) the unknowable God, and (3) the role of images in philosophical-theological thought.

1. *God, transcendent and immanent.* According to Moses ibn Tibbon, the Song's opening wish, "Let Him kiss me with the kisses of His mouth, for Your love is better than wine" (1:2), "hints" at several theological issues through its shift from third-person address ("Him") to direct personal speech ("Your love"). The first address is understood to indicate the desire of the human soul to cleave to the Divine Intellect, the ultimate goal of the spiritual quest. But this desire's object is referred to only obliquely (by the indirect pronouns "Him" and "His") since it is radically transcendent. This formulation stands in contrast to the second clause, which suddenly addresses this Divine Other in more personal

terms ("Your"). For the exegete, this grammatical variation is a theological hint of the quest itself. A seeker longs for contact with Divinity, and although that longing always respects the awesome transcendence of God (and so referred to in the third person), the passionate desire shapes a personal voice of supplication and hope. That voice comes from the human realm, which can imagine, or has experienced, moments of human and spiritual pleasure. For this reason the speaker uses the image of connection through kisses. It serves as a hint of the ultimate bliss desired: conjunction with God.

Human experience is also the reason the religious devotee uses the figure of wine, because it is an image of earthly joy. By comparing the love of God to this substance and emphasizing the superiority of the former, the commentator uses human images to construct a theological point: the love of God is distinct from all transient material pleasures (symbolized here by wine). And by articulating ultimate desire and comparing kisses to wine, the speaker also delineates three kinds of human joy: (1) earthly intoxication (through natural substances), (2) religious love (through personal emotions), and (3) spiritual bliss (through a transcendent conjunction with Divinity). These topics also delineate three stages of human development: natural pleasure, religious experience, and inner perfection (spiritual and intellectual). The entire focus of the book is thus encapsulated in its opening line.

2. *God, unknowable and unimaginable.* Philological prompts in the Song stimulate other theological speculations, even regarding the limits of speculation. A remarkable discourse by Al-Fawwāl provides an example. He teaches from 1:3, which states, "the fragrance of Your ointments is sweet, Your name is like finest oil—therefore do maidens love You." Interpreted allegorically, these phrases elicit a philosophical instruction as follows. The essence of Divinity (marked by the word "name") is beyond human comprehension, as are the divine attributes that partake of God's singular essence. No human mind can conceive of such a singularity, and so it is doomed to ultimate ignorance. At best, one can think logically and analogically about God. But even thinking has its limits. The most one can attain is a "sense" of Divinity on the basis of God's "actions" or sustenance of the world. But this is merely an inference sensed by the mind, comparable to inferring an ointment on the basis of its aroma. God's Name (True Being) is like the "finest" decanted oil, absolutely purified of any gross substance.[93] God is imponderable, and those who "love" God must love Him purely—in and through this "hidden" Truth, beyond all imagery. Accordingly, the true quest of God requires a purified passion. To attempt to know anything Divine beyond worldly traces of God is to transgress all philosophical and theological propriety. One can only wonder whether certain images might serve as these traces in that they can "draw me [the adept] *after* You" (v. 4). Al-Fawwāl found a positive hint in God's statement to Moses in Exod. 33:23: "You shall see that which comes *after* Me" (literally, "My back").[94]

3. *Divine images for thought.* Commentators focused on how the Song's images could serve philosophical ideas. Joseph ibn Aqnin asserted that this composition used concision to formulate figures and parables with abstract intellectual content ("hidden secrets"). He even remarked that the inner allegorical content was the veritable "soul" of the text.[95] Moses ibn Tibbon put the matter differently. He praised Solomon for his supreme achievement, whereby the external parables not only served the inner content but also "distance" the reader from falling into error by misunderstanding the meaning of the figures and their purpose. In his view, the Song was composed with a rhetorical adroitness proportionate to its high-minded content. For the undeveloped mind, the images have their own appeal and keep one's aesthetic spirit engaged; for the developed thinker, these images open the locks of hidden wisdom. It of course remained for the interpreter to perceive and impart this.

Al-Fawwāl felt the same way, and he specified the particular difficulty in penetrating the meanings of the figures. It was because, he said, each image of the text was doubly displaced—a representation of a representation (*dimyon dimyonim*).[96] That is, to protect the unwary or unaccomplished reader from misconstruing the Song's language, its literary images are figures of intellectual content *that are themselves* representational in various degrees (since one cannot speak of the mysteries of God directly). Hence there is no direct correspondence between content and form at any level of interpretation. But the adept has to move pedagogically from the concrete images to abstract and imageless thought; some traces of language are necessary (to guide one's conceptions) though they must be transcended as one achieves insights into the most exalted metaphysical matters. The Song's genius is that its images are correlated with these ultimate truths in the most appropriate manner, so that a person might ascend from the figures to transcendental insight. Al-Fawwāl's reading of the image of the Beloved in chapter 5 is a case in point. This figure is called "pure" because of the luminal transcendence of all divine matters. It has a "head" because truths derive from the ultimate font of a heavenly Being, and it has flowing "locks" because all reality emanates as an overflow from the supernal source of All.[97] Allegoric interpretation is thus a kind of purification of thought, stripping off externals as one penetrates to the text's inner core. Disclosing the text's true meaning is therefore a spiritual exercise, whose goal is to transform the reader into a philosopher. The Song of Songs was deemed a means to this end.

Philosophical-Spiritual Commentaries in the East (13th through 15th centuries)

The spirit of allegory and the destiny of the soul appear in various commentaries on the Song written in the Near East. A distinct Neoplatonic strain is evident in these allegories as they highlight the inherent perfection of each human soul, which has been separated from its divine origin and now wanders in the world, weighted by matter,

but ever longing for its source. Such a philosophical current entered the Jewish milieu through the influence of contemporary Islamic thought, where it often conjoined with Sufi piety and terminology. Duly inspired, interpreters considered the Song to be a manual for the peregrinations of the human soul seeking to escape its earthly exile and return to its homeland in heaven. Some Jewish commentators are known by name, others by implication or ascription, or not at all. Their two major locales were Egypt and Yemen. Their works were written in Judeo-Arabic and saturated with Sufi terms. In this way, the Song helped sponsor and authenticate a new mode of Jewish spirituality.

IN EGYPT

Several distinct commentaries are known from Egypt, stemming from different circles but with many common features. Of particular note is the work of R. Tanḥum Yerushalmi (ca. 1220–1291), which begins by setting forth the Song's basic theme: "The desire of the rational and wise soul to attain the place of intellectual greatness, which is her principle, original world and primal element," lost due to having become associated with a body and its "faculties." This earthly state, in which it is sullied, evokes a great longing and seeking of the soul to transcend this state of physical "grossness." She knows that she is "black, but comely" (1:5)—essentially pure and lovely, though now dark and disfigured—and thus pines with "remorse" at her "separation" from her "source." This source is the Divine Intellect itself, who perceives the "sincerity" of her "request" and responds by illuminating her progressively with His "radiance," insofar as she can bear it as she "advances" toward Him "from one degree to another." During this progression, the soul "inhales the fragrance" of the supernal divine world, "tastes of its fruit," and basks in its luminosity. Ultimately the soul transcends death, receives a perfected vision, and becomes a "luminous" light.[98]

What is significant here is the perception of the Song as an account of the soul's passage from worldly darkness to heavenly light, taking into account the dialogues of the soul's longing for perfection and the Intellect's support and praise of its progress. This reading also integrates into an overall progression the Song's various references to smell, taste, and luminosity. Such factors give the Song spiritual coherence. The "dark" soul smells the Beloved's fragrance of the soul in her initial awakening (1:3), then ascends in several stages (3:5) until deemed uniquely "pure" and "luminous" as the heavenly orbs (6:9–10). The Song's sequences depict "in human parlance"[99] the soul's travail and restoration.[100]

The themes of spiritual transformation and divine vision, and the notions of fragrance and light, are all elements that recur in other commentaries that treat the Song as a handbook of insight and guidance and do so in the language and spirit of contemporary Sufi manuals of vision and love.[101] Once again (as noted earlier regarding the West), commentaries on the Song serve as guidebooks for spiritual disciples, functioning as verbal elucidations of the scriptural treatise of Solomon. And just as Solomon (the Song's composer) was the first of the instructing masters, latter-day commentators and their teachers served a similar purpose. (Indeed, we may safely suppose that these texts document some of the principles, practices, and experiences that were trans-

mitted orally to adepts within certain circles.) Among such masters was R. Abraham He-Ḥasid, to whom none other than Rabbeinu Abraham Maimonides (1186–1237) referred as "our master in the Path of the LORD."[102] That "Path" (a technical Sufi term) "leads to [God's] gates . . . within . . . which is the world of spiritual entities." The "Song of Songs is [called] the 'Holy of Holies' . . . since it is a means of attaining the ultimate end . . . through the practice of . . . holiness and the extreme love of God." The supreme "vision and communion" is called "bride" and "love" in the Song, and they are experienced as "ointments [that] have a goodly fragrance" (Songs 1:3) that derive from "God and His holy Names" as it is said, "Your Name is as an ointment poured forth" (ibid.). Then will the soul, "black, but comely" attain "perfection and brilliance" from "the kisses of His mouth" (1:2). In such ecstasy, bathed in light, the soul will be utterly undone and undergo a spiritual expiry as it says, "My soul failed when he spoke" (5:6).[103]

These and other fragments are remarkable for the hints of spiritual allegory that the Song was believed to contain for diverse seekers, who all shared a common quest for ultimate illumination in the "Brilliant Light" of God. The heirs of Maimonides continued this exegetical tradition for generations, even to the last member of the dynasty, R. David b. Joshua Maimonides (ca. 1335–1415). In one of his works, which dealt with spiritual asceticism (or inner detachment), he specifies that the "highest degree" to be achieved on the "Path to God" is "alluded to in the Song of Songs in the verse 'O that you could be my brother, [as if] nursed from the breasts of my mother' (8:1)"; for the Song deals with the several stations on the way to God, "and the attainment of the ultimate goal, which is love of the Supreme Reality."[104] One of the practices on this path is the abatement of sense perceptions and the focusing on God alone. This is best done at night, when there is less external stimulation. This matter is even alluded to in the Song itself, when it states, "Upon my bed at night I sought the beloved of my heart" (3:1).[105] And we hear an echo of the end of Maimonides's *Guide* (III:51), where the master advises the true seeker to empty the mind of all but God alone when lying down at night, and to engage in meditative contemplation. But Maimonides was himself heir to an earlier tradition—which cited 3:1 for the same purpose. At the conclusion of his *Duties of the Heart*, in the climactic Gate of Love, Baḥya ibn Paquda (eleventh century, Saragossa) adduced this biblical passage and said that it "refers to the solitude in the remembrance of God, whenever the friend [the spiritual adept] is alone with his Friend [God], the lover isolated with his Beloved."[106] How significant that by the eleventh century, the Song was cited in the context of spiritual exercises for the attainment of the true love of God.

Rabbi David's devotion to these matters also is evident in the fact that he copied allegorical commentaries on the Song (if he was not, in fact, their author).[107] Once again we have reference to the "darkness" of the soul because of the effects of physical existence ("the sun," 1:6) and to the fact that this state is but temporary. To achieve release, the adept is told to "Go forth [literally: take yourself out] and follow the tracks of the flock" (v. 8)—advice that is interpreted to mean that one must "disengage" from worldliness through "solitary detachment." But haste is folly; one should proceed with disciplined care under the eye of a master and not be aroused before the proper time ("until *it* pleases," 2:7), that is, "until the winter is passed" (2:11) and all earthly obstacles

have been removed. When the soul will have "put off [its] coat" and "washed [its] feet" (5:3), it will have cleansed itself from physical defilements and can await the advent of final deliverance—when the Beloved will "put His hand through the door" and the soul will be ecstatically "stirred" in anticipation of spiritual union (v. 4). At that supreme moment there is only one truth: "I am my Beloved's and my Beloved is mine (6:3)—nothing else.

IN YEMEN

From the preceding examples we can see how the Song's language conjoins with spiritual practices to produce a new formulation of the religious life. This phenomenon is also evident in commentaries deriving from Yemen, and we conclude this section by discussing the thought of the celebrated scholar, R. Zechariah Ha-Rofei (fifteenth century).[108] His work sheds light on the way philosophical-spiritual interpretations introduce external topics—in this case derived from Greek and Islamic sources—and gives them a native setting that authorizes a new mode of Jewish piety and spiritual self-reflection. Indeed at several points R. Zechariah even makes use of the Delphic maxim ("know yourself") in the form known in its Arabic versions to make the (Sufi) point that knowledge of God may be attained by a knowledge of one's soul: "He who does not know his own soul does not know his Lord. No one knows God other than he."[109] In the author's opinion, the Song's chief concern is to exhort individuals precisely to such introspection so that the soul might realize that God alone is the "ultimate purpose of ultimate purposes, the cause of causes, and the light of lights"; and by this realization also to know that "he [the adept] knows nothing other than God." Or as R. Zechariah puts it elsewhere in a less radical way, "Know that the purpose of this book [is to portray] the desire of the rational soul to attain its spiritual world, wherein lies its essential perfection."[110] Once again, the Song of Songs is deemed a mirror of the soul's quest for perfection, guiding its initiation into the holy of holies of Divinity.

Two Other Intellectual Prisms

A LATE MEDIEVAL EXAMPLE

The Jewish exegetical tradition under review features the integration of diverse spiritual content with Scripture. Such integration enabled seekers of perfection to discover their spiritual ambitions in the Song's expressed desires and dialogues. As the (human) subject and (Divine) object of the quest changed, so did the meaning of the passages interpreted. This is particularly evident in the first case that I note here. In it, R. Solomon Alkabetz (ca. 1500–1580), the author of one of the Song's most beautiful treatments, *'Ayelet 'Ahavim*, presented the female voice as that of Torah in conversation with the male, who seeks her divine perfections. In this personal guise, the Torah is virtually the *Shekhinah*, or God's immanent and intimate presence (though Alkabetz doesn't say this explicitly in this work), assiduously seeking her human beloved and guiding him in his spiritual development. And since this Torah embodies a myriad of meanings,

Alkabetz draws from the entire range of Jewish interpretation as he gives voice to the teachings of the Torah—including the Zohar, though this source is adduced solely for spiritual advice (not for mystical content). His restraint in divulging esoteric matters to noninitiates was undoubtedly deliberate, since he was himself a master of this lore (and he indicates the need to acquire higher wisdom in a careful progression). Alkabetz was a student of the mystic R. Joseph Taitatzek (in Greece) and the teacher of R. Abraham Galante (in Turkey). He associated with such illuminati as R. Joseph Caro and R. Moshe Cordovero (in Turkey and Safed). His commentary was completed in 1532 and published in 1552.

For Alkabetz, the Torah is the true path to heavenly perfection for humans for it is divine and transmits an unbroken light from Divinity—as distinct from philosophy, which is grounded in human reason and consequently refracts heavenly wisdom in broken or bent beams.[111] Adepts must stay rooted in the orbit of native Torah traditions to achieve intellectual and spiritual perfection. All the senses of Scripture duly serve individuals as they progress toward the highest and hidden truths, rooted in God, whereas the merely human path wanders among fallen fruit and misgauges its value. The Song of Songs gives strong expression to Torah's desire that the adept turn to her from her opening appeal: "O, let him kiss Me with the kisses of his mouth"—which is interpreted (following rabbinic exegesis) as her call to the student to study Scripture and be wholeheartedly devoted to its instructions. Indeed (also following rabbinic teachings), the verb "kiss Me" enfolds the desire of Torah for the pursed and loving lips of human students, as they transmit Torah from mouth to mouth across the generations.[112] And if there is a marked shift of pronouns from "*his* mouth" to "*your* love" in the Torah's appeal to the adept, this is taken to mark the transition from an initially impersonal relationship to one of personal intimacy as the seeker engages with Torah and God with loving devotion.

From the beginning, the Torah discloses its multiform nature. "I am dark, but comely" (Song 1:6). According to Alkabetz, this passage indicates that the external content of Torah, the *peshat*, is itself complete and perfect (though it may appear both opaque or strange) since its outward verbal configurations embody all the other, deeper levels of meaning—the legal norms and theology of rabbinic *derash*, the hints of the allegorical *remez*, and the supernal secrets of the hidden *sod*. Hence one should not reject the dark "tents" of Torah (its outward expressions) but enter them as the "pavilions" of inner divine truth.[113] One should study in a steady manner, following the "tracks of sheep" and moving progressively from the revealed to the concealed meanings. In this process, humility and faith are fundamental; they are the spiritual gateway to the Torah's laws and teachings.[114] These latter constitute its practical and intellectual content. They remain binding upon all worshipers—even those advanced in wisdom and engaged in private practices and spiritual contemplation (including ascetic isolation and meditation).[115] One must take care. Sometimes the seeker tries to arouse the fullness of love before its proper time; and this can lead to excesses and crises of faith. Hence the Torah repeatedly instructs the adept ("I adjure you") not to awaken false expectations.

The proper path must lead through the physical and mental virtues. Only with their deliberate acquisition may one progress in the divinely approved manner. Even aging

and death must not be accelerated through severe ascetical practices.[116] The release of the soul from the body will come in due time; hence, all simulations of death (through various acts of self-mortification) are forbidden. Again and again, Torah (the True Guide) makes this point to the student. When the lesson sinks in, the seeker may begin to practice those activities that prepare for the most exalted of states: the acquisition of prophecy and an ecstatic vision of the supernal secrets at death.[117] Alkabetz's work closes on this high note, thus fulfilling the task of the Torah (itself called *ʾAyelet ʾAhavim*, the Beloved Doe) proclaimed (by him) at the outset: "To instruct the perfected seeker to cleave to the Creator of All by means of the Divine Torah, as he [prepares to] enter the Inner Sanctum of her most esoteric secrets and mysteries" (Introduction, 5a).

A MODERN EXAMPLE

A second instance of the integration of the Song of Songs with intellectual currents takes us to the modern period. We now explore how contemporary sensibilities (of mind and heart) may illumine the Song, and how the Song may provide a modern grounding for the spiritual quest and its ideals—for humankind in general and Judaism in particular. The example is the tour de force of R. Joseph B. Soloveitchik (1903–93), entitled *U-Viqqashtem mi-Sham* (And From There You Shall Seek).[118] This work (drafted in the 1940s but published only in 1979) reflects a combination of rabbinic erudition (especially Talmud and medieval Jewish philosophy) and Western thought (in particular, Kierkegaard and neo-Kantian philosophy), along with a strong interest in religious phenomenology (especially, the description of primary and subsequent religious experiences proposed by Rudolf Otto and Max Scheler, among others).[119]

The Song's content gives repeated expression to the maiden's longing for her Beloved, who offers praise and presence while often distancing himself in unknown places—just as she, for her part, subverts his earnest beckoning by hiding and hesitation. These topics are deemed by Soloveitchik as traces of a twofold allegory of the spiritual life: one that is both metaphysical-individual and metaphysical-national. Soloveitchik thus regards the elusive or aborted quests of the human lovers in the Song to be emblematic of both the *universal* quest of everyman for meaning and for God (impelled by a natural impulse to survive and make sense of existence) and of the Jew in *particular* (who may transcend his natural state by heeding the call of revelation and the tasks it imposes).[120] This dual dimension is a reinterpretation of both the Song's plain sense (which, because it does not refer to Israelite history explicitly, is understood in natural and universal terms) and its allegorical meaning (which, though expressive of national religious history, focuses on issues of individual spirituality for the Jewish person).

In Soloveitchik's view, the primary awakening for the creature as such (everyman) is the universal impulse to survive and to find or make meaning. This awakened creature is thus an ontological being (rooted in existence), embedded in nature but seeking to transcend that state. The desire of the maiden for higher purposes (the kiss of the Beloved) reflects that universal level of existence. The ensuing and subsequent awakening of the Jew further responds to the ongoing Divine Call to sacred transcendence—now

from within a religious community. This collective unit thus has a metaphysical destiny that goes beyond the merely ontological desire to survive and find basic meaning in life. Of fundamental concern to Soloveitchik is the way individuals may scale the metaphysical heights through commitment and deeds of spiritual devotion. Thus the Song speaks of the universal quest of all persons (in their ontological being) to transcend their merely animal condition; however, it also conceals (allegorically) a challenge to Jews to hear more in the divine call and enrich the quality of their lives with spiritual significance.

Soloveitchik's reading of the Song evinces a discernible progression, despite the swirls of existential turmoil that mark the ever-faltering path of spiritual development. He spells out this progression through the selection of verses from the Song that he cites as epigraphs to several chapters.[121] These passages serve as typological prisms—archetypal formulations of the diverse spiritual issues that mark the arduous path of spiritual achievement and growth. Thus Soloveitchik's work does not provide a running exegesis; rather he constructs it around certain key phrases, whose interconnections reveal the sequence of spiritual development to be discerned in the Song overall. We follow his lead and explore the same passages. In this way we can track Soloveitchik's own presentation of the move from the natural (universal) human condition to the ideal (particular) Jewish possibilities latent in the Song.

Stage One: "Draw me after you, let us run" (1:4). This verse is said to encode the universal desire for stability and meaning in existence. The self reaches outward from within its natural situation—seeking permanence and significance. But being finite, the self can never take the measure of the whole. It is repeatedly distraught by misunderstandings of those parts it can discern. And also because it is finite, the self is engulfed by this infinite whole and overwhelmed by its excesses. The resistance of external reality to human certitude nevertheless hints at a greater (Divine) reality beyond, and the self reaches out toward this in hope ("draw me"), ever trying to understand its discernible elements rationally (which lead to scientific postulates) and its indiscernible ones through faith assumptions (which lead to religious postulates). Caught between the finite and the infinite, the self is marked by irresolvable contradictions and tensions. This is its natural (and universal) situation.

"Sustain me with raisin cakes . . . for I am faint with love" (2:5). This verse alludes to the fact that Judaism (biblical and rabbinic traditions) validates these core human frustrations (both the search for certainty and the sense of being overwhelmed by awesome magnitudes). Jewish liturgy expresses the turbulence of existence and its fullness of bounty. But for all its benefit, such expressions only reinforce the inherent problem. "My beloved had turned and gone" (5:6): God and meaning are both evanescent and elusive. There is dark absence, and there is also a sudden presence that mysteriously turns away and hides. This, too, is a painful tension.

Stage Two: "I am asleep, but my heart is wakeful. Hark, my beloved knocks" (5:2). This passage marks a transition. From its dark night of despair (sleep), the self is aroused and surprised. Divine revelation calls to the self from beyond: to behold the

world and its fullness, the gift of God. The self is called to heed this good within existence and serve it by enhancing life and raising the self (body and mind) to a sacred service. "Submission" to this task is the true response to the "Inscrutable Will" of God, which imposes the creation and responsibility for its maintenance upon the human being. This sense of revelation arises out of "an obscure dimness." It is wholly beyond reason, compelling the attentive heart to heed its call. "The clear day—a symbol of rational existence—had disappeared, and the dread-laden night had arrived. The great vision became a mystery, a transfinite secret that cannot be fathomed."[122]

Judaism validates this reality and expresses it through halakhic living. The human heart is called to worship God, giver of the wondrous world, in a loving and devoted service, and to submit its will to God in reverential obedience. This is the new tension: the mystery of existence imposes a moral responsibility upon the person who accepts the teachings of Sinai as formulated by Moses and interpreted by generations of teachers. Seeking God thus involves accepting the shaping truths of Tradition as creatively studied and interpreted by its faithful devotees. Hence, one's love of God and creative will are both subordinate to and expressed by the tasks of serving God through the obligations of *halakhah*—whose preeminent concerns are the sustenance and enhancement of the creation and the redirection of human needs to sacred ends.

This is the allegorical truth of the verse "His left hand was under my head, and his right arm embraced me" (2:6, 8:3). God expresses His moral and creative Will in the creation, and Torah and Tradition bring it to living, cultural expression. God's seekers ever strive to conjoin their will to this Will, while realizing that through this twofold revelation (creation and Torah) the finite self may change: it may be linked to the infinite mystery of God; it may transcend itself in a transcendent service; and it even may spiritually resolve the tensions that mark its natural situation. For God's devotees, God's Will is an encompassing embrace, and they actively submit to its loving reality.

Stage Three: "Let me be a seal upon your heart, like the seal upon your arm" (8:6). This verse expresses the longing for conjunction or attachment to God by bringing to ongoing expression God's care and providential support of the creation. Through creative study and performance of the obligations of *halakhah*, the lovers of God seek to perpetuate the revelation—both by its creative enhancement and active embodiment. The significance of Sinai thus extends in time through the Oral Torah and its transmission. The loving servant of Tradition actualizes the truths of Torah and thereby remains firmly connected to God and divine creativity. The creation is a once and ever-renewed beneficence of God, which expresses divine care for existence (the "good" of each and all). Correspondingly, the revelation of Sinai is also a once and ongoing divine beneficence through the Oral Torah whereby humans can sustain and enact the God-given "goods" of the world—for the enhancement of life and the love of God. "Thus can the individual cleave completely and absolutely to God in an attachment that no longer involves either flight or retreat."[123] This is the ideal of Judaism. It is also the pinnacle of the Song in Soloveitchik's allegorical interpretation. His words illumine a path from existential despair to a supervening spiritual existence. The pivot is the all-claiming sound of the "knock," which may be heard in the silent depths of life.[124]

Sod: The Most Hidden Truth— Divinity and Divine Love in the Depths

The fourth (and supreme) level of scriptural interpretation is called *sod*, and it deals with the hidden mysteries of God in the supernal realms. This level of meaning has also been called *nistar*, and its content *ḥokhmah nisteret*, because it was a "concealed wisdom" about Divinity. Exclusive circles of adepts guarded such secrets and transmitted them orally in a whisper to the spiritual elite.[125] The content was esoteric in every sense. Only gradually (by the twelfth century) were such matters disclosed more publicly, written down, and also shown to be encoded in Scripture. In this way, oral secrets became literary hints and then also symbols of the most supernal truths. Knowing such matters (through exegetical contemplation) was also a mystical experience, related to contemplative visions of its spiritual content.

The Emergence of Esoteric Comments

Among the subjects prohibited by the Mishnah from exegetical disclosure, even in limited circles, was the mystery of Creation (*Ma'aseh Bereishit*; Genesis 1) and the mystery of the Heavenly Throne or Chariot (*Ma'aseh Merkavah*; Ezekiel 1). Mishnah Ḥag. 2:1 specifies these two topics (and the study of forbidden sexual relations). According to a list of these matters that the Church Father Origen preserved in his Song commentary (ca. 240 C.E.), the Song of Songs was included among the biblical topics "that should be reserved for study until the last"—so esoteric was its wisdom.[126] Origen also reports a Jewish tradition that "care is taken to allow no one even to hold this book in his hands, who has not reached a full and ripe age."[127] Presumably a less mature reader would be aroused by its passionate content.

THE SONG AND ANCIENT JEWISH ESOTERISM

Ancient Jewish sources also specified the Song's esoteric character and study. Recall that R. Akiva (in the discussion of *derash*) once gave a sermon based on 5:9–16 and 6:1–3, which dealt with the companions' desire to know something about the Divine Beloved and included his citation of the verse (in response), "My beloved is clear-skinned and ruddy" (5:10). I suggested that the sage was undoubtedly alluding to mystical depictions of the Divine Form based on 5:10–16. I add here that precisely these texts (from 5:9–6:3) were cited in the accounts of Divinity in the so-called Heikhalot (heavenly palaces) literature, where this Divine Form is envisioned.[128] Thus R. Akiva's sermonic allusion has fuller exemplars in purely mystical sources; and although these sources derive largely from subsequent centuries, there is little doubt that such mystical experiences were very early. Indeed, a well-known passage found in T. Ḥag. 2:1, contemporary with M. Ḥag. (noted above), refers to various spiritual events with the

caveat that only R. Akiva endured these matters "in peace" (i.e., he emerged whole in mind and body). In support of this point, Song 1:4 is cited: "Draw me after You [the King has brought me to his chambers]."[129] Quite evidently, the Rabbis understood this passage to depict a divinely inspired ascent to the heavenly palaces in late antiquity.

A second example complements this report and even links speculations on 5:10–16 with visions of the Heavenly Chariot (upon which sat a Being of an apparent human likeness). Thus R. Ezra of Gerona (and others in the thirteenth century) presented an otherwise unknown passage from a "Midrash Shir Ha-Shirim" on 5:10 that states (regarding the appearance of the Beloved figure): "His image (*demuto*) is of red, black, green, and white—like the image of God, [which was] *like the appearance of the rainbow in the cloud* (Ezek. 1:28)."[130] This is a remarkable statement, presumably based on exegeses and visionary experiences of the Beloved (some type of synesthesia). The meditation involved a mystical vision of God, based on 5:10–16, and correlated with the appearance of the Divine upon the Throne in Ezekiel 1—another vision involving the color spectrum. One can be sure that our Song passage was believed (in some circles) to contain an esoteric depiction of God. It is thus understandable that only mystics preserved the midrash in question. (For this reason, R. Akiva was also allusive in his own public references to these matters when speaking to Jews in the synagogue.)

THE SONG OF SONGS AND EARLY KABBALAH

The streams of tradition flow from antiquity, and these include the channels conveying esoteric readings. One cannot easily determine when and how mystical adepts began to see secret meanings in the Song and began to relate these meanings to the oral traditions of heavenly events in the supernal domains. We can only note their first public occurrence in texts, imagining the discussions that preceded the written formulations. An example is the Book of Bahir, which appeared in Provence around 1180. Undoubtedly, several earlier editions preceded it, which suggests ongoing oral deliberations.[131] Why certain secrets of mystic cabals found the light of day at this time is uncertain; however, what is clear is that the holds that barred the release of certain deliberations about Scripture and its esoteric content were released, and questions were posed to sages who expounded these secrets for all to read in spite of all the restrictions formulated in the ancient Mishnah (see above). The Book of Bahir is thus a work of mystical pedagogy that interprets Scripture as a work containing secret references to the supernal dynamics and gradations of Divinity.

The Development of Exegetical Commentaries

THE BAHIR AND THE SONG

In the course of extended explications of the supernal gradations and their nomenclature, we find the Song of Songs referred to several times, its terms and images given esoteric significance. With respect to the terms, it is clear that a symbolic code expounded Scripture—the external *peshat* was a vehicle to convey meanings for this world

and its natural features, whereas the internal *sod* pointed to supernatural realities in the divine worlds. Thus when discussing the emanation of the divine qualities, the supernal channel from above to below was designated "a fountain of gardens, a well of living waters, flowing from Lebanon" (Song 4:15). The authorship of the Bahir was undoubtedly tapping into prior understandings of the Song as encoding hints of the ultimate font of creative being—whose symbolic source was "Lebanon." The text explains this location to mean the gradation of Wisdom (*Ḥokhmah*), the highest sphere of Sense in the divine hierarchy, undoubtedly because this term (*levanon*) also alluded to a sense of pure luminosity or clarity (*lavan* = white) in the supernal heights.[132] This example provides further evidence that secret meanings of the Song circulated in mystical circles long before they went public.

Additional support for these contentions is in another key passage in the Bahir. In it, the discussion concerns all ten of the cosmic gradations that the supernal King decided to plant in His garden. Of the ten, nine were "male" (palm) trees; and one was "female," an *'etrog* (the citron fruit). Accordingly, a scriptural verse encodes this mysterious teaching: "fruit of a glorious (*hadar*) tree [and] palm branches" (Lev. 23:40)—which refers to the species used on the Festival of Tabernacles (Sukkot).[133] On this basis, the festival bouquet of species held by worshipers on this holiday had cosmic import. Hence, the palm branch referred to the cosmic column of divine reality that spread over six gradations (the main column and the five surrounding species that symbolized the extension of divine reality). The citron referred to the female entity required for the vitality of existence to be sustained, "for it is impossible for the upper and lower worlds to endure without a female."[134]

Not only is the feminine dimension the "glorious" recipient of all the fructifying powers from the higher domains, she is also identified with the Song's maiden, deemed "beautiful as the moon [and] radiant as the sun" (6:10). Significantly, this female modality is not a divine consort or bride (as she is later in the Zohar) but *an embodiment of the Song of Songs itself*—the queen of the sacred Scriptures! How so? On the basis of the old teaching (of R. Akiva) that stated that the Song was the "Holy of Holies." For (we now learn) if the Torah is the most "holy" work of all the other holy writings of Scripture (the "holies"), then the Song (which encodes the Torah in a special symbolic way) is the most "holy" and glorious climax of the six supernal gradations (or "holies") above her.

Despite these cryptic formulations and allusions, there is no doubt that the Song of Songs had attained an exalted and esoteric status in the circle of the Bahir. Studying this book takes one to the core of all spiritual truth (the divine gradations). Celebrating the Festival of Sukkot with the citron and palm in hand, and these mystical truths in mind, might inspire the celebrant to contemplate the integration of masculine and feminine dimensions in the Divine creation—to ascend to a mystical sense of the glory of femininity in reality and in its embodiment in the Song, the Bride of all Scripture. Since Scripture and its rituals symbolized supernal realities, there is every reason to suppose that people performed these religious practices, keeping these truths in mind. In this way people could participate in a meditative and ritual way in the higher divine dimensions. Later mystical-ritual handbooks specifically spell out such matters (including

sections on the palm and citron species). The work *Sefer ha-Rimmon* by R. Moses de León, less than a century later, is a notable case in point.[135]

COMMENTARY OF EZRA OF GERONA

From scattered and oblique comments on the Song in Provence, just a generation later we have a full-blown commentary. It appeared in the Catalonian city of Gerona—the site of a mystical circle whose most prominent member was Nachmanides. Rabbi Ezra ben Solomon (died ca. 1235) was one of the "companions" of this group, who broke the seals that kept the Kabbalah an oral secret within small groups.[136] In his bold work, with multiple introductions that provide a history of esotericism and a sketch of the symbolism in the Song, he interpreted the Song's dialogues as a series of discourses *between the divine gradations* (all spiritually personified)—especially the longing of a feminine component called the Glory (*Kavod*; sometimes also *Shekhinah*) to ascend the heights and kiss the transcendent masculine element (called Splendor, *Tif'eret*, or even the exalted Wisdom, *Ḥokhmah*) in ecstatic union and, thereby, restore the integral harmony of all Being.[137] Making this teaching public sent shock waves from the epicenter in Gerona. Perhaps Ezra's disclosure was in some measure an attempt to counter both the tide of rational philosophy and the philosophical commentaries (*remez*) on the Song at this time.[138] In any event, Ezra ben Solomon decided that the time was ripe to reveal the Song's secrets. (Based on his other writings, it seems that he composed this commentary by the 1220s, when he was over 70.) This or another similar work on the Song was the object of great antikabbalistic venom by R. Meir of Narbonne in a letter from around 1240.[139]

The origin of Jewish esotericism, according to R. Ezra, begins with Adam and Eve, continues through the patriarchs, and suffers a great decline during the Egyptian servitude. Moses recovered the inner sense of Scripture, after which it was transmitted until the exile, when the sages sealed its wisdom in their (midrashic) parables because during the exile wisdom had waned. The dislocation of this dispersion was thus not merely a historical event but a spiritual one as well. The recovery of the Song's esoteric meaning by R. Ezra and his circle was thus a retrieval of an old divine wisdom, and his decision to make that wisdom public was an act of spiritual service to those mired in the darkness of the exile. In Ezra's view Solomon the wise composed the Song in a masterful manner. Those who could penetrate and understand its secrets could join the Divine longing for cosmic repair, and they even could facilitate it through meditation and ritual practice. The stylistic key to the Song, he said, was to realize that certain symbols were the matrix of a passage and that the surrounding terminology served this overall core. For example, the figure of a "kiss" is said to symbolize the cleaving or conjunction of the divine gradations at each point of contact and integration with one another; thus, the image of "mouth" that occurs together with it functions only in a secondary and supportive capacity. Ezra also revealed the meaning of a number of other symbols in the Song, for example, "Lebanon" refers to "Wisdom." The sage offers the reader kabbalistic "hints" that bear on the Song's meaning. Because no simple correspondences exist between the Song's symbolic language and the supernal do-

mains, Ezra states that its words are designed solely to stimulate mystical speculations, which is what he also seeks to encourage through his commentary.

One of the notable features of R. Ezra's work is the way it integrates allusions to supernal states, individual mystical yearnings, and (even) national considerations.[140] These do not always jibe and often leave the reader perplexed; however, these may be intentional ambiguities, or they may derive from mystical insights that flashed to consciousness as Ezra pondered the Song. His comment on 1:2 is exemplary in this regard.

> *O, let him kiss me with the kisses of his mouth*. These are the words of the Glory, which desires and pines to ascend, to be conjoined to the light of the Supernal Light which has no image. She ascends in Thought and Idea; and thus speaks [of it] in the third person. The kiss is a figure [symbol] for the joy of the conjunction of the soul in the Source of Life and for the increase of the Holy Spirit. Thus it says *with the kisses of his mouth*, for each and every cause receives the Thought and increase from that sweet Light and luminous Splendor. And when he speaks with the Glory, which is the gateway to the entities, he speaks in the third person.[141]

This comment brings the reader into the midst of a living, mystical universe—replete with technical terms, ideals, and supernal dynamics.[142] It is also evident that philosophical conceptions that portray the Divine gradations in intellectual terms and as having such luminosity as to transcend all images infuses this reading of the Song. Being so transcendent, the Glory addresses this entity as something wholly other ("his"). The Song formulates the desire of the feminine Glory (*Shekhinah*) to conjoin with her masculine partner (*Tif'eret*) by the term "kisses." This feature is in truth a symbol of the conjunction of spiritual entities at every point along the chain of cosmic cause and effect (the "kisses" thus symbolize the interfusion of all beings). Such an esoteric teaching is remarkable. But the passage goes further and supplements the exegesis with references to the soul of the mystic, which also desires to ascend and conjoin with Divinity—which it may do through the lowest gradation of Glory, to which it turns and requests kisses. In this moment of longing, the human soul (of the mystic) takes on the persona of the feminine Glory (in the supernal realm), desiring a mystical transport and addressing the Higher Glory in the third person masculine.

These spiritual transformations show a mystical parallelism between the human seeker and the divine entities. Reading the Song is therefore not an abstract desire for esoteric wisdom but an engaged experience in which the interpreter seeks to participate in an inner divine desire to ascend its Source. Love is *the* driving force for the mystic, even as it is in the divine heights. Studying the Song reveals these intricate truths. There are no purely external theological ideas as opposed to subjective religious experiences. Rather, the objective divine ground (divine love within the divine order) is lived experientially in the depths of the self; and the subjective self is grounded in a divine truth, which is the fundamental truth of all existence. The two are one. The rest is further commentary.

IBN SAHULA'S COMMENTARY

Commentators continued to write kabbalistic interpretations to the Song in the thirteenth century—some we know of, but others are lost. A key contribution is the work of R. Yitzḥak ibn Sahula of Castile (b. 1244), a scholar of wide-ranging talent and the

author of the celebrated ethical work *Mashal Ha-Qadmoni*.[143] He composed a detailed commentary on the Song in 1283 or 1284, which is a masterpiece of succinct, if also allusive, mystical exegesis.[144] In his introduction, Ibn Sahula mentions having seen the Song commentary of the kabbalist Moses of Burgos while he was still young (ca. 1260); some have reasoned that his frequent statements "I have heard" refer to this lost work.[145] However, more evidence points to a dependence upon R. Yitzḥak ibn Laṭif's theological compendia, because many of Ibn Sahula's comments exactly parallel Ibn Laṭif's esoteric interpretations of the Song.[146] None of these relationships lessen Ibn Sahula's innovative achievement but simply help fill the gap (of a half-century) between his commentary and that of R. Ezra. We consider below other materials from this time, produced by groups that comprised the circle of the Zohar.

Ibn Sahula repeatedly emphasizes the Song's profound esoteric character. In his introduction he asserts that this Song was composed of supernal melodies sung by the angels on High, thus capable of opening the heart to the mysteries of the Torah and prophecies. In due course, this supernal Song of songs emanated to Levi and the Levites, who gave it final shape; and then Solomon came and "made a work" (*'asah sefer*) from the Song of the angels "and sealed [heavenly] wisdom within it," to be discovered by devoted adepts. The Song is thus based on a primordial prototype and, therefore, may accord the human soul a supreme cosmic attunement. Ordinary worshipers are not immediately ready for such spiritual heights, which require patience and training. Along the way, the student is "supported" by the external words of the *Peshat* "until the time of love arrives," and one can imbibe the inner truths of the words and achieve true Wisdom (comment on 2:4). Since this requires "great effort and much contemplation, and attending [to the practices of] sages and elders . . . and saints" (on 8:6), one must be "careful" not to divulge such hidden matter to the simple folk, lest it destroy the foundations of their religious life (on 4:11). And so even if Ibn Sahula decided to make his commentary public, he had all kinds of strategies to keep his intent hidden. The most common tactic was to cite seemingly innocent phrases from Scripture—which, however, point the wise (mystical initiates) to more secret content.

According to Ibn Sahula, the inclusion of esoteric matters and the encouragement of spiritual experiences is the Song's hallmark from the outset. Its opening words, "Let him kiss me," are a case in point. First, the "supernal kiss" symbolizes "the emanation of the [Divine] Spirit from its Source," and thus these words are "in truth" the beginning of the song that God sings every day as the entities of existence flow eternally from Divinity. But these words do not refer solely to these supernal dimensions of divine creativity. They also address the spiritual seeker. They are also divine words calling to the human soul to "be aroused," to "desire the supernal heights," and to become perfected (comment on 1:2). Here, the Divine Name symbolizes the flow of divine creativity, and the verse "Your Name (*shemekha*) is oil poured forth" symbolizes the whole idea. The adept learns that God and all God's names are One (for the term *shemekha*, "names," is plural) and that all of the sacred designations of God (recorded in Scripture or elsewhere) symbolize different dimensions of the Divine Mystery. Learning these "hidden" wonders, spiritual seekers "love" God all the more (reading v. 3, *'al*

kein ʿalamot ʾaheivukha, not "therefore do the maidens love you" but "therefore"—because of the "hidden" truths, *ʿalumot*—the adepts "love You").

Mystic interpretations also have ethical consequences in other places, and the *sod* interpretation of the Song addresses both issues. For example, a voice exclaims in 3:6: "Who is this who ascends from the desert (*midbar*) . . . in clouds of myrrh and frankincense (*levonah*)?" The seeker may wonder what is being said here, beyond some visage of a scented maiden. For Ibn Sahula, the first thing to observe is that the reference is made to two distinct scents: the first, myrrh, being a resin that can appear reddish (or reddish-brown); the second, frankincense, being an aromatic of white on the color spectrum (hence the name *levonah-lavan*). To his rabbinic (kabbalistic) mind, these colors refer (respectively) to the two emotional qualities of anger and mercy. Ibn Sahula goes on to say that this verse indicates the changing nature of these qualities in humans—a species famously distinguished among other animals for the ability to speak. If humans speak with anger and negativity, they diminish the quality of life; however, if they speak calmly and positively, they can enhance it. But this is also an earthly hint of higher mysteries for the source of speech lies in the divine heights, in the supernal forms of the Written and Oral Torah. When the proclamation is voiced in 3:6, it celebrates the capacity of speech (*medabber*) to ascend to these domains and to experience the spiritual fragrance that flows through (the heavenly) Torah into all existence (including the earthly Torah of Moses, whose teachings guide one on the path of justice and righteousness, judgment and mercy).

Thus, mystical meditations on the Song can open the mind to higher realities, at the same time disclosing the ethical implications of speech and emotion for everyday life. In this process, the *peshat* sense is not replaced by the *Sod*; rather, it opens the way to its transcendent significance. Contemplation thus deepens conduct but does not replace it. Mystics can thus ascend to the highest supernal realms while remaining bound to the normative behaviors of Tradition.

The Triumph of Exegetical Esoterism

ZOHARIC LITERATURES—THIRTEENTH CENTURY

Diverse collections of Zoharic teachings appear in thirteenth-century Spain, attesting to several circles of mystical meditation on Scripture with different exegetical styles and concerns. The Song's treatments in these sources confirm this. Three primary strata can be noted: (1) the so-called Midrash Ha-Neʿelam, (2) the main corpus of the Book of Zohar, and (3) the anthology known as *Zohar Ḥadash*. The Midrash Ha-Neʿelam (ca. 1275–80),[147] as its name suggests, is a corpus of writings (now scattered and in a fragmentary state in the other corpora) that construct a hidden (or esoteric) midrash. The work focuses largely on the book of Genesis, using the Song to inaugurate mystical comments (especially dealing with the soul); its language mixes Hebrew and Aramaic, and it has a distinctive narrative quality. The one unit that comments directly on the

Song (included in Zohar Ḥadash, 60c–61d) begins with the significance of its large initial letter *shin* (***Shir***), noting that it symbolizes the Heavenly Chariot—and that its three (orthographic) prongs symbolize Abraham, Isaac, and Jacob in a supernal form. The Song is thus deemed to encode supreme divine realities.

The main Book of Zohar emerged from old traditions and creative innovations in the early 1290s, with citations and interpretations of the Song found throughout this large corpus. Indeed, the preponderance of quotes and their theological uses mark this book as one of unparalleled scriptural significance.[148] Of particular importance is the long homily of R. Yose dealing with the mystery of the Tabernacle and the Song (Zohar 2:143a–147a; *parashat Terumah*); two important passages dealing with mystical "Assemblies"—the so-called Great Assembly, which focused on the Divine Form (2:176b–177b), based on Song 5:10–16, and the Small Assembly, which anticipated the death of R. Shimʿon bar Yoḥai (3:189b–192b), using a cluster of passages from the Song; and the teaching about the Lily, placed at the very beginning of the introduction to the Zohar (1:1a).[149] All these units have different theosophical concerns, which is indicative of the diversity of teachings gathered in the Book of Zohar.[150] They undoubtedly reflect many different mystical groups and the living fluidity of mystical speculations.

As stated earlier (introduction, "The Many Poetics of Love in Jewish Tradition," *sod*), central to the theosophy in the Zohar is the emanation of ten supernal gradations out of the Infinite Godhead (denominated as *'Ein Sof*, "Unending"). The gradations reflect an inner hierarchy of major qualities (though all ten qualities are contained in each gradation). In one format, imagined as a Supernal King, the highest gradation is the "Crown" (*Keter*); followed by two intellectual gradations, called "Wisdom" (*Ḥokhmah*) and "Understanding" (*Binah*); then three emotional valences, called "Mercy" (*Ḥesed* or *Raḥamim*), "Rigor" (*Gevurah* or *Din*), and "Splendor" (*Tif'eret*; a balance of the prior two); followed by three types of temporal powers, called "Eternity" (*Netzaḥ*), "Glory" (*Hod*), and "Foundation" (*Yesod*; the source of creativity and fecundity); and, finally, the royal "Kingdom" (*Malkhut*), recipient of all the bounties (also called a "Diadem," *ʿAtarah*, which has a feminine valence, being the "creative mother" of the impregnating energies). The final gradation, known as "Community of Israel" (*Keneset Yisra'el*, being the supernal embodiment of the nation), also is referred to as *Shekhinah*. This last designation is of major significance because now this (heretofore masculine) dimension of divine immanence (and worldly presence) in midrashic sources is identified with both the people *and* the feminine gradation in the heavenly hierarchy.[151] Older trends suddenly coalesce and assume a new spiritual modality within the Godhead; but to what extent these spiritual developments were primarily internal or (also) influenced by external factors is a matter of scholarly discussion.[152] Either way, there can be no doubting their import and effect upon Jewish religious consciousness ever since. All these matters (of the divine gradations overall and, especially, the femininity of the final one) take on special importance through interpretations of the Song of Songs.

The mystical and symbolic significance of Scripture assumes a special esoteric valence when the focus is the Song for several reasons: (1) Now a focus is on the drama of love, and longing for union, between Divinity's masculine element (Solomon,

Shelomoh, is God, the King of Peace, *shalom*) and its feminine element (*Keneset Yisra'el* and *Shekhinah*)—a drama expressed through the Song's dialogues and the quests for, and encounters between, the feminine and masculine elements. (2) The longing for union and the rapture of kisses express an inner divine longing for harmonious unity, which has been disrupted by the sins of Israel, whose (historical) exile prompts a dislocation within Divinity (manifested in part by Israel's exilic wandering and longing for restoration); hence, Israel's religious obedience may facilitate this inner divine union, symbolized as a Mystical Marriage. (3) The dynamics within the Godhead are now dominated by the Song's imagery, especially the topics of the Garden and Moon (symbols of the *Shekhinah*) and the Beloved's Form (symbols of the Male Face, Mind, and Body). (4) The study of the Song's dialogues and imagery enables the individual mystic (an embodiment of *Keneset Yisra'el*) to link a personal love of God to divine energies as such and thus to participate in these dynamics *and* experience them in spiritual rapture. The soul's true love of God is thus part of the restoration of all the fragments of existence to Divinity.[153]

The portion of the work Zohar Ḥadash that is devoted to the Song continues the various esoteric dynamics with its own emphases, distinguished especially from the main Zohar by virtue of the fact that the prophet Elijah reveals the mysteries to Rabbi Shim'on. As a rule in the Zohar, the fellowship of seekers discovers the mysteries by mystic inquiry into the text, or its leader Rabbi Shim'on discloses the mysteries. Here the Song's secrets are a supernal disclosure to a unique sage, who is entrusted with them and also urged to disclose their encoding in the Song. Of highest significance are mysteries of the Divine Names, which are not revealed even to the angelic host. Developing this point, the work opens with an awesome meditation on the four Hebrew words that compose the opening phrase (*shir ha-shirim 'asher li-shlomoh*; "The Song of Songs, which is of Solomon"). These four words are linked to various holy epithets of God and also to the holy tetragrammaton or four-letter name of God (*Y-H-V-H*)—the ultimate symbol of divine reality (ZḤ 61d–62a). All these are deemed components of the Mystery of the Heavenly Chariot (itself also a quaternary structure; cf. Ezek. 1:6–10, 16–17); and thus here, too (as noted above regarding the Midrash Ha-Ne'elam), there is a conjoining of the mystery of the Song with this most esoteric sphere of speculation. The same correlation between the four-letter name and the Song's four initial words occurs in the Zohar (2:144a).[154] All this may be understood to mean that the entire Divine Hierarchy (the Supernal Chariot) is integrated by the four letters of the name and the Song's opening words. Hence the Song (symbolized by the title line) is a symbolic expression of Divinity, and the initial four words reflect the longing of the lower gradations to unite in love with the upper ones. This yields the following interpretation: the song (*shir*) that *Shekhinah* sings, together with the songs (*shirim*) of other supernal princes (*sarim*), to Solomon (*Shelomoh*), the King of peace, *shelama'*—in a loving rapture that ascends to *'Ein Sof.*

The supernal Song is further disclosed as a great radiance and a channel of divine blessings into the world. This luminosity—like others in the divine realm—transcends all worldly qualities; it is a vision to be perceived only by the inner eye and an understanding heart. Many of the teachings of R. Shim'on take the form of discourses

built in the manner of the ancient Midrash, such that verses of the Song conjoin with passages from elsewhere in Scripture, to deepen the various mystical disclosures. The Zohar Ḥadash comprises a running commentary on the first eleven verses of the Song (ZḤ 61d–74d); it thus offers a more systematic presentation of passages in the Song than that found in the Zohar itself (whose focus is on the verses of the Torah, as read on the Sabbath).

EXAMPLES FROM ZOHARIC LITERATURE

The Mystery of the Song. The Song of Solomon is deemed the greatest of all the songs of Scripture, "transcending all the songs of its predecessors"—including the Song of Moses (at the Sea) and the Psalms of David. How so? Through song, the prophet Moses ascended in praise of God, "thanking the supernal King" for saving Israel (in Egypt and at the Sea); and through all his sacred songs, David was able to adorn the *Shekhinah* (also called *Matronita*, "Spiritual Matron") and her handmaidens and give them ascent through his "Songs of Ascent." But Solomon did more. Finding the Queen adorned, "he strived to conjoin her to her Groom," and through his Song sang wooing "words of love" that brought them together in a most transcendent "perfect love." Solomon's Song thus helped to stimulate and establish Divine Harmony in all the spheres of being, above and below. It is thus a supernal wedding song for the sake of all existence (2:144b–145a).

But there is even more to the Song according to the Zohar for it is also designated *kelala' de-khol 'oraita'*, the "totality of the entire Torah." This means that the Song contains not only "the totality" of all the mysteries of the creation, the patriarchs, the commandments of Sinai, and even the mysteries of the Temple and the secrets of the exile but also the "totality [of the secrets] of crowning the Holy Name in love," and also the mystery of the revival of the dead. "Whatever was, is, or ever will be . . . is all in the Song of Songs" (2:144a). And so wondrous are its words that every verse in the Song also contains supernal mysteries. It is thus the Holy of Holies and, as such, contains within it the "mystery of the Holy of Holies," which is the secret of the inner divine unions and unities, concealed beyond all comprehension (2:145b).

Knowing the Mysteries. In a penetrating interpretation found in Zohar Ḥadash, R. Shim'on says that all spiritual seeking must begin with a query, a desire to know God and the higher orders of divine wisdom. He informs the student of the requirement to contemplate the most transcendent secrets for without such knowledge, one cannot be perfected and attain eternity. This knowledge is said to include the following: learning to contemplate the mystery of God (the Master of Being); understanding one's body—its origin and destiny; meditating on the mystery of the soul—its nature and presence in the self; and learning to contemplate the world in which one lives, with all its mysteries. These matters—the query and the need for true knowledge—are specified in two verses of the Song. The true seeker must begin by turning to God, saying: "*Tell me,* [*You whom I love so well*]" (Song 1:7): tell me of the "mysteries of wisdom," and *how You pasture* and guide the hidden domains, which I do not know, so that I won't *stray* afield

or be ashamed when I come to the supernal heights after death! The answer is given immediately in the next verse: *if you do not know* the mysteries when you come to the higher worlds, you will have to *go forth* from there, banished and unaccepted. So: *Go forth and follow* the teachings—and the ways of those who understand the hidden *tracks* of the mysteries (v. 8)—and then you will come to an expanded awareness and true knowledge (ZḤ 71a).

We are thus privy to certain initiation conditions directed to the adept so that the seeker can set forth on the mystical path. Spoken by the supreme teacher R. Shimʿon, the Song's language changes from a heavenly dialogue between the *Shekhinah* and her Beloved into a spiritual guidebook for the human seeker. The Song articulates for the seeker the query of the desire for proper spiritual information, and then it offers (albeit in generalities) an answer that articulates what is required for supernal knowledge and one's inner perfection. To acquire the requisite information, the self is told to turn to the masters of esoteric wisdom. It is they alone who can unseal the locks of Scripture, initiating the seeker into the mysteries of God, the body, the soul, and the world.

The Power of Kisses and Love. According to the Zohar, the kiss is the true mystery of all union—Divine and human. For if one were to ask (as R. Yose does) why Solomon began his Song about love between the spiritual entities (in the Divine Hierarchy) with a longing for a kiss, the answer is plain. It is because "there is no true cleaving of spirit to spirit other than by a kiss," especially on the mouth. For when kisses are exchanged by the mouth, separate spiritual entities "become one" in "one love." According to the Zohar, this is a profound mystery that has an analogy with human love and kissing; for when kisses are exchanged between two persons, four spirits are involved—each one giving and receiving breath, reciprocally. These four spirits create an interfusion of love between the two entities, and they ascend on High upon the four letters of l-o-v-e (*ʾalef-heh-bet-heh* = the consonants of *ʾa-ha-va-h*, "love"). This four-letter word is, in turn, deemed to be a component of the numerical sum of the four-letter Divine Name, such that all human love strengthens and depends upon God's Name, which is mystically comprised of "Love."

As with human love, all Divine entities yearn to conjoin and interfuse with one another in infinite combinations and unities, all the way to the "Palace of Love" at the supreme height of the divine order. Thus the Bride calls out to the most concealed and unknown Divine Dimension, desiring that "He kiss me with the kisses of His mouth." Each expression of loving-longing is a cleaving to other entities so that the entities interfuse and establish chariots of love that ascend to the highest realms. Human love of persons and of God ascend these spiritual chariots of Divinity—driven upward in ever purer forms in an ultimate yearning for the Kiss of His Mouth (the most Supernal Reality), which blesses these actions and makes the many One (see Z. 2:145a–b). This is the spiritual core of Solomon's Song.[155]

The New Turn Inward

LATER HASIDIC SOURCES

The teachings of the Zohar and subsequent works (like Tiqqunei Zohar) form the Bible of Jewish mystical life and thought, and subsequent writings are in various ways the ongoing commentary. Indeed, the various trends that flow from the Zohar all crystallized in this form beginning in Safed in the sixteenth century. Particularly noteworthy of this early period is the immense (16-volume) Zohar commentary *'Or Yaqar* of R. Moses Cordovero (1522–70) and the various meditative and speculative comments of R. Isaac Luria (1534–72), found especially in his *'Etz Ḥayyim* (taught orally and diffused only in manuscript until 1772). The transmission and explication of Luria's insights continued long after his death in the many commentaries on his works by his disciples (both actual and spiritual) down to the modern period. The most well-known of such Lurianic commentaries is the so-called *Sullam* commentary by R. Yehuda Ashlag (early twentieth century). In these and other ways, the Zohar's teachings on the Song found new voices and new life.

A particularly vital renewal of this kabbalistic material is found in the writings of the Hasidic masters, beginning with R. Israel Baal Shem (the Besht) in the late eighteenth century (Ukraine). While clearly infused with Lurianic speculations and meditative practices, the Besht and his disciples addressed themselves to the wider community, thus engaging in a more popular spiritual diffusion and reinterpretation of the esoteric traditions. In particular, a strong feature of these teachings was the focus on the psychological and ethical aspects of the divine gradations, especially their dynamics (in microcosm) in the soul of the individual. Issues of inner unity and spiritual perfection dominate their comments—most often as these convey the integrity of private thoughts and the highs and lows of the spiritual life. All this is markedly evident (both the traces of older themes and their newer applications) in the teachings of these masters on the Song of Songs.

In some cases the comments on the Song by these founding teachers are brief summaries of single passages, reported by disciples of the Besht (especially R. Yaakov Yosef of Polonoye; 1710–84). In other cases, they are brief summaries of discourses delivered during the Festival of Passover when the Song was recited (collected under that holiday heading in the anthologies of their teachings). Typical of these assemblages are the teachings found in *Ginzei Yosef* (by R. Yosef Bloch, an early follower of the Besht) or the spiritual instructions found in the *Kedushat Levi* by R. Levi Yitzḥak of Berdichev (1740–1809) in a subsequent generation. The very elaborate and extensive comments on the Song taught by R. Shneur Zalman of Liadi (1745–1812) appear in his *Liqquṭei Torah*; and the long commentary by his disciple, R. Aaron Halevi of Staroselye (1852; printed with his comments on the Zohar in the Zhitomir edition of 1856), indicates that he bases his remarks on the oral teachings of his master. Among other teachings on the Song produced for Passover are the homilies of R. Yisrael (the Maggid) of Kozhnitz (1733–1814), found in his *'Avodat Yisra'el,* and fragments of teachings by R. Avraham Yehoshua Heschel of Apt (1748–1825; the Apter Rov), known

as the *'Ahavat Yisra'el* (the title of his collection of "*torahs*"). Moreover, just as various Torah teachings (as noted above) cited brief comments on the Song, there are also comments on more extended series of verses. Particularly noteworthy are the teachings on Song 1:2–9; 3:1, and 8:1 by R. Yaakov Yosef of Polonoye, found in his teachings on the Torah portion of *Be-ha'alotekha* (*Ketonet Passim*, 36a–c).

The teachings vary by master, although chains of exegetical traditions are reported. As indicated, a major focus of Hasidic homilies on the Songs is the concern with spiritual practice and levels of spiritual consciousness. I bring the following three examples to illustrate this emphasis:

1. Commenting on the phrases "Your ointments yield a good fragrance . . . Your Name is like a fine [decanted] oil . . . Draw me after you, let us run" (1:3–4), R. Levi Yitzḥak of Berdichev counseled his audience on spiritual repair. Sometimes, he said, an individual may fall in their spiritual service and lose focus or intensity. On such occasions the task of the person is to recover a trace of the "fragrance" produced by one's former (higher) service, letting it be a reminder and guide for the path to be pursued. This may help the worshiper to recover spiritual strength and "run" to God in true worship. On such occasions a person may be blessed with the higher consciousness desired and be able to aver, "The King has brought me *into* His chambers" (v. 4).[156] Reflecting a later tendency of Hasidism (when individual spiritual tasks were transferred to a *tzaddik*, "Holy Master"), the *Ma'or Va-Shemesh* (by R. Kalonymos Kalman Halevi Epstein; d. 1827) stated that if one has fallen in spiritual stature, one should go to one of the "Masters of the Generation" to imbibe the fragrance of Eden from him so that one's "soul will be aroused" toward God and desire a higher consciousness, bound to the Divine Intellect. Rabbi Kalonymos adds, commenting on the phrase "therefore the maidens (*'alamot*) love you" [v. 2], that this heavenly fragrance may even stimulate the young (*'elem*) to seek out God and come to love Him.[157]
2. Other passages in the Hasidic literature are addressed to the spiritual elite, reflecting different ideals. Based on the verse "If you do not know, O fairest of woman, then go out among the tracks of the sheep, and graze your kids by the tents of the shepherds" (1:8), R. Yaakov Yosef (*Ketonet Passim*, 36c) speaks to those who devote themselves totally to the study of Torah. He says that when one has exhausted one's mind in intense study (i.e., "if you cannot learn" any longer), go out among the people ("flock") and engage in the social needs of the community. Doing so, one may fulfill the adage of engaging in both Torah study and communal activity. For R. Yaakov had learned from the Besht's interpretation of M. Avot 2:2, "[Study of] Torah that doesn't include work results in sin," that one must take one's spiritual activity and transform it into concrete worldly deeds (ibid., 36a). In this teaching, the Besht transforms the older ideal of combining study with labor into a new Hasidic value, namely, to use the spiritual power of study when one engages in the works of the world.
3. R. Levi Yitzḥak interpreted the foregoing Song passage with other ideals in mind. For him, a key tension was the difference between persons who served

God with the hope of a reward (a utilitarian worship) and those who served God for no reason other than that God is the creator of all being and existence (a worship "in truth"). To develop his teaching, the master notices two features: the verse addresses the seeker as a female ("If you do not know, O fairest of woman"), and the counsel is to "go out," that is, beyond oneself (*tze'i lakh*) among the flocks of the field. What can these features teach? To develop his point, the master begins with the second element and uses the prism of verse 7 in Psalm 36. The plain sense (*peshat*) of that verse is that "God will save man and beast." But a bold midrashic interpretation (*derash*) found in the Talmud suggests its spiritual sense. We are instructed that "People should make themselves into an animal" in the service of God (B. Ḥul. 5b). Picking up on this point, R. Levi says that a person who serves God for ulterior motives is merely a "man" whereas one who serves God without personal motives is both a "man and beast" (and thus will achieve spiritual salvation). Why? Because the service of this second (higher) type is of a feminine kind: the person simply receives the gifts and creation of God, and in this act of passive acceptance, the self divests itself of all personal desires and comes to a pure consciousness. Totally emptied of personal concerns (i.e., thinking in terms of means and ends), the mind becomes animal-like and the person serves God in truth. This is the spiritual *sod* of our Song passage.[158]

It is evident from the foregoing examples that Hasidic masters focus on various levels of religious and spiritual consciousness.

In conclusion, we turn to a teaching of a great modern spiritual master, R. Avraham Yitzḥak Ha-Kohen Kook (1865–1935), who was concerned with precisely these matters. Rav Kook composed a series of ongoing spiritual notes and reflections that have been variously collected and edited. One of his most celebrated works is called *'Orot Ha-Qodesh*, and it comprises the core of his spiritual vision.[159] In a radical rereading of the Song's first four words as interpreted in the Zohar (see above), this master develops a teaching of four kinds of song—each focused on one of four types of persons, who reflect four orientations to reality. The first kind of song is sung by a single individual, who sings the song of his or her soul and finds therein all that is necessary. The second kind of song is that of the nation, whereby individuals transcend their separate selves and become attached to their people; for Rav Kook this means love of the people of Israel. The third kind of song transcends the concerns of one's nation and sings the song of all humankind, and this attachment expands the heart into a universal love. Fourth is the song that comprises the totality of existence, whereby a person addresses all elements in the creation and celebrates them together in one great love.

But there is yet a consummate kind of song. It is the song of a person who can integrate all these separate songs into one unity. For such an individual, "All [the songs] interfuse in him at all times and all hours; and this perfection in its fullness ascends to become a holy song: a song of God (*El*), a song of Israel." For "*Israel* is the Song (Shir) of God (*El*)"—a fourfold song: as it says, a "Song of Songs by Solomon," who is the King of Peace, God.[160]

NOTES TO THE EXCURSUS

1. For these particular matters, see E. Touitou, "Shiṭato shel Rashbam 'al Reqa' Ha-Metzi'ut Ha-Hisṭorit shel Zemano," in *E. Z. Melammed Jubilee Volume* (Ramat Gan: Tel Aviv University Press, 1982), 48–74; and also his "La Renaisssance du 12e siècle et l'exégèse biblique de Rashbam," *Archives Juives* 24 (1984): 3–12. Overall, see M. Fishbane, "Bible Interpretation."

2. S. Kamin produced a major overview of Rashi's use of *Peshat* in *Rashi: Peshuṭo shel Miqra' u-Midrasho shel Miqra'* (Jerusalem: Magnes Press, 1986).

3. The passage is from MS Parma 655 and adduced by A. Grossman in *Ḥakhamei Tzarefat Ha-Ri'shonim* (Jerusalem: Magnes Press, 1995), 197. The phrase is: *melukkad ha-davar u-myushav 'al mekhono ve'al besiso*.

4. Rashi conspicuously uses the verb *yotzei'* in both cases: any *Miqra'* (scriptural passage) can *yotzei'* several meanings, but no *Miqra'* can *yotzei'* its contextual sense. The verb has a hermeneutical force—as in classical rabbinic Hebrew.

5. I disagree with the contention of S. Kamin, "Dugma' be-Feirush Rashi," that the term marks a Jewish typological reading to counter Christian uses of theological types. The term is in the Midrash (SongsR 1.viii.1), and I think that Rashi's usage conforms to its figurative sense. The examples I bring below must stand for others. On this topic, see also the comments of I. Ta-Shma, "'Al Ha-Perush La-Piyyuṭim Ha-'Aramiyyim She-be-Maḥazor Viṭry," *Kiryat Sefer* 57 (1982): 703, where he indicates that Rashi is not the first to use the term *dugma'* or *dimyon* to connote a historical figure or parable, referring to terms already used by the poet Yannai. On this point, see M. Zulay, "'Inyanei Lashon Be-Fiyyuṭei Yannai," in *Yedi'ot Ha-Makhon Le-Ḥeiqer Ha-Shirah Ha-'Ivrit BiYrushalayim* 6 (1946): 183–84.

6. The lexical sense is called the *bei'ur*, *lashon*, or *dibbur* of a passage, and the thematic sense is called the *mashma'*, *'inyan*, or *seider ha-devarim*.

7. In SongsR 1.i.2, following a discussion in which certain details are not transmitted to R. Ishmael because he "was young" (i.e., not yet worthy of complicated or esoteric matters), there follows a version of a comment on the phrase, "lambs (*kevasim*) . . . for your clothing" (Prov. 27:26); we are told that the use of the word *kevasim* teaches that when your students are young, you should "hide [or: suppress]" (*mekhabeish*) [inappropriate] teachings of Torah; however, when they grow up (mature), you may reveal to them the secrets of Torah (*sitrei Torah*). It is this latter phrase that caught Rabbi Shlomoh's eye and that he used in an eschatological sense (as a new kiss of Torah).

8. Rashbam thus interprets the person Agur in Prov. 30:1 as Solomon, and he links this interpretation to the reference to Solomon's great "wisdom" in 1 Kings 5:9–13, said to be "greater than all the wisdom of the people of the east" (people of Kedem); this wisdom resulted in the composition of 3,000 parables and 1,005 songs. All this caught Rashbam's eye and had long since been noted in relation to the Song of Songs (see also in the commentary).

9. However, this point is alluded to at the beginning of the commentary itself.

10. This final phrase is in MS St. Petersberg 1.21 (Hebrew University microfilm 51073).

11. S. Japhet draws a similar conclusion; see her discussions in *Peirush R. Shemu'el ben Meir*, 25–27, 79–84.

12. See the commentaries of Kara and Anon. 1 noted below, as well as the work edited by Hübsch and Japhet, mentioned in n. 15 below and referred to in the commentary as MsP.

13. Ibn Ezra speaks similarly of the second type in his short commentary at v. 1.

14. See the entries on the verbal stem *ḥashaq* in E. Ben-Yehudah, *A Complete Dictionary of Ancient and Modern Hebrew*, vol. 3–4 [Hebrew] (Jerusalem: Hotza'at Laor, 1948). Cf. the observations of Japhet, "The Lover's Way," 868–69.

15. This is the "Anonymous Commentary" edited by H. J. Matthews, cited in my commentary as "Anon. I." This is a work combining acute philological analysis with remarkable physical depictions of human love. The preceding anonymous commentary (Type Two 1) was initially published by A. Hübsch in *Die Fünf Megillot* (1866), and reedited with an extensive introduction dealing with philological and thematic comparisons of contemporary commentaries by S. Japhet, "Peirush Anonimi Le-Shir Ha-Shirim" (2011). See her extensive notes.

16. H. Brody published the poem in *Diwan des Abu-l-Hasan Jehuda ha-Levi* (Berlin, 1894–1930 [reprint; Farnsborough: Greg, 1971]), 2:49. Brody identified the anonymous commentator's citation with this poem in his review of Matthew's edition of our anonymous commentator; see *Zeitschrift für Hebräische Bibliographie* 1 (1896): 43. He also noted the small variation between the commentary citation and the poem (e.g., *'al derekh* instead of *'al lekhyeikh*). Japhet, "The Lover's Way," 869, has observed these matters. There are numerous other references to the Song of Songs in the Halevi poem, and it is an excellent instance of a poem made up of a catena of scriptural citations (in this case, particularly from the song).

17. The conclusion to this line is, of course, a playful allusion to the initial blessing found in the daily *Shaḥarit* service, itself based on Isa. 45:7.

18. These are followed by a brief episode about a young girl, a reference to the thousand songs in 8:8–12, and a final coda in 8:13–14.

19. See, especially, 40–91.

20. Cf. the studies by F. Dornsieff, "Ägyptische Liebeslieder, Hohes Lied, Sappho, Theokrit"; and M. Rozelaar, "Shir Ha-Shirim 'al Reqa' Ha-Shirah Ha-Eroṭit Ha-Yevanit Ha-Hellenisṭit."

21. See G. Cohen, "The Song of Songs and the Jewish Religious Mentality," 13–14.

22. These and other terms in the biblical argot significantly were part of a common ancient Near Eastern treaty terminology. See the concise and fundamental studies of M. Weinfeld, "Ha-Berith ve-Haḥesed—'Bond and Grace'—Covenantal Expression in the Hebrew Bible and the Ancient World: A Common Heritage" [Hebrew], *Lešonnenu* 36 (1971–72): 85–105; and "Covenant Terminology in the Ancient Near East and Its Influence on the West," *Journal of the American Oriental Society* 93 (1973): 190–99. NJPS translates "with goodness and mercy" at v. 21, but this misses the technical language of love and covenant at play in the passage.

23. An exact rendition of these terms is difficult for they convey deep and obligating emotions simultaneously. In this use of older prophetic images, the reference to the "wife of youth" (v. 6) harks back to Jer. 2:3 and the terms "*ḥesed* of your youth" and the bridal espousals with God. Isaiah 50:1 states that God did not divorce Israel or give her a "bill of divorce"; Ibn Ezra notes the contradiction between this statement and Jer. 3:8.

24. The translation is formulated to highlight the responsive terminology (*na'im* is best rendered "handsome," as in the Ugaritic usage, not "beautiful" as in NJPS).

25. Cf. the comment of S. Leiberman, "Mishnat Shir Ha-Shirim," 118: "The 'day' of giving (*matan*) the Song of Songs is on the model of the 'day' of 'The Giving of the Torah' (*matan Torah*)."

26. The link in this case is both thematic and verbal. Regarding the latter, the Sifra unit begins with an explication of the word *va-yhi* ("And it was") found in both Exod. 40:17 and Lev. 9:1 (the frame events of the erection and dedication of the shrine), taken to mean "joy," which is the key emotional term in Songs 3:11. The rabbis connected the divine speech in Lev. 1:9 to the day of the erection of the tabernacle, specified in Exod. 40:17.

27. See in Pesiqta de-Rav Kahana, *Va-yhi Be-Yom* 1.3 in B. Mandelbaum, ed. (New York: Jewish Theological Seminary of America, 1962), 1:7. This unit also refers to the Tabernacle as woven with crimson threads; and earlier in 1.2, the crimson in Solomon's palanquin is correlated with the Ark hanging in the Tabernacle (thus establishing their connection).

28. See the text compiled by J. N. Epstein and E. Z. Melammed (Jerusalem: Hillel Press, 1955), 143.

29. For another instance of *meforash* in these Tannaitic sources, see below. In other instances, the verb *peireish* was used in an early Amoraic tradition to refer to the fact that certain condensed and esoteric phrases in the Torah dealing with the creation (Gen 1:1, 3) were "explicated" in the Prophets and Writings (Isa. 40:22; Job 37:6; and Ps. 104:2, respectively). See GenR 1.7; in the Theodor-Albeck edition, p. 6.

30. The formulation in Midrash Shir Ha-Shirim (ed. Grünhut) is prolix, as noted by W. Bacher in his review of this edition ("Un Midrasch sur Le Cantique," 237, n. 2). The counter term to the Song, whose style is *dehuqah*, is *meruvaḥim*, which refers to songs that are "spaced out" (i.e., with an expanded texture). For this word used in a botanic sense, see J. Shevi. 2, end.

31. See in the edition of Horovitz-Rabin, 202. I have smoothed out the dialogical references.

32. Another version of this episode occurs in SifDeut 305 (op. cit., 325). In this case the phrase used by R. Yoḥanan ben Zakkai (regarding Song 1:8) upon his chance encounter with the young woman is: "All my life I sought (the meaning of) this passage and (now) I have found it" (*kol yamai biqqashti miqra' zeh u-mtza'tiv*). In this version, moreover, the word for "lowly" nation is *shefeilah* (not *pegumah*), and the word *gediyotayikh* ("your kids") is "emended" to yield *geviyotayikh* ("your bodies")—thereby emphasizing the physical debasement that Israel would endure. The midrashic play involves the slightest orthographical manipulation (*dalet* to *vav*).

33. This source was mentioned earlier.

34. Overall, see the discussion of this material in M. Cohen, *The Shi'ur Qomah: Liturgy in Pre-Kabbalistic Jewish Mysticism* (Lanham, MD: University Press of America, 1963); cf. p. 111 for uses of the Song. On the question of the antiquity of these inquiries, see G. Scholem, *Jewish Gnosticism, Merkavah Mysticism, and Talmudic Tradition* (New York: Jewish Theological Seminary of America, 1963), ch. 6, (also referring to Origen); and S. Lieberman, "Mishnat Shir Ha-Shirim" (appendix D of Scholem's work), where he demonstrates a tannaitic dating, especially on the basis of the visions of the divine figure asserted by various ancient sages. Cf. the summation in Scholem, *The Mystical Shape of the Godhead* (New York: Schocken, 1991), 22–32.

35. See the extensive documentation provided by Lieberman in his "Mishnat Shir Ha-Shirim," Appendix D of Scholem's *Jewish Gnosticism*.

36. See the many textual references to both terms found in *Konkordanz zur Hekhalot-Literatur*, ed. P. Schäfer (Tübingen: J. C. B. Mohr, 1988), 2:443–44 and 635–36. Cf. further in the commentary.

37. Precisely this dialectal form occurs (in the singular) in Songs 1:5, "I am dark, but comely (*na'vah*)."

38. The role of the Song of Songs in the relations between early Judaism and Christianity has been the subject of serious consideration, beginning with the seminal study by E. E. Urbach, "The Homiletical Interpretation of the Sages and the Exposition of Origen on Canticles, and the Jewish-Christian Disputation." Subsequent studies were offered by R. Kimelman, "Rabbi Yohanan and Origen on the Song of Songs," and in the evaluative essay by A. Goshen-Gottstein, "Polemomania: Methodological Reflections." In addition, formulations found in Origen's commentary may also help elucidate midrashic sources, as shown by M. Hirshman, "Love and Holiness: The Midrash on Song of Songs and Origen's Homilies," in his *Rivalry of Genius*, ch. 8.

39. See the discussion of this theme in R. Le Déaut, *La Nuit Pascale; essai sur le signification dela Pâque juive à partir du Targum d'Exode XII, 42* (Rome: Pontifical Biblical Institute, 1963).

40. The entire *piska'* 5 occurs in the Mandelbaum edition, 1:78–108; the units citing Song 2:8–13 appear on pp. 88–98. These comprise a wide-ranging collection of Amoraic sermons for the occasion.

41. Pesiqta Rabbati 15 (Ish Shalom edition, 70b–76a) preserves a parallel collection of sermons.

42. At the end, the editor adds other verses: sec. 16 ends with Exod. 12:2 but is conjoined to sec. 17, which adds v. 3; and sec. 18 ends with Exod. 12:2 but is conjoined to sec. 19, which adds v. 9.

43. See in the Theodor-Albeck edition, 2:680–81.

44. For an analysis of the thematic and theological aspects of this entire pericope in SongsR, see my study "Anthological Midrash and Cultural Paideia."

45. For a discussion of Abraham's martyrdom (exegetically portrayed) and related examples, see D. Green, *The Aroma of Righteousness*, 178–96.

46. The translation here is in accord with the rabbinic interpretation of it; NJPS renders "Do not wake or rouse love until it please."

47. The phrase *yiggalu misṭorin* ("reveal mysteries") was understood by MatKeh as referring to *sodot ha-'ibbur* ("the mysteries of lunar intercalation"). Regarding the tradition in B. Sanh. 111a, see the comments of Rabbi Shlomoh and Tosafot regarding the "mysteries." See also the discussion in the Commentary.

48. NJPS turns her odd request to flee into a plea to "hurry" to the hills of spices. It thus seems to import a messianic coda into the translation.

49. See, M. B. Lerner, "The First Printing of the Five Megillot: Studies in the Work Methods of the Hebrew Printers in Constantinople and Pisaro," in *Yad Le-Heman: A Collection of Articles in Memory of A. M. Haberman* [Hebrew], ed. Z. Malachi (Jerusalem: R. Mas, 1977), 289–311.

50. A full study of manuscripts and translation techniques, with full documentation, appears in P. Alexander's work *The Targum of Canticles*, based on his earlier studies.

51. The noun *dodim* is taken as "lovers" rather than "(with) love," here and in SongsR.

52. This translation follows the sense perceived by the Targum; NJPS is interpretative in a different way (see Peshat).

53. The Judeo-Arabic translation with midrashic features of R. Saadia Gaon must be mentioned in this context as well. It had a great (and ongoing) impact on many communities; see the edition of Kafiḥ in the bibliography, with his introduction and notes. For an important new text demonstrating Saadia's use of midrashic materials with reference to the Song of Songs and other songs of Scripture, see Ḥ. Ben-Shammai, "Metzi'ah 'Aḥat She-Hi' Shtayim: Peirush Ha'azinu le-Rav Shemu'el ben Ḥofni u-Feirush Va-Yosha' Le-Rab Sa'adiah Ga'on BiKhtav Yad Nishkaḥ," in *Kiryat Sefer* 61 (1986–87): 320–26.

54. The interested student should also consult the achievements of the Karaite commentators and the presentation of their

works with selected examples and analysis by D. Frank, "Karaite Commentaries on the Song of Songs from Tenth-Century Jerusalem" and the materials in his book *Search Scripture Well*.

55. For the former, see *Rabbi Eleazar Mi-Wormayza, Derashah Le-Pesaḥ*, ed. S. Immanuel (Jerusalem: Mekize Nirdamim, 2006), 67–70; for the latter, see *Derashot R"Y ibn Shu'aib*, ed. Z. Metzger (see bibliography under Ibn Shu'aib), 223–34.

56. The work of this Hasidic circle and the teachings of other masters have entries in the bibliography and represent an important forum for the impact of the Song with its midrashic meanings.

57. For an overview with specific examples, see L. Lieber, *Let Me Sing to My Beloved*; for a detailed study of one massive poem by R. Meshullam, see my "Polysystem and Piyyuṭ." A list of *piyyuṭ* compositions bearing on the Song, with authors, appears in the bibliography.

58. My translation of the Hebrew, published in Y. Fraenkel, ed., *Maḥazor Li-Rgalim: Pesaḥ* (Jerusalem: Koren, 2003), 142. The core passage in the Midrash is SongsR 1.i.2, built around puns on the word *shir* (song); that play is found in the poem with various others. Line 3 alludes to Num. 21:18 (and in the Midrash these chieftains recited it at the dedication of the Tabernacle); the reference to its recitation in the Temple (with the verb *sadar*, provides a kind of etiology to the recitation of the Song in Piyyuṭ); the reference to (the saintly ones of) Israel in line 4 alludes to Dan. 12:4 (who, in Gen. Rabbah 68.21, recite it to God and the angels); and the final line uses Prov. 31:28 (to suggest a legal term, adduced earlier as a pun on *'asher*).

59. See in the Finkelstein edition, p. 55. I have examined the traditions there in my *Kiss of God*, 398, and discussed many of the transformations of the theme and its use in rituals in subsequent chapters. Note the reuse of this passage in Baḥya ibn Paquda's *Ḥovot Ha-Levavot*, Gate 10 (Love of God); E. de Vidas considers it exegetically in his *Rei'shit Ḥokhmah* in the first section *Sha'ar Ha-'Ahavah*.

60. J. Whitman, *Interpretation and Allegory*, 2 notes the sense of allegory as reading in the light of "something else" or to "say one thing in terms of another." On the hermeneutical issues of "double sense," see P. Ricoeur, "The Problem of the Double Sense." More broadly, see M. Bloomfield, "Allegory as Interpretation." For a consideration of allegory in Jewish sources more broadly, see M. Fishbane, "L'Allégorie dans la Pensée, la Littérature et la Mentalité Juives," in *Allégorie des Poètes, Allégorie des Philosophes: Études sur La Poétique et L'Herméneutique de L'Allegorie de L'Antiquité à La Réforme*, edited by G. Dahan and R. Goulet (Paris: Vrin, 2005), 89–112.

61. For different kinds of models, cf. the essay by P. Allen, "Plato, Aristotle, and the Concept of Woman in Early Jewish Philosophy." For the tension between soul and body in these allegories in the Middle Ages among Jewish thinkers, see H. Malter, "Personification of Soul and Body: A Study of Judeo-Arabic Literature."

62. The love poetry of Ibn Khalfon gives strong evidence of songs of "desire"; cf. *Shirei Yitzḥaq ibn Khalfon*, ed. A. Mirsky (Jerusalem, 1961), 63. The desire for a "gazelle" in the poetry of Mar Shaul is far bolder; cf. *Shirim Ḥadashim Min Ha-Genizah*, ed. Ḥ. Schirmann (Jerusalem: Israel Academy of Sciences, 1966), 158. How one should evaluate this theme is subject to diverse views. J. Schirmann, "The Ephepe in Medieval Hebrew Poetry," *Sefarad* 15 (1955): 55–68, reflects a moderated assessment; less restrained is the position of N. Roth, "'Deal Gently with the Young Man': Love of Boys in Medieval Hebrew Poetry of Spain," *Speculum* 57 (1982): 20–51. For a full discussion of the concordance between secular Hebrew love poems and their Arabic types, see I. Levin, "Biqqashti," passim.

63. See Ḥ. Schirmann, *Ha-Shirah*, 2:166 (no. 15); and *Divan Shmu'el Ha-Nagid*, ed. D. Yarden (Jerusalem: Hebrew Union College, 1966), 284 (no. 133).

64. See Ḥ. Schirmann, *Ha-Shirah*, 1:167–68 (no. 18); and *Divan Shmu'el Ha-Nagid*, 288 (no. 140). I translated *libbebhuni* as a "pierced" heart to capture the double entendre of *leibh* as "heart" (here, "enthused"), and the stem *l-b-b* as pierced—a meaning adduced by Ibn Janaḥ in his *Sefer Ha-Shorashim*, 238. Cf. Peshat.

65. See *Divan Shmu'el Ha-Nagid*, 221 (no. 75, lines 12–13). The citations are from Song 5:10 and 7:5, respectively. The Nagid specifically refers to the criticism in no. 18, lines 55–58 (p. 61) and remonstrates with his pure intent.

66. See his commentary to M. Avot 1:16, *Mishnah 'im Peirush Ha-Rambam*, vol. 2 (*Seder Nezikin*), Y. Qafiḥ edition (Jerusalem: Mosad Ha-Rav Kook, 1965), 419.

67. See the letter and response in *Iggerot Ha-Rambam*, 3rd ed., ed. Y. Shilat (Jerusalem: Shilat, 1995) 1:425–31.

68. The Arabic phrase for such love songs is *ash'ār al-ghazal*.

69. See Yisrael Moshe Ḥazzan, *Sefer Teshuvot Ha-Ge'onim 'im Haggahot 'Iyyei Ha-Yam* (Livorno, 1869), #152.

70. See *Mivḥar Ha-Shirah Ha-'Ivrit*, ed. Ḥ. Brody and M. Weiner, vol. 1, abbrev. with addenda by M. Ḥabermann (Jerusalem: Rubin Mas, 1963), appendix, 21–22. The poem is an *'ahavah* for *Shemini 'Atzeret*.

71. *Shirei Ha-Qodesh Le-Rabbi Shelomo ibn Gabirol*, ed. D. Yarden (Jerusalem, 1980), 2:468 (no. 144); my translation.

72. See famously, A. Altmann and S. M. Stern, *Isaac Israeli: A Neo-platonic Philosopher of the Early Tenth Century* (Oxford: Oxford University Press, 1958); and also S. M. Stern, "Ibn Hasday's Neoplatonist—A Neoplatonic Treatise and His Influence on Isaac Israeli and the Longer Version of the Theology of Aristotle," *Oriens* 8–14 (1961): 58–120.

73. See Ḥ. Schirmann, *Ha-Shirah*, 2:514–15 (no. 220), and *Shirei Qodesh Le-Rabbi Yehudah Halevi*, ed. D. Yarden (Jerusalem, 2000), 2:372–73 (no. 153). There is a small variant in the two publications; the former has *qumi* in line 4; the latter reads *rumi*. The poem is a *reshut* for the Intermediate Sabbath of Passover. This instance of the redemption of the soul (and the passage from the Song) was deftly adduced by B. Septimus, "He'arot Le-Divrei Ḥazal," 612–13.

74. See *Ḥay ben Meqitz*, in the edition of I. Levin (Tel Aviv, 1983), 49, 57; for a later version see *Ibn Tufayl's Hayy ibn Yaqzān*, trans. by L. Goodman (Chicago: Univ. of Chicago Press, 2003). These passages are also adduced by Rosenberg, "Ha-Parshanut," 136–37.

75. See in the *Kitâb Ma'âni*, ed. I. Goldziher, ch. 8, 26, for the list of epithets, 30–31 for the references to Song 7:1; and in the Hebrew version, *Sefer Torot Ha-Nefesh*, trans. Broydé, 33 and 38–40, respectively.

76. A careful treatment of the (adduced) title, and consideration of the background and focus of the work, appears in M. Plessner, "Kavvanato shel Kitab Ma'ani Alnafs Ha-Meyuḥas Le-R. Baḥya ibn Paquda u-Mqomo be-Toledot ha-Maḥashavah ha-Yhudit," *Kiryat Sefer* 48 (1972–73): 491–98.

77. See the full and analytic introduction in part one of the edition of Marciano, which also details philosophical features and influences (especially on Ibn Sahula).

78. These comments appear in his commentary on Ecclesiastes, trans. with an introduction by J. Robinson, *Samuel Ibn Tibbon's Commentary*. References below are to the paragraphs of that work. The forthcoming edition of the Hebrew manuscript is entitled *Sefer Nefesh Ha-Adam: Perush Qohelet li-Shmuel b. Yehudah ibn Tibbon* (Jerusalem: The World Union of Jewish Studies).

79. In his introduction, Gersonides states that he had "not found any [other] commentary on it [Song of Songs] that could be construed as a [correct] explanation of the words of this scroll"—and this despite the geographical proximity and thematic similarities with the commentary of Ibn Tibbon. On this issue, see M. Kellner, "Communication or the Lack Thereof."

80. Regarding his philosophical comments, Ibn Aqnin (Halkin ed., fol. 4b) remarks that "we have not discovered

among the predecessors anyone who has anticipated us in it or suggested any of it in the slightest; and again (at 8:4; Halkin ed., fol. 110a), he praises "God for the wisdom He revealed to us and the secrets that He divulged to us to a degree of which no predecessor of ours was aware." Cf. the preceding note for Gersonides' assertion.

81. For this date, see A. Halkin, "Ibn 'Aknin's Commentary," 404.

82. See his formulations in the Introduction to the *Guide*.

83. See his *Book of Beliefs and Opinions* (2:13)

84. The pertinent passage in Maimonides (*Guide* III: 51) suggested that the ultimate conjunction of the soul with Divinity occurred at the time of death (this being the "kiss"); but the formulation is ambiguous, and the dominant view was to regard the divinization of the soul to be postmortem when all bodily constraints had terminated. A full study of the notion of final conjunction appears in Afterman, *Deveiqut*, passim.

85. *Malmad Ha-Talmidim*, 162b (sermon on *parashat Ve-'ethannan*).

86. See Samuel's discussion in his Commentary on Ecclesiastes, para. 65–68.

87. Samuel cited Gen. 2:16, namely, "of every tree of the garden you may freely eat." As Robinson astutely notes (in his edition, 184, n. 283), "The beginning of the verse is: *And the* LORD *God commanded the man, saying*... Thus philosophy is not only permitted but required; it is, as it were, a divine command."

88. Cf. in Samuel's Commentary on Ecclesiastes, para. 41–48.

89. Ms. London 238, 2, fol. 83b 1–2; see p. 198 in Ravitzky's transcription.

90. See details in Marciano's edition (dissertation, vol. 2, 48–51); based on Ms. Livorno, 7.

91. See his *Peirush Le-Shir Ha-Shirim*, in *Sheloshah Peirushim* (Constantinople, 1544), without pagination; cited by Halkin, "Ibn 'Aknin's Commentary," 412, n. 101, from the edition of Akrish, 2a; and see in I. H. Last, *'Asarah Kelei Khesef*, Ibn Kaspi's commentary on the Song.

92. See at Song 3:1, and elsewhere.

93. See the *Peshat* commentary for philological details.

94. Cf. Targum Onqelos *de-vatrai*.

95. See in Halkin's edition, comments at 4:13, 5:11, and 8:4 (where he speaks of revealing the special treasures of this "profound" work).

96. I develop this matter at length in the Introduction. The multiple displacements are to protect the content.

97. See Al-Fawwāl's discussion, ad loc.

98. See the text (Oxford Ms. Pococke 320, fol. 7a–8a) produced by Fenton in "Peirush Mysṭi," 542–43. It was first identified and published by P. Kokovzov, "Tanḥum Yerushalmi's Commentary of the Book of Jonah," in *Festschrift Baron Rosen* (Saint-Petersburg, 1897), 163–65 (an appendix to his article). I have followed Fenton's translation in the English version of the above article, "A Mystical Commentary on the Song of Songs in the Hand of David Maimonides II," in *Esoteric and Exoteric Aspects in Judeo-Arabic Culture*, ed. B. Hary and H. Ben-Shammai (Leiden: Brill, 2006), 26–27.

99. The Arabic phrase is *bilisān al-ḥāl*.

100. The extent of Tanḥum's work (other than the manuscript noted above) is debatable. Fenton, "Peirush," 542, n. 12, contended that he is the author of the anonymous commentary (no. 4; Sassoon 1147) in Qafiḥ, "Ḥamesh Megillot," 60–85, 106–29. Langerman, in "Yemini Interpretations," 150, rejected this contention, deeming it an independent work.

101. The topics recur in the texts published by Fenton in "Peirush" and "Some Judeo-Arabic Fragments," with many citations from the Arabic literature. On the impact of contemporary Sufi love literature and practices on the Jews of Egypt, see his *Deux Traités*, 47–55.

102. See in his *Highways to Perfection*, trans. S. Rosenblatt (Baltimore: John Hopkins University Press, 1938), 2:290.

103. For these materials, see Fenton, "Some Judeo-Arabic Fragments," 44–46, 53–56; trans. and with some supplements in "Peirush," 580–83.

104. See the source and Hebrew translation in Fenton, "Peirush," 546.

105. Ibid.

106. See Baḥya's *Ḥovot Ha-Levavot*, ed. Y. Qafiḥ (Jerusalem: Feldheim, 1973), 423–24.

107. This is exactly Fenton's suggestion, "Peirush," 547; a translation into Hebrew of the rich commentary appears on 549–77. The following excerpts are taken from this corpus.

108. This commentary appears in Qafiḥ, "Ḥamesh Megillot," 17–129. The opening fragment was first published by M. Friedländer, "Teḥilat," 51–57. Qafiḥ suggests the possibility that the fourth commentary also comes from Yemen; by contrast, Fenton has proposed that this is the work of Tanḥum (see above, n. 100).

109. Cf. the Arabic formulation in Qafiḥ, "Ḥamesh Megillot," 27. Langerman, "Yemenite Interpretations," 159–66, deals with the various occurrences of this maxim in Zechariah and adduces the Koranic and Sufi citations, among others. The important study by A. Altmann, "The Delphic Maxim in Medieval Islam and Judaism," in *Studies in Religious Philosophy and Mysticism* (Ithaca: Cornell University Press, 1969), 1–40, did not adduce Zechariah's commentary.

110. Ibid., 26.

111. *'Ayelet 'Ahavim*, 5b (pagination follows the edition noted in the bibliography).

112. Ibid., 9a–11a.

113. Ibid., 15a–b.

114. Ibid., 16a–18a.

115. Ibid., 24a–25b.

116. In an unusual comment, the phrase to "leap over the hills" is interpreted as one who "acts like an old man in his [extreme ascetic] practices" (*mitnaheig ke-zaqein be-ma'asav*), ibid., 24a, and elsewhere.

117. Ibid., 60b–63b and 65a–67a.

118. Citations below follow the English translation (see bibliography).

119. He cites many of the medieval and modern influences in the text and the notes. Hermann Cohen's name is conspicuously absent, oddly so, since Soloveitchik develops a neo-Kantian epistemology toward the end of his book, and key aspects of his existentialist approach reflect his critique of Cohen's idealism in his doctoral dissertation (s.v. Josef Solowiejczyk), *Das reine Denken und die Seinskonstitutuierung bei Hermann Cohen* (Berlin: Reuther and Reichard, 1932).

120. See chapter 1 in detail, where the complex dialectics are poetically depicted and offer a foreshadowing of Soloveitchik's overall interpretation. At each juncture, he asks "What does this mean?" and then, at the end of the chapter, offers this poignant epitome of the Song (*And From There*, 5): "The Song of Songs is the most wonderful and most astonishing poem of the divine ontic dialectics. It is the poem of the creation and the Creator in general, and of the Jewish nation and its God in particular."

121. See *And From There*, chapters 2 (A and B), 4, 13, and 19.

122. Ibid., 35–37.

123. Ibid., 148.

124. In his essay "Qol Dodi Dofeiq," Soloveitchik takes up the national allegorical dimension of this verse (Song 5:2), understanding it as a series of Divine appeals to the people Israel to mark the redemptive moment then occurring (the establishment of the State of Israel and the challenge to religious Zionism); he warns his readership not to miss the call of God in their day. The essay appears in *'Ish Ha-'Emunah* (Jerusalem: Mosad Ha-Rav

Kook, 1982), 65–106; for an English translation, see *Kol Dodi Dofek: Listen—My Beloved Knocks* (New York: Yeshiva University Press, 2006).

125. See M. Idel, "'In a Whisper'," for a comprehensive survey of this topic.

126. See *Origen: The Song of Songs*, trans. R. Lawson, 23; and in W. A. Baehrens, ed., *Origenes Werke*, vol. 8 (Leipzig: Hinrichs, 1925), I.5, 62. Origen notes the opening chapters of Genesis, the reference to the cherubim in Ezekiel 1, the building of the Temple, and the Song of Songs. Cf. Scholem, *Jewish Gnosticism*, 38:"There is no doubt but that this quotation refers to the fact that esoteric teachings were connected with the four texts enumerated."

127. Such mature persons were designated as *nisi quis ad aetatem perfectam maturamque pervenit*.

128. See P. Schäfer, ed., *Synopse zur Heikhalot-Literatur* (Tübingen: J. C. B. Mohr, 1981), 75 (text 167/B, at end); 179 (text 419/M, middle); 258 (text 704/N); and other briefer references.

129. For the text, see T. *Ḥag.* 2:1 in the edition of Lieberman (New York: Jewish Theological Seminary of America, 1962), 381, sec. 4. In his commentary on this passage in *Tosefta Ki-Fshuṭah, Seder Mo'eid*, vol. 5 (New York: Jewish Theological Seminary of America, 1962), 1290, lines 21–22, Lieberman completed the citation (given here in parentheses), deeming it central to the intent of the quote; and indeed the last part of the verse is adduced in the comment on this verse in SongsR (see Lieberman, ad loc., and also 1288–89). See also J. Dan, "*Ḥedrei Ha-Merkavah*," 51.

130. The passage appears in R. Ezra's Song commentary (attributed to Nachmanides); see *Kitvei Ramban*, II, 502. It is also cited in the mystical commentary on midrashic passages by R. Azriel; see I. Tishby, ed., *Peirush Ha-'Aggadot Le-Rabbi 'Azriel* (Jerusalem: Magnes Press, 1983), 70; and by R. Todros Abulafia; see M. Oron, ed., *Sha'ar ha-Razim Le-Rabbi Todros ben Yosef Abulafia* (Jerusalem: Mosad Bialik, 1989), 128.

131. For a full discussion of the work, its emergence, and its gnostic and mythic content, see G. Scholem, *Origins of the Kabbalah*, ed. R. J. Zwi Werblowsky, trans. Allan Arkush (Philadelphia: Jewish Publication Society, 1987), ch. 2, 49–198. See also the discussion of D. Abrams, *Sefer Ha-Bahir 'al pi Kitvei Ha-Yad Ha-Qedumim* (Los Angeles: Cherub Press, 1994), 1–54, and the bibliography appended.

132. For the text, see in the Abrams edition, para. 121, 205.

133. Ibid., 117.

134. The column is thus a kind of Cosmic Tree, yielding the fruit of "Being." On this symbolism in the Bahir, see E. Wolfson, "On the Tree that Is All." In para. 118, the "holy" citron is further defined as "the glory of all"—meaning, the glorious gradation of the supernal "All."

135. See his discussion of the symbolism of the species in the critical edition of the work by E. Wolfson, *The Book of the Pomegranate: Moses de Leon's Sefer Ha-Rimmon* (Atlanta: Scholar's Press, 1988), 181–82.

136. Scholem, *Origins of the Kabbalah*, 368–70, discussed the Gerona circle of 1210–60 and the place of R. Ezra within it as one of the "companions." For a review of Ezra's place in the Gerona circle and a study of his writings with a comparison of his Song commentary with that on the *Aggadot*, see I. Tishbi, *Ḥiqrei Qabbalah*, 3–10 and 11–35, respectively.

137. Although in a Parma manuscript the work was attributed to Ezra ben Solomon as early as 1387 (see Scholem, *Origins of the Kabbalah*, 371, n. 16), it was printed under the name of Nachmanides in the Altona 1794 edition. This faulty ascription still appears in C. Chavel's edition. The basis of a new text edition can be found in the work of G. Vajda, *Le Commentaire d'Ezra de Gérone sur le cantique des cantiques*. I have used the Jewish Theological Seminary's manuscript labeled Lutzki 1059.

138. M. Idel, *Kabbalah: New Perspectives* (New Haven: Yale University Press, 1988), 253, proposed "that the Kabbalah emerged in the late twelfth and early thirteenth centuries as a sort of reaction to the dismissal of earlier mystical traditions by Maimonides' audacious reinterpretation of Jewish esotericism and his attempt to replace the mystical traditions with a philosophical understanding." My comment extends this point to the commentaries on the Song.

139. See in A. Neubauer, "The Bahir and the Zohar," *Jewish Quarterly Review* 4 (1892): 357–59.

140. This comment is based on the observation (in different terms) made by E. Wolfson in "Asceticism and Eroticism in Exegesis of the Song," 96–97, in his discussion of Song 1:2 (adduced below), with which I largely agree (my translation varies at some points). I shall not attend to the historical and messianic dimension of the commentary, but this is a key component. Exile and rupture was a recurrent element in Ezra's sense of history and theosophy, undoubtedly derived from his master, Isaac the Blind.

141. *Kitvei Ramban*, II, 485.

142. R. Ezra uses terminology that reflects his own mystical tradition (thus there is a lower and higher Glory, the first being feminine, the second masculine). Other groups had different symbol systems and hierarchies (cf. the Bahir).

143. This work, from 1281, contains at the end the "oldest quotation" from the Zohar; see G. Scholem, *Major Trends in Jewish Mysticism* (New York: Schocken Books, 1941), 187; see also below, n. 147.

144. The only surviving manuscript, Oxford Neubauer 343, was published by A. Green, "Peirush Shir Ha-Shirim," with a detailed introduction that considers the influences and types of mystical exegesis. Regarding the latter, Green's point is well-taken that Ibn Sahula regularly alluded to mystical ideas using biblical proof texts; but there are other kinds of mystical comments at play, including some direct comments in the text, as suggested below.

145. The case has been asserted by G. Scholem, "Rabbi Moshe Mi-Burgos Talmido shel R. Yitzḥaq," *Tarbiz* 3 (1932): 269.

146. Ibn Laṭif's "'Iggeret Ha-Teshuvah" was published by A. Berliner, *Kovetz 'al Yad* 1 (1881). His responsum no. 35, 161, answering a query regarding the Song of Songs, gave a summary of some secrets of various verses. For a synoptic view of the parallels with Ibn Sahula's commentary, see A. Green, "Peirush Shir Ha-Shirim," 402.

147. The oldest citation is part of a comment on Genesis, preserved in a 14th-century (Cambridge University Library) manuscript, published by G. Scholem, "Parashah Ḥadashah Mi-Midrash Ha-Ne'elam," in *Jubilee Volume in Honor of Louis Ginzberg* (New York: Jewish Theological Seminary of America, 1945), Hebrew sec., 425–46. The features of the Midrash Ha-Ne'elam are discussed by G. Scholem in *Major Trends of Jewish Mysticism* (New York: Schocken Books, 1941), 181–86.

148. Recent research strongly suggests that the Zohar was the product of a circle of mystics (whose identities can be traced); see Y. Liebes, "Keitzad Nitḥabber Sefer Ha-Zohar," in *Sefer Ha-Zohar ve-Doro*, edited by Y. Dan, in *Meḥqerei Yerushalayim bi-Maḥshevet Yisrael* 8 (1989), 1–71. The entire volume deals with other aspects of the subject. Liebes has also treated the larger notion of eros in the Zohar, in its multiform dimensions, in "Zohar ve-'Eros," 67–119.

149. On the textual history of the introduction, see D. Abrams, "'Eimatai Ḥubberah Ha-Haqdamah Le-Sefer Ha-Zohar?' Ve-Shinuyim Bi-Ṭfasim Shonim shel Ha-Haqdamah she-bi-Dfus Mantova," *Asufot* 8 (1994): 211–26.

150. For analysis of the many strata of the Zohar dealing with the Song of Songs, with many major interpretative insights, see the dissertation of S. Asulin, *Ha-Parshanut Ha-Misṭit Le-Shir Ha-Shirim*, passim.

151. On the *Shekhinah* in classical Judaism, see E. E. Urbach, *The Sages: Their Concepts and Beliefs* (Cambridge: Harvard Uni-

versity Press, 1987), ch. 3; regarding the *Shekhinah* and the emergence of a feminine component with Divinity, see G. Scholem, *On the Mystical Shape*, ch. 4; and *On the Kabbalah*, ch. 3.

152. See previous note; also in A. Green, "Shekhinah," who then emphasizes this coalescence of images as "*a Jewish response to the great popular revival of Marian piety in the twelfth century Western Church*" (his emphasis) with many structural comparisons adduced. These latter cannot be doubted, and they may be parallel expressions of symbolic imagery in two cultures dealing with mystical readings of the same text. For a rejection of a comparison of the Virgin Mary with the *Shekhinah*, see Y. Liebes, "Ha-'Omnam." P. Schaefer has found other cultural reasons to suggest Christian influence in "Daughter, Sister, Bride, and Mother: Images of the Femininity of God in the Early Kabbala, *Journal of the American Academy of Religion* 68 (2000): 221–42, and subsequently in his *Mirror of His Beauty: Feminine Images of God from the Bible to the Early Kabbala* (Princeton: Princeton University Press, 2002).

153. Overall, see M. Fishbane, *The Exegetical Imagination: On Jewish Thought and Theology* (Cambridge, MA: Harvard University Press, 1998), chapter 7 ("The Book of *Zohar* and Exegetical Spirituality").

154. There is reason to suppose that this linkage was of great antiquity. In a midrash composed in Hebrew and Arabic, published by Friedländer in the Steinschneider Festschrift (see bibliography), 52, we read that when R. Akiva was expounding the Song of Songs and came to the verse *Let Him kiss me*, Rabban Gamliel broke into tears; and when he was asked why by his disciples, he said: "Because one may not expound the Work of the Chariot even before one person"—however skilled in esoteric lore. Such a prohibition is not found in the Mishnah or other early sources, but it is attached in the above text to an old injunction imposed by the sages upon the community, stating that one may recite the Song according to its straightforward sense (*ʿal pashṭeih*), but only teach its wisdom (*ḥokhmah*) to a judge or another worthy (B. Ḥag. 13a). Although the midrash is found in a 14th-century Yemenite text, it has been argued that it is an old tradition and that the rabbinic restrictions are in response to early Christian interpretations of the Song (and efforts to keep Jewish esoteric meanings secret). See S. Lieberman, *Midreshei Teiman*, 2nd ed. (Jerusalem: Wahrmann Books, 1970), 12–14.

155. Because of considerations of space, we make only a brief mention of the unique commentary on the Song, *Sefer Tashaq*, produced sometime after 1304, and with evident knowledge of portions of the Zohar. A critical edition was produced by J. Zwelling (1975), and its references are followed here; he accepts the attribution of the work to R. Joseph of Hamadan, following A. Altmann, "Le-She'elat Meḥabbero shel Sefer Ṭaʿamei Ha-Mitzvot Ha-Meyuḥas Le-R. Yosef Gikatilla," *Kiryat Sefer*, 40 (1968): 262–64; see Zwelling, x. Overall, this commentary is a complex, intertextual correlation between the building of the Tabernacle in Exodus 25 and the Song (with many unusual terms and correlations; see the discussions in Zwelling's introduction). Section 1 is a commentary on Exodus 25 and Song 1:1–2:5 (folios 1–25b). After intervening materials (sec. 2–6), a final section (fragmentary) continues the initial commentary on folios 94a–98a; this section breaks off with the correlation between Exod. 25:7–8 and Song 2:6–9. Exodus 25 is the principle emphasis, and it is related to the archetype of Ezekiel's heavenly chariot. For the writer, the Song of Songs is a wedding song chanted by the two cherubim of the Tabernacle: the King = *'Arikh 'Anpin*, and the Bride = *Ze'ir 'Anpin*; see especially Zwelling at p. 12, re: the request *yishaqeini* ("Let Him kiss Me")—this being a request of *Tif'eret* to send pure oil into the upper and lower worlds (folio 3b). The mysteries are revealed by Divine aide (*besiyuʿa . . . min ha-shamayim*; Zwelling, folio 1b). The Song is "Holy of Holies" (folios 2b–3a) and hints at the conjunction (*ha-yiḥud*) between the Bride and Groom. A newly discovered manuscript of the work has been published by C. Mopsik, "Un manuscript inconnu de *Sefer Tashak* de R. Joseph Hamadan suivi d'un fragment inédit," *Kabbalah* 2 (1997): 169–205.

156. See *Kedushat Levi*, 280b and 281a–b.

157. *Ma'or Va-Shemesh*, I, 386a.

158. *Kedushat Levi*, 283b.

159. *'Orot Ha-Qodesh*, reprint; (Jerusalem: Mosad Ha-Rav Kook, 1963–64), I–III.

160. For the teaching, see ibid, II, 444–45 (*Shir Merubaʿ*, sec. 30).

BIBLIOGRAPHY

I. Primary Sources

A. Biblical Text

Breuer, M. "Ha-Nosaḥ u-Mqorotav." In *Five Scrolls* [Hebrew], edited by A. Ḥakham, 11–14. Da'at Miqra'. Jerusalem: Mossad Ha-Rav Kook, 1973.

Canticles. In *Qumran Cave 4.XI: Psalms to Chronicles*, edited by E. Ulrich. DJD XVI. Oxford: Clarendon, 2000.

Elliger, K., W. Rudolph, and H. P. Rüger. *Biblia Hebraica Stuttgartensia*. 4th ed. Stuttgart: Deutsche Bibelgesellschaft, 1990.

Tov, E. "Three Manuscripts (Abbreviated Texts?) of Canticles from Qumran Cave 4." *Journal of Jewish Studies* 46 (1995): 88–111.

B. Midrash and Targum

Aggadath Shir Hashirim. Edited by Solomon Schechter. Cambridge: Deighton Bell, 1896.

Alexander, P. S. *The Targum of Canticles: Translated, with a Critical Introduction, Apparatus, and Notes*. Vol. 17a: The Aramaic Bible. Collegeville, MN: Liturgical Press and London: T & T Clark, 2003.

Avot De-Rabbi Natan. Edited by S. Schechter. Revised edition with Prolegomenon by M. Kister. New York: Jewish Theological Seminary of America, 1997.

Bacher, W. "Un Midrasch Sur Le Cantique Des Cantiques." *Revue des Études Juives* 35 (1897): 230–39.

Bereischit Rabbah. Edited by J. Theodor and Ch. Albeck. 2nd ed. Jerusalem: Wahrmann Books, 1965.

Ginzei Midrash. Edited by Z. M. Rabinovitz. "Shir Ha-Shirim Rabbah," 83–100. Tel Aviv: Tel Aviv University Press, 1977.

Goldstein, N. "Midrash Shir Ha-Shirim Rabbah Bi-Khtav Yad Parma 1240." *Qovetz al Yad* 9 (1980): 1–24.

Kedari, T. "Shenei Qiṭ'ei Geniza Le-Midrash Shir Ha-Shirim Rabbah." *Qovetz al Yad* 2, no. 20 (2008): 3–47.

Lerner, M. B. "A Midrashic Commentary on the Song of Songs from the Time of the Geonim" [Hebrew]. *Qovetz al Yad* 8 (1966): 143–64.

——. "Collected Exempla: Studies in Aggadic Texts Published in the Genizot Series" [Hebrew]. *Kiryat Sepher* 61 (1986–87): 867–92.

——. "Le-Tzurato Ha-Qedumah Shel Midrash Shir Ha-Shirim Rabbah (Le-Fi Qit'ei Ha-Geniza)." *Teudah* 3 (1983): 83–90.

——. "Peirush Midrashi Le-Shir Ha-Shirim Mi-Ymei Ha-Beinayim." *Qovetz al Yad* 8 (1976): 141–64.

Mann, J. "Some Midrash Geniza Fragments." *Hebrew Union College Annual* 14 (1939): 303–58.

Mekhilta De-Rabbi Ishmael. Edited by H. Horovitz and I. Rabin. Jerusalem: Bamberger and Wahrmann, 1960.

Melamed, R. H. "The Targum to Canticles according to Six Yemen Mss. Compared with the 'Textus Receptus.'" *Jewish Quarterly Review* 11, 12 (1921–22): 1–20 and 57–117.

Midrash Rabbah Ha-Mevo'ar Shir Ha-Shirim. 4 vols. Jerusalem: Machon Ha-Midrash Ha-Mevo'ar, 1994.

Midrash Rabbah, Shir Ha-Shirim, Midrash Ḥazit. Edited by S. Dunsky. Jerusalem: Dvir, 1980.

Midrash Shemot Rabbah. Parashot 1–14. Edited by A. Shinan. Jerusalem and Tel Aviv: Dvir, 1984.

Midrash Shir Ha-Shirim *('Al Pi Ketav Yad Yashan Mi-Tokh Ha-Geniza She-be-Qahir)*. Edited by E. Halevi Grünhut. Jerusalem, 1897. Reprint, 2nd ed. with introduction and critical notes by R. Y. H. Wertheimer (Jerusalem: Ketav-Yad Sefer, 1981).

Midrash Suta. Hagadische Abhandlungen über Schir Ha-Schirim, Ruth, Echah Und Koheleth. Edited by Salomon Buber. Berlin: H. Itzkowski, 1894.

Midrash Tanḥuma. Edited by Saloman Buber. Vilna: Romm, 1885.

Miqra'ot Gedolot "Haketer": Ḥamesh Megillot. Edited by M. Cohen. Ramat-Gan: Bar-Ilan University Press, 2012.

Peirush Leqaḥ Ṭov 'al Megillat Shir Ha-Shirim, R. Ṭoviah b. Eliezer. Edited by A. Greenup. London: 1909.

Pesikta De Rav Kahana. Edited by B. Mandelbaum. Vol. 1–2. New York: Jewish Theological Seminary of America, 1962.

Pesiqta Rabbati. Edited by M. Ish Shalom. Vienna: Y. Kaiser, 1880.

Rabinovitz, Z. M. *Ginzei Midrash*. Tel Aviv: Tel Aviv University Press, 1977.

Scheiber, A. "Ein Fragment Aus Der Midrasch Schir Haschirim Rabba: Aus Der Kaufmann Geniza." *Acta Orientalia* 32 (1978): 231–43.

Shir Ha-Shirim Rabbah. [Standard Vilna edition.]

Shoḥer Ṭov. Edited by Saloman Buber. Vilna: Romm, 1891.

Sifre Bemidbar. Mahadurah Mevo'eret. Annotated ed. by M. Kahana. Vols. 1–3. Jerusalem: Magnes Press, 2001.

Sifrei 'Al Sefer Devarim. Edited by L. Finkelstein. 2nd ed. New York: The Jewish Theological Seminary of America, 1965.

Siphre De'be Rav. Edited by H. S. Horowitz. Jerusalem: Wahrmann Books, 1966.

Sperber, A. "Targum Song of Songs." *The Bible in Aramaic, Based on Old Manuscripts and Printed Texts*, 127–41. Leiden: E. J. Brill, 1968.

Torat Ḥayyim: Rut–Shir Ha-Shirim. Edited by M. Katzenelenbogen. Jerusalem: Mossad Ha-Rav Kook, 2011.

Wertheimer, S. A. *Midrash Ḥazita, Unknown Manuscript of Varia Lectiones, Published as "Liqquṭei Nusḥa'ot Mi-Shir Ha-Shirim Rabbah Ketav Yad."* Vol. 1, Battei Midrash. Jerusalem: Ketav ve-Sefer, 1980.

Yalquṭ Shim'oni, traditional editions, Part 2, Song of Songs; also the manuscripts printed in the appendix of Schechter, *Aggadath Shir Ha-Shirim* (see above).

C. Liturgy and Piyyuṭ

Piyyuṭ on the Song of Songs—with entries annotated as to the verses cited, regional practices, and where relevant, the place of the unit within Passover liturgy (i.e., *Shaḥarit*; *Tefillah*; or *Musaf* service for the first, second, seventh, or eighth day of the holiday), following. Critical editions of liturgical poets given by editor, followed by name (if known) and an annotation of the poetic liturgy using the Song of Songs; similarly, Maḥzor editions listed by editor, followed by listing the poets by name and their uses of the Song (with the pages in the Maḥzor edition).

Bernstein, S., ed. "Yotzeir le-Ḥol Ha-Mo'eid Pesaḥ." In *Piyyuṭim U-Fayṭanim Ḥadashim Mei-ha-Tequfah Ha-Bizanṭinit*, 86–99. Jerusalem: Solomon Press, 1951. Poem interprets all verses of the Song of Songs.

David, Y. "Yotzeir Le-Pesaḥ Le-Avraham Ha-Mekhuneh 'Ezraḥ Bar Metatiah." In *Yad Le-Heiman: Meḥqarim Be-Sifrut Ha-'Ivrit Shel Yemei Ha-Beinayim / A. M. Haberman Jubilee Volume*, edited by Zvi Malachi, 85–106. Jerusalem: Rubin Mass, 1977.

Davidson, I., ed. "Shir Ha-Shirim de-R. Shmuel Ha-Shlishi." *Ginzei Schechter 3: Piyyuṭim Ve-Shirim*, 59–92. New York: Hermon Press, 1969. Shemu'el Ha-Shlishi. This *piyyuṭ* interprets all verses of the Song of Songs.

——, editor. "Shiv'ah. Shir Ha-Shirim Le-R. Yannai." In *Ginzei Schechter 3: Piyyuṭim Ve-Shirim*, 11–16. New York: Hermon Press, 1928; reprinted 1969. Yannai (all verses adduced).

Elitzur, Sh. *Be-Todah Ve-Shir: Shiv'atot Le-'Arba' Ha-Parashiyyot Le-Rabbi Ele'azar Bi-Rabbi Kallir*, 41–45 (#1), 100–109 (#12), respectively. Eleazar Kallir: A *Shiv'ata* for *Parashat Sheqalim*, using Song 1:15 as frame verse, and another for *Parashat Ha-Ḥodesh*, both using Song 2:8–13 in successive stanzas. Jerusalem: R. Mas, 1991.

——. "Li-Mqomo Shel Ha-Yotzeir Be-Morashto Shel R. Eleazar Biribbi Qillir." *Tarbiz* (1997): 351–97. Materials from Song 1:1–4:9 (pp. 61–66); 1:14–3:8 (pp. 68–74); 6:2–5, 6:10–8:6 (pp. 74–78); 7:4–8:12 (pp. 55–58), [R. Shmuel He-Ḥaveir, Song 6:2–5 (pp. 74 f.)].

——. "Rei'shitam Shel Piyyuṭei Y"Ḥ," *Meḥqerei Yerushalayim Be-Sifrut 'Ivrit* 5: 1984.

Epstein, Kalonymos Kalman Halevi. *Ma'or Va-Shemesh*. Volume 1, *Rimzei Shir Ha-Shirim*, 344a–352b. 1842. Reprint: Jerusalem: Machon 'Even Yisrael, 1992.

Fleischer, E. *Piyyuṭei Shlomoh Ha-Bavli* (Jerusalem: Israel Academy of Science, 1973).

1. *'Or Yesha' Me'usharim*, a *Yotzeir* poem for Passover: (i) *yotzeir* unit interprets Song 1:1–3:10 (pp. 191–203); (ii) *silluq* interprets 3:11–5:10 (pp. 204–10); (iii) *'ophan* interprets 5:11–16 (pp. 210–13); (iv) *zulat* interprets 6:1–8:14 (pp. 213–20); (v) addition to *zulat* interprets 8:14 (pp. 221–22); (vi) *ge'ulah* interprets 8:14 (pp. 222–23).
2. *'Ashirah Va-'Azammerah Shemo*, a *Yotzeir* for Passover, by R. Eleazar (Ha-Kalliri?), in Addendum 2: (i) *yotzeir* unit uses incipits from Song 1:1–2:7 (pp. 371–73); (ii) *silluq* uses incipits from 2:8–4:11 (pp. 273–74); (iii) *'ophan* uses incipits from 4:12–6:3 (p. 374); (iv) *me'orah* uses incipits from 6:4–7 (p. 375); (v) *'ahavah* uses incipits from 6:8–11 (p. 375); (vi) *zulat* uses incipits from 6:12–8:14 (pp. 375–77).

——. "Le-Fitron Shel Qamah Ba'ayot Yesod Be-Mivneh Ha-Qedushta' Ha-Qelasit." In *Sefer Zikkaron Le-Ḥanokh Yalon*, edited by Y. Kutsher, S. Lieberman, and M. Kadari, 454–67. Ramat Gan: Meḥqere Bar-Ilan, 1973. An anonymous *Qedushta'* (Geniza ms.) integrating incipits from the entire Song of Songs.

——. "Luaḥ Mo'adei Ha-Shanah Be-Fiyyuṭ Le-R. Eleazar Bi-Rabbi Qillir," *Tarbiz* 52 (1983): 237–41 and 258–71, respectively. Eleazar Kallir: *Qerovah* for *Shabbat Eichah*, with incipits from 7:5–8:14, and *Qedushta* for *Shabbat Eichah* (?), with incipits from 2:6–7:4.

Fraenkel, A., editor. *Piyyuṭei R. Yeḥi'el Mi-Roma 'Avi R. Natan Ba'al 'Ha-'Arukh.'* Jerusalem: Mekize Nirdamim, 2007, 94–119. Yeḥi'el bar Avraham Mi-Roma: *Ma'arekhet Yotzeir Le-Pesaḥ* (all verses of the Song of Songs noted).

Frankel, Jonah, editor and annotator of *Maḥazor La-Regalim—Pesaḥ*. Jerusalem: Koren, 1993.

1. Shlomoh (Haqaṭan b. R. Yehuda) Ha-Bavli, *Yotzeir* for *Shaḥarit* First Day (*'Or Yesha'*), interpreting Song 1:1–3:10; Frankel, pp. 60–69. See also Fleischer (above, *Piyyuṭei Shlomoh Ha-Bavli*), pp. 191–203.
2. Mordechai Haqatan, *Yotzeir* for First Day, interpreting Song 3:11–4:12; Frankel, pp. 69–71.
3. Shlomoh Ha-Bavli, *Yotzeir*, interpreting Song 4:13–5:10; Frankel, pp. 71–73.
4. Anonymous, *Yotzeir* for Second Day (in Mayence, the First Day), interpreting Song 1:1–3:10; Frankel, pp. 74–81.
5. Meshullam b. R. Qalonymos, *Yotzeir* for Second Day, interpreting Song 3:11–4:1; Frankel, p. 82.
6. Shlomoh (Ha-Bavli) Ḥazaq, *'Ophan* for *Shaḥarit* First Day, interpreting Song 5:11–16; Frankel, pp. 88–90.

7. Anonymous, *'Ophan* for Second Day, interpreting Song 4:12–6:3; Frankel, pp. 90–91.
8. Mordechai Haqaṭan, *Zulat* for *Shaharit* First Day, interpreting Song 6:1–8:10; Frankel, pp. 94–96; per Fleischer, all composed by Shlomo Ha-Bavli, but Frankel notes only this attribution beginning with citation from 1:5 on p. 96.
9. Shlomoh b. R. Yehudah Ḥazaq (Ha-Bavli), *Zulat* for First Day, interpreting brief selections from Song (first reference 1:5; last 8:14); Frankel, pp. 96–98.
10. (Idem; but no specific attribution), conclusion to *Zulat* (Fleischer) in the form of a *Silluq* (Frankel), interpreting Song 8:14; Frankel, pp. 98–99.
11. Meshullam b. R. Qalonymos, *Zulat* for Second Day, interpreting Song 6:12–8:7; Frankel, pp. 100–102.
12. Shlomoh Haqaṭan (Ha-Bavli), *Ge'ulah* for *Shaḥarit* First Day, interpreting Song 8:14 (with verses from 2:7–9 and 5:16; plus blends); Frankel, pp. 103–4.
13. Meshullam (b. R. Qalonymos), *Ge'ulah* for Second Day, interpreting Song 8:14; Frankel, pp. 104–5.
14. Anonymous, *Qerovah* for *Shaḥarit*, recited on the First Day in Mayence, interpreting Song 1; 1–8:14 (divided by subunits); Frankel, 139–52 (following Fleischer, in *Sefer Ḥanokh Yalon*, 1974, pp. 454 ff). (i) *Magein* (Song 1:1–8; Frankel, pp. 139–140); (ii) *Meḥayyeh* (1:9–16; pp. 140–41); (iii) *Meshallesh* (1:17–2:5; pp. 141–42); (iv) *Piyyuṭ* 4 (1:1; p. 142); (v) *Piyyuṭ* 5 (2:6–14; p. 143); (vi) *Rihiṭ* (2:15–4:8; pp. 144–45); (vii) *Silluq* (4:9–5:14); (viii) *Qedushah* (5:15–6:10; pp. 149–50); *Qedushah* (6:11–7:11; pp. 150–51); *Qedushah* (8:10–14; p. 152).
15. Shim'on b. Yitzḥaq, *Yotzeir* for *Shaḥarit* on Sabbath of *Ḥol Ha-Mo'eid*, interpreting Song 3:11–5:9; Frankel, 299–300.
16. Anonymous, ibid., interpreting Song 1:1–3:10; Frankel, 304–10.
17. Binyamin b. R. Shemuel, ibid., interpreting Song 3:11–5:1; Frankel, pp. 311–13.
18. Idem, ibid., interpreting Song 5:2–8; Frankel, p. 314.
19. Shim'on b. Yitzḥaq, *'Ophan* for *Shaḥarit* on Sabbath of *Ḥol Ha-Mo'eid*, interpreting Song 5:10–6:3; Frankel, pp. 316–17.
20. Binyamin (b. R. Shemuel) Payyeṭan, ibid., interpreting Song 5:9–6:3; Frankel, p. 318.
21. Anonymous, *Me'orah* for *Shaḥarit* on Sabbath of *Ḥol Ha-Mo'eid*, interpreting Song 6:4–7; Frankel, p. 319.
22. Anonymous, *'Ahavah* for *Shaḥarit* on Sabbath of *Ḥol Ha-Mo'eid*, interpreting Song 6:8–11; Frankel, p. 320.
23. Shim'on b. Yitzḥaq, *Zulat* for *Shaḥarit* on Sabbath of *Ḥol Ha-Mo'eid*, interpreting Song 6:12–8:6; Frankel, pp. 322–23.
24. Idem., ibid., interpreting 8:7–14; Frankel, p. 324.
25. Binyamin b. R. (Shemu'el), ibid., interpreting Song 6:4–8:10; Frankel, pp. 325–27.
26. Shim'on (b. Yitzḥaq), *Ge'ulah* for *Shaḥarit* on Sabbath of *Ḥol Ha-Mo'ed*, interpreting Song 8:14; Frankel, pp. 328–30.
27. Kallir, R. Eleazar, *Yotzeir le-Pesaḥ*, interpreting Song 1:1–8:14, appendix B in Fleisher, *Piyyuṭei Shlomoh Ha-Bavli*, pp. 371–77.
28. Meshullam b. R. Qalonimos "Me'orah Ve-Ahavah and Piyyuṭim Le-Aḥar Ha-Zolat for Yotzer Le-Pesaḥ ('Afiq Renen)," interpreting Song 6:4–11 and 8:8–14, respectively [see full reference in 5], *Tashlum Ma'arekhet Ha-Yotzer*, edited by A. Frankel, 559–60.

Padwa, V. "Ve-Eretz 'Atzhil Be-Shirot Menushaqot'—Qedushta' Le-Pesaḥ Li-Shlomoh Suleiman." *Qovetz al Yad* 11 (1989): 1–61.

Rabinovitz, Zvi M. *Maḥazor Piyyuṭei Rabbi Yannai La-Torah Ve-la-Mo'adim*. Vol. 1–2. Jerusalem: Mosad Bialik, 1987.

Spiegel, S. "Shiv'ata Le-Yom 1 De-Pesaḥ She-Ḥal Be-Shabbat—Gevurot Ṭal Shabbat Eleazar." In *'Avot Ha-Piyyuṭ: Meqorot U-Meḥqarim Le-Toledot Ha-Piyyuṭ Be-'Eretz Yisrael*, edited by M. Schmelzer, 154–63. New York: Jewish Theological Seminary of America, 1996.

Van Bekkum, W. J. "Additions to Seder Shir Ha-Shirim, a Medieval Hebrew Poem for the Seventh Day of Passover." *Dutch Studies* 4 (1999): 87–94.

——. "Shir Ha-Shirim, a Medieval Hebrew Poem for the Seventh Day of Passover." *Dutch Studies* 1 (1995): 21–84.

Zulay, M., ed. "Anonymous Paytan, Piyyuṭ on Songs 2:7–3:10" [Hebrew]. In *'Eretz Yisrael U-Fiyyuṭeihah*, 149–54. Jerusalem: Magnes Press, 1996. Poet's name in the acrostic is Mosheh.

II. Traditional Medieval and Modern Jewish Sources

A. Published Works

Abraham b. Azriel. "Aus der Vaticanischen Handscriften. Abraham B. Asriels Machsor-Commentar." Edited by D. Kaufmann. *Magazin die Wissenschaft des Judenthums* 13 (1886): 129–60.

Abravanel, Don Isaac. *Peirush 'Al Ha-Torah*. Jerusalem: Benei Arba'el, 1964.

Abulafia, Todros. *Sha'ar Ha-Razim*. Edited by M. Oron. Jerusalem: Mosad Bialik, 1989.

Aharon Ha-Levi of Staroselye, *'Avodat Ha-Levi*. Vol. 1, 21a–23a (end, s.v. Derushim), 1844.

'Ahavat Qedumim. Ya'aqov Fischer. Benei Brak: Yad Moshe Tzvi, 1979.

Albo, Yosef. *Sefer Ha-'Iqqarim*. Warsaw: Goldmann, 1877.

Alemanno, Yoḥanan. "'The Song of Solomon's Ascents' by Yohanan Alemanno: Love and Human Perfection according to a Jewish Colleague of Giovanni Pico Della Mirandola." PhD diss. by A. Lesley, The University of California, 1976.

Al-Fawwāl, Yosef b. Shlomoh. "Peirush Le-Shir Ha-Shirim." In *Ha-Parshanut Ha-Philosophit Le-Shir Ha-Shirim Bi-Ymei Ha-Beinayim: R. Yosef Ben Shelomoh Al-Fuwwāl u-Farshanim 'Aḥeirim*, edited by Yosi Marciano. Part 2 of PhD diss., Hebrew University, 2005.

Alkabetz, Shlomoh Halevi. *'Ayelet 'Ahavim*. Reprint. Safed: Yeshivat Tzefat, 1889.

Alsheikh, Moses. *'Alsheikh 'Al Ha-Megillot (Commentary on Song of Songs Entitled Shoshanat Ha-'Amaqim)*. Warsaw: N. D. Zisberg, 1862. Reprint, Jerusalem: 1986.

Anatoli, Jacob b. Abba Mari b. Simson. *Malmad Ha-Talmidim*. Lyck: Mekize Nirdamim, 1866.

Anonymous. "Fragment d'un Commentaire Anonyme du Cantique des Cantiques." Edited by S. Eppenstein. *Revue des Etudes Juives* 53 (1907): 242–54.

Anonymous 1. "Anonymous Commentary on the Song of Songs." *Festschrift zum Achtzigsten Geburtstag M. Steinschneider (Tehillah Le-Moshe)*. Edited by H. J. Mathews, 238–40, and Hebrew text in Hebrew section, 164–85. Leipzig: O. Harrasowitz, 1896.

Anonymous 2. "Peirush Le-Shir Ha-Shirim," in Judeo-Arabic, published by Y. L. Naḥum, edited by Y. Tovi. *Mi-Yetzirot Sifrutiyot Mi-Teiman*. Ḥolon: Mif'al Hotza'at Ginzei Teiman, 1981, 1–26 (Hebrew pagination).

Arama, Yitzḥaq. *'Aqeidat Yitzḥaq. Sefer Vayiqra' 'im Peirush Megillat Shir ha-Shirim*. Pressburg: H. Y. Polk, 1849.

Aripul, Samuel. *Sefer Sar Shalom: Peirush Le-Shir Ha-Shirim*. Safed: Brought to press by Peretz Tishbi, 1579.

Ashkenazi, Samuel Jaffe b. Isaac. *Yefeih Qol* (commentary on *Shir Ha-Shirim Rabbah*). In *Midrash Rabbah*, Vilna edition.

Azriel of Gerona. *Peirush Ha-'Aggadot Le-Rabbi 'Azriel, Mei-Ri'shonei Ha-Mequbbalim Be-Gerona*. Jerusalem: Magnes Press, 1983.

Azulai, Yosef Ḥayyim b. Moshe Ḥayyim. In *'Even Sheleimah Ha-Shaleim 'Al Shir Ha-Shirim*, edited by R. D. Yehudiyof. Jerusalem, 1998.

Baḥya b. Asher. "Kad Ha-Qemaḥ." In *Kitvei Rabbeinu Baḥya*, edited by Ch. Chavel. Jerusalem: Mossad Ha-Rav Kook, 1970.

Berlin, Naftali Tzvi Yehudah (Netziv). *Megillat Shir Ha-Shirim, Rinah Shel Torah*. Jerusalem: Yeshivat Volozhin Press, 2003.

Berman, Issachar b. Naftali Ha-Kohen. *Mattenot Kehunnah* (commentary on Midrash Rabbah) In *Midrash Rabbah*, Vilna edition.

Binyamin Ze'ev Yitrof: Notes from Various Authors on Job, the Megilloth (except Ruth) and Ezra. Edited by H. J. Matthews. Amsterdam: Levisson Brothers, 1878.

Breuer, R. *Die Fünf Megilloth, Erster Teil, Hohelied*. Frankfurt a.M: A. I. Hofmann, 1912.

Cherlow, Y. *'Aḥarekha Narutzah: Peirush 'al Shir ha-Shirim*. Tel Aviv: Yediot Aḥaronot & Sifrei Hemed, 2003.

Cohen, M. S. "The Shi'ur Qomah: Liturgy and Theurgy." *Pre-Kabbalistic Jewish Mystics*, 51–76. Washington, DC: University Press of America, 1983.

David, Y. "Ha-Sha'ar Ha-Risho'n Mi-'Sefer Ha-Meshalim' Le-Ya'aqov Ben-'Eleazar." In *Sefer Avraham Even-Shoshan*, edited by B-Z. Lurie, 139–55. Jerusalem: Kiryat Sefer, 1988.

De Vidas, E. *Rei'shit Ḥokhmah Ha-Shaleim*, Vol. 1. Edited by Ḥ. Valdman. 3 vols. Jerusalem: 'Or Ha-Musar, 1984.

Di Trani, Isaiah. *Peirush Na"Kh Le-Rabbeinu Yish'ayah Ha-Risho'n Mi-Trani*. Edited by A. J. Wertheimer. Jerusalem, 1978.

Dov Ber, Maggid of Mezhirech. *Maggid Devarav Le-Ya'aqov*. Edited by R. Shatz-Uffenheimer. Jerusalem: Magnes, 1976.

——. *'Or Torah*. In *Rimzei Torah*. Brooklyn: Kehat Publishing House, 1972.

Eidels, Shmu'el Eliezer b. Yehuda Ha-Levi (Maharsha). *Maharsha* (commentary on *'Ein Ya'aqov*). In traditional editions of *'Ein Ya'aqov*.

Einhorn, Ze'ev Wolf b. Yisra'el 'Iser. *Maharzu* (commentary on Midrash Rabbah). In *Midrash Rabbah*, Vilna edition.

Eleazar of Worms. *Derashah Le-Pesaḥ*. Edited with introduction and notes by S. Immanuel. Jerusalem: Mekize Nirdamim, 2006.

——. *Peirush Ha-Roqeiaḥ 'Al Ha-Megillot*. Edited by Sh. Kanevsky. Bnei Brak: J. Klugman and Sons, 1985.

Eliezer b. Reuven Kahana mi-Karlin. *Siaḥ Sefunim, Ḥibbur Neḥmad Ve-Na'im 'Al Ḥamesh Megillot; 'Shirat Dodim' Al Megillat Shir Ha-Shirim*. Lemberg: J. Schneider, 1850.

Elijah, Abraham ben. *Commentary: Be'eir Avraham*. Megillat Shir ha-Shirim: reprint 1886; Bnei Brak, n.d.

Elijah de Vidas. *Rei'shit Ḥokhmah. Sha'ar Ha-Ahavah*. Edited by H. Valman. Vol. 1. Jerusalem: 1980.

Elimelekh of Lizensk, *No'am 'Elimelekh*. Edited by G. Nigal. Vol. 1–2. Jerusalem: Mossad HaRav Kook, 1978.

Eliyahu ben Shlomo Zalman Mi-Vilna (Vilna Gaon). *'Aderet 'Eliyahu*. Tel Aviv, 1962.

——. "Bei'ur Ha-Gr"a Le-N"K. Shir Ha-Shirim." *Peraqim 1–4*, addendum and notes and commentaries by Eliahu Kohen. Jerusalem: Mossad Ha-Rav Kook, 2008.

——. *Megillat Shir Hashirim (with Commentary by Rokeah and Be'er Avraham)*. 1886.

Epstein, Baruch Halevi. *Torah Temimah, Sefer Va-Yiqra'*. Vol. 3, Shir ha-Shirim. Tel Aviv: Am Olam, 1969.

Epstein, Kalonymos Kalman Halevi. *Ma'or Va-Shemesh*, 1842. Reprint: Jerusalem: Machon 'Even Yisrael, 1992. Vol. 1, pp. 344a–352b (*Rimzei Shir Ha-Shirim*).

Ezra ben Solomon, *Rabbi Ezra ben Solomon. Commentary on the Song of Songs*. Translated by Seth Brody. Kalamazoo, MI: Medieval Institute Publications, 1999.

——. "Peirush Shir Ha-Shirim." In *Kitvei Rabbeinu Moshe Ben Naḥman*. Edited by H. Chavel, 476–518. Jerusalem: Mossad Harav Kook, 1964.

Friedländer, M. "Tehillat Peirush Shir Ha-Shirim, Me-'Urav Mi-Leshon 'Ever Ve-'Arav." *Tehillah Le-Mosheh: Festschrift Zum Achtzigsten Geburtstag Moritz Steinschneider*, Hebrew section, 49–59. Leipzig: O. Harrasowitz, 1896.

Gallico, Elisha. *Peirush 'Al Shir Ha-Shirim*, 1587. Reprint, Alexander-Lodz: A. Y. Fischer, 1929.

——. *Peirush 'Al Shir Ha-Shirim*, 1587. Reprint, Jerusalem: Machon Maor Harim, 2000.

Gersonides, Levi ben Gershom (Ralbag). *Commentary on Song of Songs: Levi Ben Gershom.* Translated with introduction by M. Kellner. New Haven: Yale University Press, 1998.

——. *Peirush Le-Shir Ha-Shirim. He-Hedir Be-Tzeiruf Mavo' Ve-He'arot M. Kellner*. Ramat Gan: Bar Ilan University Press, 2001.

Gikatilla, Joseph. *Ginnat 'Egoz*. Jerusalem: Yeshivat Ha-Ḥayyim Vaha-Shalom, 1989.

——. "Beirurim Be-Kitvei R. Yosef Gikatilla." Edited by E. Gottlieb. *Tarbiz* 39 (1970): 78–80.

Ginzei Yosef. Vol. 1. Lvov, 1972. Reprint, Jerusalem, 1987. 334a–339b.

Ha-Gershuni, Avraham b. Solomon. *Sefer Shir Ha-Shirim 'im Peirush Rabbi Shlomoh ve-'im Bei'ur Ḥadash Be-Shem 'Avodat Ha-Gershuni), Commentary by R. Avraham, Brother of Gaon R. Elijah of Vilna.* Warsaw, 1866; reprint Jerusalem, 1982.

——. *Shir Ha-Shirim 'im Peirush Rabbi Shlomoh U-Vei'urim Mei-Ḥakhmei Vilna Bi-ymei Ha-Gra: 'Avodat Ha-Girshuni; Shir Ḥadash*. Jerusalem: Feldheim Publishers, 2011.

Ha-Ketavim Ha-'Ivriyyim Shel Ba'al Tiqqunei Zohar Ve-Ra'aya' Meheimna'. Edited with notes by E. Gottlieb. Jerusalem: Israel Academy of Sciences and Humanities, 2003.

Ḥakham, A. *Ḥameish Megillot*. Da'at Miqra. Jerusalem: Mossad Harav Kook, 1973.

Ha-Nagid, Shemuel. *Divan Shmu'el Ha-Nagid. Ben Tehillim*. Edited by Dov Yarden. Jerusalem: Hebrew Union College Press, 1966.

Ha-Shoshani, Shema'yah. "R. Shema'yah HaShoshani u-Feirusho 'Al-Shir Ha-Shirim." Edited by Avraham Grossman. In *Sefer Ha-Yovel Le-Rav Mordechai Breuer*, edited by M. Bar-Asher. Vol. 1. Jerusalem: Academon Press, 1993.

Ḥayyim of Volozhin. *Bei'urei Ḥayyim Mi-Volozhin*. Jerusalem: Naḥliel, 2000; s.v. "Shir Ha-Shirim," 128–38.

Ḥayyun, Yosef ben Avraham. In A. Gross, *R. Yosef ben Avraham Ḥayyun. Manhig Kehillat Lisbon Viytzirotav*. Ramat-Gan: Bar-Ilan University Press, 1993. Appendix 3, pp. 183–91.

Hollender, Elisabeth. "Ms. Parma 655 on 'Afiq Renen Ve-Shirim (= Biblioteca Palatina Cod. Parma 3205 [De Rossi 655], F. 89r–101v." *Piyyuṭ Commentary in Medieval Ashkenaz*, *41–*86. Berlin: Walter de Gruyter, 2008.

Hübsch, A. *Die Fünf Megillot*. Prague: Senders & Brandeis, 1866.

ibn Aqnin, Joseph b. Judah b. Jacob. *Divulgatio Mysteriorum Luminumque Apparentia. Commentarius in Canticum Canticorum = Peirush 'al Shir ha-Shirim*. Edited by A. S. Halkin. Jerusalem: Meqize Nirdamim, 1964.

ibn 'Attar, Ḥayyim b. Moshe. *Shir Ha-Shirim 'Im Peirush 'Or Ha-Ḥayyim*. Commentary entitled 'Ri'shon Le-Tziyyon.' Benei Berak: Kollel Naḥalat Tzvi, 2008.

ibn Ezra, Abraham. *Commentary on the Canticles. (First Recension of the Song of Songs Commentary)*. Edited by H. J. Mathews. London: Trübner, 1874.

——. *Yesod Mora' Ve-Sod Torah*. Edited by Yosef Cohen and Uriel Simon. Ramat Gan: Bar-Ilan University Press, 2002.

ibn Janaḥ, Yonah. *Sefer Ha-Riqmah*. Translated by Y. ibn Tibbon. Edited by M. Wilenski. Jerusalem: Ha-Akademiah La-Leshon Ha-'Ivrit, 1964.

——. *Sefer Ha-Shorashim*. Edited by Wilhelm Bacher. Berlin: Itzikowski, 1896.

ibn Kaspi, Joseph. *Ḥatzotzerot Kesef. Bei'ur Shir Ha-Shirim*. Constantinople, 1577; reprinted in *'Asarah Kelei Kesef* (*Zehn Schriften des R. Josef ibn Kaspi*), edited by Y. J. Last. Pressburg: Alkelai, 1903; reprint: Jerusalem, 1970. 1:183–84.

ibn Parḥon, Solomon. "Maḥberet He-'Arukh Le-he-Ḥakham R. Shlomoh b. R. Avraham, Ha-yadu'a Ibn Parḥon." *Maḥberet He-'Arukh*. Edited by Sh. Rapaport. Pressburg, 1844.

ibn Sahula, Yitzḥak. "Peirush Shir Ha-Shirim Le-R. Yitzḥak ibn Sahula." Edited by A. Green. *Meḥqerei Yerushalayim be-Maḥashevet Yisrael* 6 (1987): 393–491.

ibn Shu'aib, Yehoshua. *Derashot 'al ha-Torah U-Mo'adei Ha-Shanah*. Edited by Z. Metzger. Jerusalem: Machon Lev Sameiaḥ, 1992.

ibn Tibbon, Moses. *Moses ibn Tibbons Hohelied-Kommentar*. Edited by Otfried Fraisse. Übersetzung und Analyse ed. Berlin: W. de Gruyter, 2005.

ibn Tibbon, Samuel. *Samuel ibn Tibbon's Commentary on Ecclesiastes*. Edited by James T. Robinson. Tübingen: Mohr-Siebeck, 2007.

ibn Yaḥye, Yosef b. David. *Peirush Shir Ha-Shirim*. In *Miqra'ot Gedolot "Qehillot Moshe"* (Amsterdam, 1724); reprinted in Miqra'ot Gedolot "'Orim Gedolim." Jerusalem: Machon Ab"i, 1992.

ibn Zimra, David (Radbaz). *Sefer Migdal David. Peirush 'al Shir Ha-Shirim*. First transcription of manuscript in library of R. Menahem Mendel of Viznitz. Brooklyn, NY: Emunah Publishing, n.d.

'Iggeret Ha-Teshuvah. Attributed to Yitzhak ibn Laṭif. *Qovetz al Yad* 1 (1885): 45–70.

Immanuel b. Shlomoh Ha-Romi. *Maḥberet 'Immanuel Ha-Romi*. Edited by D. Yarden. 2 vols. Jerusalem: Mosad Bialik, 1957.

——. *Peirush 'Al Shir Ha-Shirim*. Edited by Eschwege. Frankfurt am Main: Y. L. Golde, 1905; reprint Jerusalem, 1970.

——. "R. Immanuel b. Shlomoh (Immanuel of Rome). Commentary to the 'Song of Songs'." I. Ravitzky, Master's thesis, Hebrew University of Jerusalem, 1970.

Israel b. Shabbetai of Koznitz. *'Avodat Yisrael*. Jerusalem: Machon Siftei Tzadiqim, 1999; s.v. Le-Pesaḥ 137b–141b.

Jacob of Lissa. *Ḥamesh Megillot. Sefer Tzeror Ha-Ner 'al Megillat Shir Ha-Shirim*. Reprint: Jerusalem, 1991.

Japhet, S. "Peirush Anonimi Le-Shir Ha-Shirim Bi-Khtav Yad Prag (Ḥumash Eiger): Mavo' u-Mahadurah Biqortit." In *Le-Yashev Peshuṭo shel Miqra: Asufat Meḥqarim Be-Farshanut Ha-Miqra*, edited by S. Japhet and E. Weisel, 206–47. Jerusalem: Magnes, 2011.

Joseph of Hamadan. "Sefer Tashak." Critical text edition with introduction by J. Zwelling. PhD diss., Brandeis University (Ann Arbor, MI: University Microfilms, 1975). Commentary on Song of Songs 1:2–2:5, fols. 1–25b; on 2:5–9, fols. 94a–98a.

——. "Un Manuscrit Inconnu de Sefer Tashak de R. Joseph de Hamadan, Suivi D'un Fragment Inédit." Edited by C. Mopsik. *Kabbalah* 2 (1997): 169–88.

Katz, Avigdor. *Peirush Shir Ha-Shirim Le-Rabbeinu Avigdor Kohen Tzedeq*. Edited by Y. Bamberger. Frankfurt, 1859; reprint, Y. H. Wertheimer. Jerusalem: Ketav-Yad Sefer, 1981.

Kimḥi, David (Radak). *Sefer Ha-Shorashim*. Edited by J. Biesenthal and F. Lebrecht. Berlin, 1847.

Kitâb Ma'ânî Al-Nafs. Buch Von Wesen Der Seele. Edited by I. Goldziher. Berlin: Weidmann, 1907.

Kook, Avraham Y. HaKohen. "Shir Ha-Shirim." *Seder Tefillah 'Im Peirush 'Olat Ra'ayah*. Vol 1: 1–9. Jerusalem: Mossad HaRav Kook, 1996.

Krimsky, Y. *Yahel 'Or (Super-Commentary on A. ibn Ezra's Songs Commentary)*. Vol. 3 (Leviticus), Ḥumash Meḥoqeqei Yehuda; reprint, Bnei Brak: Ḥorev, n.d.

Labrat, Dunash ben. *Sefer Teshuvot Dunash Ben Labrat 'im Hakhra'at Rabbeinu Ya'akov Tam = Criticae Vocum Recensiones Donasch Ben Librat, Levitae . . . Cum Animadversionibus Criticus Jacobi Ben Mejer Tam*. Edited by Herschel Filipowski. London: Ḥevrat Me'orerei Yesheinim, 1855.

——. *Sefer Teshuvot Dunash Halevi Ben Labrat 'al Rabbi Saadia Gaon = Kritik des Dunasch Ben Labrat über enzelne Stellen aus Saadia's Arabischen Uebersetzung Des Alten Testament und aus dessen grammatischen Schriften (nach einem Codex des Professor S. D. Luzzatto)*. Edited by Robert Schröter. Breslau: Schletter'sche Buchhandlung, 1866.

Levi Yitzḥak of Berdichev. *Kedushat Levi Ha-Shalem 'Al Ha-Torah Ve-ha-Mo'adim*. Vol. 1. 289–95. Brooklyn: Machon Kedushat Levi, 1995.

Lo'antz, Elijah b. Moshe. *Sefer Rinat Dodim*. Basel: Konrad Waldkirch, 1600.

Luria, David (Radal). *Ḥiddushei Ha-Radal* (commentary on Midrash Rabbah). In *Midrash Rabbah*, Vilna edition.

Luzzatto, S. D. *Sefer Yesha'yah. Il Profeta Isaia*. Padova: Antonio Bianchi, 1855.

Machsor Vitry. Edited by S. Hurvitz. Vol. 1. Nürnberg, 1923.

Maharal of Prague (Judah Loeb). *Siddur Maharal Mi-Prag Le-Shalosh Regalim* Jerusalem: Machon Yerushalayim, 2007; s.v. *Shir Ha-Shirim* (comments collated from author's works), 250–65.

Maimonides, Moses. *The Guide of the Perplexed*. Edited and translated by S. Pines. Chicago: University of Chicago Press, 1963.

Moses de León. *The Book of the Pomegranate. Moses De Leon's Sefer Ha-Rimmon*. Text edition with introduction and notes by Elliot Wolfson. Atlanta: Scholar's Press, 1988.

Nachmanides, Moses. *Kitvei Ramban*. Edited by C. Chavel. 2 vols. Jerusalem: Mossad HaRav Kook, 1964.

Nathan b. Yeḥiel. *Aruch Completum*. Reprint Hebrew edition. Jerusalem: Makor, 1969–70.

Nathan of Gaza. "'Al Ha-'Ahavah Ha-Ruḥanit,' Mi-Divrei Natan Ha-'Azati." *Qovetz Hotza'at Schoqen Le-Divrei Sifrut*. Edited by H. Wirshubski, 180–91. Tel Aviv: Schocken Publishing House, 1941.

Negroponte, Shemariah b. Elyah [Ikriti]. *Commentary on the Song of Songs* [Hebrew]. In *Ḥameish Megillot*. Edited by Y. Kafiḥ. Jerusalem, 1961.

Peirush Shel Dibberot. Edited by S. Hurwitz. Machsor Vitry. Vol. 1. Nürnberg: J. Bulka, 1923.

Pinḥas of Koretz. *'Imrei Pinḥas Ha-Shalem*. Edited by Y. S. Frenkel, nos. 240–42. Bnei Brak: Mishor, 1988; s.v. *Shir Ha-Shirim* 38a.

Ratzhabi, Y. "New Geniza Fragments from the Commentary on the Song." *Sinai* 125 (2001): 1–8.

——. "Targum Megillat 'Shir Ha-Shirim' Le-Rav Saadia." *Beit Mikra* 43 (1998): 256–62.

Rotenberg, M. *Ki Ṭovim Dodekha Mi-Yayin. Peirush Meqori Le-Shir Ha-Shirim*. Jerusalem: Carmel, 2007.

Saadia Gaon (Saadia b. Joseph). *Commentary on the Song of Songs* [Hebrew]. In *Ḥameish Megillot*, edited by Y. Qafiḥ. Jerusalem, 1961.

——. "Peirush Rav Saadyah Gaon li-Mgillat Shir ha-Shirim." In *Kitvei-Yad Ha-Geniza Ginzei Yerushalayim*, edited by S. Wertheimer, 163–203. Jerusalem: Makhon le-'Arikhat ve-Hotza'at Sefari ve-Kitvei Yad, 1993.

Samuel b. Meir (Rashbam). *The Commentary of Samuel Ben Meir on the Song of Songs*. PhD diss. by Y. Thompson, Jewish Theological Seminary, 1988. University Microfilms, 1989.

——. *Der Kommentar zu Kohelet und dem Hohen Liede von R. Samuel Ben Meir*. Edited by A. Jellenik. Leipzig: L. Schnauss, 1855.

——. "Peirush R. Shmuel Ben Meir (Rashbam) le-Shir Ha-Shirim." Edited by S. Japhet. Jerusalem: The World Union of Jewish Studies, 2008.

Saruq, Menaḥem ben. *Maḥberet Menaḥem = Antiquissimum Linguae Hebraicae Et Chaldaicae Lexicon Ad Sacras Scripturas Explicandas a Menahem Ben Saruck Hispaniensi*. Edited by Herschel Fillopowski. London: Ḥevrat Me'orerei Yesheinim, 1854.

Sefas 'Emes. Sefer Shir Ha-Shirim 'im Peirush Rabbi Shlomoh ve-'im Peirush Sefas 'Emes ve-'im Liqquṭei Yehudah. Edited by Yehuda Aryeh Leib Heine (private printing 1955, with additions in 1980 by Avraham Heine). Jerusalem: Nidpas be-Siyu'a Ma'yan Ḥokhmah.

Sefer Ba'al Shem Tov. Edited by Shimon Gevorchov. Reprint: Jerusalem, 1962.

Sefer Ha-Bahir. Edited by R. Margulies. 1951. Jerusalem: Mossad HaRav Kook, 1994.

Sefer Ha-Bahir 'Al Pi Kitvei-Yad Ha-Qedumim. Edited by D. Abrams. Los Angeles: Cherub Press, 1994.

Sefer Ha-Zohar. Edited by R. Margoliot. 4th corrected ed., with commentary *Nitzotzei Zohar*. Jerusalem: Mossad HaRav Kook, 1964.

Sefer Ha-Zohar 'im Peirush 'Ha-Sullam' 'al Shir Ha-Shirim. Edited by Y. Ashlag. Vol. 1–2. Bnei Brak: Machon Ateret Shelomoh, 2006.

Sefer Torot Ha-Nefesh. Translated by I. Broydé. Paris: J. Levinsohn-Kilemnik, 1896.

Sforno, Ovadiah. *Megillat Shir Ha-Shirim*. Königsberg: Hartungschen Hofbuchdruckerei, 1845.

Shlomoh b. Meir. "Fragments of Comments, D. Kaufmann." *Magazin des Judentums* 1 (1886): 152–60.

Shlomoh b. Yitzḥak (Rashi). *Peirush Rashi ʿal Shir Ha-Shirim*. Edited by Yehudah Rosenthal, with commentary. In *Sefer ha-Yovel li-Khvod Shemuel Kalman Mirsky*, edited by Simon Bernstein and Gerson Churgin. New York: Vaʿad Ha-Yovel, 1958.

Shne'ur Zalman of Liadi, *Sefer Liqquṭei Torah*. Brooklyn: Kehot Publication Society, 1998, s.v. Shir Ha-Shirim, 2, 1–102.

Soloveitchik, Joseph B. *And from There You Shall Seek*. Jersey City: Toras HaRav Foundation-Ktav Publishing House, 2008. Translation of *U-Vikkashtem mi-Sham*. First Published in *Ha-Darom* 47 (1979); reprinted in *Ish Ha-Halakhah-Galuy ve-Nistar*. Jerusalem: Ha-Histadrut Ha-Tziyonit Ha-Olamit (1979): 115–235.

Tamakh, Abraham b. Isaac ha-Levi. "Abraham b. Isaac ha-Levi TaMaKH. Commentary on the Song of Songs, Based on Mss and Early Printings with an Introduction, Variants and Comments." Edited by Leon Feldman. *Studia Semitica Nederlandica* 9 (1970): 249–53.

——. *R. Abraham B. Isaac Ha-Levi Tamakh: Commentary on the Song of Songs*. Critical edition. Leon A. Feldman: Assen Van Gorcum, 1970.

Tibbon, Moshe ibn. *Peirush ʿal Shir Ha-Shirim*. Lyck: Vereins Mekize Nirdamim/R. Siebert, 1874.

Tiqqunei Zohar. Edited by M. Margoliot. Tel Aviv-Jerusalem: Mossad HaRav Kook, 1948.

Tosafot Ha-Shalem. 'Otzar Perushei Baʿalei Ha-Tosafot. Ḥamesh Megillot. Shir Ha-Shirim-Rut. Edited by Jacob Gellis. Jerusalem: Makhon H. Fischel, 1991.

Vajda, G. *Le Commentaire D'Ezra de Gérone sur le Cantique des Cantiques*. Paris: Aubier-Montaine, 1969.

Yaʿaqov Yosef of Polonoye. *Keṭonet Passim*. Edited by G. Nigal, 36a–c. Jerusalem: Machon Peri Ha-Aretz, 1985.

Yehudah Halevi. *Diwan Des Abu-L-Hasan Jehuda Ha-Levi*. Edited by H. Brody. Berlin 1894/1940. Reprint: A. M. Habermann. 4 volumes. Farnsborough: Greg, 1971, 2, 49.

Ze'ev Wolf of Zhitomer. *Sefer 'Or Ha-Me'ir, Moreh Be-ʿOmeq Shir Ha-Shirim*. 1797. Reprint: Jerusalem, 2000.

Zekharyah Ha-Rofe'. "Midrash (Peirush) Le-Shir Ha-Shirim." In *Ḥasifat Genuzim Mi-Teiman*, edited by S. Gridi, 202–36. Ḥolon: Mifʿal Ḥasifat Ginzei Teiman. Published by Y. L. Naḥum, 1971.

Zhlozhitz (Zlozetz), Benjamin of. *'Ahavas Dodim: Peirush ʿal Shir Ha-Shirim*. Lemberg, 1793; reprint: Jerusalem: ʿEin Yaʿaqov, 1978.

Zohar, Le. Cantique Des Cantiques. Translated by Charles Mopsick. Paris: Verdier, 1999.

Zohar Ḥadash ʿim Nitzotzei Zohar. Edited by Reuven Margoliot, 60c–74d. Jerusalem: Mossad HaRav Kook, 1953.

B. Manuscripts Consulted

Al-Fuwwāl, Yosef. Ms. Livorno 7 (published by Y. Marciano).

Ezra b. Solomon. Ms. Jewish Theological Seminary of America, L 1059.

Immanuel b. Shlomoh Ha-Romi. Ms. London 238, 2; supplemented by Ms. Vatican 250 (published by I. Ravitzky).

——. Hebrew Union College, Cincinnati, Ms. 167 (=Institute of Microfilms Jerusalem, Ms. 47524).

Shlomoh b. Yitzḥak (Rabbi Shlomoh). Jewish Theological Seminary of America, Ms. L 778 (published by S. Kamin and A. Saltman; see below under *Secundum Salomonem*; pp. 81–99, Hebrew pagination).

III. *Christian Commentaries*

A. *Primary Sources*

Bede. *The Venerable Bede: On the Song of Songs and Selected Writings*. Trans. and edited by A. Holder. Mahwah, NJ: The Paulist Press, 2011.

Bernard of Clairvaux. *On the Song of Songs*. Translated by K. Walsh and I. M. Edmonds. Kalamazoo, MI: Cistercian Publications, 1971–80.

Gregory of Nyssa. *Commentary of the Song of Songs*. Translated with an introduction by C. McCambley. Brookline, MA: Hellenic College Press, 1987.

Madame Guyon. *The Song of Songs of Solomon with Explanations and Reflections Having Reference to the Interior Life*. Trans. by J. Metcalf. New York: Dennett, 1879.

Nicholas of Lyra. *The Postilla of Nicholas of Lyra on the Song of Songs*. Edited by J. Kieker. Milwaukee: Marquette University Press, 1998.

Origen. *The Song of Songs: Commentary and Homilies*. Edited by R. P. Lawson. Ancient Christian Writers 26. Westminster, 1957.

Secundum Salomonem. A 13th Century Commentary on the Song of Songs. Edited by Sarah and Avrom Saltman Kamin. Ramat Gan: Bar-Ilan University Press, 1989.

Teresa of Avila. "Meditations on the Song of Songs." In *The Collected Works of Teresa of Avila* vol. 2, pp. 205–60. Trans. by K. Kavanaugh and O. Rodriguez. Washington, DC: Institute of Carmelite Studies, 1980.

William of St. Thierry. *Exposition on the Song of Songs*. Translated by Columbus Hart. Spencer, MA: Cistercian Publications, 1970.

B. *Secondary Literature*

Asiedu, F. B. A. "The Song of Songs and the Ascent of the Soul: Ambrose, Augustine, and the Language of Mysticism." *Vigilae Christianae* 55 (2001): 299–317.

Astell, A. *The Song of Songs in the Middle Ages*. Ithaca: Cornell University Press, 1990.

Blanpain, J. "Langage Mystique, Expression du Désir dans les Sermons sur le Cantique des Cantiques de Bernard de Clairvaux." *Collectanea Cisterciensia* 36 (1874): 226–47.

Cohen, J. "'Synagoga Conversa': Honorius Augustodunensis, the Song of Songs, and Christianity's 'Eschatological Jew.'" *Speculum* 79 (2004): 309–40.

Cottier, O. P., and P. Georges. "Désir Naturel de Voir Dieu." *Gregorianum* 78 (1997): 679–98.

Danielou, J. *Bible Et Liturgie*. Paris: Cerf, 1950.

De Certeau, M. "L'énonciation Mystique." *Revue des sciences religieuses* 64 (1976): 183–215.

Elliott, M. *The Song of Songs and the Early Church*, 381–451. Tübingen: Mohr Siebeck, 2000.

Fulton, R. *From Judgment to Passion. Devotion to Christ and the Virgin Mary*, 800–1200. New York: Columbia University Press, 2002.

——. "Mimetic Devotion, Marian Exegesis, and the Historical Sense of the Song of Songs." *Viator: Medieval and Renaissance Studies* 27 (1996): 85–116.

Kaske, R. E., in collaboration with A. Groos and M. Twomey. *Medieval Christian Literary Imagery: A Guide to Interpretation*. Toronto: University of Toronto Press, 1988.

Leclerq, J. "St. Bernard and the Metaphor of Love." In *Monks on Marriage: A Twelfth-Century View*, 73–86. New York: The Seabury Press, 1982.

——. "St. Bernard et la Tradition Biblique d' Après le Sermon sur les Cantiques." *Sacris Eridiri* 2 (1960): 225–48.

Marinov, D. "Exegesis and Mysticism in Gregory of Nyssa's and Ambrose of Milan's Commentaries on the Song of Songs." PhD diss., Hebrew University of Jerusalem, 2008.

Matter, A. E. *The Voice of My Beloved: The Song of Songs in Western Medieval Christianity*. Philadelphia: The University of Pennsylvania Press, 1990.

McGinn, B. *The Foundations of Mysticism: Origen to the Fifth Century; Volume 1 of "The Presence of God: A History of Christian Mysticism."* New York: Crossroads, 1991.

——. *The Growth of Mysticism: Gregory the Great through the 12th Century; Volume 2 of "The Presence of God."* New York: Crossroads, 1994.
——. *The Flowering of Mysticism: Men and Women in the New Mysticism*, 1200–1350; *Volume 3 of "The Presence of God."* New York: Crossroads, 1998.
——. *The Harvest of Mysticism in Medieval Germany:* 1300–1500; *Volume 4 of "The Presence of God."* New York: Crossroads, 2005.
——. *The Varieties of Vernacular Mysticism:* 1300–1550; *Volume 5 of "The Presence of God."* New York: Crossroads, 2012.
——. "Women Reading the Song of Songs in the Christian Tradition." In *Scriptural Exegesis. The Shapes of Culture and the Religious Imagination: Essays in Honour of Michael Fishbane*, edited by D. A. Green and L. S. Lieber, 281–96. Oxford: Oxford University Press, 2009.
McGuckin J. A. "Symeon the New Theologian's Hymns of Divine Eros: A Neglected Masterpiece of the Christian Mystical Tradition." *Spiritus: A Journal of Christian Spirituality* 5:2 (2005): 182–202.
Miller, P. C. "'Pleasure of the Text, Text of Pleasure': Eros and Language in Origen's Commentary on the Song of Songs." *Journal of the American Academy of Religion* 54:2 (1986): 241–53.
Moore, S. D. "The Song of Songs in the History of Sexuality." *Church History* 69:2 (2000): 328–49.
Nygren, A. *Agape and Eros*. Philadelphia: Westminster Press, 1953.
Ohly, F. *Hohelied-Studien: Grundzüge Eine Geschichte Der Heheliedauslegung Des Abendlandes Bis Um* 1200. Weisbaden: Franz Steiner, 1958.
——. *Sensus Spiritualis. Studies in Medieval Significs and the Philology of Culture*. Edited by Samuel P. Jaffe. Chicago: University of Chicago Press, 2005.
Otten, W. "Nature and Scripture: Demise of Medieval Analogy." *Harvard Theological Review* 88 (1995): 257–84.
Stock, B. *The Implications of Literacy: Written Language and Models of Interpretation in the Eleventh and Twelfth Centuries*. Vol. 4, no. 3: Bernard of Clairvaux. Princeton: Princeton University Press, 1983.
Stroumsa, G. "Clement, Origen, and Jewish Exoteric Traditions." *Origeniana Sexta. Origène Et La Bible/Origen and the Bible*, 53–69. Leuven: University Press, 1995.
Turner, D. *Eros and Allegory. Medieval Exegesis of the Song of Songs*. Kalamazoo, MI: Cistercian Publications, 1995.

IV. Modern Commentaries

Alon, G. *Bei'ur La-Ketuvim*. Tel Aviv, n.d., 251–53.
Bloch, Ariel and Chana Bloch. *The Song of Songs*. New York: Random House, 1995.
Breuer, R. *Zur Abwehr*. Frankfurt a.M: Gebrüder Knauer, 1912.
Delitzsch, Franz. *Das Hohelied*. Leipzig: Dörffling und Franke, 1851.
Ehrlich, A. B. *Randglossen Zur Hebräischen Bibel*. Hildesheim: Georg Olms, reprint 1968.
Exum, J. C. *Song of Songs: A Commentary*. Louisville: Westminster John Knox Press, 2005.
Falk, M. *The Song of Songs. A New Translation and Interpretation*. San Francisco: HarperCollins, 1990.
Feliks, J. *The Song of Songs: Nature, Epic, and Allegory* [Hebrew]. Jerusalem: Ha-Ḥevrah Le-Ḥeqer Ha-Miqra' Be-Yisrael, 1964.
Fox, M. V. *The Song of Songs and the Ancient Egyptian Love Songs*. Madison: University of Wisconsin Press, 1985.
Ginsburg, C. D. *The Song of Songs and Coheleth*. Edited by H. M. Orlinsky, 1857 and 1861. Reprinted New York: KTAV, 1970.

Gordis, R. *The Song of Songs and Lamentations: A Study, Modern Translation, and Commentary*. Revised and Augmented ed. New York: KTAV, 1974.
Goulder, M. D. *The Song of Fourteen Songs*. Journal for the Study of the Old Testament Supplement Series 38. Sheffield: JSOT Press, 1986.
Graetz, H. *Schir Ha-Schirim oder das Solomonische Hohelied*. Breslau: W. Jacobsohn, 1885.
Haupt, P. *Biblische Liebeslieder: Das sogennante Hohelied Salomos unter steter Berücksichtigung der Übersetzungen Goethes und Herders*. Leipzig: J. C. Hinrichs, 1907.
Hitzig, F. *Das Hohe Lied: Kurtzgeffastes Exegetisches Handbuch Zum Alten Testament*. Liepzig: J. C. Hinrichs, 1855.
Jastrow, M. *The Song of Songs, Being a Collection of Love Lyrics of Ancient Palestine* Philadelphia: J. B. Lippincott Company, 1921.
Juöon, P. *Le Cantique de Cantiques: Commentaire Philologique et éxègtique*. Paris: Gabriel Beauchesne, 1909.
Keel, O. *The Song of Songs*. Minneapolis: Fortress Press, 1994.
Kingsmill, E. *The Song of Songs and the Eros of God: A Study in Biblical Intertextuality*. Oxford Theological Monographs. Oxford: Oxford University Press, 2009.
Levinger, E. *Shir Ha-Shirim*. Jerusalem: Rubin Mass, 1944.
Longman, T. *The Song of Songs (New International Commentary on the Old Testament)*. Grand Rapids, MI: Wm. B. Eerdmans Publishing Company, 2001.
Murphy, R. E. *The Song of Songs: A Commentary on the Book of Canticles or the Song of Songs*. Hermeneia. Minneapolis: Fortress Press, 1990.
Pope, M. H. *Song of Songs: A New Translation with Introduction and Commentary*. Vol. 7C, Anchor Bible. Garden City: Doubleday, 1977.
The Song of Songs: A Feminist Companion to the Bible. Edited by A. Brenner and C. R. Fontaine. Sheffield: Sheffield Academic Press, 2000.
Tur-Sinai, N. *Ha-Lashon Ve-ha-Sepher*. Vol. 2, *Shir Ha-Shirim 'Asher Lishlomoh*. Jerusalem: Mosad Bialik, 1951.
Zakovitch, Y. *Shir Ha-Shirim 'im Mavo' u-Feirush*. Miqra' Le-Yisrael. Tel Aviv: Am Oved, 1992.

V. Secondary Literature: Themes and Studies

Abrams, D. *Sexual Symbolism and Merkavah Speculation in Medieval Germany. A Study of the Sod Ha-Egoz Texts*. Tübingen: Mohr-Siebeck, 1997.
Abramsky, S. "Ha-'Ishah Ha-Nishqefet Ba'ad Ha-Ḥalon." *Beth Mikra* 25 (1980): 114–24.
Abusch, T. "Gilgamesh's Request and Siduri's Denial." *The Tablet and the Scroll: Near Eastern Studies in Honor of William W. Hallo*, edited by D. C. Snell, M. E. Cohen, and D. B. Weisberg, 1–14. Bethesda, MD: Capital Decisions Ltd, 1993.
Afterman, A. *Deveiqut Hitqasherut 'Intimit Bein 'Adam La-Maqom Be-Hagut Ha-Yehudit Bi-ymei Ha-Beinayim*. Los Angeles: Cherub Press, 2011.
Aḥituv, S. "Semadar." *Leshonnenu* 39 (1975–1976): 37–40.
Albright, W. F. "Archaic Survivals in the Text of Canticles." In *Hebrew and Semitic Studies Presented to G. R. Driver*. Edited by D. W. Thomas and W. D. McHardy. Oxford: Clarendon, 1963.
Alexander, P. "The Song of Songs as Historical Allegory: Notes on the Development of an Exegetical Tradition, in Targumic and Cognate Studies: Essays in Honour of Martin McNamara." *Journal for the Study of the Old Testament Supplement* 230 (1996): 14–29.
Alexander, P. S. "Textual Criticism and Rabbinic Literature: The Case of the Targum of the Song of Songs." *Bulletin of the John Rylands Library* 75:3 (1993): 159–73.

——. "Tradition and Originality in the Targum of the Song of Songs." In *The Aramaic Bible. Targums in Their Historical Context*, edited by D. R. Beattie and M. J. McNamara, 318–39. Sheffield: Sheffield Academic Press, 1994.

Allen, Sr. P. "Plato, Aristotle, and the Concept of Woman in Early Jewish Philosophy." *Florilegium* 9 (1987): 89–111.

Alster, B, *Human Love and its Relationship to Spiritual Love in Jewish Exegesis on the Song of Songs* [Hebrew]. PhD diss., Bar-Ilan University (Ramat-Gan, 2006).

Alter, R. *The Art of Biblical Narrative*. New York: Basic Books, 1990.

Altmann, A. "Eleazar of Worms' Chokhmat Ha-Egoz." *Journal of Jewish Studies* 11 (1960): 101–13.

——. "Moses Narboni's Epistle on 'Shi'ur Qoma.'" *Jewish Medieval and Renaissance Studies*, edited by A. Altmann. Cambridge, MA: Harvard University Press, 1967.

Amado Lévy-Valensi, E. *La Poétique du Zohar.* Paris: L'Éclat, 1996.

Angénieux, J. "Le Cantiques Des Cantiques En Huit Chants À Refrains Alternants." *Ephemerides theologicae lovanienses* 44 (1973): 87–140.

Asulin, S. Ha-Parshanut Ha-Mysṭit Le-Shir Ha-Shirim Be-Sefer Ha-Zohar Ve-Riq'ah. PhD diss., Hebrew University of Jerusalem, 2006.

Audet, J-P. "Le Sens Du Cantique Des Cantiques." *Revue Biblique* 62 (1955): 197–221.

Avishur, Y. "Le-Ziqqah Ha-Signonit Bein Shir Ha-Shirim ve-Sifrut Ugarit." *Beth Miqra* 59 (1970): 508–25.

Avitzur, Y. "Shir Ha-Shirim." *Beth Mikra* 43 (1998): 256–62.

Bacher, S. "Ha-Bosem be-Shir Ha-Shirim: Motiv 'Eroti ve-Tziyyun Ḥeiqer Ma'amadi." *Shnaton Le-Ḥeqer Ha-Miqra' ve-Hamizraḥ Ha-Qadum* 15 (2005): 39–52.

Bacher, W. "Das Merkwort Prds in Der Jüdischen Bibelexegese." *Zeitschrift für die alttestamentliche Wissenschaft* 13 (1893): 294–305.

——. "L'exégèse Biblique Dans Le Zohar." *Revue des Études Juives* 22 (1891): 33–46, 219–29.

Baer, Y. "Israel, the Christian Church and the Roman Empire" [Hebrew]. *Zion* 21 (1956): 1–49.

Bakon, S. "Song of Songs." *Jewish Bible Quarterly* 22 (1994): 211–20.

Banitt, M. "Les Poterim." *Revue des Ètudes Juives* 125 (1966): 21–33.

Bar-Ilan, M. "Beḥinat Ha-Nusaḥ, 'Inyanim 'Erotiyyim U-ma'asei Keshafim Bi-mgillat Shir Ha-Shirim." *Shenaton La-Mikra' ule-Ḥeqer Ha-Mizraḥ Ha-Qadum* 9 (1987): 31–53.

Barfield, O. *Poetic Diction: A Study in Meaning*. Hanover: Wesleyan University Press, 1973.

Ben-David, Abba. *Leshon Miqra' u-Lshon Ḥakhamim*. Vol. 1–2. Tel Aviv: Dvir, 1967.

Ben-Shammai, H. "Metzi'ah Aḥat She-Hi' Shetayim: Peirush Ha'azinu Le-Rav Shemuel Ben Hofni U-Feirush Ve-Yosha' Le-Rav Se'adiyah Gaon Bikhtav Yad Nishkah." *Kiryat Sefer* 61 (1986–87): 313–32.

Bergant, D. "'My Beloved Is Mine and I Am His' (Song 2:16)." *Semeia* 68 (1996): 23–40.

Bernat, D. "Biblical Waṣfs Beyond Song of Songs." *Journal for the Study of the Old Testament* 28:3 (2004): 327–49.

Blanpain, J. "Langage Mystique, Expression du Désir." *Collectanea Cisterciensia* 36 (1976).

Bloch, J. A. "A Critical Examination of the Text of the Syriac Version of the Song of Songs." *American Journal of Semitic Languages and Literatures* 38 (1922): 103–39.

Bloomfield, M. "Allegory as Interpretation." *New Literary History* 3 (1972): 301–17.

Blowers, P. M. "Origen, the Rabbis and the Bible: Towards a Picture of Judaism and Christianity in Third-Century Caesaria." *Origen of Alexandria: His World and His Legacy* edited by C. Kannengiesser and W. L. Peterson, 96–116. Notre Dame: University of Notre Dame Press, 1988.

Blumenberg, H. *Paradigms for a Metaphorology*. Ithaca: Cornell Uniersity Press, 2010.

Blumenthal, D. "Maimonides' Intellectual Mysticism and the Superiority of the Prophecy of Moses." In *Approaches to Judaism in Medieval Times*, edited by D. Blumenthal, 27–51. Brown Judaic Studies 54. Chico: Scholars Press, 1984.

Booth, W. C. "Metaphor as Rhetoric: The Problem of Evaluation." *On Metaphor*, edited by Sheldon Sacks, 47–70. Chicago: University of Chicago, 1979.
——. *The Rhetoric of Fiction*. Chicago: University of Chicago Press, 1961.
Boyarin, D. "Shenei Mevo'ot Le-Midrash Shir Ha-Shirim." *Tarbiz* 56 (1986–87): 479–500.
Braslavi, J. *Meida' Ha-'Aretz La-Mikra'*. Tel Aviv: Ha-Kibbutz Ha-Me'uḥad, 1970.
Brenner, A. "A Note on Bat-Rabbim (Song of Songs vii 5)." *Vetus Testamentum* 42 (1992): 113–15.
——. "Aromatics and Perfumes in the Song of Songs." *Journal for the Study of the Old Testament* 25 (1983): 75–81.
——. "The Scroll of Love by Immanuel of Rome: A Hebrew Parody of Dante's Vita Nuova." *Prooftexts* 32 (2012): 149–75.
——. "To See Is to Assume: Whose Love Is Celebrated in the Song of Songs?" *Biblical Interpretation* 1 (1993): 265–84.
Brod, M. "Love as a This-Worldly Miracle: The Song of Songs." *Paganism-Christianity-Judaism: A Confession of Faith*, 141–68 (with rearrangements and translation 56–68). Tuscaloosa: University of Alabama Press, 1968.
Brody, H. *Zeitschrift für Hebraische Bibliographie*. Vol. 1, 1896.
Brown, J. "The Mediterranean Vocabulary of the Vine." *VT* 19 (1969): 146–70.
Broyde, M. J. "Defilement of the Hands, Canonization of the Bible, and the Special Status of Esther, Ecclesiastes, and Song of Songs." *Judaism* 173 (1995): 65–79.
Brückman, J., and J. Couchman. "Du 'Cantiquedes Cantiques' Aux 'Carmina Burana' Amour Sacré Et Amour Érotique." *L'érotisme Au Moyen Âge: Etudes Présentées Au Troisimème Colloque De L'insitut D'études Médiévales*, edited by B. Roy, 35–50. Paris: Éditions de l'Aurore, 1977.
Buzy, D. "Allégory Matrimoniale de Jahvé Et d' Israël et Le Cantique des Cantiques." *Vivre Et Penser, Recherces d'exegésis et d'histoire, 3e Série*, 77–90. Paris: Lecoffre, 1945.
Carr, D. "Ancient Sexuality and Divine Eros: Rereading the Bible through the Lens of the Song of Songs." *Union Seminary Quarterly Review* 54:3–4 (2000): 1–18.
——. "Gender and the Shaping of Desire in the Song of Songs." *Journal of Biblical Literature* 119 (2000): 233–48.
Carson, A. *Eros. The Bittersweet*. Champaign, IL: Dalkey Archive Press, 1998.
Certeau, M. de. "L'Énonciation." *Revue de science religieuse* 64 (1976): 183–215.
Cheyne, T. K. "New God Names." *Journal of Biblical Literature* 30 (1911): 104–5.
Chodowski, Solomon. *Observationes Criticae in Midrash Schir Haschirim, Secundum Cod. Monac. 50 Orient.* Dissertation Inauguralis, Halis Saxonum, 1877.
Christos, Y. *Variations on the Song of Songs*. Brookline: Holy Cross Orthodox Press, 2005.
Claudel, P. *Le Cantique Des Cantiques*. Paris: Gallimard, 1948.
Clifford, G. *The Transformations of Allegory*. London: Routledge & Kegan Paul, 1974.
Cogan, M. "From the Peak of Amanah." *Israel Exploration Journal* 34 (1984): 255–59.
Cohen, G. "The Song of Songs and the Jewish Religious Mentality." *The Samuel Friedland Lectures 1960–66*, 1–21. New York, 1966. Reprint ed. in G. Cohen, *Varieties of Jewish Culture*. Philadelphia: The Jewish Publication Society of America, 1991.
Conan, M. *Essais de Poetique des Jardins*. Florence: Leo S. Olschki, 2004.
——. *Gardens and Imagination: Cultural History and Agency*. Cambridge: Harvard University Press, 2008.
Cook, A. S. *The Root of the Thing*. Bloomington: Indiana University Press, 1968.
Cooper, J. S. "Heilige Hochzeit." *Reallexikon der Assyriologie* 259–69. Berlin: Walter De Gruyter Inc., 1972–75.
——. "New Cuneiform Parallels to the Song of Songs." *Journal of Biblical Literature* 90 (1971): 157–62.
Cottier O.P., and P. Georges. "Désir Natural de Voir Dieu." *Gregorianum Colloque Henri de Lubac* (1997): 679–98.

Culley, R. C. *Studies in the Structure of Hebrew Narrative*. Philadelphia: Fortress Press, 1976.

D'Arcy, M. C. *The Mind and Heart of Love*. New York: Meridian Books, 1956.

Daiches, S. *Bible Studies*. London: Goldston & Son, 1950.

Dales, G. "Necklaces Bands and Belts on Mesopotamian Figurines." *Revue d'assyriologie et d'archéologie orientale* 57 (1963): 21–40.

Dalman, G. "Die Blume Habasselet Der Bibel." *Beihefte Zum Alten Testament Vom Alten Testament: Karl Marti zum siebzigsten Geburtstage gewidmet* 42 (1925): 62–68.

Dan, Y. "Ḥedrei Ha-Merkavah." *Tarbiz* 47 (1977–78): 49–55.

Decter, J. "Landscape and Culture in the Medieval Hebrew Rhymed Narrative." *Jewish Studies Quarterly* 14 (2007): 257–85.

Détienne, M. *The Garden of Adonis: Spices in Greek Mythology*. Princeton: Princeton University Press, 1994.

Dickie, J. "The Hispano-Arab Garden: Its Philosophy and Function." *Bulletin of the School of Oriental Studies* (1968): 237–48.

Dijkstra, M. "The Myth of Astarte, the Huntress (KTU 1.92). New Fragments." *Ugarit-Forschungen* 26 (1994): 113–26.

Dirksen, P. B. "Song of Songs 3 6–7." *Vetus Testamentum* 39 (1989): 219–24.

Dobbs-Allsopp, F. W. "Late Linguistic Features in the Song of Songs." *Beihefte zum Alten Testament. Perspectives on the Song of Songs—Perspektiven der Hoheliedauslegung* (2005): 27–77.

Dornseiff, F. "Ägyptischer Liebeslieder, Hoheslied, Sappho, Theokrit." *Zeitschrift der deutschen morgenländischen Gesellschaft* 90 (1931): 588–601.

Dorsey, D. "Literary Structuring in the Song of Songs." *Journal for the Study of the Old Testament* 46 (1990): 81–96.

Driver, G. R. "Hebrew Notes on 'Song of Songs' and 'Lamentations.'" *Festschrift Alfred Bertholet*, edited by Walter Baumgartner, 134–46. Tübingen: J. C. B. Mohr, 1950.

Dronke, Peter. "The Song of Songs and Medieval Love-Lyric." *The Bible and Medieval Culture*, edited by W. Lourdaux and D. Verhelst, 236–62. Louvain: Leuven University Press, 1979.

Dubrau, I. "Motiv 'Iqonografi Shel Re'im 'Ahuvim Be-Maḥazorim 'Ashkenaziyim Mi-Be'Ad Le-Darkhei Ha-Parshanut Shel Torat Ha-Sod Be-'Ashkenaz Bi-ymei Ha-Beinayim." *Kabbalah* 24 (2011): 209–40.

Durand, G. *L'Imagination Symbolique*. Paris: Presses Universitaires de France, 1964.

Einstein, B. *R. Josef Kara und sein Commentar zu Kohelet.* Berlin: Mampe, 1886.

Ellenbogen, M. *Foreign Words in the Old Testament: Their Origin and Etymology*. London: Luzac, 1962.

Epstein, A. "R. Schemaja, Der Schüler und Secretär Raschi's." *Monatschrift für die Geschichte und Wissenschaft des Judentums* 41 (1897): 257–63, 96–312.

Eppenstein, S. "Recherches sur les Comparaisons de l'hebreu avec l'arabe chez les éxegetes du Nord de la France." *Revue des Ètudes Juives* 47 (1903): 47–56.

Exum, J. C. "A Literary and Structural Analysis of the Song of Songs." *ZAW* 85 (1973): 47–79.

——. "Asseverative 'Al in Canticles 1, 6?" *Biblia* 62 (1981): 416–19.

——. "How Does the Song of Songs Mean? On Reading the Poetry of Desire." *Svensk Exegetisk Årsbok* 64 (1999): 47–63.

——. "In the Eye of the Beholder: Wishing, Dreaming, and Double Entendre in the Song of Songs." In *The Labour of Reading: Desire, Alienation, and Biblical Interpretation*, edited by R. Boer, F. Black, and E. Runions, 71–86. Atlanta: Society of Biblical Literature, 1999.

——. "The Poetic Genius of the Song of Songs." *Beihefte zum Alten Testament. Perspectives on the Song of Songs—Perspektiven der Hoheliedauslegung* (2005): 78–96.

Ezrahi, S. D. "'To What Shall I Compare You': Jerusalem as Ground Zero of the Hebrew Imagination." *Proceedings of the Modern Language Association* 122 (2007): 220–34.

Feliks, J. *Fauna and Flora of the Bible*. 2nd edition. London: United Bible Societies, 1972.

——. *'Olam Ha-Tzomeiaḥ Ha-Miqra'i*. Ramat-Gan: Masada, 1968.

——. *Shir Ha-Shirim. Teva', 'Alilah, Ve-'Alegoria*. Jerusalem: Ha-Ḥevrah Le-Ḥeqer Ha-Miqra, 1974.

——. *The Animal World of the Bible*. Tel Aviv: Sinai, 1962.

Fenton, P. *Deux Traités de Mystique Juive*. Paris: Lagrasse, 1987.

——. "Deux Traités Musulmans d'Amour Mystique en Transmission Judéo-Arabe." *Arabica* 37 (1990): 47–55.

——. "Peirush Mysṭi le-Shir Ha-Shirim be-Yado Shel R. David Ben Yehoshu'a Maimuni." *Tarbiz* 69 (2000): 539–89.

——. "'Od 'al R. Ḥanan'el b. Shemu'el, Gedol Ha-Ḥasidim." *Tarbiz* 55 (1986): 77–107.

——. "Some Judeo-Arabic Fragments by Rabbi Abraham He-Ḥasid, the Jewish Sufi." *Journal of Semitic Studies* 26 (1981): 47–72.

Fisch, H. "Song of Solomon: The Allegorical Imperative." *Poetry with a Purpose: Biblical Poetics and Interpretation*. Bloomington: Indiana University Press, 1988.

Fishbane, M. "L'Allégorie dans la Pensée, la Littérature et la Mentalité Juives." In *Allégorie des Poètes, Allégorie des Philosophes. Études sur la Poétique et L'Herméneutique de L'Allegorie de L'Anitquité à La Réforme*, edited by G. Dahan and R. Goulet, 89–112. Paris: Vrin, 2005.

——. "Anthological Midrash and Cultural Paideia: The Case of Songs Rabba 1.2." In *Textual Reasonings: Jewish Philosophy and Text Study at the End of the Twentieth Century*, edited by P. Ochs and N. Levene, 32–66. London: SCM Press, 2002.

——. "Bible Interpretation." In *The Oxford Handbook of Jewish Studies*, edited by M. Goodman, 680–704. Oxford: Oxford University Press, 2002.

——. *Biblical Interpretation in Ancient Israel*. Revised edition. Oxford: Clarendon Press, 1985.

——. *Biblical Myth and Rabbinic Mythmaking*. Oxford: Oxford University Press, 2003.

——. *The Exegetical Imagination: On Jewish Thought and Theology*. Chapter 7, "The Book of *Zohar* and Exegetical Spirituality." Cambridge, MA: Harvard University Press, 1998.

——. *Haftarot. The JPS Bible Commentary*. Philadelphia: The Jewish Publication Society, 2002.

——. *The Kiss of God. Spiritual and Mystical Death in Judaism*. Seattle: University of Washington Press, 1994.

——. "Polysystem and Piyyuṭ: The Poetics of a Yotzer by R. Meshullam B. Qalonimos." In *Festschrift for Peter Schäfer*, edited by R. Boustan et al. Tübingen: Mohr-Siebeck, 2012.

——. "The Song of Songs and Ancient Jewish Religiosity: Between Eros and History." *Von Enoch Bis Kafka: Festschrift Für Karl E. Grözinger Zum 60. Geburtstag*, edited by M. Voigts, 69–81. Wiesbaden: Harrasowitz, 2002.

Flint, Peter W. "The Book of Canticles (Song of Songs) in the Dead Sea Scrolls [Perspektiven Der Hoheliedauslegung]." *Beihefte zur Zeitschrift für alttestamentliche Wissenschft* 346 (2005): 96–104.

Foster, B. O. "Notes on the Symbolism of the Apple in Classical Antiquity." *Harvard Studies in Classical Philology* 10 (1899): 39–55.

Fox, M. "Love, Passion, and Perception in Israelite and Egyptian Love Poetry." *Journal of Biblical Literature* 102 (1983): 219–28.

Frank, D. "Karaite Commentaries on the Song of Songs from Tenth-Century Jerusalem." In *With Reverence for the Word: Medieval Scriptural Exegesis in Judaism, Christianity, and Islam*, edited by Jane Dammen McAuliffe, Barry D. Walfish, and Joseph W. Goering. New York: Oxford University Press, 2003.

——. *Search Scripture Well: Karaite Exegetes and the Origin of the Jewish Bible Commentary in the Islamic East*. Leiden: E. J. Brill, 2004.

Frankel, A. "Tashlum Ma'arekhet Ha-Yotzer 'Afiq Renen Ve-Shirim' Le-R. Meshullam Bar Qalonimos." *Higgayon Le-Yonah. Hebeiṭim Ḥadashim Be-Ḥeqer Sifrut Ha-Midrash, Ha-Aggadah Ve-ha-Piyyuṭ (Festschrift for Y. Frankel)*, edited by J. Elbaum, J. Levinson, and G. Hazan-Rokem, 551–65. Jerusalem: Magnes Press, 2007.

Friedman, S. "The Holy Scriptures Defile the Hands: The Transformation of a Biblical Concept in Rabbinic Theology." In *Minḥah Le-Naḥum: Biblical and Other Studies Presented to Nahum M. Sarna in Honour of His 70th Birthday*, edited by M. Brettler and M. Fishbane, 117–32. Sheffield: Sheffield University Press, 1993.

Galli, B. "The Loving Body in Time and Space: Rosenzweig and the Song of Songs." *The Journal of the Faculty of Religious Studies* 26 (1998): 51–61.

Gault, B. "The Fragments of Canticles from Qumran: Implications and Limitations for Interpretation." *Revue de Qumran* 24 (2010): 351–71.

Geiger, A. "Die Nordfranzösische Exegeten-Schule im 12 Jahrhundert." *S. L. Heilberg, Nit'ey Ne'emanim* 1–44. Breslau, 1847.

Gesenius' Hebrew Grammar. Edited by W. Gesenius, E. Kautzsch, and A. E. Cowley. 2nd ed. Oxford: Clarendon Press, 1910.

Gilson, E. *The Spirit of Medieval Philosophy*. London: Sheed & Ward, 1936.

Girón-Blanc, L. F. "Exégèse et Homilétique dans le Cantique des Cantiques Rabbah." In *Rabbi Shlomoh 1040–1990, Hommages À Ephraïm E. Urbach*, edited by G. Sed Rajna (4: *E Congrès Européen des Études Juives, Paris-Troyes 6–13 Juillet*), 291–99. Paris, 1990.

Goitein, S. D. "Ayumma Kannidgalot (Song of Songs 6.10) 'Splendid Like the Brilliant Stars.'" *Journal of Semitic Studies* 10 (1965): 220–21.

——. "'Ofyo Ha-Sifruti U-Feirusho shel Shir Ha-Shirim." *'Iyunim Be-Miqra'*, 283–317. Tel Aviv, 1967.

Goodman, M. "Sacred Scripture and 'Defiling the Hands.'" *Journal of Theological Studies* 41 (1990): 99–107.

Gordis, R. *The Song of Songs*. New York: Jewish Theological Seminary of America, 1961.

——. "The Root D-G-L in the Song of Songs." *Journal of Biblical Literature* 88 (1969): 203–4.

Gordon, P. "The Erotics of Negative Theology: Maimonides on Apprehension." *Jewish Studies Quarterly* 2 (1995): 1–38.

Goshen-Gottstein, A. "Love as a Hermeneutic Principle in Rabbinic Literature." *Journal of Literature and Theology* 8:3 (1994): 247–67.

——. "Polemomania: Methodological Reflection on the Study of the Judeo-Christian Controversy between the Talmudic Sages and Origen over the Interpretations of the Song of Songs" [Hebrew]. *Jewish Studies* 42 (2004): 119–90.

Goshen-Gottstein, M. H. "Philologische Mizcellen zu den Qumrantexten," part 4: "Die Schoenheit Saras (1Q Genesis Midrash) und der Wasf in Hohenliede." *Revue de Qumran* 2 (1959): 46–48.

Gottlieb, E. *Meḥqarim Be-Sifrutha-Kabbalah*. Tel Aviv: University of Tel Aviv Press, 1976.

Gottlieb, I. B. "The Jewish Allegory of Love: Change and Constancy." *Journal of Jewish Thought and Philosophy* 2 (1992): 1–17.

Green, A. "Shekhinah, the Virgin Mary, and the Song of Songs: Reflections on a Kabbalistic Symbol in Its Historical Context." *Association for Jewish Studies Review* 26 (2002): 1–52.

——. "The Song of Songs in Early Jewish Mysticism." *Orim* 2 (1987): 49–63.

Green, D. *The Aroma of Righteousness: Scent and Seduction in Rabbinic Life and Literature*. University Park: Pennsylvania State University Press, 2011.

Griess, Z. "Ha-Perushim Ha-Qabbaliyyim Ha-Qedumim Le-Shir Ha-Shirim." *Mar'ah* 1 (2001): 18–24.

Gross, Avraham. *R. Yosef Ben Avraham Ḥayyun: Manhig Kehilat Lisbon Vi-ytzirato*. Ramat Gan: Bar-Ilan University Press, 1993.

Grossberg, D. "A Centrifugal Structure in Biblical Poetry." *Semiotica* 58 (1986): 139–50.

——. *Centripetal and Centrifugal Structures in Hebrew Poetry*. Atlanta: Scholars Press, 1989.

——. "Nature, Humanity, and Love in the Song of Songs." *Interpretation* 59 (2005): 229–42.

——. "Noun/Verb Parallelism: Syntactic or Asyntactic." *Journal of Biblical Literature* 99 (1980): 481–88.

——. "Sexual Desire: Abstract and Concrete." *Hebrew Studies* 22 (1981): 59–60.

——. "Two Kinds of Sexual Relationships in the Hebrew Bible." *Hebrew Studies* 35 (1994): 7–25.

Grossman, A. "Haggahot R. Shema'yah Ve-Nusaḥ Peirush Rabbi Shlomoh La-Torah." *Tarbiz* 60 (1991): 67–98.

——. "Ha-Reqa' Le-Tzimiḥat Parshanut Ha-Piyyuṭ Be-Ashkenaz U-ve-Tzarfat Ba-Me'ah Ha-Y"G." In *Sefer Ha-Yovel Li-Shlomoh Simonson*, edited by D. Carpi et al., 45–72. Tel Aviv: Tel Aviv University Press, 1993.

——. "R. Shema'yah Ha-Shoshani U-Feirusho Le-Shir Ha-Shirim." In *Sefer Ha-Yovel Le-Rav Mordechai Breuer*, edited by M. Bar-Asher, 27–62. Jerusalem: Academon-Hebrew University, 1992.

——. "Ziqqatah shel Yahadut 'Ashkenaz Ha-Qedumah 'el 'Eretz Yisrael." *Shalem* 3 (1981): 57–92.

Gurion, P. *Grammar de l'Hebrew Biblique*. 2nd ed. Rome: Pontifical Biblical Institute, 1923.

Gutzwiller, K. *Poetic Garlands. Hellenistic Epigrams in Context*. Berkeley: University of California Press, 1998.

Hacohen, E. "Shir Ha-Shirim Ve-Shirav—'Iyyun Be-Fiyyuṭei Shir Ha-Shirim Be-'Ashkenaz." In *Sefer Ha-Yovel Le-Rav Mordechai Breur*, edited by M. Bar-Asher, 399–416. Jerusalem: Academon-Hebrew University, 1992.

Hagedorn, A. "Perspectives on the Song of Songs." *Beihefte zum Alten Testament* 346 (2005).

Halbertal, M. *Concealment and Revelation. Esoterism in Jewish Thought and Its Philosophical Implications*. Princeton: Princeton University Press, 2007.

Halkin, Abraham. "Ibn Aknin's Commentary on the Song of Songs." *Alexander Marx Jubilee Volume*, 389–424. New York: Jewish Theological Seminary of America, 1950.

Harl, M. "La Version LXX du Cantique des Cantiques et le groupe Kaige-Theodotian—Quelques Remarques Lexicales." *Textus* 18 (1995): 101–20.

Harrison, R. P. *Gardens: An Essay on the Human Condition*. Chicago: University of Chicago Press, 2008.

Harvey, K., ed. *The Kiss in History*. Manchester: Manchester University Press, 2005.

Harvey, S. "The Meaning of Terms Designating Love in Judaeo-Arabic Thought and Some Remarks of the Judaeo-Arabic Interpretation of Maimonides." In *Judaeo-Arabic Studies: Proceedings of the Founding Conference for the Society of Judaeo-Arabic Studies*, edited by N. Golb. Netherlands: Harwood Press, 1997.

Harvey, W. Z. "On Maimonides' Allegorical Readings of Scripture." In *Interpretation and Allegory. Antiquity to the Modern Period*, edited by J. Whitman. Leiden: Brill, 2000.

Haupt, P. "The Book of Canticles." *American Journal of Semitic Languages and Literature* 18 (1902): 193–245; and 19 (1902): 1–32.

Heath, M. *Ancient Philosophical Poetics*. Cambridge: Cambridge University Press, 2013.

Hecker, J. "Kissing Kabbalists: Hierarchy, Reciprocity, and Equality." *Studies in Jewish Civilization*, 171–208. Omaha, NE: Creighton University Press, 2008.

Heinemann, I. *Altjüdische Allegoristik*. Beilage Zum Jahresbericht Des Jüdisch-Theologischen Seminars. Breslau: 1936.

——. "Die Wissenschaftliche Allegoristik Des Jüdischen Mittelalters." *Hebrew Union College Annual* (1950–51): 611–43.

Heinemann, J. "Targum Shir-Ha-Shirim U-Mqorotav." *Tarbiz* 41 (1962): 125–29.

Hirshman, M. *Rivalry Genius: Jewish and Christian Biblical Interpretation in Late Antiquity*. Albany: SUNY Press, 1996.

Hollander, E. *Piyyuṭ Commentary in Medieval Ashkenaz*. Berlin: Walter de Gruyter, 2008.

Honeyman, A. M. "Two Contributions to Canaanite Toponomy." *Journal of Theological Studies* 50 (1949): 50–52.

Horst, F. "Die Formen Des Althebräischen Liebesliedes." In *Gottes Recht*, edited by H. W. Wolff, 176–87. Munich: C. Kaiser, 1961.

Huss, B. "Sefer Ha-Zohar as a Canonical, Sacred, and Holy Text. Changing Perspectives of the Book of Splendor between the Thirteenth and Eighteenth Centuries." *The Journal of Jewish Thought and Philosophy* 7 (1998): 257–307.

Hyde, W. "Greek Analogies to the Song of Songs." In *The Song of Songs: A Symposium*, edited by W. Schoff, 31–42. Philadelphia: The Commercial Museum, 1924.

Idel, M. *Absorbing Perfections. Kabbalah and Interpretation*. New Haven: Yale University Press, 2002.

——. "'In a Whisper': On Transmission of Shiʿur Qomah and Kabbalistic Secrets in Jewish Mysticism." In *Il Mantello De Elia. Trasmissione E Innovazione Nella Cabala; Estratto Da: Rivista Di Storia E Letteratura Religiosa*, edited by L. S. Olschki, 443–88. Firenze: L. Olschki, 2011.

——. *Kabbalah and Eros*. New Haven: Yale University Press, 2005.

——. "Types of Redemptive Activity in the Middle Ages." In *Meshiḥiyut Ve-'Esthatologia: Qovetz Ma'amarim [Messianism and Eschatology: A Collection of Articles]*, edited by Zvi Baras, 253–79. Jerusalem: Merkaz Zalman Shazar, 1983/84.

Ishay, H. *U-ve-Gan 'Eittim U-Khtavim Nitʿalsah Ba-'Ahavim. Sifrut Ha-'Ahavah Be-Ḥalal Ha-Siaḥ Ha-Tarbuti Ha-'Ivri-'Aravi Bi-ymei Ha-Beinayim*. Jerusalem: Ben-Tzvi Institute, 2011.

Israelit-Groll, S. "Ostracon Nash 12 and Chapter 5 of Song of Songs." *Proceedings of the Tenth World Congress of Jewish Studies: Jerusalem, August 16–24, 1989*, 131–35. Jerusalem: World Union of Jewish Studies, 1990.

Jakobson, R. *Language and Literature*. Edited by K. Promorska and S. Rudy. Cambridge: Harvard University Press, 1987.

Japhet, S. "Exegesis and Polemic in Rashbam's Commentary on the Song of Songs." In *Jewish Biblical Interpretation and Cultural Exchange*, edited by N. B. Dohrmann and D. Stern, 182–95. Philadelphia: University of Pennsylvania Press, 2008.

——. "'Lebanon' in the Transition from Derash to Peshat: Sources, Etymology and Meaning (with Special Attention to the Song of Songs." In *Emanuel: Studies in the Hebrew Bible, Septuagint, and Dead Sea Scrolls in Honor of Emanuel Tov*, edited by R. Kraft and S. Paul, 707–24. Leiden-Boston: Brill, 2003.

——. "'The Lovers' Way': Cultural Symbiosis in a Medieval Commentary on the Song of Songs." In *Birkat Shalom. Studies in the Bible, Ancient Near Eastern Literature, and Post-biblical Judaism Presented to Shalom M. Paul on the Occasion of His Seventieth Birthday*, edited by C. Cohen, 863–80. Winona Lake: Eisenbrauns, 2008.

——. "Rabbi Shlomoh's Commentary on the Song of Songs." In *Mein Haus wird ein Bethaus für alle Völker Genannt Werden (Jes 56,7): Judentum Seit der Zeit des Zweiten Tempels in Geschichte, Literatur und Kult; Festschrift für Thomas Willi zum 65. Geburtstag*, edited by J and T. Riprisch Mannchen. Neukirchen, 2007.

——. *Tei'urei ha-Guf ve-Dimuyei ha-Yofi be-Farshanut ha-Peshaṭ le-Shir ha-Shirim Bi-ymei Ha-Beinayim: Davar Davur 'al 'Ofanav. Meḥqarim be-Farshanut ha-Miqraʿ ve-ha-Qoran bi-ymei ha-Beinayim Mugashim le-Ḥaggai Ben-Shammai*. Edited by S. Hopkins M. Bar-Asher, et al. Jerusalem: Makhon Ben-Tzvi, 2007.

——. "Two Introduction by Rabbi Samuel Ben Meir (Rashbam), to the Song of Songs and Lamentations." In *Transforming Relations. Essays on Jews and Christian Throughout History in Honor of Michael A. Signer*, edited by Franklin Harkins, 205–23. Notre Dame: University of Notre Dame Press, 2010.

Jolles, A. *Einfache Formen*. 3rd ed. Tübingen: Niemeyer, 1965.

Kadari, T. "Li-Mlekhet Ha-'Arikhah Be-Midrash Shir Ha-Shirim Rabbah." PhD diss., Hebrew University of Jerusalem, 2004.

——. "Rabbinic and Christinan Models of Interaction on the Song of Songs." In *Interaction between Judasim and Christianity in History, Religion, Art and Literature*, edited by J. Schwartz, M. Poortius, and J. Turner, 65–82. Leiden: Brill, 2009.

——. "'Tokho Ratzuf 'Ahavah': 'Al Ha-Torah Ke-Ra'ayah bi-Drashot Tanna'im Le-Shir Ha-Shirim." *Tarbiz* 71 (2002): 391–404.

Kamin, S. "Dugma' be-Feirush Rashi le-Shir ha-Shirim." *Bein Yehudim le-Notzrim be-Farshanut ha-Miqra'*, 13–30. Jerusalem: Magnes, 1991.

——. "Peirush Rashi 'Al Shir Ha-Shirim Ve-ha-Vikuaḥ Ha-Yhudi-Notzri." *Bein Yehudim La-Notzrim Be-Farshanut Ha-Miqra'*, 31–61. Jerusalem: Magnes Press, 1991.

Kaplan, J. "A Divine Love Song. The Emergence of the Theo-Erotic Interpretation of the Song of Songs in Ancient Judaism and Early Christianity." PhD diss., Harvard University, 2010.

Kearney, R. "The Shulammite's Song: Divine Eros, Ascending and Descending." In *Towards a Theology of Eros: Transfiguring Passion at the Limits of Discipline*, edited by V. Burrus and C. Keller, 306–40. New York: Fordham University Press, 2006.

Kellner, M. "Communication or the Lack Thereof among 13th–14th Century Provencal Jewish Philosophers: Moses ibn Tibbon and Gersonides on the Song of Songs." In *Communication in the Jewish Diaspora*, edited by S. Menache, 227–46. Leiden: E. J. Brill, 1996.

——. "Gersonides on the Song of Songs and the Nature of Science." *Journal of Jewish Thought and Philosophy* 4 (1994): 1–21.

——. "'Gersonides' Commentary on Song of Songs: For Whom Was It Written and Why?" In *Gersonides Et Son Temps*, edited by G. Dahan, 81–107. Paris: Cerf, 1991.

——. "Haqdamat Ha-Ralbag le-Feirusho le-Shir Ha-Shirim." *Daat* 23 (1989): 15–32.

——. *Torah in the Observatory: Gersonides, Maimonides, Song of Songs*. Boston: Academic Studies Press, 2010.

Kessler, R. *Some Poetical and Structural Features of the Song of Songs*. Oriental Society Monograph Series 8. Leeds: Leeds University, 1957.

Kimelman, R. "Rabbi Yochanan and Origen on the Song of Songs: A Third Century Jewish-Christian Disputation." *Harvard Theological Review* 73 (1980): 567–95.

Kosman, A. *Massekhet Nashim: Ḥokhmah, 'Ahavah, Teshuqah, Yofi, Min, Qedushah* [*Women's Tractate: Wisdom, Love, Faithfulness, Passion, Beauty, Sex, Holiness*]. Jerusalem: Keter, 2007.

Kozodoy, M. "Messianic Interpretation of the Song of Songs in Late-Medieval Iberia." In *The Hebrew Bible in Fifteenth-Century Spain. Exegesis Literature, Philosophy, and the Arts*, edited by J. Decter and A. Prats, 117–47. Leiden: E. J. Brill, 2012.

Krauss, S. "The Archeological Background of Some Passages in the Song of Songs." *Jewish Quarterly Review* 32 (1941): 115–37.

Kristeva, J. *Tales of Love*. New York: Columbia University Press, 1987.

Kuhl, C. "Das Hohelied und Seine Deutung." *Theologische Rundshau* 9 (1937): 137–67.

Lachs, S. T. "Prolegomena to Canticles Rabba." *Jewish Quarterly Review* 55 (1965): 235–55.

Lambert, W. G. "Devotion: The Language of Religion and Love." *Figurative Language in the Ancient near East*, 25–39. London, 1987.

——. "Divine love Lyrics from Babylon." *Journal of Semitic Studies* 4 (1959): 1–15.

Landsberger, F. "Poetic Units within the Song of Songs." *Journal of Biblical Literature* 73 (1954): 203–16.

Landy, F. "On Metaphors, Play, and Nonsense." *Semeia* 61 (1993): 219–37.

——. "The Song of Songs and the Garden of Eden." *Journal of Biblical Literature* 98 (1979): 513–28.

Langermann, Tzvi. "Saving the Soul by Knowing the Soul: A Medieval Yemini Interpretation of Song of Songs." *Journal of Jewish Thought and Philosophy* 12:2 (2003): 147–66.

Leiman, S. Z. *The Canonization of Hebrew Scripture: The Talmudic and Midrashic Evidence (Transactions of the Connecticut Academy of Arts and Sciences, 47)*. Hamden, CT: Archon Books, 1976.

Lemaire, A. "Zāmīr dans la Tablette de Gezer et le Cantique des Cantiques." *Vetus Testamentum* 35 (1975): 15–26.

Lerner, M. B. "Collected Exempla: Studies in Aggadic Texts Published in the Genizot Series" [Hebrew]. *Kiryat Sepher* 61 (1986–87): 867–92.

——. "The First Printed Edition of the Midrash on the Five Scrolls: Studies in Working Methods of the First Hebrew Printers in Constantinople and Pesaro" [Hebrew]. In *Yad le-Heman: Qovets Meḥqarim le-Zekher A.M. Haberman,* edited by T. Z. Malachi, 289–311. Lod: Mekhon Haberman Le-Meḥqere Sifrut, 1983.

Levin, I. "'I Sought the One Whom My Soul Loveth': A Study on the Influence of Erotic Secular Poetry on Hebrew Religious Poetry" [Hebrew]. *Hasifrut* 3 (1971): 116–49.

Lévy-Valensi, E. *La Poétique du Zohar*. Paris: Éditions de l'éclat, 1996.

Lieber, L. "'Let Me Sing for My Beloved': Transformations of the Song of Songs in Synagogal Poetry." PhD diss., University of Chicago, 2003.

——. *A Vocabulary of Desire: The Song of Songs in the Early Synagogue*. London: Brill, 2014.

Liebes, Y. "Ha-'Omnam Betulah Hi' Ha-Shekhinah?" *Pe'amim* 101–2 (2005): 303–13.

——. "Keitzad Nitḥabber Sefer Ha-Zohar." In *Sefer Ha-Zohar ve-Doro*, edited by Y. Dan, in *Meḥqerei Yerushalayim be-Maḥashevet Yisrael* 8 (1989): 1–71.

——. *Torat Ha-Yetzirah shel Sefer Ha-Yetzirah*. Tel Aviv: Schocken, 2000.

——. "Zohar ve-'Eros." *'Alpayim* 9 (1994): 67–119.

Lieberman, S. "Mishnat Shir Ha-Shirim." In G. Scholem, *Jewish Gnosticism, Merkavah Mysticism and Talmudic Tradition*, 118–26. New York: Jewish Theological Seminary, 1960.

Liebreich, L. J. "The Benedictory Formula in the Targum to the Song of Songs." *Hebrew Union College Annual* 18 (1944): 177–97.

Loewe, R. "Apologetic Motifs in the Targum to the Song of Songs." In *Biblical Motifs: Origins and Transformations*, edited by A. Altmann, 159–96. Cambridge: Harvard University Press, 1966.

Long, G. "A Lover, Cities, and Heavenly Bodies: Co-Text and the Translation of Two Similes in Canticles (6:4c; 6:10d)." *Journal of Biblical Literature* 115 (1996): 703–709.

Loprieno, A. "Searching for a Common Background: Egyptian Love Poetry and the Biblical Song of Song." *Beihefte zum Alten Testament. Perspectives on the Song of Songs—Perspektiven der Hoheliedauslegung* (2005): 97–104.

Loretz, O. "Zum Problem des Eros im Hohenlied." *Biblische Zeitschrift* 8 (1964): 191–216.

Lys, D. "Notes Sur Le Cantique." *Vetus Testamentum Supplement*, Congress volume: *Rome* 1968 18 (1969): 170–78.

Malter, H. "Personifications of Soul and Body. A Study of Judaeo-Arabic Literature." *The Jewish Quarterly Review* 2 (1912): 453–79.

Marcus, I. "The Song of Songs in German Hasidism and the School of Rabbi Shlomoh: A Preliminary Comparison." In *The Frank Talmage Memorial Volume*, edited by B. Walfish, 181–89. Haifa, 1994.

Margolis, M. L. *The Hebrew Scriptures in the Making*. Philadelphia: The Jewish Publication Society of America, 1922.

——. "How the Song of Songs Entered the Canon." In *The Song of Songs. A Symposium*, edited by W. Schoff, 9–17. Philadelphia: The Commercial Museum, 1924.

Mariaselvan, A. *The Song of Songs and Ancient Tamil Love Poems: Poetry and Symbolism*. Rome: Pontifical Biblical Institute, 1988.

Martineau, R. "2: The Song of Songs." *The American Journal of Philology* 13:3 (1892): 307–28.

Mazor, Y. "The Song of Songs or the Story of Stories." *Scandinavian Journal of the Old Testament* 1 (1990): 1–29.

McAuliffe, J. D., B. D. Walfish, and J. W. Goering, eds. *With Reverence for the Word: Medieval Scriptural Exegesis in Judaism, Christianity, and Islam*. New York: Oxford University Press, 2003.

McGinn, B. "Language of Love in Christian and Jewish Mysticism." In *Mysticism and Language*, edited by S. Katz, 202–35. New York: Oxford University Press, 1992.

Meek, T. "Canticles and the Tammuz Cult." *American Journal of Semitic Languages and Literature* 39 (1922): 1–14.

——. "The Song of Songs and the Fertility Cult." In *A Symposium on the Song of Songs*, edited by W. H. Schoff, 48–79. Philadelphia: Commercial Museum, 1924.

——. "Babylonian Parallels to the Song of Songs." *Journal of Biblical Literature* 43 (1924): 245–52.

Melamed, E. Z. "Targum Shir Ha-Shirim." *Tarbiz* 40 (1970–71): 201–15.

Mendes-Flohr, P. "Between Sensual and Heavenly Love: Franz Rosenzweig's Reading of the Song of Songs." In *Scriptural Exegesis: The Shapes of Culture and the Religious Imagination: Essays in Honour of Michael Fishbane*, edited by D. Green and L. Lieber, 310–18. Oxford: Oxford University Press, 2009.

Menn, E. "Targum of the Song of Songs and the Dynamics of Historical Allegory." In *The Interpretation of Scripture in Early Judaism and Christianity: Studies in Language and Tradition*, edited by C. A. Evans, 423–45. Sheffield: Sheffield University Press, 2000.

Meroz, R. "Zoharic Narratives and Their Adaptations." *Hispania Judaica Bulletin* 3 (2000): 3–63.

Meyers, C. "Gender Imagery in the Song of Songs." *Hebrew Annual Review* 19 (1986): 209–23.

——. "'To Her Mother's House': Considering a Counterpart to the Israelite bêt 'ab." In *The Bible and the Politics of Exegesis*, edited by David Jobling et al., 39–51, 304–7. Cleveland: Pilgrim Press, 1991.

Milikowsky, C. "Reflections on Hand-Washing, Hand-Purity and Holy Scripture in Rabbinic Literature." In *Purity and Holiness: The Heritage of Leviticus*, edited by M. Poorthuis and J. Schwartz, 149–62. Leiden: E. J. Brill, 1999.

Minnis, A. *Medieval Theory of Authorship. Scholastic Literary Attitudes in the Later Middle Ages*. 2nd ed. Philadelphia: University of Pennsylvania Press, 2010.

Mopsik, C. "The Body of Engenderment in the Hebrew Bible, the Rabbinic Tradition and the Kabbalah." In *Fragments of a History of the Human Body*, edited by M. Feher with R. Nadaff and N. Tazi, 48–73. New York: Zone Books, 1989.

Moyn, S. "Divine and Human Love: Franz Rosenzweig's History of the Song of Songs." *Jewish Studies Quarterly* 12 (2005): 194–212.

Muffs, Y. *Love and Joy: Law, Language and Religion in Ancient Israel*. New York City: Jewish Theological Seminary of America, 1992.

Müller, H. P. "Die Lyrische Reproduktion des Mythischen im Hohenlied." *Zeitschrift für Theologie und Kirche* 73 (1976): 23–41.

Munk, R. "'And to Cleave to Him': The Conjunction between God and Man." *The Rationale of Halakhic Man: Joseph B. Soloveitchik's Conception of Jewish Thought (Amsterdam Studies in Jewish Thought)*, 104–23. Amsterdam: J. C. Gieben, 1996.

——. *The Rationale of Halakhic Man: Joseph B Soloveitchik's Conception of Jewish Thought*. Amsterdam: J. C. Gieben, 1996.

Munro, J. M. "Spikenard and Saffron: A Study in the Poetic Language of the Song of Songs." *Journal for the Study of the Old Testament. Supplement Series*. Sheffield: Sheffield Academic Press, 1995.

Naeh, S. "'Ṭovim Dodeykha Mi-Yayin': Mabaṭ Ḥadash 'Al Mishnat 'Avodah Zarah 2, 5." In *Meḥqarim be-Talmud u-Midrash. Sefer Zikaron le-Tirtzah Lipshitz*, edited by J. Levinson, M. Bar-Asher, B. Lipshitz, 411–34. Jerusalem: Mosad Bialik, 2005.

Nahon, G. "A Propos de l'Amour Intellectuel dans les Oeuvres de Moïse ibn Ezra." *Revue des Études Juives* 126 (1967): 191–204.

Neubauer, A. "Joseph Ben Aknin." *Monatschrift für die Geschichte und Wissenschaft des Judentums* (1870).

Nissinen, M. "Love Lyrics of Nabû and Tašmetu: An Assyrian Song of Songs?" In *Und Mose Schrieb Dieses Lied Auf. Studien zum Alten Testaments und zum Alten Orient. Festschrift für Oswald Loretz. Studien zum Alten Testament und zum Alten Orient 250*, edited by Manfried Dietrich and Ingo Kottsieper, 585–634. Münster: Ugarit-Verlag 1998.

Noegel, S and G. Rendsburg. *Solomon's Vineyard: Literary and Linguistic Studies in the Song of Songs*. Atlanta: Society of Biblical Literature, 2009.

Oberhänsli-Widmer, G. "Schir Ha-Schirim Rabba—Ein Spätantik-Frühmittelalterlischer Midrasch Zum Hohenlied." *Kirche und Israel* 36 (2011): 163–77.

On Metaphor. Edited by Sheldon Sacks. Chicago: University of Chicago Press, 1979.

Oppenheim, A. "On Royal Gardens in Mesopotamia." *Journal of Near Eastern Studies* 24 (1965): 328–33.

Ott, H. "Theologie als Gebet und als Wissenschaft." *Theologische Zeitschrift* 14 (1958): 120–32.

Pardee, D. "As Strong as Death." In *Love and Death in the Ancient Near East: Essays in Honor of Marvin H. Pope*, edited by John H. Marks and Robert M. Good, 65–69. Guilford, CT: Four Quarters, 1987.

Paul, S. "A Lover's Garden of Verse: Literal and Metaphorical Imagery in Ancient near Eastern Love Poetry." In *Tehillah Le-Moshe: Biblical and Judaic Studies in Honor of Moshe Greenberg*, edited by Barry Eichler and Jeffrey Tigay, 99–110. Winona Lake, IN: Eisenbrauns, 1996.

——. "An Unrecognized Medical Idiom in Canticles 6, 12 and Job 9, 21." *Biblica* 59 (1978): 545–47.

——. "The 'Plural of Ecstasy' in Mesopotamian and Biblical Love Poetry." In *Solving Riddles and Untying Knots. Biblical, Epigraphic, and Semitic Studies in Honor of Jonas C. Greenfield*, edited by S. Gitin, Z. Zevit, and M. Sokoloff, 585–97. Winona Lake: Eisenbrauns, 1995.

Pelletetier, A-M. "Lectures du Cantiques des Cantiques." In *De L'enigma Du Sens Aux Figures De Lecture*. Rome: Pontifical Biblical Institute, 1989.

Perella, J. *The Kiss: Sacred and Profane*. Berkeley: University of California Press, 1969.

Perry, T. A. *Erotic Spirituality: The Integrative Tradition from Leone Ebreo to John Donne*. Tuscaloosa: University of Alabama Press, 1980.

Pines, S. "The Philosophical Purport of Maimonides' Halakhic Works and the Purport of the Guide of the Perplexed." In *Maimonides and Philosophy*, edited by S. Pines and Y. Yovel, 1–14. Dordrecht-Boston: Nijhoff Publishers, 1986.

Plüss, T. "Das Gleichnis in Erzählender Dichtung: Ein Problem für Philologen und Schulmänner." In *Festschrift zur 49: Versammlung Deutscher Philologen und Schulmänner in Basel im Jahre 1907*, 40–64. Basel: E. Birkhäuser, 1907.

Rabin, C. "Qesharim Hodiyim shel Shir Ha-Shirim." *Sefer Baruch Kurtzveil*, 264–74. Jerusalem: Schocken Books and Bar-Ilan University Press, 1965.

——. "The Song of Songs and Tamil Poetry." *Sciences Religieuses/Studies in Religion* 3 (1973/74): 205–19.

Rapp-de Lange, B. "The Love of Torah: Solomon Projected into the World of R. Aqiba in the Song of Songs Rabbah." In *Recycling Biblical Figures: Papers Read at a Noster Colloquium in Amsterdam, 12–13 May 1997*, edited by A. and Willem van Henten Brenner, 272–92. Leiden: Deo Publishing, 1999.

Ratzhaby, Y. "Ha-'Ahavah Be-Shirei R. Shmuel Ha-Nagid." *Tarbiz* 39 (1970): 137–69.

Reich, B. "The Beauty and the King? An Interpretation of Song of Songs 7:6" [Hebrew]. *Shnaton HaMiqra'* 13 (2003): 173–74.

Rendsburg, G. "A Comprehensive Guide to Israelian Hebrew: Grammar and Lexicon." *Orient* 38 (2003): 5–35.

——. "Talpiyyôt" (Song 4:4)." *Journal of Northwest Semitic Studies* 20 (1994): 13–19.

Ricoeur, P. "The Metaphorical Process as Cognition, Imagination, and Feeling." *Critical Inquiry* 5 (1978): 143–59.

——. "The Nuptial Metaphor." In *Thinking Biblically: Exegetical and Hermeneutical Studies*, edited by A. LaCoque and P. Ricoeur, 265–303. Chicago: University of Chicago Press, 1998.

——. "The Problem of the Double-Sense as Hermeneutic Problem and as Semantic Problem." In *Myths and Symbols: Essays in Honor of Mircea Eliade*, edited by J. Kitagawa and C. Long, 63–79. Chicago: University of Chicago Press, 1969.

——. *The Rule of Metaphor: Multidisciplinary Studies or the Creation of Meaning in Language*. Toronto: University of Toronto Press, 1977.

Ricoeur, P., and E. Jüngel. *Metapher. Zur Hermeneutik Religiöser Sprache*. München: C. Kaiser, 1974.

Ringgren, H. "The Marriage Motif in Israelite Religion." In *Ancient Israelite Religion: Essays in Honor of Frank Moore Cross*, edited by P. Miller, P. Hanson, and S. Dean McBride, 421–28. Philadelphia: Fortress Press, 1987.

Rosenberg, S. "Ha-Parshanut ha-Philosophit le-Shir Ha-Shirim: He'arot Mavo'." *Tarbiz* 59 (1990): 133–51.

Rosenthal, F. "A Judeo-Arabic Work under Sûfic Influence." *Hebrew Union College Annual* 15 (1940): 433–84.

Rosenzweig, F. *The Star of Redemption*. New York: Holt, Rinehart and Winston, 1971.

Roth, N. "My Beloved Is Like a Gazelle': Imagery of the Beloved Boy in Religious Hebrew Poetry." *Hebrew Annual Review* 8 (1984): 143–65.

Rozenlaar, M. "Shir Ha-Shirim 'Al Reqa' Ha-Shirah Ha-'Erotit Ha-Yevanit Ha-Hellenistit." *Eshkolot* 1 (1954): 33–48.

Ruggles, D. F. *Gardens, Landscape, and Vision in the Gardens of Islamic Spain*. University Park, PA: Pennsylvania State University Press, 2000.

Salfeld, S. *Das Hohelied Salomo's bei den jüdischen Erklärern des Mittelalters*. Berlin: J. Benzian, 1879.

Salters, R. B. "The Medieval French Glosses of Rashbam on Qoheleth and Song of Songs." *Studia Biblica* 1 (1978): 249–52.

Sandler, P. "Le-Ba'ayat Pardes." In *Sefer Ha-Yovel Le-'Eliyahu Auerbach*, 222–35. Jerusalem: Kiryat Sefer, 1955.

Sasson, J. M. "A Further Cuneiform Parallel to the Song of Songs?" *Zeitschrift für die Alttestamentliche Wissenschaft* 85:3 (1973): 359–60.

——. "On M. H. Pope's Song of Songs [Ab 7c]." *A Journal for the Study of the Northwest Semitic Languages and Literatures* 1:2 (1978–79): 177–96.

Scheindlin, R. *The Gazelle*. Philadelphia: The Jewish Publication Society, 1991.

——. "Redemption of the Soul in Golden Age Religious Poetry." *Prooftexts* 10 (1990): 49–67.

Scherer, R. "Das Symbolische: Eine philosophische Analyse." *Philosophisches Jahrbuch der Görres-Gesellschaft* 48:2–3 (1935) (Festgabe zu . . . H. Finke): 210–57.

Schirmann, J. "L'Amour Spirituel dans la Poésie Hébraïque du Moyen Âge." *Les Lettres Romanes* 15 (1961): 315–25.

Schoff, W., ed. *The Song of Songs: A Symposium*. Philadelphia: The Commercial Museum, 1924.

Scholem, G. *Major Trends of Jewish Mysticism*. New York: Schocken Books, 1941.

——. *On the Kabbalah and Its Symbolism*. New York: Schocken Books, 1965.

——. *On the Mystical Shape of the Godhead*. New York: Schocken Books, 1991.

Schwartz, D. "The Phenomenology of Faith. R. Soloveitchik's Analysis in 'And From There You Shall Seek.'" In *Jewish Philosophy: Perspectives and Retrospectives*, edited by R. Jospe and D. Schwartz, 279–314. Boston: Academic Studies Press, 2012.

——. "He'arot 'al Peirushei Shir Ha-Shirim le-R. Shemaria Ha- 'Iqriṭi." In *Sefer Zikkaron Le-Rav Yosef Ben David Kafiḥ*, 319–33. Ramat Gan: Lishkat Rav ha-Kampus shel Universitat Bar-Ilan, 2001.

Scolnic, B. "Why Do We Sing the Song of Songs on Passover?" *Conservative Judaism* 48.4 (1996): 53–72.

Sefati, Y. *Love Songs in Sumerian Literature: Critical Edition of the Dumuzi-Inanna Songs*. Ramat-Gan: Bar-Ilan University Press, 1998.

Segal, M. H. *Mavo' Ha-Miqra'*. Vol. 2, 668–84. Jerusalem: Qiryat Sefer, 1967.

——. "The Song of Songs." *Vetus Testamentum* 12 (1962): 470–90.

Sells, M. "Guises of the Ghul: Dissembling Simile and Semantic Overflow in the Classical Nasib." In *Reorientations: Arabic and Persian Poetry*, edited by S. P. Stetkevych, 130–64. Bloomington: Indiana University Press, 1994.

Septimus, B. "He'arot Le-Divrei Ḥazal Be-Shirat Sefarad." *Tarbiz* 53 (1984): 607–14.

Shalev-Eyni, S. "Iconography of Love: Illustrations of Bride and Bridegroom in Ashkenazi Prayerbooks of the Thirteenth and Fourteenth Century." *Studies in Iconography* 26 (2005): 27–57.

——. "'Itti Milvanon Kallah." *Rimonim* 6–7 (1999): 6–20.

Shea, W. H. "The Chiastic Structure of the Song of Songs." *Zeitschrift für die Alttestamentliche Wissenschaft* 92 (1980): 378–96.

Shirman, Ḥ. *Ha-Shirah Ha-'Ivrit Bisfarad Uve-Provans*. 2nd corrected ed. 1–4 vols. Jerusalem: Mosad Bialik & Dvir, 1961.

Shpigal, Y. "'Od 'Al 'Midrash Shir Ha-Shirim' ve-'Shi'ur Qomah.'" *Tarbiz* 47 (1978): 253.

Signer, M. "God's Love for Israel: Apologetic and Hermeneutical Strategies in Twelfth-Century Biblical Exegesis." In *Jews and Christians in Twelfth-Century Europe*, edited by M. A. Signer and J. Van Engen, 123–49. Notre Dame: Notre Dame University Press, 2001.

Sirat, C. "La Pensée Philosophique De Moise ibn Tibbon." *Revue des Études Juives* 138 (1979): 505–15.

Sonne, Isaiah. "Sifrut Ha-Musar Ve-ha-Filosophia be-Shirei Imannuel Ha-Romi." *Tarbiz* 5 (1934): 324–40.

Soulen, R. N. "The Wasfs of the Song of Songs and Hermeneutic." *Journal of Biblical Literature* 86 (1967): 183–90.

Sparks, H. F. D. "The Symbolical Interpretation of Lebanon in the Fathers." *Journal of Theological Studies* 16 (1955): 254–79.

Steiner, G. *On Difficulty and Other Essays*. New York & Oxford: Oxford University Press, 1978.

——. "Philosophical Allegory in Medieval Jewish Culture: The Crisis in Languedoc (1305–6)." In *Interpretation and Allegory. Antiquity to the Modern Period*, edited by J. Whitman, 189–209. Leiden: Brill, 2000.

Steiner, R. "The Aramaic Text in Demotic Script: The Liturgy of a New Year's Festival Imported from Bethel to Syene by Exiles from Rash." *Journal of American Oriental Society* 111 (1991): 362–63.

Steinschneider, M. "Die Jüdischen Erklärer des Hohenliedes, 9.-16. Jahrh." *Hebräische Bibliographie* 9 (1869).

Steller, H. E. "Preliminary Remarks to a New Edition of Shir Hashirim Rabbah." In *Rabbi Shlomoh 1040–1990, Hommages À Ephraïm E. Urbach*, edited by G. Sed Rajna (IV *E Congrès Européen Des Études Juives, Paris-Troyes 6–13 Juillet*), 301–11. Paris, 1990.

Stemberger, G. "Die Megillot als Festlungen der Jüdischen Liturgie." *Jahrbuch für biblische Theologie* 18 (2003): 261–76.

Stern, D. "Ancient Jewish Interpretation of the Song of Songs in a Comparative Context." In *Biblical Interpretation and Cultural Exchange*, edited by N. Dohrmann and D. Stern, 87–107. Philadelphia: University of Pennsylvania Press, 2008.

Stevens, W. *The Necessary Angel: Essays on Reality and the Imagination*. New York: A. Knopf, Inc., 1942.

Stronach, D. "The Garden as a Political Statement: Some Case Studies from the Near East in the First Millennium B.C." *Bulletin of the Asia Institute* 4 (1990): 171–80.

Talmage, F. "Apples of Gold: The Inner Meaning of Sacred Texts in Medieval Judaism." In *Jewish Spirituality I: From the Bible to the Middle Ages*, edited by A. Green, 313–55. New York: Crossroads, 1986.

Tishby, I. "Kitvei Ha-Muqubbalim R. Ezra ve-R. 'Azriel Mi-Gerona." In *Ḥiqrei Qabbalah ve-Sheluḥoteyha*, 11–16. Jerusalem: Magnes Press, 1982.

Tuell, S. S. "A Riddle Resolved by an Enigma: Hebrew Glš and Ugaritic Glt." *Journal of Biblical Literature* 112 (1993): 99–104.

Urbach, E. E. "The Homiletical Interpretation of the Sages and the Exposition of Origen on Canticles, and the Jewish-Christian Disputation." *Scripta Hierosolymitana* 22 (1971): 247–75.

Vajda, G. "En Marge du Commentaire sur Le Cantiques des Cantiques de J. ibn Aqnin." *Revue des Études Juives* 127–128 (1968–69): 187–99.

——. *L'Amour de Dieu dans la Théologie Juive du Moyen Age*. Paris: Vrin, 1957.

Van der Heide, A. "Pardes: Methodological Reflections on the Theory of Four Senses." *Journal of Jewish Studies* 34 (1983): 147–59.

Van Dijk-Hemmes, F. "The Imagination of Power and the Power of Imagination: An Intertextual Analysis of Two Biblical Love Songs: The Song of Songs and Hosea 2." *Journal for the Study of the Old Testament* 44 (1989): 75–88.

Vermes, G. "Lebanon: The Historical Development of an Exegetical Tradition." In *Scripture and Tradition*, 26–39. Leiden: Brill, 1961.

Von Grünebaum, G. "The Early Development of Islamic Religious Poetry." *Journal of the American Oriental Society* 60 (1940): 23–29.

Walfish, B. "Bibliographiyah Mu'eret Shel Ha-Parshanut Ha-Yehudit 'Al Shir Ha-Shirim Mi-ymei Ha-Beinayim." In *Ha-Mikra Bi-Re'i Mefarshav. Sefer Zikkaron Le-Sarah Kamin*, edited by S. Japhet, 518–71. Jerusalem: Magnes Press, 1994.

Waltke, B. K., and M. O'Connor. *An Introduction to Biblical Hebrew Syntax*. Winona Lake, IN: Eisenbrauns, 1990.

Watson, W. G. E. "Some Ancient Near Eastern Parallels to the Song of Songs." In *Words Remembered, Texts Renewed*, edited by J. Davies et al. Sheffield: Sheffield Academic Press, 1995.

Webster, E. C. "Pattern in the Song of Songs." *Journal for the Study of the Old Testament* 22 (1982): 73–93.

Weinfeld, M. "Feminine Features in the Imagery of God in Israel: The Sacred Marriage and the Sacred Tree." *Vetus Testamentum* 46 (1996): 515–29.

Westenholz, J. G. "A Forgotten Love Song." In *Language, Literature, and History: Philological and Historical Studies Presented to Erica Reiner, American Oriental Society*, 415–25. New Haven: 1987.

——. "Love Lyrics from the Ancient Near East." In *Civilizations of the Ancient Near East*, edited by Jack M. Sasson, 4:2471–84. New York: Charles Scribner's Sons, 1995. Reprint, Peabody, MA: Hendrickson Publishers, 2000.

——. "Metaphorical Language in the Poetry of Love in the Ancient near East." In *La Circulation des Biens, des Personnes et des Idées dans le Proche-Orient Ancient: Actes de la 37 Rencontre Assyriologique Internationale*, edited by D. Charpin and F. Joannès, 381–87. Paris, 1992.

——. "Symbolic Language in Akkadian Narrative Poetry: The Metaphorical Relationship between Poetical Images and the Real World." In *Mesopotamian Poetic Language: Sumerian and Akkadian*, edited by M. E. Vogelzang and H. L. J. Vanstiphout. Cuneiform Monographs 6; Gröningen: Styx, 1996.

Westenholz, J. G., and A. Westenholz. "Help for Rejected Suitors: The Old Akkadian Love Incantation MAD V 8." *Orientalia* 46 (1977): 198–219.

Wetzstein, J. G. "Die Syrische Dreschtafel." *Zeitschrift für Ethnologie* 5 (1873): 270–302.

White, J. B. *A Study of the Language of Love in the Song of Songs and Ancient Egyptian Love Poetry*. Missoula, MT: Scholars Press, 1975.

Whitman, J. *Allegory. The Dynamics of an Ancient and Medieval Technique*. Cambridge: Harvard University Press, 1987.
——. *Interpretation and Allegory. Antiquity to the Modern Period*. Leiden: Brill, 2000.
Wilder, A. *Theopoetic: Theology and the Religious Imagination* Philadelphia: Fortress Press, 1976.
Willis, J. T. "On the Text of Micah 2: Aα-β." *Biblica* 48 (1967): 534–41.
Wolfson, E. "Asceticism and Eroticism in Medieval Jewish Philosophical and Mystical Exegesis of the Song of Songs." In *With Reverence for the Word: Medieval Scriptural Exegesis in Judaism, Christianity, and Islam*, edited by J. D. McAuliffe, B. D. Walfish, and J. W. Goering, 92–118. New York: Oxford University Press, 2003.
——. "Female Imaging of the Torah: From Literary Metaphor to Religious Symbol." In *From Ancient Israel to Modern Judaism: Intellect in Quest of Understanding: Essays in Honor of Marvin Fox*, edited by J. Neusner et al., 271–307. Atlanta: Scholars Press, 1989.
——. *Language, Eros, Being: Kabbalistic Hermeneutics and Poetic Imagination*. New York: Fordham University Press, 2005.
——. "Mirror of Nature Reflected in the Symbolism of Medieval Kabbalah." In *Judaism and Ecology*, edited by H. Tirosh-Samuelson, 305–31. Cambridge: Harvard University Press, 2002.
——. "The Tree That Is All: Jewish-Christian Roots of a Kabbalistic Symbol in Sefer Ha-Bahir." *Journal of Jewish Thought and Philosophy* 3 (1993): 31–76.
Yahalom, Y. "Ha-Rambam Ve-ha-Melitzah Ha-'Ivrit." *Pe'amim* 81 (1999): 4–18.
Yannaras, C. *Variations on the Song of Songs*. Brookline: Holy Cross Orthodox Press, 2005.
Yitzḥaki, M. *'Elei Ginnat 'Arugot: Shirat ha-Gan ve-ha-Peraḥim Ha-'Ivrit bi-Sfarad*. Tel Aviv: Notzah Ve-Qeset, 1988.
Young, I. "Notes on the Language of 4Q Cant B." *Journal of Jewish Studies* 52 (2001): 122–31.
Zakovitch, Y. "Song of Songs 8:6–7 Connection to Proverbs 6:20–35" [Hebrew]. *Beth Mikra* 3 (1965): 366–68.
——. "Song of Songs in Relation to Israelite Poetry of the Biblical Period." In *Proceedings of the Tenth World Congress of Jewish Studies: Jerusalem, August 16–24, 1989*, 123–30. Jerusalem: World Union of Jewish Studies, 1990.
Zohary, M. *Plants of the Bible*. Cambridge: Cambridge University Press, 1982.

MW00805039